the inclusive hebrew scriptures

volume ii: the prophets

the
inclusive
hebrew
scriptures

volume ii: the prophets

ALTAMIRA
PRESS

A Division of
ROWMAN & LITTLEFIELD PUBLISHERS, INC.
Walnut Creek • Lanham • New York • Toronto • Oxford

220.520 9
PnI
(II)

ALTAMIRA PRESS
A division of Rowman & Littlefield Publishers, Inc.
1630 North Main Street, #367
Walnut Creek, CA 94596
www.altamirapress.com

Rowman & Littlefield Publishers, Inc.
A wholly owned subsidiary of The Rowman & Littlefield Publishing Group, Inc.
4501 Forbes Boulevard, Suite 200
Lanham, MD 20706

PO Box 317
Oxford
OX2 9RU, UK

Cover illustration by Melissa Cooper

British Library Cataloguing in Publication Information Available

Library of Congress Catalog Card Number: 99-74682

ISBN 0-7591-0762-9 (alk. paper)
ISBN 0-7591-0763-7 (pbk: alk. paper)

Printed in the United States of America

⊖™ The paper used in this publication meets the minimum requirements of American
National Standard for Information Sciences—Permanence of Paper for Printed Library
Materials, ANSI/NISO Z39.48–1992.

table of contents

the prophets

the earlier prophets

the later prophets

continued

the twelve

acknowledgements

We would like to acknowledge the following people who made this book possible:

Rev. Joseph A. Dearborn, whose pioneering Kansas spirit and dedication to equality in the Church echoes the prophets of old. His was the vision behind the inclusive language translation work and the voice that kept us going. Now in retirement, we proudly dedicate this book to him.

The board and staff of the Quixote Center, who shepherded this project over the years: Nancy Allen (board), Regina Anderson (staff—Interfaith Voices), Carol Binstock (staff—Business Manager), Jack Bresette (board), Jim Burchell (part-time staff—Quest for Peace), Bill Callahan (staff—Quixote Center/Quest for Peace), Rose Marie Canty (volunteer), Eugenia Charles (staff—Haiti Reborn), John Clark (staff—Computer Operations Manager), William D'Antonio (board), Frank DeBernardo (board), Jan DeRight (staff—Nicaraguan Cultural Alliance), Caleb Downin (part-time staff), Joe Duplan (volunteer), Jack Engle (volunteer), Maureen Fiedler, SL (staff—Interfaith Voices), Jane Henderson (staff—Equal Justice, USA), Jeff Garis (board), Noelle Hanrahan (board), Rea Howarth (staff—Catholics Speak Out), John Judge (part-time staff), Trisha Kendall (staff—Administration), Njoki Njehu (board), Melinda Miles (staff—Haiti Reborn), Dolly Pomerleau (staff—Quixote Center/Quest for Peace), Josephine Reed (staff—Interfaith Voices), Carol Ries (part-time staff—Quest for Peace), Shari Silberstein (staff—Equal Justice, USA), Natacha Thys (board), Dan Walsh (board), Kathy Wright, SL (board), Lisa Zimmerman (board), and Saul Wolf (intern—Quest for Peace).

Our reviewers and editors, who provided such a vital service to the project: the Rev. Elizabeth Anderson, Kate Barfield, Esq., Barbara Marian, Dr. Gail Rekers, and Dr. Thomas Reed West; and our eagle-eyed proofreaders:

Jennifer Buckley, Rea Howarth, Trisha Kendall, Jerry Pederson, Tom Ricker, and Tom West.

Our friends at AltaMira Press, particularly Erik Hanson.

And the many people who have contributed toward The People's Scripture Campaign and made this book possible:

Bernardine and Joseph Abbott, David W. Abbott, Flavio J. Acosta, Robert H. Adams, Leslie Alphen, Effie K. Ambler, Robert L. Anstey, the Rev. Patricia Arledge-Benko, Dorothy Armbruster, Angela C. Backman, Regina Bannan, Mary Jane Barkett, Ellen W. Barth, Michael O. Bartz, Jean Ann Basinger, Annette Batzer, Betty and Herbert Bazur, Ann P. Becherer, Dolores Becker, BVM, Evelyn M. Becker, Mary Beckfeld, Gary B. Beebe, Jo Bell, Benedictine Monks, Jacquelyn H. Benjamin, Abigail M. Benkeser, Fran Beshada, Sharon Beshoar, Timothy Biel, Christopher Bingham, Alfred F. Blancato, Connie Blumenthal, Mary K. Boggs, Margaret Boler OSF, Mary M. Boone, Georgann T. Brophy, John H. Bruggeman, Douglas L. Brunk, Natalie J. Brunson, Harriet Bryan, Fr Jerome Brzezinski, Rev. Eugene Buhr, the Rev. Alta M. Burnett, Sr. Eileen T. Burns, SND, Mary and Carlo Busby, Bill Callahan, Sr. Therese M. Camardella, Jevene Campbell, Michael J. J. Campbell, ThD, Ann M. Carberry, Dennis Carlson, Valerie J. and Gordon Carlton, Sr. Barbara Carr, Rokki Carr, Madeline and Ed Casey, Winifred Cawley, Martha Chapman, Rev. Paul Chateau, Monica and Rudy Cherniak, Susan A. Cheston, Rosalie E. Cieply, Patricia and Donald Clausen, Rev. Richard E. Cleary, OSFS, Allanah Cleary Beh, Rev. Victor Clore, Marilyn Ward Coll, Sr. Jane Ann Comerford, CSJ, M. Eileen Conlin, Fr Edmund Coppinger, Marguerite M. Corcoran, Eugenio Corpuz, G. Lisa Corum Fox, Fr. Samuel L. Craig, Rev. Senter C. Crook, Janet Halley Crosby, Sr. Heloise Cruzat, Katherine Cudlipp, Anne T. Daly, Jean M. Daniels, Marianne B. Danks, Harriet Dart, Dorothy C. Davies, Paula K. Dawson, Adele and Bill De Line, Joan M. DeGregorio, Sheila Durkin Dierks, Edward J. Dobransky, Erin and Terry Donahue Cousins, David Donovan, Margaret M. Dostal, Grace Drake, Diane Drufenbrock, OSF, Norbert J. Duda, Sr. Mary Catherine Duerr, Rosanne M. Dummer, Mary Ellen and Dan Duran, Erma M. Durkin, the Rev. Amy Egan, Christine Eheman, Janice and Neil Eiden, John J. and Martha L. Eischeid, Carolyn Emery, Sherry M. Enserro, Sarah L. Esgate, Helen Fay, Patricia E. Fettig, Helen Ann Fisher, William H. Fisher, Esther R. Flebbe, Anne M. Flynn, Margie A. Ford, Sr. Victoria Forde, Daniel K. Fox, Sr. Ruth Ann Fox, RSM, Deborah Gavrin Frangquist, Fr. John Frederic, Mary Clare Freeman, Sr. Mary Noel Frey, RSM, Joseph F. Friend, Robert G. Fuller, Henrietta L. Gallagher, Patricia A. Gamache, Elaine M. Gasser, Deborah R. Geelsdottir, Timothy G. Geen, Rev. B.J. George, Lucille A. Gervase, Sr. Patricia Gimblett, RSM, Mary and Kenneth Gleason, Stanley F. Glowiak, Leticia Gomez, Anne and Tom Gonsoulin,

Kathy Goodman, Liisa Granfors-Hunt, Rev. Dominic J. Grassi, Rosanne M. Greco, Jeanette and Kenneth Grenz, Joseph Grilliot, Conrad T. Gromada, Fr. Ralph C. Gross, Ron Grossi, Lucille J. Grow, Dr. Alexandra Guliano, Sr. Elaine Hagedorn, CHM, Anne Hall, Christie B. Halvor, Rev. William D. Hammer, Edward Harding, Rev. Paul A. Harman, Joan T. Harrington, CSJ, Roberta Harrington, Francesca C. Hartnett, Vincent A. Haselhorst, Jeanne M. Hassenzahl, Jane Hatheway, Rita L. Haugh, Kathleen and Richard Hauke, Avis C. Hayden, Mark L. Hayes, Eloise Heimann, Laurie A. Helgoe, Ellen R. Hendrix, Margaret L. Herman, Dennis E. Hetrick, Sr. Mary Hettich, Linda Sue Hewitt, Lina B. Hill, Marie A. Hill, the Rev. Mary Louise Hintz, Peg Hoffmiller, Michael J. Holasek, Holy Cross Catholic Church, Holy Union Sisters, Betty Howell, John and Roberta Hydar, Rosemary H. Jackson, William T. Jacobks, Rev. Msgr. Balthasar Janacek, Katherine R. and Ed Janes, Christopher B. Janezic, Bruce Jarstfer, Sr. Maureen M. Jessnik, RSM, Andrea and Spencer Johnson, Mary Beth Jones, Rev. Samuel T. Kaetzel, Edward J. Kansa, Marianne H. Kaple, Anna M. Kelly, Nancy Lou Kelly, Kathleen R. Kennedy, Mary Kiernan, Rev. Eugene M. Kilbride, Helen Kipa, Patricia B. Koechlin, Fr. Myron Kowalsky, Ruth F. and Robert N. Kremer, Jodi Kremiller Kingdon, Joseph J. Kuciejczyk, Jr, Rev. Eugene C. Kutsch, Carol Labonte, Julia M. Ladner, Sullins M. Lamb, Richard J. Lang, Norbert J. Langer, III, Cynthia Lapp, Kay Larrieu, R. W. Larroque, Chele Lavalla, Katherine M. Leighton, Margaret K. Leinbach, Eleanor V. Lewis, Linda D. Lewis, Mary and John Lindstrom, Robert Link, Judith Liro, Ann and David Lodge, Janet H. Lowry, Carol Ludwig, Rev. Patrick M. Lyons, Sr. Patricia Mahoney, SP, Mary Mallon, Betty Mannlein, Wendy and Stanley Marsh, Steve Marston, Margaret and James Martin, Rev. Joseph Mattern, Mary W. Matthews, Mary K. Maulucci, Barbara A. Maurer, Vicki Mayster, Margaret and Myles McCabe, the Rev. Ruth E. McCarty, J. Justin McCormick, Sr. Joan McDermott, PBVM, Sr. Kathryn E. McDermott, SC, Mary C. McDonagh, RSM, Carol McGuire, Thomas and Susan McGuire, Sr. Roberta McInerney, Rose M. McKillips, Rev. Ernan McMullin, Rev. Douglas A. McNeill, Julie A. Melton, Rev. Paul F. Menke, Miriam Meyers, Lois A. Michelin, Clara L. Milko, Margaret Peggy Mohler, Lucille Monti, Rosemary and Ronald Moon, Alice C. Moore, Elizabeth P. Moore, the Rev. Grace Jones Moore, James and Roberta Moran, David L. Morse, Mary Dolores Moses, Julie Mudd, Fr. Joseph A. Mulcrone, Neil M. Mulock, Josefa Theresia Munch, Frank Murphy, J. P. Murphy, Susan E. Murphy, Rev. Lawrence J. Murtagh, David A. Neal, Jr, Mary Jo and Jack Neal, Patricia Nemec, the Rev. Susan Norris, Teresa Norton, Diane K. O'Donnell, Walter R. O'Neil, Mark W. Olson, Sr. Dorothy Oursler, CSJ, the Rev. Carol Parish, Jan F. Parker, Barbara Parsons, Agnes Pastorino, Richard E. Patenaude, Jack Payden-Travers, Larry Peacock, Frank

W. Perreault-Kuebel, Dr. Lisa C. Pesavento, C.P.R.P., Sr. Joy Peterson, Elaine and Rick Pfaff, Elizabeth B. Phillips, Angie Pihlman, Sharon Pikula, Ann R. Plogsterth, J. William Potter, Jr, Mary Reynolds Powell, Felicia Pratto, Donna Prince, Rosemary A. Rader, Bob Rankin, Elisabeth A. Rareshide, Geri Raszkowski, Elizabeth Ravenscroft, Karen Ray, Pamela Ray, Kathy and Robert Redig, James B. Reed, Jr, Elisabeth Rees, Barbara B. Regulinski, Lawrence A. Reh, Sr. Elizabeth M. Reis, SSJ, Paul V. Reithmaier, Dorothy L. Renner-Grodek, Rev. Daniel Reynolds, Katherine A. Rhoda, Carol Ries, SNJM, Loreta M. and Ronald Riffel, Sr. Beth Rindler, SFP, Joyce and Robert E. Rittman, Sr. Frances Roberts, SSJ, Gayle N. Rosenkrantz, Alberta B. Ross, Janis and Edward Ross, Norma L. Rudinsky, Dr. John R. Russell, Audrey and Bernard Rutkowski, Jean and Jack Ryan, Br. John H. Ryan, OCP, Louise and Donald Sandercock, Elizabaeth A. Schoeni, Fr. Paul A. Schumacher, Steve Scott, Marilyn C. Sendek, Joanne Shackelford, Timothy Shaw, Gretchen and Joseph Shilts, Kana Shimasaki, Cathy Siegl, Michael Sirany, Sisters Of Charity, Sisters Of St Joseph Of Carondelet, Sisters Of The Holy Redeemer, Sisters of Mercy, Sr. Deidre Sitko, James M. Small, Albert J. Smith, OSFS, Suzanne J. Smith, Margaret and Paul Soergel, Deborah Sokolove, Lois Ann Sorensen, Leroy Spaniol, St Francis Church Tithing Committee, St Julia Church, Sr. Mary Stasia Stafford, BVM, Stanley D. Starr, Sr. Mary Lou Steele, SC, Sr. Irma Steffen, Nancy G. Stein, Hugh Stephenson, Marlis V. Stoner, Sr. Maleada Strange, SNJM, Donna M. Strong, Charlotte B. Sullivan, Kathleen C. Sullivan, Richard F. Sullivan, Jo Ann M. Summer, Karen A. Summers, Robert G. Sweet, Gregory C. Swiderski, Edith Sylvester, Elizabeth Taneyhill, Norman D. Taylor, Roslyn Taylor, Thayer C. Taylor, The Women's Office, BVM, Leona M. Thorpe, Sr. Catherine Tighe, Jan Tooker, Shirley Tung, Sr. Mary Turgi, CSC, Helen E. Umphrey, Grace M. Vagnini, Sr. Barbara Valuckas, SSND, E. Jane Via, Stephanie Visokay, Rev. Wilbur J. Votraw, Roger A. Waha, Sally Kay Waite, Sr. Doris T. Walbridge, Mary and Bob Walden, Joanne Ward, Rev. John F. Ward, Carrie Watson, Mary Anne Weiner, Sarah E. Wellinger, Wilma and Richard White, Martha J. Wicklund, Mary C. Wilborn, Marian Wilcox, Eleanor K. Willhard, Gerald Wilmsen, Halcyon and Leland Wilson, Elizabeth Winslea, Brian Wren, Rev. John Wutscheck, Julie Yarborough, Mark Zaborney, and Loretta and Dan Zehe.

about the translators

Craig R. Smith has been a biblical scholar and writer for over a quarter century. During his undergraduate program at Lake Forest College in Illinois, he studied history, psychology, and religion, and was tutored in biblical Hebrew, Aramaic, and *koiné* Greek by a Jesuit priest who is a scholar and author in his own right. Smith then pursued his continuing studies in biblical languages independently. In addition to Hebrew and Greek, he is fluent in French and has studied German and Latin.

In addition to his translation and editing work, Smith has published numerous articles on issues affecting contemporary religious life in journals and newspapers. He won the 1994 Polly Bond Award for Excellence in Communications for "The Word in Our Hearts," an article published in *The Witness* magazine that examined the love-hate relationship many 20th century Christians—lay and clergy alike—have with the Bible.

Mark D. Buckley studied for the Catholic priesthood between 1980 and 1985. His interest and training in Biblical Theology developed during his graduate studies and continues to this day. Besides biblical Hebrew and *koiné* Greek, he is knowledgeable in Latin, French, and Irish Gaelic. He has worked with Priests for Equality since 1987 and is one of the original planners of PFE's Inclusive Language Project.

introduction

What are the Prophets?

"The words that prophets utter are not offered as souvenirs. Their speech to the people is not a reminiscence, a report, hearsay. Prophets not only convey; they reveal. They almost do unto others what God does unto them. In speaking, prophets reveal God. This is the marvel of the prophets' work: in their words the invisible God becomes audible. They do not prove or argue. The thought they have to convey is more than language can contain. Divine power bursts in the words. The authority of the prophets is in the Presence their words reveal."

Abraham Joshua Heschel
The Prophets (Harper, 1962), rev.

The Prophets (or *Nevi'im* in Hebrew) is the second of the three sections of the Hebrew Bible: the *Torah, The Prophets,* and *The Writings.* In some ways, it is a continuation of the *Torah,* recounting the history of the People of Israel and their relationship to God through the Covenant. The Prophets cannot be separated from the Torah—it is their point of reference, their certain, guiding star. The prophet looks at history, reads the signs of the times, and speaks and acts through and within the Covenant.

Several Hebrew words describe the prophets. Taken together, they unfold for us a complete picture of what the ancient prophets of Israel were.

The Hebrew word for prophet, *navi,* comes from the term *niv sefatayim,* meaning "fruit of the lips." This gives a major clue to the role of the prophet as "speaker," who speaks for God. By far the most common and basic phrase translated as "prophet" is *navi htcb*. Among a number of possible ways of understanding the meaning and origin of this term, a clear definition can be constructed from observing its use in Exodus 7:1-2:

> YHWH said to Moses, "Look, I have made you like a god to Pharaoh, with Aaron, your brother, as your prophet. Tell Aaron everything I command you to say, and your brother will tell Pharaoh, so that he will let the Israelites leave Egypt.

Two other common words used to discuss the biblical prophets are the Hebrew terms *ro'eh vtr* and *hozeh vzj*. These terms seem to be synonymous. Their root meanings are "to see." The word *navi* emphasizes the prophet's utterances, whereas *ro'eh* and *hozeh* point to the method by which the prophet receives those utterances from God. I Samuel 9:9 clearly indicates that the offices of seer and prophet were identical:

> In the old days in Israel, when people had questions of God, they would say, "Come, let us go to the seer." For what is now called a prophet (*navi*) used to be called a seer (*ro'eh*).

The prophet is both an actor and an passive recipient: Two verb forms frequently appear (*pi'el* and *hitpa'el*), both meaning "to play the *navi* role," "to act the *navi* part." It is a good guess, but only a guess, that the lost Hebrew root is related to cognate Accadian and Arabic words meaning "to call" or "to announce." The underlying meaning of the Hebrew noun might be, then, "an announcer," or "the one who announces" the purpose and activity of God. This is the prophetic action. In the passive sense, the prophet is the listener who receives the announcement of God, and is then one who is "called" (*ro'eh*). The Greek translation of this verse in the Septuagint presupposes a slightly different text, conveying the sense that the term "seer" was in the past simply a common, popular name for prophet.

Even if we were certain of the original meaning of the root underlying the Hebrew noun, we could hardly take this as conclusive evidence of the basic understanding of the Hebrew prophet in the middle centuries of the first millenium B.C.E. Rather, we will have to understand the sense of the word *navi* from the character of the prophets themselves as they appear and function in the community of ancient Israel.

From what we have said so far, a primary meaning of "prophet" would be "to speak for." Rabbi Abraham Joshua Heschel described prophets as sharing in the *pathos* of God's heart. This means that to be prophetic is to be, first of all, a listener—one who shares heart to heart with God and in prayerful intimacy and whose heart echoes God's own. Hence, a prophet listens to and speaks from the very heart of God, proclaiming forth the divine message.

Other terms for a prophet include the phrases "Godly one," stressing the prophet's moral character and divine ministry; "Servant of YHWH," the title Moses carried and passed on to Joshua, emphasizing the close and holy relationship between God and the prophet; and "Messenger of YHWH," which could also be understood as "angel of God," one of those agents sent to deliver God's proclamations to people.

Structure of *The Prophets*

The Prophets is divided into three distinct parts: *Nevi'im Ri'shonim*, or Earlier Prophets—Joshua through Kings; the *Nevi'im Acharonim*, or Later Prophets—Isaiah through Ezekiel; and the *Trei-Asar* or The Twelve, often referred to as the "Minor" Prophets because their books are shorter than those of the other prophets. The books of Samuel and Kings are often each counted as one book, as are The Twelve. In the order in which they appear, the names of the books making up *The Prophets* are:

Yehoshua' (Joshua)
Shoftim (Judges)
Shmu'el א (1 Samuel)
Shmu'el ב (2 Samuel)
Malkhim א (1 Kings)
Malkhim ב (2 Kings)

Yesha'yahu (Isaiah)
Yirmiyahu (Jeremiah)
Yechezq'el (Ezekiel)

Hoshea' (Hosea)
Yo'el (Joel)
Amos
'Ovadyah (Obadiah)
Yonah (Jonah)
Mikhah (Micah)
Nachum (Nahum)
Chabaquq (Habakkuk)
Tsfanya (Zephaniah)
Chagai (Haggai)
Zkharya (Zechariah)
Malakhi (Malachi)

The books included in the canon of the Prophets do not exhaust the number of prophets of Israel. The Talmud says that there were twice as many prophets as the number of people who left Egypt—60,000. Most prophets, however conveyed messages that were meant only for their particular time and place, and their message was lost as the generation for which it was intended passed on to the next. There were other prophets whose messages spoke from one generation to the next—their words and deeds living on in the memory of the people. Scripture identifies fifty-five prophets, only a few of whom have whole books dedicated to their prophecies. Among these prophets are a number of prominent women: Sarah, Miriam, Deborah, Hannah, Abigail, Huldah, and Esther.

The Purpose of the Prophets

The prophets of the People of Israel are called by God for at least two main purposes. One is to call the descendents of Abraham—both Israel and Judah—back to faithfulness: faithfulness to YHWH and to the Torah, forsaking idolatry and sin. Sometimes the prophets make attempts to warn the people of the dire consequences they face if they do not repent. Another aim of the prophets was to encourage the remnant, who needed to be heartened as they watched their people fall by the wayside and forsake God, and as times of great national distress befell Israel and Judah—because, according to the prophets, of the people's own waywardness.

Sometimes the prophets spoke words directed at the nations surrounding Israel. There were often words of stern rebuke and warning. However, as with the Israelites, there was also a faithful remnant from among the nations who needed encouragement to continue following the God of Israel. The prophets provided God's words of encouragement.

Characteristics of the Prophetic Writings

Most of the original messages of the prophets were sermons delivered publicly. Sometimes the prophets had their own scribes, whose task it was to write their sermons in a scroll. One such example is Baruch, Jeremiah's scribe. That many of the prophecies were first spoken orally helps explain the strange language or references in their messages.

Another characteristic of the prophets that their messages sometimes come through seemingly strange actions. An example is Ezekiel's lying on one side, then turning over to his other side. The very action was also part of the message.

The prophets are actors within history. Theirs is not some ethereal nebulous proclamation. All of the messages of the prophets related to what was going on within Israel, outside of Israel, or both. They are God's mouthpiece to explain the actions of God at any given moment in history. That is why we cannot study the prophets without knowing what was happening at the time of their speeches.

The prophets are distinguished also for their artistic use of the Hebrew language. Most of their messages are delivered in poetry and, possibly, song. They also employ the entire gamut of idioms, wordplays, root plays, and metaphors that the Hebrew language possesses. That is one reason why many of the prophetic passages are difficult to translate and to exegete. They freely employed all forms of the intricate, yet beautiful, Hebrew parallelism, so characteristic of ancient Semitic poetry.

Hebrew (and Semitic) poetry employs at least three types of parallelism. In what is called Synonymous Parallelism, the second or third line of a passage essentially repeats the same thought as the first line. In Antithetical Parallelism, a parallelism by contrast, the second line of a verse communicates something that is the opposite of the statement in the first. Each succeeding line in Synthetic Parallelism builds on the thought expressed by the first line. Subsequent lines may simply complete the thought begun by the first line, or draw analogies, or provide arguments. Scholars also identify Climactic Parallelisms, in which subsequent words build on the same word, and Emblematic Parallelisms employing simile or metaphors. The hard and sometimes frustrating work of understanding the system of parallelism and recognizing their uses in the Scripture is essential to coming to an accurate understanding of what a given text means.

Themes of the Prophets

There are many messages in *The Prophets*, and indeed, each prophet has a message particular to the time and community to which he or she is speaking. Several volumes could be filled just identifying the particular messages. Yet, underlying the words of the prophets are three meta-themes: the uniqueness of God, a call to faithfulness to the Covenant, and the primacy of justice and kindness.

Uniqueness of God

In every word the prophet speaks and in every act the prophet performs, we hear echo the Jewish statement of faith found in Deuteronomy: *"Sh'ma Yisroel, YHWH Elohainu, YHWH Echad,"* one translation of which is "Hear, O Israel, YHWH is our God, YHWH alone." This is fundamental to the prophets, for it is YHWH alone who is the God of Israel. The reliance on any other god is a betrayal. Indeed, apostasy, in one form or another (whether through the actual worship of other gods and goddesses, or through a hardening of the heart to YHWH's word), is the major sin of Israel. Israel is unique because of its special relationship with YHWH. While all other gods belong to the nations, Israel is a people because of the Covenant with YHWH. This self-understanding often lead to defensiveness in national identity and to violence against those found in the land of Canaan. The early history of Israel, particularly in Joshua, exemplifies this understanding.

Yet even as the prophets preached the uniqueness of YHWH to the People of Israel, we see a growing understanding through the Hebrew Scriptures of who God is and how God relates to the other nations. Throughout the Prophets, the understanding of who YHWH is shifts from being exclusively Israel's God to being a universal God. The further along one goes in the prophetic timeline, the more one can see the prophets recognizing that YHWH is not just the tribal god of Israel, but the God of all peoples and nations. This echoes the other translation of the *Shema:* "Hear, O Israel, YHWH our God, YHWH is One"—or, as the Muslim statement of faith puts it, "There is no God but God."

Faithfulness to the Covenant

The message of the prophets is rooted in Israel's Covenant with YHWH. This defined Israel's relationship to God. On the basis of the requirements laid out in the Torah, the prophets called the people back to faith. Prophets sometimes recalled Israel's covenantal roots to reaffirm the truth of God and to ground God's faithfulness. At other times they recalled those traditions to demonstrate how God was going to do something new and even more wonderful than what had been done in the past. In any case, the prophets carried on their ministry against the background of God's covenantal relationship with Israel.

The prophets tried to shape the faith of the people so that they would think and act rightly. This often placed them in conflict with the leaders of both the religion and the state. While critiquing particular religious practices and governmental policies, the prophets never categorically condemned religious ritual practices or formal worship but only opposed such things when they promoted religious self-satisfaction, complacency, and social injustice. In fact, some prophets were also priests, and all true prophets were informed by the best principles of Israel's priestly tradition, including the reality of sin and the need for sacrifice, purification, and holiness. The prophet Micah summarized eloquently and for all time the requirements at the heart of the Covenant:

"What shall I bring when I come before YHWH,
 and bow down before God on high?" you ask.
"Am I to come before God with burnt offerings?
 With year-old calves?
Will YHWH be placated by thousands of rams
 or ten thousand rivers of oil?
Should I offer my firstborn for my wrongdoings—
 the fruit of my body for the sin of my soul?"
Listen here, mortal:

God has already made abundantly clear
what "good" is, and what YHWH needs from you:
simply do justice,
love kindness,
and humbly walk with YHWH.

These words lead us to the third important theme of the prophets.

Primacy of Justice and Kindness

There are times that the prophet's message seems to be one of anger and vengeance rather than hope and compassion (the book of *Amos* and Jeremiah 5:4-6 are two good examples). The image of God in *The Prophets* is, at times, one of a vengeful, angry God who is ready to destroy the people because of their unfaithfulness to the Covenant. Yet underlying the words of anger is justice and compassion. The God of the prophets is one who is passionate about the people, jealous to protect the intimate relationship that God had formed with Israel.

YHWH has a special love for those on the margins, the poor, and those most vulnerable in society. The widowed and orphaned, for example, are under God's special protection, and those who harm them fall under the wrath of God. The prophets speak on behalf of those under God's special care and protection. They do not accept things as they are, because knowing the heart of God, they cannot abide injustice. Prophets revive our capacity to feel and draw our attention to what we would rather not see. In Rabbi Heschel's words, "They take us to the slums."

Inclusive Language

Human beings can be said to be creatures of language. We are born into a world of language. We come to know ourselves, others, and the world in and through language. Language gives structure and shape to our experience. Language gives us not only the means to describe our experience, but also prescribes our views, values, and norms of the way the world should be. Through language, we also perpetuate biases, fears, resentments, and frustrations. Sexism, racism, and classism are perpetuated in our language, and words are often used as weapons.

In developing scripture translations today, translators still bring in the biases of their own culture. For two millennia standard biblical translations have reflected Western, male-centered attitudes and prejudices. Words and phrases such as "brotherhood of man," which are claimed to include all people, carry with them the implication that maleness is the standard for being human. The language used in such translations does not merely describe sexual biases and prejudices; it also prescribes a course of behavior that fits into such an understanding. Biblical translations have been used to justify patriarchal and exclusionary practices and oppressive measures against women.

This male-centered approach to language is changing rapidly in our own culture as a growing consciousness of human equality develops. As women of faith became more conscious of their exclusion, they have sought to recover their place in the religious traditions. For them, inclusive language—using words and phrases that are not sexist or classist—is a vital and attitude-changing tool in the church. And as inclusive language becomes more accepted in general use—particularly in the media and in public speech—the need for inclusive language in religious texts becomes more apparent than ever.

With this shift in consciousness came a shift in language. Inclusive language is more than a corrective to the language of patriarchy—it is a form of language that expresses a vision of inclusion. Inclusive language is itself an issue of social justice as well as a means of achieving it. To use inclusive language is to challenge deeply ingrained biases and educate people in the habit of equality. In short, inclusive language is an essential consciousness-raising tool that can foster change in the Church and in society at large.

Developing Inclusive Language Translations

When we first started working on inclusive language texts back in 1987, we struggled with learning to speak the language of inclusion. We faltered and fell many times in our initial efforts—as we still sometimes falter. Thanks primarily to the encouragement and suggestions of women and men who share our vision of equality, we began to develop a degree of confidence, and we felt more at ease with the language of equality.

Along the way, we developed a set of guiding principles to make sure that we were consistent in our use of inclusive language. These principles are:

❖ **To create a "critical feminist biblical interpretation" of sacred Scripture that is inclusive in both content and style.**

From the beginning of the project, our efforts have involved grassroots feedback, the guidance of feminist theology and scripture scholarship, and an editorial process that involves women and men who are skilled in both the theological and the social aspects of feminist, pastoral, and scriptural critique.

❖ **To present the text in a layout that enhances the flow of the text, emphasizing the particular literary form that the text uses, while retaining the traditional chapters and verses.**

The modern division of the Bible into chapters most likely happened in the 13th century; separating the text into numbered verses occurred in the 16th century. While we have retained the traditional chapter and verse numbering throughout *The Prophets*, we have sought to present the text in its appropriate literary style: poetry looks like poetry, stories look like stories, genealogies are recognizable as genealogies, etc.

❖ **To make a clear distinction between linguistic convention and overt bias in passages that appear sexist, and to distinguish between those passages that simply exclude women and those that actively vilify women.**

This is probably the most difficult problem we have had to face in our translation work. Nonetheless, we have sought to determine whether the text is using a mere linguistic convention that seems sexist to our modern sensibilities, or whether the underlying meaning of the text is inherently sexist.

In all circumstances, we seek to recover the original meaning of the text without perpetuating the sexist or classist idiom. To do this, we have employed some of the most current biblical scholarship and feminist critique available today.

❖ **To use terminology that acknowledges the many forms in which God appears in our lives, and to restore the role of women and of feminine images of God in Scripture.**

Through our many surveys and countless written responses, people who use our inclusive language texts have told us that the biggest concern in inclusive scripture is "God language"—words and images that describe the Divine Mystery. God is spirit, and the words and images we use to describe God are approximations, drawn from our experience, to describe a Mystery. Drawing upon imagery that is exclusively male violates both our experience and the Divine Mystery. We simply do not rely on exclusively male role models as the standard for human experience—why then would we limit God to exclusively male images?

In referring to God, we have sought in all circumstances to be gender-neutral yet personal. This at times means using the Hebrew names of God in referring to God or in direct address. One area where we have changed our minds over the years has been in the use of the fourfold name of God, spelled with the letters י (Yod), ה (Heh), ו (Waw or Vav), and ה (Heh). This name, sometimes called the Tetragrammaton, is the most sacred Name of God and was only pronounced once a year by the high priest; at other times, the devout would employ circumlocutions to avoid saying the Name, substituting other words such as Adonai ("sir" or "Lord") or Ha-Shem ("the Name") whenever they encountered the Tetragrammaton in the text.

English translations most often use "LORD" as a stand-in for the Name; a few use "Yahweh," even though scholars are uncertain as to how the Tetragrammaton was actually pronounced, or "Jehovah," which is a peculiar amalgam, the German form of YHWH (JHVH) interspersed with the Hebrew vowel pointings for the word "Adonai." We have chosen to retain the Name in its form of four letters, transliterated from the Hebrew, with the recommendation to the reader that, when you approach the four-lettered Name of God, you pause for a moment in prayerful reflection. When reading the scriptures aloud, you may choose to pronounce the Name as "Yahweh," or substitute such epithets as Holy One, Our God, the Most High, Ha-Shem, the I Am, or other names that speak to your heart and communicate your understanding of the Divine Mystery. Whatever you choose, however, choose with reflection and reverence.

❖ **To maintain a preferential option for those relegated to society's margins.**

The God of Scripture is one who stands for those who are most vulnerable and those who have been relegated to the margins of society. We are, too, called to stand for those who are at the margins of society. Our goal is to humanize individuals and declare God's preferential option for those on the margins of society. To that end, we strive to acknowledge the dignity of each individual by the simple expedient of how we address that person.

One way we do this in our translation is to prefer terms which emphasize social justice over moral rectitude. For example, the same Hebrew word can be translated "justice" and "righteousness"; "wickedness" can just as easily be translated "corruption." While traditional translations have preferred terms underscoring morality and virtue (or lack there of), we believe the original Hebrew concepts are more correctly translated by terms which talk about personal ethics, the quality of interpersonal relationships, and just (or unjust) social structures.

❖ **To stress an underlying mutuality and equality in human relationships.**

Another area of the translation work that proved somewhat problematic was how to handle what is often referred to as "power language." This is language that reflects power relations among human beings and between human beings and the divine. Such language has been used to perpetuate such injustices as sexism, classism, and ethnocentrism. Use of power language reflects the inequalities in society where individuals and groups dominate other individuals and groups.

The ancient world was filled with inequalities that are reflected in the text: there were kings and servants, masters and slaves. God is portrayed as a ruler very much like the despots of the ancient world.

Over the past few years, there has been a growing concern about the role of power language in the perpetuation of sexist and classist structures. People of conscience have begun to work with substitutes, many of which we have incorporated in our translation.

In our translation, we have attempted to eradicate power language that might be used to perpetuate forms of injustice such as sexism and racism, and to find ways of mitigating it in other circumstances. In our text, we have attempted to find "functional" substitutes for social roles—terms that describe what a person does, but don't define who the person is. For example, we have in most cases translated "kings" as "rulers" or "leaders." "Masters" and "servants" frequently become "employers" and "laborers."

Where we were describing historical conditions and events, we wanted to reflect these circumstances as they were—even with the inequalities built into the society. We have attempted to use language that describes the social roles and conditions then present, rather than prescribe the way things ought to be, but even here we may not have done this to the extent that would make everyone happy. Our intention is always to provide a text that is both faithful to the original *and* reflective of the values of justice and equality that we hold so dear. We humbly leave it to the reader to determine whether we have fulfilled in our intent.

Conclusion

Translating scripture into inclusive language is not an easy task, but it is a necessary one. In order for people today to hear the Liberating Word of Scripture, it is necessary that the words used in translation themselves be liberated from the shackles of sexism. We cannot deny our sexist past, but we must not repeat that sexist past in either word or deed.

As noted scripture scholar Phyllis Trible put it, "Since no exegesis is exempt from the experience of the exegete, no interpretation is fixed once and for all. Clearly the hermeneutical task requires understanding the Bible as dynamic literature engaged with continued experience." Every translation is an interpretation and reflects the views and experiences of the translators. What we have presented here in *The Inclusive Hebrew Scriptures—The Prophets* is guided by our commitment to make them accessible to women and men today. Our dedication to produce quality texts is what impels us to study the texts carefully, and uncover the intention behind each passage so that we might faithfully render it. And our bond of solidarity with women and men struggling to build just churches and social structures has been our constant touchstone for this translation. If this book can help deepen faith, open eyes, or strengthen commitment to effect change, then we have more than attained our goal.

A Chronology of the Prophets

Below is a timeline of the prophetic era, showing the rulers and events that many of the prophecies concerned. Please note that the dates before about 800 B.C.E. are somewhat tenuous, with scholars disagreeing more vociferously the older the date.

Approx. Date	Significant Events	Israelite Rulers		Foreign Rulers and Powers	Prophets
		Early Prophets and Judges			
1394	Joshua dies				
1350-1200				Hittite Empire dominant	
1140	Deborah and Barak defeat Jabin of Hazor			Barak	Deborah
1191	Gideon defeats the Midianites			Gideon	
1049	Samson dies in the Philistine temple of Dagon			Samson	
1047	Israel repents under Samuel and the Philistines are defeated at the battle of Ebenezer				Samuel
		United Monarchy			
1043-922		Saul, David, Solomon			Samuel, Nathan
921	Division of Israel into northern (Israel/Samaria) and southern (Judah) realms				
		Divided Monarchy			
		Israel	Judah		
921		Jeroboam	Rehoboam		
850		Ahab			Elijah, Elisha
830				Uzziah	Joel?
780					Jonah
750-730	Syrian-Israelite League against Judah	Jeroboam II			Amos, Hosea

Date	Event	Kings of Judah	Foreign Rulers	Prophets
742-695	Assyrian Crisis	Jotham, Ahaz	Tiglath-Pileser III	Isaiah of Jerusalem (First Isaiah)
730-721		Hezekiah		Micah
721	**Destruction of Samaria/Israel**			
	Judah			
721-701		Hezekiah, Manasseh		Micah
701	Assyrian attack on Jerusalem	Hezekiah	Sennacherib	
663-612	Babylonian Crisis	Manasseh		Nahum
630-622	Deuteronomic Reform	Josiah		Zephaniah
622		Jehoiakim		
609	Death of Josiah	Jehoiachin		Jeremiah, to 580; Obadiah
605-600				Habbakuk
598 to 570	First Deportation	Zedekiah	Nebuchadnezzar	Ezekiel
587	**Destruction of Jerusalem/Judah**	Zedekiah	Nebuchadnezzar	
	Babylonian Exile			
586-570			Nebuchadnezzar	Ezekiel
540			Nabonidus, Cyrus	Second Isaiah
539	**Cyrus captures Babylon**			
	Restoration of Judah			
538	Edict of Cyrus; Sheshbazzar and First Return to Jerusalem		Cyrus	
520	Zerubbabel and Second Return to Jerusalem	Zerubbabel	Darius I	Haggai
515	Second Temple completed			
515-445				Zechariah, Third Isaiah
458	Return of Ezra: covenant renewal			Malachi
445	Return of Nehemiah: Jerusalem's walls rebuilt			

the earlier prophets

joshua

After moses the servant of yhwh
died, YHWH said to Joshua ben-Nun,* Moses' second in command:
² "Moses, my Servant, is dead. Now prepare to cross the Jordan—you and
all this People, the Children of Israel†—and go to the land I give to them.
³ As I promised Moses, I give you every place on which you set foot. ⁴ Your

---

* The book of *Joshua* is the first book of the Prophets, but it can also be seen as the sixth book of what
scholars call the Hexateuch (the Torah, or Five Books of Moses, form the Pentateuch, or "five scrolls";
Joshua continues the story of the formation of the people of Israel, and essentially completes the journey
from slavery to the Promised Land). The book most likely came together through the work of several
authors and editors. While talmudic tradition says that "Joshua wrote his own book," at no point in
Joshua does the author claim to be Joshua himself. There are references to events after the time of
Joshua, and many scholars believe that the composition of the book spans hundreds of years.
† The phrases "Children of Israel" and "People of Israel" appear throughout the book of *Joshua*. Its
significance should not be lost on the reader: there are many nations, but it is through the Covenant
with YHWH that Israel becomes a people, and its collective identity depends on its faithfulness to that
Covenant. When the people break the Covenant, they become like the nations. Much of the Prophets is
an account of how the Children of Israel became the nation of Israel—one nation among the others.

domain will run from the Negev in the south to Lebanon in the north, and from the Euphrates in the east—all the land of the Hittites—to the Mediterranean in the west. ⁵ No one will pose a serious challenge to you as long as you live. I will be with you as I was with Moses. I will not leave you. I will not abandon you.

⁶ "Be strong! Be courageous! You will lead this People to take possession of the land I swore to your ancestors that I would give them. ⁷ But you must be strong and very courageous, and put into full practice the entire Torah* that Moses, my Servant, gave you. Be careful not to deviate from it—neither to the right nor to the left—and you will have success everywhere you go. ⁸ Keep what is written in the Torah on your lips at all times. Recite it day and night, so that you will be sure to do all that it says. Only then will you be successful on your journey; only then will you act with wisdom. ⁹ So I charge you: be strong; be courageous! Don't be afraid or discouraged, for YHWH your God is with you wherever you go."

¹⁰ Then Joshua ordered the leaders of the people, ¹¹ "Go through the camp and give these orders to the people: 'Pack food and supplies. In three days you will cross the Jordan at this spot and take possession of the land that YHWH your God is giving you as your very own.'"

¹² Then Joshua told the Reubenites, the Gadites, and the half-tribe of Manasseh, ¹³ "Remember what Moses, the Servant of YHWH† instructed you: 'YHWH your God is giving you rest: you are granted this land as your own.' ¹⁴ Your spouses, your children, and your livestock will remain here in the land east of the Jordan that Moses gave you. But all your strongest warriors, in full battle array, must cross over ahead of your sisters and brothers to help them. ¹⁵ You will fight until YHWH gives rest to your sisters and brothers as well as to you, and they take possession of the land that YHWH your God is giving them. After this you may return to the land east of the Jordan, which Moses, the Servant of YHWH, gave you."

¹⁶ They answered Joshua, "We will do all you command us to do, and we will go wherever you send us. Just as we followed Moses in all things, so now we will follow you. ¹⁷ May YHWH your God be with you, as God was

---

* The Torah is more than simply a set of laws and commandments. It is a treaty or covenant with God, as well as God's instructions to the people about who they are (origins) and how they are to act (law and ethics).

† The phrase "Servant of YHWH," which appears throughout the book as a specific title of Moses, is understood in a several senses. It refers to Moses as the one to whom God talks directly, the one who has seen the face of God. It signifies Moses' role as God's "first in command"—the person to whom God give the instructions for the Children of Israel, and through whom the purpose of God is accomplished. The title also suggests that Moses possesses a more direct priesthood over and above the cultic, Aaronic–Levitic priesthood. Joshua, who is Moses' successor, will bear the same title and will speak directly to God, just as Moses did. The author of the book is careful to establish Joshua as the legitimate successor of Moses.

with Moses! [18] Whoever rebels against your orders or does not obey your commands will be put to death. Only be strong! Be courageous!"*

[2:1] Then Joshua ben-Nun secretly sent out two spies from Shittim, ordering them, "Go, scout out the territory—especially Jericho."

The two spies set off and went to Jericho. There they went to the house of an innkeeper† named Rahab, where they spent the night. [2] When the word reached the ruler of Jericho that two Israelites had arrived that evening to scout the territory, [3] the ruler sent this message to Rahab: "Bring me the two who are lodging in your house, for they are here to spy on my land."

[4] But Rahab took the two spies and hid them, then told the ruler, "Yes, they did come here, but I didn't know where they were from. [5] And after dark, knowing that the gate would be closed soon, they left. I don't know where they went. But you might catch up to them if you hurry." [6] As a matter of fact, Rahab had taken them up to the roof and hidden them under stalks of flax stored there.‡ [7] The ruler's posse set off in pursuit, down the road that crosses the Jordan at a ford. But as soon as the posse had left, they shut the gate.

[8] The spies had not yet bedded down when Rahab came to them on the roof. [9] She said to them, "I know that YHWH has given you this land. Dread of you has fallen on us, and the inhabitants of this land are terror-stricken. [10] We have heard how YHWH dried up the waters of the Sea of Reeds ahead of you when you came out of Egypt, and what you did to Sihon and Og, the Amorite rulers east of the Jordan whom you utterly destroyed.§ [11] We heard all this, and we lost heart. Because of you, no one has any courage left. For YHWH your God is truly God, in heaven above and the earth below. [12] Please, swear to me by YHWH that you will show mercy to my family, as I have shown mercy to you. Give me a sign of good faith: [13] promise me that you will spare the lives of my mother and father, sisters and brothers, and all who belong to them. Deliver us from death."

[14] The spies replied, "We pledge our lives for yours, as long as you do not disclose our mission. When YHWH gives us this land, we will be show true loyalty to you."

---

* Echoing YHWH's words to Joshua at the beginning of the book.
† While the Hebrew word, zonah, usually denotes a sex worker (deriving it from zanah, "to be a prostitute"), it would appear in this case that Rahab was a woman who simply kept a public house (derived from zun, "to feed"), and Joshua's spies felt they would be more inconspicuous there. At the same time, such inns frequently hosted illicit activities, so the traditional designation may not be completely off the mark.
‡ The flax on her roof and the scarlet cord (v. 17) make it likely that she manufactured and dyed linen, as did the Phoenicians. Jericho was an important trading crossroads between Phoenicia, Babylon, and Egypt, which is how Rahab knew the facts of the exodus, the passage through the Sea of Reeds, and the overthrow of Sihon and Og.

¹⁵ Then Rahab let them down through the window with a rope—she lived in a house built against the city's outer wall.* ¹⁶ Then she said to them, "Go up into the hills and hide out there from your pursuers. Stay there for three days until the posse returns. Then you can go on your way."

¹⁷ The two then warned her, "When we invade the country, we will keep this oath you made us swear, ¹⁸ provided you tie this scarlet cord to the window through which you let us down. You must also gather your mother and father, your sisters and brothers—your entire family—into this house. ¹⁹ Should any of them pass through the doors of the house and go into the street, their blood will be on their own heads, and we will be released from our oath; but if they stay in the house with you, and anyone lays a hand on them, their blood will be on our heads. ²⁰ If, however, if you betray us and tell anyone our plans, we will be free of the oath you made us take."

²¹ "Let it be as you say," Rahab replied, and sent the spies on their way. And she tied the scarlet cord to the window.

²² The spies took to the hills and hid there for three days until their pursuers turned back, having searched all along the road for them without success.

²³ Then the two left the hill country and crossed the Jordan, and reported back to Joshua ben-Nun. They related all that had happened to them. ²⁴ They assured Joshua, "YHWH has delivered the whole land into our hands, and all its inhabitants are terror-stricken before us."

3:1 Early in the morning, Joshua and all the Children of Israel set out from Shittim and went as far as the Jordan, where they set up camp before crossing over. ² At the end of three days, officers passed through the camp ³ issuing instructions to the people: "When you see the Ark of the Covenant of YHWH your God being carried by the Levitical priests, you are to break camp and follow it. ⁴ But be sure to stay some distance from it—about 3,000 feet—and don't approach it. It will show you the route to follow, for you have never traveled that way."

⁵ Joshua also commanded the people, "Purify yourselves, for tomorrow YHWH will do extraordinary things among you."

---

* Surrounding the city of Jericho was an impressive fortification, as recent archaeological discoveries attest. Jericho was built on a mound about forty feet above ground level; the wall that surrounded the city was made of mudbricks, and was six feet thick and about twenty-four feet high. Outside the wall, the mound sloped downward until it was about fifteen feet above ground level, at which point it became a vertical drop. This was then strengthened by a stone retaining wall about ten feet thick. On top of this retaining wall was built a second mudbrick wall, of approximately the same dimensions as the inner wall. Between the inner and the outer wall, and on top of the earthen rampart, were built domestic structures consistent with the description of Rahab's quarters.

⁶ Then Joshua said to the priests, "Take up the Ark of the Covenant and advance to the head of the people." So they took up the Ark of the Covenant and went before the people.

⁷ YHWH said to Joshua, "Today I will begin to make you great in the eyes of all Israel so that the Children of Israel will understand that I am with you just as I was with Moses. ⁸ Tell the priests who carry the Ark of the Covenant, 'When you come to the edge of the Jordan's waters, wade into the middle of the Jordan itself, and stand still.' "

⁹ Joshua said to the Children of Israel, "Gather close, and hear the words of YHWH your God!" ¹⁰ Joshua continued, "By this you will know that the living God is in your midst, who at your approach will completely dispossess the Canaanites, Hittites, Hivites, Perizzites, Girgashites, Amorites, and Jebusites: ¹¹ watch what happens when the Ark of the Covenant of the Sovereign of all the earth crosses the Jordan ahead of you.* ¹³ When the feet of the priests carrying the Ark of YHWH, Sovereign of all the earth, touch the water of the Jordan, it will stop flowing: the water flowing from upstream will be restrained as if it were dammed up."

¹⁴ So when the people set out from their encampment to cross the Jordan, the priests carrying the Ark of the Covenant led them to the water. ¹⁵ The Jordan was now at flood stage, for it was harvest time. But no sooner had the priests set their feet in the edge of the river ¹⁶ than the water upstream stopped flowing. It piled up for a great distance, as far away as Adam, the town next to Zarethan. The water flowing down to the Sea of Arabah—that is, the Salt Sea†—was completely cut off. And the people crossed over at the spot opposite Jericho. ¹⁷ The priests carrying the Ark of the Covenant of YHWH stood firm on dry land in the middle of the Jordan until the entire nation had crossed the river.

4:1 Once the entire nation had completed the crossing of the river, YHWH told Joshua, ² "Choose twelve people from the tribes of Israel, one from each tribe, ³ and instruct them as follows: 'Take twelve stones from the middle of the Jordan—from where the feet of the priests stood firm—and carry them across the river. Place them in the camp where you will spend the night.' "

⁴ Joshua summoned the twelve selected from the twelve tribes of the Children of Israel, one from each tribe. ⁵ Joshua said to them, "Go up to the Ark of YHWH your God, in the middle of the Jordan. Each of you is to lift up a stone and carry it on your shoulder, one for each tribe of the Children

---

* We have deleted verse 12; it is a scribal error, repeating in its entirety 4:2, where it more naturally belongs.
† In later periods, the Salt Sea came to be called the Dead Sea.

of Israel. ⁶ These stones are to stand as a memorial among you. When your children ask what these stones stand for, ⁷ tell them, 'The waters of the Jordan stopped flowing before the Ark of the Covenant of YHWH when it crossed the Jordan. These stones serve as a perpetual memorial to the Children of Israel.' "

⁸ The Children of Israel did as Joshua instructed: they took twelve stones from the middle of the Jordan, one for each tribe of the Children of Israel, as YHWH had commanded Joshua, and carried them over to the camp, where they set them them down. ⁹ Joshua then erected a monument from the twelve stones taken from the middle of the Jordan as the spot where the priests who carried the Ark of the Covenant had stood. Those stones remain there to this day.

¹⁰ The priests carrying the Ark remained in the middle of the Jordan until everything that YHWH had commanded Joshua to tell the people was accomplished. And the people crossed hurriedly, just as Moses had once commanded Joshua to do.* ¹¹ Once everyone had crossed the river, the Ark of YHWH and the priests advanced to the head of the people.

¹² The warriors of Reuben, Gad, and the half-tribe of Manasseh, in battle formation, marched in front of the Children of Israel, as Moses had charged them to do. ¹³ About forty thousand warriors in full battle array† crossed to the desert plains of Jericho in the presence of YHWH. ¹⁴ That day YHWH made Joshua great in the eyes of all Israel. The Children of Israel stood in awe of Joshua, just as they had stood in awe of Moses all the days of his life.

¹⁵ Then YHWH said to Joshua, ¹⁶ "Command the priests carrying the Ark of the Testimony to come up out of the Jordan."‡ ¹⁷ Joshua passed the word to the priests. ¹⁸ And when the priests carrying the Ark of the Covenant came up from the Jordan and stepped on dry land, the waters of the Jordan began to flow and it resumed its course, flowing over the entire river bed as before.

¹⁹ The people came up from the Jordan on the tenth day of the first month, and encamped in Gilgal, on the eastern border of Jericho. ²⁰ At Gilgal Joshua set up the twelve stones taken from the Jordan ²¹ and said to the Children of Israel, "In the future when your descendants ask their parents, 'What is the meaning of the stones?' ²² tell them, 'It was here that Israel crossed the Jordan on dry ground. ²³ YHWH your God dried up the waters of the Jordan in

---

* This makes explicit the parallel between Moses' leading the people across the Sea of Reeds and Joshua's leading the people across the Jordan.

† Essentially, they were shock troops.

‡ This is in direct contradiction to verse 11, which has the priests already out the Jordan and leading the people. Clearly we have two traditions here, artlessly merged by a later redactor. A similar conflict of literary traditions occurs between verses 9 and 20, where the story of the twelve monument stones is told in two different ways.

front of you until you crossed over, just as YHWH your God dried up the Sea of Reeds in front of us until we crossed over ²⁴ so that all peoples of the earth will realize that YHWH's hand is powerful, and so that you will stand in awe before YHWH your God forever.' "

5:1 When all the rulers of the Amorites to the west of the Jordan, and all the rulers of the Canaanites by the sea, heard how YHWH had dried up all waters of the Jordan in order for the Children of Israel to cross over, their strength vanished, and they lost all courage to fight the Children of Israel. ² At that time YHWH told Joshua, "Make flint knives, then go back and circumcise the Children of Israel once again." ³ So Joshua had flint knives made and all the Israelite men were circumcised at Gilbeath-haaraloth.* ⁴ Joshua did so because all the male able-bodied warriors had died in the wilderness on the journey out of Egypt. ⁵ Those who came out of Egypt had been circumcised, but not those born in the desert during their pilgrimage. ⁶ The Children of Israel roamed in the wilderness for forty years until the whole generation that departed from Egypt—that is, the warriors—had died out, because they did not listen to YHWH's voice. YHWH had sworn that none of them would see the land promised on oath to their ancestors, a land flowing with milk and honey.† ⁷ And so it was that their descendents, whom God raised up in their place, were the ones Joshua circumcised, for they still had foreskins, not having been circumcised while in the desert.

⁸ Once the circumcision of the whole nation was completed, it remained encamped until everyone had recovered. ⁹ Then YHWH said to Joshua, "Today I rolled away from you the reproach of Egypt." And the place is called Gilgal to this day.‡

¹⁰ During their encampment at Gilgal, the Children of Israel offered the Passover sacrifice at sunset on the fourteenth day of the month on the plains of Jericho. ¹¹ On the day after the Passover they ate the produce of the land, unleavened cakes and roasted grain. On that same day, ¹² after the Passover on which they ate the unleavened cakes and roasted grain, the manna stopped falling for the Children of Israel. They ate the crops of Canaan from that year on.

---

* A play on words: the name means "hill of foreskins." Why the ritual of circumcision was allowed to lapse during their wilderness journeys is uncertain, but it was necessary to reinstitute the practice for at least two reasons: to make any uncircumcised Israelites eligible to take part in the upcoming Passover, and to have a fully covenanted people prepared to fight the wars and conquer the land.

† The phrase "flowing with milk and honey" has definite sexual connotations; in Hebrew, milk and honey are euphemisms for the male and female sexual fluids, respectively. The image, then, is of a paradisical land of physical joy.

‡ Gilgal literally means "circle," as a circle of stones, but the word is a close cognate of the word for "rolling." The "reproach of Egypt" refers to the shame of being uncircumcised like Egyptians.

¹³ When Joshua was nearing Jericho, he looked up and saw a warrior holding a drawn sword. Joshua approached the warrior and asked, "Are you with us, or with our enemies?"

The warrior replied, "Neither! I come to you as commander of the army of YHWH!"

Joshua fell face down on the ground and said, "What command do you give to your Servant?"

¹⁴ The commander of YHWH's army told Joshua, "Remove your sandals, for where you stand is holy ground."* And Joshua obeyed.

⁶ᐟ¹ Jericho† had barricaded itself against the Children of Israel. No one could come in or go out. ² YHWH said to Joshua, "Listen! Into your hands I have delivered Jericho, its ruler, and its brave warriors. ³ Have all your troops encircle the city and march around it once a day for six days. ⁴ Seven priests carrying seven shofars made from rams' horns are to go before the Ark. On the seventh day you are to march around the city seven times, with the priests blowing their shofars. ⁵ When the last long blast is sounded on the rams' horns—when you hear those shofars sound—the entire army must make a deafening noise by shouting. The city wall will come crashing down to the ground, and the people will advance with everyone surging forward straight ahead."

⁶ Joshua ben-Nun summoned the priests and commanded them, "Take up the Ark of the Covenant and have seven priests with seven shofars go before it." ⁷ Then Joshua ordered the people, "Move out! March around the city! Let the armed guard take a place in front of the Ark of the Covenant."

⁸ Once Joshua gave this command to the people, the seven priests who carried the seven shofars of rams' horns before YHWH moved ahead of the Ark and blew the shofars. The Ark of the Covenant of YHWH followed them. ⁹ The armed guard marched in front of the priests who blew the trumpets, and the rearguard took their place behind the Ark, the trumpets sounding as they all marched.

¹⁰ Joshua commanded the people, "Do not shout yet. March in complete silence until the day I command you to shout. When I do, raise a mighty war cry."

¹¹ So Joshua ordered the Ark of YHWH to be carried around the city once. Then the marchers returned to camp for the night.

¹² Joshua woke everyone early the next morning, and the priests took up the Ark of the Covenant. ¹³ The seven priests carrying the seven rams' horns marched in front of the Ark of YHWH, and blew their shofars. The armed

---

* An echo of Moses' calling at the burning bush.
† The name comes from a root meaning either "the moon" (*yare'ach*), for its serving as the seat of Canaanite moon worship, or "broad," for its location in a plain bounded by the Jordan.

guard marched ahead of them and the rearguard followed the Ark, the horns sounding as they marched. ¹⁴ That second day, they marched once around the city, then returned to camp, and so on for six days.

¹⁵ On the seventh day they rose at daybreak and marched around the city as before, only on this day they marched around the city seven times instead of once. ¹⁶ The seventh time around, as the priests blew their shofars, Joshua commanded the people, "Now, shout! YHWH has given you the city! ¹⁷ The city—and everything in it—is devoted to YHWH for destruction.* Only Rahab the innkeeper and everyone in her house are to be spared, for she hid our two spies. ¹⁸ But beware that sacred curse! Be careful that you do not in your greed take something that has been devoted to destruction. If you do, you will bring the camp of Israel under the same curse and bring disaster down upon us. ¹⁹ All the silver and gold, all the bronze and iron are consecrated to YHWH. They are to go to YHWH's treasury."

²⁰ Then the shofars blew, and as soon as the people heard the sound of the shofars, they raised a tremendous war cry and the walls came crashing to the ground. The people rushed into the city, everyone surging straight ahead, and captured it.† ²¹ They placed everything in the city under the sacred ban, putting every living thing to the sword—the women and the men, the young and the old, and the cattle, the sheep, and the donkeys.

²² Joshua told the two spies who scouted the land, "Go to the innkeeper's house and bring her out, and everyone in her family as well, in keeping with the oath you made to her." ²³ They brought out Rahab, her mother and father, her sisters and brothers, and all her relatives, and put them in a secure location outside the camp of Israel.

²⁴ The city and everything in it was burned to the ground, except for the silver, the gold, and the copper and iron vessels, which were put in the treasury of God's house. ²⁵ Only Rahab the innkeeper, her household, and all her family were spared by Joshua, for she had hidden the two spies Joshua sent out to scout the land. She and her family settled in Israel and their descendants reside there to this day.

---

* This is the concept of *cherem*, the utter and irrevocable devotion of things, individuals, or entire peoples over to God, generally translated as "sacred ban" or "divine curse." It usually entailed the annihilation of whatever (or whoever) was thus devoted—theoretically to be consumed by God's glory, though in the later conquests of Canaan, towns, cities, and entire peoples were declared *cherem* and completely wiped out. It was also sometimes used to contain disease, such as a plague. From the same root comes the word "harem" (literally, "sacred or forbidden," emphasizing the separateness and inviolability of the women in such an arrangement.

† In one part of the city of Jericho, archeologists found large piles of bricks at the base of both the inner and outer walls, indicating a sudden collapse of the fortifications. The collapsed bricks formed a ramp by which an invader might easily enter the city.

²⁶ Then Joshua pronounced a solemn oath: "The curse of YHWH be upon anyone who attempts to rebuild Jericho: may their firstborn be laid down as its foundation and their youngest set up as its gates!"

²⁷ So YHWH was with Joshua, and Joshua's fame spread throughout the land.

⁷:¹ In an act of treachery, the Children of Israel violated the sacred ban: Achan ben-Carmi ben-Zerah, from the tribe of Judah, plundered some of the devoted items. And YHWH's anger smoldered against the Children of Israel.

² Joshua sent agents from Jericho with orders to go up to Ai—"the ruin"—near Beth-Aven, east of Bethel, telling them, "Go scout out the region." So the agents went up and spied on Ai.

³ When they returned they reported to Joshua, "Don't send all the troops up there. Two or three thousand warriors would be sufficient to defeat Ai. Don't weary all of our soldiers there, since the population is so small."

⁴ So about three thousand soldiers were chosen from among the people, and they marched on Ai. But they fled in retreat before the warriors of Ai. ⁵ The people of Ai killed struck down thirty-six of them, and chased the rest from the city gate as far as the stone quarries, cutting them down along the descent. The people's courage melted like water.

⁶ Joshua tore his clothes and fell face down on the ground before the Ark of YHWH, and remained there until evening, along with all the elders of Israel, throwing dust on their heads.

⁷ Joshua cried, "Ah! Sovereign YHWH, why did you insist on bringing this People across the Jordan? Was it to place us under the power of the Amorites? To destroy us? If only we had been content to remain on the eastern shore of the Jordan! ⁸ Forgive me, God, but how else can I say it, now that Israel has made such a cowardly retreat from its enemy? ⁹ Once the Canaanites and all the other inhabitants of the land hear about this, they will surround us and wipe our name off the face of the earth. Then what will you do for the honor of your great Name?"

¹⁰ YHWH answered Joshua, "Get up! Why do you grovel with your face to the ground? ¹¹ Israel has sinned. The people have violated the covenant by which I bound them. They took some of the devoted things—they stole, then they lied about it! They've even hidden the items inside their own tents. ¹² This is why the Children of Israel are unable to stand up to their enemies. They can only retreat from the face of their enemies, for they are now under the curse. And I will not remain with you unless you remove from your midst whoever brought you under the curse.

---

* Most likely through the casting of lots.

¹³ "Stand up! Consecrate the people! Command them, 'Consecrate yourselves for tomorrow. For thus says YHWH, the God of Israel—Something that was devoted to destruction is in your midst. You will not be able stand up to your enemies until you have removed it. ¹⁴ In the morning, you will be called forth by tribe. The tribe that YHWH designates* will come forward family by family. The family that YHWH designates will come forward household by household. And the household that YHWH designates will come forward person by person. ¹⁵ All who are caught with the devoted item must be burned, along with all that belongs to them.* Whoever has violated the covenant of God has disgraced Israel!' "

¹⁶ Early the next morning Joshua called Israel forth tribe by tribe, and the tribe of Judah was designated. ¹⁷ Then Joshua called forth the families of Judah, and the family of Zerah was designated. Then Joshua called forward the family of Zerah by households, and Zabdi's was designated. ¹⁸ Finally Joshua called forward the household of Zabdi person by person, and Achan ben-Carmi ben-Zabdi ben-Zerah of the tribe of Judah was designated.

¹⁹ Joshua said to Achan, "My child, give glory to YHWH, the God of Israel, and praise God by telling me what you did. Do not hide anything from me."

²⁰ Achan answered Joshua, "Yes, I have sinned against YHWH, the God of Israel. It happened like this: ²¹ I found among the spoils a fine Shinar cloak, two hundred shekels of silver, and a wedge of gold weighing fifty shekels.† I got greedy and stole them. They are buried under my tent, with the silver at the bottom."

²² Joshua selected messengers who ran to the tent, and there it was, hidden in the tent, with the silver at the bottom. ²³ They took the things from the tent, brought them to Joshua and all the Children of Israel, and spread them out before YHWH.

²⁴ Then Joshua took Achan ben-Zerah, the silver, the fine cloak, and the bar of gold, as well as Achan's daughters and sons, oxen, donkeys, sheep, tent, and all his possessions, and led them off to the Valley of Achor. All of Israel followed.

²⁵ Joshua said, "Why have you brought this calamity upon us? YHWH will bring calamity upon you today!" And all Israel stoned Achan to death. They set his family on fire and stoned them. ²⁶ Then they buried his body under a great mound of stones, which remains to this day, and YHWH's anger was assuaged. It is for this reason that the place is called the Valley of Achor—"the Valley of Calamity."

---

* The person who took the item that was under the *cherem* becomes one with it, and is similarly "devoted" to God by being completely destroyed.
† The silver weighed five pounds, and the gold nearly two pounds—a considerable sum.

⁸⁻¹ YHWH then said to Joshua, "Do not be afraid or discouraged. Take all your warriors and march on Ai. Listen! I will deliver the ruler of Ai into your hands, along with the citizenry, the city, and all their territory. ² Treat Ai and its ruler just as you treated Jericho and its ruler, with one exception: you may keep the livestock and other spoil for yourselves. Take up a concealed position behind the city."

³ Joshua prepared the all the warriors for the attack on Ai. He chose thirty thousand great warriors. They left after dark ⁴ with these orders: "Listen! Lie in ambush behind the city. Don't place yourself too far away from the city, though; and be ready. ⁵ I will approach the city with the rest of the people who are with me, and when the warriors come out to engage us, as they did the last time, we will retreat from them. ⁶ We will let them pursue us until they are some distance from the city. We will lure them into thinking we are fleeing from them the way we did before. ⁷ Then you are to rush in from your position and capture the city. For YHWH your God will deliver it into your hands. ⁸ Once the city has been occupied, set it on fire, in obedience to YHWH's word. See to it! You have my orders!"

⁹ Once Joshua sent them on their way, they set up their ambush between Bethel and Ai, to the west of Ai. Joshua stayed behind with the rest of the people.

¹⁰ Early the next morning Joshua mustered the troops. Together with the elders of Israel, he marched ahead of the troops toward Ai. ¹¹ Once all the troops had made the ascent and approached the city, they set up their camp to the north of Ai, with a valley between them and the city. ¹² Then Joshua took five thousand warriors and set up an ambush between Bethel and Ai, to the west of the city. ¹³ Everything was in readiness, with the main body north of the city, and the ambush west of the city. Joshua waited overnight with the troops in the valley.

¹⁴ Very early the next morning, when the ruler of Ai saw that Joshua was there, the militia of the town banded together and rushed out to do battle with Israel on the slope facing the Arabah.* They were unaware that an ambush had been set up for them west of the city.

¹⁵ Joshua and all Israel, feigning defeat, fled down the road toward the desert. ¹⁶ With all of the warriors of Ai drawn in pursuit of Joshua, they were maneuvered away from the city; ¹⁷ no one was left in Ai or Bethel who had not gone after Israel. The city was left open and unprotected.

¹⁸ Then YHWH said to Joshua, "Take the spear that is in your hand and point it toward Ai. I am delivering the city into your hands." Joshua pointed the

---

* A desert valley running south from the Sea of Galilee.

spear toward Ai [19] and at his signal, the troops in ambush rose up and rushed into the city. They captured it and immediately set it on fire.

[20] When the warriors of Ai looked back, they saw smoke from their city rising to the sky. They were trapped and powerless to escape in any direction, for the troops who they thought had fled down the desert road now turned back upon their pursuers. [21] When Joshua and all Israel saw that the city had been captured and was burning, they turned back and attacked the warriors of Ai.

[22] The warriors who had come out to do battle with all Israel were now surrounded on every side. They ran in every direction and all Israel cut them down until there wasn't a single survivor. [23] Only the ruler of Ai was taken alive and brought to Joshua.

[24] When all Israel had finished slaughtering the warriors of Ai—those who had chased them through the plains and into the valley—they marched into Ai and put rest of the city's inhabitants to the sword. [25] Twelve thousand women and men, the entire population of Ai, were killed that day.

[26] Joshua continued to point his spear until all the inhabitants of Ai had been annihilated under the sacred ban. [27] The Children of Israel plundered the livestock and the took the spoils the city had to offer, just as God had commanded Joshua.

[28] Joshua ordered Ai to be burned and made an eternal ruin,* and it remains so to this day. [29] Then Joshua ordered the ruler of Ai to be hung from a tree until evening.† At sunset Joshua ordered the body removed from the tree and thrown down at the city gates. A large pile of stones was placed over it, which remains to this day.

[30] Then Joshua built on Mount Ebal an altar to YHWH, the God of Israel, [31] as Moses the Servant of YHWH had commanded the Children of Israel. The altar was built according to instructions written in the Torah of Moses: an altar of uncut stones, upon which no iron tool was used. There the priests sacrificed burnt offerings to YHWH and made peace offerings.

[32] There, in the presence of the Children of Israel, Joshua inscribed upon the stones a copy of the Covenant written by Moses. [33] And all Israel, including their elders, officers, and judges, as well as the resident aliens and natives of the land,‡ stood on either side of the Ark facing the Levitical priests who carried the Ark of the Covenant of YHWH. Half of them stood facing Mount

---

* Ai, "The Ruin," was made into "an eternal ruin," a permanently uninhabited mound.
† According to the Torah, anyone executed was to be hung from a tree but buried the same day. One thus executed was deemed cursed by God, and to leave the body exposed overnight was to invite the curse of God on the land and its people since, as scholar Jeffrey Tigay has noted, even a criminal is created in the image of God.
‡ The resident aliens were Hebrews who had remained in Canaan, while the natives of the land were Canaanites loyal to Israel.

Gerizim, with the other half facing Mount Ebal, to fulfill the command of Moses, the Servant of God, for the first blessing of the Children of Israel.

³⁴ Then Joshua read aloud all the stipulations of the Law—the blessing and the curse—exactly as it is written in Book of the Torah. ³⁵ There was not a word Moses commanded that Joshua did not read to the whole assembly of the Children of Israel, to parents and children alike, as well as to the foreigners dwelling among them.

ରେ ରେ ରେ

⁹·¹ When news of these events reached all the rulers west of the Jordan—in the hill country, along the coast of the Great Sea up to Lebanon, and the rulers of the Hittites, Amorites, Canannites, Perizzites, Hivites, and Jebusites— ² they all banded together to make war against Joshua and Israel.

³ When the inhabitants of Gibeon heard what Joshua had done to Jericho and Ai, ⁴ they concocted a scheme: they loaded their donkeys with worn-out sacks and old wineskins needing repair, ⁵ they wore patched sandals on the feet, their clothing was old, and there were only stale crusts of bread in their provisions bag.*

⁶ They came to Joshua in the camp at Gilgal and said, "We come from a faraway land. Please make a peace treaty with us."

⁷ But the Children of Israel replied to these Hivites, "Maybe you're really from the territory we now inhabit. How, then, can we make a treaty with you?"

⁸ But they answered Joshua, "We are now your vassals."

And Joshua asked, "Who are you? Where did you come from?"

⁹ They answered, "We, your vassals, have come came from a faraway land. We come because of the legend of YHWH your God. We heard reports of all the things your God did in Egypt, ¹⁰ and what your God did to the two Amorite rulers beyond the Jordan—to Sihon, ruler of Heshbon, and Og, ruler of Bashan, who lived in Ashtaroth. ¹¹ Our elders everyone living in our land instructed us, 'Take provisions for your journey. Go meet with Israel and say, "We are your vassals. Please make a treaty with us." '

¹² "Look at our bread. It was fresh when we packed it back home on the day we left to come here. See how dry and crumbly it is! ¹³ Look at our wineskins. They were new when we filled them before leaving. Look how

---

* In other words, even though Gibeon, one of the three main cities inhabited by the Hivite people, was only a short distance away, the delegation from Gibeon disguised themselves as travelers from a faraway land. They pretended they were not Hivites because Israel was under orders to exterminate them, and they sought a treaty of peace with Israel, albeit through trickery.

they have cracked! See how our clothes and sandals are worn out from our very long journey."

¹⁴ The people took the word of their visitors because of the provisions. But they did not seek YHWH for a decision. ¹⁵ Joshua gave the Gibeonites hospitality and entered into a treaty with them, guaranteeing their lives. And the leaders of the assembly ratified it with an oath.

¹⁶ But three days after making the treaty with the Gibeonites, Israel learned that they were really people from a nearby territory. ¹⁷ So the Children of Israel broke camp and marched on the Hivite towns of Gibeon, Chephirah, Beeroth, and Kiriath-Jearim. ¹⁸ But the Children of Israel did not attack them for the leaders of the assembly had sworn an oath to them by YHWH the God of Israel.

The entire assembly grumbled about their leaders.

¹⁹ The leaders answered, "We gave our oath by YHWH, the God of Israel. We can't touch them now. ²⁰ We must spare their lives. We don't want to incur God's anger by violating an oath we swore to them. ²¹ But because we have spared their lives, they must now cut wood and carry water for the assembly." The assembly agreed to this arrangement.

²² Joshua summoned the Gibeonites and asked of them, "Why did you play this trick on us? You told us you lived a long distance from us, but you actually live in this territory! ²³ You are now under a curse: You will always be our vassals and will never cease to cut wood and carry water in the house of God!"

²⁴ They answered, "It was made very clear to us, your vassals, that YHWH your God had commanded Moses, the Servant of God, to give you the entire land and to wipe out all its inhabitants. We feared for our lives. That is why we did what we did. ²⁵ Now we are in your hands. Whatever you think is right and just to do to us—do it."

²⁶ That is how Joshua delivered them from the hands of the Children of Israel so that they were not killed. ²⁷ That day, Joshua made them woodcutters and water carriers for the assembly and for the altar of YHWH. And to this day their descendants continue to do so, at the location God would select for the altar.*

10:1 Adoni-zedek, the ruler of Jerusalem,† learned that Joshua captured Ai, putting it under the sacred ban and treating its ruler the same way that the ruler of Jericho had been treated. Then he learned that the citizens of Gibeon had entered into a treaty with Israel and now dwelt among them as

---

* That is, Shiloh, though the Children of Israel haven't reached there at this point in the story.
† In this era, Jerusalem was an Amorite stronghold.

vassals. ² Upon hearing these things, Jerusalem was terrified. Gibeon was as powerful as any royal city, it was larger than Ai, and all its warriors were brave. ³ So the ruler of Jerusalem sent this message to the rulers of neighboring city-states: "To Hoham of Hebron, Piram of Jarmuth, Japhia of Lachish, and Debir of Eglon: ⁴ Come up and help me defeat Gibeon, for it has made a treaty with Joshua and the Children of Israel."

⁵ So the five rulers of the Amorite city-states—Jerusalem, Hebron, Jarmuth, Lachish, and Eglon—joined forces and prepared for the attack on Gibeon.

⁶ The Gibeonites sent word to Joshua, now camping at Gilgal: "Don't abandon your subjects! Come quickly and save us! Help us, for the Amorite rulers of the hill country have joined forces against us."

⁷ As Joshua, with the whole army, went up from Gilgal, ⁸ YHWH said to him, "Don't fear the enemy. I am giving them into your hands. Not even one of them will be able stand up to you."

⁹ Joshua took them by surprise, marching all night from Gilgal. ¹⁰ YHWH threw them into a panic at Israel's advance, and Joshua's troops had a complete victory over them at Gibeon. They pursued them down the pass of Beth-Horon and kept up the assault all the way to Azekah and Makkedah.

¹¹ While they were on the road down from Beth-Horon to Azekah, as they retreated before the Children of Israel, YHWH hurled large hailstones down on them from the sky. More of them died from the hail than were killed by the swords of the Children of Israel.

¹² The day YHWH delivered the Amorites over to Israel, Joshua commanded in the presence of Israel:

"Sun, stand still over Gibeon!
    Moon, stand still over the valley of Aijalon!"
And the sun stood still,
    and the moon stopped in its tracks,
    until the nation had taken vengeance
    on all its enemies.

—as it is recorded in *The Book of Yashar.** The sun stopped in the middle of the sky and delayed setting for nearly an entire day. ¹⁴ Never has there been a day like it before or since, a day when YHWH listened to the voice of a human being—for YHWH fought for Israel that day.

Then Joshua and all Israel returned to camp at Gilgal.

¹⁶ In the meantime the five rulers ran and hid in a cave at Makkedah, ¹⁷ Joshua was told, "The five rulers are hiding in a cave at Makkedah." ¹⁸ Joshua

---

* *The Book of Yashar*, or *Upright One*, was probably a collection of war songs.

ordered, "Place some large stones over the mouth of the cave and set up a sentinel there. ¹⁹ But don't stop with that. Pursue the retreating army! Attack them from the rear and don't let them reach their cities, for YHWH your God is putting them into your hands."

²⁰ After Joshua and the Children of Israel completely vanquished them, with the exception of a few stragglers who escaped into their fortified cities, ²¹ the whole army returned safely to Joshua, who was camped at Makkedah. No one dared slander the Children of Israel.

²² Joshua said, "Open the mouth of the cave and bring the five rulers to me."

²³ They did so, removing from the cave the five rulers—from Jerusalem, Hebron, Jarmuth, Lachish, and Eglon—and bringing them to Joshua. ²⁴ Once this took place, Joshua summoned all the warriors of Israel, ordering their commanders, "Come forward! Place your feet on the necks of these five rulers." The commanders came forward and placed their feet on the necks of the five rulers. ²⁵ Joshua said to them, "Do not fear them! Do not loose heart! Be strong and courageous! This is what YHWH will do to all your enemies whom you fight."

²⁶ Joshua delivered a fatal blow to each ruler. Afterward, the bodies were hung on five trees and left there until evening.

²⁷ At sunset Joshua ordered the bodies of the five rulers to be lowered from the trees and thrown into the cave where they had sought refuge. Large stones were placed on the mouth of the cave. They are there to this day.

²⁸ On that same day, Joshua took the city of Maqqedah. Its ruler and all its inhabitants were placed under the sacred ban and put to the sword; no one survived. And Joshua did to the ruler of Maqqedah what he had done to the ruler of Jericho.

²⁹ Then Joshua and the Children of Israel moved on from Maqqedah to Libnah and attacked it. ³⁰ YHWH delivered the city and its inhabitants into the hands of Israel. Everyone in the city was put to the sword. There were no survivors. And Joshua did to the ruler of Libnah what he had done to the ruler of Jericho.

³¹ Then Joshua and all Israel moved on from Libnah to Lachish and took up positions for attack. ³² On the second day, YHWH delivered the city into their hands. Everyone in the city was put to the sword, just as had been done at Libnah. ³³ In the meantime, Horam, the ruler of Gezer, came to the aid of Lachish with an army, but Joshua captured them and put them to the sword as well. There were no survivors.

³⁴ Then Joshua and the Children of Israel moved from Lachish to Eglon. After taking up positions against it, they attacked. ³⁵ They captured it

that same day and put all its inhabitants to the sword, just as they did to Lachish.

³⁶ Then Joshua and all Israel went up from Eglon to Hebron to attack it. ³⁷ They captured the city and put it to the sword: its ruler, its villages, and its inhabitants. As in Eglon, they left no survivors. Joshua placed the city and everyone in it under the sacred ban.

³⁸ Then Joshua and all Israel turned back to attack Debir. ³⁸ They captured the city, its ruler and its villages, and put all of its inhabitant to the sword. Everyone was included. It was totally destroyed. There were no survivors. The Children of Israel did to Debir and its ruler what they had done to Hebron, and to Libnah and its ruler.

⁴⁰ In time, Joshua conquered the entire land, including the hill country, the Negev, the western foothills and the mountain slopes, as well as their rulers. Joshua left no survivors, totally annihilating anything that breathed, just as YHWH, the God of Israel, had commanded. ⁴¹ Joshua prevailed from Qadesh-Barnea to Gaza, and from the whole land of Goshen to Gibeon. ⁴² Joshua conquered in one campaign all the rulers and their lands for YHWH, their God, fought for Israel. ⁴³ Then Joshua and all Israel returned to the camp at Gilgal.

11:1 When Jabin, the ruler of Hazor,* heard about these events, he sent word of it to Jobah the ruler of Madon, to the rulers of Shimron and Acshaph, ² to the rulers in the north, in the hill country, in the Arabah south of Kinnereth, in the Shephelah, and in Naphath-dor to the west. ³ He also sent word to the Canaanites both in the east and in the west, to the Amorites, Hittites, Perizzites, and Jebusites in the hill country, and to the Hivites below Hermon in the region of Mizpah.

⁴ They sent out all their troops and many horses and chariots. It was a huge assembly, as numerous as the sands of the seashore. ⁵ All the rulers joined forces and pitched their camp at the Waters of Merom to fight against Israel.

⁶ Then YHWH said to Joshua, "Do not fear them! By this time tomorrow, I will deliver all of them to Israel, dead. You are to hamstring their horses and set fire to their chariots."

⁷ So Joshua and his warriors launched a surprise attack by the Waters of Merom. ⁸ YHWH delivered the foe into the hand of the Israel, who defeated them and pursued them all the way to Greater Sidon, to Misrephoth-maim, and eastward to the valley of Mizpeh, striking all of them down. There

---

* Hazor was the dominant urban center in the north—"the New York City of Canaan," as scholar Yigael Yadin puts it.

were no survivors. ⁹ Joshua did to them what YHWH had commanded: he hamstrung their horses and set fire to their chariots

¹⁰ Joshua then reversed course and captured Hazor, which had served as the capital of all the neighboring city-states, and put its ruler to the sword. ¹¹ Everything there was put to the sword, placed under the sacred ban. The people of Israel spared nothing that breathed. Then they burned Hazor.

¹² Joshua captured these cities and their rulers and placed them under the ban, destroying them all, as Moses, the Servant of YHWH, had commanded. ¹³ But with the exception of Hazor, Israel did not burn those cities still standing on their mounds. Joshua saw to it that Hazor alone was destroyed by fire. ¹⁴ Those other cities the Children of Israel plundered, pillaging all their livestock. They cut down the people until none survived—not a soul remained alive.

¹⁵ Moses, the Servant of YHWH, had received these commands from God. Moses gave these commands to Joshua, and Joshua carried them out. Not one of the commands that YHWH had given Moses was left undone.

¹⁶ So Joshua conquered all of the land: the hill country of Judah, all of the Negev, all of Goshen, the western foothills, the Arabah, and the mountains and foothills of Israel. ¹⁷ Joshua's conquest extended from Mount Halaq, which overlooks the region of Seir, to Baal-Gad in the Valley of Lebanon below Mount Hermon. Joshua captured all their rulers and put them to the sword.

¹⁸ Joshua waged war against all the rulers. ¹⁹ No town, with the exception of the Hivites dwelling in Gibeon, made a treaty with the Children of Israel; all were taken in battle. ²⁰ For YHWH had hardened their hearts for war against Israel so that they would be put under the sacred ban, which ensured that no mercy would be shown them and they would be completely annihilated, just as YHWH had commanded Moses.

²¹ During this period Joshua wiped out the Anakim* from the hill country—from Hebron, Debir, Anab, all the hill country of Judah, and all the hill country of Israel. Joshua placed them and their cities under the sacred ban. ²² No Anakim remained in the land of the Children of Israel, though some survived in Gaza, Gath, and Ashdod.

²³ Thus Joshua controlled the whole country. Then, just as YHWH had commanded Moses, Joshua divided up the land as an eternal inheritance to the Children of Israel, and gave an allotment to each tribe. And all the land was at rest from war.

12:1 These are the rulers of the countryside east of the Jordan whom the Children of Israel defeated and whose land they occupied, from the Arnon

---

* The Anakim were mythic giants; the Canaanites, who were tall of stature, were reputed to have descended from them.

River to Mount Hermon, including all the eastern side of the Arabah:

² Sihon, ruler of the Amorites. Sihon lived in Heshbon and ruled from Aroer, which sits on the bank of the Arnon River and includes the river itself and all the land to the north through half of Gilead to the Jabbok River, the Ammonite frontier. ³ Sihon also ruled over the eastern Arabah from the Sea of Kinnereth* to the Arabah Sea, that is, the Salt Sea, as well as the route to Beth-Jeshimoth and the region south of the slopes of Pisgah.

⁴ Og, ruler of Bashan, who was one of the last of the Rephaim.† Og lived in Ashtaroth and Edrei, ⁵ and reigned over Mount Hermon, Salecah, all of Bashan to the border of the Geshurites and Maacahites, and half of Gilead to the border of Sihon, ruler of Heshbon.

⁶ These two were defeated by Moses, YHWH's Servant, and the Children of Israel. And Moses, YHWH's Servant, gave the land to the tribes of Reuben and Gad and the half-tribe of Manasseh as their inheritance.

⁷ These are the rulers of the city-states that Joshua and the Children of Israel conquered on the west side of the Jordan, from Baal-Gad in the valley of Lebanon to Mount Halak, which lies near Seir. Joshua divided their land, allotting it to the tribes of Israel— ⁸ the hill country, the lowlands, the Arabah, the slopes, the desert, the Negev, and the territories of the Hittites, Amorites, Canaanites, Perizzites, Hivites, and Jebusites. ⁹ They were:

the ruler of Jericho	1
the ruler of Ai, near Bethel	1
¹⁰ the ruler of Jerusalem	1
the ruler of Hebron	1
¹¹ the ruler of Jarmuth	1
the ruler of Lachish	1
¹² the ruler of Eglon	1
the ruler of Gezer	1
¹³ the ruler of Debir	1
the ruler of Geder	1
¹⁴ the ruler of Hormah	1
the ruler of Arad	1
¹⁵ the ruler of Libnah	1
the ruler of Adullam	1
¹⁶ the ruler of Makkedah	1
the ruler of Bethel	1
¹⁷ the ruler of Tappuah	1

---

* The Sea of Kinnereth became known as the Sea of Galilee.
† Also reputed to be extremely tall.

the ruler of Hepher	1
¹⁸ the ruler of Aphek	1
the ruler of Lasharon	1
¹⁹ the ruler of Madon	1
the ruler of Hazor	1
²⁰ the ruler of Shimron Meron	1
the ruler of Acshaph	1
²¹ the ruler of Taanach	1
the ruler of Megiddo	1
²² the ruler of Kedesh	1
the ruler of Joqneam in Carmel	1
²³ the ruler of Dor in Naphath-dor	1
the ruler of Goiim in Gilgal	1
²⁴ the ruler of Tirzah	1
Total number of rulers:	31

13:1–21:45

*W*hen Joshua was old, well advanced in years, YHWH said to him, "Even though you have grown old, there is still much land to conquer. ² This is the remaining land: All the territory of the Philistines and all the territory of the Geshurites, which is considered Canaanite territory; ³ the area from the River Shihor east of Egypt to the territory of Ekron on the north, which belongs to the five regents of the Philistines in Gaza, Ashdod, Ashkelon, Gath, and Ekron; the Avvite territory in the south; ⁴ all the land of the Canaanites, from Mearah of the Sidonians to Aphek, as far as the Amorite frontier; ⁵ the territory of the Gebalites; and all of Lebanon to the east, from Baal-gad at the foot of Mount Hermon to Labo Hamath.

⁶ "The inhabitants of the mountain regions from Lebanon to Misrephoth-maim, including all the Sidonians, I myself will drive out before the Children of Israel.

⁷ "Meanwhile, divide up this territory among the other nine Israelite tribes and the other half of Manasseh. You are to give them the land from the Jordan to the Great Sea* in the west; the Great Sea will be the border."

⁸ The other half-tribe of Manassah and the tribes of Reuben and Gad had already received their inheritance—they were given the territory east of the

Jordan, as Moses the Servant of YHWH had ordained. [9] It extends from Aroer on the bank of the River Arnon, includes the river itself, and runs through the plateau of Medeba as far as Dibon; [10] it also encompasses all the cities of Sihon, the ruler of the Amorites who reigned in Heshbon, to the Ammonite border, [11] along with Gilead and the territory of the Geshurites and Maacahites. It also includs all of Mount Hermon and all of Bashan as far as Salcah— [12] that is, all of the former realm in Bashan of Og, a descendant of the Rephaim who lived in Ashtaroth and Edrei. Even though Moses conquered these territories, [13] the Children of Israel did not dispossess the Geshurites and the Maacathites. So Geshur and Maacath survive among the Children of Israel to this day.

[14] The tribe of Levi received no inheritance, for the offerings made by fire to YHWH the God of Israel are its inheritance, as God had promised.

[15] This is what Moses alloted to the tribe of Reuben for their families: [16] The southern boundary that extends from Aroer on the bank of the Arnon River; the plateau halfway along the river, including the plateau as far as Medeba; [17] Heshbon and all its cities on the plateau—Dibon, Bamoth-baal, Beth-baal-meon, [18] Jahaz, Kedemoth, Mephaath, [19] Kiriathaim, Sibmah, Zerath-Shahar on the valley hillside, [20] Beth-Peor, the slopes of Pisgah, and Beth-Jeshimoth— [21] all the towns on the plateau, and the entire realm of Sihon, ruler of the Amorites, who ruled at Heshbon. Moses defeated and put Sihon to the sword, together with the Midianite chiefs who settled the land: Evi, Redem, Zur, Hur, and Ruba. [22] Along with those put to the sword, the Children of Israel also killed the soothsayer Balaam ben-Beor. [23] The boundary of the tribe of Reuben will be the shores of the Jordan and its adjacent land. These cities, along with their surrounding villages, are the inheritance of the families of the tribe of Reuben.

[24] Moses alloted the following territory to the tribe of Gad for its families: [25] all the territory of Jazer, all the towns of Gilead, and half the Ammonite country as far as Aroer, near Rabbah. [26] The territory extends from Heshbon as far as Ramath-mizpeh and Betonim, and from Mahanaim as far as the boundary of Lo-debar. [27] It includes the valley cities of Beth-Haram, Beth-Nimrah, Succoth, and Zaphon—the rest of the realm of Sihon, ruler of Heshbon. Its boundary is the shore of the Jordan to the southeastern tip of the Sea of Kinnereth. [28] These cities and their outlying villages are the inheritance of the families of the tribe of Gad.

[29] Moses allotted the following territory to the half-tribe of Manasseh: [30] Their inheritance included Mahanaim, all of Bashan, the entire realm of Og, ruler of Bashan, and all the villages of Jair—sixty cities in Bashan. [31] Half

---

* The Mediterranean.

of Gilead, along with Ashtaroth and Edrei—at one time royal cities of Og in Bashan—went to the descendants of Makir ben-Manasseh, for half the Gileadite clans descended from Makir. [32] This is the allotment Moses gave to the tribes as their inheritance when Moses was in the plains of Moab, beyond the Jordan east of Jericho.

[33] But Moses gave no inheritance to the tribe of Levi, for YHWH, the God of Israel, is its promised inheritance.

[14.1] Eleazer the priest, Joshua ben-Nun, and the leaders of the families of the tribes of Israel allotted these lands to the Children of Israel as their inheritance in the land of Canaan: [2] They apportioned the land to the remaining nine-and-a-half tribes by lot, according to YHWH's instructions to Moses. [3] Moses had granted the two-and-a-half tribes their holdings east of the Jordan, but had not given the Levites an inheritance among the other tribes. [4] The descendants of Joseph made up two tribes—Manasseh and Ephraim. The tribe of Levi received no land except cities to live in, and pastures for its herds and livestock. [5] So the Children of Israel assigned the land just as YHWH had commanded Moses.

[6] Members of the tribe of Judah approached Joshua at Gilgal, and Caleb ben-Jephunneh, the Kennizzite, said to him, "Remember what YHWH said about you and me to Moses, the Servant of YHWH, at Kadesh Barnea? [7] I was forty years old then when Moses, the Servant of YHWH, sent me from Kadesh Barnea to scout out the land. And I brought back to Moses an honest report. [8] The other spies who accompanied me gave the people a discouraging report, but I was completely loyal to YHWH, my God. [9] On that occasion Moses made this oath to me: 'The land you explored will become your inheritance and that of your descendants forever, because you loyally carried out the will of YHWH my God.' [10] Now then, YHWH preserved me as promised while Israel journeyed through the wilderness for the forty-five years since the oath was made. Here I am at eighty-five, [11] still as healthy today as I was the day Moses sent me spying. I am as vigorous now as I was then, whether for battle or for work. [12] Therefore, I am asking for this hill country, which YHWH promised me long ago as you yourself heard. Yes, the Anakim are there with large fortified cities, but if YHWH is with me I will be able to dispel them, as YHWH promised."

[13] Joshua blessed Caleb ben-Jephunneh, and gave him Hebron as his allotment. [14] To this day Hebron is the heritage of Caleb ben-Jephunneh the Kenizzite, for Caleb wholeheartedly followed YHWH, the God of Israel. [15] Previously Hebron was called the city of Arba, named for Arba, the greatest of the Anakim.

And the land was at rest from war.

15:1 The inheritance of Judah, family by family, extended down into the territory of Edom, to the wilderness of Zin in the Negev. 2 The southern boundary began at the tip of the Salt Sea, from the bay that projects southward. 3 It went south below Scorpion Pass, continued over to Zin, and ascended to the south of Kadesh-Barnea. Then it ran across to Hezron, up to Addar, and from there looped around Karka. 4 It crossed to Azmon and then joined the Wadi of Egypt,* ending at the sea. This was the southern boundary of Judah.

5 The eastern boundary was the Salt Sea up to the mouth of the Jordan.

6 The northern boundary went up from the bay where the Jordan meets the sea, up to Beth-Hoglah, and ran north of Beth-Arabah, up to the stone of Bohan ben-Reuben. 7 From there it climbed to Debir, north of the Valley of Achor, in the direction of Gilgal that faces the Pass of Adummim, on the south side of the river, and from there crossed to the waters of En-shemesh and came out at En-rogel. 8 It then ran up the Hinnom Valley to the southern flank of the Jebusites (that is, Jerusalem). From there it ascended to the top of the hill west of the Hinnom Valley at the northern end of the Valley of Rephaim. 9 From that hilltop the boundary ran toward the spring of the waters of Nephtoah, and came out at the cities of Mount Ephron and continued to Baalah (that is, Kiriath-Jearim). 10 From Baalah the boundary curved to the west toward Mount Seir (that is, Chesalon), then down to Beth-Shemesh and on to Timnah. 11 It then ran north to the slope of Ekron, continued through Shikkeron and across to Mount Baalah and came to Jabneel. The boundary ended at the sea. 12 The western boundary is the coastline of the sea.

In accord with the command YHWH gave Joshua, Caleb ben-Jephunneh received a portion in Judah—the city of Arba, that is, Hebron. Arba was the forebear of the Anakim, 14 and Caleb drove the three Anakite clans out of Hebron—the Sheshai, Ahiman, and Talmai clans, all descendants of Anak. 15 From there Caleb marched against the inhabitants of Debir, formerly known as Kiriath-sepher. 16 Caleb let it be known that whoever attacked and captured the city would be allowed to marry his daughter Achsah. 17 Othniel ben-Kenaz, Caleb's nephew, won both the city and Achsah's hand in marriage.

18 On the day of the wedding ceremony, Achsah cajoled her father into giving her some land. Then, as she alighted from her donkey, Caleb asked her, "Is there anything I can do for you?"

19 She replied, "You can give me a little present. Since you assigned me land in the arid Negev, you could give me a source of water as well." So Caleb gave her the Upper and the Lower Springs.

---

* Not the Nile, but the Wadi el-Arish, a streambed (which becomes a brook in the rainy season) that likely formed the border between Egypt and Canaan.

²⁰ Following is the inheritance of the tribe of Judah, family by family.

²¹ The towns belonging to the tribe of Judah:
At the southernmost part of their territory, near the border of Edom, were Kazbeel, Eder, Jagur, ²² Kinah, Dimonah, Adadah, ²³ Kedesh, Hazor, Ithnan, ²⁴ Ziph, Telem, Bealoth, ²⁵ Hazor-Hadattah, Kerioth-Hezron (that is, ²⁶ Hazor-Amam), Shema, Moladah, ²⁷ Hazar-Gaddah, Heshmon, Beth-Pelet, ²⁸ Hazar-Shual, Beersheba, Biziothiah, ²⁹ Baalah, Iim, Ezem, ³⁰ Eltolad, Kesil, Hormah, Ziklag, Madmannah, Sansannah, ³² Lebaoth, Shilhim, Ain, and Rimmon—a total of twenty-nine cities and their surrounding villages.*

³³ In the western foothills were Eshtaol, Zorah, Ashnah, ³⁴ Zanoah, En-gannim, Tappuah, Enam, ³⁵ Jarmuth, Adullam, Socoh, Azekah, ³⁶ Shaaraim, Adithaim, Gederah (or Gederothaim)—a total of fourteen cities and their surrounding villages; ³⁷ Zenan, Hadashah, Migdal-gad, ³⁸ Dilean, Mizheh, Joktheel, ³⁹ Lachish, Bozkath, Eglon, ⁴⁰ Cabbon, Lahmam, Chilish, ⁴¹ Gederoth, Bethdagon, Naaham, and Makkedah—a total of sixteen cities and their surrounding villages; ⁴² Libnah, Ether, Ashan, ⁴³ Iphtah, Ashnah, Nezib, ⁴⁴ Keilah, Achzib, and Mareshah—a total of nine cities and their surrounding villages; ⁴⁵ Ekron, with its surrounding cities and villages; ⁴⁶ west of Ekron, all the cities near Ashdod and their surrounding villages; ⁴⁷ Ashdod, with its surrounding cities and villages; Gaza, with its surrounding cities and its surrounding villages; and as far west as the Wadi of Egypt and the coast of the Sea.

⁴⁸ In the hill country were Shamir, Jattir, Socoh, ⁴⁹ Dannah, Kiriath-Sannah (that is, Debir), ⁵⁰ Anab, Eshtemoh, Anim, ⁵¹ Goshen, Holon, and Giloh—eleven cities and their surrounding villages; ⁵² Arab, Dumah, Eshan, ⁵³ Janim, Beth-Tappuah, Aphekah, ⁵⁴ Humtah, Arba City (that is, Hebron). and Zior—a total of nine cities and their surrounding villages; ⁵⁵ Maon, Carmel, Ziph, Juttah, ⁵⁶ Jezreel, Jokdeam, Zanoah, ⁵⁷ Kain, Gibeah, and Timnah—a total of ten cities and their surrounding villages; ⁵⁸ Halhul, Beth-Zur, Gedor, ⁵⁹ Maarath, Beth-Anoth, and Eltekon—a total of six cities and their surrounding villages; and Kiriath-Baal (that is, Kiriath-Jearim) and Rabbah—a total of two cities and their surrounding villages.

⁶¹ In the wilderness were Beth-Arabah, Middin, Secacah, ⁶² Nibshan, Ir-maelach, and En Gedi—a total of six cities and their surrounding villages.
Judah could not dislodge the Jebusites residing in Jerusalem. To this day the Jebusites dwell there with the people of Judah.

16:1 The portion that fell by lot to the descendants of Joseph ran from the Jordan at Jericho—that is, from the waters of Jericho east of the wilder-

---

* There are thirty-five cities listed, not twenty-nine, which may be due to a scribal error or to the additions of a later editor; it is possible that this list includes the villages as well as the cities, though the other lists do not follow the same pattern.

ness—then up from Jericho into the hill country at Bethel. ² It ran from Bethel to Luz and crossed over to the territory of the Archites at Ataroth. ³ It then descended to the west to the territory of the Japhletites as far the border of Lower Beth-Horon and Gezer, ending at the sea. ⁴ This was the inheritance of the descendants of Joseph—Manasseh and Ephraim.

⁵ This is the inheritance of Ephraim, family by family:

The eastern border ran from Ataroth-addar up to Upper Beth-Horon. ⁶ It continued to the west to the Sea. From Michmethath on the north, the boundary curved easterly around Taanath-shiloh, and continued by it on the east side to Janoah. ⁷ From Janoah it descended from Ataroth and Naarah, skirting Jericho, it continued on to the Jordan. ⁸ From Tappuah the border ran west to the Wadi Kanah and ended at the sea. This was the portion of the families of Ephraim, ⁹ including all the cities and their surrounding villages that were set aside for Ephraim within the territory of Manasseh. ¹⁰ The people of Ephraim failed to drive out the Canaanites dwelling in Gezer; but while the Canaanites live among the people of Ephraim to this day, they now serve Ephraim as forced laborers.

17:1 This is the inheritance alloted to the tribe of Manasseh, Joseph's first-born: The descendants of Makir (Manasseh's firstborn and the father of Gilead), who were warriors, had already been alloted the land of Gilead, and the territory that had belonged to Bashan. ² Now allotments were made to the rest of the people of Manasseh: the families of Abiezer, Helek, Asriel, Shechem, Hepher, and Shemida—the other heirs of Manasseh ben-Joseph, family by family.

³ Zelophehad ben-Hepher ben-Gilead ben-Machir ben-Manasseh had no male heirs, only daughters. Their names were Mahlah, Noah, Hoglah, Milcah, and Tirzah. ⁴ They approached the priest Eleazer and Joshua ben-Nun, and said, "YHWH told Moses to grant us an inheritance among our relatives." So Joshua granted them an allotment along with their relatives, as YHWH had commanded. ⁵ Manasseh's share was ten tracts of land (not including Gilead and Bashan east of the Jordan), ⁶ since the daughters of the tribe of Manasseh received an inheritance along with the sons. The land of Gilead was assigned to the rest of Manasseh's descendants.

⁷ The territory of Manasseh reached from Asher to Michmethath east of Shechem. The border ran to the south toward those dwelling in En-Tappuah.

⁸ The district of Tappuah belonged to Manasseh, but Tappuah itself belonged to the tribe of Ephraim, which bordered Manasseh. ⁹ The border continued down to the Qanah Gorge. The cities south of the city belonged

to Ephraim as an enclave among the cities of Manasseh. The border of Manasseh lay north of the Gorge and ended at the Sea.

¹⁰ On the south side, the land belonged to Ephraim. On the north side, the land belonged to Manasseh. And their common boundary ended at the Sea. This territory bordered Asher on the north and Issachar on the east.

¹¹ Within the territories of Issachar and Asher, Manasseh was assigned Beth-Shean and its villages; Ibleam and its villages; and the peoples of Dor, Endor, Taanach, and Megiddo, together with their surrounding villages. These consisted of three regions. ¹² The tribe of Manasseh could not conquer these cities, however, for the Canaanites put up strong resistance. ¹³ As the Children of Israel grew stronger, they were able to put the Canaanites into forced servitude, but were never able to expel them.

¹⁴ These descendants of Joseph went to Joshua and asked, "Why have you assigned us only one tribal allotment? There are so many of us because YHWH had blessed us greatly."

¹⁵ Joshua replied, "If there are so many of you, and if the hill country of Ephraim is too small for you, go up into the forest, in the hill country of the Perizzites and Rephaites, and clear the land."

¹⁶ The descendants of Joseph rejoined, "Even that hill country is too small for us. And the Canaanites living in the valley regions have iron-wheeled chariots, especially those in Beth-Shean and its surrounding villages, and those in the Valley of Jezreel."

¹⁷ So Joshua said to Ephraim and Manasseh—that is, the house of Joseph— "You are indeed a numerous people, and strong militarily. So you will have not only your tribal allotment, but the Perizzite and Rephaite hill country as well—though it is now covered in forest. Clear it and it will be yours to its farthest limits. Despite the Canaanites' strength and their iron-wheeled chariots, you will be able to drive them out."

¹⁸⁺¹ Once they had subdued the land, the whole community of the Children of Israel came together at Shiloh to set up the Tent of Meeting. ² Seven of the tribes had not yet received their allotments.

³ So Joshua said to the Children of Israel, "How long will you wait before you take possession of the land that YHWH, the God of your ancestors, gave you? ⁴ Choose three leaders from each tribe. I will send them out to survey the land and describe its suitability for occupation. They will report back to me, ⁵ and will divide the land into seven parts. Judah will retain its territory in the south, and the house of Joseph its territory in the north. ⁶ You will bring to me the written descriptions of the seven territories, and

I will cast lots for you here before YHWH our God.* ⁷ As for the Levites, they do not have a portion among you, for the priesthood of YHWH is their inheritance. As for Gad, Reuben, and the half-tribe of Manasseh, they have already received their portion east of the Jordan, which Moses, the Servant of God, gave them."

⁸ Once those selected to scout out the territory were ready, Joshua instructed them to survey the land, prepare a description of it, and return to him. Then Joshua would cast lots for them before YHWH their God in Shiloh. ⁹ So they left and went through the land and described seven territories, city by city, listing them on a scroll. Then they returned to Joshua at camp at Shiloh. ¹⁰ Joshua then cast lots for them in Shiloh in the presence of YHWH, and there apportioned the land for the Children of Israel into their allotted shares.

¹¹ The first lot fell to the families of the tribe of Benjamin. The territory allotted them lay between the territories of Judah and Joseph. ¹² Its northern boundary began at the Jordan, passed the northern slope of Jericho, and continued to the west into the hill country, until it reached the wilderness of Beth-Aven. ¹³ From there it crossed over to the southern slope of Luz (that is, Bethel), and proceeded down to Ataroth-addar, over the hill country south of Lower Beth-Horon. ¹⁴ For the western border, the boundary then extended to the south along the western side from the hill country opposite Beth-Horon until it reached Kiriath-Baal, that is, Kiriath-Jearim, a city of Judah. This was the boundary on the west side. ¹⁵ The southern boundary began at the outskirts of Kiriath-Jearim and ended at the spring of waters of Nephtoah. ¹⁶ It ran down to the edge of the hill near the Valley of Ben-hinnom, north of the Valley of Rephaim. It continued down the Hinnom Valley along the southern slope of the Jebusites to En-rogal. ¹⁷ Curving to the north, it went to En-Shemesh, continued to Gelilogh, which faces the Adummim Pass, and ran down to the stone of Bohan ben-Reuben. ¹⁸ It continued northerly to the slope of Beth-Arabah and down into the Arabah. ¹⁹ From there it continued across the northern slope of Beth-Hoglah and came out at the northern inlet of the Salt Sea, at the southern end of the Jordan. This is the southern boundary. ²⁰ The Jordan formed the eastern boundary. This, then, is the inheritance of the tribe of Benjamin and the description of its borders.

²¹ The cities of the tribe of Benjamin, family by family, are these: Jericho, Beth-Hoglah, Emeq-Keziz, ²² Beth-Arabah, Zemaraim, Bethel, ²³ Ha-Av-

---

* The casting of lots determined which tribe got which territory. Lot-casting, usually done by throwing specially marked stones, was an ancient method of determining the will of God. It was believed that the gods revealed themselves through apparently random things, because ultimately nothing is random and all things are dictated by fate or divine will.

vim, Parah, Ophrah, ²⁴ Kephar-Ammoni, Ophni, and Geba—twelve cities and their surrounding villages; ²⁵ and Gibeon, Ramah, Beeroth, ²⁶ Mizhap, Kephirah, Mozah, ²⁷ Rekem, Irpeel, Taralah, ²⁸ Zelah, Haeleph, the Jebusite city (that is, Jerusalem), Gibleah, and Kiriath—fourteen cities and their surrounding villages. This is an accounting of the inheritance of Benjamin, family by family.

¹⁹:¹ The second lot fell to the families of the tribe of Simeon. Their inheritance lay within the territory of Judah. ² It included Beersheba, Moladah, ³ Hazar-Shual, Balah, Ezem, ⁴ Eltolad, Bethul, Hormah, ⁵ Ziklag, Beth-Marcaboth, Hazar-Zusah, ⁶ Beth-Lebaoth, and Sharuhen—thirteen cities and their surrounding villages; ⁷ Ain, Rimmon, Ether, Ashan—four cities and their surrounding villages, ⁸ including all the villages surrounding the cities as far as Baalath-beer (that is, Ramath in the Negev). This is an accounting of the inheritance of the descendants of Simeon, family by family.

⁹ The inheritance of the tribe of Simeon was taken from the inheritance of Judah, because Judah's portion was too large. So the tribe of Simeon received its inheritance within the territory of Judah.

¹⁰ The third lot fell to the families of the tribe of Zebulun. The boundary of their inheritance extended as far as Sarid. ¹¹ Their boundary went west to Maralah, touching Dabbesheth and the wadi east of Jokneam, ¹² then turned east from Sarid toward the sunrise up to the border of Kisloth-Tabor, and continued on to Daberath and up to Japhia. ¹³ From there it went eastward to Gath-hepher and to Eth-Kazin, then on to Rimmon, where it turned towards Neah. ¹⁴ The northern boundary then turned toward Hannathon, and ended at the Valley of Iphtahel. ¹⁵ Included were Qattah, Nahalal, Shimron, Idalah, and Bethlehem—in all, twelve cities and their surrounding villages. ¹⁶ This is the inheritance of Zebulun, family by family.

¹⁷ The fourth lot fell to the families of the tribe of Issachar, family by family. ¹⁸ Their boundaries extended as far south as Jezreel, and included Kesulloth, Shunem, ¹⁹ Hapharaim, Shion, Anaharath, ²⁰ Daberion, Qishion, Ebez, ²¹ Rement, En-Gannim, En-Haddah, and Beth-Pazzez. ²² The boundaries met those of Tabor, Shahazumah, and Beth-Shemesh, ending at the Jordan. There were sixteen towns and their fortifications, along with the surrounding villages. ²³ This is the inheritance of Issachar, family by family, with their towns and villages.

²⁴ The fifth lot fell to the families of the tribe of Asher. ²⁵ Within their boundaries were the towns of Helqath, Hali, Beten, Achshaph, ²⁶ Allammelech, Amad, and Mishal. In the west, it reached Carmel and Shihor-Libnath. ²⁷ It then turned to the east in the direction of Beth-Dagon, and reached Zebulun and the Valley of Iphtahel. It then ran north to Beth-Emek and Neiel,

passing Cabul on the left. [28] It continued on to Abdon, Rehob, Hammon, and Kanah, as far as Greater Sidon. [29] The boundary then turned back toward Ramah and to the fortress city of Tyre. Finally, it ran back again to Hosah, and ended at the Sea. Other cities included Mahalab, Achzib, Ummah, [30] Acco, Aphek, and Rehob—twenty-two cities with their surrounding villages. [31] This is the inheritance of the tribe of Asher, family by family, with their towns and villages.

[32] The sixth lot fell to the descendants of Naphtali, family by family. The boundary of the clans of Naphtali [33] extended from Heleph and the Sacred Oak of Zaanannim, passing Adami-Nekeb and Jabneel to Lakkum and ending at the Jordan. [34] The boundary then turned west through Aznoth-tabor and from there on to Hukkok. It touched the border of Zebulun on the south, Asher on the west, and the Jordan on the east. [35] The fortified cities are Ziddim, Zer, Hammath, Rakkath, Chinnereth, [36] Adamah, Ramah, Hazor, [37] Kedesh, Edrei, En-hazor, [38] Yiron, Migdal-el, Horem, Beth-Anath, and Beth-Shemesh—in all, nineteen cities with their surrounding villages. [39] This is an accounting of the inheritance of Naphtali, family by family, with their towns and villages.

[40] The seventh lot fell to the decendants of the tribe of Dan. [41] Their inheritance was the territory of Zorah, Eshtaol, Ir-shemesh, [42] Shaalabbin, Aijlon, Ithlah, [43] Elon, Timnah, Ekron, [44] Eltekeh, Gibbethon, Baallath, [45] Jehud, Bene-berak, Gath-rimmon, [46] Me-jarkon, and Rakkon, at the border facing Joppa. [47] This is an accounting of the inheritance of the tribe of Dan, family by family, with their towns and villages. But the Danite territory slipped out of their grasp,* so they marched against Leshem, captured it and put its inhabitants to the sword, moved in, and settled the place. And they renamed it Dan after their ancestor. [48] This is an accounting of the inheritance of the descendants of Dan, family by family, with their towns and villages.

[49] When the last of the tribes finished dividing the land, and each received its portion, the Children of Israel gave Joshua ben-Nun an inheritance among them, [50] as YHWH their God commanded. They gave Joshua the city he requested—Timnath-serah in the hill country of Ephraim. And Joshua rebuilt the city and settled there.

[51] These are the inheritances assigned by lot to the tribes of Israel by Eleazar the priest, Joshua ben-Nun, and the heads of the tribal families. They cast the lots in Shiloh in the presence of YHWH their God, at the entrance to the Tent of Meeting.

---

* The Hebrew could also indicate that they had not yet conquered the territory.

²⁰:¹ Then YHWH told Joshua, ² "Say this to the Children of Israel: 'Designate which will be your cities of refuge, as I instructed you about through Moses, ³ so that someone who kills another accidentally and unintentionally may flee to them for protection from a blood-avenger.* ⁴ Those who seek sanctuary in one of these cities are to stand at the entrance to the city gate and plead their case before the elders of the city. Then the elders are to admit them and provide them a place to live there. ⁵ Should the blood-avenger pursue them, the elders of the city are not to surrender the accused, for they killed unintentionally and not out of prior enmity. ⁶ Those who seek asylum are to remain in the city until a fair trial can be held in front of the whole assembly—and until the death of whoever is the high priest at the time. Then the accused may return to their home city.' "†

⁷ The cities designated were Kedesh in Galilee, in mountain region of Nephtali; Shechem, in the hill-country of Ephraim; and Kiriath-arba, that is, Hebron, in the hill-country of Judah. ⁸ On the other side of the Jordan, east of Jericho, they designated these cities: Bezer on the plateau, for the tribe of Reuben; Ramoth in Gilead, for the tribe of Gad; and Golan in Bashan, for the tribe of Manasseh.

⁹ These cities were selected for all the Children of Israel and the foreigners living among them, so that whoever killed another accidentally could seek refuge from a blood-avenger in these designated cities and not be killed before standing trial in front of the assembly.

²¹:¹ The chieftains of the families of Levi approached Eleazar the priest, Joshua ben-Nun, and the leaders of families of the Children of Israel. ² They approached them at Shiloh in Canaan and said, "YHWH commanded Moses to provide us with cities to live in, including pastures for our livestock." ³ So, the Children of Israel gave the Levites the following cities and pastures out of their original inheritance.

⁴ The first lot was cast among the Levites went to the Qohathite families. Those Levites, descendants of Aaron, were allotted thirteen cities from among the tribes of Judah, Simeon, and Benjamin. ⁵ The rest of the descendants of Qohath were allotted, family by family, ten cities from

---

* Because Israelite society had no police force to investigate crimes, it was the responsibility of the family member closest to the victim—the "blood-avenger"—to investigate the homicide and exact justice. The cities of refuge provided protection from family members whose grief and anger might be so clouding their judgment as to keep them from taking into account whether the death was premeditated or accidental; they also prevented the clan feuds that would otherwise result when such accidents happened.

† In effect, a trial was held, and if it was determined that the killing was indeed accidental, the individual returned to the city of refuge and stayed there until the death of the high priest. Several rabbinical commentators have viewed this process as a general pardon or clemency granted upon the death of the high priest and the appointment of a new high priest, since they were in charge of the cities of refuge.

the tribes of Ephraim, Dan, and half of Manasseh. ⁶ The descendants of Gershon were allotted thirteen cities from the families of the tribes of Issachar, Asher, Naphtali, and the half-tribe of Manasseh that lived in Bashan. ⁷ The descendants of Merar were allotted, family by family, twelve cities from the tribes of Reuben, Gad, and Zebulun. ⁸ So the Children of Israel allotted the Levites these cities and pastures by lot, as YHWH had commanded Moses.

⁹ The Children of Israel allotted the following cities out of the tribes of Judah and Simeon, ¹⁰ and assigned them to the descendants of Aaron, members of the Qohathite family of the Levites, since the first lot fell to them. ¹¹ First, they gave them the city of Arba the father of Anak, that is, Hebron, along with its surrounding pastures in the hill country of Judah. ¹² The elders had already ceded the fields and villages surrounding the city to Caleb ben-Jephunneh. ¹³ So to the descendants of Aaron the priest they ceded Hebron, the city of refuge for those accused of murder; Libnah; ¹⁴ Jattir, Eshtemoa, ¹⁵ Holon, Debir, ¹⁶ Ain, Juttah, and Beth-Shemesh; along with their surrounding pasture lands—nine cities from these two tribes.

¹⁷ From the tribe of Benjamin the descendants of Aaron received the four cities of Gibeon, Geba, ¹⁸ Anathoth, and Almon, all with their surrounding pasture lands. ¹⁹ The cities and surrounding pasture lands given the priestly descendants of Aaron numbered thirteen.

²⁰ The rest of the Qohathite families among the Levites were ceded towns from the tribe of Ephraim, four cities: ²¹ Sechem, a city of refuge, located in the mountain region of Ephraim; Gezer; ²² Kibzaim; and Beth-Horon; all with their surrounding pasture lands. ²³ From the tribe of Dan they were ceded Eltekeh, Gibbethon, ²⁴ Aijalon, and Gibbethon, together with their surrounding pasture lands—four cities. ²⁵ And from the half-tribe of Manaseh they were ceded Taanach and Garth Rimmon, together with their surrounding pasture lands—two cities. ²⁶ All these cities with their surrounding pasture lands were ceded to the rest of the Qohathite families. There were ten cities in all.

²⁷ The family of Gershon of the Levites was ceded two cities: Golan, a city of refuge in Bashan, and Beth-Astharoth, both with their surrounding pasture lands. ²⁸ From the tribe of Issachar, they were ceded the four cities of Kishion, Daberath, ²⁹ Jarmuth, and Engannim, all with their surrounding pasture lands. ³⁰ From the tribe of Asher, they were ceded the four cities of Mishal, Abdon, ³¹ Helkath, and Rehob, all with their surrounding pasture lands. ³² And from the tribe of Naphtali, three cities were ceded: Kedesh, a city of refuge in Galilee, Hammath, and Rakkath, all with their surrounding pasture lands. ³³ These thirteen cities along with their surrounding pasture land belonged to the family of Gershon.

³⁴ The family of Merari, the remaining group of Levites, were ceded four cities from the tribe of Zebulun: Joqneam, Kartah, ³⁵ Rimmon, and Nahalal, all with their surrounding pasture lands. ³⁶ East of the Jordan at Jericho, from the tribe of Reuben, they were ceded four cities: Bezer, a city of refuge, Jahaz, ³⁷ Qedemoth, and Mephaath, all with their surrounding pasture lands. ³⁸ And from the tribe of Gad they were the ceded the four cities of Ramoth, a city of refuge in Gilead, Mahanaim, ³⁹ Heshbon, and Jezer, all with their surrounding pasture lands. ⁴⁰ The cities ceded to the Merari family, the remaining group of Levites, were twelve in all.

⁴¹ The cities given to the Levites within the territory of the Children of Israel numbered forty-eight in all. ⁴² Each of these cities was surrounded by its own pasture lands, as was the case with all the cities in Israel.

⁴³ In fulfillment of the oath sworn to their ancestors, YHWH gave Israel all the land. And the people of Israel took possession of it and settled down. ⁴⁴ In fulfillment of the promise to their ancestors, YHWH gave them peace and security in every way. None of their enemies had withstood them; YHWH had put all their enemies in their power. ⁴⁵ Not a single word of the promise that YHWH made to them was unfilfilled; every one came to pass.

*T*hen Joshua called together the tribes of Reuben and Gad and the half tribe of Manasseh ² and said to them. "You have faithfully carried out all the commands that Moses, the Servant of God, gave you. And you faithfully carried all the commands I gave you. ³ For a very long time now you, up to this very day, you have not deserted your sisters and brothers; you have faithfully carried out the mission that YHWH gave you. ⁴ Now that God has given them the promised security, return to your homes, to your lands that Moses, the Servant of God, assigned to you on the far side of the Jordan. ⁵ But you must thoroughly keep the commandments and the Torah that Moses, the Servant of God, gave you: To love YHWH your God, walk in God's way and keep God's commandments, and serve God with your whole heart and soul."*

---

* The Jordan was, and continues to be, a major geographical division in the land. The two-and-a-half tribes whose holdings were on the eastern side of the Jordan, in the land of Gilead (now called Transjordan), were effectively cut off from the ritual worship of the rest of Israel—at Shiloh in that era, and later in Jerusalem—on the western side of the river in the land of Canaan, and so were given the admonishment to adhere to the worship of YHWH even while so far away.

⁶ Then Joshua blessed them and sent them on their way to their own homes.

⁷ To half the tribe of Manasseh, Moses had assigned land in Bashan, but to the other half-tribe, Joshua assigned land on the west side of the Jordan with the rest of the Israelites. ⁸ Joshua dismissed them with this blessing: "You are returning to your homes with great wealth—much livestock, silver and gold, bronze and iron, and a large quantity of clothing. Share the spoil from your enemies with the rest of your tribe."

⁹ So the tribes of Reuben and Gad and the half-tribe of Manasseh left the Children of Israel at Shiloh in Canaan to return to their holdings in Gilead, which belonged to them according to the command of YHWH through Moses.

¹⁰ Once they arrived at Geliloth† near the Jordan in Canaan, the tribes of Reuben and Gad and the half-tribe of Manasseh built an enormous altar on that spot.

¹¹ When the Children of Israel learned of the building of the altar on the border of Canaan at Geliloth by the Jordan, they sent round a proclamation: "Hear this! The tribe of Reuben, the tribe of Gad, and the half-tribe of Manasseh have built an altar opposite the land of Canaan, near the territories of the Jordan, close to the territories of the Children of Israel!"

¹² When the rest of the Children of Israel heard this, the entire assembly of the Children of Israel met at Shiloh to wage war against them.

¹³ At the same time the Children of Israel sent Phinehas ben-Eleazer the priest to Gilead to the tribes of Reuben, Gad, and the half-tribe of Manasseh. ¹⁴ Accompaning Phinehas were ten tribal leaders with military experience, one from each tribe.

¹⁵ When they came to the three tribes in the land of Gilead, they declared, ¹⁶ "We speak in the name of the entire assembly of YHWH. How dare you break faith with the God of Israel this way! Is this your way of breaking away from YHWH—building your own altar in defiance of God? ¹⁷ Recall the sin of Peor and the plague that struck our people! To this very day we haven't purified ourselves from that sin. Must you now add to it? ¹⁸ Your rebellion against YHWH today will certainly raise God's wrath against the whole community of Israel tomorrow!

¹⁹ "Now, if you have raised this altar because you believe that the land you received is unclean, come over to the land of YHWH's own possession, where YHWH's tabernacle stands, and share the land with us. But you must not rebel against YHWH or involve us in your rebellion by building your

---

* This may be the same as the town of Gilgal; or it may be not a place name, but rather a stone circle left behind by the previous inhabitants of the land.

own altar in addition to the altar of YHWH our God. ²⁰ Call to mind when Achan ben-Zerah violated the curse, and the entire assembly suffered for it. Didn't Achan die for his crime?"

²¹ The tribes of Reuben, Dan, and the half-tribe of Manasseh replied to the delegation sent from the families of Israel, ²² "El! God! YHWH! El! God! YHWH!* Let God make known and Israel learn: If it is by rebellion or by disobedience against YHWH that we have built this altar, may God strike us down.† ²³ If we have built this altar in order to turn away from YHWH and to offer burnt offerings and grain offerings, or to sacrifice fellowship offerings on it, let YHWH call us to account for it!

²⁴ "We did this out of our concern that, in times to come, your children should say to our children, 'What is the bond between you and the God of Israel? ²⁵ YHWH made the Jordan a boundary between us and you. You of the tribe of Reuben and you of the tribe of Gad have no share in YHWH,' that your children would prevent our children from worshipping YHWH.

²⁶ "It is because of this that we said, 'Let us, on our own initiative, build an altar—not for burnt offerings and sacrifices, ²⁷ but as a testimony between us and you, and between our descendants in generations to come, that we are free to worship YHWH and come into God's presence with our burnt offerings, sacrifices, and fellowship offerings. Then in the future your children cannot say to our children, 'You have no share in YHWH.' ²⁸ Our thought was that even if in the future they should say this to our descendants, we will point to this replica of the altar of YHWH that we constructed, not for burnt offerings or for sacrifices, but as a testimony between you and us. ²⁹ We have no intention of defying YHWH or turning away from God by building an altar for burnt offerings, grain offerings, and sacrifices to compete with the altar of YHWH our God, which stands before God's Tent of Meeting."

³⁰ When Phinehas the priest and the ten tribal chieftains heard what the tribe of Reuben, the tribe of Gad, and the half-tribe of Manasseh had to say, they were satisfied. ³¹ Phinehas ben-Eleazar the priest said to them, "Now we know that YHWH dwells in our midst, because you did not act treacherously against YHWH but have kept the Children of Israel free from God's wrath."

³² Phinehas ben-Eleazar the priest and the tribal chieftains returned from the tribes of Reuben and Gad in the land of Gilead to the Children of Israel

---

† El, "god," is the singular form of elohim, "gods" or "God." El was another name for the Canaanite god Ba'al, but it was also a frequent construction in Hebrew names for God, such as El Elyon, "God Most High." Hebrew rarely uses the verb "to be" explicitly, and otherwise leaves the hearer to understand it from the context. This phrase El Elohim YHWH could mean "El is God is YHWH," indicating that there is no god but God, and that God can be worshipped anywhere and by any means; or it may mean "God of all gods is YHWH," affirming faith in YHWH as the supreme deity.
† Literally, "do not save us."

in the land of Canaan, and reported all this to them. ³³ Their report was satisfactory to the Children of Israel, who then blessed God and gave up the idea of going to war against them and ravaging the territories of Reuben and Gad. ³⁴ The tribes of Reuben and the tribe of Gad named the altar "Witness," short for "A witness between us that YHWH is God."

ᘉ   ᘉ   ᘉ

²³⁻¹ When Joshua was very old, a long time after God gave the Children of Israel security from all their enemies surrounding them, ² Joshua summoned all of Israel—the elders, leaders, judges, and officers—and said, "I am old and advanced in years. ³ You have seen everything that YHWH your God did for you against your these nations. It was YHWH your God alone who fought for you. ⁴ Remember that I allotted to you as an inheritance, tribe by tribe, the land of all the nations I conquered and of the nations I destroyed, from the Jordan and the Great Sea. ⁵ YHWH your God alone drove them out as you advanced. It was YHWH who dispossessed them to make room for you, and you took the land, that YHWH your God promised you.

⁶ "So be strong! Be courageous!* Put into full practice all that is written in the book of the Law of Moses. Be careful not to deviate from it—neither to the left nor to the right. ⁷ Do not mingle with the nations that still live among you. Never invoke their gods, swear by them, serve them, or worship them. ⁸ You must cling to YHWH your God, as you have done up to this day.

⁹ "God drove out great and powerful nations before you. And to this day, not one of them poses a serious threat. ¹⁰ Each one of you tramples over an entire village battalion, for YHWH your God is the one who fights for you, as God promised you.

¹¹ "For your own sake, therefore, take great care to love YHWH your God. ¹² For if you ever abandon God and attach yourselves to the remnants of the nations that still live among you—if you intermarry with them and have relations with them, and they with you— ¹³ then you can be sure that YHWH your God will no longer drive out these peoples on your behalf. Rather, they will become snares and traps for you. They will be whips on your backs and thorns in your eyes, until the day you perish from this good land that YHWH your God entrusted to you.

¹³ "Now, as you can plainly see, I am going the way of all flesh. All of you know in your hearts and in the depths of your soul that not one of the promises that YHWH your God made to you has failed. Every promise made to you has been fulfilled, without a single exception. ¹⁵ But just as all the

---

* Echoing once again YHWH's words to Joshua at the beginning of the book.

good promises of YHWH your God have come true, so too can God bring upon you everything evil until you have been wiped off this good land that YHWH your God gave you. ¹⁶ If you deviate from the covenant that YHWH your God enjoined upon you and go off to serve other gods and worship them, then YHWH's anger will be roused against you, and you will quickly disappear from the good land you received."

²⁴:¹ Joshua gathered together all the tribes of Israel at Shechem, and called a summit of the elders, leaders, judges, and officials of Israel. Once they presented themselves before God, ² Joshua said to the whole assembly, "This is the word of YHWH, the God of Israel:

" 'Long ago your ancestors, including Terah, the father of Abraham and Nahor, lived beyond the Euphrates and worshiped other gods. ³ But I took your ancestors Sarah and Abraham from the land beyond the Euphrates and led them through the entire region of Canaan. I made Sarah and Abraham's descendants numerous: there was Isaac, ⁴ and to Rebecca and Isaac I gave Jacob and Esau. To Esau I assigned the hill country of Seir, while Jacob and his family went down to Egypt.

⁵ " 'Later I sent Moses and Aaron, where I struck the Egyptians with plagues—you know well what I did to them— ⁶ and after that I liberated you from Egypt. By the time your ancestors reached the Sea of Reeds, the Egyptians were in hot pursuit with their chariots and cavalry. ⁷ When your ancestors cried out for my help, I put darkness between them and the Egyptians and made the sea engulf them. You saw with your own eyes what I did to the Egyptians.

" 'You dwelt in the wilderness for a long time, ⁸ and then I brought you into the land of the Amorites living on east side of the Jordan. They greeted you with hostility, but I delivered them into your power. And you took possession of their land. ⁹ Balak, the ruler of Moabben-Zippor, waged war against Israel. Balak sent for Balaam ben-Beor to curse you, ¹⁰ but I refused to listen to Balaam. On the contrary, Balaam was forced to bless you, and I saved you from his power. ¹¹ Once you crossed the Jordan and came to Jericho, the citizens of Jericho went to war against you, as did the Amorites, Perizzites, Canaanites, Hittites, Girgashites, Hivites, and Jebusites. And I delivered them all into your power. ¹² I sent hornets ahead of you, which drove the two rulers of the Amorites out of your way. And it was this—not your sword and bow—that destroyed the Amorites. ¹³ I gave you land that you had not tilled, and cities you had not built, and you have settled in them. You now take the fruit of vineyards and olive groves that you did not plant.' "

¹⁴ Joshua then said, "I now call upon you to revere and serve YHWH completely and sincerely. Cast off the gods that your ancestors worshiped

beyond the Euphrates and in Egypt, and worship YHWH alone. ¹⁵ If you do not want to worship YHWH, then make the decision today whom you will worship, even if it is the gods of your ancestors beyond the Euphrates or the gods of the Amorites in whose country you live. As for me and my household, we will worship YHWH."

¹⁶ Then the people responded, "Far be it from us to abandon YHWH to worship other gods. ¹⁷ It was YHWH our God who brought us and our ancestors up and out of the land of slavery. YHWH performed those great signs before our eyes. YHWH protected us on the entire journey and among all the peoples whose lands we passed through. ¹⁸ YHWH drove out before us the Amorites and all the people dwelling in the land. We too will serve YHWH, who is our God."

¹⁹ Joshua said to the people, "You will not be able to serve YHWH. This is a God most holy, a jealous God, a God who doesn't forgive your transgressions and your sins. ²⁰ If you desert YHWH and serve foreign gods, after all God has done for you, you will bring disasters—fatal ones—upon yourselves."

²¹ But the people protested, "No! We will serve YHWH!"

²² Then Joshua said, "You are your own witnesses that you are chosing to serve YHWH."

"Yes, we are witnesses," they replied.

²³ "Now then," said Joshua, "throw away the alien gods among you and turn your hearts to YHWH, the God of Isreal."

²⁴ Then the assembly said to Joshua, "We will serve and obey YHWH our God!"

²⁵ On that day Joshua ratified the covenant with the people and drew up statutes and ordinances for them at Shechem, ²⁶ which were recorded in the book of God's law. Then Joshua took a large stone and set it up there under the oak tree close by the sanctuary of YHWH. ²⁷ Joshua said to the assembly, "See this stone? It will be a witness against us. For it heard all the words that YHWH spoke to us. If you renounce your God, it will be a witness against you." ²⁸ The Joshua dismissed the people, each to their own holdings.

²⁹ After this, Joshua ben-Nun, the Servant of YHWH,* died at the age of one hundred and ten. ³⁰ Joshua was buried on his own in Timnath-serah, north of Mount Gaash in the hill-county of Ephraim. ³¹ Israel had served YHWH throughout Joshua's entire lifetime and the lifetimes of the elders who outlived Joshua and experienced everything YHWH did for Israel. ³² And Joseph's bones, which the people had transported up from Egypt, were

buried at Shechem in the plot of land Jacob had purchased for one hundred pieces of silver from the children of Hamor, Shechem's father. This became the inheritance of Joseph's descendants.

³³ Eleazar ben-Aaron died and was buried at Gibeah, which was alloted to Phinehas, his son, in the hill country of Ephraim.

---

* For the first time, the term that has been applied to Moses throughout the book is now given to Joshua.

júdges

After joshua died, the israelites sought
guidance from Yʜwʜ, asking, "Which tribe should be the first to march
against the Canaanites and attack them?" *

² Yʜwʜ answered, "Judah is to go first. I will deliver the land into their
hands."

³ Judah said to Simeon, "Follow me into the territory allotted to us. There
we will do battle against the Canaanites. After that we will follow you into
your allotted territory." The Simeonites followed them.

⁴ When the troops of Judah attacked, Yʜwʜ delivered into their hands
the Canaanites and the Perizzites. They routed 10,000 warriors at Bezek.

---

* As the book of *Judges* opens, the land of Canaan is the scene of tremendous political instability, with
many groups vying for supremacy. The once-great empires of the Egyptians and the Hittites have
been trying to control Canaan because of the importance of its trade routes, but their dominance
has started to wane, and a stalemate between them has created a virtual free-for-all among the
lesser nations. A group of "sea peoples"—the Philistines in particular—are moving from west to
east, trying to dominate the lands between the Mediterranean and the Jordan River. The tribes of
Israel, having received their allotments of land from Yʜwʜ, are pushing from east to west toward
the Jordan, claiming the land for themselves. Caught in the middle are the indigenous Canaanite
population, who are unwilling accept a wholesale takeover of their territory.

⁵ On the field of battle they engaged Adoni-bezek in battle, and defeated the Canaanites and Perizzites. ⁶ Adoni-bezek fled but was quickly captured. The victors cut off his big toes and thumbs. ⁷ "Seventy rulers with their thumbs and big toes cut off used to pick up my table scraps," said Adoni-bezek. "Now God has done to me what I have done to others." The victors brought him back to Jerusalem, where he eventually died.

⁸ The Judahites then attacked Jerusalem* and captured it. Their troops put its people to the sword and set fire to the city. ⁹ Judah then turned south to attack the Canaanites dwelling in the hill country, the Negev, and the coastal plains. ¹⁰ Judah attacked the Canaanites in Hebron, formerly known as Kiriath-arba, and overran Sheshai, Ahiman, and Talmai. ¹¹ Then their troops marched off to confront the inhabitants of Debir, once known as Kiriath-sepher.

¹² Caleb† said, "I offer the hand of my daughter Achsah to the warrior who attacks and captures Kiriath-sepher." ¹³ Othniel ben-Caleb's younger brother Kenaz captured the city, and Caleb blessed the union of Achsah and Othniel.

¹⁴ Achsah cajoled her father into giving her some land. Then, as she alighted from her donkey, Caleb asked her, "Is there anything I can do for you?" ¹⁵ She replied, "Please give me a little present. Since you are putting me in this arid Negev, give me a source of water." And Caleb gave her the Upper and Lower Springs.

¹⁶ The descendants of Moses' father-in-law, the Kenite, joined with Judahites from the City of the Date Palms and journeyed to the wilderness of Judah at Arad in the Negev.

¹⁷ Then the people of Judah set out with their cousins the Simeonites to attack the Canaanites in Zephath. They put Zephath under the sacred ban and annihilated it, so they named that place Hormah, "Annihilated." ¹⁸ Judah took Gaza, Ashkelon, Ekron, and their surrounding territories. ¹⁹ YHWH was with the Judahites, who also took possession of the hill country. But Judah failed to drive the people from the plains, for the defenders had ironclad chariots.

²⁰ As Moses promised, Hebron was given to Caleb, who drove out the three Anakim.

---

* Jerusalem was at this time called Jebus, the capital of the region held by the Jebusites, a Canaanite people. Sometime after this attack, the Jebusites reestablished their control until David defeated the Jebusites and captured the city some two hundred years later. Verse 21 says that the Benjamites also attacked Jerusalem but were unable to drive out the Jebusites; this may reflect the blending of two different histories, or it may indicate that the time span of these events is much longer than this simple recounting would imply.

† Caleb ben-Jephunneh was the leader of the tribe of Judah, and was one of only two to survive the period in the wilderness after the Exodus and enter Canaan.

²¹ The Benjaminites were unable to drive out the Jebusites inhabiting Jerusalem, who live there along with the Benjaminites to this day.
²² For their part, the House of Joseph attacked Bethel, and YHWH was with them. ²³ When they sent agents to spy on Bethel—or, as it was called in those days, Luz— ²⁴ they approached someone with the request, "Show us a way into the city and we will treat you well." ²⁵ He showed them a way into the city and the agents put the city to the sword, but spared him along with his family. ²⁶ He went into the Hittite country and eventually founded a city. He named it Luz after his old hometown, and that has been its name ever since.

²⁷ Manasseh failed to take possession of Beth-shean, Taanach, Dor, Ibleam, and Megiddo as well as their surrounding villages. The Canaanites held firmly to their territory. ²⁸ At a later time, when Israel was stronger, the Israelites subjected the citizens of these towns and villages to forced labor but never drove them out completely. ²⁹ Ephraim also failed to drive out the Canaanites dwelling in Gezer. The Canaanites lived among the Israelites there. ³⁰ Zebulun failed to dislodge the townspeople of both Kitron and Nahalol. The Canaanites lived among the invaders and eventually were subjected to forced labor.

³¹ Nor did the tribe of Asher dislodge the inhabitants of Acco or Sidon or Ahlab or Aczib or Helbah or Aphek or Rehob. ³² So the people of Asher settled among the Canaanites already established there.

³³ Naphtali also failed to overcome the natives of Beth-shemesh and Beth-anath, but subjected them to forced labor. ³⁴ The Amorites contained the tribe of Dan to the hill country and did not let its people settle on the plains. ³⁵ The Amorites held their ground at Mount Heres, Aijalon, and Shaalbim. But as the tribe of Joseph continued to grow there, it was able to subject them to forced labor.

³⁶ The territory of the Amorites began at the Akrabbim Pass and extended to Sela and beyond.

²·¹ An angel from YHWH* set out from Gilgal to Bochim, and announced to the Israelites, "I brought you out of Egypt and into the land I swore to give to your ancestors. I told you, 'I will never break my Covenant with you. ² For your part, you must never make covenants with the people of this country. You must destroy their altars.' You have disobeyed me—but for what reason? ³ So from now on I will not drive the inhabitants out before you. They will become your oppressors and their gods will snare you."

---

* "Angel" simply means messenger, "one who is sent." In general, angelic representatives speak the words of God, like human prophets, and are often referred to as if they were the very manifestation of God.

⁴ When the angel of YHWH finished saying these things to the Israelites, they wailed in despair. They called this place Bochim, "Weepers." ⁵ There they offered sacrifices to YHWH.

*W*hen Joshua dismissed the people, each of the tribes of Israel moved out to take possession of its own inheritance. ⁷ They were faithful to YHWH God throughout Joshua's lifetime and the times of the elders who survived him—everyone, that is, who was witness to the great deeds that YHWH had done for Israel.

⁸ At the age of 110, Joshua ben-Nun, the servant of God, died ⁹ and was buried on the land of his inheritance, in Timnath-Heres in the hill country of Ephraim, north of Mount Gaash.

¹⁰ All of Joshua's generation were likewise gathered to their ancestors. The generation that replaced them failed to acknowledge YHWH and what God had done for Israel. ¹¹ Then the Israelites compounded their treachery toward YHWH by serving the ba'als. ¹² They deserted YHWH, the God of their ancestors who had brought them out of Egypt, and went after other gods, the gods of the peoples around them, and worshiped them, which provoked YHWH to anger. ¹³ They abandoned YHWH and served Ba'al and Ashtoreth.*

¹⁴ At this point YHWH's anger against Israel flared up, and God made its people the prey to raiders and plunderers. YHWH handed them over to their neighboring enemies, whom they were unable to overcome. ¹⁵ Everything they did to defend themselves turned into disastrous defeats, just as YHWH had told them.

¹⁶ Then YHWH raised up chieftains† who delivered them out of the hands of the plunderers. ¹⁷ Yet once more they refused to listen to their chieftains and prostituted themselves, worshipping other gods and bowing down before them. How quickly they returned to their pagan ways, abandoning

---

* Ba'al was both the chief god of the Canaanites and one of many local manifestations of that divinity, often called "the ba'als." *Ashtoreth* is a deliberate corruption of the name of the Mesopotamian lunar mother goddess Ishtar or Astarte, blending the name with *bosheth*, "shameful"; adding to the confusion, the same Hebrew letters (but with different vowel points) spell *ashtaroth*, the plural of Ashtart, the Canaanite spelling of Astarte. The ba'als represented the masculine and the ashtaroth the feminine divine principles in manifestation.

† The word *shapatim* is usually translated "judges," though they were not judicial figures. While some of these chieftains occasionally arbitrated disputes (Deborah in particular), they were first and foremost tribal leaders and governors, defenders of the people. The twelve chieftains described in this book came to be known as judges because they applied God's judgment to Israel's enemies, and because they stood up for the oppressed and the afflicted.

judges 2   46

the way of obedience to YHWH's commands that their ancestors had taught them! [18] Every time God set up a chieftain over them, God kept the people safe from their enemies as long as the chieftain lived. In this way God took pity on the people's cries for mercy. [19] But when the chieftain died, the people turned to their pagan practices, practices more corrupt than the behavior of their ancestors. They served foreign gods, prostrated before them, and refused to abandon these evil practices and vile conduct.

[20] Then again YHWH's anger flared out against Israel, and God said, "Once again this nation has violated the Covenant I had laid upon its ancestors; once again the people disobey me. [21] For my part, I will no longer drive out before them any nations Joshua left at the time of his death." [22] For YHWH let those nations remain as a test—to see whether the Israelites would keep the way of YHWH as their ancestors had done. [23] That is why God did not drive those nations out quickly or give them into Joshua's hand.

[3:1] YHWH left several nations in the land to test the Israelites who had not taken part in the early battles for Canaan. [2] God's purpose was to train these new generations of Israelites in the art of warfare, for they had not experienced the battles with Canaan. [3] Those left in the land included the five city-states of the Philistines, and all the Canaanites, Sidonians, and Hivites who inhabited the hill country of Lebanon between Mount Ba'al-Hermon and Lebo-Hamath. [4] God's other purpose was to test whether this new generation of Israel would obey the commandments YHWH had given to its ancestors through Moses.

[5] So the Israelites lived among the Canaanites, the Hittites, the Amorites, the Perizzites, the Hivites, and the Jebusites. [6] They intermarried with them and embraced their intermarriage with Israelite daughters and sons. And they worshiped the gods of their neighbors.

3:7–16:31

because the Israelites forgot YHWH their God and worshiped the ba'als and the asherahs,* [8] YHWH's anger so flared up against them that they

---

* Much controversy surrounds the word *asherah*. A "high place" or shrine of the ba'al (*bamah*) consisted of an altar, a *mazzebhah* or stone pillar, and an *asherah*, which was either a sacred tree or grove, or a wooden pole in the shape of a phallus. But while some scholars believe that the asherah became the goddess Asherah only after the Exile, essentially subsuming the worship of Ashtar and the ashtaroth, others contend that Asherah was the ancient Canaanite name for the Great Goddess and the partner of the primal god El; and while most scholars associate Asherah with Astarte or Ishtar, others believe she was Astarte's mother.

were allowed to fall into the hands of Cushan-rishathaim, ruler of Aram Naharaim, who enslaved them for eight years.

⁹ But the anguished cries and moans of the people brought YHWH to relent and raise up for them a liberator, Othniel ben-Kenaz, Caleb's younger brother, who saved them. ¹⁰ The Spirit of YHWH came upon Othniel so powerfully that he became Israel's governor with the power to call for war. And into Othniel's hands YHWH delivered Cushan-rishathaim, ruler of Aram, ¹¹ and the land was at peace for forty years. Then Othniel ben-Kenaz died.

¹² Once more the Israelites did evil in the sight of YHWH, who for this offense gave Eglon the ruler of Moab power over Israel. ¹³ With a coalition of Ammonites and Amalekites, Eglon led an attack on Israel, capturing the City of the Date Palms. ¹⁴ For eighteen years Israelites were subjects of Eglon, ruler of Moab.

¹⁵ Then the Israelites cried out to YHWH, pleading for deliverance, and YHWH raised up a liberator for them: Ehud ben-Gera the Benjamite, who was left-handed. The Israelites sent him to carry their tribute to Eglon, ruler of Moab. ¹⁶ Now Ehud had constructed a double-edged sword eighteen inches long that he strapped to his right thigh under his clothes. ¹⁷ Ehud presented the tribute to Eglon, who was very fat. ¹⁸ After presenting the tribute, Ehud and the tribute bearers left for home. ¹⁹ Near the stone quarries at Gilgal, Ehud left his travel companions and returned to Eglon, and said, "I have a secret message for you, my ruler." Eglon dismissed all his attendants from the room.

²⁰ Then Ehud approached Eglon as the ruler sat alone in the upper room of his summer residence, and said, "I have a message from God for you." As the ruler rose from his seat, ²¹ Ehud reached with his left hand, drew the sword from his right side and drove it into Eglon's belly. ²² The sword sank into the body over the hilt and ended protruding out of the back. ²³ Then Ehud went out onto the porch, where he locked the door shut on Eglon.

²⁴ After a while, Eglon's attendants came up and, finding the doors locked, thought, "He must be relieving himself in the cool room." ²⁵ They waited a long time, but when the door remained locked, they grew anxious. So they took out a key, unlocked the door, and entered the room to discover the dead ruler.

²⁶ Ehud escaped while the attendants waited; passing Pesilim, he took refuge in Seirah. ²⁷ Once he arrived home, he sounded the shofar in the hill country of Ephraim, and the Israelites followed him down from the hill country as their leader. ²⁸ "Follow me," he said to them, "for YHWH gave us Moab, our enemy, into your hands." They followed Ehud and took possession of the fords of the Jordan that led to Moab. No one could cross over

there. ²⁹ On that occasion they counted 10,000 dead Moabites, all of them strong and able-bodied. Not one of them escaped. ³⁰ On that day Moab became subjugated to Israel. And the land was at peace for eighty years.

³¹ After Ehud there was Shamgar ben-Anath. Shamgar once killed 600 Philistines with an ox goad. He too was a liberator of Israel.

છ   છ   છ

4:1 After Ehud died, the Israelites once again did evil in the sight of YHWH. ² And once again YHWH allowed them to fall under the power of a foreign ruler: this time, the Canaanite ruler Jabin, who reigned in Hazor. Sisera, the commander of Jabin's army, was stationed at Harosheth Haggoyim ³ and, equipped with 900 ironclad chariots, cruelly harassed the Israelites for twenty years. They cried out to YHWH for relief.

⁴ At this time the prophet Deborah, who was married to Lappidoth, was the governor of Israel. ⁵ She held court under Deborah's Palm between Ramah and Bethel in the hill country of Ephraim. The Israelites came to her for arbitration.

⁶ One day she sent for Barak ben-Abinoam, from Kedesh in Naphtali, and instructed him, "YHWH, the God of Israel, commands this: 'You are to lead 10,000 Israelites from Naphtali and Zebulun to Mount Tabor. ⁷ I will lure Sisera, Jabin's commander, with his chariots and troops to the Kishon River and you will defeat him there.'"

⁸ Barak said to Deborah, "If you come with me, I will go. And if you do not go with me, I will not go."

⁹ "Very well, I will go with you," she replied, "but then you won't have the honor of victory from this battle—for YHWH will deliver Sisara into the hands of a woman!"

So Deborah joined up with Barak and journeyed to Kedesh. ¹⁰ Then Barak mobilized Zebulun and Nephtali and drew 10,000 soldiers. Deborah went with them.

¹¹ Now Heber the Kenite, who had separated himself from the other Kenites—all of them descendants of Hobab, Moses' father-in-law—had pitched his tent by the Oak of Zaanannim, which was near Kedesh.

¹² When Sisera learned that Barak ben-Abinoam was encamped on Mount Tabor, ¹³ he assembled his troops and all 900 ironclad chariots, and marched from Harosheth Haggoyim to the River Kishon. ¹⁴ Then Deborah instructed Barak, "Arise! This is the day YHWH gives Sisera into your hands. YHWH leads us at the head of your column!" And Barak marched off to Mount

Tabor followed by 10,000 soldiers, ¹⁵ and YHWH God routed Sisera and all 900 ironclad chariots before the onslaught. Sisera abandoned his own ironclad chariot, and fled from the field of battle on foot. ¹⁶ Barak pursued Sisera's chariots and army as far as Harosheth Haggoyim. Sisera's troops were put to the sword. No one survived the encounter.

¹⁷ While this was happening, Sistera found refuge in the tent of Jael, the wife of Heber the Kenite, because Jabin the ruler of Hazor and the family of Heber the Kinite were on friendly terms. ¹⁸ Jael stepped outside the tent to meet Sisera, saying, "Enter, sir! Come in, and have no fear." Sisera entered the tent and Jael hid him under a blanket.

¹⁹ He said, "I am thirsty. Give me a drink of water." She opened a skin of milk and gave him some to drink, then covered him once more.

²⁰ "Stand in the tent entrance," he said. "If anyone comes and asks whether a man is here, say No." ²¹ The exhausted Sisera immediately fell into a deep sleep.

Then Jael took a tent peg, picked up a mallet, and crept closely to the general and drove the peg through his temple and into the ground, killing him. ²² When Barak came by searching for the fugitive, Jael went out to greet him, and said, "Come, I will show you the person you seek." So he entered the tent after her and found Sisera dead with a tent peg through his temple.

²³ On that day God subdued Jabin the Canaanite ruler before the Israelites. ²⁴ Their power over Jabin kept growing stronger and stronger, until he was finally destroyed.

5:1 On that day Deborah and Barak ben-Abinoam sang this song:

2 "When the leaders of Israel lead courageously,
   when the Israelites dedicate themselves,
   bless YHWH!
3 Listen, rulers! Listen, commanders!
   I will sing the praises of YHWH, I will sing!
   I will sing hyms to YHWH,
   the God of Israel.
4 YHWH, when you moved out from Seir,
   when you marched from the land of Edom,
   the earth quaked and the heavens shook,
   the clouds opened their gates.
5 Mountains shook before YHWH of Sinai,
   before YHWH, God of Israel!
6 In the days of Shamgar ben-Anath,
   in the days of Jael,
   the crime-ridden travel routes lay desolate,
   and travelers took roundabout paths to avoid robbers.

7 Village life died a lonely death until you rose up,
Deborah, the great mother of Israel.
8 When the people chose new gods,
war came to the city gates.
But neither spear nor shield was found
among forty thousand in Israel.
9 My heart is with the leaders of Israel,
who responded to the call.
For this, bless YHWH!
10 You who ride upon white donkeys,*
seated on rich carpets for the trip,
and you who walk along the road,
declare the news!
11 Listen to the shepherds at the watering holes,
who sing of YHWH's gracious deeds—
God's gracious deliverance of Israel.
Then YHWH's people
marched to the gates and shouted,
12 'Awake! Awake, Deborah!
Rise up! Rise up! Break out in song!
Arise, Barak!
Take your captives prisoner,
ben-Abinoam!'
13 Then the survivors triumphed
over the mighty.
The people of YHWH
were victorious over trained warriors.
14 Some came from Ephraim,
whose roots were in Amalek;
Benjamin was among
the people who followed you.
The captains came down from Makir,
the bearers of the command staff came from Zebulun.
15 Chieftains from Issachar were with Deborah,
and Issachar was with Barak.
Down the valley
they pursued the foe.

---

* Or possibly zebras; the word for "white," *zachor*, is similar to the Ethiopian word for zebra, *zechora*. These are the wealthy caravan merchants, once again able to travel the trade routes now that they have been made safe from brigands and outlaws. The watering holes in the next verse are wells located just outside of towns; in unstable times, these were often dangerous places, but in times of peace they became communal gathering places.

But with the tribe of Reuben,
   there was much searching of the heart.
16 Reuben, why do you huddle around your campfires
   listening to the lowing of the herd?
   Among the tribe of Reuben
   there was much searching of the heart.
17 Gilead lingered beyond the Jordan.
   And Dan, why did you tarry by the ships?
   Asher stayed close to the seashore,
   and remained in the harbors.
18 But you, Zebulun—you stared death in the face!
   Naphtali, too, on the heights of the battlefield!
19 Rulers came and faced you in battle.
   They fought, those rulers of Canaan,
   at Taanach near the waters of Megiddo;
   But this time they carried off no silver, no plunder.
20 The very stars of the heavens fought;
   from their courses, they defied Sisera.
21 The river Kishon swept them away.
   the ancient river, the river Kishon.
   March on, my soul!
   Be strong!
22 Next came the thunder of horses' hoofs,
   galloping, relentlessly galloping
   went the beautiful steeds.
23 'Curse Meroz,' says the angel of YHWH.
   'Curse the dwellers there
   Because they never came to YHWH's aid,
   to YHWH's aid against the mighty!
24 But blessed be Jael among women,
   the wife of Heber the Kenite!
   Among all tent-dwelling women,
   she is most blessed!'
25 He asked for water, she gave him milk.
   In a bowl fit for royalty, she brought him curds.
26 Her left hand had held the tent peg,
   her right right hand the mallet;
   she struck Sisera and crushed his head,
   shattering and splitting his skull.
27 He fell at her feet, dead before hitting the floor.
   At her feet he dropped,

and where he dropped,
    there he fell dead.
²⁸ Sisera's mother peered through the window;
    behind the lattice she cried out,
'Why is his chariot so long in coming?
Why is there no sound of his chariots?'
²⁹ The wisest of her attendants answered her—
indeed, she repeated the attendant's words to herself:
³⁰ 'They are sharing the spoils:
the women, one or two for every soldier;
beautiful dyed and embroidered cloth for Sisera,
and one scarf—no, two, and embroidered—for you!'
³¹ May all your enemies
    perish like this, YHWH!
But let whoever loves you
    be like the sun when it rises in all its glory."

And the country was at peace for forty years.

ᙢ   ᙢ   ᙢ

⁶·¹ Once more, Israel did evil in the sight of YHWH, and for seven years YHWH gave the people into the hands of the Midianites. ² They were so oppressive that the Israelites found refuge in the mountains, in caves and dens. ³ Whenever the Israelites sowed crops, the Midianites, Amalekites, and other eastern tribes would arrive to attack them, ⁴ pitching tents opposite them and destroying their crops as far as the outskirts of Gaza. They would leave nothing living, not sheep, oxen, or donkeys. ⁵ They would come up with their livestock and their tents, swarming like locusts; they and their camels were beyond counting, invading the land and ravaging it. ⁶ Midian so impoverished the Israelites that they cried out to YHWH for help.

⁷ When the Israelites cried out to YHWH because of Midian, ⁸ YHWH sent them a prophet, who told them, "These are the words of YHWH, the God of Israel: 'I led you from the land of Egypt, the land of slavery. ⁹ I rescued you from the Egyptians and all your other oppressors, whom I drove out before you to provide you with your land. ¹⁰ I said to you, I am YHWH, your God. Do not worship the gods of the Amorites in whose country you are settling. But you failed to listen to me.' "

¹¹ An angel from YHWH arrived and sat under the oak in Ophrah that belonged to Joash the Abiezrite. As Gideon ben-Joash thrashed wheat in the winepress (he did this to keep out of the sight of the Midianites), ¹² the angel appeared to him and said, "You are brave, and YHWH is with you."

¹³ Gideon replied, "Yes, but if YHWH is really with us, why are we being treated like this? Where are the wonders our parents told us about when they said, 'Did not YHWH bring us out of Egypt?' Why has YHWH now abandoned us and delivered us into the hands of the Midianites?"

¹⁴ Then YHWH turned to Gideon and said, "Go! Use your strength to liberate Israel from the Midianites. It is I who send you."

¹⁵ But Gideon replied, "How can I free Israel? My family is the weakest in Manasseh, and I am the most insignificant in my parents' household."

¹⁶ YHWH said, "I will be with you, and you will slay every person in Midian." *

¹⁷ Gideon replied, "If I have found favor in your eyes, give me a sign that it is you who talk to me. ¹⁸ Please don't leave this place until I return and bring my offering and set it before you."

And God answered, "I will stay until you get back."

¹⁹ Gideon hurried inside, prepared a young goat and formed an ephah of flour into unleavened bread. He put the meat in a basket, poured the broth into a pot, and brought it to the angel waiting under the oak. As Gideon came near, ²⁰ the angel instructed, "Place the meat and the bread here on the rock and pour out the broth." When he did this, ²¹ the angel of YHWH extended a staff, touching the bread and the meat. Fire erupted from the rock and consumed the meat and the bread. Then the angel of YHWH vanished into air.

²² When Gideon realized that his visitor was an angel, he exclaimed, "Alas, Sovereign YHWH! I have seen an angel from YHWH face to face!" †

²³ And YHWH said to Gideon, "Peace be with you. Fear not. You are not going to die." ²⁴ Gideon built an altar to YHWH there and named it "YHWH is Peace." To this day it stands at Ophrah of the Abiezrites.

²⁵ That night YHWH said to Gideon, "Take the young bull in your father's herd, and a second bull, the seven-year-old, and pull down the altar to Ba'al that is on your parents' property and cut down the Asherah pole beside it. ²⁶ Then replace it with a proper altar to YHWH your God atop the mound. Take the second bull—the seven-year-old—and offer it as a whole offering using the wood of the Asherah pole you cut down." ²⁷ So Gideon took household attendants and did what YHWH had told him. But he did not know how his family and the people of the village might react, so he did it at night.

²⁸ In the morning the people of the village discovered that the altar to Ba'al had been demolished, the Asherah pole cut down, and the second bull

---

* Or "You and I will slay the Midianites as if we were one person."
† In Exodus 33, YHWH told Moses that no one can see God face to face and live, so Gideon's fear is understandable.

sacrificed on a newly-built altar. ²⁹ Asking one another who had done this, they investigated and were told that Gideon ben-Joash was the culprit.

³⁰ They demanded that Joash bring Gideon to them: "He must die because he tore down altar of Ba'al and cut down the Asherah pole that stood beside it!"

³¹ But Joash defended Gideon, "Are you speaking on Ba'al's behalf? Does Ba'al need you plead his cause? Whoever stands up for Ba'al will be put to death by morning. If Ba'al is really a god, let him defend himself when someone tears down his altar."

³² From that day on, Gideon's father called him Jerubbaal, that is, "Let Ba'al Defend," for he had torn down Ba'al's altar.

³³ At this time the Midianites, Amalekites, and other eastern tribes joined forces, crossed the river, and encamped in the valley of Jezreel. ³⁴ Then the Spirit of God took possession of Gideon, and Gideon sounded the shofar, summoning the family of Abiezer to follow him. ³⁵ He also sent messengers throughout Manasseh, calling them to arms. He did the same with Asher, Zebulun, and Naphtali. They, too, came up to meet him.

³⁶ Gideon said to God, "Are you truly the one who is promising to save Israel through me? ³⁷ I will set this woollen fleece on the threshing floor. If there is dew on the fleece while all the ground around it is dry, then I will understand that it is through me that you will deliver Israel as you promised." ³⁸ And that is what happened: when Gideon rose early the next morning and wrung out the fleece, he squeezed enough dew from it to fill a bowl with water.

³⁹ Then Gideon said to God, "Don't be angry with me. Allow me to do one more test with the fleece. This time, keep the fleece dry and cover the ground with dew." ⁴⁰ God did as Gideon had requested. This time only the fleece was dry, and there was dew all around the ground.

7:1 Early the next morning Jerubbaal—that is, Gideon—and all his troops camped at the spring of Harod. The Midianite encampment was north of them in the valley close by the hill of Moreh. ² YHWH said to Gideon, "You have too many warriors for me to deliver Midian into your hands. The Israelites would be tempted to claim victory for themselves and presume that the triumph had been by their own strength. ³ Announce to all your troops that anyone who is anxious or too afraid to continue is to leave Mount Gilead immediately and go home." So 22,000 people left; 10,000 stayed behind.

⁴ "There are still too many," said YHWH to Gideon. "Take them down to the water so that I can separate them there. I will tell you which are to go with you and which are to stay." ⁵ When Gideon brought the troops down to the water, YHWH instructed him, "Separate the ones who lap the water with their tongues from the ones who kneel down to drink." ⁶ Three hundred

soldiers lapped the water, bringing their hand to their mouth. And all the rest knelt to drink.*

[7] YHWH said, "With the 300 who lapped their water I will save you and put the Midianites into your hand." [8] So Gideon dismissed the rest of the warriors of Israel and kept the 300, who took the shofars and and the provisions that the other soldiers had brought with them.

The camp of the Midianites was below them in the valley. [9] During the night, YHWH said to Gideon, "Get up. Go down the valley to their camp, for I have delivered them into your hands. [10] If you are afraid to attack, first go down with your attendant, Purah, [11] and eavesdrop on them. Then you will have the courage to attack the camp."

So Gideon and his attendant Purah descended into the valley to the outposts of the camp. [12] The Midianites and the Amalekites, along with all the eastern tribes there, were assembled like a swarm of locusts. There were countless camels, innumerable like the grains of sands on the seashore.

[13] As Gideon approached he heard a soldier describing a dream to the others, saying, "I dreamed that I saw a round loaf of barley bread rolling into the Midianite camp. It came to a tent, striking it with such force that the tent collapsed and turned upside down."

[14] Another soldier responded, "This can be none other than the sword of Gideon ben-Joash the Israelite. God has delivered Midian and our whole army into his hands."

[15] As Gideon listened to the account of the dream and its interpretation, he fell on his knees in worship. Then he returned to the camp and ordered, "Let us be off. YHWH has delivered the camp of the Midianites into our hands." [16] Gideon divided the soldiers into three companies of 100 each, and handed each a shofar and a jar containing nothing but a torch. [17] "Watch me," he said, "and follow me. When I get to the edge of the camp, do exactly what I do. [18] When my group and I sound our shofars, all of you around the camp do the same, shouting, 'For YHWH and for Gideon!'"

[19] When Gideon and his company of 100 reached the outskirts of the camp at the beginning of the middle watch, it was just after the changing of the guard. They blew their shofars and shattered the jars they were carrying, [20] and the other two companies also blew their shofars and shattered their jars. Then, holding their torches in their left hand and their shofars in their right, they all shouted, "A sword for YHWH and for Gideon!"

---

* The 300 bent over and used their cupped hands to get water, then lapped it, drinking quickly the way a dog sensing danger might; the rest knelt and put their faces down to the water to drink. The 300 proved themselves to be more attuned to their surroundings, and more able to move quckly should the need suddenly arise.

²¹ All the soldiers encircling the camp held their ground, and the camp erupted into panic and fled. ²² As the 300 sounded their trumpets, YHWH set all the Midianite soldiers fighting one another. They fled as far as Beth-Shittah in the direction of Zerereah, near the border of Abel-Meholah at Tabbath.

²³ The warriors of Israel from Naphtali, Asher, and all Manasseh were called out to pursue the Midianites. ²⁴ Gideon also sent messengers throughout the hill country of Ephraim with this order: "Go down ahead of the Midianites and seize access to the waters of the Jordan as far as Beth-Barah."

So all the Ephraimites came out and took control of the banks of the Jordan as far as Beth-Barah. ²⁵ Capturing two Midianite chieftains, Oreb and Zeeb, they killed Oreb at Raven's Rock, and killed Zeeb near the Winepress of the Wolf.* On the other side of the Jordan they delivered to Gideon the heads of Oreb and Zeeb.

⁸:¹ In anger the Ephraimites said to Gideon, "Why didn't you call us when you put out the order to fight against Midian?" And they upbraided him severely.

² Gideon replied, "Look what little I have accomplished compared with you! Ephraim's gleanings are better than Abiezer's entire grape harvest. ³ God delivered the Midianite chieftains Oreb and Zeeb into your hands. What did I do, compared with your accomplishments?" When he said this, their anger abated.

⁴ Gideon and the three companies of 100 continued the pursuit in spite of their exhaustion. Reaching the Jordan, they crossed it. ⁵ Gideon said to the people of Succoth,† "See to it that my troops get bread. They are tired and famished. I will continue in pursuit of Zebah and Zalmunna, the rulers of Midian."

⁶ But the officials of Succoth said, "Give bread to your three companies? Are Zebah and Zalmunna already in your possession?"

⁷ Gideon replied, "Very well, then. When YHWH delivers Zebah and Zalmunna into our hands, I will return and tear your flesh off with the thorns and briars of the desert."

⁸ Gideon went from there up to Penuel and made the same request. The people of Penuel gave the same answer as had the people of Succoth. ⁹ Gideon said to them, "When I return victorious, I will tear down your tower."

¹⁰ In the meantime the rulers Zebah and Zalmunna reached Karkor with a force of about 15,000 warriors, all that was left of the army of the eastern

---

* *Oreb* means "Raven" and *Zeeb* means "Wolf." The rock may have been on Oreb's property and the winepress may have belonged to Zeeb, or the writer may be making a play on words.

† Succoth, which means "booths" or "huts," was a town in the Israelite territory of Gad named for the temporary structures Jacob and his people erected when he returned from Aram. The town of Penuel in the next verse, also on the western bank of the Jordan, was in Ephraimite territory.

peoples; the slain numbered 120,000. ¹¹ Gideon marched up the road of the nomads east of Nobah and Jogbehah and attacked the camp, which was taken off guard. ¹² The rulers of Midian, Zebah, and Salmunna, after briefly escaping, were captured, and their army destroyed.

¹³ Gideon ben-Joash then returned from the battle near the Pass of Heres. ¹⁴ He was going by way of the Pass of Heres when he captured a young straggler originally from Succoth. The youth, under interrogation, provided the names of the rulers of Succoth and its elders, a total of seventy-seven.

¹⁵ Then Gideon returned to Succoth and said, "Here are Zebah and Zalmunna, about whom you taunted me. Remember saying, 'Are Zebah and Zalmunna already in your hands, that we should give bread to your exhausted troops?' ¹⁶ He gathered the elders of the city, took desert thorns and briers, and ground them into their flesh. ¹⁷ He pulled down the tower of Penuel and put its men to death.

¹⁸ Gideon asked Zebah and Zalmunna, "Describe the men you killed in Tabor."

They replied, "They looked like you. Every one of them had the look of nobility."

¹⁹ "They were my brothers," Gideon said, "the sons of my mother. I swear by YHWH that if you had spared them, I would not have killed you."

²⁰ Then he said to his eldest son Jether, "Kill them!" But Jether, who was young and timid, could not to draw his sword.

²¹ Then Zebah and Zalmunna said, "Do it yourself. You are strong enough." So Gideon stepped forward and executed the two, and he removed the crescent moon-shaped ornaments from the necks of their camels.*

²² The Israelites said to Gideon, "You saved us from the Midianites. Now rule over us—you and your children and your grandchildren."

²³ But Gideon declined. "I will not rule over you, nor will my children rule over you. YHWH alone must rule over us." ²⁴ Gideon continued, "I do have a favor to ask of you. Each of you give me an earring from your booty." (The vanquished enemy were Ishmaelites, and it was customary for Ishmaelites to wear gold earrings.)

²⁵ They responded, "It would give us joy to do so." So they spread a garment on the ground and each tossed an earring onto it. ²⁶ The gold earrings weighed fifty-three pounds—not counting the ornaments, the crescents, and the purple garments worn by the rulers of Midian, or the gold collars worn by the camels.

---

* The crescent moon-shaped ornaments were symbols of the goddess Astarte.

²⁷ Gideon make the gold into an ephod* that he set up in his hometown, Ophrah. But all Israel paid idolatrous homage to it there, and it caused the ruin of Gideon and his family.

²⁸ The Midianites were humbled by the Israelites, and could no longer hold their heads up high. And for the next forty years, the land had peace, thoughout Gideon's lifetime.

²⁹ Then Jerubbaal ben-Joash returned home to stay. ³⁰ Gideon had many wives, and they bore him seventy children of his own issue. ³¹ A concubine, a resident of Shechem, also bore him an heir whom they named Abimelech. ³² Gideon ben-Joash died at a full old age and was buried in his father's tomb at Ophrah of the Abiezrites.

³³ After Gideon's death the Israelites again strayed from the path. They abandoned themselves to the ba'als by making Ba'al-Berith their god.† ³⁴ They forgot YHWH their God, who had rescued them from the hands of their enemies time and again. ³⁵ They also failed to show loyalty to the family of Jerubbaal—that is, Gideon—for all the good he had done for Israel.

ରେ ରେ ରେ

⁹:¹ Abimelech ben-Jerubbaal traveled to Shechem to the house of his mother's brothers and spoke to them and to his maternal grandfather's entire family clan, and said, ² "Poll the citizens of Shechem with this question: 'Which is better for you: that seventy children of Jerubbaal rule over you, or just one?' Keep in mind that I am your own flesh and blood."

³ When his relatives shared this with all the citizens of Shechem, they were sympathetic to Abimelech. "Isn't he one of us?" they asked. ⁴ They also gave him seventy shekels for the temple of Ba'al-Berith. But he used the money to hire hooligans and mercenaries as followers. ⁵ He then went to his ancestral home at Ophrah and murdered his siblings, the seventy children of Jerubbaal, on a single stone‡—all except for one named Jotham, the youngest, who hid himself and survived. ⁶ Then all the citizens of Shechem and all Beth Millo came together to make Abimelech ruler under the great tree at the memorial pillar in Shechem.

⁷ When Jotham learned of this he climbed to the top of Mount Gerizim, and cried out to the people, "Hear me, people of Shechem, so God may listen

---

* The ephod was a priestly garment made of linen that contained the Urim and Thummim, the oracular stones used by priests to divine the will of God; this ephod seems to have been a model made of hammered gold and used as an oracle in and of itself.
† The name means "Ba'al of the covenant."
‡ Likely by sacrificing them all on the same stone altar, in revenge for the demolition of Ba'al's altar by their father, Gideon.

to you. [8] One day, the trees gathered to anoint a ruler for themselves. They said to the olive tree, 'Be our ruler.' [9] The olive tree replied, 'But I would have to give up my rich oil, by which both the gods and the people are honored, to go and hold sway over the trees.' [10] Then the trees said to the fig tree, 'Be our ruler.' [11] But the fig tree replied, 'But I would have to give up my sweetness and my excellent fruit, to hold sway over the trees.' [12] Then the trees said to the vine, 'Be our ruler.' [13] But the vine replied, 'But I would have to give up my wine that cheers the gods and the people, to hold sway over the trees.' [14] Then the trees said to the thornbush, 'Be our ruler.' [15] But the thornbush replied, 'If your desire to anoint me ruler over you is in good faith, then come and take refuge in my shade. But if not, may fire come from the thornbush and devour the cedars of Lebanon!'

[16] "A question for you: Have you acted in good faith and honorably in appointing Abimelech as your ruler? Have you dealt honorably with Jerubbaal and his family, and treated them as he deserved to be treated? [17] Just remember how my father fought battles for you, risking his life when he delivered you from the power of Midian. [18] Yet today you rose up against his family and murdered his seventy legitimate children upon one stone. And you appointed Abimelech—the child of his handmaid!—to be ruler over the people of Shechem, simply because he is related to you. [19] Now, if then you have acted honorably and in good faith toward Jerubbaal and his family today, may Abimelech be your joy and may you revel in him. [20] But if not, let fire come from Abimelech and consume you, people of Shechem and Beth Millo. And may fire come out from you, people of Shechem and Beth Millo, and consume Abimelech!"

[21] Then Jotham fled to Beeroth, and dwelt there out of fear of his half-brother Abimelech. [22] After Abimelech ruled for three years, [23] God sent an evil spirit to create ill will between him and the people of Shechem, and they rebelled against him. [24] This was a just punishment for the murder of the seventy children of Jerubbaal: it avenged their blood upon their brother Abimelech, who had murdered them, and upon the people of Shechem, who had encouraged him in his deed. [25] The people of Shechem then set ambushes on the hilltops to rob travellers, and news of this was reported to Abimelech.

[26] Now Gaal ben-Ebed came with his companions to Shechem, and they won the trust of the people of Shechem. [27] That year, after going out into the fields and gathering in the grapes and treading them, they held a harvest festival in the temple of their god, where they ate and drank and cursed Abimelech. [28] During the festivities, Gaal ben-Ebed asked, "Who is this Abimelech, and who are these Shechemites, that they should rule over us? This same son of Jerubbaal, along with his deputy Zebul, once served Hamor,

Shechem's father. So why are we subjects of him? ²⁹ If only these people were in my charge, I would know how to be rid of Abimelech! I would challenge him to gather his forces!"

³⁰ When Zebul the governor of the city learned what Gaal had said, he was furious. ³¹ He sent this message to Abimelech in Arumah: "Gaal ben-Ebed and his companions came to Shechem to stir up the city against you. ³² Come after dark, you and your forces, and lie in ambush out in the fields. ³³ At sunrise, attack the city. When Gaal and his companions come out to fight you, do whatever circumstances dictate."

³⁴ So Abimelech and his troops made up four companies, and set out after dark and took up concealed positions opposite Shechem. ³⁵ Gaal ben-Ebed marched forth and had arrived at the city gate when Abimelech and his troops revealed themselves. ³⁶ Gaal, viewing the troops emerging from their camouflage, said to Zebul, "Look at those people coming down from the hilltops!"

But Zebul replied, "You are mistaking the shadows of the hills for people."

³⁷ But Gaal said once more, "No, look, people are coming down from the center of the ridge, and more are coming from the direction of the soothsayers' tree."

³⁸ Then Zebul said, "Where are your brave words now? You said, 'Who is Abimelech that that he should rule over us?' Aren't these the very people you scorned? Go out and engage them!"

³⁹ So Gaal led the people of Shechem into the battle against Abimelech. ⁴⁰ But Gaal fled from the engagement with Abimelech in pursuit. Many casualties covered the ground all the way to the gate entrance. ⁴¹ Abimelech returned to Arumah, and Zebul drove out Gaal and his companions.

⁴² The next day, when the people Shechem went out to the fields, Abimelech was informed of these events. ⁴³ So he took his troops, divided them into three companies, and lay in wait in the open country. As the people left the city, he attacked. ⁴⁴ Abimelech and one company advanced quickly and took up positions at the entrance of the city gate. In the meantime, the other two companies rushed the people working in the fields, striking them down. ⁴⁵ Abimelech kept up the attack on the city all that day. He captured the city, and massacred the people inside it; then he razed the town and sowed the ground with salt.

⁴⁶ When news of this reached the people who had taken shelter in the tower of Shechem, they went to the crypt in the temple of El-Berith.* ⁴⁷ Upon learning this, Abimelech ⁴⁸ and his soldiers went up Mount Zalmon. There

---

* This may be the same as Ba'al-Berith, since El and Ba'al were often treated as the same god.

he took an ax and cut up some branches, hoisting them on his shoulders and saying to the others, "See what I am doing? You do the same." [49] The others cut brushwood and followed Abimelech to the crypt, where they placed it against the crypt's entrance. Then they set fire to the crypt with the people inside. All of them, about 1,000, burned to death.

[50] Abimelech moved on to Thebez, surrounding and capturing it. [51] Now there was a strong tower in the middle of the town. All the people, both men and women, took refuge there. They shut themselves in and went up to the roof. [52] Abimelech arrived at the tower and attacked it. As he approached the entrance of the tower to set fire to it, [53] a woman threw a millstone down on his head and fractured his skull. [54] Quickly, he called for his armor-bearer and ordered him, "Draw your sword and run me through, so that no one can say that a woman killed me." The armor-bearer dispatched him.

[55] When the Israelites saw that Abimelech was dead, they went home. [56] In this way God repaid Abimelech for the evil he had done to his father when he murdered his seventy siblings. [57] It was also repayment for the wrongdoing of the people of Shechem. Jotham ben-Jerubbaal's curse upon them had been fulfilled.

[10:1] After Abimelech, Tola ben-Puah ben-Dodo of the tribe of Issachar arose to liberate Israel. He lived in Shamir, in the hill country of Ephraim. [2] He led Israel for twenty-three years and was buried in Shamir.

[3] Tola was followed by Jair of Gilead, who led Israel for twenty-two years. [4] Jair had thirty children, who rode on thirty donkeys. They controlled thirty towns in Gilead, which to this day is known as Havvoth Jair, "Jair's Tent Villages." [5] When Jair died, he was buried in Kamon.

ငၽ   ငၽ   ငၽ

[6] Once more Israel did evil in the sight of YHWH. The people worshipped the ba'als and the ashtaroth, as well as the gods of Aram, the gods of Sidon, the gods of Moab, the gods of the Ammonites, and the gods of the Philistines. And because the Israelites abandoned the worship of YHWH, [7] God became enraged against Israel and turned the people over to the power of the Philistines and the Ammonites, [8] who for eighteen years oppressed all the Israelites living on the east side of the Jordan in Gilead, the land of the Amorites. [9] The Ammonites also crossed the Jordan to fight against Judah, Benjamin, and the house of Ephraim. Israel was in desperate straits. [10] So the Israelites cried out to YHWH, saying, "We have committed offenses against

you, abandoning YHWH our God to serve the ba'als."

¹¹ YHWH replied, "When the Egyptians, the Amorites, the Ammonites, the Philistines, ¹² the Sidonites, the Amalekites, and the Midianites oppressed you and you cried out to me for help, did I not deliver you? ¹³ But still you abandoned me to serve other gods! So I will not come to your rescue again. ¹⁴ Go to your gods and cry for help from them. Let them deliver you in your time of need."

¹⁵ But the Israelites implored YHWH, "We stand guilty. Treat us as you wish. We beg you, only deliver us today!" ¹⁶ They did away with their foreign gods and served YHWH alone. And God could no longer bear Israel's suffering.

¹⁷ When the Ammonites gathered for war and set up camp in Mizpah, ¹⁸ the leaders of the people of Gilead said to one another, "Whoever strikes the first blow at the Ammonites will be chieftain over all the inhabitants of Gilead."

11:1 Jephthah of Gilead* was a skilled warrior. Jephthah's mother was a prostitute. ² Gilead had sired other children who, when they grew up, drove Jephthah away, saying, "Because you are born of a prostitute you have no right to an inheritance." ³ So Jephthah left and settled in the land of Tob, where a group of malcontents bonded with him, and they lived the life of bandits.

⁴ Some time later, the Ammonites went to war against the Israelites. ⁵ When this happened the elders of Gilead went to the land of Tob to enlist Jephthah. "Come," they pleaded, "lead us in our fight against the Ammonites."

⁷ Jephthah said to them, "Didn't you drive me away from our homestead? Why do you turn to me when trouble arrives?"

⁸ The elders replied, "We need you. Come, lead us against the Ammonites and we will make you leader over all of Gilead."

⁹ Jephthah replied, "Very well, if I take command of the fight against the Ammonites and YHWH delivers them to me, I will become your leader."

¹⁰ The elders swore, "As YHWH is our witness, we will do what you say."

¹² So Jephthah went with the elders of Gilead, and the people made him their commander-in-chief. As they marched on Mizpah, Jephthah in the presence of YHWH repeated all the conditions he had laid down.

¹² Then Jephthah sent messengers to the Ammonite ruler, saying, "What

---

* Or "Jephthah ben-Gilead." Gilead, which denotes a cairn, a mound of stones erected as a memorial or marker, is the name of a region, a mountain, and a city (possibly associated with the modern city of Jil'ad)—all in the same general area on the east side of the Jordan. Jephthah's father may also have been named Gilead, but it is more likely that since his mother was a prostitute, his "sire" is the personification of the region itself.

do you have against us to justify a war against me?"

¹³ The ruler of the Ammonites replied, "When the Israelites came up out of Egypt, they siezed my land from the Arnon to the Jabbok, all the way to the Jordan. Now give it back peaceably."

¹⁴ Once more Jephthah sent messengers to the ruler of the Ammonites, ¹⁵ saying, 'Thus says Jephthah: Israel did not take the land of the Ammonites. ¹⁶ When Israel came up out of Egypt, its people went through the desert to the Sea of Reeds and from there on to Kadesh. ¹⁷ Then Israel sent a message to the ruler of Edom, and said, 'Permit us to go through your territory,' but the ruler of Edom refused the request. Then the Israelites petitioned the ruler of Moab, who also refused them passage. So Israel remained in Kadesh. ¹⁸ Then the Israelites journeyed through the desert, skirting Edom and Moab, keeping to the eastern border of Moab. They set up camp along the Arnon River, also Moab's border, and did not enter Moabite territory.

¹⁹ "Then the Israelites sent messengers to Sihon, ruler of the Amorites, who ruled at Heshbon. The Israelites asked, 'Please allow us to pass through your territory to our own territory.' ²⁰ Sihon, however, distrusted the Israelites and refused passage. He then mobilized his army, encamped the troops at Jahaz, and opened hostilities with Israel. ²¹ Then YHWH, the God of Israel, gave Sihon and the Amorite army into Israel's hands, and the troops defeated them. So Israel took possession of all the land of the Amorites dwelling in that region, ²² which included all of the territory from the Arnon River to the Jabbok River and from the desert to the Jordan River.

²³ "Consider this," continued Jephthah. "Since YHWH, the God of Israel, dispossessed the Amorites for the benefit of the Israelites, what right do you have to occupy it? ²⁴ You should keep the land that your god Chemosh gave you, and we will keep the land YHWH gave us. ²⁵ Are you mightier than Balak ben-Zippor, ruler of Moab? Did he ever challenge Israel? ²⁶ For 300 years Israel occupied Heshbon, Aroer, the surrounding villages, and all the settlements along the Arnon River. Why didn't you retake them at that time? ²⁷ We have not sinned against you; you wrong us by warring against us. YHWH our Judge will decide this day between the Israelites and the Ammonites."

²⁸ But the ruler of the Ammonites did not heed the message Jephthah had sent him.

²⁹ Then the Spirit of YHWH came upon Jephthah. He crossed Gilead and Manassah, passing through Mizpah of Gilead, and from there moved against the rear of the Ammonites.

³⁰ And Jephthah made this vow to YHWH: "If you will really deliver the

Ammonites into my hands, ³¹ the first creature to come out of my house to meet me when I return victorious over the Ammonites will belong to YHWH, and I will sacrifice it as a burnt offering." *

³² Then Jephthah's troops crossed into Ammonite territory and attacked its people, and YHWH gave them into his hands. ³³ Jephthah struck them with a very great slaughter, completely destroyed twenty towns from Aroer as far as Minnith, all the way to Abel Keramim. And the Ammonites were made to submit to the Israelites.

³⁴ Then Jephthah came home to Mizpah. At that very moment his daughter came out of his house to meet him, dancing to the sound of tamborines. She was still a girl, and Jephthah's one and only child.

³⁵ Seeing her, he tore his clothes, crying out, "Ah, my daughter! You have torn my heart! You have become my calamity!† For I have opened my mouth to YHWH and I cannot turn back."

³⁶ "Papa," she replied, "you gave your word to YHWH. Do to me just as you promised, especially now that YHWH has avenged your enemies, the Ammonites. ³⁷ But do grant me one request! Let me have two months to roam the hills and mourn my virginity with my female companions." †

³⁸ "Go," he replied, and she and her friends wept for her virginity in the hills. ³⁹ After the two months, she returned to her father. And he carried out his vow. She died a virgin.

From this incident it became a custom throughout Israel ⁴⁰ for young women in Israel go out for four days every year, to mourn and tell the story of the daughter of Jephthah of Gilead.

12:1 The Ephraimites mobilized their forces, crossed over to Zaphon, and said to Jephthah, "Why did you take on the Ammonites without calling upon us to go with you? For that we'll burn down your house—with you in it!"

---

* As the renowned scholar and theologian Phyllis Trible notes, "A certain vagueness lurks in these words of Jephthah, and we do well to let it be. Did he intend a human sacrifice, male or female? A servant perhaps? Or an animal?" Trible also writes, "[Here] the savior figure has spoken on his own, for neither Yahweh nor the people of Gilead require the vow....[He presses] for divine help that ironically is already Jephthah's through the spirit of Yahweh. The making of the vow is an act of unfaithfulness. Jephthah desires to bind God rather than embrace the gift of the spirit. What comes to him freely, he seeks to earn and manipulate. The meaning of his words is doubt, not faith; it is control, not courage. To such a vow the deity makes no reply." (Phyllis Trible, *Texts of Terror: Literary-Feminist Readings of Biblical Narratives*, Philadelphia: Fortress Press, 1984.)

† "That time is to be filled," says Trible, "with lamentation, not for death, but for unfulfilled life." She goes on to compare the story with Abraham's sacrifice of Isaac: "[There the] suspense is bearable because Isaac is to be spared. At the last moment, the angel of [YHWH] degates the divine imperative....But in the story of the daughter of Jephthah, no angel intervenes to save the child. The father carries out the human vow precisely as he spoke it; neither God nor man nor woman negates it....Though the son was saved, the daughter is slain."

² Jephthah replied, "My people and I were engaged in a bitter conflict with the Ammonites, and although I appealed to you for help, you did not rescue me from their hands. ³ When I saw that no one was responding I took my life into my own hands and marched against the Ammonites. And YHWH handed them over to me. Now why do you attack me?"

⁴ Jephthah then mobilized his Gileadites and struck down the Ephraimites for their persistence in claiming, "You people of Gilead are nothing but fugitives from Ephraim, in territory that belongs to Ephraim and Manasseh."

⁵ The Gileadites overran the fords of the Jordan near Ephraim. When the fleeing Ephraimites asked permission the cross over, the Gileadites would ask, "Are you an Ephriamite?" Whoever answered "no" ⁶ was asked to pronounce the word "shibboleth." * Anyone who mispronounced the word as "sibboleth" was seized and killed at the fords of the Jordan. And 42,000 Ephraimites were put to death at that time.

⁷ After serving as chieftain of Israel for six years, Jephthah the Gileadite died and was buried in the city of Gilead.

ଓ   ଓ   ଓ

⁸ After Jephthah came Ibzan of Bethlehem, who served as governor of Israel. ⁹ He had thirty sons and thirty daughters, all of whom married outside the familial clan.† ¹⁰ Ibzan died, and was buried in Bethlehem.

¹¹ After Ibzan, Elon the Zebulunite led Israel for ten years. ¹² Then Elon died and was buried in Aijalon in the land of Zebulun.

¹³ The next governor of Israel was Abdon ben-Hillel, from Pirathon. ¹⁴ He had forty children and thirty grandchildren, each of whom owned and rode donkeys. Adbon led Israel for eight years. ¹⁵ Then Adon ben-Hillel died and was buried in at Pirathon in Ephraim, in the hill country of the Amalekites.

---

* The Jordan River ranges from 230 feet above sea level at its headwaters in the north to about 1,290 feet below sea level in the south. It often travels through deep and nearly inaccessible ravines, and the valley's quick descent creates swift currents and dangerous rapids in many places. (The word *shibboleth* actually means a torrent of water.) This made the river a natural boundary—so much so that the tribes living east of the Jordan, separated for many generations from those on the west, gradually came to adopt different speech patterns, one of which was the inability to pronounce the "sh" sound. The Jordan was such a serious obstacle in any east-to-west movement in Canaan that control of the fords—those few places where crossings were possible—became extremely important militarily.

† The Hebrew says that they married "outside," leading some scholars to speculate that they married outside the tribe, not just the clan.

13:1 Once more the Israelites did evil in the sight of YHWH, and YHWH delivered them into the hands of the Philistines for forty years.
2 A man named Manoah of Zorah, from the tribe of Dan, was married and childless. 3 The angel of YHWH appeared to his wife and said, "You and your husband have never been able to have children, but you are going to conceive and bear a son. 4 From now on, take care not to drink any wine or other liquor, and do not eat anything unclean, 5 for you will conceive and give birth to a son. No razor is to touch his hair: he is to be a Nazarite,* consecrated to God from the womb. The child will strike the first blow for Israel's freedom from the power of the Philistines."

6 The woman went to her husband and said, "A godlike figure came to me, someone like an angel of YHWH, an awesome being. I didn't ask where it came from, and it didn't tell me its name. 7 But I was told, 'You will conceive and bear a son. In the meantime drink no wine or other fermented drink and do not eat anything unclean, for the child is to be a Nazarite of God from birth until the day he dies.' "

8 Then Manoah prayed to YHWH, "God, I beg you, let the angel of YHWH you sent to us return to us to teach us how to raise the child who is to be born!"

9 God heard Manoah's prayer, and the angel of YHWH came to Manoah's wife when she was out in a field alone, 10 and she ran and told her husband, "The angel who appeared to me earlier is here!" 11 Manoah followed his wife, and when they reached the angel of YHWH, Manoah said, "Is it you who talked to my wife?"

The angel answered, "I am."

12 Then Manoah asked, "When your words are fulfilled, what rules do we need to follow for him, and what will be his life's work?"

13 The angel of YHWH replied, "Your wife is to do carefully all that I instructed. 14 She must not taste anything that comes from the vine, or to take other fermented drinks. And she is not to eat anything unclean. She is to do all that I told her to do."

15 Manoah said to the angel of YHWH, "We would like you to stay while we prepare a young goat for you."

---

* *Nazir* means "consecrated or devoted," and signified a complete dedication to God similar to the Hebrew priesthood. Men, women, and even servants could take the Nazarite vow; the vow was generally for thirty days, though it could be renewed indefinitely. People became Nazarites in gratitude for being cured of illness, or after the birth of a child or the fulfillment of some other prayer, or as a mark of piety or asceticism. The vow entailed drinking no alcohol, touching no dead bodies (not even a parent's), and keeping the hair uncut until the term of the vow ended, after which the hair was cut and offered as a sacrifice.

¹⁶ But the angel of YHWH replied, "Even though you detain me, I will not eat with you. But prepare a burnt offering, if you will, and offer it to YHWH." Manoah did not realize who with the stranger was.

¹⁷ Then Manoah asked the angel of YHWH, "What is your name? For we certainly will want to honor you when your words are fulfilled."

¹⁸ The angel replied, "Why do you ask for my name? It is *peli.*" *

¹⁹ Then Manoah took a young goat together with a grain offering and sacrificed them on a rock to YHWH. While Manoah and his wife watched, a wondrous thing happened: ²⁰ as the flame blazed up from the sacrifice on the rock towards heaven, the angel of YHWH ascended in the flames of the altar. Upon witnessing this, the couple prostrated themselves on the ground.

²¹ The angel of YHWH never again appeared to Manoah and his wife, but Manoah was certain that it was the angel of YHWH. ²² "Surely we're going to die now," cried Manoah, "for we have seen God!"

²³ But his wife replied, "If YHWH had meant for us to die, our burnt offering and grain offering would never have been accepted from us, nor would we have been allowed to see all this or have been told such things."

²⁴ The woman gave birth to a boy and named him Samson.* ²⁵ He grew up in the encampment of Dan, between Zorah and Eshtaol, and it was there that the Spirit of God first began to stir inside him.

14:1 Once Samson journeyed down to Timnah and there one of the young Philistine women caught his eye. ² Upon returning home he said to his parents, "While in Timnah I saw a Philistine woman I would like to marry."

³ They protested, "Isn't there a woman within your clan or within our tribe for you to marry? Must you go to those heathen Philistines for a spouse?"

But Samson insisted, "Father, get her for me, for she's the one I'm attracted to."

⁴ Neither parent knew that YHWH's hand was at work in this. For it was an opportunity to strike a blow against the Philistines, who at that time held dominion over Israel.

⁵ Samson went down to Timnah with his parents. As he approached the Timnah vineyards, a full-grown lion attacked him. ⁶ The Spirit of God seized

---

* The word *peli* means "incomprehensible, mysterious, wonderful, or beyond understanding." Most versions translate the reply as a rebuff ("Why bother asking, since my name is beyond your comprehension?"), but it may also have been a pun on the angel's part ("I don't see why you'd want to know, but my name is Peli").

† The name means "sun-like" (the Arabian sun god was named Shams-On), and he was born near the important city of Beth Shemesh, which means "house of the sun." Samson was virtually identical with Ra-Harakhti, the Egyptian sun god, and his deeds seem to duplicate those of the demigod Heracles from Greece.

him, and he tore the lion to pieces with his bare hands as if it were a young goat, but he never told his parents what he had done. ⁷ Then he went down and spoke to the woman, and he knew that she was the right one.

⁸ Some time later, when he went back to marry the woman, he spotted the remains of the lion, and noticed that a hive of bees had settled in its carcass, and there was honey. ⁹ So he scooped up a handful of the honey and ate it on the way. When he came to his parents, he gave them some of it to eat, but did not tell them where he had found it.

¹⁰ Samson's father went down to see the woman. And Samson threw a feast, as was customary for bridegrooms. ¹¹ The Philistines arranged for thirty young men from the village to keep him company. ¹² At the banquet, Samson said to them, "Let me tell you a riddle. If you can solve it within the seven days of the feast, I will give you thirty linen tunics and thirty festal robes. ¹³ But if you cannot solve the riddle, you give me thirty linen tunics and thirty festal robes!"

"Tell us the riddle," they said. "Let's hear it."

¹⁴ So Samson said to them,

"Out of the eater, something to eat;
out of the strong, something sweet."

At the end of three days, his companions had not solved the riddle. ¹⁵ On the fourth day they approached Samson's wife: "Coax your husband into explaining the riddle to you, or we will burn you and your father's house. Did you invite us here to reduce us to poverty?"

¹⁶ Then Samson's wife threw herself on him, sobbing, "You must hate me! You don't love me, for you proposed a riddle for my people without telling me the answer."

He replied, "I haven't even told it to my mother and father. Why should I explain it to you?"

¹⁷ She cried throughout the rest of the week that the feast lasted, and nagged him so persistently that on the seventh day he told her the answer, and she told it to her people. ¹⁸ So on the seventh day, just before sunset, the men of the city said to Samson,

"What is sweeter than honey?
What is stronger than a lion?"

¹⁹ Samson replied, "If you had not plowed with my heifer, you would not have solved my riddle!" * Then the Spirit of YHWH overcame him. And he went down to Ashkelon and killed thirty men, stripped them, and gave

---

* Farmers typically used their own animals to plow a field, not someone else's. Samson is saying that the Philistines had utilized a source of information that should have been off-limits to them.

their clothes to the men who had answered the riddle. Then, burning with rage, he returned to his own family.

²⁰ Samson's wife then married one of Samson's wedding companions.

¹⁵:¹ Some time later, during the wheat harvest, Samson set out to visit his wife with a young goat for a present. But when he said, "I am going to meet with my wife in our bridal chamber," her father refused him entry, and said, ² "I was so certain that you hated her that I let her marry your wedding companion. But her younger sister is more beautiful than she, so why don't you marry her instead?"

³ Samson said, "This is the time for me to settle accounts with the Philistines. And I will do them some real harm." ⁴ He then went out and caught 300 foxes and prepared torches. He tied the foxes tail to tail and fastened a torch to each pair. ⁵ He then lit the torches and turned to foxes loose in the standing grain of the Philistines. The torches set fire to the standing grain and sheaves, as well as to the vineyards and olive groves.

⁶ The Philistines inquired, "Who did this?" And when they learned that it was Samson, because his father-in-law the Timnite had taken his wife and given her to the wedding companion, they took her and her father and burnt them to death.

⁷ Samson said to them, "I will wreak vengeance on you for what you have done. I swear that I will not rest until I have my revenge." ⁸ He attacked them and put many of them to death. Then he went down and took refuge in a cave in the Rock of Etam.

⁹ The Philistines went up and camped in Judah, spreading out over Lehi. ¹⁰ The people of Judah asked, "Why have you encamped here? To fight us?"

They replied, "We are here to capture Samson, and do to him what he did to us." ¹¹ Then 3,000 Judahites left Judah and went down to the cave in the Rock of Etam. They met with Samson and said, "Don't you realize that we are vassals of the Philistines? Why have you done this?"

He replied, "I merely did to them what they had done to me."

¹² They responded, "We came here to take you prisoner and turn you over to the Philistines."

Then Samson said, "Swear to me that you will not execute me."

¹³ "No, we won't execute you. We will only bind you and deliver you to them." So they restrained him with two new ropes and led him away from the Rock.

¹⁴ When Samson came to Lehi, the Philistines met him with shouts of triumph. But the Spirit of YHWH came over him. The ropes on his arms turned into charred strings and the binding fell away from his hands. ¹⁵ Nearby lay

the fresh jawbone of a donkey. He reached out, grabbed it and used it to kill a thousand Philistines. ¹⁶ He declared,

> "With the jawbone of an ass
> I piled them in a heap;
> With the jawbone of an ass
> I lay a thousand Philistines in a heap;
> With the jawbone of an ass
> I slew a thousand Philistines."

¹⁷ When he had finished speaking, he threw away the jawbone. After that the place was called Ramath Lehi, "Lehi's Jawbone."

¹⁸ Samson felt very thirsty and called out to YHWH, "You gave your servant this great victory. Must I now die of thirst or fall into the hands of heathens?" ¹⁹ God opened a hollow in the ground at Lehi, and water poured out of it. As Samson drank, his strength returned and he revived. So the spring was named En Hakkore, "The Spring of the Caller," and is there to this day in Lehi.

²⁰ Samson led Israel for twenty years in the time of the Philistines.

¹⁶:¹ Samson went to the Philistine city of Gaza. There he saw a prostitute, and went to spend the night with her. ² When the people of Gaza learned that Samson was there, they surrounded the house and set guards at the city gate. They took no action during the night, and said, "We'll kill him at dawn."

³ But Samson lay in bed only until midnight, whereupon got up, took hold of the city gates and the two gateposts, and tore them loose, bar and all. He hoisted them onto his shoulders and lugged them all the way to the top of the hill east of Hebron.

⁴ Some time later, Samson fell in love with a Philistine woman from the Sorek Valley whose name was Delilah. ⁵ The chiefs of the five Philistine cities went to her and said, "Coax him so he'll tell you what makes him so strong. With that information we can overpower him, tie him up, and humiliate him. Each one of us will give you 1100 shekels of silver." *

⁶ So Delilah said to Samson, "Tell me, what is the source of your great strength? Could anyone tie you up or make you helpless?"

⁷ Samson replied, "If I were restrained with seven bowstrings—fresh ones, not dried—then I would be as weak as anyone else."

---

* Eleven hundred shekels is about 28 pounds of silver. Gideon had a third as much after routing the Midianite rulers, and Levites received only ten shekels per year as their salary, so 1100 shekels represents more than most people would see in a lifetime. Delilah is being offered five times that amount.

⁸ The Philistine chiefs brought Delilah seven fresh bowstrings, not yet dried, and she tied Samson with them. ⁹ With an ambush waiting in her room, she cried out, "Samson, the Philistines are upon you!" In a flash he snapped the bowstrings as easily as a piece of string snaps when it is lighted by a flame. So the secret of his strength remained unknown.

¹⁰ Then Delilah said to Samson, "You fooled me! You lied to me! This time, really tell me how you can be bound!"

¹¹ He said, "If I am restrained by new rope, rope never used before, I will be as weak as anyone else."

¹² So Delilah took new rope and bound him with it. Then she called out, "Samson, the Philistines are upon you!" In a flash he snapped the ropes as if they were thread.

¹³ Then Deiliah said to Samson, "You have been fooling me all along and lying to me! Tell me how you can be bound."

He replied, "If you took seven locks of my hair and wove them into the fabric of the loom and fastened it with the peg, I would be as weak as anyone else." As he slept Delilah took the seven locks of his hair, wove them into the fabric ¹⁴ and tightened them with the pin. Again she called out, "Samson, the Philistines are upon you!" He woke up and pulled out the peg, the loom, and the fabric.

¹⁵ Then she pleaded with him, "How can you say you love me, when you won't take me into your confidence? This is the third time you have deceived me, and you still won't tell me the secret of your great strength!" ¹⁶ She pressed him night and day, haranguing him relentlessly until he grew sick to death of her nagging.

¹⁷ So he told her his secret: "No razor has touched my head, for I am a Nazirite, consecrated to God from the day of my birth. If my head were shaved, I would lose my strength, and be no stronger than anyone else." ¹⁸ Delilah realized that she had finally learned Samson's secret.*

She notified the rulers of the Philistines. They came quickly and brought the money with them. ¹⁹ She lulled Samson to sleep on her lap, and then

---

* Read casually, Samson is a dupe and Delilah is a seducer, a betrayer, and a shrew. But understood mythologically, Samson is the sun and Delilah the dark of the year that whittles away the sun's power; the loss of Samson's hair and the gouging out of his eyes is analogous to the cutting of the sun god's rays in autumn. The feminist scholar Barbara G. Walker has pointed out that just as Heracles was controlled by Omphale and Ra was "made weak" by Isis, so Samson was deprived of strength by Delilah, whose name may mean "She Who Makes Weak." Hair-cutting was a mythic symbol of castration; each year many agrarian cultures performed a ceremonial reenactment of the death of the sun god, in which a strong hero rose up at the spring equinox, took many lovers throughout the spring and summer, and was castrated and sacrificed—symbolically, at least, with the cutting of the hero's hair—at the harvest.

summoned a Philistine to shave off the seven locks of his hair. [20] Then she called out, "Samson, the Philistines are upon you!"

He woke up and thought, "I'll get out of here as before," but he did not realize that YHWH had abandoned him. [21] The Philistines quickly captured him, then they gouged out his eyes. They took him down to Gaza. He was bound with bronze shackles, and he was put to work grinding grain in the prison. [22] But though his hair had been shaved off, it was now beginning to grow back.

[23] The rulers of the Philistines gathered at the temple of their god Dagon* to offer a great sacrifice and celebrate. They said, "Our god delivered our enemy Samson into our hands."

[24] When the people saw their god's idol, they shouted his praise, chanting,

"Our god delivered our enemy into our hands,
the ravager of our land who multiplied our dead."

[25] After the people got drunk, they said, "Bring out Samson, and make him entertain us!"

When they brought out Samson to perform for them, standing him among the pillars, [26] Samson told the deputy holding his hand, "Put me where I can feel the pillars that support the temple, so that I can lean against them."

[27] By this time the temple was full of men and women; the chieftains of the Philistines were there, along with about 3,000 men and women on the roof watching Samson entertain. [28] Then Samson prayed to YHWH, "Sovereign YHWH, please remember me! Give me strength, God, just one more time, and let me strike one blow to get revenge on the Philistines for my two eyes."

[29] Then Samson reached out to the two central pillars supporting the temple and braced himself, one with his right arm, the other with his left. [30] Samson said, "Let me die with the Philistines!" Then he pushed with all his strength. The temple crashed down on the chieftains and all the people inside it. So in one stroke Samson killed many more when he died than when he had lived.

[31] All his family and all his relatives went down and carried Samson's body up to the grave of his father Manoah between Zorah and Eshtaol and buried him there. He had led Israel for twenty years.

---

* Dagon was the god of grain, a Semitic deity adopted by the Philistines after their invasion of Canaan; this celebration in his temple has all the earmarks of a harvest festival, making explicit the connection to Samson as the personification of the sun god being sacrificed at the autumn harvest. The Hebrew word *dagan*, "grain," is probably derived from the name of the god.

Ín the hill country of Ephraim lived a man named Micah.* ² He said to his mother, "Do you remember the 1100 shekels of silver that were stolen from you, and your pronouncing a curse over anyone who knew where they were? You repeated that curse in my hearing. I have the shekels—I took them. I now return them you."

His mother said, "May YHWH bless my son!"

³ He returned the 1100 shekels of silver, but his mother said, "I consecrate this silver to YHWH, for my son's benefit. I will have an artisan make a sculpted idol, and an idol in cast metal, and the rest of the money I now give back to you."

⁴ So of the money he had returned, his mother took 200 shekels and gave them to a silversmith, who made a sculpted idol and an idol in cast metal. These were kept in Micah's residence, ⁵ so Micah made himself a sanctuary. He also made an ephod and some household idols, and consecrated one of his sons, who became his priest.

⁶ In those days, Israel was without a ruler, so all people acted as they pleased.

⁷ There was a young Levite from Bethlehem, the clan seat of Judah, who was staying there temporarily. ⁸ He left Bethlehem in search of another place to live. On the journey he came to Micah's house in the hill country of Ephraim.

⁹ Asked by Micah where he was from, the traveler replied, "I am a Levite from Bethlehem in Judah, and I am looking for a place to stay."

¹⁰ Then Micah said, "Stay with me and be my advisor and priest, and I will pay you ten shekels of silver a year, and provide you with clothing and food."

¹¹ So the Levite agreed to live with Micah, and was treated as a member of the family. ¹² Then Micah consecrated the Levite, who became his priest and served at Micah's shrine. ¹³ "Now I know that YHWH will make me prosperous," Micah said, "for I have a Levite as my priest."

---

* This last section contains unrelated stories that took place much earlier in time, soon after the death of Joshua, during the days of Phinehas ben-Eleazar, but that the editors of *Judges* apparently felt would interrupt the flow of the main narrative and so included them as a sort of appendix. The 1100 shekels in the next verse, like the 1100 shekels with which Delilah was bribed to betray Samson, are symbolic numbers; eleven hundred represents sin on a massive scale. There were eleven goat's hair curtains on the Tabernacle, where sin offerings were accepted, and eleven was the number of incompleteness, disorganization, disintegration—going beyond the perfection of ten, yet falling short of the fulfillment of twelve.

18:1 In those days, Israel was without a ruler. And in those days the tribe of Dan was seeking a place to occupy. Its members had not migrated far enough to take possession of the territory allotted to them among the tribes of Israel. 2 So the Danites sent five valiant warriors from Zorah and Eshtaol to spy on the country and survey it. Following their instructions, they came to Micah's place in the hill country of Ephraim and spent the night there.

3 While visiting there, they recognized the dialect of the young Levite, and asked, "Who brought you here? What are you doing here? Why are you here?"

4 He told them what Micah had done for him, saying, "Micah hired me, and I am his priest."

5 They said to him, "Seek God on our behalf to find out whether our mission will succeed."

6 The priest replied, "Go in peace. YHWH looks with favor on your mission."

7 The five valiant warriors continued on their way and came to Laish. They found the inhabitants free of care just like the Sidonians, peaceful and trusting, with no one making trouble in the land or trying to dispossess them. They lived far from the Sidonians and had no contact with anyone.

8 When the warriors returned to Zorah and Eshtaol, and the people asked them 9 what they had found out, they replied, "Come, we should occupy the territory. We have seen the land and it is very good. 10 When you get there you will find a trusting people living a carefree life in wide open spaces of country. And the soil is very good. God has put the land into your hands, a land lacking nothing whatever."

11 Six hundred Danites set out from Zorah and Esthaol, armed for war. 12 Along the way they set up camp near Kiriath-Jearim in Judah. It is for this reason that the place west of Kiriath-Jearim is called Dan's Camp to this day. 13 From there the migrants moved into the hill country of Ephraim and came to Micah's house.

14 Then the five who had led the first expedition to spy out the land of Laish said to their relatives, "We learned that one of the houses has an ephod, other household gods, a sculpted idol, and a cast metal idol. You know what to do."

15 So they turned down that road and went to the young Levite's shrine at Micah's home and greeted the Levite peacefully. 16 As the 600 armed Danites stood at the gate threshold, 17 the five who had led the expedition went inside and removed the sculpted idol, the ephod, the other household gods, and the cast metal idol.

The priest, meanwhile, was standing at the gate entrance with the 600 armed Danites. ¹⁸ When he realized that the five scouts had entered Micah's house and were removing the sculpted idol, the ephod, the other household gods, and the cast metal idol, the priest said, "What are you doing?"

¹⁹ They silenced him, "Be quiet! Don't say a word! Come with us, and be our advisor and priest. Isn't it better to be a priest for a tribe and a clan than to be a priest for a single household?" ²⁰ This pleased him, so he gathered together the ephod, the household gods, the sculpted idol, and the cast metal idol, and he left with the people. ²¹ They set out once more, with their dependents, herds, and possessions going before the soldiers.

²² When they had gone some distance from Micah's house, Micah's neighbors set out together to overtake them. ²³ As they approached the Danites, they shouted to them to stop. But the moving Danites shouted back to Micah, "Why have you called out your warriors?"

²⁴ Micah replied, "You took the gods I had made, and you went off with my priest as well. What is left for me? How dare you ask what I want of you?"

²⁵ "Don't keep shouting at us," the Danites said, "for we are a desperate people, and if we have to fight you, it will mean the death of you and your family." ²⁶ So the Danites continued on their journey, and Micah, seeing the size of the Danite army, went back home.

²⁷ Carrying off the items Micah had fashioned and taking the priest with them, the Danites then attacked Laish, a quiet and trusting people, putting them to the sword and burning down the town. ²⁸ There was no one to come to their rescue, for they were a long way from Sidon and had no treaties with others nearby.

The city was in a valley near Beth-Rehob. The Danites rebuilt the city and inhabited it. ²⁹ Though the city had once been called called Laish, they renamed it Dan after their ancestor Dan ben-Israel.

³⁰ The Danites set the idols up for themselves, and Jonathan ben-Gershom ben-Moses and his sons were priests for the tribe of Dan until the time of the captivity. ³¹ For as long as the house of God was in Shilah, they set up for themselves the idol Micah had made.

ભ ભ ભ

¹⁹:¹ In those days, when Israel was without a ruler, there was a man, a Levite who lived in a remote area of the hill country of Ephraim. The Levite

took for himself a woman, a concubine from Bethlehem in Judah.* ² But she left him in a fit of anger and went back to her father's home.

After four months ³ the Levite set out with an attendant and two donkeys, went after her, attempting to speak to her heart and bring her back. She invited him into her home, and her father gladly welcomed him. ⁴ His father-in-law, the father of the young woman, prevailed upon him to stay, so the Levite stayed for three days; they ate and drank and spent the nights there.

⁵ On the fourth day, the guests rose early and the Levite prepared to leave. But the father suggested, "Have some food for the journey, and then you can leave." ⁶ So they sat down and feasted together. The young woman's father said to the Levite, "Please stay another night, and enjoy yourself." ⁷ The Levite rose to leave, but his father-in-law kept urging him to stay, so he stayed one more night, eating and drinking.†

⁸ They rose early on the fifth day to leave, but the young woman's father said, "Just gather your strength for the journey and have something to eat," so they stayed on and dined until late afternoon. ⁹ Then the man, his concubine, and his attendant started to leave, but his father-in-law, the young woman's father, insisted, "It will soon be evening. Do stay one more night. Look, the day is almost over—spend the night here and enjoy yourself. You can get an early start on your journey tomorrow." ¹⁰ But the Levite refused to stay for the night. He set off with a pair of saddled donkeys, the concubine and an attendant, until they came within sight of Jebus—that is, Jerusalem.

¹¹ As they approached Jebus at dusk, the attendant asked the Levite, "Please let us stop in this Jebusite town and spend the night there."

¹² "No," he said to his attendant, "we don't enter towns of foreigners, of non-Israelites. We will head for Gibeah. ¹³ Come on, we'll try to reach either Gibeah or Ramah and spend the night there."

¹⁴ So they moved on, and the sun had set as they entered Gibeah in Benjamin. ¹⁵ Intent on spending the night, they stopped at the town square, but no one offered to take them in for the night.

---

* This introduces one of the most horrific stories in the Bible. But as Phyllis Trible says so powerfully in her book *Texts of Terror*, "The betrayal, rape, torture, murder, and dismemberment of an unnamed woman is a story we want to forget but are commanded to speak. It depicts the horrors of male power, brutality, and triumphalism; of female helplessness, abuse, and annihilation. To hear this story is to inhabit a world of unrelenting terror that refuses to let us pass by on the other side." Concubines were usually house servants who had all of the responsibilities of a wife with none of the rights or privileges; poverty usually forced women into such arrangements, and here the Levite clearly treats her as property.

† Note the focus is on the power struggle between the two men, while totally ignoring the woman. "Unlike her father," says Trible, "the daughter has no speech; unlike her master, the concubine has no power. A journey 'to speak to her heart' has become a visit to engage male hearts, with no speech to her at all."

¹⁶ At nightfall an old man originally from the hill country of Ephraim, though he lived among the Benjaminites in Gibeah, was returning from working in his field ¹⁷ when he spotted the Levite in the town square, and asked the traveler's origin and destination. ¹⁸ The Levite said, "We are traveling from Bethlehem in Judah to the hill country of Ephraim, which is where I live. I journeyed to Bethlehem in Judah, and now I am on my way to the House of YHWH, and no one has offered to take me in for the night. ¹⁹ We have straw and fodder for our animals, and wine and food for me, and your handmaid, and the young man traveling with me, your servant. We have all we need."

²⁰ "I welcome you," said the old man. "Let me take care of all your needs. You must not spend the night in the square." ²¹ He took them inside, gave them fodder for the animals, water for cleaning up, and food and drink.

²² As they enjoyed their mutual company some local degenerates showed up, surrounded the house and started pounding on the door. They shouted to the old man, "Bring out the man, we want to have sex* with him."

²³ The owner of the house went out to remonstrate with them: "My brothers, don't commit such a wrong! He is my guest, and he falls under my protection, so don't commit this vile thing. ²⁴ Look, here is my daughter, a virgin—and here is his concubine. I'll bring them out to you. Violate them, do to them whatever is good in your eyes. But to this man don't do such a vile thing." †

²⁵ When the men refused to listen to the old man, the Levite grabbed his concubine and pushed her outside. They took her away and raped her repeatedly all night long until morning, letting her go only when dawn was breaking.

²⁶ At daybreak she came to the house of the old man and collapsed at his door and lay there until morning. ²⁷ When the Levite woke up at daybreak and opened the door to start his journey home, there lay his concubine, at the entrance of the house, with her hands on the threshold. ²⁸ "Get up," he said to her, "it's time to leave." But there was no answer. So he placed her on a donkey and set out for home.

²⁹ When he arrived home he picked up the knife, took hold of his concubine, cut her limb from limb into twelve pieces,‡ and sent them throughout all of Israel. ³⁰ He instructed his messengers, "Say this to all the Israelites:

---

* Literally, "to know," which is often a euphemism for intercourse—in this case, they want to rape and sexually humiliate him. Men in many ancient near eastern cultures raped male strangers, trespassers, and their conquered enemies to indicate their subordinate status; essentially, they want to "turn them into women," graphically demonstrating the abased status of women in those societies.

† Trible notes that "If done to a man, such an act is a vile thing; if done to women, it is 'the good' in the eyes of men.... Conflict among [males] can be solved by the sacrifice of females."

‡ One piece for each tribe.

'Has anything like this been done from the time the Israelites came out of Egypt until now? Take this to heart, discuss it; then speak up.'"*

And all who saw it cried out, "Nothing like this has ever been done or been seen since the Israelites came out of Egypt until now."

20:1 All the children of Israel came together as one, from Dan to Beer-sheba, and from the land of Gilead. They left their homes and assembled before YHWH at Mizpah. 2 The leaders of the people and all the tribes of Israel presented themselves at this assembly of God's people: there were 400,000 foot soldiers, armed with swords.

3 In the meantime, the Benjaminites learned that the rest of the Israelites were gathered at Mizpah. The Israelites confronted them and said, "Tell us how this loathsome incident took place." 4 So the Levite, the murdered woman's husband, described what had happened: "My concubine and I spent the night Gibeah in Benjamin. 5 In the middle of the night, the men of Gibeah rose up against me and surrounded the house. They tried to kill me, and they raped my concubine until she died. 6 So I took her body, cut it into pieces, and sent a piece to each region of Israel's territory. For all should learn of this abominable act of depravity that has been committed in Israel. 7 Now that we are all gathered here, people of Israel, what action will you take?"

8 All the people rose up as one, and said, "We won't go back to our tents, we will not enter our homes. 9 But this is what we will do to Gibeah: We will draw lots for the attack, 10 taking from all the tribes of Israel ten soldiers out of every hundred, a hundred out of every thousand, a thousand out of every ten thousand. And the army will collect provisions for the troops. These will go to the warriors mobilized against Gibeah in Benjamin to avenge this outrage committed in Israel."

11 And all the Israelites came together and were massed against the city for one purpose. 12 The tribes of Israel sent messengers throughout the tribe of Benjamin with the question, "How can you justify this terrible evil committed among you? 13 Turn over to us the perpetrators in your midst, so that we can put them to death and remove this evil from Israel."

But the Benjaminites refused to listen to their fellow Israelites. 14 Instead, the Benjaminites left their towns and gathered in Gibeah, to take up arms

---

* One last comment from Phyllis Trible's peerless analysis: "Of all the characters in scripture, she is the least. Appearing at the beginning and close of a story that rapes her, she is alone in a world of her own. Neither the other characters nor the narrator recognizes her humanity. She is property, object, tool, and literary device. Without name, speech, or power, she has no friends to aid her in life or mourn her in death. Passing her back and forth among themselves, the men of Israel have obliterated her totally....In the end, she is no more than the oxen that Saul will later cut in pieces and send throughout all the territory of Israel as a call to war (1 Samuel 11:7)." Perhaps we should heed the Levite's command: "Take this to heart, discuss it; then speak up."

against the other Israelites. ¹⁵ The Benjaminites mobilized from all their cities 26,000 sword-bearing infantry, besides the citizens of Gibeah. Seven hundred of them were carefully selected— ¹⁶ 700 slingshooters, all of them left-handed*—selected because they could sling a stone and not miss by so much as a hair's breadth.

¹⁷ The other tribes, not counting Benjamin, mustered 400,000 sword-bearing warriors. ¹⁸ They went up to Bethel to consult with God. When the Israelites asked God who should be first to attack Benjamin, YHWH said, "Judah is to be first."

¹⁹ The following day the Israelites moved out at dawn and advanced against Gibeah. ²⁰ They took the field against the Benjaminites, drawing up in battle formation just outside the town. ²¹ The Benjaminites came out swinging and cut down 22,000 Israelites that day. ²² But the Israelites encouraged one another, and took up their positions as before. ²³ Then the Israelites went up and wept before YHWH until evening. They asked whether they should engage the Benjaminites once more, and YHWH said, "Yes." ²⁴ Once more they engaged the Benjaminites, ²⁵ who came out from Gibeah and struck down 18,000 armed soldiers.

²⁶ So the entire Israelite army retreated up to Bethel, where they wept and fasted before YHWH until evening and presented burnt offerings and fellowship offerings to YHWH. ²⁷ The Israelites again inquired of YHWH—in those days, the Ark of the Covenant of God was there, ²⁸ and Phinehas ben-Eleazar ben-Aaron ministered before God—and they asked, "Should we take up arms again today?"

And YHWH said, "Attack! Tomorrow I will deliver them into your hands." †

²⁹ So the armies of Israel set up an ambush around Gibeah. ³⁰ Then the armies of Israel—this was on the third day—formed their battle lines at Gibeah as before. ³¹ The Benjaminites rushed out to engage them, but allowed themselves to be drawn away from the city. They began to strike down the Israelites just as they had done before. On the main road between Bethel and Gibeah and in open country, they killed about thirty Israelites.

³² The Benjaminites thought, "We are defeating them, just as we did before," but drawing the Benjaminites away from town and onto the roads was part of the Israelites' plan. ³³ While the main body of the Israelites was

---

* This is not some odd coincidence. "Left-handed" in Hebrew actually means "bound in the right hand," a training method in which use of the right hand was restricted from an early age so the left hand would become dominant, since lefthanders have a distinct military advantage when attacking city gates.

† Following are two separate accounts of the same battle, artlessly edited together: Verses 29-36a form the first account, which is repeated with more detail in 36b-46. Verse 47 then picks up the first account again, repeating some material that the middle section had already stated in 44-45. Chapter 21 appears similarly pieced together.

moving away from its positions and drawing the Benjaminites out to Baal-tamar, an Israelite ambush was springing from its position just outside of Gibeah. ³⁴ Then the main body—10,000 soldiers, Israel's best—turned and made a frontal attack, and the battle was fierce, though the Benjaminites did not realize that disaster was approaching. ³⁵ Then YHWH struck Benjamin before Israel, and that day the Israelites killed 25,100 armed Benjaminites. ³⁶ The Benjaminites then knew that they had been defeated.

The Israelite troops started by yielding ground to the Benjaminites, relying on the ambush they had set at Gibeah. ³⁷ The ambushing troops made a sudden dash into Gibeah. Fanning out, they put all its inhabitants to death. ³⁸ In their planning they had agreed on a signal: when the ambushers sent up a column of smoke from the town, ³⁹ the rest of the Israelites would stop yielding ground and would turn around and engage them again in battle. The Benjaminites began by killing some thirty Israelites, giving themselves the impression they were winning as they had done in the first and the second battles; ⁴⁰ but now, the Benjaminites looked back and saw the column of smoke rising from the city, and thought their whole city was in flames. ⁴¹ Just then the Israelite army turned back and attacked them. The Benjamites were panic-stricken, and realized that disaster had overtaken them.

⁴² So they fled before the Israelites in the direction of the desert, but they could not escape the battle: the ambushers now charged out from city and cut them down from the rear. ⁴³ They surrounded the Benjaminites, and chased them and trod them down from Nohah all the way back to Geba on the east. ⁴⁴ Eighteen thousand valiant Benjaminites fell that day. ⁴⁵ The survivors fled into the desert toward the Rock of Rimmon. The Israelites pursued them, picking off 5,000 stragglers on the road, and continued to pursue them until they captured 2,000 more. ⁴⁶ The total number of armed Benjaminites who fell that day was 25,000, all of them valiant warriors.

⁴⁷ The 600 who survived the ordeal turned and fled through the desert to the Rock of Rimmon, and they stayed there for four months.

⁴⁸ The Israelites went back through the territory of Benjamin. Along the way they put to the sword all the towns, people, and livestock they encountered—everything that they came upon. And they set fire to all the towns they passed through.

21:1 The Israelites took an oath at Mizpah: "Not one of us will let our children marry anyone from the tribe of Benjamin." ² And the Israelite leaders went to Bethel and stayed there in God's presence until sunset, wailing and weeping bitterly. ³ "YHWH, God of Israel," they cried, "how is it that one of our tribes should this day be missing from Israel?"

⁴ Early the next morning the people built an altar and offered whole offerings and communion offerings. ⁵ Then they asked of themselves, "Who

among all the tribes of Israel did not come up to YHWH for the assembly?" For all of them had taken a solemn oath that anyone who had not come up to YHWH at Mizpah would be put to death.

⁶ The Israelites were disconsolate over Benjamin and said, "Today one of the tribes of Israel has been cut off from Israel. ⁷ How can we find wives for the Benjaminite survivors? For we swore by YHWH not to give them any of our people in marriage."

⁸ And when they asked whether anyone among the tribes of Israel had not come up to YHWH in Mizpah, ⁹ they found that none of people of Jabesh Gilead had been there. ¹⁰ So the assembly ordered 12,000 warriors to go there, commanding them, "Go and put the citizens of Jabesh Gilead to the sword—men, women, and children. ¹¹ This is what you are to do: put every male, and every woman who has ever slept with a male, under the sacred ban." ¹² They found among the citizens of Jabesh Gilead 400 female virgins, and took them to the camp at Shiloh in Canaan. ¹³ The whole community sent messengers to the Benjaminite soldiers at the Rock of Rimmon, offering them peace. ¹⁴ So the Benjaminites returned, and they were given the young women of Jabesh Gilead whose lives had been spared, but there were not enough of them for all of the soldiers.*

¹⁵ The people were still remorseful over Benjamin for the breach that YHWH had created in the tribes of Israel. ¹⁶ The community elders asked, "How can we find wives for the rest of the soldiers, inasmuch as so many Benjaminite women were wiped out? ¹⁷ The survivors of Benjamin must have sons," they continued, "so that a tribe of Israel will not die out. ¹⁸ Yet we cannot let them marry our daughters, because we swore that there will be a curse on whoever gives a spouse to a Benjaminite."

¹⁹ Then someone remembered the annual festival of YHWH in Shiloh, north of Bethel, east of the highway from Bethel to Shechem and to the south of Lebonah. ²⁰ The Benjaminites were instructed to go there and hide in the vineyards. ²¹ "When you see the young women of Shiloh dancing in the vineyard," they were advised, "each of you should seize one of them for a spouse, and come back to the land of Benjamin. ²² If their relatives come to complain to us, we can say, 'Do us a kindness—we couldn't provide any of them with wives because of the war. Besides, you couldn't give your daughters in marriage to them willingly, or you'd break your oath not to let them intermarry with Benjaminites.' " ²³ So this is what the Benjaminites did. They carried off as many young women as they needed by abducting them from the vineyard during their dancing.

---

* Note that here, and in the next paragraphs, women are once again treated as chattel, taken by men and given to men as property. In verse 23, the verb "abducting" is *gazal*, which means "to tear away, to take violent possession of, or to plunder."

Then the Benjaminites returned to their own territory, where they rebuilt their towns and settled in them. ²⁴ The other Israelites also dispersed and left that place and returned home to their tribes and clans, all to their own territory.

²⁵ In those days, Israel was without a ruler, so all people acted as they pleased.

1 samuel

$t$here was a certain person from Ramathaim, a Zuphite from the hill country of Ephraim, named Elkanah ben-Jeroham ben-Elihu ben-Tohu, an Ephraimite. ² Elkanah had two wives, one named Hannah and the other Peninnah. Peninnah had children, but Hannah was childless.

³ Elkanah made an annual pilgrimage from Ephraim up to Shiloh to worship and sacrifice to YHWH, the God of Israel.* The two sons of Eli, Hophni and Phinehas, served as priests of YHWH there. ⁴ When the time came for Elkanah to sacrifice, he would give portions to Peninnah and her children, ⁵ and a double portion to Hannah, for he loved Hannah, even though YHWH made her childless. ⁶ And because YHWH closed her womb, her rival con-

---

* Of all the books of the Hebrew scriptures, *I Samuel* may provide one of the clearest examples of the weaving together of the scriptures from multiple sources—most notably in this case, the Yahwistic narrative, which primarily uses the name YHWH to refer to God, and the Elohistic narrative, which uses Elohim. There are many duplicate and sometimes contradictory traditions regarding similar events, such as two different accounts of Saul's rejection as ruler; David being Saul's musician in ch. 16, but a stranger to him in ch. 17; two accounts of Saul trying to kill David with a spear; two stories of Saul caught up in prophetic ecstasy; etc. In addition to the Yahwistic and Elohistic threads, some scholars see an early source that is in favor of the monarchy, and a late one that is antagonistic to it.

stantly taunted her. As a result, she grew gravely depressed. ⁷ This went on for years. Every year they made the pilgrimage to YHWH's Tent of Meeting, her rival taunted her to tears and she refused to eat.

⁸ Elkanah, her husband would ask, "Hannah, why do you cry, and why do you refuse to eat? To grieve? Am I not more to you than ten sons?"

⁹ Hannah rose after one such meal at Shiloh, and presented herself to God. At the time, the priest Eli was sitting on a chair by the door of YHWH's Tent of Meeting.

¹⁰ Hannah, deeply distressed, wept greatly, ¹¹ vowing, "YHWH Omnipotent, look with pity on your handmaid. Don't forsake me. Remember me. If you will give me a child, a male, I will dedicate him to you. For all the days of his life, he will neither drink wine nor liquor, and no razor will ever touch its head."

¹² As she kept praying to YHWH, Eli noticed her lips. ¹³ Hannah was praying silently—her lips moved but they made no sound. Seeing this, Eli decided she was drunk, ¹⁴ and said to her, "How long will you continue to remain in this drunken state? Sober up!*

¹⁵ Hannah replied, "Oh no! It isn't that! I am a woman with a broken heart! I have drunk neither wine nor liquor. But I have been pouring out my heart before YHWH. ¹⁶ Don't judge me as a terrible person. I am simply pouring out my feelings of grief and misery."

¹⁷ Eli said "Go in peace. And may the God of Israel grant you your wish."

¹⁸ Hannah replied, "You are most kind." Then she left.

¹⁹ Early the next morning they arose early and worshiped before YHWH and then returned to Ramah, their home.

When Elkanah made love to Hannah, YHWH remembered her. ²⁰ She conceived, and gave birth to a son. She named him Samuel, for she had asked for him.†

²¹ Elkanah and the whole family made the annual trip to sacrifice to YHWH and make his vows. ²² Hannah did not go, however, telling Elkanah, "Once the child is weaned I will take him up and present him to YHWH in the Tent of Meeting. He will remain there always."

²³ Elkanah said, "Do what you think best. Stay here until the child is weaned. For only YHWH may see your vow fulfilled." And she stayed home, nursing the child until she weaned it.

---

* It was probably not unusual for participants at the feast to be intoxicated, since drinking was a part of the ritual. At times, the High Priest had to be the "bouncer," and kept watch over the activities in the Tent of Meeting for any suspicious activity. Hannah's breaking of customary prayer forms by praying silently raised his suspicions enough to confront her. His admonition to "sober up" is met with Hannah's clear and sober answer.

† The name Samuel means "The one over whom the Name of God is pronounced."

²⁴ Once weaned, she took the boy with her. She also took a three-year-old bull, an ephah of flour and a skin of wine, and presented him at the Tent of Meeting of YHWH, the God of Israel in Shiloh. ²⁵ After the boy's father sacrificed the young bull, Hannah brought it to Eli, ²⁶ saying, "Sir, as sure as you live, I am the woman who stood her beside you praying to YHWH. ²⁷ I asked YHWH for this boy and God granted my request. ²⁸ Now I give him to YHWH, for his entire life is given to YHWH." And they prostrated themselves there before YHWH.

²·¹ Then Hannah prayed:

My heart delights in YHWH,
    to YHWH I lift my horn high.
I gloat over my foes,
    I rejoice in your deliverance!
2 There is no one holier than you.
    No one is holier than YHWH;
    there is no Rock like YHWH.
3 All bragging must cease.
    Boastful arrogance must come to an end.
For YHWH is all-knowing,
    and weighs all mortal deeds.
4 The bows of warriors are broken,
    while those who stumble gain renewed strength.
5 Those who had their fill now sell themselves for crusts of bread
    while those who were hungry are now sated.
Childless women bear seven children
    while mothers of many are forsaken.
6 It is YHWH who deals out both life and death;
    it is YHWH who casts down to Sheol, and raises up again.
7 It is YHWH who makes both the poor and the wealthy.
    It is YHWH who both humbles and exalts.
8 YHWH lifts the weak from the refuse dump
    and raises the poor from the cesspool,
to place them among the mighty
    and promotes them to seats of honor.
The foundations of the earth belong to YHWH,
    and YHWH sets the world upon them.
9 YHWH lights the ways of the just
    and delivers the evildoer to darkness.
It is not by strength that the just prevail:
10   it is YHWH who shatters foes.
The Most High thunders against them in the skies;
    YHWH judges the ends of the earth.

Now Y<small>HWH</small> will endow the ruler with strength
and exalt the head of the anointed one."*

¹¹ Then Elkanah returned to Ramah, and the child remained in the service of Y<small>HWH</small> under Eli the priest.

¹² Eli's sons were thugs.† They had no regard either for Y<small>HWH</small> ¹³ or for the duties of the priests toward the people. This is how the priests would deal with people: once someone offered a sacrifice, an attendant of the priests would be there with a three-pronged fork. As the meat boiled, ¹⁴ the attendant would plunge it into the cauldron or the pan or the kettle or the pot. The attendant would take whatever came out on the fork.

This should have been the practice whenever Israelites came to sacrifice at Shiloh. But now, ¹⁵ even before the fat was burned, the priest's attendants would arrive and say to the person sacrificing, "Give me meat to roast for the priest." The attendant would not accept boiled meat, only raw meat. ¹⁶ And if the person sacrificing protested, and said, "Let the fat be burned first, and then take whatever you wish," the attendant would answer, "No, hand it over. And if you don't, I will take it by force."

¹⁷ This sin, the sin of the sons of Eli, was extremely offensive in the eyes of Y<small>HWH</small>. For they treated offering to Y<small>HWH</small> with contempt.

¹⁸ Samuel, on the other hand, would minister before Y<small>HWH</small> wearing a linen ephod around his waist.‡ ¹⁹ Each year Samuel's mother would bring him a small cloak, when she went up to sacrifice with Elkanah. ²⁰ Eli would bless Elkanah and Hannah, and say, "May Y<small>HWH</small> grant you children by Hannah in place of the one you gave to Y<small>HWH</small>." Then they would return to their home. ²¹ Y<small>HWH</small> took care of Hannah, for she conceived and gave birth to three sons and two daughters. Meanwhile Samuel grew up in the presence of Y<small>HWH</small>.

²² Eli was very old. When he learned the truth of how his sons treated all the people of Israel—particularly how they seduced the women serving at the entrance of the Tent of Meeting— ²³ he said to them, "Why do you do such things? I've heard from all the people about your evil deeds. ²⁴ No, my sons! You must stop this! The report I hear the people of Y<small>HWH</small> spreading about you is not good. ²⁵ If one person sins against another, a third person

---

* The mention of the ruler in this poem points to a later authorship; "anointed one" should be understood as synonymous with "ruler" in the previous line.
† There is an interesting contrast here between the children of Eli and Samuel: Samuel's piety is contrasted with the depraved acts of Eli's son. As Samuel's star rises, that of the corrupt children of Eli falls. This is a literary foreshadowing of the rise of the house of David and the fall of the house of Saul.
‡ Samuel's wearing of the ephod indicates that he was performing the functions of the priest.

can intercede with YHWH. But when a person sins against God, who is there to intercede?"

But they ignored Eli's rebuke, for YHWH had other plans to bring about their deaths.

²⁶ As young Samuel grew up, he increasingly grew in stature and in favor with God and the people.

²⁷ One day, a prophet* of God came to Eli and said, "Hear the word of YHWH: You know that I revealed myself to your ancestors' house when you and your ancestors where slaves under the Pharaoh. ²⁸ I chose your ancestors out of all the tribes of Israel to be my priests, to go up to the altar, to burn incense and to wear the ephod in my presence. I also gave your ancestors' family all the burnt offerings made by the people of Israel. ²⁹ Why, then, do you keep such an avaricious eye on the sacrifices and the offerings that I have commanded? And why do you honor your sons more than me by fattening yourselves on the choice parts of every offering made by my people Israel?

³⁰ "Therefore, YHWH the God of Israel declares: I promised that you and your family and your ancestors' family would minister before me forever. But now YHWH declares: Away with you! I will honor those who honor me. But those who reject me will be cursed. ³¹ Yes, the time is coming when I will break your power and the power of your ancestor's house, so that no one in your house will reach old age. ³² You will even resent the prosperity I give to Israel. Never again will anyone in your house reach old age. ³³ Every one of you that I don't cut off from my altar will be spared only to blind your eyes with tears and make your heart grieve. All your descendants will die in the prime of life. ³⁴ The fate of your two sons, Hophni and Phinehas, will be a sign to you—both of them will die on the same day. ³⁵ And I will raise up for myself a faithful priest, who will act according to what is in my heart and in my mind. I will firmly establish his family line, and he will walk before my anointed one forever. ³⁶ And any of your family remaining will come and bow humbly before this person to beg for a piece of silver and a loaf of bread and plead, 'Appoint me to some priestly office so that you can have food to eat.'"

3:1 Now young Samuel was in the service of YHWH under Eli. In those days, the voice of YHWH was rarely heard—prophesy was uncommon. ² One night Eli, whose eyes had grown so weak that he could no longer see, was sleeping in his bed. ³ The lamp of God had not gone out, and Samuel was sleeping in the Tent of Meeting, near the Ark of the Covenant.

---

* This passage was likely inserted into the text at a later date, since, according to 3:1, prophecy was rare at the time. Within a single generation, however, there were entire groups of prophets spontaneously falling into ecstatic rapture, as in 19:20.

⁴ Then YHWH called to Samuel.

Samuel answered, "Here I am!" ⁵ and ran to Eli saying, "You called. Here I am!"

Eli said, "I didn't call you. Now go back to sleep." He went back to sleep.

⁶ A second time, YHWH called Samuel, and he got up and went to Eli.

"Here I am!" Samuel said, "You called me."

Eli repeated, "I did not call you. Go back to sleep."

⁷ At that time Samuel had not yet encountered YHWH, and the word of YHWH had not yet been revealed to him.

⁸ YHWH called Samuel a third time, and Samuel got up, went to Eli, and said once more, "Here I am. You called me."

⁹ Then Eli realized that YHWH was calling the boy.

So he said to Samuel, "Go back and go to sleep, and if you are called, say, 'Speak, YHWH, for your servant is listening.' " So Samuel went back to sleep.

¹⁰ And YHWH called, "Samuel! Samuel!"

And Samuel replied, "Yes, YHWH, I am listening."

¹¹ Then YHWH said to Samuel, "I am going to do things in Israel that will make the ears of all who hear about them ring. ¹² I am going to fulfill all the dreadful things I told Eli I would do against his family—from the beginning to the end. ¹³ You are to tell Eli that I condemn his family forever because he knew of the blasphemies of his sons against God which he ignored. ¹⁴ Therefore, I swear it to the house of Eli, neither sacrifice nor offering will ever expiate the guilt of the House of Eli."

¹⁵ Samuel lay down to rest till morning, when he opened the doors of the Tent of Meeting. He feared to tell Eli about the vision, ¹⁶ but Eli called to Samuel, who answered, "Here I am."

¹⁷ "Samuel, come here, what did God say to you? Don't hide it from me. May YHWH curse you if you conceal from me one word of what you were told."

¹⁸ Then Samuel told Eli everything, concealing nothing. Eli said, "YHWH reigns. YHWH will do what must be done."

¹⁹ As Samuel grew, YHWH was with him. None of Samuel's words remained unfulfilled. ²⁰ From Dan to Beersheba, all Israel recognized that Samuel was a prophet of YHWH. ²¹ YHWH continued to appear in Shiloh, for Samuel first encountered YHWH there.

4:1 Samuel's renown spread throughout Israel.

CR CR CR

At this time, the Philistines banded together to attack Israel, and the people of Israel marched out to engage them. The armies of Israel camped at Ebenezer and the Philistines camped at Aphek. ² The Philistines drew up their battle lines to engage Israel, and when the battle was over, the Philistines had defeated the armies of Israel. There were about 4,000 Israelite casualties.

³ When the army returned to camp, the elders of Israel said, "Why did YHWH allow the Philistines to defeat us today? Let's carry the Ark of the Covenant of YHWH from Shiloh to accompany us on the field of battle to protect us and shield us from the power of our enemies."

⁴ So they sent envoys to Shiloh to bring back the Ark of the Covenant, where YHWH is enthroned upon the cherubim. Eli's sons, Hophni and Phineas, were there with the Ark.

⁵ When the Ark of the Covenant of YHWH came into the camp, all Israel raised such a loud shout that the ground shook. ⁶ Hearing the noise, the Philistines asked, "Why all the shouting in the camp of Israel?"

On learning that the Ark of the Covenant of YHWH had come into the camp, ⁷ the Philistines were struck with fear and cried out, "Gods have come into their camp! Woe to us! This has never happened before. ⁸ Woe to us! Who can deliver us from the power of these majestic gods? These are the gods who struck down the Egyptians with all those plagues and pestilence! ⁹ Be strong! Take courage!* Do you want be enslaved by the Hebrews? Carry on!"

¹⁰ The Philistines fought bravely and defeated the armies of Israel once more. The armies of Israel fled to their homes. It was a huge defeat: Israel lost 30,000, ¹¹ the Ark of the Covenant was captured, and Eli's two sons, Hophni and Phineas, were killed.

¹² A Benjaminite retreated from the battlefield and reached Shiloh later that day. His clothes were torn and his head was covered with dirt. ¹³ When he arrived Eli was sitting in his chair near the road, watching, for he feared in his heart for the Ark of the Covenant of YHWH. When the soldier entered the town with the bad news the people were in an uproar. ¹⁴ Hearing the uproar, Eli inquired of those standing nearby, "What is the meaning of all this commotion?" ¹⁵ Eli was ninety-eight years old, and his eyes were dim.

¹⁶ The messenger quickly came up to Eli saying, "I have just returned from the field of battle. I fled from it today."

Eli asked, "What happened?"

---

* The words here echo the admonition that Joshua gave to the people of Israel.

¹⁷ And the messenger said, "Israel retreated from the battlefield, in fact, we suffered heavy losses. Your two sons, Hophni and Phineas, are dead, too. And the Ark of the Covenant of YHWH has been captured."

¹⁸ At the mention of the Ark of the Covenant of YHWH, Eli fell backward from the chair and into the gateway. Because he was elderly and heavy, he died of a broken neck. Eli had judged Israel for forty years.

¹⁹ Eli's daughter-in-law, the wife of Phineas, was pregnant and very close to her term. When she heard the bad news about Phineas and Eli she went into labor and gave birth. ²⁰ She was about to die when the midwives attending her said, "Never fear! You just gave birth to a son!" Yet she neither answered nor paid attention to them. ²¹ She named the child Ichabod,* that is, "Glory Has Departed from Israel," referring to the capture of the Ark of the Covenant of YHWH and the deaths of her father-in-law and husband. ²² She said, "Glory has departed from Israel, because the Ark of the Covenant of YHWH has been captured."

⁵:¹ When the Philistines captured the Ark of the Covenant of YHWH, they transferred it from Ebenezer to Ashdod, ² where they carried it into the temple of Dagon, setting it beside Dagon's statue.† ³ When the Ashdodites rose the next morning, they found Dagon on the floor face down before the Ark of the Covenent of YHWH. So they picked up Dagon and replaced it. ⁴ But early the next morning when they rose, they found Dagon on the floor face down before it the Ark of the Covenant of YHWH, this time with its head and hands broken off lying on the threshold. Only the trunk remained intact. ⁵ It is for this reason that the priests of Dagon and all those who enter the temple of Dagon at Ashdod never step on the threshold; they always leap over it.

⁶ The hand of YHWH weighed heavily on the Ashdodites. God threw them into despair by plaguing them with boils and swarms of rats throughout their territory.‡ Death and destruction reigned throughout the city. ⁷ When the citizens of Ashdod saw what was happening, they said, "The Ark of the God of Israel must not remain here, for the hand of their God lies heavy on us and on Dagon our god."

---

* The name literally means "No Glory" or "Dishonor."

† Dagon was not an original god of the Philistines, but a Semitic god adopted by them after their invasion of Canaan. Many scholars believe that Dagon was originally a vegetation deity (the name possibly derived from the Hebrew *dagan*, meaning "grain"), but this is not clear from other existing evidence. There is some evidence to suggest that the cult of Dagon can be traced back to the third dynast of Ur (25th Century BCE).

‡ The description here suggests an outbreak of bubonic plague. This plague recalls the plagues of Egypt. Even though the Ark is in captivity, just as the people of Israel were in Egypt, God's power breaks all bonds and overwhelms the enemies of the people of Israel. Even the Philistine's god, Dagon, falls prostrate and is broken before the God of Israel.

⁸ So they convened all the rulers of the Philistines and asked them, "Please take the Ark away from us and bring it with you to Gath." And they did so. ⁹ The moment it arrived, YHWH inflicted its citizens, young and old, with boils, which caused a great panic there.

¹⁰ So they sent the Ark of God to Ekron. But as it entered the city the citizenry cried out, "Why have you brought the Ark of the God of Israel here to murder us and our families?"

¹¹ They sent messengers and called the rulers of the Philistines to an assembly once more, pleading, "Get the Ark of the God of Israel out of here! Let it be placed where it belongs, or it will murder us and our families!" A fatal panic had seized the whole city for the hand of God weighed heavily on it. ¹² Those who did not die were plagued with boils, and their cry rose to the heavens.

⁶·¹ By now the Ark of YHWH had been in Philistine territory for seven months. ² The Philistines summoned the priests and the diviners and said, "What are we to do with the Ark of the God of Israel? Tell us how we should go about sending it back to where it belongs."

³ They replied, "If it is your desire to send the Ark of the God of Israel back, do not send it alone. You must, by all means, make a guilt offering to their God. Then you will be healed and you will know why God's hand has been lifted from you."

⁴ When they were asked, "What should we send?" they answered, "Send five gold boils and five gold rats, one for each of the Philistine rulers, for the same plague afflicted both you and the rulers. ⁵ Make models of your boils and the rats that ravage the land, and give honor to the God of Israel. Perhaps their God will lift the divine hand which oppresses you, your god, and your land. ⁶ Why suffer from stubbornness like Pharaoh and the Egyptians? Recall how their God made sport of them until they let Israel go.

⁷ "After you have done this, prepare a new wagon. Hitch two unyoked cows that have calved, pen up the calves, and hitch the cows to the wagon. ⁸ You will next place the Ark of the Covenant of YHWH in the wagon. Place in a box the golden items you are offering, as amends for your guilt. Place the box in the wagon, then let the cows take the wagon where they will.

⁹ "Keep a sharp eye! If the wagon wanders up the road to its own territory, toward Beth-Shemesh, then it was the God of Israel who did us this injury. On the other hand, if it doesn't, we will know it was not the God of Israel who struck us down, but that what happened occurred by chance."

¹⁰ So these instructions were carried out. They took two cows, hitched them to a wagon, but shut up their calves indoors. ¹¹ Then they placed the Ark in the wagon, along with the box containing the golden rats and golden

boils.* ¹² The cows went straight up the road to Beth-Shemesh, lowing as they went and turned neither right or left. The Philistine rulers followed as far as the border of Beth-shemesh.

¹³ The people of Beth-shemesh were in the process of harvesting wheat in the valley. When they looked up and saw the Ark, they greeted it joyfully. ¹⁴ The wagon came to the field of Joshua the Beth-shemite, and stopped there, near a large stone. The people chopped up the wood of the wagon and offered the cows as a whole burnt offering to YHWH. ¹⁵ The Levites unloaded the box containing the golden offerings and placed them on the large stone. On that day the people of Beth-Shemesh offered burnt offerings and sacrifices to YHWH. ¹⁶ The five Philistine rulers witnessed all of this and returned to Ekron that same day.

¹⁷ The gold boils which the Philistines sent back as an offering to YHWH were for Ashdod, Gaza, Ashkelon, Gath, and Ekron—one for each city. ¹⁸ The gold rats were for all the towns of the Philistines governed by the five leaders, both fortified cities and open settlements. The great stone upon which they set the Ark of YHWH is still in the field of Joshua the Beth-shemesh to this day.

¹⁹ But God struck down some of the people of Beth-shemesh because they looked into the Ark of YHWH; God struck down seventy of them, five percent of the population.¹² The people went into mourning because God struck them down so fiercely. ²⁰ The people of Beth-shemesh asked, "Who can stand in the presence of YHWH, this holy God? To whom will the Ark go from here?" ²¹ Then they sent messengers to the inhabitants of Kiriath-jearim, and said, "The Philistines returned the Ark of YHWH. Come down and get it."

⁷:¹ So the citizens of Kiriath-Jearim came for the Ark of YHWH and delivered it to the hillside house of Abinadab, and consecrated Eleazar ben-Abinadab to be guardian of the Ark.

² The Ark rested in Kiriath-jearim for quite a while—some twenty years in all. At that time, a movement to return to the ways of YHWH swept over

---

* The people of Beth-Shemesh looked into the ark presumably to inspect it to see if the Philistines had taken or damaged anything, though to do so was forbidden to all except the Levites. How many were killed (Josephus says they were struck by lightning) is in question; the text literally reads, "and God struck down seventy people, fifty thousand people," provoking much debate over its meaning. This small village could hardly have a population of 50,070, and the text says that only "some" of its people were struck down, so there is clearly a scribal error of some sort; some believe the "fifty thousand" should be read as "fifty for a thousand" (that is, five percent), which means that if seventy were struck, the population of village would be a more manageable 1,400. This verse is markedly different in the Septuagint: "The descendants of Jeconiah did not join in the celebration with the people of Beth-shemesh when they greeted the Ark of YHWH; seventy of them were struck down." This Jeconiah is unknown to history.

Israel, ³ and Samuel said to the people of Israel, "If you are single-hearted about returning to YHWH, you must get rid of your foreign gods and the Ashtareth.* Then you must devote yourselves to YHWH, and worship YHWH alone. Then God will deliver you from the power of the Philistines."

⁴ So the people of Israel put away their Ba'als and their Ashtareths, and worshipped YHWH alone. ⁵ Then Samuel ordered, "Let all of Israel gather at Mizpah, and I will pray to YHWH for you."

⁶ When they gathered at Mizpah, they drew water and poured it out before YHWH, and fasted that day, confessing, "We have sinned against YHWH." It was at Mizpah that Samuel became Israel's judge.†

⁷ When the Philistines learned that the people of Israel had assembled at Mizpah, their rulers prepared to attack them. When the people of Israel learned this, ⁸ they said to Samuel, "Plead with YHWH to rescue us from the power of the Philistines!"

⁹ Samuel took a suckling lamb and sacrificed it whole as a burnt offering to YHWH. Then Samuel cried out to YHWH on behalf of Israel, and YHWH heard Samuel's prayers.

¹⁰ As Samuel offered the burnt offering to God, the Philistines advanced to attack. That day, however, YHWH thundered mightily against the Philistines and created among them such confusion that they fled in panic before the people of Israel, ¹¹ who set out from Mizpah in pursuit of the Philistines, slaughtering them along the way to a point below Beth-Car.

¹² It was there that Samuel took a stone and set it up as a monument between Mizpah and Jeshanah, naming it Ebenezer, "Stone of Help," explaining, "YHWH has helped us to this point."‡ ¹³ It was here that the Philistines were subdued, never again to invade the territory of Israel. The hand of YHWH was against them for the rest of Samuel's life. ¹⁴ The cities from Edron to Gath which the Philistines took from Israel were restored to them. Israel also freed the territory of these cities from the dominance of the Philistines. Moveover there was peace between the people of Israel and the Amorites.

¹⁵ Samuel governed Israel for the rest of his life, ¹⁶ and every year traveled the circuit to Bethel, Gilgal, and Mizpah to dispense justice. ¹⁷ But he always returned home to Ramah. It was home, and the place from which he governed Israel. It was there that Samuel built an altar to YHWH.

---

* The name is derived from the Mesopotamian goddess Ishtar; she was also known as Astarte.
† While the word *shapat* literally means "to judge," the judges of Israel were actually more akin to governors and leaders of the people.
‡ Ebenezer was also the name of the place where the armies of Israel encamped before being defeated by the Philistines encamped at Aphek (4:1; 5:1). It is doubtful that they are the same place, or if they are, the name used in 4:1 may have been inserted at a later time.

⁸ʲ When Samuel grew old, he appointed his two sons as judges over Israel. ² The firstborn, Joel, and the second, Abijah, sat as judges in Beer-sheba. ³ But they did not follow Samuel's ways: they desired wealth, they took bribes, and they distorted justice. ⁴ So the body of elders of Israel came to Samuel at Ramah, ⁵ and said, "You are old, and your sons pervert your ways. Appoint a ruler to lead us as all the other nations do."

⁶ Samuel was not happy when the asked for a ruler to judge them. He prayed to YHWH, however, ⁷ who responded, "Give to the people whatever they ask for. They are not rejecting you, they reject me as your ruler. ⁸ As they did from the day I brought them up from Egypt to this day. They desert me and worship other gods, as they are doing to you. ⁹ Listen to them carefully. But warn them solemnly and let them know the rights of the ruler who will rule them."

¹⁰ Samuel reported to those asking for a ruler all that YHWH said to him. "This is the type of ruler who will rule over you," ¹¹ Samuel said, "Your ruler will take your youths and make them serve as charioteers or with the cavalry, while others will be made to run in front of the chariots. ¹² Your ruler will appoint some of them as commanders of troops of 1,000 and of divisions of 100. Others will be forced to plow and harvest the royal fields. Still others will work making weapons of war and equipment for chariots. ¹³ Your daughters will be taken as cooks, bakers and makers of perfume. ¹⁴ Your ruler will take the best of your fields, your vineyards and your olive groves and give them to various governing officials and attendants.

¹⁵ "You will have to tithe your crops and your vineyards for the ruler to use these funds in support of the eunuchs and slaves. ¹⁶ The ruler will take the male and female workers, your best cattle and donkeys and take them for personal use. ¹⁷ Your ruler will take a tenth of your flocks and you yourselves will become slaves. ¹⁸ On that day you will cry out against the very ruler you chose. But YHWH will not answer your pleas on that day."*

¹⁹ The people refused to listen to Samuel's warning, and said, "No! We must have a ruler over us. ²⁰ Then we will be like other nations who have rulers to lead us and to lead us in warfare and fight our battles."

²¹ After Samuel listened to what all the people had to say, he relayed it to YHWH, ²² who responded, "Listen to them and give them a ruler."

---

* More than one feminist scholar has noted that the development of the monarchy paralleled the ascendancy of a more patriarchal view of God, the need to suppress, subvert, or overthrow matriarchal religions and cultures, and systemic injustice, particularly toward the poor; the tension between the religion of Israel and the faiths of the people who lived in the land (which frequently included goddess-worship) is a continuing theme throughout *The Prophets*.

And Samuel reported back to the people, "All of you are to return to your own towns."

⁹·¹ There was an influential person from the territory of Benjamin named Kish ben-Abiel ben-Zeror ben-Bechorath ben-Aphiah, a Benjaminite. Kish, a person of rank, ² had a very tall and handsome son named Saul. No one in Israel was more handsome than he, and he stood head-and-shoulders above everyone else.

³ One day Kish's donkeys wandered off, and he told Saul, "Take one of the workers and search for the stray donkeys." ⁴ They started by searching the hill country of Ephraim, then through the area around Shalisha, but to no avail. Then they went into the district of Shaalim without success, then through the land of Benjamin. Nothing.

⁵ When they reached the district of Zuph, Saul said to the worker, "Let's go back, for my father might stop worrying about the donkeys and start worrying about us."

⁶ Then the worker suggested, "I have an idea. There's a prophet in this city, one who is held in high esteem. Everything the prophet says comes true. Maybe we can get advice on which way to travel."

⁷ But Saul said, "If we do go, what can we offer the prophet? We have no bread in our bags. And we have no present. What do we have?"

⁸ Then the worker said, "I have a quarter of a silver shekel. We can give it to the prophet." ⁹ (In the old days in Israel, when people had questions of God, they would say, "Come, let us go to the seer." For what is now called a prophet used to be called a seer.)

¹⁰ Saul said, "Great! Let's go!" So they set out for the town where the prophet resided.

¹¹ As they ascended the hill to the town, they met some young women going out to draw water, and asked, "Is the seer here?"

"Yes," they responded, ¹² "but hurry. He just arrived ahead of you. He is here because the people have a sacrifice at the shrine today. ¹³ As soon as you enter the town you may find him before he goes up to the shrine to eat. The people will not eat until he arrives. Only after the seer blesses the sacrifice will the invited guests eat. Hurry up, for you should find him at once."

¹⁴ So they went up to the town, and, just as they entered it, there was Samuel approaching them on his way to the shrine.

¹⁵ Just the day before this happened, YHWH gave this revelation to Samuel: ¹⁶ "About this time tomorrow I will send you a Benjaminite. Anoint him leader of the people of Israel. For this person will deliver my people from the Philistines. I have seen the suffering of my people, and their cry has reached my ears."

¹⁷ The moment Samuel caught sight of Saul, YHWH said, "Samuel, this is the one I spoke to you about. He will govern my people."

¹⁸ Saul approached Samuel in the gateway and asked, "Can you give me directions to the seer's house?"

¹⁹ "I am the seer," Samuel replied. "Go up ahead of me to the shrine and eat with me today. In the morning I will set you on your way, after I tell what you have on your mind. ²⁰ Don't worry about the donkeys you lost three days ago. They have been found. For whom does Israel yearn if not for you and your whole family?"

²¹ Saul answered, "Am I not from the tribe of Benjamin, of one the smallest tribes of Israel, and my family is the least important of all the families of the tribe of Benjamin. Why do you say all this to me?"

²² Samuel brought Saul and the worker into the dining hall and gave them a place at the head of the invited guests, about thirty of them. ²³ He said to the cook, "Bring out the portion I gave you and told you to set aside." ²⁴ The cook took up the leg and what was set aside and set it before Saul. Samuel continued, "Here is the portion of meat kept for you. Eat it: it has been reserved for you at this feast to which I have invited the people."

And Saul dined with Samuel that day.

²⁵ After they came down from the shrine to the town, Samuel talked with Saul on the roof of his house. Saul slept there that night. ²⁶ Early the next morning Samuel called up to Saul on the roof: "Get ready, and I will send you on your way."

Then Saul rose, and he and Samuel went outside together, ²⁷ and as they neared the edge of town, Samuel said to Saul, "Tell the worker to go on ahead." So the worker went on ahead. Then Samuel said, "Stay here for a moment, and I will give you a message from God."

10·¹ Samuel took a flask of oil and poured it over Saul's head. He kissed Saul, and said, "YHWH anoints you ruler over this people Israel. You are to rule God's own people and deliver them from their enemies near and far. There will be a sign for you that YHWH appoints you ruler and commander of God's heritage. ² When you leave me today, you will meet two emissaries near Rachel's tomb at Zelzah on the border of Benjamin, who will say, 'The donkeys you went searching for have been found. Kish is no longer worried about the donkeys, but is anxious about you and sends this message: What shall I do about my son?'

³ "From there move forward until you arrive at the terebinth of Tabor. There you will meet three pilgrims going up to meet God at Bethel. One will be bringing three kids, another three loaves of bread, and the third a skin of wine. ⁴ They will greet you and offer you two loaves of bread, which you will take with you.

⁵ "After that you will come to Gibeath-elohim, where there is a garrison of Philistines. As you enter that city, you will meet a group of prophets coming down from the shrine, led by lyres, tambourines, flutes, and harps, and filled with prophetic rapture. ⁶ Suddenly you will be possessed with the Spirit of YHWH. And you, too, will prophesy with them. And you will become a different person. ⁷ Once these signs are fulfilled, do whatever your hand finds to do, for God is guiding you.

⁸ "Go down ahead of me to Gilgal. I will definitely come down to you to sacrifice burnt offerings and fellowship offerings, but you must wait seven days until I come to you and tell you what you are to do."

⁹ As Saul turned to leave Samuel, God changed Saul into a different person,* and all these signs were fulfilled that day. ¹⁰ When they arrived at Gibeath there was a company of prophets coming to meet him, and the Spirit of God quickly took possession of him, so that he as well was filled with prophetic rapture. ¹¹ When the people who formerly knew him saw Saul speaking in rapture like the prophets, they said to each other, "What is happening to the son of Kish? Is Saul one of the prophets?"†

¹² One of the locals there answered, "But who is their father?"

So it became a proverb: "Is Saul also among the prophets?" ¹³ After Saul prophesied, he went home.

¹⁴ Saul's uncle inquired of Saul and the worker, "Where have you been?"

Saul replied, "To look for the donkeys. And when we could not find them, we went to Samuel."

¹⁵ Then the uncle inquired again, "Tell me: what did Samuel say to you?"

¹⁶ Saul said to the uncle, "Samuel assured me that the donkeys had been found." But he chose not to mention anything about what Samuel said concerning ruling.

¹⁷ Samuel called the people of Israel to YHWH at Mizpah ¹⁸ and said to them, "This is what YHWH the God of Israel says: 'I brought Israel up out of Egypt, and I delivered you from the power of Egypt and all the dominions that oppressed you.' ¹⁹ But now you reject your God, who rescues you from of all your calamities and distresses. And you said, 'No! Set a ruler over us.' So now present yourselves before YHWH, by your tribes and your families."

---

* Literally, "gave Saul another heart."
† Here we see that one way the gift of prophecy was given was through trance states and ecstatic utterance—a technique of accessing the divine that is still found today in tribal cultures and modern shamanic practice. At the same time, note that "prophecy" has little to do with the prophet's moral character; there were many prophets in Israel about whom YHWH said, "I didn't send them." The odd retort in the next verse probably means, "What does one's parentage have to do with the prophetic gift?"

²⁰ When Samuel brought all the tribes of Israel near, the tribe of Benjamin was chosen. ²¹ Then he brought forward the tribe of Benjamin, family by family, and Matri's family was chosen. Finally, Saul ben-Kish was chosen. But when they searched for Saul, he was not to be found. ²² So they inquired further of YHWH, "Has the person arrived yet?"

And YHWH said, "Yes, Saul is hiding among the baggage."

²³ Some of them ran and brought him out from among the baggage, and when Saul stood among the people he was a head taller than the others. ²⁴ Samuel said to all the people, "Behold the one YHWH chose for us. There is no one like Saul among all the people."

Then all the people shouted, "Long live Saul!"

²⁵ Samuel explained to the people the rules of the monarchy. He wrote them down on a scroll and deposited it before YHWH. Then Samuel dismissed all to their homes. ²⁶ Saul also went home to Gibeah, accompanied by virtuous warriors whose hearts God had touched. ²⁷ But there were troublemakers who said, "How can this fellow save us?" They thought nothing of Saul and brought no gifts to the ruler.

¹¹·¹ Just one month later the Ammonite Nahash attacked and besieged Jabesh-Gilead. The citizens of Jabesh said to Nahash, "Make a treaty with us, and we will be your subjects." ² But Nahash responded, "I will negotiate with you on one condition: that I gouge out everyone's right eye as an insult to all Israel."

³ The elders of Jabesh-gilead said, "Give us seven days to consult throughout Israel. And if no one comes to rescue us, we will surrender to you." ⁴ Messengers arrived at Gibeah, where Saul lived, and delivered the message. It caused the people to break into lamentations and weeping. ⁵ At that moment, Saul, driving the oxen, returned from doing field work. He asked why the people were lamenting and weeping. The people informed him of the demands of the Ammonites.

⁶ When Saul heard this, the Spirit of God seized him and he became enraged. ⁷ Saul took a pair of oxen, cut them into pieces, and sent the pieces throughout Israel with the message, "This is what will happen to your oxen if you choose not to follow Samuel and Saul into battle." Then the fear of YHWH overtook the people who mustered as one. ⁸ When Saul called for the assembly, 300,000 able-bodied warriors reported from Israel, and 30,000 from Judah.

⁹ Saul told the messengers, "Tell the Ammonites of Jabesh-gilead, 'You will be saved tomorrow morning by the time the sun is hot.'"

When they heard this message, the people of Jabesh sighed a sigh of relief,

¹⁰ but they said to Nahash, "We will surrender to you tomorrow and then you may do whatever you wish with us."

¹¹ The next day, Saul, with three columns of troops, overran the enemy camps during the morning watch and eliminated the Ammonites as the day grew hot. The survivors scattered so furiously that no two of them were left together.

¹² Then the people asked Samuel, "Who was it that asked, 'Will Saul reign over us?' Bring them to us and we will put them to death."

¹³ But Saul intervened, "No one will be put to death today, for today YHWH has rescued Israel."

¹⁴ Then Samuel said to the people, "Come, it is the time for us to go to Gilgal to establish our reign anew." ¹⁵ So the people went to Gilgal and proclaimed Saul ruler before YHWH at Gilgal. They sacrificed a peace offering before YHWH. And Saul with all the Israelites celebrated the event with great joy.

12:1 Samuel said to the people of Israel, "I listened to your request and installed a ruler for you. ² The ruler is now your leader. As for me, I am old and gray, and my sons are among you. I lived with you from my youth to this day. ³ Here I stand. Testify against me in the presence of YHWH and the anointed ruler. Did I take your ox? Did I take your donkey? Did I cheat you? Did I oppress you? From whose hand did I accept a bribe by closing my eyes? Tell me! for I will make restitution to you."

⁴ They replied, "You have not cheated us. You have not oppressed us."

⁵ And Samuel said, "YHWH witnesses us today, for you did not find anything in my hands."

"YHWH is our witness," they replied.

⁶ Then Samuel addressed the people: "Our witness is YHWH, the One who appointed Moses and Aaron and Miriam and delivered your ancestors up from Egypt. ⁷ Now stand here in the presence of YHWH for I am going to make the case against you by reciting all the acts of mercy YHWH did for you and your ancestors. ⁸ After Jacob went to Egypt, they cried out to YHWH for relief, and God sent Moses and Aaron and Miriam, who brought your ancestors out of Egypt and settled them here. ⁹ But they forgot YHWH their God, who sold them into the hands of Sisera, the commander-in-chief of the army of Hazor, and into the hands of the Philistines and the ruler of Moab, who fought against them. ¹⁰ Then your ancestors cried out to YHWH once more, 'We sinned, we abandoned YHWH and served the Ba'als and the Ashtoreths. But deliver us from the hands of our enemies, and we will serve you.' ¹¹ Then God sent Jerubbaal and Barak, Jephthah and Samson, who delivered you from your enemies on every side. And you lived in security.

¹² Yet, when you saw Nahash, ruler of the Ammonites, advancing against you, you said to me, 'No, we want a ruler to govern us,' even though YHWH was your ruler. ¹³ Now YHWH has set a ruler over you. I present you the ruler you chose, the one you asked for.

¹⁴ "If you revere YHWH and provide true and loyal service; if you are obedient and do not rebel against YHWH's commands; if you and your ruler who rules over you are faithful to YHWH, your God, well and good; ¹⁵ but if you do not obey YHWH and if you rebel against YHWH's orders, YHWH will deal severely with you and your ruler, and destroy you.

¹⁶ "Now then, stand ready to witness the marvelous wonder that YHWH will accomplish before your eyes. ¹⁷ It is now wheat harvest time. I call upon YHWH who will delivery thunder and rain. And you will understand how displeasing it is to YHWH for you to petition for a ruler. ¹⁸ So Samuel called on YHWH, and YHWH sent thunder and rain that day. And all the people stood in awe of both YHWH and Samuel.

¹⁹ All the people said to Samuel, "Pray for us sinners lest we die, for we added to all our other sins, the sin of asking for a ruler."

²⁰ Samuel calmed the people, "Do not be afraid. Although you are fearful because of your sinfulness, do not forsake your worship of YHWH. Serve YHWH with your heart and soul. ²¹ Do not turn to the worship of sham gods which can neither help nor save you. For they are shams. ²² For the sake of YHWH's great Name, YHWH will not reject us, for YHWH is pleased to make us 'God's Own.'

²³ "As for me, far be it from me that I should sin against YHWH by failing to pray for you. And I will teach you the way that is right and good. ²⁴ But be sure to revere YHWH and serve YHWH with your heart and soul. Think about all the good things God has done among you. ²⁵ On the other hand, if you persist in your sinfulness, both you and your ruler will be swept away."

13:1–31:12

Saul became the ruler of Israel at the age of thirty, and ruled for forty years. ² Saul chose 3,000 able-bodied warriors, of whom 2,000 remained with Saul in Michmash and the hill country of Bethel; and 1,000 were assigned to Saul's son Jonathan in Gibeah of Benjamin. The rest of the army were furloughed and went home.

³ And Jonathan immediately attacked the Philistine garrison in Gibeah, and as the word spread through the country the Philistines surmised that the Israelites were revolting. And Saul had the trumpet sounded throughout the land with the message, "Let the Hebrews get the news."

⁴ So all the Israelites got this message: "Saul has attacked the Philistine garrison and Israel has brought disgrace upon the Philistines." And the people were summoned to join Saul at Gilgal.

⁵ The Philistines also sent out a call to arms. They had 3,000 chariots and 6,000 charioteers. They also had infantry as numerous as the sand on the seashore. They went up and set up camp at Michmash, east of Beth-aven. ⁶ When the Israelites realized that their situation was critical and that the army was hard pressed, they hid in caves, among thickets, among the rocks and in pits as well as in cisterns. ⁷ Some crossed the Jordan into the land of Gad and Gilead.

Saul remained at Gilgal, in spite of the fears of the troops. ⁸ He waited there for seven days—the time Samuel set. But Samuel did not come to Gilgal, and when Saul's troops began to slip away, ⁹ Saul ordered, "Bring me the burnt offering and the fellowship offering."

¹⁰ At the moment Saul finished the sacrifice, Samuel arrived, and Saul went out to greet him. ¹¹ "What have you done?" Samuel asked.

Saul answered, "When I realized that the troops were slipping away and that the Philistines were assembling at Michmash, and since you had not arrived at the set time, ¹² I said to myself, 'Now the enemy will attack me at Gilgal, and I have not yet sought YHWH's blessing,' so I felt compelled to sacrifice the burnt offering.

¹³ Samuel responded, "You are a fool!" Had you kept the command YHWH gave you, YHWH would have established your dynasty over Israel for all time. ¹⁴ But as things stand now, your sovereignty will not stand. YHWH has sought out one who reflects the heart of YHWH, who will be appointed leader of all the people of Israel, for you did not keep YHWH's command."

¹⁵ Then Samuel left Gilgal, going his own way. The rest of the people followed Saul moving from Gilgal towards the Philistines. At Gibeath of Bethlehem, he counted the troops accompanying him. They were about 600. ¹⁶ Saul, accompanied by Jonathan and his entourage, stayed in Gibeah in Benjamin, while the Philistines quartered in Mishmash.

¹⁷ Meanwhile, raiding parties left the Philistine camp in three companies: one company moved off to Ophrah in the vicinity of Shual, ¹⁸ a second towards Beth Horon and the third towards the range of hills overlooking the valley of Zeboim and the desert beyond.

¹⁹ In the whole of Israel, no blacksmiths were to be found, because the Philistines said, "Otherwise the Hebrews will fashion swords and spears!" ²⁰ So all of the Israelites went down to the Philistines to have their plowshares, mattocks, axes, and sickles sharpened.* ²¹ The price was two-thirds of a shekel for sharpening plowshares and mattocks, and one-third of a shekel for sharpening axes and sickles and for re-pointing goads.

²² So when hostilities broke out, not one soldier with Saul and Jonathan were armed. Only Saul and Jonathan were armed.

²³ An attachment of Philistines set up an outpost at the pass of Michmash.

^{14:1} One day Jonathan ben-Saul said to the youth who was his armor-bearer, "Come, we will scout out the Philistine outpost over there." But Jonathan failed to notify Saul. ² Saul was quartered on the outskirts of Gilbeah under the pomegranate tree in Migron and accompanied with the 600 troops. ³ Ahijah ben-Ahitub, brother of Ichabod ben-Phineas ben-Eli, YHWH's priest in Shiloh. No one realized that Jonathan was absent.

⁴ Cliffs guarded each side of the pass Jonathan intended to cross to reach the Philistines. One was called Bozez and the other Seneh. ⁵ One faced to the north toward Michmash and the other faced to the south toward Geba. ⁶ Jonathan said to the young armor-bearer, "Come, let us visit the outpost of those heathen warriors. Perhaps YHWH will do us a favor. Nothing can stop YHWH from winning a victory whether by a few or by many."

⁷ The armor-bearer replied, "Do what you think you have to do. I will match your resolve."

⁸ Jonathan said, "Off we go. We will cross over toward them to let them see us. ⁹ If they say, 'Wait there until we come to you,' we will stay where we are. ¹⁰ But if they say, 'Come over to us,' we will climb over, for that will be our sign that YHWH has given them into our hands."

¹¹ So they stepped out into the open to be viewed by the Philistines. "Look, said one of the Philistines, "the Hebrews are crawling out of the holes they were hiding in."

¹² The warriors shouted to Jonathan and the armor-bearer, "Come up so we can teach you a lesson." Jonathan said. "Climb up behind me, for YHWH is giving them into the hands of Israel."

¹³ Using his hands and feet, Jonathan climbed up with the armor-bearer right behind. The Philistines fell back from the onslaught of Jonathan and the armor-bearer. ¹⁴ In that first attack they killed twenty Philistines;

---

* By this time the Philistines controlled the land. The practice of disarming conquered peoples was often followed in the ancient world. For repairing any serious damage to their agricultural implements, the Israelites had no choice but to visit the Philistine settlements and pay their exhorbitant prices. A mattock is a kind of pick used for digging with a flat blade set at right angles to the handle.

it was as if they were cutting a furrow across a small field. ¹⁵ Panic broke out within the whole army, spreading through their camp, the country-side, the outpost and the raiding parties—the ground quaked, for it was a panic sent by God.

¹⁶ Saul's sentinels at Gibeah in Bethlehem saw the panicking army melting away in all directions. ¹⁷ Saul ordered a count of the troops to gauge who was missing. The count turned up the information that Jonathan and the armor-bearer were missing.

¹⁸ Saul said to Ehijah, "Bring the ephod here." Ehijah was wearing the ephod before the Israelites at the time of the rout.

¹⁹ As Saul spoke to the priest, the terror in the Philistine camp kept in-creasing. So Saul said to the priest, "Withdraw your hand!" ²⁰ Then Saul and all the troops, shouting and rushing, joined in the rout. The confused Philistines continued to stab each other.

²¹ Then the Hebrews who previously had gone up with them to the Philistines camp, turned against the Philistines and joined up with Saul and Jonathan. ²² Likewise, all the Israelites hiding in the hill country of Ephraim, learning that the Philistines were being routed, joined in the pursuit. ²³ So YHWH Omnipotent rescued Israel that day and the battle continued beyond Beth Aven.

²⁴ The Israelites, driven to exhaustion from day-long battles, compounded their distress because Saul bound the people with a rash vow, "A curse on anyone who eats food before evening and before I have avenged myself on my enemies!" So no one ate food that day.

²⁵ There were honeycombs in the countryside; ²⁶ but when all the people of the land came upon one, dripping with honey, no one would stoop down to eat it, for they feared the curse.

²⁷ Jonathan, who had not heard about the curse of Saul, stretched out his staff and dipped its tip in the honey. When he raised it to his lips his eyes lit up. ²⁸ Seeing this one of the soldiers said, "Saul strictly forbade this," and continued, "he put a curse on the person who eats food today. And we are all faint with hunger."

²⁹ Jonathan replied, "Saul has done the people great harm. See how my eyes lightened by the mere taste of this honey. ³⁰ How much better it would have been if the people had eaten freely today of the enemy's booty. For then there would have been much more energy with which to fight the enemy."

³¹ Once the Philistines were routed from Michmash to Aijalon, the people were exhausted. ³² They pounced on the booty and took sheep, cattle, and calves, butchered them on the ground, and ate the meat, along with the blood. ³³ Then someone said to Saul, "Look, they are sinning against YHWH by eating meat with blood in it."

"They broke their faith. Roll that large stone here," ³⁴ Saul said. "Go out among the people and tell them, 'All of you are to bring your oxen and sheep here. In this way they will not sin against YHWH by eating meat with blood on it.' " So as night fell they came, driving their own ox, and slaughtered it there. ³⁵ Then Saul erected an altar to YHWH. This was a first for Saul.

³⁶ Let us go down and pursue the Philistines after dark, to plunder them until daybreak and to kill all of them."

They replied, "Do what you think best."

But the priest said, "Let us consult God."

³⁷ So Saul consulted God, "Should I go down in pursuit of the Philistines? Will you give them into the hands of Israel?"

But Saul received no answer this time. ³⁸ So he said, "Let all the leaders of the people come forward and let us find out where the sin lies today. ³⁹ As YHWH the deliverer of Israel lives, even if the sin resides in Jonathan, he will die." Not a soul responded to Saul. ⁴⁰ Then he said to all the Israelites, "All of you stand at one side, and let Jonathan stand opposite you."

The people replied, "Do what you think best."

⁴¹ And Saul said to YHWH, the God of Israel, "Why do you not answer what your servant asks here? If the blame resides in me or in Jonathan, respond with Urim. But if it lies in your people Israel, let it be Thummim."*

Jonathan and Saul were selected and the people were cleared.

⁴² Saul said, "Cast lots between me and Jonathan." And Jonathan was selected.

⁴³ Saul asked Jonathan, "What have you done?"

"I merely tasted a little honey with the end of my staff. Now must I die?"

⁴⁴ Then Saul swore a solemn oath that Jonathan should die.

⁴⁵ But the people said to Saul, "Is Jonathan to die? Jonathan, who won this great victory for Israel? Never! As surely as YHWH lives, not a hair of his head will fall onto the ground, for Jonathan did this today with the help of God." So the people rescued Jonathan, and he was not executed.

⁴⁶ Then Saul called off the pursuit of the Philistines. And they were allowed to retreat to their own territory.

⁴⁷ Once Saul assumed rule in Israel, he fought against their foes on every side, the Moabites, the Ammonites, the Edomites, the ruler of Zobah, and

---

* These are objects for divining the will of God, though their appearance and use are a great mystery—perhaps deliberately so. *Urim* means "lights" or "manifestations," and *Thummim* means "perfections" or "the truth." Most scholars feel they were stones for casting lots (as in verse 42), but in the book of 1 *Samuel*, the Urim were equated with dreams and prophets as a means of answering questions, so they may have been some other oracular device. It is also possible, since the words begin with the first and last letters of the Hebrew alphabet, respectively, that the names are merely symbolic.

the Philistines. Every time Saul called out the militia they were victorious. ⁴⁸ Special victories were those against the Amalekites and the freeing of Israel from hostile raids.

⁴⁹ Saul's sons were named Jonathan, Ishvi, and Malki-Shua. His first daughter was named Merab and his youngest was named Michal. ⁵⁰ Saul's wife was Ahinoam, daughter of Ahimaaz. The commander of the army was Abner ben-Ner, and Ner was Saul's uncle. ⁵¹ Saul's father Kish and Abner's father ben-Ner, were children of Abiel.

⁵² All the days of Saul were days of bitter wars with the Philistines. Whenever Saul came across strong or brave warriors, he took them into his service.

15:1 Samuel said to Saul, "I am the person YHWH sent to anoint you ruler over God's own, the Israelites. Now listen to this message from YHWH. ² YHWH Omnipotent says, 'I will punish the Amalekites for what they did to the Israelites when they harassed them on their way up from Egypt. ³ Go now. Attack them and destroy everything they possess and put their property under the ban. Spare no one. Put all of them to death: women and men, children and toddlers, herds and flocks, camels and donkeys."

⁴ Saul called out the troops and reviewed them at Telaim: 200,000 infantry plus 10,000 troops from Judah. ⁵ Saul went to the city of Amalek and set up an ambush in the valley. ⁶ Meanwhile he sent a message to the Kenites: "Leave the Amalekites so that I don't destroy you along with them. For you were kind to the Israelites when they came up out of Egypt." So the Kenites moved away from the Amalekites. ⁷ Once the Kenites were gone, Saul attacked the Amalekites all the way from Havilah to Shur on the Egyptian border. ⁸ Their ruler, Agag, was captured; but Saul put to the sword all the people under the ruler. ⁹ Agag was spared, as were the prime sheep and cattle, the fat calves and lambs—everything worth keeping. But any useless thing, anything not valuable, was destroyed.

¹⁰ Then the word of YHWH came to Samuel: ¹¹ "I am grieved that I made Saul ruler, for he has turned away from me and has not obeyed my instruction." The angry Samuel spent the night crying out to YHWH.

¹² Early the next morning Samuel went to meet with Saul, but was told that Saul went to Carmel, for he had set up a monument to himself there; and from there he journeyed down to Gilgal. ¹³ Samuel met up with Saul there and greeted Samuel, "May YHWH bless you! I have carried out YHWH's instructions."

¹⁴ But Samuel replied, "What is this bleating of sheep? What is this lowing of oxen I hear?"

¹⁵ Saul answered, "Our troops spared the best sheep and oxen for sacrifices to YHWH. But we carried out the ban on the rest."

¹⁶ Samuel declared, "Stop it! Let me tell you what YHWH Omnipotent said to me last night."

"Tell me," replied Saul.

¹⁷ Samuel said, "There was a time, once, when you thought little of yourself Are you not the leader of the tribes of Israel now? YHWH appointed you leader of the tribes of Israel. ¹⁸ And YHWH sent you on a mission with these instructions, 'Go and completely destroy these corrupt people, the Amalekites. Declare war on them until they have been completely wiped out.' ¹⁹ Why? Why did you disobey YHWH? Why did you pounce on the plunder, committing an act displeasing to the eyes of YHWH?"

²⁰ "But I did obey YHWH," said Saul. "I went on the mission assigned to me by YHWH. I completely destroyed the Amalekites and brought back their ruler Agag. ²¹ Our troops took the choicest of the sheep and the cattle from the detritus of the war. It was slated for sacrifices to YHWH at Gilgal."

²² But Samuel replied:

"Is it not true that YHWH desires burnt
burnt offerings and sacrifices
as much as obeying the voice of YHWH?
To obey is better than to sacrifice,
listening to YHWH is better than the fat of rams.
²³ Rebellion is a sin of sorcery,
presumption a sin of idolatry.
Because you rejected the word of YHWH,
YHWH rejects you as our ruler."

²⁴ The Saul said to Samuel, "I have sinned! I violated YHWH's command and your instructions. Our of fear of the people I gave in to them. ²⁵ I beg you, forgive my sin and return with me that I may worship YHWH."

²⁶ But Samuel said, "I will not go with you. You rejected the word of YHWH, and YHWH rejects you as ruler over Israel."

²⁷ As Samuel turned to leave, Saul caught hold of the hem of Samuel's robe, and it tore. ²⁸ And Samuel said, "YHWH tore the rulership of Israel from you today and gave it to a neighbor—to a person better than you. ²⁹ The Glory of Israel never deals falsely or regrets a decision; it does not change its mind the way human beings do."

³⁰ But Saul answered, "I am a sinner, at least honor me before the elders of my people and before Israel. Return with me that I may worship YHWH." ³¹ And Samuel returned with Saul, who worshipped YHWH.

³² Then Samuel said, "Bring me Agag, ruler of the Amalekites."

The trembling Agag came and said, "Surely, death is a bitter thing."

³³ Samuel said,

"Just as your sword made women childless,
so shall your mother be made childless among women."

Then Samuel cut down Agag before YHWH in Gilgal.
³⁴ Samuel departed for Ramah, and Saul went home to Gibeah of Saul.
³⁵ Until the day he died, Samuel did not see Saul. Yet Samuel grieved over Saul, for YHWH regretted making him ruler of Israel.*

^{16:1} YHWH said to Samuel, "How long will you grieve for Saul since I rejected him as ruler of Israel? Fill your horn with oil, and be on your way. For I am sending you to Jesse in Bethlehem, for I have chosen my ruler from among his children."

² But Samuel replied, "How can I go? For if Saul learns about it, I will be murdered.

YHWH replied, "Take a heifer with you: I am sending you to Jesse. Tell him that you came to offer a sacrifice to YHWH, ³ and invite Jesse to the sacrifice. Then I will show you what to do. You are to anoint for me my selection."

⁴ Samuel did what YHWH said. When he arrived at Bethlehem, the elders of the town trembled when they met Samuel. They asked, "Do you come in peace?"

⁵ Samuel said, "Yes, in peace; I have come to sacrifice to YHWH. Consecrate yourselves and come to the sacrifice with me." Then he consecrated Jesse and his children and invited them to the sacrifice.

⁶ When they arrived, and Samuel saw Eliab, and said to himself, "Surely, God's anointed stands here before YHWH."

⁷ But YHWH said to Samuel, "Pay no attention to appearance and height; I have rejected him. YHWH does not see as mortals see; mortals see only appearances but YHWH sees into the heart."

⁸ Then Jesse called Abinadab to pass before Samuel, who said, "No. YHWH has not chosen this one."

⁹ Next came Shammah, but Samuel said, "Not this one either."

¹⁰ Seven sons were presented to Samuel by Jesse, who said, "YHWH has not chosen any of these."

¹¹ Samuel asked, "Are these all the sons you have?"

"There is still the youngest," Jesse said, "but he is tending the sheep."

---

* The word translated "regret" in this verse and in verse 29 is *nacham*, which means to be sorry, to grieve, to repent, or to change one's mind. The contradiction between the two verses may be resolved by seeing that Samuel was similarly conflicted—in verse 29 he felt he had to be hard and unyielding in rejecting Saul, but here it is revealed that Samuel privately grieved over him.

Samuel said, "Send for him; we will not begin the sacrificial banquet until the lad arrives."

¹² So they sent for the boy, a ruddy youth with bright eyes, and handsome to behold. YHWH said, "Rise and anoint this one."

¹³ Then Samuel took the horn of oil and anointed the boy in the presence of his brothers, and from that day forward the Spirit of YHWH came upon David and was with him. Then Samuel set out on his way to Ramah.

¹⁴ The Spirit of YHWH then departed from Saul, and an evil spirit from YHWH tormented him.* ¹⁵ Saul's attendants said to Saul, "See, an evil spirit from God torments you. ¹⁶ You should order your attendants to search for someone who can play the harp, which will sooth your mind when the evil spirit from God is upon you. And you will feel better."

¹⁷ Saul put out the word, "Find someone who plays well and bring him to me."

¹⁸ One of the attendants spoke up, "There is a boy, David ben-Jesse of Bethlehem, who plays the harp well. He is also a brave warrior. He is a handsome person who speaks well. And YHWH is with him."

¹⁹ So Saul sent messengers to Jesse, and said, "Send me your son, David, who tends the sheep."

²⁰ So Jesse took a donkey loaded with bread, a wine skin and a kid goat and sent them with David to Saul.

²¹ David came to Saul and entered his service. Saul was immediately struck with this talented fellow, and David became one of his armor-bearers. ²² Then Saul sent word to Jesse, "Allow David to remain in my service, for I am pleased with the boy."

²³ Whenever the evil spirit from God would fall upon Saul, David would take up the harp and play. Then Saul would be relieved, would feel better and the evil spirits would vanish.

৩   ৩   ৩

17:1 Once more the Philistines rallied their forces for war. They gathered at Socoh in Judah. They pitched their tents between Socoh and Azekah at Ephes-dammim. ² Saul and the Israelites also mustered and camped in the

---

* The idea of God sending an evil spirit upon someone is shocking until we remember the words of Isaiah 45:7, "I form light and create darkness. I make peace and create evil. It is I, YHWH, who do all these things." Israel saw God as doing whatever was necessary to bring about a change in the people's hearts, minds, or behavior, even if it meant sending (and removing) evil spirits. Note that many psychological disorders are often experienced as something external to us, and certainly "evil" in its effects; for example, we sometimes speak of a "cloud of depression" that comes on at unforeseen moments.

valley of Elah. It was there that they drew up their battle lines to meet the Philistines. ³ The Philistines occupied one hill and the Israelites another. The valley lay between them.

⁴ A nine-foot-tall champion known as Goliath of Gath came out of the Philistine camp. ⁵ He wore a bronze helmet, and bronze armor plates that weighed 125 pounds. ⁶ He wore bronze greaves on his legs with a bronze javelin slung over his back. ⁷ The spear shaft could serve as a weaver's rod, and its iron point alone weighed fifteen pounds. His shield-bearer marched ahead of him.

⁸ The champion, standing before his forces, shouted to the ranks of the Israelites, "I dare you to come out in battle formation! I am a Philistine, and you are attendants of Saul. Choose one of your best warriors to come down to me. ⁹ If he defeats me and kills me in a fair fight, we will be your subjects. But if I overcome your warrior, you will become our subjects and serve us."

¹⁰ Then the Philistine said, "Today, I defy your ranks, Israelites! Send over a warrior to fight me." ¹¹ On hearing the Philistines challenge, Saul and the Israelites were dismayed and terrified.

¹² Now David was the son of an Ephrathite named Jesse. Jesse had eight sons, and was already advanced in years when Saul took the throne. ¹³ The three eldest sons followed Saul into battle. The eldest was named Eliab, the next Abiandab, and the third Shammah. ¹⁴ David was the youngest. ¹⁵ When the three eldest mobilized with Saul, David would move from attending Saul to tending the family flocks at Bethlehem.

¹⁶ Morning and evening for forty days, the Philistine came forward and challenged the Israelites. ¹⁷ Then one day Jesse said to David, "Take an ephah of this roasted grain and these ten loaves of bread to your brothers at their camp. ¹⁸ Take with you these ten cheeses for the commander of their unit. Take notice of how they are faring and bring back a memento from them. ¹⁹ Saul and your brothers and all the Israelites were in the Valley of Elah, at war with the Philistines."

²⁰ Early the next morning David, having left the care of the sheep with a shepherd, loaded up and set out, as Jesse directed. He reached the camp just as the army moved out, shouting battle cries. ²¹ The Israelites and the Philistines drew up opposite each other in battle array. ²² David, leaving his things in the charge of the quartermaster, ran to the battle line and greeted his brothers. ²³ As they chatted with each other, Goliath, the champion from Gath, came out and shouted his challenge in the same words as before. And David heard the challenge.

²⁴ When the Israelites saw the champion they fell back before him in fear. ²⁵ "Look at this champion who comes out daily to defy Israel," they said.

"The ruler will give a rich reward to the person who kills him. The ruler will also give a daughter in marriage and will exempt his family from service due in Israel."

²⁶ David asked the warriors nearby, "What is to be done for the one who kills the Philistine and wipes out this disgrace? And who is this, this uncircumcised Philistine, to defy the army of the living God?"

²⁷ The warriors, repeating what had been said before, told him what was to become of the one who kills the Philistine.

²⁸ Eliab overheard this conversation with the soldiers and angrily demanded, "What are you doing here? And whom have you left to look over our few sheep in the wilderness? I know how conceited you are and how corrupted your heart is. Why did you come down here to watch a battle?"

²⁹ Now David answered, "Now what have I done? I only asked a question."

³⁰ And he turned away to someone else and repeated the question, but everyone gave the same answer.

³¹ David's words were overheard and reported to Saul, who sent for him.

³² David said to Saul, "Don't anyone lose heart! I will fight the Philistine!"

³³ But Saul replied to David, "You cannot go up to fight against this Philistine. You are just a lad, and he has been fighting all his life."

³⁴ David said to Saul, "I am my father's shepherd. Whenever a lion or a bear carries off one of our flock. ³⁵ I go after it, attack it and rescue the sheep from its jaws. Then if it turns on me I seize it by its fur, strike it, and kill it. ³⁶ I have killed lions and bears, and this uncircumcised Philistine will fare no better than they, for this 'champion' has defied the ranks of the living God. ³⁷ YHWH who saved me from the lions and the bears will save me from this Philistine."

"Go then," Saul said, "and may YHWH go with you."

³⁸ Saul put his own tunic on David, placed a bronze helmet on his head, and gave him a coat of mail to wear. ³⁹ Then Saul fastened his sword on David over the tunic. But David held back, saying, "I can't go in these. I am not used to them." So David took them off.

⁴⁰ Then David took up his staff, chose five smooth stones from the stream, put them in the shepherd's bag which served as his pouch, and with his sling in hand, went out to meet the Philistine. ⁴¹ The Philistine, preceded by his shield-bearer, approached David. ⁴² He looked David over, up and down, and had nothing but disdain for the lad with the ruddy cheeks and bright eyes.

⁴³ He said to David, "Am I a dog, that you come at me with sticks?" And he cursed David in the name of his gods, ⁴⁴ saying, "Come, I will give your flesh to the birds and the beasts!"

⁴⁵ David answered, "You come against me with sword, spear, and dagger, but I come against you in the name of YHWH Omnipotent, the God of the armies of Israel whom you insulted. ⁴⁶ Today YHWH will deliver you into my hands, for I will strike you down and cut off your head and leave your carcass and the carcasses of the Philistines to the birds of the air and the beasts of the wilderness. The whole world will know that there is a God in Israel. ⁴⁷ All those gathered here will be witness that YHWH saves without sword or spear. This battle is YHWH's, who will put all of you into our power."

⁴⁸ When the Philistine moved closer to attack, David ran quickly to engage him. ⁴⁹ Reaching into his bag and taking out a stone, he put it into his sling, slung it, and struck the Philistine on the forehead—it penetrated his forehead, and Goliath fell face down onto the ground.

⁵⁰ So David triumphed over the Philistine with a stone and a sling. He struck down the Philistine without carrying a sword. ⁵¹ David ran up to the Philistine and standing over him, grasped his sword, drew it out of the scabbard, killed him and cut off his head.*

When the Philistines witnessed the fate of their champion, they turned away in flight. ⁵² The warriors of Israel and of Judah immediately raised the battle cry and closely pursued the Philistines all the way to Gath and up to the gates of Ekron. Their dead were strewn along the Shaaraim road to Gath and Ekron. ⁵³ When the Israelites returned from chasing the Philistines, they plundered their camp. ⁵⁴ David took the Philistine's head and carried it to Jerusalem, and put the Philistine's weapons in his own tent.

⁵⁵ As Saul watched David going out to meet the Philistine, he asked Abner, the commander of the army, "Abner, whose child is that lad?"

Abner replied, "I don't know. But I will find out."

⁵⁶ Saul said, "Find out whose child this boy is."

⁵⁷ As soon as David returned from killing the Philistine, Abner took him to Saul, with David still carrying the Philistine's head. "Whose child are you?" Saul asked.

David said, "I am the child of your servant, Jesse of Bethlehem."

18:1 Once David finished speaking with Saul, the souls of Jonathan and David became intertwined, and Jonathan loved David with all his heart and soul. ² Seeing this, Saul took David in, and wouldn't allow him to return home. ³ And Jonathan and David made a solemn covenant with one another, for they loved each other as much as they loved themselves. ⁴ Then Jonathan

---

* 2 Samuel 21:19 says that Goliath was killed by Elhanan, not David (though it also says that David and his attendants killed four other Philistines in Gath who were descended from giants)—another example of multiple source narratives in the books of Samuel.

took off his robe and his tunic, and gave them to David; he also gave him his sword, his bow, and his belt.*

⁵ David, succeeding so well in the missions Saul ordered, was put in charge of the fighting forces. This pleased the people and Saul's officers as well.

⁶ When the troops were returning from the event in which David slew the giant, the people from all the towns and cities of Israel came out singing and dancing to meet the ruler Saul, rejoicing with tambourines and lutes. ⁷ As they danced they sang,

> "Saul slew his thousands,
> but David slew tens of thousands."

⁸ Then Saul, filled with rage and resentment, said, "They ascribe to David ten thousands, and only ascribe to me thousands. What else can happen to this one but to replace me as ruler?" ⁹ And from that day on Saul envied David.

¹⁰ The next day an evil spirit from God seized Saul. And it forced the ruler into a state of rage. David was present, as usual, playing the harp. Saul, holding a spear, ¹¹ hurled it, thinking to himself, "I will pin David to the wall." But once more David eluded the ruler.

¹² Saul feared David for now YHWH was with him and not with Saul. ¹³ Saul dismissed David by making him a field officer in charge of 1,000 troops. ¹⁴ And David led the troops in successful campaigns; everything he did was a success because YHWH was with him. ¹⁵ Saul saw how successful David was in everything he did. And this made the ruler more fearful than ever. ¹⁶ But all Israel and Judah loved David for leading the troops in their successful campaigns.

¹⁷ Saul said to David, "Here is my firstborn daughter, Merab. I will let you propose marriage to her on one condition: you must serve me bravely and fight YHWH's battles." For Saul surmised, "I will not raise a hand against him. But I will let the Philistines do it!"

¹⁸ David answered Saul, "Who am I and what are my parent's people, my kin, in Israel, that I should become the son-in-law of the ruler?" ¹⁹ So when the time came for Saul's daughter Merab to be engaged to David, she became engaged to Adriel of Meholah instead.

---

* This is a symbolic act. For the son of a ruler to divest himself of his royal garb and the symbols of military leadership, and give them to a shepherd, was shocking; Jonathan is making David his equal in all respects, and suggests emotional intimacy as well, essentially saying, "I stand naked and powerless before you." Erotic friendship and love between hero warriors was a rather common theme in antiquity, examples include Gilgamesh and Enkidu, Achilles and Patroclus, and Alexander the Great and Hephaestion.

²⁰ In the meantime Saul's daughter Michal had fallen in love with David. When Saul learned of Michal's love, he was pleased. ²¹ For Saul thought, "I will have her marry David. Then she'll become a snare that lures him to his death at the hands of Philistines!"

So Saul told David, "Today you will become my son-in-law a second time!"*

²² Saul ordered his attendants to speak to David privately, "The ruler is well disposed to you and all the attendants highly respect you. Now is the time for you to become the ruler's son-in-law."

²³ But when the attendants briefed David, he replied, "Do you think it's a small matter to become the son-in-law of the ruler? I am only a poor person, and hardly known."†

²⁴ When the attendants related this to Saul, ²⁵ he replied, "Tell David that all the ruler wants as a marriage settlement is the foreskins of 100 Philistines. In this way Saul will be taking revenge on the enemy." Saul was counting on David's death at the hands of the enemy.

²⁶ When the attendants reported this offer, David was pleased with the prospect of becoming the son-in-law of the ruler. ²⁷ So, before the allotted time, David and the troops slew 200 Philistines. David brought their fore-skins and counted them out in the presence of Saul. This doubly fulfilled Saul's condition for David to become his son-in-law, so he gave permission for Michal and David to marry.

²⁸ Saul saw clearly that YHWH was with David. ²⁹ And he was certain that Michal loved David. But in time he grew more and more fearful of David, and came to see David as an enemy, which continued for the rest of his life.

³⁰ The Philistine commanders continued to raid the Israelites, and as often as they did, David was more and more successful and famous against them than any other of Saul's officers.

19:1 Saul told Jonathan and his attendants to murder David. Jonathan, however, delighted greatly in David— ² so much so that he alerted David:

---

* Our translation of this phrase is somewhat controversial; it literally reads, "You will become my son-in-law through two." Some translations interpret this verse as meaning that Saul "said for the second time," or that David has a "second opportunity" to become Saul's son-in-law. But assuming Saul is telling David that he will become his son-in-law for the second time, what did he mean? The first offer Saul made to David for a wife was Merab, but she married Adriel instead and was never even engaged to David. The only other covenant made between Saul's family and David was between David and Jonathan in 18:3, which is not a covenant of business or politics, but of love.

† Becoming "son-in-law of the ruler" was such an issue because in most of the nations that Israel was familiar with, the rulers were chosen through matrilinear succession, and as there was no monarchy in Israel before this, there was no other pattern to follow. Jonathan, then, would not be the heir-apparent, but whoever married the ruler's daughter and proved himself qualified militarily—in this case, David.

"Saul is looking for a chance to murder you. So be on your guard tomorrow morning. Go, hide yourself and remain hidden. ³ I will go out and stand near Saul, close to where you are hiding, and I'll try to change his mind. If I learn anything, I will let you know."

⁴ Jonathan advocated on David's behalf to his father Saul. He said, "Your majesty, do not wrong your faithful David, for David has not wronged you. In fact, his achievements have been greatly to your advantage. ⁵ David took his life into his own hands when he killed the Philistine. YHWH won a great victory for all Israel, and when you saw it you were happy. Why then would you wrong an innocent person like David by murdering him without reason?"

⁶ Once Jonathan made his case, Saul took an oath, "As surely as YHWH lives, David will not be put to death."

⁷ Jonathan called out to David and explained what had happened. Then Jonathan brought David to Saul, and David remained in attendance to Saul as before.

⁸ War broke out once more, and David led the troops into battle with such fury that the defeated Philistines retreated before him. ⁹ Once more an evil spirit from YHWH came upon Saul as he sat at home holding a spear. Nearby David was playing the harp. ¹⁰ Saul attempted to pin him to the wall with the spear, but David escaped as Saul drove the spear into the wall. David fled and made good his escape.

¹¹ That same night Saul sent messengers to watch David's house with the intention of killing him in the morning. But David's wife, Michal, said, "If you don't flee tonight, you will be dead in the morning." ¹² So she let David down through a window to slip away and escape. ¹³ Then Michal took their household idol, putting it in their bed, with a goat's hair rug for the head, and covered with a blanket.

¹⁴ When Saul's messengers arrived to arrest David, Michal said, "He is ill." ¹⁵ Then Saul sent messengers back to bring David to him, bed and all. ¹⁶ And when they arrived, there was the household idol, with the goat's hair rug as its head.

¹⁷ Saul asked Michal, "Why did you deceive me and let my adversary escape?"

Michal replied, "He threatened to kill me if I did not help him to escape."

¹⁸ Now a fugitive, David went to Samuel at Ramah and described how Saul attempted to murder him. Once David's briefing of Samuel took place, they decided to take refuge in the huts at Ramah. ¹⁹ When Saul learned that David was in the huts at Ramah, ²⁰ he sent messengers to arrest David. But

when they saw a group of prophets prophesying—Samuel standing there leading—the Spirit of God fell on the messengers and they also prophesied. ²¹ Once this was reported to Saul, he sent more messengers, and they too prophesied. A third party of messengers prophesied as well. ²² Finally, Saul went to Ramah and came to the great sistern in Secu. He inquired about Samuel and David and learned they were at the huts at Ramah. ²³ And as Saul set out, the Spirit of God fell on the ruler, too, and he was prophesying until he arrived at the huts of Ramah. Then Saul stripped off his clothes and also prophesied in Samuel's presence. He lay there all that day and night. It is for this reason that people say, "Is Saul among the prophets, too?"

20:1 David fled from the huts at Ramah and went to Jonathan, asking, "What have I done? What crime did I commit that Saul would hold against me that he tries to take my life?"

² Jonathan replied, "Heaven forbid! There is no thought of putting you to death. I am certain that the ruler does nothing, large or small, without confiding in me. Why should Saul hide this from me? It's not so!"

³ But David swore, "I am certain that Saul is aware that I enjoy your favor and thinks to himself, 'Jonathan must not know lest he resent it.' Nevertheless, as YHWH lives, I am only one step away from death."

⁴ Jonathan asked David, "Whatever you desire, I will do for you."

⁵ David answered, "We have a new moon tomorrow, and I am to dine with the ruler. But let me return to the fields to hide there until the third evening, ⁶ and if Saul misses me, say, 'David asked me to leave on short notice to go to Bethlehem, for the whole clan is holding its seasonal sacrifices there.' ⁷ If the ruler says, 'Very well,' it will be well for me. But if he flies into a rage, we will know that Saul is determined to harm me. ⁸ Do me this favor, Jonathan, for we have struck a solemn covenant before YHWH. And if I am guilty, strike the deadly blow yourself. But, by no means, don't let me fall into Saul's hands."

⁹ Jonathan exclaimed, "God forbid! If I see that Saul is set on harming you, I will tell you."

¹⁰ David answered, "How will you alert me if he answers harshly?"

¹¹ Jonathan said, "Come, let us go into the fields."

¹² There Jonathan told David, "I promise you, as YHWH the God of Israel lives, I will sound out Saul about this time tomorrow. If he is favorably disposed towards you, I will not send you word to let you know. ¹³ But if Saul is inclined to harm you, may YHWH do the same to me and more if I don't let you know and I send you on your way in peace. May YHWH be with you, as YHWH used to be with my father! ¹⁴ I am still alive, show me

YHWH's loving kindness. But even if I die, ¹⁵ never withdraw your faithful love from my family. And when YHWH eliminates all of the enemies of David from the face of the earth, ¹⁶ the name of Jonathan must never be allowed by the family of David to die out from among you; for YHWH will make you answer for it."

¹⁷ Jonathan pledged his love to David once again,* for he loved David as he loved himself.

¹⁸ Jonathan said, "Tomorrow is the new moon, and you will be missed for your seat will be empty. ¹⁹ Toward evening on the day after tomorrow, go to your hiding place when this trouble began, and wait near the heap of stones there. ²⁰ I will shoot three arrows toward it, as if I were shooting at a target. ²¹ Then I will send a youth to pick up the arrows. If I say to the youth, 'Look, you will find the arrows on the side of you, bring them here.' Then come, for, as surely as YHWH lives, you are safe. There is no danger. ²² But if I say to the youth, 'Look, the arrows are beyond you,' then you must go, for YHWH sends you away. ²³ Concerning the matter you and I discussed—recall, YHWH is witness between us forever." ²⁴ So David went back into hiding.

On the day of the new moon, the ruler sat at his customary seat for dining, ²⁵ taking his usual place against the wall, while Jonathan sat facing Saul, and Abner sat at Saul's side.

David's seat was vacant. ²⁶ However, Saul said nothing about it, thinking, "Maybe he did something to make himself ritually unclean." ²⁷ The next day, the second day of the month, David's place remained vacant. Saul inquired of Jonathan, "Why has the son of Jesse missed meals both yesterday and today?"

²⁸ Jonathan replied, "David asked permission to go to Bethlehem. ²⁹ 'Please let me go,' he begged, 'for we are having a clan sacrifice in our city, and family insists that I be there. Therefore, if I have found favor in your eyes let me slip away to see my sisters and brothers.' That is why he is not present at the table."

³⁰ And Saul was enraged with Jonathan, and said, "You child of a perverse and rebellious woman! Do you think I don't know that you are choosing the son of Jesse—to your own shame, and to the shame of your mother's nakedness? ³¹ As long as the son of Jesse dwells on this earth, neither you nor your dynasty will be established.* Now go and bring him to me, for he must die!"

---

* Our translation recalls the covenant Jonathan and David made with one another in 18:3, and referred to in 20:42. However, the text literally reads, "And again Jonathan caused to swear an oath to/upon David out of love," which could also mean that Jonathan asked David to swear an oath, arising from the love that David felt for Jonathan, to deal kindly with Jonathan's family in the event of Jonathan's death.

³² "Why must David die? What has he done?" asked Jonathan.

³³ Then Saul hurled his spear at Jonathan, intending to kill him. It was then that Jonathan was certain that Saul intended to murder David. ³⁴ Jonathan, fiercely angry, left the table; the next day, the second day of the festival, he fasted from food, for he was grieved at the way Saul had treated David.

³⁵ The next morning he went out to the field for his meeting with David. With him was a youth; ³⁶ and he instructed the lad, "Run and find the arrows I will shoot." ³⁷ When the lad came to the place where Jonathan's arrows fell, ³⁸ Jonathan called after him, "Hurry! Be quick! Don't Stop!" He picked up the arrows and returned them to Jonathan, ³⁹ for the lad did not understand what had happened; only Jonathan and David knew. ⁴⁰ Then Jonathan handed the bow and the arrows, and said, "Go, carry these back to town."

⁴¹ After the lad left, David got up from the side of the mound and prostrated himself on the ground three times before Jonathan. Then they kissed each other and cried together until David's grief exceeded Jonathan's. ⁴² Then Jonathan said to David, "Go in peace; the two of us have pledged ourselves to one another in the name of YHWH. May YHWH be between you and me, and between your descendants and mine, forever."

Then David went on his way, and Jonathan went back to town.

²¹·¹ David came to Nob, to the priest Ahimelech; the trembling cleric met David with, "Why are you alone? Shouldn't you be accompanied?

² David answered Ahimelech, "I am under orders from the ruler that my mission be carried out alone and in secret. When I took leave of my troops I told them to meet me at a certain place. No one is to know about your mission or your instructions. ³ Now then, I need five loaves, or whatever you can spare."

⁴ Ahimelech said, "I am out of ordinary bread. There is some consecrated bread here; but are your troops ritually pure?

⁵ David replied, "Because we are on a campaign, my young troops are ritually pure; and they will be much holier today!"

⁶ So the priest gave five consecrated loaves to David which had been removed from the presence of YHWH and replaced by hot bread on the day it was removed. ⁷ One of Saul's attendants, Doeg the Edomite, the ruler's chief shepherd, was detained there before YHWH,† and saw what David did.

⁸ David said to Ahimelech, "Do you have a spear or a sword here? I am without my own weapons because the ruler's business was urgent."

---

* Saul uses carefully coded language here. "You child of a perverse and rebellious woman" is essentially the Hebraic form of the phrase, "You son of a bitch!" Moreover, throughout the Hebrew scriptures, referring to the nakedness of one's parents always indicates a sexual relationship.
† He may have been at the Tabernacle to fulfill a vow, or to be cleansed from ritual impurity.

⁹ The priest replied, "The sword of Goliath the Philistine, whom you killed in the Valley of Elah, is here. It is wrapped in a cloth behind the ephod. Take it if you need it. It is the only one here."

David said, "There is none like it. I will take it."

¹⁰ Then David moved on, in flight from Saul, and went to Achish, ruler of Gath. ¹¹ But Achish's attendants said, "Isn't this David, the ruler of the land, the one they sing about in their dances:

'Saul slew his thousands,
but David slew tens of thousands'?

¹² These comments were not lost on David, and he became afraid of Achish of Gath. ¹³ So, knowing he was being watched, David feigned madness before all the people there, drumming on the doors of the gates and drooling saliva onto his beard. ¹⁴ Achish said to his attendants, "Look at this madman! He is insane! Why do you even let him in? ¹⁵ Am I so short of maniacs, that you bring in one more to carry on before me? Must this maniac come into my house?"

²²⁻¹ David escaped from Gath and went to the stronghold of Adullam,* and when his sisters and brothers learned what happened, they went down and joined him there. ² All those in distress, in debt, or embittered joined him. And David became their leader—he had about about 400 followers.

³ From there David went to Mizpah in Moab, and said to the ruler of Moab, "May I leave my mother and father with you, until I learn what God wants of me"? ⁴ They stayed with the ruler of Moab, and they stayed there as long as David remained in his stronghold.

⁵ But the prophet Gad said to David, "Leave your stronghold, and go into the land of Judah." So David left the stronghold and journeyed to the forest of Hareth.

⁶ News that David and his followers were discovered came to Saul. And Saul, sitting under the tamarisk tree of the hill at Gibeah, surrounded by his court, ⁷ said to them, "Listen, women and men of Benjamin, will the son of Jesse give all of you fields and vineyards? Will he give you commanders of thousands and commanders of hundreds? ⁸ Is this why all of you have conspired against me? No one told me that my son has made a covenant with the son of Jesse! None of you are concerned about me or tells me that my son has set my attendant against me, who lies in wait for me this very minute."

⁹ Doeg the Edomite, standing with Saul's attendants, spoke up: "I saw Jesse's son approaching Nob, toward Ahimelech's ben-Ahitub. ¹⁰ Ahimelech

---

* The Hebrew has "cave," which may include a network or region of caves rather than one large enough to shelter 400 followers, but it is more likely a scribal error for "stronghold" (v. 5). The city of Adullam was a Canaanite capital; it was later fortified by Rehoboam, David's grandson.

consulted YHWH on David's behalf and then gave David food and the sword of Goliath the Philistine."

¹¹ Saul sent for Ahimelech and his whole family, who were priests at Nob, and they came to the ruler. ¹² Saul said, "Listen to me, ben-Ahitub."

"Yes, your majesty," replied Ahimelech.

¹³ Saul said, "Why have you conspired against me, you and this son of Jesse, giving him bread and a sword and consulting God for him, so that now David rises against me and at this very moment is lying in wait for me?"

¹⁴ Abimelech replied, "And who among all your attendants can measure up to David, one who can be trusted, the son-in-law of the ruler, appointed to your staff and holds an honorable place in your household? ¹⁵ Have I done something profane for consulting God on his behalf? God forbid! Let not the ruler accuse your servant or any of my family, for I know nothing at all about this whole affair!"

¹⁶ But the ruler said, "You will surely die, Ahimelech, you and your whole family!"

¹⁷ Then Saul ordered the guards next to him, "Kill the priests of YHWH, for they, too, side with David. They knew he was fleeing, yet they did not tell me." But the guards were not willing to raise a hand to strike the priests of YHWH.

¹⁸ Then Saul ordered Doeg, "You kill the priests." So Doeg the Edomite struck them down. He killed eighty-five men wearing the linen ephod that day. ¹⁹ That day he killed every living thing in Nob, the town of the priests: women and men, children and babies, oxen, donkeys, and sheep.

²⁰ But Abiathar ben-Ahimelech ben-Ahitub, escaped and fled to join David. ²¹ He briefed David how it came about that Saul had his father and the other priests of YHWH killed.

²² "That day, when Doeg the Edomite was there, I knew he would surely tell Saul," David said. "I am responsible for the death of your whole family. ²³ Stay with me. Don't fear. The person who seeks to kill you wants to kill me as well. You will be safe with me."

²³·¹ When David learned that the Philistines were attacking Keilah and looting the threshing floors, ² he asked YHWH, "Shall I attack the Philistines in return?"

YHWH replied, "Go, attack these Philistines and save Keilah."

³ But David's troops said, "We are fearful here in Judah. How much more, then, if we go to Keilah against the Philistines?"

⁴ Once more David inquired of YHWH, and YHWH replied, "Go down to Keilah, for I am going to give the Philistines into your hands." ⁵ So David and the troops went to Keilah and fought the Philistines and carried off

their livestock. They inflicted heavy casualties on them and relieved the citizens of Keilah.

⁶ When Abiathar ben-Ahimelech fled and joined David at Keilah, he carried an ephod with him.

⁷ It was reported to Saul that David had entered Keilah, and he said, "YHWH has delivered David into my hands, for he has walked into a trap by entering a town with bars and gates." ⁸ Saul then put all the people on a war alert, in order to go down to Keilah and besiege David and his entourage.

⁹ When David learned that Saul planned a seige, he told Abiathar the priest, "Bring forth the ephod."* ¹⁰ Then David said, "YHWH, God of Israel, your faithful one learned that Saul definitely will come to besiege us and destroy the town because of me. ¹¹ Will the citizens of Keilah surrender me to them? Will Saul attack, as I have heard? YHWH, God of Israel, answer my prayer."

And YHWH said to David, "He will."

¹² Once more David asked, "Will the citizens of Keilah surrender me to Saul?"

And YHWH replied, "He will."

¹³ So David, with about 600 followers, left Keilah and kept moving from place to place. When Saul learned that David abandoned Keilah he called off the attack. ¹⁴ David moved about in the desert strongholds and in the hills of the Desert of Ziph. Day by day Saul searched for them, but God did not give David into the hands of Saul.

¹⁵ David was at Horesh in the desert of Ziph when he learned that Saul came out to seek his life. ¹⁶ Jonathan ben-Saul came to David at Horesh, and strengthened his hand in God.† ¹⁷ "Don't be afraid," he said, "Saul's hand will not touch you. For you will become the ruler of Israel and I will rank below you."

¹⁸ After they renewed their solemn covenant to one another before YHWH, David remained in Horesh and Jonathan returned home.

¹⁹ Some of the Ziphites came to Saul in Gibeah with information about David, saying, "David is hiding among us in the caves of Horesh on the hill of Hachilah, south of Jeshimon. ²⁰ Therefore, whenever Saul wishes to come down, let him do so. It will be our task to deliver him into the hands of the ruler."

---

* The Urim and Thummim were likely kept in a pocket in the breastpiece of the ephod, which is why YHWH's answers in the next few verses sound like oracular responses: they were essentially casting lots to determine the future.
† This may mean "helped him find strength in God," or "gave him powerful encouragement."

²¹ Saul replied, "May YHWH bless you for your sympathy to our cause. ²² Go now and make sure once more! Notice the place where he is and who saw him there. They tell me he is very crafty. ²³ Learn all his hiding places he uses and return to me with accurate information. Then I will go with you, and if he is in the area, I will track him down among all the clans of Judah."

²⁴ So they set out and journeyed to Ziph ahead of Saul. Now David and his followers were in the Desert of Maon, in the Arabah south of Jeshimon. ²⁵ Saul and his followers began to search, and when David learned this, he went down to the cave in the rocks, and he stayed there in the desert of Maon. On learning this, Saul went into the desert after David. ²⁶ He was on one side of the hill while David was on the other side of the hill. While David and his people were trying desperately to escape, with Saul and his people closing in for a capture, ²⁷ a messenger brought a message to Saul, "Come at once! For the Philistines are invading the land." ²⁸ Saul called off the pursuit of David and turned back to face the Philistines. This is why that place is known as the Dividing Rock. ²⁹ David went up from there and dwelt in the strongholds of En Gedi.

24:1 When Saul returned from pursuing the Philistines, they told him, "David is in the desert of En Gedi." ² So Saul took 3,000 chosen troops from all Israel and set out to find David and his entourage near the Rocks of the Mountain Goats. ³ When he came to some sheepfolds next to the road, where there was a cave. Saul went in it to relieve himself.

David and his followers were also there, but further back. ⁴ David's people said, "This is a day YHWH spoke of when you were told, 'I will give your foe into your hands for you to deal with as you wish.'" Then David, unnoticed, crept into the cave and cut off a corner of Saul's robe.

⁵ After Saul left, David regretted that he had cut off the corner of Saul's robe. ⁶ He said to his followers, "God forbid that I should harm my sovereign, YHWH's anointed, or lift my hand against him. For he is the anointed of YHWH." ⁷ With these words David rebuked the others and refused to order them to attack Saul.

And Saul left the cave and went his way. ⁸ David followed and called out to Saul, "My ruler and my sovereign!"

When Saul turned around, David bowed down and prostrated himself on the ground. ⁹ And he said to Saul, "Why do you listen when people say, 'David is bent on harming you'? ¹⁰ You can see for yourself how YHWH put you into my own hands in the cave: Some of my people urged me to murder you, but I spared you. I said to them, 'I will not lift my hand against my sovereign, for he is YHWH's anointed.' ¹¹ See, my ruler, look at this piece of your robe in my hand! I cut it off the corner of your robe but chose not to kill you. Understand and recognize that I am not guilty of wrongdoing or rebellion. I have not wronged you, yet you hunt me down in order to kill me. [12] May YHWH judge between us! And may YHWH avenge the wrongs you have done to me, though my hands will not touch you. [13] There is an old adage, 'From evildoers come evil deeds,' so my hand will never touch you. [14] Against whom has the ruler of Israel come out? What are you pursuing? A dead dog? A flea? [15] May YHWH be judge between us! May YHWH consider my cause and uphold it; may YHWH vindicate me by delivering me from your hands!"

[16] Once David finished, Saul asked, "Is that your voice, David my son?" And he burst into tears. [17] "You are more righteous than I," the ruler said. "You treated me well, and I treated you badly. [18] Just now you told me of the good you did to me. YHWH put me into your hands, and you did not murder me. [19] When a person captures an enemy, does he let the captured one go free? May YHWH reward you well for the way you treated me today. [20] I now know that you surely will be ruler and that the kindom of Israel will be well established in your hands. [21] Now swear to me by YHWH that you will not cut off my descendants or wipe out my name from my parents' families."

[22] So David gave his oath to Saul. Then Saul returned to Jerusalem, but David and his followers returned to their caves.

[25:1] Samuel died, and all of Israel came together to mourn. They buried their prophet at Ramah, where Samuel made his home.

[2] Meanwhile David went down to the Desert of Maon. There was a wealthy property owner in Carmel who had a flock of 300 sheep and 1,000 goats. It was shearing time. [3] The owner was named Nabal, and his wife was named Abigail. Abigail was an intelligent and attractive woman, while Nabal, a Calebite, was surly, mean, and hard to deal with.

[4] Now David, learning that Nabal was shearing, [5] sent ten younger attendants with greetings, [6] saying, "Long life and good health to you and your household! And good health to all your flocks! [7] I see that you are shearing. When your shepherds were in our area, we were hospitable to them, and never did they find anything missing while they were staying in Carmel. [8] Ask your herders and attendants and they will confirm what we say. Be kind to our lads, for this is a festive season. Please donate to them what you can manage."

[9] When David's followers arrived and delivered David's message, they paused for a response. [10] Nabal answered, "Who is this David? Who is this child of Jesse? Nowadays lots of indentured workers escape from their owners. [11] Am I to take my bread, my water, and the meat I slaughter for my shearers and give it to people coming from who-knows-where?"

¹² David's followers turned around immediately and went back to David and reported what the wealthy herder said. ¹³ David responded immediately by strapping on his sword, and commanded, "Everyone, strap on your swords!" About 400 went up with David, while 200 stayed back to guard their supplies.

¹⁴ One of the attendants said to Nabal's wife, Abigail, "David sent a delegation of attendants from the desert with greetings to Nabal. But he insulted them. ¹⁵ And they were very good to us when we had our herds in their territory. We found nothing missing, they did not mistreat us, ¹⁶ and the whole while we were in their territory, they formed a protective wall around us night and day. ¹⁷ Think about it! What can we do? For it is certain that disaster beckons to Nabal. Nabal is so stubborn no one can reason with him, even at a time such as this."

¹⁸ Abigail quickly collected 200 loaves and two skins of wine, five dressed sheep, five measures of roasted grain, 100 bunches of raisins, and 200 cakes of dried figs, which she loaded on donkeys. ¹⁹ Saying nothing to Nabal, she instructed her attendants, "Move out ahead of me, and I will follow you."

²⁰ As she traveled on her donkey, hidden by the hills, David and his followers met her on the road. ²¹ David said, "It is a waste of our time to protect Nabal's property in the desert. He repaid us with evil for our goodness. ²² David swore a solemn oath, "May God do the same to me and more if I leave him one male alive by morning."

²³ As soon as Abigail spotted David approaching she dismounted prostrated before David in homage. ²⁴ As she prostrated she said, "Sovereign One, blame me, and please allow me, your humble handmaid, to speak my piece. ²⁵ How can you even take notice of this wretched person? He is the embodiment of the meaning of his name, 'Fool', and fool he is. I, your handmaid, missed seeing your young messengers when they arrived.

²⁶ "Your highness, as YHWH lives and as you live, it is YHWH who has restrained you from shedding blood and avenging yourself personally. As YHWH lives, may your enemies and all who desire you ruined become like Nabal. ²⁷ Behold the presents which I, your humble attendant, bring to you. Give them to the ten youths under your command. ²⁸ Do forgive me, your highness, for my presumptuousness, for YHWH will establish your family forever, because you fight YHWH's battles so well. Calamity will not overtake you as long as you live! ²⁹ If anyone attempts to approach you with foul motives, YHWH your God will wrap up your life and put it among the divine treasures. But the lives of your enemies will be hurled away as if slung from a sling.

³⁰ "And when YHWH carries out for you the promise of success, and appoints you commander over Israel, ³¹ you will not have this incident as a

burden on your conscience, my sovereign, for shedding innocent blood or for avenging yourself personally. When YHWH does make all you do prosper, remember me, your attendant!"

³² David said to Abigail, "Blessed be YHWH, the God of Israel, who today sends you to meet with me. ³³ Blessings to you for your good sense; blessings to you for saving me today from the guilt of bloodshed and from avenging myself with my own hands. ³⁴ Otherwise, as surely as YHWH the God of Israel lives, who kept me from harming you, if you had not come quickly to meet me, not one male of Nabal's household would have been alive by daybreak."

³⁵ Then David accepted from her what she had brought, and said, "Return to your home in peace! For I have heard your wise counsel and granted your request."

³⁶ When Abigail returned home, Nabal was hosting a drinking party in the house like a drunken ruler. Nabal was merry and very drunk. Under the circumstances she chose not to relate what had just occurred. ³⁷ In the morning, when Nabal had sobered up, she told him everything that happened. Hearing this, he had a heart attack and fell into a coma.* ³⁸ Nabal died ten days later.

³⁹ When David learned that Nabal died he said, "Blessed be YHWH who avenged the insult I received at Nabal's hands and restrained me from doing evil. YHWH personally brought Nabal's sinfulness down upon his own head."

Then David sent a message to Abigail proposing marriage. ⁴⁰ Then his attendants came to her at Carmel, and said, "David sent us to bring you him, to be his wife."

⁴¹ She stood, then prostrated herself on the ground and said, "Behold, your handmaid becomes your lowly bondservant, to wash the feet of my sovereign's servants." ⁴² Abigail then stood and immediately prepared to go to David, riding a donkey. With five women in attendance, she followed David's messengers, and married David.†

---

* Literally, "his heart died within him and he became like a stone."

† The story of Abigail is especially remarkable because of its frequent misuse by antifeminists. They see a woman who first submits herself to a drunken and abusive husband, and who, once God frees her from the husband's control because of her kindness to David, is willing to subject herself to the lowliest form of servitude and become David's new wife; they applaud her submissiveness. Feminists, however, see a fiercely independent woman who calls her husband a fool, overrules her husband's insulting rudeness, and honors the sacred code of hospitality; and who, when offered marriage to David, first stands, then performs a carefully choreographed humility ritual (the submission of a subject to a ruler, even though David at this point had not yet ascended the throne), then stands again—evidence of her great dignity and self-determination—before going to meet David with five servants of her own. Abigail was a woman of power.

⁴³ David also married Ahinoam of Jezreel. ⁴⁴ Meanwhile, Saul arranged that his daughter Michal, David's first wife, would marry Palti ben-Laish of Gallim.*

²⁶ˑ¹ The Ziphites came to Saul at Gibeah with news that David was hiding on the hill of Hacilah overlooking Jeshimon. ² Saul immediately journeyed down to the desert of Ziph with 3,000 Israelite troops chosen to search out David. ³ Saul set up camp beside the road on the hill of Hachilah, and the edge of the desert.

David, now living in the desert, saw Saul setting up camp in the desert, too. ⁴ So David sent out scouts and confirmed that Saul had arrived. ⁵ David then went to the place where Saul set up camp and observed where Saul and Abner ben-Ner, the general, had set up their sleeping quarters. Saul lay within the lines within the camp and the army was encamped around him.

⁶ David asked Ahimelech the Hittite, and Abishai, son of Zeruiah and brother of Joab, "Who will go down into the camp with me to Saul?"

Abishai replied, "I will."

⁷ Abishai and David entered the camp after dark and found Saul asleep with the lines with his spear thrust into the ground near his head. Abner and the army slept all around him. ⁸ Abishai whispered to David, "God has delivered your enemy into your hands today. Let me nail him to the ground with one thrust of the spear. I won't even need a second thrust."

⁹ But David said to Abishai, "Don't harm Saul, for who can lay hands on YHWH's anointed one and remain unpunished?" ¹⁰ David continued, "As YHWH lives, it must be YHWH alone who strikes Saul down, whether the time comes for him to die, or Saul goes out and dies in battle. ¹¹ But God forbid that I touch YHWH's anointed one! Just take the spear at Saul's head and his water jug, and let us be on our way." ¹² So David took the spear and the water jug sitting just near to Saul's head; they were able to get away without anyone being seen, or known or awakened.

¹³ David crossed over to the opposite slope and stood on remote hilltop at a great distance of Abner ben-Ner and the troops. ¹⁴ Then he shouted, "Give me an answer, Abner!"

Abner answered, "Who is it who calls me?"

¹⁵ David said to Abner, "Do you call yourself a man? Is there anyone like you in Israel? When, then, did you not keep watch over your sovereign, your ruler, when someone came to harm him? ¹⁶ What you did was not a good

---

* The lack of any divorce language suggests that Saul, as ruler, simply annulled the marriage. Saul was afraid that David, Saul's son-in-law, would be the presumptive heir to the throne, and hoped that the annulment would remove David's claim and thwart any opportunity for him to rise to power.

thing. As surely as YHWH lives, you and your troops deserve to die, for you did not guard your sovereign, YHWH's anointed. Look around you—where is the ruler's spear and water jug that were near the ruler's head?"

¹⁷ Saul recognized David's voice and said, "Is that your voice, David, my son?"

David replied, "Yes it is, my sovereign and ruler." ¹⁸ Then David added, "Why do you pursue your faithful attendant? What have I done, and what wrong am I guilty of? ¹⁹ Listen, my sovereign: If it is YHWH who sets you against me, I am sure God will be appeased with an offering; but if people have turned you against me, a curse on them in YHWH's name! For they have driven me from my share in YHWH's possessions and have said, 'Go serve other gods!' ²⁰ And don't let my blood be shed on foreign soil, far from the presence of YHWH, just because the ruler of Israel came out to look for a flea, as one might hunt a partridge in the mountains."

²¹ Then Saul responded, "I have sinned. Come back, David my son. Because you considered my life precious today, I will stop trying to kill you. Surely I am acting like a fool and have erred greatly!"

²² "Here is the ruler's spear," David answered. "Let one of your attendants come over to get it. ²³ YHWH rewards all people for their righteousness and faithfulness. YHWH gave you into my hands today, but I would not lay a hand on YHWH's anointed. ²⁴ As surely as I valued your life today, so may YHWH value my life and deliver me from all trouble."

²⁵ Then Saul said to David, "May you be blessed, David my child. You will do great things and you will surely triumph."

So David went up his way, and Saul went home.

²⁷:¹ David was alone and in a reflective mood. "One of these days," he thought, "Saul will murder me. So the best thing for me to do is to escape into Philistine territory. Then Saul will give up searching for me anywhere in Israel, and I will be out of my ruler's clutches."

² So David, with a regiment of 600 troops, set out for the frontier and crossed the border at Gath, whose ruler, Achish ben-Maoch, welcomed David and the regiment.* ³ David settled there along with the regiment and their families, together with Ahioam the Jezrellite and the widow Abigail of Carmel, his two wives.

⁴ When Saul learned that David had fled to Gath, he gave up his search.

---

* Recall that Gath is one of the five Philistine strongholds, and the home of Goliath, whom David killed several years earlier. Achish likely welcomed David more as a political gesture than any great feeling of warmth.

⁵ David said to Achish, "If I have won your favor, please allow me to be placed in one of your country towns. Why should I remain in your royal city with your majesty?"

⁶ So Achish assigned David to Zilgad that day. And the city belongs to the rulers of Judah to this day. ⁷ In all, David dwelt there for sixteen months.

⁸ David and the 600 went up to make raids on the Geshurites, the Girzites, and the Amalekites, who who lived on that land from antiquity, from the edge of the desert of Shur as far as Egypt. ⁹ David's raids laid the countryside to waste, and neither male or female remained alive. They took flocks, herds, donkey, camels, and clothes before they returned to Achish.

¹⁰ Every time David returned from a raid, Achish would ask, "Where did you raid today?"

And David would reply, "Southern Judah" or "the southern Jerahmeelite region" or "the southern Kenite region." ¹¹ He let no one alive to survive the raid, fearing that they might denounce the raiders for what they did. This was the norm as long as David and the raiders remained with the Philistines. ¹² Achish trusted David, thinking, "He has made himself so hated by his own people, the Israelites, that he will remain my vassal forever."

28:1 At that time the Philistines mustered their army to attack Israel, and Achish said to David, "You understand that you and your 300 must take the field with me."

² "Then you will see what your servant can do!" David replied.

Then Achish said to David, "In that case, I appoint you as my personal body guard for life."

³ Now, Samuel was dead (all of Israel mourned; the prophet was buried in Ramah, his hometown), and Saul had driven out the mediums and fortunetellers* from the land.

⁴ Once more the Philistines mustered and marched on Shunem, and set up camp there; Saul gathered all Israel, and they encamped at Gilboa. ⁵ Saul's heart was in his mouth when he viewed the assembled Philistines.

⁶ Saul's only option was to consult YHWH, but YHWH did not respond—not in dreams, by the Urim, or through the prophets. ⁷ Then Saul said to his attendants, "Find me a female medium with whom I can consult."

"There is one in Endor," they said.

⁸ After dark, Saul disguised himself and set out with two companions to meet with the medium. They came to her home, and Saul said to her, "I need to know the future. You are a medium; please call up the person I name."

---

* "Medium" is 'owb, literally a water skin bottle; the image is of someone being merely a vehicle for the spirit to enter and speak through. "Fortuneteller" is yidde'oniy, a "knower" of the future.

⁹ But the woman said, "You know that Saul did away with the mediums and the fortunetellers throughout the land. You're just trying to trap me, and it will lead to my death."

¹⁰ Saul swore to her by YHWH: "As YHWH lives, you will not be punished by doing this."

¹¹ The woman asked for the name of the person being called up. "Call up Samuel."*

¹² When the woman saw Samuel, she shrieked, and said to the ruler, "Why have you deceived me? You are Saul!"

¹³ The ruler said to her, "Don't be afraid. What do you see?"

She said, "I see a divine being coming up out of the ground."

"What does it look like?" he asked.

"An old man wearing a robe."

¹⁴ Then Saul, realizing that it was Samuel, fell face down on the ground.

¹⁵ And Samuel asked Saul, "Why do you disturb me by bringing me up?"

The ruler replied, "I am in great trouble. While the Philistines fight against us, God turns away from me. God no longer answers me, either by the prophets or by my dreams. So I called you up to tell me what I should do."

¹⁶ Samuel said, "Why then do you ask me, since YHWH has turned away from you and is your enemy? ¹⁷ YHWH did what was foretold through me: YHWH tore the reign from your hands and gave them to your neighbor, David. ¹⁸ You did not carry out YHWH's fierce wrath against the Amalekites. This is why YHWH did this to you today. ¹⁹ YHWH will hand over both Israel and you to the Philistines; and tomorrow, you and your sons will be with me. YHWH will also hand over Israel's army to the Philistines."

²⁰ At that instant, Saul fell face down onto the ground, filled with fear due to Samuel's words; the ruler had no strength left, for he had not eaten all that day and night.

²¹ When the woman went to Saul, noticing how deeply shaken he was, she said, "I listened to what you said and I risked my life to obey you. ²² Now listen to me: let me set before you a little food to strengthen you for the journey."

²³ The ruler refused to eat anything, but Saul's attendants urged him on, and Saul, finally listening to them, got up from the ground and sat on a couch. ²⁴ The woman had a fattened cow on hand, which she slaughtered at once. Then she took flour, kneaded it, and baked bread without yeast. ²⁵ Then she set it before Saul and the attendants, who ate it all. And when they had eaten, they set out that same night.

---

* Saul asked to speak to Samuel because they had had such a close relationship while Samuel was alive, and never failed to speak God's words.

29:1 The Philistines gathered their entire army at Aphek. The Israelites camped by the spring in Jezreel. 2 As the leaders of the Philistines moved forward in units of hundreds and thousands, David and his troops occupied the rear of Achish's column.

3 Some Philistines among Saul's troop hollered above the din, "What are those Israelites doing here?"

And Achish hollered back, "This is David, the attendant of Saul, the ruler of Israel, who has been with me for over a year. Since David has been with me, I have found no fault in him."

4 "Send him back to his assigned place," the Philistine officers shouted angrily. "He must not fight with us, for he could turn against me in the midst of battle. What better way to buy your superiors favor by executing us? 5 Isn't this the David they sing about in their dances,

'Saul slew his thousands,
but David slew tens of thousands'?"

6 So Achish called for David, and said, "As surely as YHWH lives, you are a reliable person. And I would be pleased to have you serve with me in my army. From the day you came to me until today, I find no fault in you, but the other leaders don't approve of you. 7 So go back home in peace, and don't antagnize the Philistine leaders."

8 "But what have I done?" David asked. "What have you found against me from the day I came to until now, that I shouldn't go and fight against the enemies of you, my sovereign?"

9 Achish said, "I am certain that you have been as pleasing in my eyes as one of God's angels. Nevertheless, the Philistines said, 'He must not go up with you into the battle.' 10 Get up early tomorrow morning alone with your troops you brought with you, and leave at daybreak."

11 So David and the 600 made an early start at daybreak. They went back to the land of the Philistines, while the Philistines moved onto Jezreel.

30:1 On the third day David and the 600 reached Zillag. Meanwhile, the Amalekites sent out raiding parties into the Negev and Zillag. After attacking Zillag, they burned it 2 and took captive all the women and children; they did not kill any of them, but carried them off and went on their way. 3 David and his troops found Zillag destroyed by fire with everyone—wives, daughters, sons—missing. 4 David and his entourage wept aloud until they could weep no more. 5 Ahinoam of Jezreel and Abigail, the widow of Nabal of Carmel, David's two wives, were among them.

6 David found himself in great danger because the troops were talking of stoning him. They were distraught over their children and spouses.

But David found renewed strength by trusting in YHWH his God. ⁷ He instructed the priest, Abiathar ben-Abiathar, to bring the ephod. Abiathar brought the ephod, ⁸ and David sought out YHWH: "Will I pursue the raiding party? And if so, will I overtake it?"

The answer came, "Pursue it, for you will overtake it and you will rescue everyone!"

⁹ David and the 600 came to the wadi of Besor. ¹⁰ Two hundred of them who were too exhausted to cross the wadi stayed behind, and David and the other 400 pressed on in pursuit.

¹¹ While in open country his troops came upon an Egyptian, and took him to David. They gave him food and drink, ¹² as well as part of a cake of pressed figs and two cakes of raisins. The food revived the Egyptian, for he'd had nothing to eat or drink for three days and three nights.

¹³ David asked, "To whom do you belong, and where do you come from?"

He said, "I am an Egyptian, indentured to a Amalekite. My overseer abandoned me when I became ill three days ago. ¹⁴ We had raided the southern Kerethite region, which is part of Judah; and the southern region of Caleb. We also put Zilgag to the torch."

¹⁵ David asked the Egyptian, "Can you take us to the raiding party?"

The Egyptian said, "Swear to me by your God that you will not kill me or deliver me to my owner, and I will lead you to the raiding party."

¹⁶ He led them down, and they found the Amalekites scattered all over the place, eating and drinking and celebrating over the plunder they took from the Philistine and Judean territories.

¹⁷ David attacked them from before dawn until the evening of the next day. The only survivors were 400 youths, who mounted camels and fled. ¹⁸ David rescued all of whom the Amalekites captured, including his two wives. ¹⁹ No one was missing, young and old, sons or daughters, nor was any of the booty or anything else they took missing. David returned with everything. ²⁰ They took all the Amalekite flocks and herds; David's followers drove them ahead of the other livestock, and said, "This is David's plunder."

²¹ Then David came back to the exhausted group of 200 left behind at the Besor wadi. They came out to greet David and the 400. As the large group approached them, David came forward with the troops and greeted them. ²² But some troublemakers and scoundrels among David's fighers interrupted: "Since they did not go with us, we will not share any of the booty with them; they can have their spouses and children, but nothing else."

²³ But David said, "No, comrades, you must not do that, because of what YHWH gave us, and how YHWH protected us, and how YHWH handed over

to us our enemies. ²⁴ Who can agree with what you propose? Those of us who stayed back to protect our stores are to have an equal share with those of us who went into battle. Everyone is to share and share alike."

²⁵ From that time on, this was to become the custom in Israel down to this day. ²⁶ When they reached Ziklag, David sent some of the booty to the elders of Judah and his friends, with this message, "This is a present for you out of the spoil taken from the enemies of YHWH." ²⁷ It was sent to the elders in Bethel, in Ramoth Negev and Jattir; ²⁸ to those in Racal; to those in Hormah, Bor Ashan, Athach ³¹ and Hebron; and to all those in the other places David and his followers had roamed.

³¹ᐟ¹ Meanwhile the Philistines once more engaged the Israelites in combat, and once more the Israelites were routed, leaving their dead on Mount Gilboa.

² The Philistines closed in on Saul and his sons, and they killed Jonathan, Abinadab and Malchishua. ³ The battle turned fierce around Saul, and when they surrounded him, they inflicted severe wounds.

⁴ Saul said to his armor-bearer, "Draw your sword and run me through, so that these heathen brutes cannot taunt me and make sport of me." But the terrified armor-bearer refused to do it. So Saul took his sword and fell on it. When the armor-bearer saw Saul dead, he too fell on his sword and killed himself. 6 So Saul, his three sons, his armor-bearer, and all his warriors died together on the same day.

⁷ When the Israelites in the neighborhood of the valley and the Jordan learned that Saul and his sons were dead, they abandoned their towns and fled. And the Philistines moved in and occupied them.

⁸ The day after the battle, the Philistines returned to strip the dead, and came upon Saul and his sons on Mount Gilboa. ⁹ They cut off Saul's head and stripped him of his armor. Then they sent messengers the length and breadth of the land of the Philistines to proclaim the news in their temples and among the people. ¹⁰ They set up Saul's armor in the temple of the Ashtoreths and fastened his body to the wall of Beth-shan.

¹¹ When the people of Jebesh Gilead heard what the Philistines did to Saul, ¹² all their warriors among them journeyed through the night to recover the bodies of Saul and his sons from the wall of Beth-shan. They brought them back to Jabesh and cremated them. Then they took the ashes and buried them under the tamarisk tree in Jabesh, and they fasted for seven days.

2 samuel

1:1–8:18

After saul's death, david returned
from his victory over the Amalekites and spent two days in Ziklag. ² On the
third day a messenger arrived from Saul's camp, his clothes torn and his
hair full of dirt.* He fell down before David and paid homage.

³ "Where did you come from?" David asked.

⁴ The messenger answered, "I escaped from the camp of Israel."

David asked, "What happened? Tell me everything!"

"Our troops retreated from the field of battle. Many of them fell and died.
Saul and Jonathan are dead."†

⁵ Then David said to the messenger, "How do you know that Saul and
Jonathan are dead?"

⁶ The messenger replied, "It was just by chance that I ended up on Mount
Gilboa and witnessed Saul leaning on his spear surrounded by chariots and
cavalry closing in on him. ⁷ When he noticed me he called to me, and I asked,
'What can I do?' ⁸ He said, 'Who are you?' and I answered, 'An Amalekite.'

---

* These are common symbols of grief in the Middle East.
† This version of Saul's death differs greatly from the version in I Samuel 31:1-13.

⁹ Then he said, 'Come here to me and finish me off, for I am barely alive and in agony.' ¹⁰ So I went over and delivered a fatal blow, for I saw that he was near death. And I took the crown from his head and his arm band from his arm and brought them here to you."

¹¹ Then David and all with him tore their clothes. ¹² They mourned and wept and fasted until evening for Saul, Jonathan, for YHWH's army, and for the house of Israel, for they had fallen by the sword.

¹³ David said to the messenger who had brought the report, "Where are you from?"

"I am the child of a resident alien, an Amalekite," he answered.

¹⁴ Then David said, "How dare you raise your hand and kill YHWH's Anointed?" ¹⁵ Summoning one of his entourage, he ordered the attendant to strike down the Amalekite. The youth did as ordered and killed the messenger ¹⁶ as David said, "May your blood be on your own head. Your words testify against you, when you said, 'I killed YHWH's Anointed.'"

¹⁷ David took up this lament for Saul and Jonathan, ¹⁸ and ordered that "The Song of the Bow" be taught to the Judeans. It is written in *The Book of Jashar:**

19 "Saul, your glory, Israel, lies slain,
   How the mighty have fallen!
20 Do not announce it in Gath,
   do not proclaim it in the streets of Ashkelon,
   lest the daughters of the Philistines rejoice,
   lest the daughters of the heathen exalt.
21 Heights of Gilboa:
   may neither dew nor rain refresh you,
   nor deep springs make your fields lush.
   For there the tarnished shields of warriors lie.
   Saul's shield glimmers no more.
22 From the blood of the dead,
   from the flesh of the fallen,
   Jonathan's bow did not fail,
   nor did Saul's sword return unstained.
23 Saul and Jonathan—
   loved and cherished in life,
   never apart in life or in death!
   Both swift as eagles
   and as strong as lions!
24 Daughters of Israel,
   weep for Saul,

---

* This was probably a collection of poems.

who clothed you in scarlet
    and adorned you in gold!
25 How the mighty have fallen!
    In the heat of battle
    Jonathan lies slain on your heights!
26 I grieve for you, my brother, my Jonathan;
    you were my delight, my sweet!
    Your love was marvellous to me,
    more wonderful than the love of women!
27 How the mighty have fallen!
    The war machines have perished!*

2:1 Sometime afterward, David asked YHWH, "Shall I go up to one of the towns of Judah?"

YHWH replied, "Yes."

Then David asked, "Where shall I go?"

YHWH replied, "Go to Hebron."

2 So David, accompanied by his two wives—Ahinoan, and Abigail the widow of Nabal of Carmel—traveled to Hebron. 3 David also brought his faithful warriors and their families. They settled in Hebron and its surrounding villages. 4 Then the people of Judah came to Hebron and anointed David ruler of the house of Judah.

A report reached David that the people of Jabesh-gilead had buried Saul. 5 So David sent a message to them, "May YHWH bless all of you for your act of faithfulness by burying Saul, your sovereign. 6 May YHWH show faith in kind to you for your good deed. For my part, I will be favorable to you for what you did. 7 Now then, be strong, take courage, for Saul your sovereign is buried, and the people of Judah have anointed me ruler over them."

8 In the meantime, Abner ben-Ner, commander of Saul's army, took Saul's son Ish-bosheth† to the city of Mahanaim, 9 where he set him up as ruler of Gilead, the Ashurites, Jezreel, Ephraim, Benjamin and the rest of Israel. 10 Ish-bosheth ben-Saul was forty years old and ruled over Israel for two years. The tribe of Judah, however, followed David. 11 David reigned in Hebron as ruler of Judah for seven years and six months.

12 Abner ben-Ner took the troops of Saul's successor, Ish-bosheth, and left Mahanaim and marched on Gibeon. 13 Joab ben-Zeruiah and David's soldiers

---

* "War machines" refers to Saul and Jonathan.
† The name literally means "man of shame." It is probably a deliberate corruption of Ish-Ba'al or "man of Ba'al." The name was changed to eliminate the name of Ba'al and at the same time to disparage this pretender to the throne. The same defamation technique was applied to the name of Jonathan's son Mephibosheth, originally named Meribba'al.

left Hebron and headed for Gibeon to confront them. The two groups met up at the pool of Gibeon and took their positions, one force on one side of the pool and the other force on the other side.

¹⁴ Abner said to Joab, "Let your young warriors come forward and join in single combat before us." Joab agreed to this.

¹⁵ So they approached, one by one, and took their places—twelve youths from Benjamin and Ish-bosheth, and twelve from David's warriors. ¹⁶ Each warrior seized an opponent by the head and thrust a dagger into his opponent's side; and each pair fell together, dead. It is because of this incident that the battlefield in Gibeon is known as the Field of Blades.

¹⁷ That day a fierce battle ensued, and Abner and his warriors were defeated by David's troops. ¹⁸ All three sons of Zeruiah were there—Joab the army captain, and his brothers Abishai and Asahel.

Asahel, who was as swift as a gazelle, ¹⁹ chased after Abner, turning neither to the right nor to the left. ²⁰ Abner glanced behind and shouted, "Is that you, Asahel?"

He answered, "Yes!"

²¹ Then Abner said, "Turn to the right or the left, seize one of my warriors, and you can keep his weapons for yourself." But Asahel would not take the bait. ²² Once more Abner urged him to give up the chase, and asked, "Why should I kill you? How could I look your brother Joab in the face?" ²³ But Asahel still kept up the pursuit. So Abner thrust his spear into Asahel's stomach, with the spear coming out his back. Asahel was dead before he hit the ground. And whenever soldiers came to the spot where he had died, they stopped right there.

²⁴ But Joab and Abishai continued the pursuit of Abner, and as the sun set, they came to the hill of Ammah, near Giah on the road leading to the pastures of Gibeon.

²⁵ Then the Benjaminites rallied behind Abner. Forming themselves into a single unit, they took their stand on the top of a hill. ²⁶ Abner called to Joab, "Must the slaughter go on for all time? Don't you realize how bitter we will become because of this day? How much longer will you continue your pursuit of your brothers?"

²⁷ Joab answered, "As YHWH lives, if you had not spoken, they would have continued the pursuit until dawn." ²⁸ Then Joab sounded the trumpet, and all the warriors halted. They abandoned their pursuit of the Israelites, and the fighting stopped.

²⁹ All that night Abner with his troops moved through the Arabah. They crossed the Jordan and continued all morning until they came to Mahanaim.

³⁰ Then Joab returned from pursuing Abner and assembled the whole army. Not counting Asahel, nineteen of David's troops were missing. ³¹ But David's warriors had killed 360 Benjaminites who were with Abner. ³² They buried Asahel in Saul's tomb at Bethlehem. Then Joab and the warriors marched all night and arrived at Hebron by daybreak.

 ³·¹ The hostilities between the house of Saul and the house of David lasted a long time. As David's grew stronger and stronger, Saul's house grew weaker and weaker.

 ² Sons were born to David at Hebron: The eldest was Amnon, whose mother was Ahinoam from Jezreel; ³ the second was Chileab, whose mother was Abigail the widow of Nabal from Carmel; the third was Absalom, whose mother was Maacah, daughter of Talmai ruler of Geshur; ⁴ the fourth was Adonijah, whose mother was Haggith; the fifth was Shephatiah, whose mother was Abital; ⁵ and the sixth was Ithream, whose mother was David's wife Eglah. The sons were born to David at Hebron.

 ⁶ During the war between the house of Saul and the house of David, Abner strengthened his own status in the house of Saul. ⁷ Now Saul had a concubine* named Rizpah bat-Aiah. Ish-bosheth challenged Abner, and said, "Why did you sleep with my father's concubine?"

 ⁸ Outraged by the accusation, Abner said, "Do you take me for a Judean dog? Up to this moment I have been loyal to the house of your father Saul, to Saul's family and friends. I have not betrayed you to David. Yet you choose this moment to charge me with an offense over a woman! ⁹ But now, I swear to God that I will do everything in my power to bring about what YHWH swore to do for David: ¹⁰ I will put an end to the reign of Saul, and establish the throne of David over Israel and Judah from Dan to Beer-sheba!"

 ¹¹ Ish-bosheth was so afraid of Abner that he couldn't even speak a word to the commmander.

 ¹² Abner sent envoys on his own behalf to David with the message, "To whom will this land belong? Make a treaty with me, and I will help you bring all of Israel over to your side."

 ¹³ David's immediate reply was, "Good. I will make a pact with you. But I demand one thing of you: Do not come into my presence unless you bring Michal, Saul's daughter, when you come to see me."

 ¹⁴ Then David sent messengers to Ish-Bosheth ben-Saul, with the demand, "Give me back my wife Michal, whom I betrothed to myself for the price

---

* A concubine, or *pilegesh*, was generally a house servant who became the householder's lover, occasionally just for sex, but most often to bear more children for him. Such children had equal rights with the offspring of the legitimate wife; the chief distinction seems to be that a wife had a higher social status, and received a marriage contract that stipulated a settlement that was payable if her husband died or divorced her, whereas a concubine had few rights but also fewer social penalties.

of one hundred Philistine foreskins." ¹⁵ So Ish-Bosheth gave the order and had her taken away from her husband Paltiel ben-Laish. ¹⁶ Paltiel followed her as far as Bahurim, weeping all the way, until Abner ordered him to turn back, which he did.

¹⁷ Abner conferred with the elders of Israel. "For some time now," he said, "you wanted David to be your ruler. ¹⁸ Now is the time to act, for this is the word of YHWH about David: 'By the hand of my servant David, I will deliver my people Israel from the Philistines and from all their enemies.'" ¹⁹ Abner spoke to the Benjaminites as well, and then went to report to David at Hebron that the Israelites and the Benjaminites were in agreement. ²⁰ When Abner arrived, attended by twenty bodyguards, David gave a feast for them. ²¹ Abner said to David, "I will now go and bring the whole of Israel over to your majesty. They will make a covenant with you, and you will rule over everything that your heart desires." David dismissed Abner, granting him safe conduct.

²² Then David's warriors and Joab returned from a raid, bringing a great quantity of plunder with them. Abner was no longer with David since he had just been dismissed and given safe passage. ²³ Joab and his forces were greeted upon their arrival with the news that Abner ben-Ner had been with the ruler and departed with safe passage. ²⁴ Joab went to David and said, "What have you done? You had Abner in your reach. How could you let him leave and get away? ²⁵ You must know that Abner ben-Ner's only goal in coming was to deceive you, to learn about your movements and to find out everything that you are doing."

²⁶ After Joab left David's presence, he sent messengers after Abner, and they brought him back from the Pool of Sirah. Now David knew nothing of this.

²⁷ When Abner returned to Hebron, Joab drew him aside in the gateway, as though to speak privately with him, and there, he stabbed him in the belly in revenge for his brother Asahel. Abner died there in the gateway.

²⁸ When David learned the news of Abner, he said, "I swear in the sight of YHWH that I and my domain are forever innocent of the blood of Abner ben-Ner. ²⁹ May his blood fall on the head of Joab and upon his whole family! May Joab's family never be without someone who has a running sore or leprosy or leans on a crutch or falls by the sword or goes hungry."

³⁰ Joab and his brother Abishai murdered Abner because he had killed their brother Asahel in the battle of Gibeon.

³¹ Then David said to Joab and all his family, "Tear your clothes and dress in sackcloth and walk before Abner's body in mourning, and I myself will walk behind the bier." ³² They buried Abner in Hebron and David wept aloud at the tomb. The people wept with David. ³³ Then David sang this lament for Abner:

³⁴ "Should Abner have died
    the death of a dog?
Your hands were not tied,
    your feet not chained.
Yet you fell as a victim falls
    at the hands of criminals."

And the people continued to weep.

³⁵ Those nearby came up to David and urged him to eat something while it was still daylight. But David took an oath, and said, "May YHWH deal with me, be it ever so severely, if I taste bread or anything before the sun sets." ³⁶ The people noted this and were pleased. In truth, almost everything he did pleased them. ³⁷ So on that day all the people and all of Israel knew that David had no part in the murder of Abner ben-Ner.

³⁸ Then David said to his attendants, "Do you not realize that a prince and a great person fell in Israel today? ³⁹ And today, though I am the anointed ruler, I am weak, and this brood of Zeruiah is too strong for me. May YHWH repay these thugs according to their evil deeds!"

^{4:1} When Ish-Bosheth ben-Saul learned that Abner had been killed in Hebron, he lost all courage, and all Israel was alarmed. ² Now Ish-Bosheth had two officers, captains of raiding parties: Baanah and Rechab. They were sons of Rimmon the Beerothite, and Benjaminites (since Beeroth was considered part of Benjamin, ³ and the Beerothites had fled to Gittaim and have lived there as resident aliens to this day).

⁴ Jonathan ben-Saul had a son whose feet were crippled. He had been five years old when word arrived Jezreel that Saul and Jonathan were dead; the news so panicked the lad's nurse that she dropped him while fleeing, and the fall crippled him. His name was Mephibosheth.

⁵ Now Rechab and Baanah ben-Rimmon the Beerothite set out for the house of Ish-Bosheth. They arrived there in the heat of the day while Ish-Bosheth was taking his midday rest. ⁶ The woman who kept the door had been sifting wheat, but she was sleeping in her chair. So Rechab and Baanah slipped into the inner part of the house.* ⁷ Once they located the bedroom they stabbed Ish-Bosheth to death and decapitated him. They took his head and traveled all night by way of the Arabah to Hebron.

---

* For this verse we follow the Septuagint, since the Masoretic Text is especially troublesome. It reads, "And they come inside the house as if to take wheat, and stabbed him [Ish-Bosheth] under the fifth rib. Then Rechab and Baanah escaped." Presumably "they come inside the house as if to take wheat" means that they slipped in as stealthily as if they were stealing wheat, though that is awkward phrasing; and this does not explain why, after the mention of their escape, the statement about the murder is repeated in the next verse with different details.

⁸ When they arrived, they presented Ish-Bosheth's head to David, saying, "This is the head of Ish-Bosheth ben-Saul, your foe, who sought your life. Today YHWH has avenged our sovereign against Saul and his progeny."

⁹ But David replied to the brothers Rechab and Baanah ben-Rimmon the Beerothite, "As surely as YHWH lives, who delivered me from every trouble: ¹⁰ I took the life of the messenger in Ziklag who brought me the news of Saul's death. He considered it to be news good enough to merit a reward. I killed him in Ziklag. That was the reward I gave the courier for his news! ¹¹ How much more will I reward murderers who slay an innocent person on his own bed in his own house! Shouldn't I at this moment demand an account of his blood from you, and wipe you from the face of the earth?"

¹² So at a command from David, the soldiers killed them, cut off their hands and feet, and hung the bodies beside the pool in Hebron. But they took the head of Ish-Bosheth and buried it in Abner's tomb in Hebron.

5:1 All the tribes of Israel gathered at Hebron and said to David, "We are your own flesh and blood. ² In the days when Saul ruled, it was you who led Israel on our military campaigns. And YHWH said to you, 'You will shepherd my people Israel and be our commander of Israel.'"

³ All the elders of Israel came to David at Hebron, and David made a pact with them before YHWH. Then they anointed David ruler of Israel. ⁴ David was thirty years old and his reign lasted for forty years. ⁵ He ruled in Hebron in Judah for seven-and-a-half years, and later reigned over all Israel and Judah for thirty-three years in Jerusalem.

⁶ David and his army took Jerusalem by attacking its inhabitants, the Jebusites. The Jebusites said to David, "You cannot enter here: even the lame and blind will trounce you." They said this to make it clear that even they could defend the city against David. ⁷ Nevertheless, David captured the hilltop fortress of Zion, and it is now called the City of David.*

⁸ David said on that day, "Anyone who conquers the Jebusites will have to use the water tunnel to reach 'the lame and the blind,' that is, David's enemies." That accounts for the saying, "The lame and the blind will not enter the Temple of YHWH."

⁹ So David took the fortress and renamed it "City of David." He built a wall around it, from the supporting terraces and working inward. ¹⁰ And David became more and more powerful, for YHWH was with him.

---

* The acceptance of David's sovereignty united the two realms in the person of David. The two, however, remained distinct, with David's house sovereign over both. David's choice of Jerusalem (originally named Salem, and while under Jebusite control, Jebus) as the capital of the two realms was politically astute: Jerusalem was at the border of both Judah and Israel, and neither side had a claim on it. Zion means "signpost" or "monument."

¹¹ Hiram, the ruler of Tyre, sent envoys to David with gifts of cedar wood, along with carpenters and stonemasons to build a residence for David. ¹² Thus David knew that YHWH had established him as ruler and had exalted David's reign for the sake of the people of Israel.

¹³ After leaving Hebron, David took more concubines and wives in Jerusalem; and many more children were born to the ruler: ¹⁴ Shammua, Shobab, Nathan, Solomon, ¹⁵ Ibhar, Elishua, Nephe, Japhia, ¹⁶ Elishama, Eliada, and Eliphelet.

¹⁷ Once the Philistines learned that David was anointed ruler of Israel, they mobilized their full forces against him. David learned of it and went down to the stronghold.* ¹⁸ When the Philistines arrived they deployed their forces throughout the Valley of Rephaim.

¹⁹ Learning this, David consulted YHWH, "Shall I attack the Philistines? Will you deliver them into my hands?"

YHWH replied to David, "Attack, for I will most certainly deliver the Philistines into your hands." ²⁰ David then went to Ba'al-Perazim, where he defeated them. Then David said, "YHWH has scattered our enemies before me like a river breaching its banks." That is why the place was named Ba'al-Perazim—"controller of the breaches." ²¹ The Philistines abandoned their idols there, and David with his troops carried them off.

²² Once more the Philistines arrived and deployed their forces throughout the Valley of the Rephaim, ²³ and once more David consulted YHWH, and YHWH answered, "No frontal assaults this time, but circle to their rear and come at them opposite the balsam trees. ²⁴ As soon as you hear a rustling sound in the trees attack at once, for this will mean that YHWH is in front of you to strike the Philistines."

²⁵ David did as YHWH commanded and routed the Philistines all the way from Geba to Gezer.

⁶·¹ David again called up all the warriors of Israel and picked 30,000 elite fighters. ² Then David and the whole force set out for Ba'alah† in Judah to return the Ark of God, which bears the name of YHWH who sits enthroned above the cherubim. ³ The Ark of God was placed on a new cart and removed from the house of Abinadab on the hill. ⁴ Uzzah and Ahio walked before it, ⁵ while David and all the people of Israel celebrated to their hearts' content before YHWH, with songs, harps, lyres, tambourines, rattles, and cymbals.

---

* "The stronghold" probably refers to the city of Adullam (1 Samuel 22:1-5, 2 Samuel 23:13), David's refuge after he fled from Gath. At Adullam he wrote a number of his psalms.

† This appears to be another name for Kiriath-jearim. The movement of the Ark to from Baalah in Judah to Jerusalem signifies that Jerusalem has become the religious as well as the political center of unity between the north and south.

⁶ When they came to the threshing floor of Nacon, one of the oxen stumbled, and Uzzah reached out and took hold of the Ark to steady it. ⁷ YHWH's anger so burned against Uzzah because of his violation* that he was struck dead there beside the Ark of the Covenant. ⁸ David was upset because of YHWH's wrath against Uzzah, and to this day the place is called Uzzah's Breach.

⁹ David was afraid of YHWH that day, and said, "When will the Ark of the Covenant ever come to me?" ¹⁰ For he was unwilling to take the Ark of YHWH to the City of David. So he diverted it to the house of Obed-edom the Gittite. ¹¹ The Ark of YHWH remained there for three months. During this time, YHWH blessed Obed-edom and his whole household.

¹² When David heard that YHWH had blessed Obed-edom's family and household, David went down and brought the Ark up from the house of Obed-edom to the City of David with rejoicing. ¹³ When the bearers of the Ark of YHWH took their first six steps, he sacrificed a bull and a fatted calf. ¹⁴ David, wearing a linen ephod, danced before YHWH with all his might, ¹⁵ while he and his whole house of Israel brought up the Ark of YHWH with shouts and the sound of trumpets.

¹⁶ As the Ark entered the City of David, Saul's daughter Michal looked down through the window and saw David leaping and dancing before YHWH, and his display disgusted her.† ¹⁷ The Ark of the Covenant was brought in and set in its place within the tent David had set up for it. Then David made burnt offerings and peace offerings before YHWH. ¹⁸ Finishing the burnt offerings and peace offerings, the ruler blessed the people in the name of YHWH. ¹⁹ Then he distributed among the people of Israel present—to each woman and man—a loaf of bread, a cake of dates, and a cake of raisins. And all the people returned to their homes.

²⁰ When David returned home to greet his household, Michal met him and said, "Well, didn't the ruler of Israel put on a show of dignity today—exposing himself in front of his servants' handmaids, as any vulgar clown might expose himself!"

²¹ David replied, "But it was done in the presence of YHWH, who chose me instead of your father and your family by appointing me ruler over Israel,

---

* The Ark was not to be touched by any except the priests. When an object was made holy, either by the presence of God or for some special use in the Tabernacle or Temple, touching it was tantamount to touching God; it was believed that only people who had themselves been sacralized could touch the holy and live. Rrather like touching electricity, it was more a matter of physical capacity than legal stricture. Note that the Latin *sacer*, the root of our word "sacred," means "untouchable."

† The ephod, the primary garment of a priest, was a simple linen shift or apron covering the front and back of the wearer but not the sides; it had a woven belt of some sort, but its length is unknown. We may infer that David here wore an ephod but nothing else; when carrying out their sacred duties, priests usually wore an ankle-length blue tunic underneath the ephod.

the people of YHWH. Yes, I will dance for joy before YHWH. ²² And I'm sure I will earn even more disgrace and demean myself further in your eyes. But those handmaids of whom you speak—they will honor me for it."

Michal bat-Saul was childless to her dying day.

⁷·¹ When David finally settled into the palace, and YHWH gave him rest from enemies on every side, ² he said to the prophet Nathan, "Here I am living in this house of cedar while the Ark of God sits in a tent!"

³ Nathan replied to David, "Go, do whatever you have in mind, for YHWH is with you."

⁴ That night the word of YHWH came to Nathan, and said, ⁵ "Go and tell my servant David that this is what YHWH wants: 'Are you the one to build me a Temple? ⁶ I have been without a Temple from the day I brought the Israelites up out of Egypt to this day. I have been moving from place to place with a Tent as my dwelling place. ⁷ Wherever I traveled with the people of Israel, did I ever say to the governors whom I commanded to shepherd my people Israel, "Why have you not built me a Temple made out of cedar?"'

⁸ "Now then, tell my servant, David, 'This is what YHWH Omnipotent says: I took you from the pastures and from following sheep to be the ruler of my people Israel. ⁹ I have been with you wherever you went, and destroyed all your enemies in your path. I will give you fame like the fame of the great ones on the earth. ¹⁰ I will provide a place for my people Israel. I will plant them where they will have a home of their own—a place where they will never be disturbed. Never again will the sinners oppress them as they did in the past ¹¹ ever since the time I appointed judges to lead my people Israel. I will give you security from all your enemies.

" 'Furthermore, I alone will establish your house. ¹² And when your time comes and you rest with your ancestors, I will raise up your offspring to succeed you. Your successor will come from your own body, and I will establish your dynasty. ¹³ It is you who will build a Temple to honor my Name, and I will establish your throne for an eternal dominion. ¹⁴ I will be mother and father to you, and you will be my child. When you err, I will use the rod as any parent might, and I will not spare the rod. ¹⁵ But I will never withdraw my love as I withdrew it from your predecessor Saul, whom I removed from my presence. ¹⁶ Your family and your dynasty will last forever.' " ¹⁷ Nathan reported to David everything: all the words and the entire revelation.

¹⁸ Then David the ruler entered into the presence of YHWH, and said, "Who am I, Sovereign YHWH, and who is my family, that you brought me this far? ¹⁹ As if this were not enough in your sight, Sovereign YHWH, you also promised a future for the house of your servant. Is this your usual

manner when working with people, Sovereign YHWH? [20] What more can I say, Sovereign YHWH? For you know your servant David. [21] For the sake of your promise and according to your intentions, you did this great thing and made it known to your servant.

[22] "You are great, YHWH God! No other equals you. There is no God but you, as we heard with our own ears. [23] Your people Israel are unique over all the earth—they are the one nation on earth whose YHWH sets out to free them, making them your own, making them renowned over all the earth and driving out nations with their gods before your people, whom you set free from Egypt. [24] You established your people Israel as your own forever, and you, YHWH, have become their God.

[25] "And now, YHWH God, fulfill the promise you made concerning your servant's house, and do as you promised. [26] Your Name will be praised forever. People will say, 'YHWH is God over Israel!' May the house of your servant David be established in your presence. [27] YHWH Omnipotent, YHWH of Israel, you have shown me your purpose when you say to your servant, 'I will build a house,' and therefore I have made bold to offer this prayer to you. [28] Now, YHWH, you are God and your promises will come true; you have made these lofty promises to your servant. [29] Be pleased now to bless my house so that it may continue always in your sight, as you, YHWH God, promised. May your blessings rest on your servant's house forever."

[8.1] Some time later, David attacked the Philistines and brought them into submission. Then he took control of the mother-city[13] away from them. [2] David also defeated the Moabites. He made them lie down on the ground and measured them off with a length of cord. Every two lengths of them were put to death and a third length of them were spared. The Moabites were made subject to David, paying tribute. [3] In addition, David fought Hadadezer ben-Rehob, ruler of Zobah, when he went to restore the boundary markers along the Euphrates River. [4] David captured 1,000 chariots, 7,000 charioteers, and 20,000 infantry. David ordered all but 100 chariot horses to be hamstrung.

[5] When the Arameans from Damascus came to the aid of Hadadezer ruler of Zobah, David struck down 22,000 of them. [6] He stationed garrisons in the Aramean dominion of Damascus, and they were subject to David and paid tribute to him. YHWH gave David victories wherever he went. [7] David took the gold shields that belonged to the officers of Hadadezer and brought them to Jerusalem. [8] He also removed a great quantity of bronze from Hadadezer's

---

* The Hebrew reads *Metheg Ammah*, and many translations see it as a place name, but such a place is unknown. The words literally mean "bridle of the mother," with "mother" being understood as "mother-city," essentially a term that means "metropolis"—in this case, the Philistine's stronghold, Gath.

cities, Betah and Berothai. ⁹ When Toi, ruler of Hamath, learned that David had defeated the entire army of Hadadezer, ¹⁰ he sent his son Joram to David to greet him and congratulate the victor of the battle with Hadadazer, since Hadadezer had been at war with Tou. Joram brought David items of silver, gold, and bronze.

¹¹ David dedicated these articles to YHWH, just as he did with the silver and gold from all the nations he conquered: ¹² Edom and Moab, the Ammonites and the Philistines, and Amalek. He also dedicated the plunder taken from Hadadezer ben-Rehob, ruler of Zobah. ¹³ After he slew 18,000 Edomites in the Valley of Salt, his reputation spread even more. ¹⁴ David stationed garrisons throughout Edom, and the Edomites became his subjects. YHWH gave victory to David wherever he went.

¹⁵ David reigned over all of Israel, and maintained law and justice among the people. ¹⁶ Joab ben-Zeruiah commanded the army. Jehoshaphat ben-Ahilud was scribe. ¹⁷ Zadok ben-Ahitub and Abirthar ben-Ahimelech were priests; Seraiah was adjutant-general. ¹⁸ Benaiah ben-Jehoiada commanded the Kerethite and Pelethite guards. David's sons were priests.

9:1–20:25

David asked, "Are there any members of Saul's family still alive to whom I can show kindness for Jonathan's sake?"*

² Now there was an attendant of Saul's household named Ziba, who was brought to David. "Are you Ziba?" David asked.

"At your service," Ziba replied.

³ Then David asked, "Are there any members of Saul's family still alive to whom I can show kindness?"

Ziba said, "There is still a son of Jonathan—the one whose feet are withered."

⁴ David asked, "Where is he?"

Ziba answered, "He is living with Makir ben-Ammiel in Lo Debar."

⁵ So David had him brought from Lo Debar, from the house of Makir ben-Anniel. ⁶ When Mepibosheth ben-Jonathan came to David, he greeted him by bowing down to pay homage.

---

* David's motives here appear to be mixed: on the one hand, he wanted to honor Jonathan's memory; on the other, he wanted to make sure that, in the event of a revolt, there would be no one in the house of Saul around whom potential insurgents could rally—"I keep my friends close and my enemies closer."

David said, "Mephibosheth?"

"At your service," he replied.

[7] David said, "Have no fear, for I desire to be kind to you for Jonathan's sake. And I will restore to you the whole estate of your grandfather Saul, and you will always eat at my table."

[8] Mephibosheth bowed low and said, "Who am I that you should show favor to a dead dog like me?"

[9] Then David summoned Ziba, Saul's attendant: "I give to Saul's grandson everything belonging to Saul and his family. [10] You and your family and attendants are to farm his land and bring in the crops, which will provide provisions for the household. But Mephibosheth, Saul's grandson, will always eat at my table."

[11] Ziba, who had fifteen sons and twenty workers, said to David, "Your attendant will do just as you command." And so Mephibosheth ate at David's table along with the ruler's children. [12] Mephibosheth had a young son named Mica, and the members of Ziba's household were Mephibosheth's attendants [13] And even though both his feet were withered, while Mephibosheth lived in Jerusalem he had a regular place at David's table.

[10:1] Eventually, the ruler of the Ammonites died, and was succeeded by his son, Hanun. [2] David said, "I must maintain the loyal friendship I had with Nahash, the Ammonite ruler, who was kind to me."* And David sent envoys to console Hanun, the heir apparent.

[3] But when the envoys arrived, the Ammonite leaders said to Hanun, "Don't trust David's delegation to honor your father with words of sympathy. This delegation is here to figure out how to overthrow the city."

[4] So Hanun seized the delegation, shaved off half of each delegate's beard, cut off the lower half of their garments at the buttocks, and sent them away.

[5] When he learned what had happened to the delegation, David sent messengers to meet them, for they were deeply humiliated. He told them to stay in Jericho until their beards filled out; then they were to return.

[6] The Ammonites, realizing they had offended David, hired 20,000 Aramean foot soldiers from Beth-Rehob and Zobah, as well as 1,000 soldiers from the ruler of Maacah and 12,000 soldiers from Tob.

[7] Learning this, David sent Joab out with his entire army. [8] The Ammonites came out and formed into battle formation at the entrance of their city gates,

---

* Nahash was Saul's enemy. I Samuel 11 gives an account of his threat against Jabesh-gilead and how Saul united Israel to defeat Nahash's armies. Whatever "friendship" developed between Nahash and David was probably a political alliance against Saul.

while the Arameans of Zobah and Rehob, along with the troops from Tob and Maacah, took up their positions in open country.

⁹ Joab saw the battle formations before him and behind him. So he selected the elite troops of Israel and positioned them against the Arameans. ¹⁰ He put the rest under the command of his brother Abishai, and deployed them against the Ammonites. ¹¹ Joab reasoned, "If the Arameans are too strong for us, then you come to our rescue. But if the Ammonites are too strong for you, I will come to your rescue. ¹² Be strong! May we fight bravely for our people and the cities of our God. YHWH will do what is good and proper."

¹³ Then Joab and his troops moved out against the Arameans, who fled before them. ¹⁴ When the Ammonites saw that the Arameans were in flight, they fled from Abishai and retreated into the city. So Joab returned from fighting the Ammonites and returned to Jerusalem.

¹⁵ Once the Arameans realized they had been routed by the people of Israel, they regrouped. ¹⁶ Hadaezer had Arameans brought from the Great Bend of the Euphrates, and they advanced to Helam under Shobach, commander of Hadaezer's army. ¹⁷ These movements were reported to David, who immediately gathered all Israel, crossed the Jordan, and went to Helam. The Arameans formed their battle lines to meet David and fight against him. ¹⁸ But they fled before Israel, and David killed 700 of their charioteers and 40,000 of the infantry. He also struck down Shobach, commander of their army, who died on the battlefield. ¹⁹ When all the rulers who were vassals of Hadadezer saw that Israel had defeated them, they made their peace with the Israelites and became their subjects. So the Arameans were afraid to help the Ammonites in the future.

11:1 In the spring, that time of the year when rulers go off to war, David sent Joab out along with this officers and troops. They massacred the Ammonites and laid siege to Rabbah.

David, however, stayed in Jerusalem. ² As evening approached, David rose from his couch and strolled about on the flat roof of the palace. From the roof he saw a woman—a very beautiful woman—bathing. ³ David made inquiries about her and learned that her name was Bathsheba,* and that she was the daughter of Eilam and the wife of Uriah the Hittite. ⁴ Then David sent messengers to fetch her. She came to him, and he slept with her, at a time when she had been declared ritually clean after her monthly period. Then she returned to her house. ⁵ But she conceived, and sent this message to David: "I'm pregnant."

---

* Her name means "daughter of an oath."

⁶ Then David sent a message to Joab, "Send me Uriah the Hittite." And Joab sent him to David.

⁷ When Uriah came, David asked him how Joab and the troops were doing and how the campaign was going. ⁸ Then he said to Uriah, "Go home and wash your feet after your journey." As he left the palace, attendants followed him with a gift from the ruler's table.*

⁹ Uriah, however, did not go home that evening. Instead, he lay down by the palace gate with all the ruler's officers.

¹⁰ Learning that Uriah had not gone home, David said, "Uriah, you had a long journey, why did you not go home?"

¹¹ Uriah answered, "Israel and Judah are under attack. So is the Ark. Joab and your officers are camping in the open. How can I go home to eat and drink and to sleep with my wife? As YHWH lives, and as you yourself live, I will do no such a thing!"

¹² Then David said to Uriah, "Stay here another day, and tomorrow I will let you go." So Uriah stayed in Jerusalem another day. ¹³ On the following day David invited Uriah to eat and drink with him and got him drunk. But in the evening Uriah went out to lie down in his blanket among the ruler's officers and did not go home.

¹⁴ In the morning David wrote a letter to Joab and sent it with Uriah. ¹⁵ The letter said, "Put Uriah opposite the enemy where the fighting is fiercest, and then back off, leaving Uriah exposed so that he will meet his death." ¹⁶ So Joab, during the siege of the city, stationed Uriah where he knew the strongest soldiers would be attacking. ¹⁷ When the soldiers of the city rallied and fought against Joab, some of David's troops fell, and so did Uriah the Hittite.

¹⁸ Joab sent David a full account of the battle. ¹⁹ He sent these instructions with the messenger: "When you have finished briefing the ruler with this account of the battle, ²⁰ it might happen that the ruler's anger will be provoked, and he might ask you, 'Why did you get so close to the city to fight? Didn't you know they would shoot arrows from the wall? ²¹ Don't you realize that was how Abimelech ben-Jerubbesheth was killed? Didn't a woman throw a millstone on him from the wall, causing his death in battle at Thebez? Why then did you get so close to the wall?' If he asks you this, say to him, 'Your servant Uriah the Hittite is dead as well.' "

²² The messenger set out, and when he arrived he told David everything Joab had sent him to say. ²³ The messenger said to David, "The defenders

---

* The gift was likely food and drink to put Uriah in such a festive mood that he would sleep with Bathsheba; her pregnancy would naturally then be attributed to Uriah, letting David off the hook.

overpowered us and came out against us in the open, but we drove them back to the entrance of the city gate. ²⁴ But then the archers shot down at us from the wall and some of your soldiers fell. And your servant Uriah the Hittite is dead as well."

²⁵ David told the messenger to say this to Joab: " 'Don't let the matter upset you. The sword devours one as well as another; press the attack against the city and destroy it.' Say this to encourage Joab."

²⁶ When Bathsheba heard that her husband was dead, she mourned for him. ²⁷ After the time of mourning was over, David had her brought to the palace, and she became his wife and bore him a son.

But David's actions displeased YHWH.

12:1 YHWH sent Nathan to David. Nathan went to David, and said, "Let me present you with a case for your judgment: There were two people in a certain town; one was rich and the other was poor. ² The rich person had very large herds of cattle and sheep, ³ but the poor person had only one recently-purchased little ewe lamb. The poor person raised it, and it grew with the family, adults and children alike. They shared their food with it; it drank from its own cup, and even slept with family. It was like another child to the family.

⁴ "Now a traveler came to the rich person, who went about giving hospitality to the traveler. But rather than taking one of his own livestock to prepare a meal for the traveler, the rich person took the little ewe lamb from the poor family to serve to the traveler."

⁵ When David heard the story, he became livid, and burst out, "As YHWH lives, the rich person who did this must die! ⁶ The rich person must pay for the lamb four times over! To do such a thing is evil!"

⁷ Then Nathan said to David, "You are that corrupt person! This is what YHWH of Israel, says: 'I anointed you ruler over Israel. And I delivered you from the hand of Saul. ⁸ I gave you your palace, along with your many wives in your arms. I gave you the tribes of Israel and Judah. And if all this had been too little, I would have added other favors as well. ⁹ Why did you despise the word of YHWH by doing what you did, which is evil in YHWH's eyes? You struck down Uriah the Hittite with the sword and took his wife as your own. You murdered Uriah with the sword of the Ammonites. ¹⁰ Now, therefore, the sword will never be far from your house; for you showed contempt of me and took Bathsheba to be your own.'

¹¹ "This is what YHWH says, 'I will stir up evil for you out of your own house. Before your very eyes I will take your wives and give them to your neighbor; and your neighbor will lie with your wives in broad daylight. ¹² You did it secretly, but I will do it in broad daylight before all Israel.' "

¹³ Then David said to Nathan, "I have sinned against YHWH."

¹⁴ Nathan replied, "YHWH forgives your sin and you will not die. ¹⁴ But because you outraged YHWH by doing this, the child who is to be born to you will die." Then Nathan went home.

¹⁵ YHWH struck down the child that Bathsheba had borne and it fell gravely ill. ¹⁶ David pleaded with YHWH for the child. He fasted, he went home and slept lying on sackcloth, and he refused to eat. ¹⁷ The older members of the household encouraged him to rise and to eat with them. But he refused.

¹⁸ On the seventh day the child died, and David's attendants were afraid to tell him the bad news. For they thought, "While the child was alive, we could talk with David but he would not listen. How can we now tell him the child is dead? He may do something desperate."

¹⁹ But David realized the child was dead when he noticed the attendants whispering among themselves. Then he asked them, "Is the child dead?"

"Yes," they replied.

²⁰ Lifting himself up from the ground, David bathed and anointed himself and changed his clothes. Then he went to worship in the house of YHWH. Then he returned to his quarters, asked for food, and ate it.

²¹ David's surprised attendants said, "What are you doing? While the child was alive you fasted and grieved. But now that the child is dead, you get up and eat."

²² David replied, "While the child was alive I fasted and grieved, thinking that perhaps YHWH would be gracious to me and let the child live. ²³ But now that the child is dead, I have no need to fast. I can't bring the child back. I could go to the child, but the child cannot come to me."

²⁴ Then David went to Bathsheba to comfort her, and they slept together. She conceived and gave birth to a boy whom she named Solomon—"Peace." YHWH's love for the child was such ²⁵ that YHWH sent a message through the prophet Nathan with instructions that the child be named Jedidiah—"Beloved of YHWH."

²⁶ In the meantime Joab took up arms against Rabbah of the Ammonites and captured their royal city. ²⁷ Then Joab sent messengers to David, to announce, "I stormed Rabbah and captured its water tower. ²⁸ So now mobilize the rest of the troops to besiege the city and capture it. Otherwise, I will capture the city myself and name it after me!"

²⁹ So David mobilized the entire army, attacked the city and captured it. ³⁰ David removed the crown from the head of their ruler, and it was placed on his own head. The crown weighed over seventy-five pounds; it was made of gold and was set with precious gems. David also removed a huge amount

of plunder from the city and emptied its [31] setting its inhabitants to work with saws, picks, axes, and other iron tools. They also were put to work at brick-making. David treated all Ammonite cities in the same way. Then he and the whole army returned to Jerusalem.

ଓ ଓ ଓ

13:1 Some time later, David's son Amnon fell in love with his half-sister Tamar, the sister of David's son Absalom. 2 Amnon was frustrated to the point of illness over Tamar; she was a virgin, and his sister, and he felt it would be impossible to do anything with her.

3 Now Amnon and his cousin Jonadab, the son of David's brother Shimeah, were good friends, and Jonadab was very clever. 4 Jonadab said, "Amnon, why are you sulking around every morning? Tell me what it is that bothers you."

Amnon replied, "I am in love with Tamar, my brother Absalom's sister."

5 Jonadab said, "Go to bed and pretend to be ill. When your parents come to see you, say to them, 'I would like my sister Tamar to come and give me something to eat. I want to watch her preparing the food and then have her feed me.' "

6 So Amnon went to bed pretending to be ill. When David visited him, Amnon said, "I would like my sister Tamar to come and make some special bread so that I can watch her preparing it and eat it from her hand."

7 David sent word to Tamar in the palace, "Go to the residence of your brother Amnon and prepare some food for him." 8 So Tamar went to Amnon's house, where he was laying in bed. She took dough, kneaded it, made the bread before him and baked it.

9 She took the pan and set the bread on the table, but he refused to eat it. "Send everyone away," Amnon said, so they emptied the room. 10 Then Amnon said to Tamar, "Bring the food into my bedroom so that I may eat it from your hands." And Tamar took the bread she prepared and took it into the Amnon's bedroom. 11 But when she handed it to him, he grabbed her, and said, "Come to bed with me, sister!"

12 "Brother, don't!" she cried. "Don't force yourself onto me. This must not be done in Israel. Don't do such a vile thing! 13 Think of me—where could I go to hide from my disgrace? And what about you? You would become as low as the most infamous in Israel! Speak to the ruler for me. David would not refuse to let you marry me." 14 But Amnon refused to listen to her, and since he was the stronger, he overpowered her and raped her.

15 Then Amnon was filled with intense revulsion; it was stronger than the love he had once felt for her; he said, "Get up! Get out of my sight!"

¹⁶ Tamar replied, "No, brother, to send me away is worse than everything you did to me."

But he would not listen to her. ¹⁷ He summoned an attendant and said, "Get rid of this woman. Put her out and bolt the door after her." ¹⁸ So the attendant put her out and bolted the door behind her.

She was dressed in a richly ornamented robe—the kind of garment the virgin daughters of the ruler wore. ¹⁹ Tamar put ashes on her head and tore her richly ornamented robe. She covered her face with her hands as she left, weeping loudly.

²⁰ Absalom said to her, "Is it your brother Amnon who has been with you? For now, sister, keep quiet about it; he is your brother. Don't brood about it." Forlorn and desolate, Tamar remained in Absalom's house. ²¹ When David the ruler learned about this incident he was furious.* ²² And Absalom never said a word to Amnon, either good or bad, but he hated Amnon for disgracing his sister Tamar.

²³ Two years later, when Absalom's sheep shearers were at Ba'al-Hazor near the border with Ephraim, he invited all the ruler's children to his sheepshearing. ²⁴ He went to David and said, "I am shearing. Will you and your ministers honor me by joining me?"

²⁵ David declined, and said, "With all of us there, we would only be in the way." But Absalom urged him to come. Once more David declined and dismissed him with a blessing.

²⁶ Then Absalom asked for a favor, "If not you, please let my brother Amnon come with us."

David replied, "Why should Amnon go with you?"

²⁷ But Absalom insisted, so David sent Amnon and the rest of David's children.

²⁸ Absalom prepared a feast fit for a ruler, and ordered his attendants, "Listen carefully. When Amnon gets drunk on the wine, I will give you a signal, and you are to stike Amnon down and put him to death. Have no fear—I'm the one ordering you to do it; I am the responsible party."

²⁹ So Absalom's attendants killed Amnon as ordered. Then all of David's daughters and sons ran out, mounted their mules and fled. ³⁰ While they were still in flight, a report reached David that Absalom had murdered all of his children—that not one of them had survived. ³¹ David stood up, tore his robes, and threw himself on the ground. And all the attendants who were standing around the ruler tore their clothes as well.

---

* The Septuagint adds, "But he did not want to hurt his son Amnon, whom he favored because he was the firstborn."

³² Then Jonadab, the son of David's brother Shimeah, said, "Your majesty, it is not true that all your sons were killed. Only Amnon is dead. This assassination has been Absalom's express intention ever since Amnon raped his sister Tamar. ³³ Your majesty should ignore the report that all your sons are dead; only Amnon is dead."

³⁴ Meanwhile, Absalom went into hiding.

Now the guard standing watch looked up and saw a number of people down the hill from Horonaim. ³⁵ Jonadab said to David, "Here come your sons, just as I said they would!" ³⁶ As he finished speaking, the boys entered wailing loudly. David, as well as all the attendants, wept bitter tears.

³⁷ Then Absalom fled and stayed with Talmai ben-Ammihud, the ruler of Geshur.* But David mourned for Absalom every day ³⁸ of the three years that Absalom remained in Geshur; ³⁹ David longed to go to Absalom, for he had reconciled himself to Amnon's death.

14:1 Joab ben-Zeruiah noticed that David was heartsick for Absalom, ² so he sent a messenger to Tekoa to find a wise woman.† Joab said to her, "Pretend that you are in mourning. Dress in mourning clothes and don't groom yourself; carry on as if you have been in mourning for a long time. ³ Then go to David and repeat what I tell you." And Joab told her exactly what to say.

⁴ When the woman from Tekoa went to the ruler, she fell flat on her face saying, "Save me, ruler!"

⁵ David asked her, "What is it that troubles you?"

"Your majesty, I am a widow; my husband is dead. ⁶ I had two sons, and they came to blows out in the fields, where there was no one to intervene; and one struck the other with a fatal blow. ⁷ Now the whole clan confronts me with the demand, 'Hand over the brother who delivered the fatal blow, that we may execute him for the life of the other. Then we will cut off succession in that family!' But if they do this, they will put out the only burning coal I have left, leaving me and my husband neither name nor descendants on the face of the earth."

⁸ David said to the woman, "Go home, and I will settle the case."

⁹ But the woman from Tekoa said, "Let the guilt be on me and on my ancestral house; let the ruler and the throne be without guilt."

---

* Talmai was Absalom's grandfather; Maacah, Talmai's daughter, was one of David's wives. Geshur was an independent nation on the southern border of Aram (modern Syria).

† The word translated "wise" can also mean clever or shrewd; some believe it means Joab was looking for a skilled improvisational actress. But Tekoa, a town south of Bethlehem, was likely a symbolic choice on Joab's part. The town was renowned for its olive oil, and olive oil was emblematic of wisdom—when someone was commissioned for God's service, the olive oil used in the anointing represented the wisdom of God. Joab was hoping that such wisdom would be with this woman while she spoke to David's heart.

¹⁰ David replied, "Bring to me anyone who says anything to you. I'll keep you from being harmed."

¹¹ And she said, "Then may the ruler call upon YHWH, so that the blood-avenger* may not do even greater harm and destroy my sons."

David swore, "As YHWH lives, not a hair on your son's head will fall to the ground."

¹² The woman continued, "Would you please allow your servant to say a word more, your majesty?"

"Continue," the ruler said.

¹³ So she said, "Why then has the ruler—who, in making this decision, convicts himself—not returned his banished son? This is an injustice against the people of God! ¹⁴ We all must die; we are like water spilled on the ground that can't be gathered up again, nor does God raise dead people. So please devise a plan to let the one who has been banished no longer remain in exile! ¹⁵ I say this, my sovereign, because the people frightened me. I thought to myself, 'I will speak to the ruler; ¹⁶ perhaps your majesty will agree to deliver me from the hand of those who would end our existence in Israel.' "

¹⁷ The woman concluded, "Finally I have this to say: May the word of my sovereign ruler give me rest, for you are like an angel of God in discerning good and evil. May YHWH your God be with you."

¹⁸ Then David said to the woman, "Tell me no lies. I will now ask you a question."

"Ask me anything, sovereign one," she answered.

¹⁹ The ruler asked, "Is the hand of Joab behind you in all this?"

The woman replied, "As surely as you live, my sovereign and ruler, no one can turn to the right or to the left from anything my sovereign says. Yes, your attendant Joab instructed me to do what I did, and told me what to say. ²⁰ He did it in order to let you see the issue from a different perspective. Your majesty is as wise as an angel of God who understands all that happens in this land."

²¹ David said to Joab, "Yes, I will bring my boy Absalom back home."

²² Joab fell face down on the ground and blessed David, saying, "Today I know that I have found favor in your eyes, my sovereign and my ruler, because you granted your servant's request."

²³ Then Joab traveled to Geshur and brought Absalom back to Jerusalem. ²⁴ But David said, "He must go to his own quarters. He must not see my face." So Absalom went to his own quarters and did not see the face of David.

---

* Since Israelite society had no police force to investigate crimes, it was the responsibility of the family member closest to the victim—the "blood-avenger"—to investigate the homicide and exact justice.

²⁵ There was not a person in all Israel who was as handsome as Absalom. He was flawless from the top of his head to the sole of his foot. ²⁶ When he cut his hair—he would cut his hair once a year, because it would get too heavy—he would weigh it. It weighed almost six-and-a-half pounds.

²⁷ Absalom fathered a daughter and three sons. The daughter was named Tamar after his sister, and she became a beautiful woman.

²⁸ Absalom dwelled in Jerusalem two years without seeing the ruler's face. ²⁹ Then Absalom sent for Joab to arrange a meeting with his father. But Joab refused to see him. So he sent a second request, but Joab continued to refuse to meet with Absalom. ³⁰ Then Absalom said to his attendants, "Listen, Joab has a barley field next to mine. Set it on fire." The attendants set fire to the barley field.

³¹ Joab went immediately to Absalom's house, and said, "Why did you set fire to my barley field?"

³² Absalom said to Joab, "Look, I sent you word requesting a meeting with you! I want you to go to my father and ask, 'Why did you bring me back from Geshur? It would have been better for me to stay there!' I want to see the ruler's face. If I am guilty of something, let him put me to death."

³³ So Joab went to David to deliver the message. Then the ruler summoned Absalom, who bowed to the ground in homage. And David kissed him.

15:1 After this Absalom provided himself with a chariot and horses, and fifty soldiers to run ahead of him. ² He also made it a practice to rise early and station himself on the road leading into the city gate. Whenever people went through the gate intending to present their cases before the ruler for arbitration, Absalom would call out, 'What town do you come from?" When they said they were from such-and-such a tribe of Israel, ³ Absalom would reply, "You have a good and just suit; unfortunately there is no representative of the ruler to hear your case."* ⁴ Then Absalom would add, "If only I were appointed judge in the land! Then if everyone who had a case or a complaint came to me, I could see to it that justice would prevail."

⁵ Moreover, he would kiss the hand of anyone who approached him to bow down and pay homage. ⁶ Absalom conducted himself like this to all the Israelites who came to see the ruler asking for justice; before long he had stolen the affection of the people.

⁷ Four years later, Absalom said to David, "Let me go to Hebron to fulfill a vow I made to YHWH. ⁸ While I was staying at Geshur in Aram, I made

---

* It is unclear as to whether Absalom means that there are not enough representatives available to hear all the cases, or whether he is implying that the ruler is refusing to hear some cases, perhaps out of bias against certain tribes.

this vow: 'If YHWH brings me back to Jerusalem, I will worship YHWH in Hebron.'"

⁹ The ruler replied, "Go in peace."

So Absalom went to Hebron. ¹⁰ But Absalom secretly sent agents throughout the tribes of Israel, and told them, "As soon as you hear the trumpets sounding, you are to proclaim, 'Absalom is the ruler of Hebron!'"

¹¹ Two hundred soldiers accompanied Absalom from Jerusalem. They had been invited as guests, and knew nothing of the conspiracy. ¹² While he was there offering sacrifices, Absalom sent for David's advisor Ahithophel, who lived in Gilon, and asked him to come and join the rebellion. So the conspiracy grew in strength, and Absalom's strength increased.

¹³ A messenger came to David with this message: "The people have shifted their allegiance to Absalom." ¹⁴ Then the ruler gathered all his officials with him in Jerusalem and said, "We need to leave town immediately, or none of us will be able to escape from Absalom. We have to get away quickly, or he will overtake us, bring ruin on us, and put the city to the sword!"

¹⁵ David's officials said, "Your attendants are ready to do whatever our sovereign ruler decides."

¹⁶ So David set out with the entire household, leaving only ten concubines to care for the palace.

¹⁷ So David set out on foot with all his followers. They halted at a house some distance away. ¹⁸ With his officers at his side, all of his troops marched by in review, along with the Kerethites and Pelethites, and the 600 Gittites who had accompanied David from Gath.

¹⁹ The ruler said to Ittai the Gittite, "Why are you coming with us? Go back and join up with Absalom,* for you are a foreigner, an exile from your homeland. ²⁰ You joined up with us just yesterday. And today I made you wander around with us when I don't even know where I am going. Go back home and take your people with you. May mercy and truth be with you."

²¹ But Ittai replied to the ruler, "As YHWH lives, and as my sovereign the ruler lives, wherever you go, whether it means my life or my death, I your attendant will be beside you."

²² David said to Ittai, "All right, then, march on!"

So Ittai the Gittite marched on with his troops and their families accompanying them. ²³ The whole countryside moaned and wailed as the retinue passed by. Then David took his stand at the Kidron Valley and all the people marched past him toward the wilderness.

---

* The Hebrew says, "join up with the ruler," indicating that David is assuming that the coup is complete.

²⁴ Zadok was there, and all the Levites with him, carrying the Ark of the Covenant of God. They set it down beside Abiathar until all the troops had finished leaving the city. ²⁵ Then David said to Zadok, "Take the Ark of God back into the city. For if I find favor with YHWH, God will let me see the Ark and its dwelling place once more. ²⁶ But if YHWH says, 'I don't want you,' then here I am. Let YHWH do with me whatever should be done."

²⁷ When David saw Zadok the priest, he said, "Don't you realize what is happening here? Return to the city quietly, you and Abiathar, and take your son Ahimaaz and Abiathar's son Jonathan with you. ²⁸ I will wait at the Fords of the Wilderness until you can send word to me." ²⁹ So Zadok and Abiathar took the Ark of God back to Jerusalem and remained there.

³⁰ David wept as he ascended the Mount of Olives, walking barefoot with his head covered. All the people accompanying the ruler covered their heads as well, weeping as they went. ³¹ On the way up, David was told that Ahithophel was one of the Absalom's co-conspirators. David prayed, "Please, YHWH, turn Ahithophel's counsel into foolishness!"

³² As David approached the top of the ridge where people customarily prostrated themselves before YHWH, David saw his friend Hushai of Arki waiting for him. Hushai's robe was torn from grief and there was dirt in his hair. ³³ David said to Hushai, "If you accompany me, you'll only be a burden to me. ³⁴ But if you return to the city and say to Absalom, 'My ruler, I will be your attendant; I was David's attendant in the past, but now I will be your attendant,' you will be able to thwart Ahithophel's advice for me. ³⁵ Zadok and Abiathar the priests will be there with you—tell them anything you hear in the ruler's palace. ³⁶ Along with them, you will find Ahimaaz, Zadok's son, and Jonathan, Abiathar's son. Through them you are to pass along to me any information you learn." ³⁷ So David's friend Hushai arrived in the city as Absalom was entering Jerusalem.

16:1 When David moved a little beyond the summit, Ziba the attendant of Mephibosheth met him with a pair of saddled donkeys carrying 200 loaves of bread, 100 cakes of raisins, 100 cakes of figs, and a skin of wine. ² David asked Ziba, "What are you doing here?"

Ziba replied, "The donkeys are for you and your household. The bread and summer fruit are for your attendants, and the wine is for any who become weary while in the wilderness.

³ The ruler asked, "Where is Mephibosheth?"

Ziba replied, "He is staying in Jerusalem. He's thinking, 'Today the house of Israel will return my grandfather Saul's realm to me.'"

⁴ "In that case," David said, "all that belongs to Mephibosheth is now yours."

Ziba prostrated himself and said, "I am your humble servant, my sovereign ruler. May I always find favor with you."

⁵ As the ruler approached the town of Bahurim, a man named Shimei ben-Gera, of the same clan as Saul's family, was leaving the town, hurling curses at the ruler, ⁶ pelting David and his retinue with stones, even with all his troops and bodyguard standing right next to David. ⁷ Shimei screamed, "Get out! Get out, you sinner and murderer! ⁸ YHWH has brought down on you all the blood of the house of Saul, whose sovereignty you usurped. And YHWH now transfers that same sovereignty to your son Absalom. You are a murderer, and this is your downfall!"

⁹ Abishai ben-Zeruiah said to the ruler, "Why should this dead dog curse you, Sovereign One? Let me go over and cut off his head."

¹⁰ But the ruler said, "What does this have to do with you and your family? If he curses because YHWH told him to curse the ruler, who can question it?" ¹¹ Turning to the assembled crowd, David continued, "If my very own child is out to murder me, who can wonder at this Benjaminite? Let him be, let him curse, for YHWH told him to. ¹² Perhaps YHWH will take note of my suffering and repay me with goodness for the cursing I receive today."

¹³ David and the others continued on their journey, and Shimei kept pace with the ruler along the ridge of the hill opposite them, cursing and throwing stones and dirt along the way. ¹⁴ The ruler and the others were exhausted when they arrived at their destination, and there they rested and refreshed themselves.

¹⁵ In the meantime, Absalom and everyone with him arrived at Jerusalem. Ahithophel was with him. ¹⁶ Then Hushai the Arkite, David's friend, approached Absalom saying, "Long live the ruler! Long live the ruler!"

¹⁷ Absalom asked Hushai, "Is this the way you show loyalty to your friend? Why didn't you go with your friend?"

¹⁸ Hushai replied to Absalom, "No, the person chosen by YHWH, by these people and by all the Israelites—there I will stay. ¹⁹ After all, whom should I serve? Should I not serve the son? Just as I served your father, so I will serve you."

²⁰ Absalom said to Ahithophel, "What is your advice? What should we do?"

²¹ Ahithophel replied, "Lie with David's concubines, whom he left to take care of the palace. Once all of Israel hears of this act—how odious you made

yourself to David—it will confirm the resolution of your followers." ²² So a tent was pitched on the roof for Absalom, and he lay with David's concubines in sight of all Israel.

²³ In those days, the counsel that Ahithophel gave was embraced like an oracle from God. That was how highly both David and Absalom regarded his advice.

17:1 Ahithophel said to Absalom, "Let me select 12,000 warriors and set out tonight in pursuit of David. ² If I overtake the ruler when he is tired and dispirited, I can cut him off from his followers so that they will scatter. I will not kill the followers. I will kill only David. ³ Then I can bring all the people back to you. You seek the life of only one person; then the rest of the people will be at peace."

⁴ Absalom and all the elders of Israel gave their approval to the plan. ⁵ Then Absalom hesitated, and said, "Before we do anything, let us consult with Hushai of Arki."

⁶ When Hushai came forward, Absalom said, "This is what Ahithophel has proposed to do. Should we follow his advice? If not, do you have any other proposal?"

⁷ Hushai replied, "For once Ahithopel's advice is less than the best advice. ⁸ You know your father and his hardened warriors; they can be as fierce as a wild bear robbed of her cubs. Moreover, David is an expert in warfare; he will not spend the night with his troops. ⁹ At this moment he is hiding in a cave or some such place. If the ruler should be the first to attack and you suffer some casualties, the word would go out, 'Disaster has struck Absalom's troops!' ¹⁰ Then even your bravest and most resolute warriors will lose courage. For all Israel knows that David is a warrior and is surrounded with seasoned fighters.

¹¹ "My advice is to let all Israel, from Dan to Beersheba—as numerous as the sand of the sea—be gathered around you, with you leading them into battle. ¹² Then we will attack the foe wherever they are to be found, and they will fall like dew settling on the ground. Neither David nor any of his followers will survive. ¹³ If he withdraws into a city, then all Israel will bring ropes to that town, and we will drag its stones into a ravine until not even a pebble will remain."

¹⁴ Absalom and all the troops of Israel said, "Hushai's advice is better than Ahithophel's." For YHWH was determined to thwart the good advice of Ahithophel in order to bring disaster on Absalom.

¹⁵ Hushai reported to the priests Zadok and Abiathar, "Ahithophel advised Jonathan and the elders of Israel to do such-and-such. ¹⁶ Now, be quick about

it, take this message to David: 'Don't camp in the plains of the wilderness tonight. But cross over the river as quickly as you can, or you and your whole army will be annihilated.' "

¹⁷ Jonathan and Ahimaaz were staying at En Rogel to avoid being seen entering and leaving the city. Arrangements had been made for an attendant to deliver the latest information to them. They, in turn, were to relay the information to David. ¹⁸ But an attendant saw them and reported it to Absalom. So they hurried to Bahurim, to the house of a couple who had a cistern in the courtyard, and they hid in it. ¹⁹ The wife covered the cistern with a cloth, then she scattered grain over it to dry in the sun so that nothing showed.

²⁰ Absalom's agents came to the house and asked the wife, "Where are Ahimaaz and Jonathan?"

She replied, "They crossed over the brook."

The attendants searched the area, found no one, then returned to Jerusalem. ²¹ After they left, the two climbed out of the cistern to report to David. They told David, "Cross the river at once." Then they told the ruler what Ahithophel planned to do against him. ²² So David and all the followers set out to cross the Jordan. By daybreak, no one was left who had not crossed the Jordan.

²³ When Ahithophel realized that his advice had not been heeded, he saddled his donkey and left to return to his home in his hometown. Then, after setting his house in order, he hanged himself. He was buried in his father's tomb.

²⁴ By the time Absalom crossed the Jordan with all the Israelites, David had reached Mahanaim.

²⁵ Absalom appointed Amasa commander of the army in place of Joab. Amasa was the son of Jether, the Israelite who had married Abigail, the daughter of Nahash and sister of Zeruiah, Joab's mother. ²⁶ The Israelites and Absalom camped in the land of Gilead.

²⁷ When David arrived at Mahanaim he was met by Shobi ben-Nahash from Rabbah of the Ammonites, Machir ben-Ammiel from Lodebar, and Barzillai, the Gileadite from Rogelim. ²⁸ They brought mattresses and blankets, bowls and jugs. They also brought wheat and barley, flour and roasted grain, beans and lentils, ²⁹ honey, cheese, sheep, and fattened cattle, and offered them to David and his followers to eat, knowing that they must be hungry, thirsty, and weary in the wilderness.

^{18:1} David reviewed the soldiers gathered around him, and appointed officers over battalions of 1,000 and troops of 100. ² He then put a third of the

army under the command of Joab, another third under Abishai ben-Zeruiah, Joab's brother, and the rest under Ittai the Gittite.

Then he informed the army, "I will personally lead you into battle."

³ But the troops replied, "You must not do that. For if we are forced to flee, the enemy will not give us a thought; and even if half of us are killed they will not give us a thought. For you are worth ten thousand of us. Besides, it is better for you to be prepared to reinforce us from the town."

David said, "I will do what you think is best." ⁴ So the ruler stood by the gate as the troops marched out by their hundreds and their thousands.

⁵ Meanwhile, David instructed Joab, Abishai, and Ittai, "Deal gently with young Absalom for my sake." And all the troops heard David giving the commanders orders about Absalom.

⁶ The army marched out to take the field of battle against Israel; the battle was joined in the Forest of Ephraim. ⁷ The Israelites were routed there with a great loss of life—20,000 died. ⁸ The rout spread throughout the countryside, and the forest claimed more lives that day than the sword. ⁹ Some of David's troops spotted Absalom fleeing on his mule. As the mule ran under the thick branches of a large oak tree, Absalom's head was caught in its branches, while the mule ran out from under him. ¹⁰ One of the warriors who had seen what happened said to Joab, "I saw Absalom hanging from an oak tree."

¹¹ As Joab listened, he broke in, "You saw Absalom? Why didn't you strike him to the ground then and there? I would have given you ten pieces of silver and a belt!"

¹² But the soldier replied to Joab, "If you were to put a thousand pieces of silver into my hands, I would not lift a finger against the ruler's child. We all heard David giving orders to you and Abishai and Ittai to take care of young Absalom. ¹³ If I had delivered the fatal blow—and nothing is hidden from our ruler—you would have dissociated yourself from me."

¹⁴ Joab replied, "That's a lie! I can't waste my time arguing with you!" And he took three spears and thrust them into Absalom's heart as he struggled to be free of the oak tree. ¹⁵ Then Joab's ten armor-bearers cut him down and delivered the fatal blows.

¹⁶ At this point, Joab sounded the trumpet, and the troops halted their pursuit of the Israelites. ¹⁷ They took Absalom's body, threw it into a large pit in the forest, and piled a large heap of rocks over it. In the meantime, all the Israelites fled to their homes.

¹⁸ During his lifetime, Absalom had commissioned a pillar which was erected in the Ruler's Valley. He named it after himself, saying, "I have no heir to carry on my name." And to this day it is called Absalom's Monument.

¹⁹ Ahimaaz ben-Zadok said, "Let me run to the ruler with the news that YHWH has delivered him from the hands of the enemy."

²⁰ "You are not to take the news this time," Joab said. "You may bring news some other day, but you must not do it today, for David's son is dead."

²¹ Then Joab said to a Cushite, "You go, tell the ruler what you witnessed." The Cushite bowed low before Joab and ran off.

²² Ahimaaz ben-Zadok again said to Joab, "Come what may, I want to run behind the Cushite."

But Joab asked, "Why do you want to run, my lad? You don't have any news that will bring you a reward."

²³ He said, "Come what may, I want to run."

So Joab said, "Go, run." Then Ahimaaz ran by the road through the plain of the Jordan and outran the Cushite.

²⁴ As David sat between the inner and the outer gate, the lookout went up to the roof of the gate above the city wall. As he looked about, he saw a lone runner. ²⁵ The lookout reported it to David.

David said, "If the runner is alone, it must be good news."

But as the runner came nearer, ²⁶ the lookout saw a second runner, and called down to the gatekeeper, "Look, a second runner!"

David said, "The second runner must be bringing good news, too."

²⁷ The lookout said, "It looks to me that the first runner runs like Ahimaaz ben-Zadok."

David said, "He is a good runner. He comes with good news."

²⁸ Then Ahimaaz called out to the ruler, "All is well!" He bowed down with his face to the ground, and said, "Praise be to YHWH, who delivered up those who lifted their hands against our Sovereign and ruler."

²⁹ David asked, "Is the young Absalom safe?"

Ahimaaz replied, "Just as your servant Joab was about to send me off, I saw a great commotion, but I don't know what it was."

³⁰ David said, "Stand aside and wait here." So Ahimaaz stepped aside to wait.

³¹ Then the Cushite arrived, saying, "Sovereign ruler, I have good news. For YHWH delivered you today from all who rose up against you." ³² David asked the Cushite, "Is young Absalom safe?"

The Cushite replied, "May all the enemies of the ruler and all rebels intent on harming you have the same fate as that young man."

³³ David was deeply shaken and went up to the roof chamber over the gate and wept, crying out as he went, "My child! Absalom, my son! My child Absalom! If only I had died instead of you! Absalom, my son, my son!"

19:1 Joab learned that David was weeping and mourning for Absalom. 2 And for the whole army the victory that day was turned into mourning, for on that day the troops heard the report, "The ruler grieves for young Absalom." 3 The troops crept back into the city like warriors ashamed to show their faces after losing a battle. 4 The ruler covered his face and cried out, "Absalom my son! Absalom, my son! My son!"

5 Joab entered David's quarters and said, "Today, you covered with shame all your attendants, your daughters and sons, your wives and your concubines. 6 For you showed love for those who hate you, and hate for those who love you. Today you made it clear to your officers and your warriors alike that we are nothing to you. I have concluded that if Absalom were alive and all of us were dead, you would be content. 7 Now go immediately to your attendants with some encouragement. If you don't, I swear by YHWH that not a single warrior will remain with you come nightfall—and that would be a worse disaster than any you have suffered since your earliest days."

8 At that David rose and took his seat at the gate. And when the army learned that the ruler was sitting at the city gate, they assembled before him there.

Meanwhile, the Israelites fled to their homes. 9 Throughout all the tribes of Israel people were discussing it and saying, "David saved us from our enemies and freed us from the power of the Philistines, and now he has fled the country because of Absalom. 10 And now Absalom, whom we anointed to reign over us, is dead. So why not do something to restore David as ruler?"

11 The talk of all Israel reached David in his quarters. So the ruler sent this message to the priests, Zadok and Abiathar: "Ask the elders of the tribe of Judah, 'Why should you be the last to restore the ruler to the palace? 12 You are closely related to me, my own flesh and blood. So why should you be the last to bring the ruler home?' 13 And tell Amasa, 'Are you not my own flesh and blood? So why should you be the last to restore the ruler? I swear by YHWH that you will be my commander-in-chief from now on, in place of Joab.'"

14 David won over the hearts of all the women and men of Judah. They sent word to David, "We welcome your return, you and all your followers."

15 When the ruler reached the Jordan on the trip home, the women and men of Judah came to Gilgal to meet the ruler, to escort him across the Jordan. 16 Shimei ben-Gera, the Benjaminite from Bahurim, hurred down to meet David the ruler among all these people from Judah, 17 and brought with him 1,000 warriors from Benjamin. Ziba was there, too, the attendant of Saul's family, with his fifteen children and twenty attendants. They ar-

rived at the Jordan before David; and rushing into the Jordan river before the ruler's eyes, [18] crossed to and fro conveying his household in order to win David's favor. Shimei ben-Gera, having crossed the river, threw himself down before the ruler, [19] and said, "I beg your majesty not to remember how disgracefully your attendant behaved when you left Jerusalem. Please! Don't hold it against me! [20] I humbly acknowledge that I was wrong, and today I am the first of all the house of Joseph to come down to meet you."

[21] Abishai ben-Zeruiah objected, "Shouldn't Shimei be put to death for this? He cursed YHWH's Anointed!"

[22] David replied, "What business is this of yours, you brood of Zeruiah, that you would create enmity for me today? Should anyone be put to death in Israel this day? Today I know I am again ruler over Israel!"

[23] So David said to Shimei, "I will spare your life." And the ruler confirmed it with an oath.

[24] Saul's grandson Mephibosheth also went down to meet the ruler. He had not cut his toenails, trimmed his mustache, or washed his clothes from the day David left to the day he returned peacefully. [25] When he came from Jerusalem to meet the ruler, David asked him, "Why did you not go with me, Mephibosheth?"

[26] Mephibosheth answered, "My sovereign and ruler, since I, your attendant, am lame, I said to myself, 'I will have my donkey saddled and will ride on it, in order to go with my ruler.' But my own attendant, Ziba, betrayed me, [27] and his lies set you against me. Your majesty is like an angel of God; and you must do what you think is the right thing to do. [28] All of my grandfather's descendants deserved nothing but death from you; and you gave me, your attendant, a place at your table. So what right do I have to make more appeals to you?"

[29] David replied, "Say no more. I order you and Ziba to divide your fields."

[30] But Mephibosheth said to the ruler, "Let him take everything, now that my sovereign and ruler has come home safely."

[31] Brazillai the Gileadite also came down from Rogelim to escort David across the Jordan. [32] Barzillai was very old, eighty years of age; it was he who had provisioned David while the ruler was at Mahanaim, for he was very wealthy. [33] David said to Barzillai, "Cross the Jordan with me and remain during your old age in Jerusalem."

[34] Barzillai replied, "Your attendant is far too old to go up with you to Jerusalem. [35] I am now eighty years old and I cannot tell what is pleasant and what is not. I cannot taste what I eat or drink; I can no longer listen to

the voices of women and men singing. Why should I be a burden on you? ³⁶ Allow me to accompany you for a short while across the Jordan. But why should your majesty reward me so handsomely? ³⁷ Let me go back, and let me die in my own town, where my mother and father are buried. But here is your attendant, Chimham; let him go with you. Do for him what you think is best."

³⁸ The ruler answered, "Let Chimham accompany me, and I will do for him what I think is best. And I will do for you whatever you request."

³⁹ Then all the people crossed the Jordan, including the ruler. David kissed Barzillai and blessed him, and Barzillai went home. ⁴⁰ When the ruler crossed over to Gilgal, Chimham went along. All the Judean troops and half of the troops of Israel crossed over as well.

⁴¹ Then all the Israelites approached David and said, "Why did our sisters and brothers of the tribe of Judah steal you away and escort you and your household across the Jordan, along with all your troops?"

⁴² All the people of Judah answered the Israelites, "We did this because the ruler is closely related to us. Why does this anger you? Did we eat any of the ruler's provisions? Have we taken anything for ourselves?"

⁴³ The Israelites retorted, "We have ten times more interest in the ruler and, what's more, we are your elders. Why then do you despise us? Were we not the first to speak out concerning restoring the monarchy?"

Then the people of Judah responded even more fiercely than the Israelites.

^{20.1} At this, a troublemaker named Sheba ben-Bichri, a Benjaminite, sounded the shofar and cried out,

> "We have no share in David,
> no share in ben-Jesse!
> Everyone to your tents, Israel!"

² So the Israelites deserted David to follow Sheba ben-Bichri. But the people of Judah remained with their ruler, David, all the way from the Jordan to Jerusalem.

³ When David returned to the palace in Jerusalem, he moved to new quarters the ten concubines he had left behind in charge of the residence, and posted a guard over them. He provided for their upkeep but never had intercourse with them again. They were kept in confinement as if they were widows until the day they died.

⁴ Then David said to Amasa, "Call out all the people of Judah to come to me within three days, and you be here, too."

⁵ But when Amasa went to call up the people of Judah, he took longer than the time the ruler had appointed for him.* ⁶ So David said to Abishai, "Sheba ben-Bichri is likely to do us more harm than Absalom did. Take the royal bodyguards and follow him closely in case he takes shelter in a fortified city as we look on."

⁷ So Joab and the Herethites, the Pelethites, and all the bodyguards marched out under the command of Abishai. They left from Jerusalem in pursuit of Sheba ben-Bichri.

⁸ When the paused at the great stone in Gibeon, Amasa met up with them. Joab wore a military tunic with a belt, and strapped to the belt, concealed in a sheath next to his thigh, was a sword that could be drawn in a downward movement. ⁹ Joab said to Amasa, "I pray that you are well, comrade," and with his right hand grabbed Amasa's beard as if to kiss him. ¹⁰ Amasa never saw the sword as Joab drove it into his belly. His entrails spilled onto the ground, and no second blow was necessary. With Amasa taken care of, Joab and Abishai moved on in pursuit of Sheba ben-Bichri.

¹¹ One of Joab's officers stood over the dying Amasa and shouted, "Follow Joab, all who are for Joab and David!" ¹² Amasa's blood-soaked body lay in the middle of the road, and when the officer noticed that the people stopped at the sight of the body, he rolled it into the field and covered it with a cloak. ¹³ Once it was moved from the road, the army followed Joab in pursuit of Sheba ben-Bichri.

¹⁴ Sheba passed through all the tribes of Israel until he arrived at Abel-Beth-maacah, and all the clan of Bichri rallied around and followed him into the city. ¹⁵ Joab's forces arrived and besieged the city. While the troops and Joab labored at building siege ramps against the city walls, ¹⁶ a wise woman called down from inside the walls, "Listen! Listen! I must talk to Joab!"

¹⁷ When Joab came forward the woman asked, "Are you Joab?"

Joab replied, "Yes, I am he."

"Listen to what I have to say," she said.

"I'm listening," Joab replied.

¹⁸ "In the old days," she said, "people used to say, 'If you have a question, you'll find your answer at Abel,' and they would settle their disputes by coming to us. ¹⁹ Our town is one of the most peaceful and loyal in Israel. She is one of Israel's mother-cities, and you seek to kill her! Would you swallow up YHWH's own possession?"

²⁰ Joab replied, "God forbid! Far be it from me to swallow up or to destroy! ²¹ That is not our intention. A Benjaminite named Sheba has raised

---

* When Amasa didn't return promptly, David concluded that he had defected to Sheba's side.

a hand against our ruler, David. If you hand him over, we will withdraw from the city."

The woman said to Joab, "Sheba's head will be thrown over the wall." ²² Then the wise woman went to her people and gave them sage advice, and they cut off Sheba's head and threw it to Joab. Then Joab sounded the shofar, and his soldiers withdrew from the city and returned to their own towns. And Joab returned to Jerusalem and the ruler.

²³ Joab commanded the entire Israelite army. Benaiah ben-Jehoiada commanded the Kerethites and the Pelethites. ²⁴ Adoniram was in charge of forced labor. Jehoshaphat ben-Ahilud was the historian, ²⁵ and Sheva was the expert on the Law. Zadok and Abiathar were priests, ²⁶ and Ira the Jarite was David's priest.

21:1–24:25

famine struck the land for three straight years. So David consulted YHWH, who replied, "There is blood-guilt resting on Saul and on Saul's family because they put the Gibeonites to death." ² The Gibeonites were not Israelites, but a remnant of the Amorites to whom the Israelites had bound themselves by oath. But Saul in his zeal for Israel and Judah had attempted to annihilate them.

³ David asked the Gibeonites, "What can I do for you? How can we make amends so that you can call down a blessing on YHWH's own people?"

⁴ The Gibeonites replied, "Our feud with Saul and Saul's family cannot be settled with silver or gold, and we have claim on the life of no one else in Israel."

"Then what do you want me to do for you?" asked David.

⁵ The Gibeonites answered, "As for the person who massacred us and planned to annihilate us so that we should no longer exist within the borders of Israel— ⁶ hand over to us seven of his male descendants to be executed; we will dismember them before YHWH in Gibeah, the town of Saul, YHWH's chosen one."

And the ruler said, "I will give them to you."

⁷ David spared Mephibosheth ben-Jonathan ben-Saul because of the oath before YHWH that bound David and Jonathan ben-Saul to each other, ⁸ but David took Armoni and Mephibosheth,* the two sons whom Rizpah bat-Aiah had borne to Saul, together with the five sons whom Saul's daughter

Merab had borne to Adriel ben-Barzillai of Meholah. ⁹ David handed them over to the Gibeonites, who dismembered them before YHWH on a hilltop. The seven perished together in the first days of harvest, at the beginning of the barley harvest.

¹⁰ Rizpah bat-Aiah took sackcloth and spread it out for herself on a rock. From the beginning of the barley harvest until rain fell from the sky on the bodies, she did not allow the birds of heaven to touch them during the day or the wild animals during the night. ¹¹ When David learned what Rizpah bat-Aiah, Saul's concubine, had done, ¹² he went and removed the bones of Saul and Jonathan from the people of Jabesh-gilead, who had stolen them from the public square at Beth-shan; the Philistines had hung them there on the day they defeated Saul at Gilboa. ¹³ David removed the bones of Saul and Jonathan from that place, as well as the bones of the dismembered, ¹⁴ and they were buried in the tomb of Saul's father Kish, at Zela in Benjaminite territory. David's orders were carried out to the letter. After that, God was moved by prayers for the land.

¹⁵ Once more war broke out between Israel and the Philistines. David went down with the troops to engage the Philistines; but in the heat of battle the ruler collapsed from exhaustion. ¹⁶ And Ishbi-Benob, a descendant of the Rephaim,† was wearing new armor and had a bronze spear weighing over nine pounds and, he was confident that he could kill David. ¹⁷ But Abishai ben-Zeruiah came to the ruler's aid, cut down the Philistines, and killed Ishbi-Benob. Then David's officers admonished him, saying, "You must never again go into battle with us, lest the lamp of Israel be extinguished!"

¹⁸ Some time later, in Gob, there was another battle with the Philistines. In that battle Sibbecai the Hushathite killed Saph, another Rephaim descendant. ¹⁹ In still another battle with the Philistines at Gob, Elhanan ben-Jaare-oregim of Bethlehem killed Goliath of Gath,‡ whose spear was the size of a weaver's beam. ²⁰ In Gath the Israelites engaged a giant with six fingers on each hand and six toes on each foot, twenty-four in all. He too was descended from the Rephaim. ²¹ When he challenged Israel, Jonathan ben-Shimeah, David's cousin, killed him. ²² These four were descended from the Rephaim in Gath; they all fell at the hands of David and his bodyguards.

ᘓ   ᘓ   ᘓ

---

* This Mephibosheth is the uncle of Mephibosheth ben-Jonathan, whom David is protecting.
† The Rephaim were legendary giants.
‡ In 1 Samuel 17 tells the more familiar version of the story; there it is David who kills Goliath. And in 1 Chronicles 20:5, Elhanan kills Lahmi, Goliath's brother, not Goliath. Multiple versions of the same story reveal the work of editors who cobbled together material from numerous sources.

²²˙¹ David sang YHWH the words of this song when God delivered him from the hand of all his enemies and from the hand of Saul.* ² He sang:

2 "YHWH, my mountain crag,
    my fortress, my rescuer,
3 my God, my rock
    behind whom I take refuge,
    my shield, my horn of deliverance,
    my stronghold!
4 The One whom I praise,
    upon whom I call,
  is YHWH—
    and from the enemy I am saved!
5 The waves of Death enclosed me,
    the torrents of Destruction devoured me;
6 the snares of Sheol entangled me,
    the traps of Death drew me down.
7 In my distress I called you, YHWH;
    to you, my YHWH, I cried for help.
  From your Temple you heard my voice,
    and my cry to you reached your ears.
8 Then the netherworld reeled and rocked;
    the mountains trembled to their foundations
    in the presence of your anger.
9 Smoke billowed from your nostrils
    and a consuming fire spewed forth from your mouth;
    glowing coals erupted into flames.
10 You tore through the heavens and came down;
    thick darkness was under your feet.
11 You rode upon the backs of the cherubim,
    and soared on the wings of the wind.
12 You made the night your cloak;
    you covered yourself in a canopy of storm clouds.
13 From the brightness before you
    your clouds surged forth
    your hailstones and lightning bolts.
14 You thundered in the heavens,
    and your voice, YHWH, resounded
    with hailstones and bolts of lightning.
15 You shot your arrows and scattered my enemies;
    you scattered your lightning bolts and routed them.

---

* This is virtually a duplicate of Psalm 18.

16 Then the channels of the sea were exposed,
    and the foundations of the world were laid low
at your rebuke, YHWH,
    at a snort from your nostrils.
17 You reached from on high and took hold of me,
    and pulled me out of deep water.
18 You rescued me from my strong enemy,
    and from my foes who were too powerful for me.
19 They fell upon me in the day of my calamity,
    but you, YHWH, were my support.
20 You brought me out of the vast netherworld;
    you rescued me, because you delighted in me.
21 YHWH, you set everything right again because I was just;
    you rewarded me because my hands were clean.
22 For I kept your ways, YHWH:
    I didn't do evil—I didn't leave you, my God.
23 For all your laws were in front of me,
    and I didn't turn away from a single decree.
24 I was blameless before you,
    and I kept myself from evil—
25 You rewarded me because I was just,
    because I kept my hands clean.
26 To those who love,
    you show yourself loving;
to those who are blameless,
    you show yourself blameless;
27 to those who are single-hearted,
    you show yourself single-hearted;
to those who are crooked,
    you show yourself . . . shrewd!
28 You save humble people,
    but force the arrogant to lower their eyes.
29 You are my ever-burning lamp, YHWH!
    My God, you lighten my darkness!
30 Yes, with you I can crush a brigade,
    and with my God I can scale ramparts.
31 YHWH, your way is perfect;
    your promise, YHWH, proves true;
    you are a shield for all who take refuge in you.
32 For who is God, but you?
    And who is a rock except YHWH—

³³ the God who arms me with strength
and makes my path perfectly safe,
³⁴ who gives me the sure footing of a mountain goat,
and sets me on heights of my own,
³⁵ who trains my hands for battle
so that my arms can bend a bow of bronze?
³⁶ You have given me your shield of victory
and your strong hand supported me;
you stoop down to make me great.
³⁷ You make my road wide and smooth,
so that I never twist an ankle.
³⁸ I pursued my enemies and overtook them,
and did not relent until they were destroyed.
³⁹ I crushed them, so they couldn't rise;
they fell beneath my feet.
⁴⁰ For you armed me with strength for the battle;
you made my assailants sink beneath me.
⁴¹ You made my enemies turn back and run,
and I destroyed my opponents.
⁴² They cried for help, but there was none to save them;
they cried to YHWH, but God didn't answer them.
⁴³ I beat them as fine as dust in the square;
I stamped on them like mud in the streets.
⁴⁴ You delivered me from the attacks of an unbelieving people;
you made me a leader of the nations.
A people whom I had not known
are now subject to me.
⁴⁵ As soon as they hear of me, they obey me—
nations come cringing!
⁴⁶ The nations come cowering,
and come trembling from their strongholds.
⁴⁷ YHWH lives! Blessed be my rock!
And let the God of my salvation be exalted—
⁴⁸ the God who gave me vengeance
and subdued my attackers under me,
⁴⁹ who rescued me from my enemies,
lifted me clear of my foes,
and delivered me from defamers!
⁵⁰ For this I will extol you among the nations, YHWH,
and sing praises to your Name.

⁵¹ You give great victories to your leader,
and show unfailing love to your Anointed,
to David and his descendants forever."

23:1 These are the last words of David:

"The oracle of David ben-Jesse,
the oracle of the person God raised up
the one anointed by the God of Jacob,
the favorite of the songs of Israel:
² The Spirit of YHWH has spoken through me;
God's word was on my tongue.
³ The God of Israel spoke,
the Rock of Israel said to me:
'Rulers who govern with justice,
who rule in the reverence of YHWH,
⁴ are like the light of mornings at sunrise,
a cloudless morning after a rain shower,
that makes the grass of the earth sparkle.'
⁵ Yes, my house is right with YHWH!
YHWH has made an everlasting covenant with me,
its terms spelled out and faithfully obeyed;
God will ensure my complete success,
and bring my every desire to fruition.
⁶ But the ungodly are rootless,
they are like abandoned thorns;
none dare put out a hand to pick them up,
⁷ none touch them but with a tool or a piece of wood;
they are fit only for burning where they lie."

∞ ∞ ∞

⁸ These are the names of David's three greatest warriors:* First, Josheb-basshebeth, a Tahchemonite, leader of the three; it was he who wielded a battle-axe against 800, whom he killed in one encounter. ⁹ Under him was Eleazar ben-Dodo, the Ahohite, one of three great warriors who were with David at Pas-dammim when the Philistines mustered for battle there and the Israelites retreated before them. ¹⁰ But Eleazar stood his ground and struck down the Philistines until his hand was so numb that it stuck to the sword.

---

* The last two sections in 2 *Samuel* are pieces that the editor(s) apparently did not know what to do with, fragments of stories that clearly belong elsewhere but which would likely have broken the flow if placed among the other stories in the book.

YHWH brought about a great victory that day, and though the army rallied behind Eleazar, it was only to plunder. ¹¹ After Eleazar there was Shamma ben-Elah, the Hararite. The Philistines had mustered at Lehi. There was a field full of lentils there; the army took flight before the Philisitines, ¹² but Shamma ben-Elah positioned himself in the middle of the field, defending it, and struck down the Philistines. So YHWH brought about a great victory.

¹³ Once, at the beginning of the harvest, these three (out of the thirty chiefs of David's army) went down and came to David at the stronghold of Adullam, while a company of Philistines was encamped in the Valley of the Rephaim. ¹⁴ David was then in the stronghold, and there was a Philistine garrison in Bethlehem. ¹⁵ "Oh," David sighed, "if only someone would fetch me a drink of water from the well standing by the gate at Bethlehem!" ¹⁶ At this the three champions, forcing their way through the Philistines' camp, drew water from the well standing by the gate at Bethlehem, carried it back to the stronghold, and presented it to David. But he would not drink any of it and poured it out as a libation to YHWH: ¹⁷ "God forbid that I should drink this! This is the blood of warriors who went at the risk of their lives!" And so he would not drink. Such were the deeds of the three champions.

¹⁸ Abishai, the brother of Joab and ben-Zeruiah, was leader of the thirty. It was he who wielded his spear against the 300 whom he killed, winning himself a name among the thirty. ¹⁹ He was more famous than the thirty and became their captain, but he was no rival for the three.

²⁰ Benaiah ben-Jehoiada, a hero from Kabzeel, a man of many exploits, struck down the two champions of Moab and, one snowy day, went down and killed the lion in the cistern. ²¹ He was also the soldier who killed an Egyptian of great stature. The Egyptian had a spear in his hand, but Benaiah went down against him with a staff, tore the spear from the Egyptian's hand and killed him with it. ²² Such were the exploits of Benaiah ben-Jehoiada, winning him a name among the thirty chiefs. ²³ He was more famous than the thirty, but he was no rival for the three. David put him in command of his bodyguard.

²⁴ Among the thirty* were:

Asahel the brother of Joab;
Elhanan ben-Dodo, from Bethlehem;
²⁵ Shammah from Harod;
Elika from Harod;
²⁶ Helez from Beth-pelet;
Ira ben-Ikkesh, from Tekoa;
²⁷ Abiezer from Anathoth;

---

* "The thirty" is apparently a loose designation: this list includes the three champions, Abishai the leader, Benaiah the hero, thirty-one chiefs, and Uriah the Hittite, whom David arranged to fall in battle.

	Sibbecai from Hushah;
28	Zalmon from Ahoh;
	Maharai from Netophah;
29	Heled ben-Baanah, from Netophah;
	Itti ben-Ribai, from Gibeah of Benjamin;
30	Benaiah from Pirathon;
	Hiddai from the brooks of Gaash;
31	Abialbon from Beth-arabah;

28 Zalmon from Ahoh;
   Maharai from Netophah;
29 Heled ben-Baanah, from Netophah;
   Itti ben-Ribai, from Gibeah of Benjamin;
30 Benaiah from Pirathon;
   Hiddai from the brooks of Gaash;
31 Abialbon from Beth-arabah;
   Azmaveth from Bahurim;
32 Eliahba from Shaallbon;
   the two sons of Jashen;
33 Jonathan ben-Shammah, from Harar;
   Ahiam ben-Sharar, from Harar;
34 Eliphelet ben-Ahasbai, from Beth-maacah;
   Eliam ben-Ahithophel, from Gilo;
35 Hezro from Carmel;
   Paarai from Arab;
36 Igal ben-Nathan, from Zobah;
   Bani the Gadite;
37 Zelek the Ammonite;
   Naharai from Beeroth, Joab ben-Zeruiah's armor-bearer;
38 Ira from Jattir;
   Gareb from Jattir;
39 and Uriah the Hittite—
   thirty-seven in all.

ଔ   ଔ   ଔ

24:1 YHWH's anger once more blazed out against the Israelites, and God incited David against them by prompting him to take a complete census of Israel and Judah.*

2 So the ruler said to Joab and the army commanders, "Go throughout

---

* 1 Chronicles 21 offers a fascinating parallel version of this story. There it is Satan, not YHWH, who incites David to take the census. A more mundane explanation, however, is that a nearby nation was growing hostile, and David wanted to assess his military capabilities. Why this particular census was considered a sin is never stated; most commentators say it was because David was relying on his own strength instead of trusting God to protect the people in time of war. But note that in 2 *Samuel's* version, David is faced with an intolerable dilemma: if he obeys God's prompting to take the census, he sins; if he disobeys God's command, he sins by *not* taking the census. This gives us new insight into God's "anger," which is often assumed to be what lies behind certain events. Here the people receive from the ruler an inexplicable decree that places on them an unreasonable hardship, so they figure God must be angry at them for some reason, that it is God who has pushed David into action. Then a devastating plague hits the country, so David must have sinned and made YHWH angry. Such stories paint a rather disturbing image of an arbitrary and volatile God.

the tribes of Israel from Dan to Beersheba and take a census of the people. I wish to know the size of our population."

³ Joab said to the ruler, "May YHWH multiply the population one hundred times over, and may your eyes see it. But why does my sovereign ruler want such a thing?"

⁴ But David's word prevailed, and Joab and the army commanders left the presence of the ruler to take a census of the people of Israel.

⁵ After crossing the Jordan, the commanders started with Aroer and the towns at the streams, then moved on to Gad and Jazer. ⁶ Then they came to Gilead and to Kadesh in the territory of the Hittites. The next stop was Dan, and from Dan, they made their way toward Sidon. ⁷ They then arrived at the fortress of Tyre and all the towns of the Hivites and Canaanites, ending up in the Negev of Judah and in Beersheba. Having covered the entire country, they returned to Jerusalem after nine months and twenty days.

⁹ Joab gave David the figures of the census of the people. In Israel there were 800,000 armed warriors capable of drawing a sword, and Judah had 500,000 armed soldiers.

¹⁰ After commissioning the census, David was overcome with remorse and said to YHWH, "In numbering the people, I have sinned greatly. Now, YHWH, I beg you to remove the guilt of your servant. I did a very foolish thing."

¹¹ Before David got up the next morning, the word of YHWH came to the prophet Gad, the ruler's seer: ¹² "Go tell David, 'This is what YHWH says: I offer you three options; choose one and I will bring it upon you.'" ¹³ So Gad went to David and said, "Do you prefer three years of famine in your land, three months of fleeing from your enemies, or three days of plague in your land? Think it over and decide how I should answer the One who sent me."

¹⁴ David said to Gad, "This is a hard choice. But let us rather fall into the power of YHWH, whose mercy is great, and not into the power of mortals." ¹⁵ So David chose plague.

It was the season of the wheat harvest. YHWH sent a plague on Israel from that morning until the time appointed; the epidemic ravaged the people from Dan to Beersheba, and 70,000 Israelites died. ¹⁶ The angel stretched out a hand toward Jerusalem to destroy it, but YHWH thought better of this evil and said to the angel destroying the people, "Enough! Withdraw your hand." The angel of YHWH was then at the threshing floor of Araunah the Jebusite.

¹⁷ When David saw the angel striking down the people, he said to YHWH, "I am the one who sinned. I am the one who did this horrible thing. But these people, this flock, what have they done? Let your hand lie heavy on me and my family."

¹⁸ Gad went to David that day and said, "Go up and build an altar to YHWH on the threshing-floor of Araunah the Jebusite."* ¹⁹ So David went up, as YHWH commanded through Gad. ²⁰ When Araunah looked up and saw the ruler and the royal officials approaching, he went out and bowed with his face touching the ground. ²¹ Araunah said, "Why has my sovereign the ruler come to his attendant?"

"To buy your threshing-floor," David answered, "so that I can build an altar to YHWH, that the plague on the people may be stopped."

²² Araunah said to David, "Let my sovereign ruler take it, and offer up whatever he wishes. I have oxen for the burnt offering, and we can use the threshing sled and the oxen's yoke for the wood." ²³ Araunah gave it all to the ruler, saying, "May YHWH your God accept your offering."

²⁴ But David said to Araunah, "No, I will purchase it from you. For I am not going to offer up to YHWH my God burnt offerings that cost me nothing." So David bought the threshing-floor and the oxen for fifty shekels of silver. ²⁵ There he built an altar of YHWH and offered burnt offerings and communion offerings. YHWH was moved by David's prayer for the land, and the plague in Israel was lifted.

---

* The site of the altar, the threshing floor of Araunah, later became the site of the Temple in Jerusalem.

1 kings

1:1–11:43

When david was old and well up in years, he could not keep warm even when he was wrapped in blankets. ² So his attendants said, "Let us find a young woman to take care of you, sovereign one, and nurse you. If she sleeps with you, her body will keep you warm." ³ The attendants looked all over the land of Israel to find the right person, and found Abishag of Shunem, and brought her to David. ⁴ She was very beautiful. And she looked after David and kept him comfortable. But they did not have intercourse.

⁵ Meanwhile, Adonijah, whose mother was Haggith,* boasted, "I will the next to rule!" Accordingly Adonijah acquired horses and chariots, and fifty runners to precede him. ⁶ Yet his father never corrected him or asked why he did what did. Like his brother Absalom, to whom he was near in age, Adonijah was handsome.

---

* David had ten sons and one daughter; he had eight wives and numerous concubines. Adonijah was his fourth son, and Haggith his fifth wife; Solomon, Adonijah's rival, was his youngest son.

⁷ Adonijah lobbied Joab ben-Zeruiah* and Abiathar the priest, and won their support. ⁸ But Zadok the priest, Benaiah ben-Jehoiada, Nathan the prophet, Shemei, Rei, and David's house guards did not support Adonijah.

⁹ Adonijah then held a sacrifice of sheep, oxen, cattle and fattened calves at the Stone of Zoheleth, or "Serpent's Stone," near En-rogel. He invited all his brothers—David's sons—and all the officials of Judah. ¹⁰ Adonijah did not invite Nathan the prophet, Benaiah, David's house guards, or his brother Solomon.

¹¹ Nathan asked Bathsheba, Solomon's mother, "Did you hear that Adonijah ben-Haggith has announced that he is the ruler, without the assent of our sovereign David? ¹² For your personal safety, and for the safety of Solomon, I advise you ¹³ to go immediately to David and say, 'Did you not swear to me, the one who has been loyal to you, that Solomon would succeed you as ruler, and that Solomon would sit on your judgment seat? How then can Adonijah claim the judgment seat?' ¹⁴ While you are still there talking to David, I will come in and confirm what you said."

¹⁵ So Bathsheba went to the aged ruler's room, where Abishag was in attendance. ¹⁶ Bathsheba bowed low to pay homage to David, who asked her, "Do you want something?"

¹⁷ She replied, "Did you not, O sovereign one, swear by YHWH your God to me, your most loyal subject, that Solomon would succeed you as ruler and sit on the judgment seat? ¹⁸ But now Adonijah is ruling, and you, O sovereign one, don't even know about it! ¹⁹ He has sacrificed great numbers of cattle, fatted calves, and sheep, and invited all your sons, as well as Abiathar the priest and Joab the commander of the army, but not Solomon. ²⁰ O sovereign ruler, the eyes of all Israel are on you, to learn from you who will sit on the judgment seat. ²¹ Otherwise, when you rest with your ancestors, Solomon and I will be treated as criminals."

²² While she was speaking with David, Nathan the prophet arrived, ²³ and David's guards announced him. Nathan went up to the ruler and bowed low with his face to the ground, ²⁴ then said, "Have you, O sovereign ruler, declared that Adonijah will be ruler after you, and that he will sit on your judgment seat? ²⁵ Today he went down and sacrificed great numbers of cattle, fattened calves, and sheep. He has invited all of your sons, the commander of the army, and Abiathar the priest. At this very moment they are eating and drinking together, saying, 'Long live Adonijah the ruler!' ²⁶ But I, your faithful one, Zadok the priest, Benaiah ben-Jehoiada, and Solomon were not invited. ²⁷ Is there something you did, O sovereign ruler, without informing your faithful ones who should sit on the judgment seat after you?"

---

* Joab was one of the leaders of David's army, and David's nephew as well; Zeruiah was David's sister.

²⁸ Then David said, "Call Bathsheba back in." So she came into the ruler's presence and stood there before him. ²⁹ David swore an oath, "By the living YHWH, who delivered me from all my troubles, ³⁰ I will carry out the oath I made to you, the oath I swore by YHWH the God of Israel: Solomon will succeed me and sit on the judgment seat in my place!" ³¹ Bowing to the floor in homage to the ruler, Bathsheba said, "May my sovereign, David the ruler, live forever!"

³² David said, "Summon Zadok the priest, Nathan the prophet, and Benaiah ben-Jehoiada," and when they came before the David, ³³ he said to them, "Take the attendants of the household with you, set Solomon on a mule, and take him down to Gihon.* ³⁴ There let Zadok the priest and Nathan the prophet anoint Solomon as ruler over Israel. Then sound the shofar and shout, 'Long live Solomon the Ruler!' ³⁵ You are to escort Solomon home again and let him sit on my judgment seat and reign in my place. For I designate Solomon to be ruler of over Israel and Judah."

³⁶ Benaiah ben-Jehoiada answered David, "Amen! And may YHWH, the God of my sovereign and ruler, confirm it! ³⁷ As YHWH has been with your majesty, so may God be with Solomon. May YHWH make Solomon's judgment seat even greater than the judgment seat of our sovereign David the Ruler!"

³⁸ So Zadok the priest, Nathan the prophet, Benaiah ben-Jehoiada, and the Kerethites and Pelethites† went down and put Solomon on David's mule, escorting him to Gihon. ³⁹ Zadok the priest took the horn of oil from the Tent‡ and anointed Solomon. Then they sounded the shofar and all the people shouted, "Long live Solomon the Ruler!" ⁴⁰ Then all the people escorted Solomon home in a procession, with great rejoicing and the playing of pipes, so that the very earth shook with the sound.

⁴¹ As they finished their feast, Adonijah and all the guests who were with him heard the sounds. On hearing the sound of the shofar, Joab asked, "What is the meaning of all this noise in the city?"

⁴² As he spoke, Jonathan ben-Abiathar the priest arrived. Adonijah said, "Come in. A worthy person like yourself must be bearing good news!"

⁴³ "Not at all!" Jonathan replied. "Our sovereign ruler, David, has made Solomon ruler. ⁴⁴ David sent with him Zadok the priest, Nathan the prophet, Benaiah ben-Jehoiada, and the Kerethites and Pelethites, and they sat him on the ruler's donkey. ⁴⁵ Zadok the priest and Nathan the prophet anointed

---

* Gihon was a stream near Jerusalem.
† The Kerethites were David's foreign-born bodyguard, and the Pelethites were his personal palace guard.
‡ The Tent of Meeting, that is, the Tabernacle that was used to house the Ark of the Covenant before Solomon built the Temple.

him at Gihon. From there they are in a procession with cheers, and the city reverberates with it. That is the noise you hear. ⁴⁶ Solomon is now seated on the judgment seat. ⁴⁷ And all the officials of the household came to congratulate David, saying, 'May God make the name of Solomon more famous than your own and the throne ever greater than yours.' And David bowed in worship from his couch. ⁴⁸ Beyond that, the ruler said, 'Praise be to YHWH, the God of Israel, who has allowed my eyes to see a successor on my judgment seat today.'"

⁴⁹ At this point, all of Adonijah's guests rose in panic and dispersed. ⁵⁰ But Adonijah, fearing Solomon, went at once to the altar and took hold of its horns.*

⁵¹ When Solomon learned the fate of Adonijah—that he was clinging to the horns of the altar and pleading, "Let Solomon the Ruler swear to me here and now that he will not put me to sword"— ⁵² he replied, "If Adonijah proves to be an honorable person, not a hair of his head will fall to the ground. But if it is found that he is a troublemaker, he must die." ⁵³ Then Solomon ordered him removed from the altar. He came and prostrated himself before the ruler, and Solomon said, "Go home."

2:1 As David grew closer to dying, he gave a charge to Solomon: ² "I am about to go the way of all flesh. Be strong and courageous. ³ Fulfill your duties to YHWH your God. Conform yourself to God's ways, keep God's statutes, commands, ordinances, and decrees as they are written in the Law of Moses. By doing this, you will succeed in whatever you do, wherever you turn. ⁴ And YHWH will keep the divine promise made to me: 'If your descendants are careful to walk faithfully in my sight with all their heart and with all their soul, you will never lack a successor on the judgment seat of Israel.'

⁵ "Now, you yourself know that what Joab ben-Zeruiah did to me—what he did to the two commanders of Israel's armies, Abner ben-Ner and Amasa ben-Jether. He killed them, shedding their blood in peacetime as if in battle, and with that blood stained the belt around his waist and the sandals on his feet. ⁶ Act as your wisdom prompts you, but do not let his gray hair go down to the grave peacefully.

⁷ "Show kindness to the children of Barzillai of Gilead and let them be among those who eat at your table. They stood by me when I fled from your brother Absalom. ⁸ And remember, you must deal with Shimei ben-Gera, the Benjaminite from Bahurim, who called down bitter curses on me the day I

---

* This is the ancient practice of seeking sanctuary, of claiming sacred and inviolable asylum when in danger—though, as 2:34 demonstrates, that claim was not always respected.

went to Mahanaim. When he came down to the Jordan, I swore to him by YHWH, 'I will not put you to death by the sword.' ⁹ But now, do not let him remain unpunished. You are wise—you will know what to do to him. Bring his bloodied gray head down to the grave."

¹⁰ Then David rested with his ancestors and was buried in the City of David.* ¹¹ He had reigned for forty years over Israel—seven years in Hebron and thirty-three years in Jerusalem. ¹² So Solomon sat on the judgment seat of David, and his rule was firmly established.

¹³ Now Adonijah, whose mother was Haggith, went to Bathsheba, Solomon's mother.

She asked, "Do you come in peace?"

He replied, "Yes, peacefully." ¹⁴ Then he added, "I have something to say to you."

"What is it?" she asked.

¹⁵ "As you know," he replied, "the realm was mine. All Israel looked to me as their ruler. But things changed, and the realm has gone to my brother, for it has come to him from YHWH. ¹⁶ Now I have one request to make of you—please do not refuse me."

"You may make it," she said.

¹⁷ So he continued, "Please ask Solomon the ruler—he will not refuse you—to give me the hand of Abishag the Shunammite in marriage."

¹⁸ "Very well," Bathsheba replied, "I will speak to the ruler for you."

¹⁹ When Bathsheba went to Solomon the ruler to speak to him for Adonijah, the ruler stood up to greet her, bowed down to her, and sat down on his judgment seat. He had a second judgment seat set up for the ruler's mother, and she sat down at his right hand.†

²⁰ "I have one small request to make of you," she said. "Do not refuse me."

The ruler replied, "Make it, mother; I will not refuse you."

²¹ So she said, "Let Abishag the Shunammite be betrothed to your brother Adonijah."

²² Solomon the ruler answered her, "Why do you request Abishag the Shunammite for Adonijah? You might as well request the entire realm for him—after all, he is my older brother, and Abiathar the priest and Joab ben-Zeruiah are on his side!"‡

---

* In this case, "City of David" indicates Jerusalem (specifically, the fortress of Zion), not Bethlehem, David's birthplace.
† In this era, queens were the kings' mothers rather than their wives.
‡ Solomon felt that Adonijah's desire for Abishag, his father's attractive nurse, was the height of insult to David's memory.

²³ Then Solomon swore by YHWH: "May God deal with me, be it ever so severely, if Adonijah does not pay with his life for this request! ²⁴ And now, as surely as God lives—who established me securely on the judgment seat of my father David and has founded a dynasty for me as promised—Adonijah will be put to death today!" ²⁵ So Solomon the ruler gave the order to Benaiah ben-Jehoiada, and he struck down Adonijah, and he died.

²⁶ To Abiathar the priest the ruler said, "Go back to your fields in Anathoth. You deserve to die, but I will not put you to death now, for you carried the Ark of Sovereign YHWH before David and shared in all of his hardships." ²⁷ So Solomon removed Abiathar from the priesthood of YHWH, fulfilling the word of YHWH spoken at Shiloh about the house of Eli.

²⁸ When the news reached Joab, who had conspired with Adonijah but not with Absolom, he fled to the tent of YHWH and took hold of the horns of the altar. ²⁹ Solomon the ruler was told that Joab had fled to the Tent of YHWH and was beside the altar. Then Solomon ordered Benaiah ben-Jehoiada, "Go, strike him down!"

³⁰ So Benaiah entered the tent of YHWH and said to Joab, "The ruler says, 'Come out!' "

But Joab answered, "I will die here."

Benaiah reported to the ruler what Joab had said in reply.

³¹ Then the ruler commanded Benaiah, "Do as he wishes. Strike him down and bury him, and so clear me and my family of the guilt of the innocent blood that Joab shed. ³² YHWH will repay him for the blood he shed, attacking two officers without David's knowledge and killing them with the sword. Both of them—Abner ben-Ner, commander of Israel's army, and Amasa ben-Jether, commander of Judah's army—were better soldiers and more upright than he. ³³ May the guilt of their blood rest on the head of Joab and his descendants forever. But on David and his descendants, his house and his judgment seat, may YHWH's peace rest forever."

³⁴ So Benaiah ben-Jehoiada went up and struck down Joab, killing him, and he was buried on his own land in the wilderness. ³⁵ Solomon put Benaiah ben-Jehoiada over the army in Joab's position and replaced Abiathar with Zadok the priest.

³⁶ Then Solomon sent for Shimei and said to him, "Build yourself a house in Jerusalem and live there, but do not go anywhere else. ³⁷ The day you leave and cross the Kidron Valley, you can be sure you will die—your blood will be on your own head."

³⁸ Shimei responded to Solomon, "What you say is good. I will do as you say." And Shimei stayed in Jerusalem for a long time. ³⁹ But three years later, two of Shimei's attendants ran off to Achish ben-Maacha, ruler of Gath, and Shimei was told, "Your attendants are in Gath." ⁴⁰ So Shimei saddled his

donkey and went to Achish at Gath in search of them, and returned with them from Gath. ⁴¹ When Solomon learned that Shemei had left Jerusalem to bring his attendants back from Gath, ⁴² he summoned Shimei, saying, "Didn't I make you swear by YHWH and warn you, 'On the day you leave Jerusalem you will surely die?' At the time you said, 'What you say is good. I will obey.' ⁴³ Why then did you not keep your oath to YHWH and obey the command I gave you?"

⁴⁴ Solomon continued, "You know in your heart all the wrong you did to my father David. Now YHWH will repay you for your wrongdoing. ⁴⁵ But Solomon the ruler will be blessed, and David's judgment seat will remain secure before YHWH forever." ⁴⁶ Then Solomon gave the order to Benaiah ben-Jehoiada, and he went out and executed Shimei.

The reign was now firmly established in Solomon's hands.

ℭ℈ ℭ℈ ℭ℈

³·¹ Solomon allied Israel with Egypt by marrying the Pharaoh's daughter. They took up housing in the City of David until construction of the royal residence, the Temple of God, and the wall around Jerusalem could be completed. ² But the people continued to sacrifice at the hilltop shrines, because the Temple had not yet been built for the Name of YHWH. ³ Solomon showed his love for YHWH by following the precepts of David, except that he still offered sacrifices and incense at the shrines.

⁴ Solomon went to Gibeon, since the chief shrine was located there, to offer sacrifice. There he offered one thousand burnt offerings on its altar. ⁵ At Gibeon God appeared in a dream to the ruler during the night, saying, "Ask what you would like me to give you."

⁶ Solomon replied, "You have shown great kindness to your servant, David, who was faithful, righteous, and obedient to you. And you have generously maintained this constant love toward us and now you have appointed a successor to sit on the judgment seat this very day. ⁷ Now, YHWH my God, you have continued this kindness to David's successor, placing me on the judgment seat this very day. ⁸ Here I am in the midst of your chosen people, a people so numerous they cannot be counted. ⁹ Give me, your servant, a discerning heart, so that I may distinguish good from evil and govern your people with wisdom."

¹⁰ YHWH was much pleased with what Solomon had requested. ¹¹ So God said to Solomon, "Because this is what you asked for and not for a long life, or for wealth, or for the lives of your foes, but for discernment in administering justice, ¹² I grant your request. And I give you a heart so wise and so understanding that there has been no one like you before your time, nor will

there be after your time. [13] Furthermore, I give you those items which you did not ask for: wealth and glory which no ruler in your time can match. [14] If you keep my ways, keep our laws and commandments as David followed them, I will grant you long life."

[15] Solomon woke up, and realized that it was a dream. Then he returned to Jerusalem and stood before the Ark of the Covenant of God, where he sacrificed whole offerings and share offerings, and provided a banquet for the whole household.

[16] One day, two women who were sex workers came to Solomon and requested a hearing. [17] The first one said, "We share a house. I had a child while she was there with me. [18] On the third day after I gave birth she too gave birth to a child. We were the only two adults in the house.* [19] During the night this woman's child died because she had lain on it. [20] So she got up in the middle of the night and took my baby from my side while I, your subject, was asleep. She put it to her breast, and put the dead child to my breast. [21] The next morning, when I got up to nurse the baby, I discovered the dead baby."

[22] The other one said, "No! The living child is mine! The dead child is yours!"

But the first woman insisted, "No! The dead child is yours! The living child is mine!" And they argued before the ruler.

[23] Then Solomon spoke: "This one says, 'My child is alive and your child is dead,' while the other one says, 'No! your child is dead and my child is alive.' "

[24] Then Solomon said, "Bring me a sword." So they brought him a sword. [25] Then the ruler gave an order: "Cut the living child in two and give half to one of the woman and give the second half to the other woman."

[26] The woman whose baby had lived was overcome with compassion for her child and said, "Please, my sovereign, give her the living baby. Don't kill the child!"

But the other woman said, "Neither you or I will have the baby. Cut it in half!"

[27] Then Solomon made the ruling: "Give the baby to the first woman. Do not kill it—she is the mother."

[28] When all Israel heard the verdict the ruler had made, they were awe-struck at his decision. For they saw that Solomon had the wisdom from God to administer real justice.

---

* There were no other witnesses to testify as to who gave birth to which baby.

⁴:¹ And Solomon ruled over all Israel. ² These were Solomon's chief officials:

Azariah ben-Zadok—the priest;
³ The brothers Elihoreph and Ahijah ben-Shisha—scribes;
Jehoshaphat ben-Ahilud—secretary;
⁴ Benaiah ben-Jehoiada—commander of the army;
Zadok and Abiathar—priests;
⁵ Azariah ben-Nathan—in charge of district officers;
Zabud ben-Nathan—priest and personal advisor to Solomon;
⁶ Ahisar—in charge of the royal residence;
Adoniram ben-Abda—in charge of forced labor.

⁷ Solomon also had twelve district governors over all Israel, who supplied provisions for the ruler and the royal residence. Each had to provide supplies for one month of the year. ⁸ Their names are:

Ben-Hur—in the hill country of Ephraim;
⁹ Ben-Deker—in Makaz, Shaalbim, Beth Shemesh
and Elom Bethhanan;
¹⁰ Ben-Hesed—in Arubboth
(Socoh and all the land of Hepher were his);
¹¹ Ben-Abinadab—in Naphoth Dor
(who was married to Taphath, one of Solomon's daughters);
¹² Baana ben-Ahilud—in Taanach and Megiddo, and in all of
Beth Shan next to Zarethan below Jezreel, from Beth Shan to
Abel Meholah across from Jokmeam;
¹³ Ben-Geber—in Ramoth Gilead
(the settlements of Jair ben-Manassah in Gilead were his,
as well as the district of Argob in Bashan and its sixty large
walled cities with bronze gate bars);
¹⁴ Ahinadab ben-Iddo—in Mahanaim;
¹⁵ Ahimaaz—in Naphtali
(he had married another of Solomon's daughters, Basemath);
¹⁶ Baana ben-Hushai—in Asher and in Aloth;
¹⁷ Jehoshaphat ben-Paruah—in Issachar;
¹⁸ Shimei ben-Ela—in Benjamin;
¹⁹ Geger ben-Uri—in Gilead
(the country of Sihon ruler of the Amorites and the country of Og
ruler of Bashan). He was the only governor over the district.

²⁰ The people of Judah and Israel were as numerous as the sands of the seashore. They ate and drank and were as happy as could be.

⁵·¹ Solomon ruled over the entire realm from the Euphrates River to Philistia and as far as the frontier of Egypt. These countries paid tribute and
were Solomon's subjects as long as the ruler lived.*

² The daily provisions for Solomon† were 180 bushels of fine flour and 365
bushels of meal, ³ ten fattened oxen, twenty pastured oxen, and one hundred
sheep; as well as stags, gazelles, roebucks, and fattened poultry.

⁴ Solomon ruled over all the realms west of the Jordan River, from Tiphsah
to Gaza. And peace reigned. ⁵ Throughout Solomon's life, peace reigned in
Judah and Israel, from Dan to Beersheba, and all prospered under their
own vines and fig trees. ⁶ Solomon had 4,000 stalls for chariot horses, and
12,000 cavalry horses.

⁷ The regional governors, each taking a month in turn, supplied the provisions for Solomon the ruler and all who came to his table. They never fell
short in their deliveries. ⁸ They also provided to the appropriate place their
quota of barley and straw for the chariot and cavalry horses.

⁹ God gave Solomon immense wisdom and understanding, with an
open heart—as vast as the sands on the seashore. ¹⁰ The ruler's wisdom
was greater than the wisdom of all the people of the East, greater than the
wisdom of Egypt. ¹¹ He was the wisest person of his era, wiser than Ethan
the Ezrahite—wiser than Heman, Calcol, and Darda, the heirs of Mahol.
And this fame spread to all the surrounding nations. ¹² Solomon composed
3,000 proverbs and 1,005 songs. ¹³ He gave discourses on plant life—everything from the cedars in Lebanon to the hyssop growing in the wall. And
he taught about animals, birds, reptiles, and fish. ¹⁴ People from all nations,
sent by all the world's rulers who had learned of his wisdom, came to hear
Solomon speak.

¹⁵ When Hiram, the ruler of Tyre, learned that Solomon had been anointed
ruler to succeed David, he sent envoys because he had always been on good
terms with David. ¹⁶ Solomon returned the gesture with this message:

¹⁷ "You understand that because of the hostile nations surrounding Israel,
my father David could not build a Temple to honor the Name of YHWH his
God until YHWH made them our subjects. ¹⁸ But now YHWH God gives me
peace on every side. There is no one to challenge me, and I don't fear attack.
¹⁹ So I propose to build a Temple to honor the Name of YHWH my God, just
as God promised David: 'Your child, whom I will set on the judgment seat
in your place, will build a house for my Name.' ²⁰ So now I ask that you cut

---

* The verse numbering varies greatly from version to version. We follow the numbering system of
 most Jewish translations.
† That is, for the royal palace.

down the cedars of Lebanon for me. My workers will work alongside yours, and I will pay for the hiring of your workers at whatever rate you fix. As for now, we have no one as skilled in felling trees as you Sidonians."

²¹ When Hiram received Solomon's message, he was much pleased, and said, "Praise be to YHWH God who today has given David a wise successor to rule over this great people." ²² Hiram sent Solomon this reply:

"I received your message and I will fulfill your requests for cedars and cypress logs. ²³ My workers will haul them down from Lebanon to the sea, and I will float them in rafts by sea to the place you specify. There I will separate them and you can move them to your site. In return, I ask that you provide the food to my royal household."

²⁴ So Hiram supplied Solomon with all the cedar and cypress logs that he wanted, ²⁵ and Solomon gave Hiram 121,000 bushels of wheat to feed his household, in addition to 97,000 gallons of pressed olive oil, and continued to do so year after year. ²⁶ And YHWH continued to make Solomon wise, as promised. Meanwhile, the relations between Solomon and Hiram were peaceful, and the two of them made a treaty.

²⁷ Solomon conscripted 30,000 laborers from all Israel. ²⁸ They were sent off to Lebanon in shifts of 10,000 a month, so that they would spend one month in Lebanon and two months at home. Adoniram was in charge of the draft. ²⁹ Solomon had 70,000 porters and 80,000 stonecutters in the hills, ³⁰ apart from the 3,300 overseers who supervised the project and directed the work. ³¹ At the ruler's orders they quarried huge costly stones for the laying of the foundation of the Temple. ³² The skilled workers of Solomon, Hiram, and Gebal cut and prepared the timber and stone for the building of the Temple.

6:1 In the 480th year after the people of Israel came out of Egypt, in the fourth year of Solomon's reign over Israel, in the month of Ziv, the second month, he began to build the Temple of YHWH God.

² The Temple that Solomon the ruler built for YHWH was 90 feet long, 30 feet wide and 45 feet high.* ³ The portico at the front of the main hall of the Temple extended the width of the Temple—that is, 30 feet—and projected 15 feet from the front of the Temple. ⁴ Solomon made windows with recessed and latticed frames for the Temple, ⁵ and built a multi-storied structure of side chambers around the building, abutting the walls of the main hall and the inner sanctuary. ⁶ The lowest floor was 7½ feet wide, the middle floor 9 feet, and the third floor 10½—so that around the outside of the Temple, each floor overhung the one below it. This way, the supporting beams would not be inserted into the walls of the Temple itself.

---

* Note the smallish dimensions by modern standards. Hollywood depicts the Temple of Solomon as a massive edifice, when it was actually only 2700 square feet.

⁷ In building the Temple, only blocks of stone that had been finished at the quarry were used, and no hammer, chisel, or any other iron tool whatsoever was heard at the Temple site while it was being built.

⁸ The entrance to the lowest side chamber was on the south side of the Temple; a stairway led up to the middle level, and from there to the third. ⁹ So Solomon built the Temple and completed it, roofing it with beams and cedar planks. ¹⁰ Solomon built the side rooms all along the Temple. Each room was 7½ feet high, and they were attached to the Temple by beams of cedar.

¹¹ The word of YHWH came to Solomon: ¹² "As for this Temple you are building, if you follow my decrees, carry out my regulations and keep all my commands and obey them, I will fulfill through you the promise I gave to your father David. ¹³ And I will live among the people of Israel and will not abandon them."

¹⁴ So Solomon built the Temple and completed it. ¹⁵ He lined its interior walls with cedar boards, paneling them from the floor of the Temple to the ceiling, and covered the floor of the Temple with planks of cypress. ¹⁶ At the rear of the Temple he partitioned off 30 feet with cedar boards from floor to ceiling to form within the Temple an inner sanctuary, the Most Holy Place. ¹⁷ The main hall in front off this room was 60 feet long. ¹⁸ The inside of the Temple was cedar, carved with gourds and open flowers. Everything was cedar; no stone was visible.

¹⁹ The ruler prepared the inner sanctuary within the Temple to set the Ark of the Covenant of YHWH there. ²⁰ The inner sanctuary was 30 feet long, 30 feet wide and 30 feet high. Then the ruler overlaid the inside with pure gold, and overlaid the altar with cedar. ²¹ Solomon covered the inside of the Temple with pure gold, and extended gold chains across the front of the inner sanctuary, which was overlaid with gold. ²² And he overlaid the Temple with gold, then covered the altar that belonged to the inner sanctuary with gold as well. Thus the entire Temple was finished.

²³ In the inner sanctuary, a pair of 15-foot-tall cherubim* made of olive wood were attached to the wall. ²⁴ Each wing of the cherubim was 7½ feet long—15 feet from wingtip to wingtip. ²⁵ The two cherubim had the same design and were the same height; ²⁶ each cherub was 15 feet tall. ²⁷ Solomon placed the cherubim inside the innermost room of the Temple, with their wings spread out. The wing of one cherub touched one wall and the wing of the second cherub touched the other wall, and their wings touched each other in the middle of the room. ²⁸ The cherubim were overlaid with gold. ²⁹ On the walls around the Temple, in both the inner rooms and the outer rooms, there were carved reliefs of cherubim, palm trees, and open flowers.

---

* The cherubim (or, more properly, *kerubim*) were fearsome mythic creatures, great winged sphynxes or griffins—not adorable baby angels.

[30] The floors of both the inner and outer rooms of the Temple were covered with gold.

[31] The entrance of the inner sanctuary had doors of olive wood framed by five levels of recesses in the lintel and doorposts.* [32] And on the two olive wood doors were carved cherubim, palm trees, and open flowers, and all were overlaid with beaten gold. [33] The entrance to the main hall also had four-level recessed jambs of olive wood, [34] with two doors of cypress wood, each of them comprised of two folding panels on a center hinge; [35] they also had carved cherubim, palm trees, and open flowers on the doors, and were overlaid with gold hammered evenly over the carvings.

[36] And Solomon built the inner courtyard of three rows of dressed stone and one row of trimmed cedar beams. [37] The foundation of the Temple of YHWH was laid in the fourth year of Solomon's reign, in the month of Ziv. [38] In the eleventh year, in the month of Bul—the eighth month—the Temple was finished in all its details according to its specifications. Solomon spent seven years building it.

7:1 On the other hand, it took Solomon thirteen years to complete the construction of his palace. [2] The ruler built the Hall of the Forest of Lebanon, which was 150 feet long, 75 feet wide, and 45 feet high. It sat on four rows of cedar wood pillars with cedar capitals on the pillars. It was paneled in cedar on the upper part as far as the planks above the pillars. [3] It had a cedar roof extending over the beams, which rested on the columns, fifteen in each row; there were forty-five beams in all. [4] There were three rows of window frames, with three tiers of windows directly facing one another. [5] All the doorways and the windows had square frames, and window corresponded to window at three levels.

[6] Solomon built a colonnade that was 75 feet long and 45 feet wide. The colonnade—pillars and an overhanging roof—stood in front of the building. [7] Then he built the Hall of Justice, a colonnade that held the judgment seat where the ruler makes judgments. It was paneled in cedar from floor to rafters.

[8] And the royal residence was in another courtyard, set further back from the Hall of Justice, and was of the same construction. Solomon also made a residence like this hall for Pharaoh's daughter, whom he had married.

[9] All these structures, from the outside to the great courtyard and from foundation to eaves, were made of blocks of high-grade stone cut to size and trimmed with a saw on their inner and outer faces. [10] The foundations

---

* The description—literally, "the lintel, doorposts, a fifth"—is ambiguous, but likely indicates that the door frames were beveled and recessed: many doors in more luxurious structures throughout the Mediterranean world and in Mesopotamia had several recesses in the frame, forming a stairstep effect from the outer frame to the door itself.

were laid with large stones of good quality, some measuring 15 feet square and some 12 feet. [11] Above them were high-grade stones, cut to size, and cedar beams. [12] The great courtyard was surrounded by a wall of three tiers of dressed stone and one tier of trimmed cedar beams, as was the inner courtyard of the Temple of YHWH with its colonnade.

[13] Solomon sent for Hiram from Tyre. [14] Hiram's mother was a widow from the tribe of Naphtali; his father was a native of Tyre and was a skilled bronze-worker. Hiram was himself highly skilled and experienced in all kinds of bronze work. He came to the ruler and did all the work assigned to him. [15] He cast two bronze pillars, each 27 feet high and 18 feet in circumference. [16] Hiram also made two capitals of cast bronze to set on top of the pillars. Each capital was 7½ feet high. [17] A network of interwoven chains festooned the capitals on top of the pillars, seven on each capital. [18] Hiram made pomegranates in two rows encircling each network to decorate the capitals on top of the pillars. He did the same for each capital. [19] The capitals on top of the pillars in the colonnade were in the shape of lilies, 6 feet high. [20] On the capitals of both pillars, above the bowl-shaped part next to the network, were the two hundred pomegranates in a row all around. [21] Hiram erected the pillars adjacent to the colonnade of the Temple. The pillar to the south he named Jakin, and the one to the north Boaz.* [22] The capitals on top were in the shape of lilies. And so the work on the pillars was completed.

[23] Hiram made the Sea† of cast metal, circular in shape, measuring 15 feet from rim to rim and 7½ feet high, and 45 feet in circumference. [24] Gourds encircled it below the rim, ten to every foot and a half. The gourds were cast in two rows in one piece with the Sea. [25] The Sea stood on twelve bulls, three facing north, three facing west, three facing south, and three facing east. The Sea rested on top of them, and their hindquarters were toward the center. [26] It was a handbreadth thick, and its rim was like the rim of a cup, like a lily blossom. It held 9,700 gallons of water.

[27] Hiram also made ten movable basin stands in bronze. Each movable stand was 6 feet long, 6 feet wide, and 4½ feet high. [28] The moveable stands had side panels attached to uprights. [29] There were lions, bulls, and cherubim on the panels between the uprights, and on the uprights as well. Above and below the lions and bulls were wreaths of hammered work. [30] Each stand had four bronze wheels with bronze axles, and each had a basin resting on four supports, cast with wreaths on each side. [31] On the inside of the stand was

---

* Jakin means "God will establish," and Boaz means "in strength." These may have been the first words of the inscription on each pillar. Scholars have speculated that the purpose of the pillars was more than decorative. W. F. Albright suggests that they were fire-pillars, representing the pillar of smoke and the pillar of fire from the exodus.

† The Sea was a large basin that contained water for the priests to bathe themselves.

an opening that had a circular frame 1½ feet deep. This opening was round, and with its basework it measured 2¼ feet wide. Around its opening was more engraving. The panels of the stands were square, not round. ³² The four wheels were under the panels, and the axels of the wheels were attached to the stand. The diameter of each wheel was 2¼ feet. ³³ The wheels were made like chariot wheels; and the axles, rims, spokes and hubs were made of cast metal. ³⁴ Each stand had four handles, one on each corner, projecting from the stand. ³⁵ Attached to the top of the each stand was a circular support, three-quarters of a foot high. The supports and panels were attached to the top of the stand. ³⁶ On the supports and on the stands on every available space, the artisan engraved cherubim, lions, and palm trees, with wreaths everywhere. ³⁷ This is the way all ten stands were made, cast in the same molds and identical in size and shape. ³⁸ Hiram also made ten bronze basins for the stands, each of the same size and shape. The basins were 6 feet in diameter with a capacity of 195 gallons, with one basin for the top of each stand. ³⁹ Five stands were placed on the south side of the Temple and five on the north side. The Sea was placed on the south side, at the southeast corner of the Temple. ⁴⁰ Hiram also made ash containers and shovels, and sprinkling bowls.

And Hiram completed the work Solomon requested: ⁴¹ the two pillars; the two bowl-shaped capitals atop the pillars; the two ornamental networks to cover the two bowl-shaped capitals atop the pillars; ⁴² the four hundred pomegranates for the two sets of networks (two rows of pomegranates for each network, decorating the bowl-shaped capitals atop the pillars); ⁴³ the ten stands with their ten basins; ⁴⁴ the Sea and the twelve bulls under it; ⁴⁵ the containers, shovels, and sprinkling bowls.

All these furnishings made by Hiram for Solomon the ruler for the Temple were of burnished bronze. ⁴⁶ The ruler had them cast in clay molds in the foundry between Succoth and Zarethan on the Jordan plain. ⁴⁷ Solomon placed these objects in their proper places. So great was the quantity of bronze used in their making that its weight was beyond calculation.

⁴⁸ Hiram also made all the furnishing of the Temple of YHWH: the golden altar; the golden table on which the Bread of the Presence was placed; ⁴⁹ the lampstands of pure gold (five on the right and five on the left, in front of the inner sanctuary); the gold floral work and lamps and tongs; ⁵⁰ the pure gold dishes, wick trimmers, sprinkling bowls, dishes and censers; and the gold sockets for the doors of the innermost room, the Most Holy Place, and for the doors of the main hall of the Temple.

⁵¹ When all the work Solomon the ruler did for the house of God was completed, the Ruler brought in the sacred treasures of his father David, the silver, the gold, and the vessels, and deposited them in the treasuries of YHWH's Temple.

⁸·¹ Then Solomon summoned the elders of Israel, all the tribal leaders, and the heads of the families of the people of Israel to bring up the Ark of the Covenant of YHWH from the City of David, that is, Zion. ² All the people of Israel assembled in Solomon's presence at the at the time of the festival* in the month of Ethanim, the seventh month. ³ Once all the elders of Israel had arrived the priests lifted the Ark of YHWH ⁴ and brought it to the Temple; the priests and the Levites also carried the Tent of Meeting, together with all the sacred furnishings of the Tent. ⁵ In the presence of the Ark, Solomon and all Israel sacrificed sheep and oxen in numbers beyond reckoning.

⁶ The priests then brought the Ark of the Covenant of YHWH to its place in the inner sanctuary of the Temple, the Most Holy Place, under the wings of the cherubim. ⁷ The cherubim spread their wings over the place of the Ark and formed a canopy above the Ark and its carrying poles. ⁸ The poles were so long that their ends could be seen from the sanctuary immediately in front of the inner sanctuary, but from nowhere else outside. They are there to this day.

⁹ There was nothing inside the Ark but the two stone tablets which Moses had deposited there at Horeb, when God made the Covenant with the people of Israel after they left Egypt.

¹⁰ When the priests came out the sanctuary, a cloud filled the Temple of YHWH, ¹¹ and they could not continue to minister because of it, for the Glory of God filled the Temple. ¹² Then Solomon said: "YHWH, you chose to dwell among us in a thick cloud. ¹³ But now I have built you a magnificent House, a settled place where you may dwell forever."†

¹⁴ With the whole assembly present there, Solomon turned around to face those assembled and blessed them, saying, ¹⁵ "Praise be to YHWH, the God of Israel, who spoke directly to my father David, and whose promises to him have now been fulfilled. For God said, ¹⁶ 'From the day when I brought my people Israel out of Egypt, I chose no city out of all the tribes of Israel where I should build a house for my Name to be; but I have chosen David to be over my people Israel.' ¹⁷ My father David intended to build a house for the Name of YHWH, the God of Israel, ¹⁸ but God said to David, 'You intended to build for my Name, and your purpose was good. ¹⁹ Nevertheless, you are not to build it. But your heir, yet to be born to you, is the one to build the house for my Name.' ²⁰ YHWH fulfilled the promise: I have succeeded David and now I sit on the judgment seat of Israel, just as God promised, and I built the Temple for the Name of YHWH, the God of Israel. ²¹ I have provided a place there for the Ark containing the Covenant of YHWH, the covenant that God made with our ancestors when they were delivered out of Egypt."

---

* The Feast of Tabernacles, in late September or early October.
† Solomon is contrasting the nomadic life the Israelites had followed for so long with a life now firmly settled in the land.

²² Then Solomon stood before the altar of God in the presence of the whole assembly of Israel, with hands spread out to heaven, ²³ and said, "YHWH, God of Israel, there is no God like you in heaven above and on the earth below—keeping your Covenant of love with your servants who continue wholeheartedly to be faithful to you with all their hearts. ²⁴ You kept your promise to your servant David; by your deeds today, you fulfill what you said to David in words. ²⁵ So YHWH, God of Israel, keep your promise to your servant David, when you said, 'You will never lack for a person to sit before me on the judgment seat of Israel, provided your successors are careful how they behave, walking before me as you yourself did.' ²⁶ O God of Israel, may the promise you made to your attendant David come true!

²⁷ "But can God really dwell on earth? Heaven itself, the highest heaven, cannot contain you. How much less this Temple I have built! ²⁸ Hear the prayer and the plea for mercy of your servant, YHWH my God. Hear the cry and the prayer that your servant makes in your presence today. ²⁹ May your eyes watch over this Temple day and night, over this place where you said, 'My Name shall be there!' Hear the prayer your servant offers in this place.

³⁰ "Hear the plea of your servant and of your people Israel as they pray in this place. From heaven where you dwell, hear; and as you hear, forgive.

³¹ "When a person wrongs a neighbor and is required to take an oath and comes and swears the oath before your altar in this Temple, ³² hear from heaven and act. Judge between your servants, condemning the guilty and bringing their conduct down on their own heads. Declare the innocent not guilty, and so establish their innocence.

³³ "When your people Israel are defeated by the enemy because they sinned against you, if they return to you and praise your Name, and pray to you and entreat you in this Temple, ³⁴ hear from heaven and forgive the sin of your people Israel and bring them back to the land you gave to their ancestors.

³⁵ "When the heavens are shut up and there is no rain because your people sinned against you, and when they pray in this place and praise your Name and, humbled by you, repent of their sin, ³⁶ then hear from heaven and forgive the sin of your faithful ones, your people Israel. Teach them the right way to live, and send rain on the land you gave your people for an inheritance.

³⁷ "When famine or plague comes to the land, or blight or mildew, locusts or grasshoppers, or when an enemy besieges one of their cities, whatever disaster or disease may come, ³⁸ and when a prayer or a plea is made by any of your people Israel—all of them feeling remorse in their hearts and spreading their hands toward this Temple— ³⁹ hear them from heaven, your dwelling

place. Forgive and respond, dealing with each as their conduct deserves; for you alone know every heart. [40] In this way the people will revere you throughout their lives in the land you gave to our ancestors.

[41] "And the foreigners as well, those who do not belong to your people Israel, if they come from a distant country for the sake of your Name— [42] for they will hear of your Name, of your mighty hand and outstretched arm—if they come and worship in this Temple, [43] then hear from heaven where your home is, and do whatever the foreigners ask of you, so that all the peoples of the earth may know your Name and revere you, as do your people Israel, and may know that this house I built bears your Name.

[44] "When your people go to war against your enemies, wherever you send them, and when they pray to YHWH towards the city you built for your Name, [45] hear their prayer from heaven and hear their plea, upholding their cause.

[46] "Should they sin against you (and who is free from sin?), and you in your anger give them over to an enemy, and their conquerors carry them off to their own land, far or near; [47] and if they have a change of heart in the land of their captivity, and entreat you, saying, 'We are depraved sinners, we have acted wickedly,' [48] and if they turn back to you with all their hearts and souls in the land of your enemies who took them captive, and pray to you toward the land you gave our ancestors, towards the city you chose and the Temple I built for your Name; [49] then from heaven, your dwelling place, hear our prayers and our plea, and uphold our cause. [50] And forgive your people who sinned against you; forgive all the offenses they committed against you, and cause their conquerors to be merciful. [51] For they are your people and your inheritance, whom you brought out of Egypt, out of that smelting furnace.

[52] "May your eyes be open to your attendant's pleas and to the plea of your people Israel, and may you listen to them whenever they cry out to you! [53] For you singled them out from all the nations of the world to be your own inheritance, just as you declared through your attendants Moses when you, Sovereign YHWH, brought our ancestors out of Egypt."

[54] When Solomon finished all these prayers and supplications to God, he rose from before the altar of God, where he had been kneeling with hands spread out to heaven. [55] He stood up and blessed the whole assembly of Israel in a loud voice, saying, [56] "Praised be YHWH, who gave rest to the people of Israel, as promised. Of all the gracious promises that God made through Moses, not one has failed. [57] May YHWH our God be with us, as God has been with our ancestors; may God never desert us or cast us off. [58] May God turn our hearts inward so that we may follow faithfully and keep the commandants, the laws and ordinances given to our ancestors.

⁵⁹ May my words that I prayed before YHWH be near YHWH our God day and night, that they may uphold the cause of this servant and the cause of the people Israel according to each day's need, ⁶⁰ so that all the peoples of the earth may know that YHWH is God and that there is no other. ⁶¹ Make your hearts fully committed to YHWH, to live by God's decrees and obey God's commands, as you do this day."

⁶² Then the ruler and all Israel offered sacrifices before God. ⁶³ Solomon offered a sacrifice of fellowship offerings to God: 22,000 cattle and 120,000 sheep and goats. In this way the ruler and all the people of Israel dedicated the Temple of YHWH. ⁶⁴ On that same day, the ruler consecrated the middle part of the courtyard in front of the Temple of YHWH, and there offered burnt offerings, grain offerings, and the fat of the fellowship offerings, because the bronze altar before YHWH was too small to hold the burnt offerings, the grain offerings, and the fat of the fellowship offerings.

⁶⁵ So Solomon observed the festival at that time, and all Israel as well—a vast assembly, people from the entrance to Hamath to the Wadi of Egypt. For seven days and seven days more, fourteen days in all, they celebrated the feast before YHWH our God. ⁶⁶ On the fifteenth day, Solomon sent the people away. They blessed Solomon and headed for home, joyful and glad in heart for all the good things that YHWH had done for David and the people of Israel.

ଦ୍ର   ଦ୍ର   ଦ୍ର

9:1 When Solomon finished building the Temple of YHWH and the royal residence, achieving all his construction plans, ² YHWH appeared to him a second time as at Gibeon. ³ YHWH said to Solomon:

"I heard the prayers and pleas you made to me; I have consecrated this Temple you built, by putting my Name there forever. My eyes and my heart will always be there.

⁴ "As for you, if you walk before me in integrity of heart and uprightness, just as David did, and do all I command and observe my decrees and laws, ⁵ I will establish your royal judgment seat over Israel forever, as I promised David when I said, 'You will never fail to have a successor on the judgment seat of Israel.'

⁶ "But if you or your descendants turn away from me and do not observe the commands and decrees I gave you, and go off to serve other gods and worship them, ⁷ then I will cut off Israel from the land I gave them, and I will reject this Temple I consecrated for my Name. Israel will then become a byword and an object of ridicule among all peoples. ⁸ And though this Temple is now exalted, all who pass by will be appalled and scoff, saying,

'Why has YHWH done such a thing to this land and to this Temple?' ⁹ They will be told, 'Because they deserted YHWH, who brought their ancestors out of Egypt, and they embraced other gods, worshipping and serving them—that is why YHWH brought all this disaster on them.' "

¹⁰ It took twenty years for Solomon to build these two buildings—the Temple of God and the royal residence. When they were done, ¹¹ Solomon gave Hiram, the ruler of Tyre, twenty towns in Galilee because Hiram had supplied Solomon with all the cedar and cypress and gold he wanted. ¹² But when Hiram went from Tyre to see the towns that Solomon had given him, he was not pleased with what he saw. ¹³ "Just what kind of towns are you giving me here, my brother?" he asked. And he called them the Good-for-Nothing Land, a name they have to this day. ¹⁴ Hiram had sent 400 tons of gold to the ruler.

¹⁵ This is the record of the forced labor that Solomon conscripted to build God's Temple, his own royal residence, the supporting terraces, the wall of Jerusalem, and the towns of Hazor, Megiddo, and Gezer. ¹⁶ Pharaoh, the ruler of Egypt, had previously attacked and captured Gezer, put Gezer to the torch, and killed its Canaanite inhabitants, then gave Gezer as a wedding present to his daughter, one of Solomon's wives. ¹⁷ And Solomon rebuilt Gezer. He also built up Lower Beth-horon, ¹⁸ Ba'alath, the area surrounding Tamar-in-the-desert,* ¹⁹ Solomon's storage cities, and the towns where his chariots and horses were kept. He built whatever he desired to build in Jerusalem, in Lebanon, and throughout all the territory where he ruled.

²⁰ All the non-Israelites left in the land from the Amorite, Hittite, Perizzite, Hivite, and Jebusite peoples— ²¹ that is, all descendants of these peoples whom the Israelites could not annihilate—Solomon conscripted for his forced labor crews, and they continue there to this day. ²² But Solomon did not conscript into forced labor any of the people of Israel; they were his fighting forces, his government officials, his officers, captains, and commanders of the chariots and charioteers, ²³ as well as the chief officials in charge of Solomon's projects—550 officials supervising those who did the work.

²⁴ After Pharaoh's daughter came up from the City of David to the royal residence Solomon had built for her, he constructed the supporting terraces. ²⁵ Three times a year Solomon sacrificed burnt offerings and fellowship offerings on the altar he had built for YHWH, burning incense before YHWH along with them, and so fulfilling the Temple obligations.

²⁶ At Ezion, which is near Elath in Edom on the shore of the Sea of Reeds, Solomon the ruler also built a fleet of ships. ²⁷ And Hiram sent his own at-

---

* A parallel passage in 1 Chronicles substitutes "Tadmor" for "Tamar." Tadmor is the ancient name for the city the Greeks renamed Palmyra. Archaeological evidence, however, suggests that Tadmor was founded in the first or second century B.C.E., not in Solomon's era.

tendants—sailors who knew the sea—to serve in the fleet with Solomon's attendants. [28] They sailed to Ophir and brought back fourteen tons of gold, which they delivered to Solomon the ruler.

[10:1] When the queen of Sheba* learned of Solomon's fame—which was due to the Name of YHWH—she came to test Solomon with hard questions. [2] Arriving at Jerusalem with a huge retinue—camels carrying spices, great stores of gold and precious stones—she came to Solomon and opened her mind freely to the ruler. [3] And Solomon had an answer to all of her queries; not one of her questions was too obscure for the ruler to give her a reply. [4] When the queen of Sheba saw all the wisdom of the Solomon, the royal residence he had built, [5] the food on his table, the organization of his court, the service and attire his attendants, his wine service, and the burnt offerings made at the Temple of YHWH, she was left breathless.

[6] She said to Solomon, "The report I received in my own country about your wisdom and your accomplishments is true. [7] But until I came and saw it with my own eyes I could not believe what they told me; but clearly they told me less than half: for wisdom and prosperity you surpass the report I heard. [8] How happy your people must be! How happy your officials, and happy your courtiers who attend you every day and hear your wisdom! [9] Blessed be YHWH your God who delights in you and who sits you on the judgment seat of Israel! It is all because YHWH loves Israel eternally, and made you ruler to maintain law and justice." [10] Then the queen presented Solomon with four tons of gold, spices in great abundance, and precious stones. Never again did anyone bring such a quantity of spices as the queen of Sheba gave to Solomon.

[11] Besides these gifts from Sheba, Hiram's fleet of ships—which had brought Solomon gold from Ophir—brought him huge cargoes of sandlewood and precious stones from Ophir. [12] Solomon used the wood to make supports† for the Temple of YHWH and for the royal residence, as well as lyres and lutes for the singers. No such quantities of sandlewood have ever been imported or even seen since that time.

[13] All that the queen of Sheba desired and asked for, Solomon gave her; he gave her much more than she had given him. Then she left and returned with her courtiers to her own country.

---

* A sacred Ethiopian text, the *Kebra Negast*, gives the queen of Sheba's name as Makeda; other texts give her name as Bilquees or Bilqis, a name identified with the moon. Sheba (or Saba) was a large and wealthy region that reached from the southern tip of the Arabian Peninsula to ancient Ethiopia in western Africa, and it had a predominantly matriarchal government; Queen Makeda is widely regarded as the founder of the Ethiopian dynasty with Solomon's son Menyelek. Its people worshipped Astarte/Ishtar, the "queen of heaven and mother of all deities," at least until their conversion to the religion of Israel.

† The Hebrew word is obscure, and probably indicates wooden supports or pillars. The parallel passage in 2 Chronicles 9:11 uses a different word which, in context, probably indicates stairs.

¹⁴ Solomon received 23 tons of gold each year, ¹⁵ not including the revenues from merchants and traders, Arabian rulers, and governors of the land.* ¹⁶ Solomon the ruler made 200 large ceremonial shields of hammered gold; nearly four pounds of gold went into each shield. ¹⁷ He also made 300 small shields of hammered gold, with 3¾ pounds of gold going into each one, and he put them in his Lebanon Forest palace. ¹⁸ Then the ruler made a great throne inlaid with ivory and overlaid with fine gold. ¹⁹ Six steps led up to the throne, which had a golden footstool attached to it; it had armrests on either side, with a lion standing beside the arms. ²⁰ Twelve lions stood on the six steps, one on each end of each step. Nothing like it had ever been made for any other realm. ²¹ All the goblets of Solomon the ruler were made of gold, and all the household articles in his Lebanon Forest palace were made of the purest gold. Nothing was made of silver, for silver was considered of little value in Solomon's days. ²² The ruler had a fleet of Tarshish ships† at sea along with Hiram's ships. Once every three years the fleet returned carrying gold, silver, ivory, apes, and peacock tail feathers.‡

²³ Solomon the ruler was greater in riches and wisdom than all the other rulers on the earth. ²⁴ The whole world sought an audience with Solomon to hear the wisdom of God put into his heart. ²⁵ Year after year, everyone who came brought tribute—objects of silver and gold, robes, weapons, spices, and horses and mules.

²⁶ Solomon accumulated chariots and horses. He had 1400 chariots and 12,000 horses, which he allocated between the chariot cities and his own service in Jerusalem. ²⁷ The ruler made silver as common in Jerusalem as stones, and cedar as plentiful as the sycamore-fig trees in the foothills. ²⁸ Solomon's horses were imported from Muzur§ and Kuë; the royal merchants purchased them in Kuë for a fixed price. ²⁹ They imported a chariot from Muzur for 15 pounds of silver, and a horse for 3¾ pounds. They also exported them to all the rulers of the Hittites and of the Arameans.

---

* The cost of Solomon's vast bureaucracy, building projects (especially the palace complex and the Temple), standing army, and enormous harem was great, and Solomon financed it in part through taxes so high that it impoverished his people. In 2004 dollars, with gold valued at $400 per troy ounce, this part of Solomon's yearly income had a value of nearly $300 million.

† Large and powerful ships crafted in Tarshish that were made for use on the trade routes.

‡ A number of modern versions translate the Hebrew word *tukkiyim* as "baboons," but without much linguistic justification; all agree that it is an obscure word. Older versions translate it as "peacocks," which we prefer because the singular form of the word, *tukki*, is a close cognate to a word in the Tamil language, *thokei*, which means "peacock feathers"; the obscurity of *tukkiyim*, we believe, is because it is a foreign word. Tamil was spoken in southern seaports in India during Solomon's era; and we know that Phoenician traders had been bringing peacocks to Egypt from the time of the Pharaohs.

§ The Hebrew text reads "Egypt," but some commentators believe that the Hebrew word for Egypt, *Mizrayim*, is actually a scribal error for Muzur, a region of Cicilia (in modern Turkey), where Kuë, the other trading center mentioned, is also located. The Chinese called the region Ta-Kuë, which is thought to be the derivation of "Turkey."

11:1 Solomon the ruler loved many foreign women besides the Pharaoh's daughter—Moabites, Ammonites, Edomites, Sidonians, and Hittites. 2 They represented the nations about which YHWH said, "You are not to intermarry with them, because they will entice you to serve their gods." But Solomon was devoted to them, and loved them dearly. 3 The ruler had 700 wives of royal birth and 300 concubines; they turned Solomon's heart and head. 4 As Solomon aged, his wives led him astray and his heart was not as fully loyal to YHWH God as the heart of David had been.

5 Solomon became a follower of Ashtoreth, the goddess of the Sidonians, and of Milcom, the detestable god of the Ammonites.* 6 Solomon's deeds displeased YHWH, and he followed God only halfheartedly, while David had wholeheartedly worshiped God. 7 On a hill east of Jerusalem, Solomon built a shrine for Kemosh, the detestable god of Moab, and one for Milcom, the detestable god of the Ammonites.† 8 The ruler did the same for all of his foreign wives, offering burnt offerings and sacrificing to their gods.

9 YHWH was angry with Solomon for turning his heart away from the God of Israel, who had appeared to him twice. 10 In spite of the command forbidding him to follow other gods, Solomon disobeyed YHWH's order. 11 So YHWH said to Solomon, "Since this is your attitude, since you do not keep my covenant and my statutes, I will most certainly tear the realm away from you and give it to one of our your subordinates. 12 Nevertheless, for the sake of David, I will not do it during your lifetime. I will tear it out of the hand of your successor. 13 And I will not tear your whole realm from your successor, but will leave one tribe to your son, for the sake of my servant David and for the sake of Jerusalem, my chosen city."

14 Then God raised up against Solomon an adversary, Hadad the Edomite,‡ from the royal line of Edom.

15 A number of years earlier, after David crushed Edom, Joab, the commander of David's army, went up to bury the dead. 16 Joab and the entire Israelite army remained there for six months, until they eliminated every male in Edom. 17 But Hadad, then only a boy, escaped and fled to Egypt with some Edomite officials who were courtiers of his parents. 18 They set

---

* Ashtoreth is the Phoenician goddess Astarte, and Milcom is likely the fire god Molech; other parts of Palestine knew him as Ba'al, who was Astarte's consort. It is likely that Solomon's motives were political, that he started following other gods for the sake of dynastic alliances with surrounding nations.

† Kemosh is the Mesopotamian god Shamash, Ishtar's consort, thus another aspect of Ba'al. Note that Ba'al—which means "master" or "lord"—is both the proper name of the god of the Canaanites, and the name of any local deity inhabiting a specific place, which is why the Hebrew scriptures call them, "the ba'alim."

‡ This is great irony on God's part. Hadad is also one of the names of the god to whom Solomon is setting up all these shrines; and Edom is another name for Esau, Jacob/Israel's brother who had sworn vengeance upon him for being duplicitous.

out from Midian and passed through Paran, where they strengthened their numbers, then went to Egypt, where the Pharaoh, the ruler of Egypt, gave Hadad a house and land and provided him with food. ¹⁹ Hadad found great favor with Pharaoh, who arranged a marriage between Hadad and his sister-in-law, Queen Tahpenes. ²⁰ Together they had a son, Genubath. Tahpenes weaned the child in Pharaoh's royal residence, living there with the ruler's children.

²¹ When Hadad learned that David rested with his ancestors and that Joab the commander of the army was also dead, he went to Pharaoh with a request: "Let me return to my own country."

²² "What is that you find wanting in my country?" asked Pharaoh,

"Nothing," Hadad replied, "but please let me go."

²³ Meanwhile, God raised up another adversary against Solomon, Rezon ben-Eliada, who had fled from his ruler, Hadadezer of Zobah, ²⁴ while David was destroying Zobah's forces. Rezon gathered followers and became the leader of a band of rebels; they settled in Damascus, where Rezon eventually became ruler. ²⁵ As long as Solomon lived, Rezon was Israel's enemy, adding to the trouble caused by Hadad; he rejected the authority of Israel, and reigned over Aram.

²⁶ Jeroboam ben-Nebat, one of Solomon's courtiers—an Ephraimite from Zeredah whose widowed mother was named Zeredah—also rebelled against Solomon. ²⁷ This is the account of his rebellion:

Solomon was building the supporting terraces and filling in the gap in the wall of the City of David. ²⁸ Now Jeroboam was a person of many skills, and Solomon noticed the quality of his work and put him in charge of all the forced laborer of the house of Joseph.

²⁹ One day as Jeroboam was leaving Jerusalem, the prophet Ahijah from Shiloh met him on the road. The prophet was wearing a new robe; the two of them were in open country by themselves. ³⁰ Ahijah took the new robe he was wearing and tore it into twelve strips, ³¹ saying, "Take ten strips for yourself, for this is what YHWH, the God of Israel says, 'Take notice, I am about to tear the realm out of Solomon's hand and give you ten tribes. ³² But for the sake of David and the city of Jerusalem, which I chose out of all the tribes of Israel, Solomon will have one tribe. ³³ I am doing this because he abandoned me and worshiped Ashtoreth, the goddess of the Sidonians, Chemosh, the god of the Moabites, and Molech, the god of the Ammonites—because he has not walked in my ways or done what is right in my eyes, or kept my statutes and laws as David did.

³⁴ " 'But I will not take the whole realm out of Solomon's hands. I made him ruler all the days of his life for the sake of David my servant, whom I chose, who observed my commands and statutes. ³⁵ I will take the realm from his

son's hands and give you ten tribes. ³⁶ I will give one tribe to his son so that David my servant may always have a lamp before me in Jerusalem, the city where I chose to put my Name. ³⁷ But as for you, I will take you, and you will rule all that your heart desires; you will be ruler over Israel. ³⁸ If you do whatever I command you and walk in my ways and do what is right in my eyes by keeping my statutes and commands, as David my servant did, I will be with you. I will build a dynasty as enduring as the one I built for David, and will give Israel to you. ³⁹ Because of this I will humble David's descendants, but not forever.' "

⁴⁰ Solomon tried to murder Jeroboam, but Jeroboam fled to Egypt, to Shishak the ruler, and remained there until Solomon died.

⁴¹ As for the other events of Solomon's reign—all he did and the wisdom he displayed—are they not written in the book, *The Annals of Solomon?** ⁴² Solomon reigned in Jerusalem over all Israel for forty years. ⁴³ Then he rested with his ancestors and was buried in the City of David his father.

Solomon's son Rehoboam succeeded him as ruler.

12:1–16:34

Rehoboam went to Shechem,† for all the people of Israel had gone there to crown him ruler.

² Jeroboam ben-Nebat heard the news while he was still in Egypt, where he had lived ever since he fled from Solomon. ³ The people sent for Jeroboam, and he and the whole assembly of Israel went to Rehoboam and said to him, ⁴ "Your father put a heavy yoke on us, but now lighten the harsh labor and the heavy yoke he put on us, and we will serve you."

⁵ "Give me three days," he replied, "and then come back." And the people went away.

---

* This book did not survive the ancient era.

† Ever since Joshua's conquest of Canaan, Shechem had been an important religious center, one that included traditions for both the Israelite and Canaanite members of the population. It was situated between Mounts Gerizim and Ebal, where the Levites had been enjoined to recite their blessings; Joshua drew up the Mosaic statutes there, and there set up a stone as a monument to God under an oak tree; and just before his death, Joshua assembled the elders of Israel at Shechem, giving them his final exhortations. Shechem stood the test of time, and when the nation of Israel divided, it became the capital of the northern tribes (which was called Israel until the Exile, and later Samaria; the southern realm was called Judah). After the Exile, Shechem became the religious capital of the Samaritans.

⁶ Then Rehoboam consulted the elders who had served Solomon during his lifetime. "What advice would you give me to say to these people?" he asked.

⁷ The elders replied, "If today you are willing to serve these people, show yourself to be their servant now by speaking with kindness and granting their petition, and they will always follow you."

⁸ But Rehoboam rejected the advice of the elders and turned to a group of young friends with whom he had grown up. ⁹ "What is your advice?" he asked them. "How should I reply to these people who are telling me, 'Lighten the yoke your father put on us'?"

¹⁰ His friends replied, "Tell these people—who said, 'Your father put a heavy yoke on us, but make our yoke lighter'—tell them, 'You think my father was well-endowed? Why, my little finger is thicker!* ¹¹You think my father laid a heavy yoke on you? I'll make it even heavier! Solomon scourged you with whips? I'll scourge you with scorpions!' "

¹² Three days later Jeroboam and all the people came to Rehoboam on the third day, as the ruler had ordered. ¹³ Rehoboam gave them a harsh answer, rejecting his elders' advice, ¹⁴ and spoke to the people as his friends had recommended: "Solomon made your yoke heavy? I'll make it even heavier! Solomon scourged you with whips? I'll scourge with scorpions!" ¹⁵ So the ruler did not listen to the people, for this turn of events was from YHWH, to fulfill the words spoken to Jeroboam ben-Nebat through Ahijah of Shiloh.

¹⁶ When all the people of Israel saw that Rehoboam refused to listen to them, this was their reply:

"What share do we have in David?
No heritage in the son of Jesse!
Back to our own tents, Israel!
Look after your own house, David!"†

So the people of Israel went home—"back to their own tents." ¹⁷ Rehoboam ruled only over the people of Israel who lived in the cities and towns of Judah.

¹⁸ Rehoboam the ruler sent out Adoniram, who was in charge of the forced labor, but all the people of Israel stoned him to death. Rehoboam, however,

---

* As with the modern idiom, boasting about the size of one's sexual equipment was a metaphor for power over others—in this case, it represented the brazen refusal to redress the people's grievances or reduce the enormous tax burden.

† This echoes, almost word for word, a call to rebellion from David's era (2 Samuel 20:1). In the Hebrew text in that passage, however, the phrase is marked as a scribal correction (a *tiqqun sopherim*), an instance in which the scribes changed the text because they thought it sounded irreverent in some way; the original likely read, "Back to our own gods!"—which is the rendering if two letters were reversed. Here the people are rejecting the authority of the Davidic lineage, and disavowing any familial relationship.

managed to get into his chariot and escape to Jerusalem. [19] From that day to this Israel was in open rebellion against the house of David.

[20] When all the people of Israel learned that Jeroboam had returned, they called him to an assembly and made him ruler of all Israel. Only the tribe of Judah remained loyal to the house of David.

[21] When Rehoboam arrived in Jerusalem he mustered all the house of Judah and the tribe of Benjamin—180,000 seasoned warriors—to fight against the house of Israel, to restore the realm to Rehoboam ben-Solomon. [22] However, YHWH spoke to Shemaiah, a man of God, and told him, [23] "Say to Rehoboam ben-Solomon, ruler of Judah, and to the whole house of Judah and Benjamin, and to all the rest of the people, [24] 'This is what YHWH says: Do not go up to fight against your own people, the people of Israel. Go home, every one of you, for this is my doing!' " So they obeyed the word of YHWH and went home again, as God ordered.

[25] Then Jeroboam fortified Shechem in the hill country of Ephraim and lived there. From there he went out and built up Peniel.

[26] Jeroboam thought to himself, "As things stand now, the realm will revert to the house of David. [27] If these people go up to offer sacrifices at the Temple of YHWH in Jerusalem, they will again give their allegiance to their sovereign, Reheboam ruler of Judah." [28] After seeking counsel, the ruler made two golden calves,* saying to the people, "It is too much for you to go up to Jerusalem. Here are your gods, Israel, who brought you out of Egypt!"

---

* In setting up golden calves to revere, Jeroboam is following Aaron's example (Exodus 32); again we see that when the people of Israel turn away from "established religion," as it were, the calf is their first choice. While it seems nearly inconceivable that devout people would so quickly resort to what seems to us like the grossest form of idolatry and superstition, the connection is actually rather intuitive. The people of Israel are descended from a semitic group of nomads who had migrated to Canaan from Sumer (that is, from Ur, Abram's land of birth), and so the religions of those regions were deeply embedded in the consciousness of the people. For many ancient Middle Eastern peoples, bulls were symbols of strength (note the horns on the corners of Israel's sacrificial altar); cows were symbols of fertility and life (and associated with another symbol of the divine feminine, the full moon); and calves represented the manifestation of that divinity—strength and life ever-present, "God-with-us." In Canaanite mythology, the god Ba'al Hadad appeared in a storm cloud, and his clouds were called "Hadad's Calves"; this was, of course, the very form in which YHWH appeared on Mt. Sinai. And note that in verse 32 of this chapter, Jeroboam establishes the fifteenth day of the month—the day of the full moon—as a feast day; in Sumerian belief, the full moon was called Nanna, after a god who was also represented by a young calf. Archaeologists have unearthed a potsherd from Samaria that is inscribed "the bull calf of Yah," and the Sumerian god El (plural *Elohim*) was also represented by a bull. Ba'al Hadad, then, is the mighty "bull of heaven," and his consort Anat, "the Queen of Heaven," gives birth to a bull calf who appears as a storm cloud filled with thunder and lightning. It is a very short jump, then, to the worship of the representation of that calf, since it was, to these people, a palpable and enduring manifestation of God—and even, more specifically, the manifestation of YHWH. Indeed, the Catholic Encyclopedia affirms this conclusion: "It seems... probable that [the calves] were intended as symbols of Yahweh, for, thus considered, they would be more effective in attracting the pious Israelites who were accustomed to go to Jerusalem."

²⁹ One was placed in Bethel, and the other in Dan. ³⁰ This act caused the people to sin; they went even as far as Dan to worship the golden calf there.

³¹ Jeroboam built shrines on high places and appointed priests from all sorts of people, not just Levites. ³² Jeroboam instituted a festival for the fifteenth day of the eighth month, like the festival held in Judah, and offered sacrifices on the altar. This he did in Bethel, sacrificing to the golden calves. And at Bethel he also installed priests at the high places he built. ³³ On the fifteenth day of the eighth month, a month of his own choosing, he offered sacrifices on the altar he had built at Bethel. So he instituted the festival for the people of Israel and went up to the altar to make offerings.

13:1 A man of God from Judah, moved by the word of YHWH, came to Bethel, and as Jeroboam stood by the altar to offer the sacrifice, ² by YHWH's command the man of God cried out against the altar, "Altar! Altar! This is what YHWH says, 'An heir named Josiah will be born to the house of David. On you, Josiah will sacrifice the priests of the high places who now make offerings here, and human bones will be burned on you!' " ³ That same day the man of God gave them a sign. He said, "This is the sign YHWH has declared: this altar will be split apart, and the ashes on it will be scattered."

⁴ When Jeroboam heard what the man of God had cried out against the altar at Bethel, he stretched out his hand from the altar and cried, "Seize him!" But the hand he extended toward the man of God shriveled up, so that he could not pull it back. ⁵ And immediately the altar split apart and its ashes were strewn about, which was the sign the man of God had given by the word of YHWH.

⁶ Then the ruler said to the man of God, "Intercede with YHWH your God and pray for me that my hand may be restored." The man of God entreated YHWH's favor, and the ruler's hand was restored, and became as it was before.

⁷ The ruler said to the man of God, "Come home with me and have something to eat, and I will give you a reward."

⁸ But the man of God replied to the ruler, "Even if you were to give me half your possessions, I would not go with you. I will not eat bread or drink water here. ⁹ For I was commanded by the word of YHWH, "You must not eat bread or drink water, and you must not return home by the way you came.' " ¹⁰ So the man of God took another road and did not return by the way he had come to Bethel.*

¹¹ Now there was a certain old prophet living in Bethel, and his children came and told him what the man of God had done there that day. They also

---

* The implication is that Jeroboam, suspicious of this prophet from the southern realm, would have had him killed either through poisoning or by a "mishap" on the road home.

told the old prophet what he had said to the ruler. ¹² The father asked them, "Which way did he go?" And they showed him which road the man of God from Judah had traveled.

¹³ So he said to his children, "Saddle the donkey for me." And when the donkey was saddled, the old prophet mounted it ¹⁴ and rode after the man of God. He found him sitting under an oak tree and asked, "Are you the holy man of God who came from Judah?"

"I am," he replied.

¹⁵ And the prophet said, "Come home with me and eat."

¹⁶ The man of God said, "I cannot turn back and go with you, nor can I eat bread or drink water with you in this place. ¹⁷ I have been told by the word of God, 'You must not eat bread or drink water there or return by the way you came.' "

¹⁸ The old prophet said, "I too am a prophet, as you are. And an angel spoke to me by the word of YHWH, and said, "Bring him back with you to your house so that he may eat bread and drink water.' " But this was a lie. ¹⁹ So the man of God returned with him and ate and drank in the old prophet's house.

²⁰ While they were sitting at the table, the word of God came to the elderly prophet who had brought him back. ²¹ He cried out to the man of God from Judah, "This is what YHWH says, 'You have defied the word of YHWH and have not kept the command that YHWH your God gave you. ²² You came back and ate bread and drank water in the place where God had told you not to eat or drink. Therefore your body will not be buried in the tomb of your ancestors.' "

²³ When the man of God had finished eating and drinking, the prophet who had brought him back saddled his donkey for him. ²⁴ As he went on his way, a lion met him on the road and killed him. His corpse lay sprawled in the road; the donkey remained there by the body, but so did the lion. ²⁵ Some people who passed by saw the body lying in the road, with the lion standing beside the body, and they reported it in the city where the old prophet lived.

²⁶ When the prophet who had brought the man of God back from his journey heard of it, he said, "It is the man of God who defied the word of God. YHWH gave him over to the lion, which mauled and killed him, as the word of YHWH had warned him."

²⁷ The prophet said to his children, "Saddle the donkey for me," and they did so. ²⁸ Then he went out and found the body thrown down on the road, with the donkey and the lion standing beside it. The lion had neither eaten the body nor mauled the donkey. ²⁹ So the prophet picked up the body of the

man of God, laid it on the donkey, and brought it back to his own city to mourn him and bury him. ³⁰ Then he laid the body in his own tomb, and the people mourned over him and said, "Oh, my brother!"

³¹ After the burial, the old prophet said to his children, "When I die, bury me in the grave where the man of God is buried; lay my bones beside his bones. ³² For the messages he declared by the word of YHWH against the altar in Bethel and against all the shrines on the high places in the towns of Samaria will certainly come true."

³³ Even after this, Jeroboam did not change his evil ways, but once more appointed priests for the high places from all sorts of people. Anyone who wanted to become a priest he consecrated for ministry at the shrines. ³⁴ This was the sin of the house of Jeroboam that led to its downfall and to its eradication from the face of the earth.

14:1 At that time Abijah, Jeroboam's son, fell ill, ² and Jeroboam said to his wife, "Go, disguise yourself, so that you won't be recognized as my wife. Then go to Shiloh. The prophet Ahijah it there—the one who told me I would be ruler over the people. ³ Take ten loaves of bread with you, some cakes, and a jar of honey, and give them to him. He will tell you what will happen to the boy." ⁴ So Jeroboam's wife did as he said, and went to Ahihah's house in Shiloh.

Now, Ahijah was blind—age had taken his sight. ⁵ But YHWH told Ahijah, "Jeroboam's wife is coming to ask you about her son, for he is ill, and you are to give her such and such an answer. When she arrives, she will be disguised."

⁶ So when Ahijah heard the sound of her footsteps at the door, he said, "Enter, wife of Jeroboam! Why this pretense? I have been sent to you with bad news. ⁷ Go, tell Jeroboam that this is what YHWH, the God of Israel, says: "I raised you up from among the people and made you a leader over my people Israel. ⁸ I tore the realm away from the house the house of David and gave it to you, but you have not been like my servant David, who kept my commands and followed me wholeheartedly, doing only what was right in my eyes. ⁹ You have done more evil than all who lived before you. You have made for yourself other gods, idols made of metal; you have provoked me to anger and thrust me behind your back.

¹⁰ " 'Because of this, I will bring disaster on the house of Jeroboam. I will cut off from Jeroboam every last heir—slave or free—throughout Israel. I will burn down the house of Jeroboam as dung is burned, until it is all gone. ¹¹ Dogs will eat the heirs of Jeroboam who die in the city, and the birds of the air will feed on those who die in the country. YHWH has spoken!'

¹² "As for you, go home. When you set foot in your city, the boy will die. ¹³ All Israel will mourn for him and bury him. He is the only one of Jeroboam's heirs who will be buried, because he is the only one in the house of Jeroboam in whom YHWH, the God of Israel, has found anything good.

¹⁴ "YHWH will raise up a ruler over Israel who will cut off Jeroboam's family. This is the day! What? Yes, even now. ¹⁵ And YHWH will strike Israel, so that it will be a reed swaying in the water. God will uproot Israel from this good land given to its ancestors and scatter the people beyond the River, for they provoked YHWH to anger when the set up the Asherah poles. ¹⁶ And for the sins that Jeroboam committed and caused Israel to commit, God will abandon Israel."

¹⁷ Then Jeroboam's wife got up and went to Tirzah. As soon as she stepped over the threshold of the palace, the boy died. ¹⁸ They buried the lad, and all Israel mourned, as YHWH had said through the prophet Ahijah. ¹⁹ The other events of Jeroboam' reign—the wars, how he ruled—are written in the book of *The Annals of the Rulers of Israel.* ²⁰ Jeroboam reigned for twenty-two years and then rested with his ancestors. And Nabab succeeded Jeroboam as ruler.

²¹ Rehoboam ben-Solomon ruled in Judah. He was forty-one when crowned, and reigned for seventeen years in Jerusalem, the city that YHWH chose out of all the tribes of Israel in which to put God's Name. Rehoboam's mother, an Ammonite, was named Naamah.

²² Judah was corrupt in the eyes of YHWH. The sins its people committed stirred up God's jealous anger; it was beyond anything their ancestors had done. ²³ They erected shrines, sacred pillars, and Asherah poles on every high hill and under every spreading tree. ²⁴ Even worse, throughout the country, male cult prostitutes were attached to the shrines, and the people adopted the abominable practices of the nations that YHWH had dispossessed in favor of Israel.

²⁵ In the fifth year of Rehoboam's reign, Shishak, the ruler of Egypt, attacked Jerusalem, ²⁶ and carried away the treasures of the Temple of God and the treasures of the royal residence. The invaders took everything, including the gold shields Solomon had commissioned. ²⁷ So Rehoboam made bronze shields to replace them and entrusted them to the officers of the escort who guarded the entrance to the Temple. ²⁸ Whenever the ruler entered the Temple, the escort carried the shields. Afterwards they were returned to the guardroom. ²⁹ The other activities and events of Rehoboam's reign are recorded in *The Annals of the Rulers of Judah.*

³⁰ There was constant warfare between Rehoboam and Jeroboam. When Rehoboam rested with his ancestors, he was buried with them in the

City of David. His mother was Naamah the Ammonite. And his son Abijah succeeded him as ruler.

15:1 In the eighteenth year of the reign of Jeroboam ben-Nebat, Abijam was crowned ruler of Judah, ² and he reigned in Jerusalem for three years. His mother's name was Maacah, and she was the granddaughter of Absalom. ³ Abijam committed all the sins his father Rehoboam had committed before him. His heart was not fully devoted to YHWH God, as the heart of David his ancestor had been. ⁴ But for David's sake, God gave him a lamp to burn in Jerusalem by raising up an heir to succeed him and by making Jerusalem strong. ⁵ For David did what was right in the eyes of YHWH and did not fail to keep any of YHWH's commands all the days of his life—except in the matter of Uriah the Hittite.

⁶ There was constant warfare between Abijam and Jeroboam throughout Abijam's lifetime. ⁷ As for the other events in Abijam's reign and all the works he accomplished, they are written in the book of *The Annals of the Rulers of Judah*. ⁸ When Ahijam rested with his ancestors, he was buried in the City of David. Asa succeeded him as ruler.

⁹ In the twentieth year of Jeroboam ruler of Israel, Asa became ruler over Judah. ¹⁰ He reigned for forty-one years in Jerusalem; his mother's name was Maacah bat-Abishalom.

¹¹ Now, Asa did what was just in the eyes of YHWH, as his ancestor David had done. ¹² He expelled the male cult prostitutes from the land and got rid of all the idols his ancestors had made. ¹³ He even deposed his grandmother Maacah from her position as queen mother, because she had made a repulsive Asherah pole. Asa cut down the pole and burned it in the Kidron Valley. ¹⁴ Although he did not remove the shrines, Asa's heart was fully committed to YHWH all the days of his life. ¹⁵ Into the Temple of YHWH he brought the silver, the gold, and the sacred vessels that his father had dedicated, and more that he himself had dedicated.

¹⁶ There was war between Asa and Baasha ruler of Israel throughout their reigns. ¹⁷ Baasha ruler of Israel mounted an assault on Judah, and established Ramah as a military outpost to prevent anyone from leaving or entering the territory of Asa ruler of Judah.

¹⁸ So Asa took all the silver and gold that was left in the treasuries of YHWH's Temple and of his own royal residence. He entrusted it to his officials and sent them to Ben-Hadad ben-Tabrimmon ben-Hezion, ruler of Aram, who was ruling in Damascus. ¹⁹ "Let there be a treaty between me and you," he said, "as there was between my father and your father. See, I am sending you a gift of silver and gold. Now break your treaty with Baasha ruler of Israel so that he will withdraw from me."

²⁰ Ben-Hadad agreed with Asa the ruler and sent the commanders of his forces against the towns of Israel. He conquered Ijon, Dan, Abel Beth Maacah, and all of Kinnereth, in addition to Naphtali. ²¹ When Baasha heard this, he stopped fortifying Ramah and withdrew to Tirzah. ²² Asa the ruler ordered everyone in Judah—no one was exempt—to carry away from Ramah the stones and timber Baasha had been using there. With them Asa built up Geba in Benjamin, and Mizpah.

²³ As for all the other events of Asa's reign, all his achievements, all he did and the cities he built, are written in the book of *The Annals of the Rulers of Judah*.

In his old age, Asa caught a foot disease, ²⁴ and Asa rested with his ancestors and was buried with them in the City of David. Jehoshaphat succeeded Asa the ruler.

²⁵ In the second year of Asa ruler of Judah, Nadab ben-Jeroboam became ruler of Israel, and he reigned over Israel for two years. ²⁶ He did evil things in the eyes of YHWH, walking in the ways of his father, committing the same sins, and causing Israel to sin as well. ²⁷ Baasha ben-Ahijah of the house of Issachar plotted against him, and struck him down at Gibbethon, a Philistine town, while Nadab and all Israel were besieging it. ²⁸ Baasha killed Nadab in the third year of Asa ruler of Judah and succeeded him as ruler.

²⁹ As soon as he began to reign, he murdered Jeroboam's entire family. He did not leave Jeroboam anyone who breathed, but destroyed them all, according to the word that YHWH had given through his attendant Ahijah the Shilonite, ³⁰ because of the sins Jeroboam had committed and caused Israel to commit, and because he had provoked YHWH, the God of Israel, to anger. ³¹ As for the other events of Nadab's reign, and all he did, they are written in the book of *The Annals of the Rulers of Israel*.

³² There was warfare between Asa and Baasha ruler of Israel throughout their reigns. ³³ In the third year of Asa the ruler of Judah, Baasha ben-Ahijah became ruler of all Israel in Tirzah, and he reigned for twenty-four years. ³⁴ He did evil things in the eyes of YHWH God of Israel, walking in the ways of Jeroboam, committing the same sins, and causing Israel to sin as well.

16:1 Then the word of YHWH came to Jehu ben-Hanani against Baasha: ² "I lifted you up from the dust and made you leader of my people Israel, but you walked in the ways of Jeroboam and caused my people Israel to sin and to provoke me to anger by their sins. ³ So I am about to consume Baasha and his house, and I will make your house like that of Jeroboam ben-Nebat. ⁴ Dogs will eat the heirs of Baasha who die in the city, and the birds of the air will feed on those who die in the country."

⁵ As for the other events of Baasha's reign, what he did and achieved, they are written in *The Annals of the Rulers of Israel.* ⁶ Baasha rested with his ancestors and was buried in Tirzah. And Elah succeeded him as ruler.

⁷ The word of YHWH came through the prophet Jehu ben-Hanani to Baasha and his house, because of all the evil Baasha did in the eyes of YHWH, provoking God to anger by the things he did, and becoming like the house of Jeroboam, and because he killed Nadab.

⁸ In the twenty-sixth year of Asa ruler of Judah, Elah ben-Baasha became ruler of Israel, and he reigned in Tirzah for two years. ⁹ Zimri, one of his officials, commander of half of the chariots, plotted against Elah, who was in Tirzah at the time, getting drunk in the home of Arza, who was in charge of the royal palace of Tirzah. ¹⁰ Zimri came in, struck him down and killed him in the twenty-seventh year of Asa ruler of Judah. Then he succeeded Elah as ruler.

¹¹ As soon as he began to reign and took his seat on the judgment seat, he killed off Baasha's whole family. He did not spare a single male, relative or friend. ¹² So Zimri destroyed the entire family of Baasha, in fulfillment of the word of YHWH spoken against Baasha through the prophet Jehu— ¹³ because of all the sins Baasha and his son Elah had committed and caused Israel to commit, angering YHWH, the God of Israel, with their worthless idols. ¹⁴ As for the other events of Elah's reign, and all he did, they are written in the book of *The Annals of the Rulers of Israel.*

¹⁵ In the twenty-seventh year of Asa ruler of Judah, Zimri reigned in Tirzah for seven days. The army was encamped near Gibbethon, a Philistine town. ¹⁶ When the people of Israel in the camp learned that Zimri had plotted against the ruler and murdered him, that very day they proclaimed Omri, the commander of the army, to be ruler over Israel there in the camp.

¹⁷ Then Omri and all the people of Israel with him withdrew from Gibbethon and laid seize to Tirzah. ¹⁸ When Zimri saw that the city was taken, he went into the citadel of the royal palace and set the place on fire, with himself inside. He died in the fire, ¹⁹ because of his sins he had committed, doing evil in the eyes of YHWH, walking in the ways of Jeroboam, in the sin he had committed and caused Israel to commit.

²⁰ As for other events of Zimri's reign, and the rebellion he carried out, they are written in the book of *The Annals of the Rulers of Israel.*

²¹ Then the people of Israel split into two factions; half supported Tibni ben-Ginath for ruler, and the other half supported Omri. ²² But Omri's followers proved stronger than the followers of Tibni ben-Ginath. So Tibni died and Omri became ruler.

²³ In the thirty-first year of Asa ruler of Judah, Omri became ruler of Israel, and he reigned for twelve years, six of them in Tirzah. ²⁴ He purchased the Hill of Shomeron from its owner, Shemer, for 150 pounds of silver. There he built a city, which he named Samaria, after Shemer, its previous owner.*

²⁵ But Omri did evil things in the eyes of YHWH, and sinned more than all his predecessors. ²⁶ He walked in all the ways of Jeroboam ben-Nebat and in his sin, which he caused Israel to commit, so that the people angered YHWH, the God of Israel, with their worthless idols.

²⁷ As for the other events of Omri's reign, what he did and the things he achieved, they are written in the book of *The Annals of the Rulers of Israel*. ²⁸ Omri rested with his ancestors and was buried in Samaria. And Ahab succeeded him as ruler.

²⁹ In the thirty-eighth year of Asa ruler of Judah, Ahab ben-Omri became ruler of Israel, and he reigned in Samaria over Israel for twenty-two years. ³⁰ Ahab ben-Omri did more evil in the eyes of YHWH, the God of Israel, than any of his predecessors. ³¹ He not only considered it trivial to commit the sins of Jeroboam ben-Nebat, but he also married Jezebel, daughter of EthBa'al ruler of the Sidonians, and began to serve and worship Ba'al. ³² He set up an altar for Ba'al in the Temple of Ba'al that he built in Samaria. ³³ Ahab also made an Asherah pole and did more to enrage YHWH, the God of Israel, than all the rulers of Israel before him.

³⁴ In Ahab's time, Hiel of Bethel rebuilt Jericho. He laid its foundations—but at the cost of the life of his firstborn, Abiram; and he set up the gates—but at the cost of the life of his youngest son, Segub. This was in fulfillment of the word of YHWH spoken by Joshua ben-Nun.

17:1–22:53

*N*ow, Elijah the Tishbite, from Tishbe in Gilead, said to Ahab, "As YHWH lives, the God of Israel whom I serve—there will be neither dew or rain in the next few years unless I give the word!"†

---

* The "Hill of Shomeron" stands a few miles northwest of Shechem, and the city of Samaria that Omri built on its summit is only about thirty-five miles north of Jerusalem. After the Exile, the entire northern region would be called Samaria, and Shechem remained the Samaritans' religious center well into the Common Era.

† Ba'al was the god who controlled agricultural fertility by providing rain; Elijah declared a drought on the country to prove to the people that only YHWH can send life-giving rain.

² Then the word of YHWH came to Elijah and said, ³ "Leave this place and turn east. Hide yourself near the Kerith Stream, east of the Jordan. ⁴ You will drink from the stream, and I have commanded the ravens there to feed you." ⁵ Elijah did what YHWH commanded; he went to the Kerith Stream, east of the Jordan, and lived there. ⁶ The ravens brought him bread and meat every morning and evening, and he drank from the stream.

⁷ Eventually the stream dried up, for there had been no rain in the land. ⁸ Then the word of God came to him and said, ⁹ "Now go to Zarephath, a village of Sidon, and stay there. I have commanded a widow there to supply you with food." ¹⁰ So he went to Zarephath.

When he arrived at the town gate, a widow was there gathering sticks. He called to her and asked, "Could you bring me a little water in a jar for me to drink?" ¹¹ As she was going to get the water, he called out, "And please bring me a piece of bread."

¹² "As YHWH lives," she replied, "I don't have any bread—only a handful of flour in a jar and a little oil in a jug. I am gathering a couple of sticks to take home and make a meal for myself and my child. We will eat it—and then we will die."

¹³ Elijah said to her, "Don't be afraid! Go home and do what you said. But first make a small cake of bread for me from what you have and bring it to me; and then make something for yourself and for your child. ¹⁴ For this is what YHWH, the God of Israel, says: 'The jar of flour will not be used up and the jug of oil will not run dry until the day YHWH makes it rain on the land.' "

¹⁵ The widow went away and did what Elijah had told her to do. And there was food every day for Elijah and for the woman and her family. ¹⁶ The jar of flour was not used up and the jug of oil did not run dry, in keeping with the word of God spoken by Elijah.

¹⁷ Some time later the woman's child became ill. The child grew worse and finally stopped breathing. ¹⁸ The widow said to Elijah, "What do you have against me, man of God? Did you come to remind me of my sin and kill my child?"

¹⁹ "Give me your child," Elijah said.

He took the child from her arms and carried it to the upper room where he was staying, and laid the child on the bed. ²⁰ Then he cried out to YHWH: "YHWH, why did you bring such a calamity even upon this widow I am staying with, by causing the child to die?" ²¹ Then he stretched out over the child three times and called out to YHWH, "I pray, YHWH my God, let the breath of life return to the body of this child." ²² YHWH listened to Elijah's plea, and the breath of life returned to the child's body, and it revived.

²³ Elijah lifted up the child and took it down to its mother, saying, "See, your child lives!"

²⁴ The widow said to Elijah, "Now I know for certain that you are a man of God and that the word of YHWH is truly on your lips."

¹⁸·¹ Much later, in the third year of the famine, the word of God came to Elijah and said, "Go and present yourself to Ahab, and I will send rain on the land." ² So Elijah went and presented himself to Ahab.

Now, the famine in Samaria was severe, ³ and Ahab summoned Obadiah,* who was in charge of the royal residence. Obadiah revered YHWH greatly. ⁴ When Jezebel was killing the prophets of YHWH, Obadiah had taken a hundred of them and hid them in two caves, fifty prophets in each cave, and provided them with food and drink. ⁵ Now Ahab said to Obadiah, "Go through the land and search for springs and valleys. Perhaps we can find enough grass to keep the horses and mules alive so that we will not have destroy our animals." ⁶ So they divided the land they were to cover, with Ahab going in one direction and Obadiah going in another.

⁷ As Obadiah walked along, Elijah met up with him. Obadiah, recognizing the prophet, bowed down to the ground and said, "It is really you, Elijah?"

⁸ "Yes," he replied. "Go tell Ahab, 'Elijah is here.' "

⁹ "What have I done wrong," asked Obadiah, "that you are handing your servant over to Ahab to be put to death? ¹⁰ As YHWH lives, there is not a nation or realm to which Ahab has not sent someone to look for you. And whenever a nation or realm claimed you were not there, he made them swear they could not find you. ¹¹ But now you tell me to go to Ahab and say, 'Elijah is here'? ¹² As soon as I leave you, the spirit of YHWH will carry you off to who-knows-where. So I'll go and tell Ahab, and when he fails to find you, he will murder me. Yet I, your servant, have been a devout worshipper of YHWH from boyhood. ¹³ Have you not been told what I did when Jezebel put YHWH's prophets to death, how I hid a hundred of them in caves, fifty in one cave and fifty in another, and kept them alive with food and drink? ¹⁴ And now you say, 'Go and tell Ahab that Elijah is here'! He'll kill me!"

¹⁵ Elijah said, "As YHWH Omnipotent lives, whom I serve, I will surely present myself to Ahab today." ¹⁶ So Obadiah went off to find Ahab and gave him the message, and Ahab went to meet with Elijah.

¹⁷ As soon as Ahab saw Elijah, he said to the prophet, "Is it really you—Israel's troublemaker?"

---

* Not Obadiah the prophet. Obadiah, which means "worshiper of YHWH," was a name shared by thirteen different individuals in the Bible.

¹⁸ "It is not I who has brought trouble to Israel," Elijah replied, "but you and your father's family, by abandoning the commandments of YHWH and following Ba'al. ¹⁹ Now summon all Israel to meet me on Mount Carmel,* including the 450 prophets of Ba'al and the 400 prophets of Asherah who eat at Jezebel's table."†

²⁰ So Ahab sent messengers throughout the length and breadth of the Israel and had the prophets assemble on Mount Carmel.

²¹ Elijah stepped forward towards all the people there, saying, "How long will you sit on the fence? If YHWH is God, follow God; but if Ba'al is God, then follow Ba'al."

No one said a word.

²² Then Elijah said, "I am the only prophet of YHWH left, but there are 450 prophets of Ba'al. ²³ Bring two bulls for us. Let them choose one for themselves, cut it up, and lay it on the wood without setting fire to it, and I will prepare the other bull and lay it on the wood without setting fire to it. ²⁴ Then you call on the name of your god, and I will call on the name of YHWH, and the one who answers by fire is God. Agreed?"

All the people shouted their approval.

²⁵ Elijah said to the prophet of Ba'al, "Choose one of the bulls and prepare it first, since there are so many of you. Call on the name of your god, but do not light the fire." ²⁶ So they took the bull given them and prepared it. Then they called on the name of Ba'al from morning until midday. "Answer us, Ba'al!" they shouted. But there was no response; no one answered. And they did a ceremonial dance around the altar they had made.

²⁷ At noon Elijah began to taunt them. "Shout louder!" he said. "Ba'al is a god, isn't he? Maybe he's meditating, or he's off relieving himself, or he's gone on a journey! Maybe he's just asleep and needs you to wake him up!"

²⁸ So they shouted louder and slashed themselves with swords and spears, as was their custom, until they were covered in their own blood. ²⁹ Midday passed, and they continued their frantic prophesying until the time for the evening sacrifice. But there was no response. No one answered, no one paid attention.

³⁰ Then Elijah said to the people, "Come here to me." They came to him, and he repaired the altar of YHWH, which was in ruins. ³¹ Elijah took twelve

---

* Mount Carmel (*Karem El.* or "garden land of God") is a ridge thirteen miles long, with a promontory that juts out into the Mediterranean Sea. The plant life of Mount Carmel was known for its lushness, and the view is panoramic. For prophets and poets alike, Mount Carmel symbolized beauty—and judgment on the beautiful. Amos and Nahum prophesied that God would dry up the vegetation on Mount Carmel as a highly visible judgment on the apostasy of the northern realm.

† This probably means not that they were attached to Jezebel's household, but that they received financial support from her.

stones, one for each of the tribes descended from Jacob, whom YHWH had told, "Your name will be Israel." ³² With these stones he built an altar in the name of YHWH, and he dug a trench around it large enough to hold two measures of seed; ³³ he arranged the wood, cup up the bull, and laid it on the wood.

³⁴ Then he said, "Fill four jars with water and pour it on the whole offering and on the wood." This the people did. Then he said, "Do it again," and they did it again. He said, "Do it a third time." They did it a third time, ³⁵ and the water ran all around the altar and even filled the trench.

³⁶ At the hour of the regular offering, the prophet Elijah came forward and prayed, "YHWH, God of Abraham and Sarah, of Isaac and Rebecca, of Israel and Rachel and Leah, prove today that you are God in Israel and that I am your servant and have done all these things at your command. ³⁷ Answer me, YHWH, answer me and let these people know that you, YHWH, are God, and that it is you who turned their hearts back to you." ³⁸ Then fire from YHWH fell from the heavens, consuming the whole offering, the wood, the stones, and the dirt, and licking up the water in the trench.

³⁹ At this sight, the people fell face down on the ground, crying, "YHWH is God! YHWH is God!"

⁴⁰ Elijah said to them, "Seize the prophets of Ba'al! Let not one of them escape!" They were seized, and Elijah took them down to the Kishon Valley and slaughtered them there.

⁴¹ Elijah said to Ahab, "Go back now, eat and drink, for I hear the sound of a heavy rainstorm coming." ⁴² He did so, while Elijah himself climbed to the crest of Carmel, where he bowed down to the ground and put his face between his knees. ⁴³ He said to his attendant, "Go and look to the west."

The attendant went and looked, then said "There is nothing to see."

Seven times Elijah ordered him back, and seven times he went. ⁴⁴ The seventh time he said, "I see a cloud no bigger than a person's hand, coming up from the west."

"Now go," said Elijah, "and tell Ahab to harness his chariot and be off, or the rain will stop him." ⁴⁵ Meanwhile the sky grew black with clouds, the wind rose, and heavy rains began to fall.

Ahab mounted his chariot and set off for Jezreel. ⁴⁶ And the power of YHWH was upon Elijah; he tucked up his robe and ran ahead of Ahab all the way to Jezreel.

19·1 Now, Ahab told Jezebel everything Elijah had done, and how he had killed all the prophets with the sword. ² So Jezebel sent a messenger to Elijah, saying, "May the gods deal with me, be it ever so severely, if by this time tomorrow I do not make your life like that of one of them!"

³ Full of fear, Elijah fled for his life. When he came to Beersheba in Judah, he left his attendant there, ⁴ while he himself went a day's journey into the desert. He came to a broom tree, sat down under it and prayed that he might die. "I have had enough, YHWH," he said. "Take my life; I am no better than my ancestors." ⁵ Then he lay down under the tree and fell asleep.

Suddenly an angel of YHWH touched him and said, "Get up and eat."

⁶ He looked around, and there near his head was a cake of bread baked over hot coals, and a jar of water. He ate the cake and drank the water and then lay down again.

⁷ The angel of YHWH came back a second time and touched him and said, "Get up and eat, for the journey is too much for you." ⁸ So he got up and ate and drank some more. Strengthened by that food, he traveled for forty days and forty nights until he reached Horeb, the mountain of God. ⁹ There he went into a cave and spent the night.

And the word of YHWH came to him: "What are you doing here, Elijah?"

¹⁰ Elijah replied, "I have been very zealous for YHWH God Omnipotent. The people of Israel have abandoned your covenant, broken down your altars, and put your prophets to death by the sword. I am the only one left, and now they're trying to kill me, too."

¹¹ God said, "Go out and stand on the mountain in the presence of YHWH, for YHWH is about to pass by."

Then a great and powerful wind tore the mountain apart and shattered the rocks by YHWH's power—but YHWH was not in the whirlwind. After the wind there was an earthquake—but YHWH was not in the earthquake. ¹² After the earthquake came a fire—but YHWH was not in the fire. And after the fire came a gentle whisper.* ¹³ When Elijah heard it, he pulled his cloak over his face and went out and stood at the mouth of the cave.

Then a voice said to him, "What are you doing here, Elijah?"

¹⁴ Elijah replied, "I have been very zealous for YHWH God Omnipotent. The people of Israel have abandoned your covenant, broken down your altars, and put your prophets to death by the sword. I am the only one left, and now they're trying to kill me, too."

¹⁵ YHWH told Elijah, "Go back the way you came, to the Desert of Damascus. When you get there, anoint Hazael as ruler of Aram.† ¹⁶ Also anoint Jehu

---

* Other translations: "a still small voice" (KJV), "a soft murmuring sound" (JPS), "a sound of sheer silence" (NRSV); literally "a sound, a thin silence."
† Damascus, the capital of Syria (ancient Aram), is the oldest continually inhabited city in the world. Shortly after Solomon's death, the ruler of Damascus formed a powerful league with other Aramean states. This alliance resulted in many years of conflict between Israel and Damascus. Hazael's anointing had no political effect and did not in itself secure for him the position of ruler, since Syria was a foreign and hostile power; however, it was an indicator to Israel that he was YHWH's choice—and, in years to come, he would be an instrument of God's judgment upon Israel.

ben-Nimshi as ruler over Israel, and anoint Elisha ben-Shaphat, from Abel Meholah, to succeed you as prophet. ¹⁷ Jehu will put to death any who escape the sword of Hazael, and Elisha will put to death any who escape the sword of Jehu. ¹⁸ Yet I reserve 7,000 in Israel—all whose knees have not bowed down to Ba'al and all whose mouths have not kissed his images."

¹⁹ So Elijah went from there and found Elisha ben-Shaphat. He was plowing with twelve yoke of oxen, and he himself was driving the twelfth pair. Elijah went up to him and threw his cloak around him. ²⁰ Elisha immediately left his oxen and ran after Elijah.

"Let me kiss my parents good-bye," he said, "and then I will come with you."

"Go back," Elijah replied. "What have I done to you?"

²¹ So Elisha left him and went back. He took his yoke of oxen and slaughtered them. He burned the plowing equipment to cook the meat and gave it to the people, and they ate. Then he set out to follow Elijah and become his servant.

છ   છ   છ

²⁰·¹ Now Ben-Hadad, ruler of Aram, mustered his entire army. Accompanied by thirty-two rulers, their horses and chariots, he went up and besieged Samaria and attacked it. ² Hadad sent messengers into the city—to Ahab, ruler of Israel—with this message: ³ "This is what Ben-Hadad says: 'Your gold and silver are mine, and the best of your wives and children are mine.' "

⁴ The ruler of Israel replied, "It is just as you say, O Sovereign Ruler, I and all I have are yours."

⁵ The messengers returned again, saying, "This is what Ben-Hadad says, 'I told you that I would be demanding that you hand over your silver and gold, and all of your wives and your children. ⁶ But now I want more. This time tomorrow I will send my officials to search your royal residence and the houses of your officials. They will seize everything you value and carry it away.' "

⁷ The ruler of Israel summoned all the elders of the land, and told them, "You can see for yourselves how this ruler is asking for trouble! He demanded my wives and my children, my silver and my gold, and I did not refuse him. But now...."

⁸ The elders and all the people counseled, "Don't listen to him or agree to his demands."

⁹ So Ahab replied to Ben-Hadad's messengers, "Tell your ruler, 'I will do all you demanded the first time, but I will not comply with this second demand."

¹⁰ Then Ben-Hadad sent another message to Ahab: "May the gods deal with me, be it ever so severely, if enough dust remains in Samaria to give each of my followers a handful!"

¹¹ The ruler of Israel replied, "Tell him, 'A warrior who is still buckling his armor shouldn't boast like someone who is taking it off!' " *

¹² Ben-Hadad heard this message while he and the rulers were drinking in their tents, and he ordered his army, "Prepare to attack!" So they prepared to attack the city.

¹³ Meanwhile a prophet came to Ahab, ruler of Israel, and announced, "This is what YHWH says: 'Do you see their vast army? I will give it into your hands today, and then you will know that I am your God.' "

¹⁴ "But who will do this?" asked Ahab.

The prophet replied, "This is what YHWH says: 'The young officers of the provincial commanders will do it.' "

"And who will begin the assault?" Ahab asked.

The prophet replied, "You will."

¹⁵ So Ahab summoned the 232 young officers of the provincial commanders. Then he assembled the rest of the warriors of Israel, 7,000 in all. ¹⁶ They set out at noon while Ben-Hadad and the thirty-two rulers allied with him were in their tents getting drunk. ¹⁷ The young officers of the provincial commanders went out first.

Now, Ben-Hadad had dispatched scouts, who told him, "Troops are approaching from Samaria."

¹⁸ He replied, "If they have come out for peace, take them alive; if they have come out for war, take them alive."

¹⁹ The young officers of the provincial commanders marched out of the city with the army behind them, ²⁰ and each one struck down an opponent. At that, the Arameans fled, with the people of Israel in pursuit. But Ben-Hadad, ruler of Aram, escaped on horseback with some of his cavalry. ²¹ The ruler of Israel advanced and overpowered the horses and chariots, and inflicted heavy loses on the Arameans.

²² Afterwards, the prophet came to the ruler of Israel and said, "Strengthen your position and see what must be done, because next spring the ruler of Aram will attack again."

²³ Meanwhile, Aram's officials advised their ruler, "Their gods are gods of the hills. That is why they were too strong for us. But if we fight them on the plains, surely we will be stronger than they. ²⁴ Do this: remove all the leaders from their commands and replace them with other officers. ²⁵ You must also

---

* In other words, "Don't count your chickens before they're hatched!" The time for boasting is when one is home safe after a battle—not before the battle has begun.

raise an army like the one you lost—horse for horse and chariot for chariot—so we can fight Israel on the plains. Then surely we will be stronger than they." The ruler agreed with them and acted accordingly.

²⁶ The next spring, Ben-Hadad mustered the Arameans and went up to Aphek to fight against Israel. ²⁷ When the people of Israel were also mustered and given provisions, they marched out to meet the Arameans. The people of Israel camped opposite them like two small flocks of goats, while the Arameans covered the countryside.

²⁸ A man of God came up to the ruler of Israel and said, "This is what YHWH says: 'Because the Arameans think that YHWH is a god of the hills and not a god of the valleys, I will deliver this vast army into your hands, and you will know that I am your God.' "

²⁹ For seven days they camped opposite each other, and on the seventh day the battle was joined. The people of Israel killed 100,000 Aramean foot soldiers in a single day. ³⁰ The rest of them escaped to the city of Aphek, where the wall collapsed on 27,000 of them. And Ben-Hadad fled to the city and hid in an inner room.

³¹ His officials said, "Look, we have heard that the rulers of the people of Israel are merciful. Let us go to the ruler of Israel with sackcloth around our waists and ropes around our heads. Perhaps they will spare your life."

³² Wearing sackcloth around their waists and ropes around their heads, they went to the ruler of the Israel and said, "Your servant Ben-Hadad says, 'Spare my life!' "

The ruler asked, "Is he still alive? He is my brother!"*

³³ The officials took this as a good sign and were quick to pick up his word. "Yes, your brother Ben-Hadad!" they said.

"Go and get him," the ruler said.

When Ben-Hadad came out, Ahab invited him into his chariot. ³⁴ Ben-Hadad said to the ruler, "I will restore the towns that my father took from your father, and you may establish for yourself a trading quarter in Damascus, as my father did in Samaria."

"On these terms," Ahab said, "I will let you go." So he granted Ben-Hadad a treaty and freed him.

³⁵ One of the company of prophets, at YHWH's command, ordered a friend, "Strike me!" —but the friend refused.

³⁶ "Because you did not obey YHWH's order," said the prophet, "when you leave here a lion will attack you." When the friend left, a lion found him and killed him.

---

* Ahab has now defeated Ben-Hadad twice; he apparently believes his luck will not hold out a third time, and now seeks to make Ben-Hadad an ally.

³⁷ The prophet found someone else and said, "Strike me!" So the person struck the prophet and injured him.

³⁸ Then the prophet went and stood by the road waiting for Ahab. He disguised himself with a headband over his eyes. ³⁹ When the ruler passed by, the prophet called out to him, "I was in the thick of battle when a soldier came over to me with a prisoner and said, 'Take charge of this fellow. If by any chance he gets away, your life will be forfeited, or you must pay 75 pounds of silver.' ⁴⁰ While I was busy with one thing or another, the prisoner disappeared."

The ruler of Israel said to him, "You have passed sentence on yourself."

⁴¹ At that the prophet tore the bandages from his eyes, and the ruler saw that he was one of the prophets. ⁴² He said to the ruler, "This is the word of YHWH: 'Because you let Ben-Hadad go when I had given him over to destruction, your life shall be forfeited for his life, your people for his people."

⁴³ The ruler of Israel went home to Samaria sullen and angry.

21:1 Some time afterward, there was an episode concerning a vineyard that belonged to Naboth the Jezreelite. The vineyard was in Jezreel, close to the royal residence of Ahab, ruler of Samaria. ² Ahab said to Naboth, "Let me have your vineyard to use for my vegetable garden, since it is close to my royal residence. In exchange I will give you a better vineyard or, if you prefer, I will pay for the vineyard."

³ But Naboth replied, "God forbid that I should give you the inheritance of my ancestors!"

⁴ So Ahab, sullen and angry, went home because Naboth the Jezreelite had said, "I will not give you the inheritance of my ancestors." He went to bed sulking, refusing to eat.

⁵ His wife Jezebel came into the bedroom and asked, "Why are you so sullen? Why won't you eat?"

⁶ Ahab replied, "I met with Naboth the Jezreelite and said, "Sell me your vineyard, or, if you prefer, I'll give you another vineyard in exchange." He refused, saying, "I will not turn my vineyard over to you."

⁷ Jezebel said, "Is this how you carry on as ruler of Israel? Get up and eat! Stop your moping! I'll get you the vineyard of Naboth the Jezreelite."

⁸ So she wrote letters in Ahab's name, using his seal, and sent them to the elders and officials who lived in Naboth's city. ⁹ She wrote in those letters, "Proclaim a day of fasting, and seat Naboth in a prominent place before the people. ¹⁰ But seat two lowlifes opposite him and have them testify that he cursed both God and the ruler. Then take him out and stone him to death."

¹¹ So the elders and officials who lived in Naboth's city did as Jezebel ordered them in her letters. ¹² They proclaimed a fast and seated Naboth in a prominent place among the people. ¹³ Then the two lowlifes came and sat opposite him and charged him publicly with cursing God and the ruler. Then they took him outside the city and stoned him to death.

¹⁴ They sent word to Jezebel that Naboth had been stoned to death. ¹⁵ As soon as Jezebel heard the news, she told Ahab, "Go now and take possession of Naboth the Jezreelite's vineyard. He is dead." ¹⁶ When Ahab learned that Naboth was dead, he went down to take possession of the vineyard.

¹⁷ Then the word of YHWH came to Elijah the Tishbite: "Go down to meet Ahab, ruler of Israel, ruler of Samaria. He is now in the process of taking possession of Naboth's vineyard. ¹⁹ Say to Ahab, 'This is what YHWH says: You murder, and you dispossess as well?' Tell him, 'This is what YHWH says: In the place where dog's licked up Naboth's blood, dog's will lick up your blood—yes, yours!' "

²⁰ Ahab said to Elijah, "So you've found me at last, old enemy?"

"I found you," Elijah replied, "because you gave yourself over to do what is evil in the eyes of YHWH, ²¹ who says, 'I will bring disaster down upon you. I will consume your descendants and cut off every last male in Israel who is of Ahab's lineage—servant or free. ²² I will make your house like that of Jeroboam ben-Nebat and that of Baasha ben-Ahijah, for you provoked me to anger and caused Israel to sin.' ²³ And concerning Jezebel, YHWH says, 'Dogs will devour her by the wall of Jezreel. ²⁴ Dogs will eat those of the house of Ahab who die in the city, and the birds of the air will feed on those who die in the country. ²⁵ There has never been anyone as duplicitous, as willing to do what was evil in the eyes of YHWH, as you, Ahab—and all at the prompting of Jezebel. ²⁶ You have committed the grossest abominations in going after idols, like the Amorites whom YHWH drove out before Israel.' "

²⁷ When Ahab heard these words, he tore his clothes, put on sackcloth and fasted. He lay down in his sackcloth and went about moaning.

²⁸ The word of YHWH came to Eiljah the Tishbite, "Have you noticed how Ahab has humbled himself before me? Because he has humbled himself, I will not bring disaster in his time, but I will bring it on his house in the days of his successor."

22:1 For three years, there were no wars between the Aramaeans and the people of Israel. ² But in the third year, Jehoshaphat ruler of Judah came to visit the ruler of Israel. ³ Ahab said to his officials, "You know that Ramoth-gilead belongs to us, and yet we do nothing to recover it from the ruler of Aram." ⁴ And he said to Jehoshaphat, "Will you join with me to recover Ramoth-gilead?"

The ruler of Judah replied, "What is mine is yours: myself, my people, my horses. ⁵ But first," Jehoshaphat told the ruler, "let us seek direction from YHWH."

⁶ Ahab, the ruler of Israel, assembled the prophets, about 400 of them, asking, "Shall I attack Ramoth-gilead or not?"

"Go," they replied, "for YHWH will give it into the ruler's hands."

⁷ But Jehoshaphat inquired, "Is there no other prophet of YHWH here through whom we may seek counsel?"

⁸ The ruler of Israel answered Jehoshaphat, "There is still one through whom we can inquire of YHWH—Micaiah ben-Imlah. But I hate him because he never prophesies anything good about me; it is always bad."

"Your majesty should not say such a thing!" countered Jehoshaphat.

⁹ So Ahab called one of his officials and said, "Bring me Micaiah ben-Imlah immediately."

¹⁰ Dressed in their royal robes, the ruler of Israel and Jehoshaphat the ruler of Judah sat on thrones in an open space near the entrance of the gate of Samaria, with all the prophets prophesying before them.

¹¹ Zedekiah ben-Kenaanah held up horns that he had made out of iron, and proclaimed, "This is what YHWH says: 'With these you will gore the Arameans until they are destroyed.' "

¹² All the other prophets were prophesying the same thing before the rulers. "Attack Ramoth-gilead and you will be victorious," they said, "for YHWH will give it into your majesties' hands."

¹³ The messenger sent to summon Micaiah told him, "Without exception, all the other prophets are predicting success for the ruler. Let your word agree with theirs, and speak favorably."

¹⁴ But Micaiah said, "As YHWH lives, I can tell the ruler only what God tells me."

¹⁵ When he arrived at court, the ruler asked him, "Micaiah, shall we declare war against Ramoth-gilead, or should we refrain?"

"Attack and you will be victorious," he replied, "for YHWH will put victory in the ruler's hands." ¹⁶ The ruler said, "How many times must I make you swear to tell me nothing but the truth in the name of YHWH?"

¹⁷ Then Micaiah answered,

"I saw all Israel scattered on the mountains,
    like sheep without a shepherd;
and I heard YHWH say, 'They have no leader;
    let them all go home in peace.' "

¹⁸ The ruler of Israel said to Jehoshaphat, "Didn't I tell you that he never prophesies anything good about me, only bad?"

¹⁹ Michaiah continued, "Listen now to the word of YHWH: I saw YHWH seated on a judgment seat, with all the host of heaven in attendance on the right and on the left. ²⁰ And YHWH said, 'Who will entice Ahab to go up and attack Ramoth-gilead?' They talked among themselves, ²¹ and finally a spirit came forward and stood before YHWH, saying, 'I will entice him.' ²² 'How will you do it?' YHWH asked. 'I will go out and be a lying spirit in the mouth of all the prophets,' was the reply. 'You will be successful in enticing him,' said YHWH. 'Go and do it.'

²³ "So now YHWH had put a lying spirit in the mouths of all these prophets of yours. YHWH has decreed disaster for you."

²⁴ Then Zedekiah ben-Kenaanah went up and slapped Micaiah in the face, saying, "Do you really think the Spirit of YHWH has left me to speak to the likes of you?"

²⁵ Micaiah replied, "You will find out on the day you go to hide in an inner room."

²⁶ Then the ruler of Israel ordered, "Take Micaiah and send him back to Amon the governor of the city, and to Joash my son, ²⁷ and say, 'This is what the ruler says: Put Micaiah in prison and give him nothing but bread and water until I return safely.'"

²⁸ Micaiah declared, "If you ever return safely, YHWH did not speak through me." Then he added, "Mark my words, all you people!"

²⁹ So the ruler of Israel and Jehoshaphat ruler of Judah went up to Ramoth-gilead. ³⁰ The ruler of Israel said to Jehoshaphat, "I will enter the battle disguised, but you wear your royal robes." So the ruler of Israel went into battle in disguise.

³¹ Now, the ruler of Aram ordered his thirty-two chariot commanders, "Don't fight with just anyone, small or great—just go after the ruler of Israel."

³² When the chariot commanders saw Jehoshaphat, they thought, "Surely this is the ruler of Israel!" So when they turned to attack him, Jehoshaphat cried out his war cry, ³³ and the chariot commanders, realizing that he was not the ruler of Israel, called off their pursuit.

³⁴ Meanwhile, someone drew a bow at random and hit the ruler of Israel between the sections of his armor. The ruler told his chariot driver, "Wheel round and get me out of the battle—I've been wounded."

³⁵ The battle raged all day long, and the ruler was propped up in the chariot facing the Arameans. The blood from the wound covered the floor of the chariot. He died that evening. ³⁶ As the sun was setting, a cry spread through the army, "Everyone to your own town! Everyone to your own country!" ³⁷ The body of the ruler was brought to Samaria, where they

buried him. ³⁸ They washed the chariot at a pool in Samaria—the pool the prostitutes used—and the dogs licked up his blood, as the word of YHWH had declared.

³⁹ As for the other events of Ahab's reign, including all he accomplished— the royal residence inlaid with ivory and the cities he fortified—they are written in the book of *The Annals of the Rulers of Israel*. ⁴⁰ Ahab rested with his ancestors. And Ahaziah succeeded him as ruler.

⁴¹ Jehoshaphat ben-Asa had become ruler of Judah in the fourth year of Ahab ruler of Israel. ⁴² Jehoshaphat was thirty-five years old when he was crowned ruler, and he reigned in Jerusalem for twenty-five years. His mother was Azubah bat-Shilhi. ⁴³ In everything he walked in the ways of his father Asa and did not stray from them; he did what was right in the eyes of YHWH. The shrines, however, were not removed, and the people continued to offer sacrifices and burn incense there. ⁴⁴ Jehoshaphat kept the peace with the new ruler of Israel.

⁴⁵ As for the other events of Jehoshaphat's reign, the things he achieved and his military exploits, they are written in the book of *The Annals of the Rulers of Judah*. ⁴⁶ He rid the land of the male shrine prostitutes who had remained there even after the reign of his father Asa.

⁴⁷ There was then no ruler in Edom; a deputy ruled.

⁴⁸ Now Jehoshaphat built a fleet of Tarshish ships to go to Ophir for gold, but they never set sail—they were wrecked at Ezion Geber. ⁴⁹ At that time Ahaziah ben-Ahab said to Jehoshaphat, "Let my sailors sail with yours," but Jehoshaphat refused.

⁵⁰ Then Jehoshaphat rested with his ancestors and was buried with them in the city of David his ancestor. And Jehoram succeeded him.

⁵¹ In the seventeenth year of Jehoshaphat ruler of Judah, Ahaziah ben-Ahab became ruler of Israel in Samaria, and he ruled over Israel for two years. ⁵² He did evil in the eyes of YHWH, because he walked in the ways of his father and mother and in the ways of Jeroboam ben-Nebat, who had caused Israel to sin. ⁵³ He served and worshipped Ba'al and provoked YHWH, the God of Israel, to anger, just as his father had done.

2 kíngs

$\mathcal{A}$fter ahab's death, moab rebelled against Israel.

² Ahaziah fell from the balcony of his upper room in Samaria and injured himself. He sent messengers to consult Ba'al-Zebub, the god of Ekron,* to see whether he would recover from the fall. ³ But the angel of YHWH said to Elijah the Tishbite, "Go and confront the messengers of the ruler of Samaria and ask them, 'Is it because there is no God in Israel that you are going off to consult Ba'al-Zebub, the god of Ekron?' ⁴ Listen! This is what YHWH says: You will not leave the bed you are lying on. You will certainly die!' " So Elijah went.

⁵ When the messengers returned to the ruler, he asked them, "Why did you return?"

⁶ "Someone approached us and said, 'Go back to the ruler who sent you

---

* Ba'al-Zebub literally means "Ba'al of the flies," that is, the god who expels or destroys flies, or perhaps the patron or controller of flies. 1 Kings makes reference to *beth zebul*, "magnificent house" or temple; Ba'al-Zebub is likely a deliberate distortion of Ba'al-Zebul, "Lord of the magnificent temple," an appropriate name for a Canaanite deity. By the Common Era, Beelzeboul/Beelzebub was known as "prince of demons," and by the 1500s he figured prominently in various demonologies.

and say, This is what YHWH says: Is it because there is no God in Israel that you are sending messengers to consult Ba'al-Zebub, the god of Ekron? Listen! You will not leave the bed you are lying on. You will certainly die!' "

⁷ Ahaziah asked them, "Who approached you and told you this?"

⁸ They replied, "He had a garment of hair and a leather belt was around his waist."

The ruler said, "That was Elijah the Tishbite."

⁹ Then Ahaziah sent a captain with a company of fifty troops to Elijah. The captain approached the prophet, who was sitting on a hilltop, and said, "Prophet: by order of the ruler, come down from the hilltop!"

¹⁰ Elijah answered the captain, "If I am of God, let fire come down from heaven and consume you and your fifty warriors!" Then a fire fell from heaven and consumed the captain and the troops.

¹¹ After this, Ahaziah sent a second company with a captain and fifty warriors. The officer said to the prophet, "Prophet: by order of the ruler, come down at once!"

¹² "If I am of God," Elijah replied, "let fire come down from heaven and consume you and your troops!" Then the fire of God fell from the heavens and consumed the captain and the fifty troops.

¹³ So Ahaziah sent a third captain with fifty warriors. This third captain fell on his knees before Elijah. "Prophet," he begged, "please have respect for my life and the lives of my troops! ¹⁴ Fire has already fallen from heaven and consumed the first two captains and their troops. But please spare my life!"

¹⁵ The angel of YHWH said to Elijah, "Go with the captain. Don't be afraid of him." So Elijah got up and went with him to Ahaziah.

¹⁶ Elijah told Ahaziah, "This is what YHWH says: 'Is it because there is no God in Israel for you to consult that you have sent messengers to consult Ba'al-Zebub, the god of Ekron? Because you did this, you will never leave the bed you are lying on. You will certainly die!' " ¹⁷ So the ruler died, according to the word of God that Elihah had spoken.

Because Ahaziah had no heir, Jehoram ben-Jehoshaphat of Judah succeeded him as ruler. ¹⁸ All the other events of Ahaziah's reign, and what he accomplished, are written in *The Book of the Annals of the Rulers of Israel.*

ଔ ଔ ଔ

2:1 When YHWH was about take Elijah up to heaven in a whirlwind, Elijah and Elisha were on their way from Gilgal. ² Elijah said to Elisha, "Stay here. YHWH is sending me to Bethel."

"As YHWH lives, and you live," said Elisha, "I will not leave you."

So they departed together for Bethel. ³ The disciples there of the prophets approached Elisha, asking, "Do you know that YHWH is going to take Elijah from you today?"

"Yes, I know," Elisha replied, "now be silent."

⁴ Then Elijah spoke, "Stay here, Elisha. YHWH is sending me to Jericho."

And Elisha replied, "As YHWH lives, and as you live, I will not leave you."

So they went to Jericho. ⁵ The disciples of the prophets there approached Elisha, asking, "Do you know that YHWH is going to take Elijah from you today?"

"Yes, I know," he said, "now be silent."

⁶ Then Elijah said to Elisha, "Stay here. YHWH is sending me to the Jordan."

"As YHWH lives and as you live," said Elisha, "I will not leave you."

So the two of them walked on. ⁷ Fifty disciples of prophets stood off at a distance, facing the place where Elijah and Elisha stopped at the Jordan. ⁸ Elijah took his cloak, rolled it up and struck the water with it. The water divided to the right and to the left, and the two of them crossed over on dry land.

⁹ Once across, Elijah said to Elisha, "Tell me, what can I do for you before I am taken from you?"

Elisha replied, "Let me inherit two-thirds of your spirit."*

¹⁰ "You ask a difficult thing," Elijah said. "If you see me when I am taken from you, my spirit will be yours—otherwise not."

¹¹ As they were walking along and chatting with each other, suddenly a chariot of fire and horses of fire appeared and separated the two, and Elijah went up to heaven in a whirlwind. ¹² Elisha saw this and cried out, "My father! My father! The chariot and cavalry of Israel!"† And Elisha saw nothing more. Then he took hold of his clothes and tore them apart.

¹³ Elisha picked up the cloak that had fallen from Elijah and went back and stood there on the bank of the Jordan. ¹⁴ Then he struck the water with Elijah's cloak, and said, "Where is YHWH, the God of Elijah?" As he struck

---

* Two-thirds, or a double portion, of an inheritance goes to the first-born of the family. Elisha's inheritance of two-thirds of Elijah's spirit is the public sign that he is the true spiritual heir of the prophet.

† The fiery chariot and horses in the vision represent YHWH's spiritual army that fights on behalf of Israel, as in 6:17; but Elisha's exclamation may not be in response to that vision alone. In a parallel passage in 13:14, Joash the ruler uses this same phrase without having had a vision of chariots; moreover, the phrase "the chariot and cavalry of Israel" immediately follows "My father!"—a reference to Elijah as his mentor. Together they suggest that Elisha is calling Elijah the spiritual army of Israel—that without his prophetic word, Israel will be defenseless.

the water, it divided to the right and to the left, and he crossed over the river. ¹⁵ Members of the prophetic guild from Jericho were watching, and saying, "The spirit of Elijah rests on Elisha." And they went to meet him, bowing down to the ground before him, ¹⁶ and said, "We, your disciples, have fifty able bodied workers with us. Let us have them search for Elijah. Perhaps the Spirit of YHWH has picked him up and set him down on some mountain top or in some valley."

Elisha replied, "No, do not send them."

¹⁷ But they persisted until he was too worn down to refuse. So he gave the signal for them to search. The fifty able-bodied disciples searched for three days and could not find Elijah. ¹⁸ When they returned to Elisha, who was staying in Jericho, he replied, "Didn't I tell you not to go?"

¹⁹ The people of the city said to Elisha, "Please, prophet, our town is well situated, but our water is polluted and the land is not productive."

²⁰ "Bring me a new bowl," he said, "and put salt in it." So they brought the bowl to him.

²¹ The prophet went to the spring and threw the salt into it, and said, "This is what YHWH says: 'I heal this water. And never again will it cause death or make the ground unproductive.' "

²² The water has remained sweet and wholesome to this day, just as Elisha said it would.

²³ From there Elisha went to Bethel. As he walked along the road, some youths came out from the town and jeered at him. "Go away, baldy! Go away, baldy!"

²⁴ He turned around, looked at them and called down a curse on them in the name of YHWH. Then two bears came out of the woods and mauled forty-two of the youths. ²⁵ And Elisha went on to Mount Carmel and from there returned to Samaria.

³·¹ In the eighteenth year of Jehoshaphat ruler of Judah, Jehoram ben-Ahab became ruler of Israel in Samaria, and he reigned for twelve years. ² Jehoram did evil in the eyes of YHWH, though not so great as his mother and father. He did remove the sacred pillar of Ba'al that his father had made. ³ Nevertheless he clung to the sins of Jeroboam ben-Nebat, which Jeroboam had caused Israel to commit. He did not turn away from them.

⁴ Now Mesha ruler of Moab raised sheep, and he had to supply the ruler of Israel with one hundred thousand lambs and with the wool of one hundred thousand rams. ⁵ But after Ahab died, the ruler of Moab rebelled against

the ruler of Israel. ⁶ So at that time the ruler Jehoram set out from Samaria and mobilized all Israel. ⁷ He also sent this message to Jehoshaphat ruler of Judah: "The ruler of Moab has rebelled against me. Will you go with me to fight against Moab?"

"I will go with you," Jehoshaphat replied. "I am as you are, my people as your people, my horses as your horses."

⁸ "By what route will we attack?" Jehoram asked.

"Through the Desert of Edom, Jehoshaphat answered.

⁹ So the ruler of Israel set out with the ruler of Judah and the ruler of Edom. After a roundabout march of seven days, the army had no more water for itself or for its animals.

¹⁰ "What?" exclaimed the ruler of Israel. "Has YHWH called us three rulers together only to hand us over to Moab?"

¹¹ But Jehoshaphat asked, "Is there no prophet of YHWH here, through whom we may enquire of YHWH?"

An officer of the ruler of Israel answered, "Elisha ben-Shaphat is here. He used to pour water on the hands of Elijah."

¹² Jehoshaphat said, "The word of YHWH is with Elisha." So the ruler of Israel and Jehoshaphat with the ruler of Edom went down to the prophet.

¹³ Elisha said to the ruler of Israel, "What do we have to do with each other? Go to the prophets of your father and the prophets of your mother."

"No," said the ruler of Israel, "because it was YHWH who called us three rulers together to hand us over to Moab."

¹⁴ Elisha said, "As surely as YHWH Omnipotent lives, whom I serve, if I did not have respect for the presence of Jehoshaphat ruler of Judah, I would not look at you or even notice you. ¹⁵ But now bring me a harpist."

While the harpist played, the hand of YHWH came upon Elisha ¹⁶ and he said, "This is what YHWH says: 'Fill this valley with ditches.' ¹⁷ For this is what YHWH says: 'You will see neither wind nor rain, yet this valley will be filled with water, and you, your cattle and your other livestock will drink.' ¹⁸ This is an easy thing in the eyes of YHWH, who will also hand Moab over to you. ¹⁹ You will overthrow every fortified city and every major town. You will cut down every good tree, stop up all the springs, and ruin every good field with stones."

²⁰ The next morning, about the time for offering the sacrifice, there it was—water flowing from the direction of Edom! And the land was filled with water.

²¹ Now the Moabites learned that the rulers had come to fight against them. So every citizen, young and old, who could bear arms was called up and stationed on the border. ²² When they got up early in the morning, the sun

was shining on the water, and it looked red—like blood. ²³ "This is blood!" they said. "Those rulers must have fought and slaughtered each other. Now to the plunder, Moab!"

²⁴ But when the Moabites came to Israel's camp, the people of Israel rose up and fought them until they retreated. And the people of Israel invaded their land and slaughtered the Moabites. ²⁵ They destroyed the towns, and each soldier threw a stone on every good field until it was covered. They stopped up all the springs and cut down every good tree. Only Kir Hareseth was left with its stones in place, but men armed with slings surrounded it and attacked it as well.

²⁶ When the ruler of Moab saw that the battle had gone against him, he called together seven hundred troops armed with swords to break through to the ruler of Edom; but they failed. ²⁷ Then he took his firstborn son, his successor, and offered him as a whole burnt offering on the city wall. There was such consternation at this that the people of Israel struck camp and returned to their own land.

⁴:¹ The wife of one of the prophets made an appeal to Elisha: "My husband, your disciple, has died, and you know how much he revered YHWH. But now his creditors are coming to take away my two boys as bondservants."

² Elisha said to her, "How can I help you? Tell me what you have in your house?"

"I have nothing there at all," she said, "except a little oil."

³ Elisha said, "Go around your neighborhood and ask all your neighbors for empty jars, as many as you can. ⁴ Then go inside and shut yourself in with your sons. Pour oil into all the jars, and as each is filled, put it to one side."

⁵ She left Elisha and followed his instruction: the neighbors brought jars and she poured oil into them. ⁶ When all the jars were filled, she said to the boys, "Bring me another jar."

They said, "There are no more jars." And then the oil stopped flowing.

⁷ She went to the prophet and he said, "Sell the oil and pay your debts. You and your sons can live on what is left."

⁸ One day Elisha went to Shunem. There was a wealthy woman there who urged him to stay for a meal. In the course of time, whenever Elisha traveled that way he would stop for a meal. ⁹ "I have come to believe that the person who stops for a meal is a prophet of God. ¹⁰ Let us set up a small room on the roof with a bed, a table, a chair and a lamp. Then he can stay here whenever he comes to see us."

¹¹ One day when Elisha arrived, he went up to his room to rest. ¹² Once rested, he said to his disciple Gehazi, "Call the Shunammite." He called her and she came to the prophet.

¹³ Elisha said to Gehazi, "Tell her, 'You have been so generous to me. Now what can I do for you? Can we speak on your behalf to the ruler or to the commander of the army?' "

She replied, "I have a home among my own people."

¹⁴ "What can be done for her?" Elisha asked Gehazi.

He replied, "Well, she has no son and her husband is old."

¹⁵ Then Elisha said, "Call her."

She was called and she stood in the doorway. ¹⁶ "About this time next year," said the prophet of God, "you will be holding a son in your arms."

"No, prophet of God," she objected, "don't humor me!"

¹⁷ But the woman did get pregnant, and the next year about the same time she gave birth to a son, just as Elisha had told her.

¹⁸ The child grew, and one day he went to his father, who was reaping grain. ¹⁹ "My head! My head!" he said to his father, who sent the boy to his mother. ²⁰ An attendant carried the boy to her; she held him on her lap until noon, and then he died. ²¹ She went up and placed the heir on the bed of Elisha, and left him there.

²² "Please bring me an attendant and a donkey," she said to her husband, "so I can go to the prophet of God quickly and return."

²³ "Why go to him today?" the husband asked. "It's not the New Moon or the Sabbath."

"It's all right," she said.

²⁴ She saddled the donkey and said to the attendant, "Lead on; and don't slow down for me unless I tell you." ²⁵ She set out to find the prophet of God at Mount Carmel.

When he saw her at a distance, Elisha said to Gehazi, "Look! There's the Shunammite woman! ²⁶ Run to meet her and ask her, 'Are you all right? Is your husband all right? Is your child all right?' "

"Everything is all right," she said.

²⁷ When she reached the prophet of God at the mountain, she took hold of his feet. Gehazi came over to push her away, but Elisha said, "Leave her alone! She is in bitter distress, but YHWH hid it from me and has not told me why."

²⁸ "Did I ask you for a son, prophet?" said the woman. "Did I not tell you, 'Don't raise my hopes?' "

²⁹ Elisha said to Gehazi, "Tuck your cloak into your belt, take hold of my staff and run. Don't greet anyone you meet, and if anyone greets you, do not answer. Lay my staff on the lad's face."

³⁰ But the mother said, "As surely as YHWH lives and as you live, I will not leave you." So Elisha got up and followed her.

³¹ Meanwhile, Gehazi went on ahead and laid the staff on the child's face, but there was no sound or response. So Gehazi went back to meet Elisha and told him, "The child has not awakened."

³² When Elisha reached the house, the boy was lying dead on the bed. ³³ He went in, shut he door on the two of them and prayed to YHWH. ³⁴ Then he got on the bed and stretched himself on top of the child, mouth to mouth, eyes to eyes, hands to hands. As he remained stretched out, the child's body grew warm. ³⁵ Elisha turned away and walked back and forth in the room and then stretched out on the child once more. The child sneezed seven times and opened his eyes.

³⁶ Elisha summoned Gehazi saying, "Call the Shunammite woman," which he did. When she entered the room, he said, "Here is your child." ³⁷ She came in and prostrated herself before him. And she picked up her child and left.

³⁸ Elisha returned to Gilgal at a time when there was a famine in the land. While the disciples of the prophet were meeting with him, he said to Gehazi, "Put on the large pot and cook some stew for these people."

³⁹ One of them went out into the fields to gather herbs, and found a wild vine. He gathered some of it in gourds and filled the fold of his cloak. When he returned, he cut up the vine and put it into the stewpot. No one knew what they were eating. ⁴⁰ The stew was poured out for the people gathered, but as they began to eat they cried out, "Prophet of God, there is death in the pot!" And they refused to eat it.

⁴¹ Elisha said, "Get some flour." He put it in the stew pot and said, "Serve it, for there is nothing harmful in the stew."

⁴² A man came from Ba'al Shalishah, carrying twenty loaves of barley bread baked from the first ripe corn, along with some ears of new corn. "Give it to the people to eat," ⁴³ Elisha said.

"How can I serve it to one hundred people?" Gehazi asked.

But Elisha replied, "Give it to the people to eat. For this is what YHWH said: 'They will eat and have some left over.'" ⁴⁴ Then the food was set before them, and they ate and had some left over, according to the word of YHWH.

⁵:¹ Now Naaman was commander of the army of the ruler of Aram. He was a great officer and highly esteemed. It was at Naaman's hand that YHWH

gave a victory to Aram. He was a mighty warrior. And he had leprosy.

² On one of their raids the Arameans captured a young woman who was an Israelite. She served Naaman's wife. ³ One day she said to her mistress, "If only Naaman would see the prophet who is in Samaria! He would cure Naaman's leprosy."

⁴ Naaman went to the ruler and told him what the Israelite woman said. ⁵ "By all means, go," the ruler replied. "I will send a letter to the ruler of Israel."

So Naaman left, taking ten talents of silver, six thousand shekels of gold and ten sets of clothing. ⁶ The letter that he took to the ruler of Israel read, "With this letter I am sending my attendant Naaman to you so that you may cure him of leprosy."

⁷ As soon as the ruler of Israel read the letter, he tore his robes, and said, "Am I God? Can I kill and bring back to life? Why does this fellow send someone to me to be cured of his leprosy? See how he is trying to pick a fight with me!"

⁸ When Elisha the prophet of God learned that the ruler of Israel tore his robes, he sent a message to the ruler, "Why did you tear your robes? Have Naaman come to me and he will learn that there is a prophet in Israel."

⁹ So Naaman went with his horses and chariots and stopped at the door of Elisha's house. ¹⁰ Elisha sent a messenger to say to the warrior, "Go, wash yourself seven times in the Jordan, and your flesh will be restored and you will be cleansed."

¹¹ But Naaman went away angry, and said, "I thought that he would surely come out to me and stand there before me, calling on the name YHWH, and wave his hand over the spot and cure me of my leprosy. ¹² Are not Abana and Pharpar, the rivers of Damascus, better than any of the waters of Israel? Couldn't I wash in them and be cleansed?" So he turned and went away in a rage.

¹³ Naaman's attendants went to him saying, "Sir, if the prophet had told you to do some great thing, would you not have done it? How much more, then, when he tells you, 'Wash and be cleansed'?"

¹⁴ So he went down and dipped himself in the Jordan seven times, as the prophet of God told him, and his flesh was restored and became clean like that of a youth.

¹⁵ Then Naaman and his retinue went back to the prophet of God. He stood before him, and said, "Now I know that there is no God in all the world except in Israel. Please accept a gift from a grateful debtor."

¹⁶ The prophet answered, "As surely as YHWH lives, whom I serve, I will not accept a thing." And even though Naaman urged him, he refused.

¹⁷ "If you will not," said Naaman, "please let me, your servant, be given as much earth as a pair of mules can carry, for I will never again make burnt offerings and sacrifices to any other god but YHWH.* ¹⁸ But may your YHWH forgive me for just one thing: When my ruler enters the temple of Rimmon to bow down and he is leaning on my arm and I bow also—when I bow down in the temple of Rimmon, may YHWH forgive me for this."†

¹⁹ "Go in peace," Elisha said.

After Naaman had traveled some distance, ²⁰ Elisha's attendant Gehazi said to himself, "Elisha was too easy on Naaman, this Aramean, by not accepting a gift. As surely as YHWH lives, I will run after him and get something for myself." ²¹ So Gehazi hurried after Naaman.

When Naaman saw Gehazi running after him, he got down from his chariot and asked the attendant, "Is everything all right?"

²² "Everything is all right," Gehazi answered. "Elisha sent me to say, 'Two young men from the disciples of the prophet have just come to me from the hill country of Ephraim. Please give them a talent of silver‡ and two sets of clothing.'"

²³ "By all means, take two talents," said Naaman. He urged Gehazi to accept them, and then tied up the two talents of silver in two bags, with two sets of clothing. He gave them to two of his attendants, and they carried them ahead of Gehazi. ²⁴ When Gehazi came to the hill, he took the things from the attendants and put them away in the house. He sent the men away and they left. ²⁵ Then he went in and stood before Elisha.

"Where have you been, Gehazi?" Elisha asked.

"I didn't go anywhere," Gehazi replied.

²⁶ But Elisha said to him, "Was not my spirit with you when the man got down from the chariot to meet you? Is this the time to take money, or to accept clothes, olive groves, vineyards, flocks, herds, or male and female attendants? ²⁷ Naaman's leprosy will cling to you and to your ancestors forever." Then Gehazi left Elisha's presence and he was leprous, as white as snow.

6·1 The disciples of the prophet said to Elisha, "Look, the place we meet with you is too small for us. Let us go to the Jordan, where each of us can cut down trees; and let us build a place there for us to live."

Elisha said, "Go ahead."

---

* Naaman wants the dirt—the holy ground where this miracle occurred—so that he can build an altar to YHWH back home in Aram.
† Rimmon was the Aramean storm god.
‡ A talent of silver weighed around 75 pounds; informally, it was "the total load that one able person can carry."

³ Then one of them said, "Won't you please come with us?"

"I will," Elisha said, ⁴ and he went with them. When they got there and began to cut down trees, ⁵ it happened that, as one of them was felling a tree, the head of the axe flew off into the water. "Oh, no!" he cried out, "I borrowed that axe."

⁶ The prophet asked, "Where did it fall?" When he was shown the place it fell, Elisha cut a stick and threw it there, and made the iron float. ⁷ "Lift it out," he said.

So the disciple reached down and pulled it out.

⁸ Now the ruler of Aram was at war with Israel. After conferring with his officers, the ruler said, "You are to attack at such-and-such a place."

⁹ But Elisha sent word to the ruler of Israel, "Beware of approaching that place, for the Arameans are moving into that area."

¹⁰ So the ruler of Israel checked out the place indicated by the prophet. Time and again Elisha warned the ruler, so that he took special precautions every time he found himself near that place. ¹¹ This enraged the ruler of Aram. He summoned his officers and demanded of them, "Tell me, which of you is in league with the ruler of Israel?"

¹² "None of us, your majesty," said one of the officers, "but Elisha, the prophet of the people of Israel, tells the ruler of Israel the very words you speak in your bedroom."

¹³ "Go, find out where he is," the ruler ordered, "so that I can send troops to capture him."

The report came back, "He is in Dothan."

¹⁴ Then the ruler sent his cavalry, chariots, and a strong force. They went after dark and surrounded the city. ¹⁵ When the attendant got up and went out early the next morning, he saw that an army with horses and chariots had surrounded the city. Elisha's attendant said, "Oh, prophet, what shall we do?"

¹⁶ "Have no fear," he said. "Our forces are larger than theirs."

¹⁷ And Elisha prayed, "YHWH, open his eyes so that he may see." Then YHWH opened the attendant's eyes, and he saw the hills full of horses and chariots of fire surrounding Elisha. ¹⁸ As the enemy charged toward him, Elisha prayed to YHWH, "Strike these soldiers with blindness." So YHWH struck them with blindness, as Elisha had asked.

¹⁹ Then Elisha said to the blinded troops, "This is not the road, and this is not the city. Follow me, and I will lead you to the person you are looking for." And he led them to Samaria.

²⁰ After they entered the city, Elisha said, "YHWH, open the eyes of these people so that they can see." Then YHWH opened their eyes, and looking, they realized they were in Samaria. ²¹ When the ruler of Israel saw them, he

asked Elisha, "Shall I kill them, prophet? Shall I kill them?"

²² "Do not kill them," Elisha answered. "Would you kill those you captured with your own sword or bow? Set food and water before them so that they may eat and drink and then return to their ruler."

²³ So he prepared a great feast for them, and after they had finished eating and drinking, he sent them away, and they returned to their ruler. So the raiding parties never invaded the territory of Israel again.

²⁴ Some time later, Ben-Hadad ruler of Aram mobilized his entire army and marched up, laying siege to Samaria, ²⁵ and there was a terrible famine in the city. The siege lasted so long that a donkey's head sold for eighty shekels of silver, and a quart of locust beans˙ for five shekels.

²⁶ As the ruler of Israel was passing by along the wall, a woman cried out, "Help me, my ruler!"

²⁷ The ruler asked, "If YHWH does not help you, where can *I* get help for you? From the threshing floor? From the wine press?" ²⁸ Then he asked her, "What is the matter?"

She answered, "This woman said to me, 'Give up your child so that we may have something to eat, and tomorrow we will eat my child.' ²⁹ So we cooked my son and ate him. The next day I said to her, 'Give up your child so that we may eat him,' but she has hidden him."

³⁰ When the ruler heard the woman's story, he tore his robes. He walked along the wall at the time, and when the people looked, they saw that he wore sackcloth underneath the robe, next to his skin. ³¹ "May YHWH do the same to me and more," he said, "if the head of Elisha ben-Shaphat stays on his shoulders today!"†

³² At this time Elisha was sitting at home with the elders. The ruler sent a messenger on ahead. But before the messenger arrived, Elisha said to the elders, "You realize, don't you, that this assassin gave orders to cut off my head? Look, when the messenger comes, shut the door and hold it shut against him—the ruler certainly won't be far behind him."‡

³³ While was still talking to them, the ruler arrived and said, "Look, this disaster is from YHWH. Why then should I wait any longer for YHWH's promise to be fulfilled?"

---

* Literally, "dove's manure," a popular term for the nearly inedible bean pods. The locust beans would have cost about three weeks' wages, and the donkey's head nearly a year's.
† The ruler blames Elisha for the famine because Elisha had promised that YHWH would fight for Israel, and yet they are under seige.
‡ Apparently this action was to keep the messenger from beheading Elisha before the ruler arrived. In verse 33, the Hebrew text has *malak*, messenger, rather than *melek*, ruler, but either this is a scribal error, or the messenger is speaking the ruler's words to Elisha.

⁷·¹ Elisha said, "Hear the word of YHWH. This is what YHWH says: About this time tomorrow, a shekel will buy half a bushel of flour or a whole bushel of barley at the gate of Samaria."

² The officer whose arm the ruler leaned on said to the prophet, "Even if YHWH opened the floodgates of heaven, could this happen?"

"You will see it with your own eyes," Elisha answered, "but you will eat none of it!"

³ Now there were four lepers at the entrance of the city gate. "Why stay here until we die?" they said to one another. ⁴ "If we say, 'We'll go into the city,' the famine is there, and we will die. And if we stay there, we will die. So let's go over to the camp of the Arameans and surrender. If they spare us, we live; if they kill us, then we die."

⁵ At dusk they got up and went to the camp of the Arameans. When they got to the edge of the camp, no one was there, ⁶ for YHWH had caused the Arameans to hear the sounds of chariots and horses and the movement of a great army, so that they said to one another, "Look, the ruler of Israel hired the Hittites and the Egyptian rulers to attack us!" ⁷ So they had got up and fled in the dusk and abandoned their tents and their horses and donkeys. They left the camp as it was and ran for their lives.

⁸ The lepers reached the edge of the camp and entered one of the tents. They ate and drank, and carried away silver, gold, and clothes, and went off and hid them. They returned and entered another tent and took some items from it and hid these also. ⁹ Then they said to one another, "We're not doing right. This is a day of good news and we are keeping it to ourselves. If we wait until daylight, punishment will overtake us. Let's go at once and report this to the royal residence."

¹⁰ So they went out to the city gatekeepers and told them, "We went into the Aramean camp and no one was there—not a sound of anyone—only tethered horses and donkeys, and the tents left just as they were." ¹¹ The gate-keepers shouted the news, and it was reported within the royal residence.

¹² The ruler got up in the night and said to his officers, "I will tell you what the Arameans did to us. They know we are starving; so they left the camp to hide in the countryside, thinking, 'They will surely come out, and then we will take them alive and get into the city.' "

¹³ One of the officers answered, 'Have some scouts take five of the horses that are left in the city. Even if they are killed, their fate will be no different than the rest of the People of Israel—we're all perishing!* So let us send them to find out what happened."

---

* This sentence could also be rendered, "Those few horses are like what is left of the multitude of Israel, that once vast multitude that has now perished."

¹⁴ So they selected two chariots with their horses, and the ruler sent them after the Aramean army. He commanded the drivers, "Go and find out what has happened." ¹⁵ They followed the army as far as the Jordan, and they found the whole road strewn with the clothing and equipment that the Arameans had thrown away in their headlong flight. So the messengers returned and reported to the ruler.

¹⁶ Then the people went out and plundered the camp of the Arameans. So a half-bushel of flour sold for a shekel, and a full bushel of barley sold for a shekel, as YHWH had said.

¹⁷ Now the ruler put in charge of the gate the officer on whose arm he leaned, and the people trampled the officer in the gateway, and he died, just as the prophet had foretold when the ruler came down to his house. ¹⁸ It happened as the prophet had said to the ruler: "About this time tomorrow, a shekel will buy half a bushel of flour or a whole bushel of barley at the gate of Samaria." ¹⁹ The officer had said to the prophet, "Look, even if YHWH unlocked the floodgates of heaven, could this happen?" The prophet replied, "You will see it with your own eyes, but you will not eat any of it!" ²⁰ And that is exactly what happened to him, for the people trampled him in the gateway, and he died.

8:1 Now Elisha said to the Shunammite woman, "Go away with your family and stay away for a while wherever you can, for YHWH has decreed that there will be a famine in the land that will last for seven years." ² The Shunammite woman proceeded to do what the prophet of YHWH said. And she and her family went away and stayed away in the land of the Philistines for seven years.

³ At the end of seven years she returned from the land of the Philistines and went to the ruler to beg from him her house and her land. ⁴ The ruler was talking to Gehazi, the attendant of the prophet of God, and he inquired, "Tell me about all the great things Elisha has done."

⁵ Just as Gehazi was telling the ruler how the prophet of God had restored the dead to life, the woman whose child Elisha had brought back to life came in to beg the ruler for her house and land.

⁶ Gehazi said, "This is the woman, my ruler, and this is her child whom Elisha restored to life." The ruler asked the woman about it, and she verified everything Gehazi had said.

Then the ruler assigned an official to her case, and said to him, "Give back everything that belonged to her, including all the income from her land from the day she left the country until now."

⁷ Elisha went to Damascus, and Ben-Hadad, the ruler of Aram, was ill. When the ruler was told, "The prophet of God has come all the way up

here," [8] he said to Hazael, "Take a gift with you and meet the prophet of God. Consult YHWH through him; ask him, 'Will I recover from this illness?'"

[9] Hazael went to meet Elisha, taking with him a gift of forty camel-loads of all the finest wares of Damascus. He went in and stood before him, and said, "Your son Ben-Hadad,* the ruler of Syria, sent me to you to ask whether he will recover from his illness.

[10] Elisha answered, "Go and say to the ruler, 'You will certainly recover'— though YHWH has in fact revealed to me that he will die."

[11] Elisha stared at him with a fixed gaze until Hazael felt uneasy. Then Elisha began to weep.

[12] "Why do you weep?" asked Hazael.

"Because I know the damage you will do to the people of Israel," he replied. "You will set fire to their fortresses, kill their young with swords, dash their children to the ground, and rip open their pregnant women."

[13] Hazael said, "But I am a dog, a mere nobody. How can I do such a depraved thing?"

"YHWH told me that you will become the ruler of Aram," answered the prophet.

[14] Then Hazael left Elisha and returned to the ruler. When Ben-Hadad asked, "What did Elisha say to you?" Hazael replied, "He told me that you will certainly recover."

[15] The next day, Hazael took a thick blanket, soaked it in water and spread it over the ruler's face, murdering him. Then Hazael succeeded Ben-Hadad as ruler.

[16] In the fifth year of Jehoram ben-Ahab ruler of Israel, Jehoram ben-Jehoshaphat succeeded Jehoshaphat on the throne and began his reign over Judah.† [17] He was thirty-two when he was crowned ruler, and he reigned in Jerusalem for eight years. [18] But he walked in the ways of the rulers of Israel, as the house of Ahab did, for he married one of Ahab's daughters. He did evil in the eyes of YHWH. [19] But YHWH was not willing to destroy Judah out of respect for David, God's servant: YHWH had promised to maintain a lamp for David and his ancestors forever.

---

* Ben-Hadad was not Elisha's son; Hazael is merely demonstrating the ruler's profound respect for Elisha.
† In other words, there were two rulers named Jehoram, one ruling over Israel (the son of Ahab and Jezebel), the other ruling over Judah (the son of Jehoshaphat). Jehoram of Judah created a political alliance with Israel by marrying Athaliah, the daughter of Ahab and sister of Jehoram of Israel; their son Ahaziah (named for Athaliah's late brother, the former ruler of Israel), continued the alliance with Israel when he became ruler of Judah.

²⁰ In the time of Jehoram, Edom rebelled against Judah and set up its own ruler. ²¹ So Jehoram went to Zair with his chariots. The Edomites surrounded him and his chariot commanders, but he rose up and broke through after dark. His army, however, fled to their homes. ²² To this day Edom has remained independent of Judah. Libnah also revolted at the same time.

²³ The other events of Jehoram's reign, and all he did, are written in *The Book of the Annals of the Rulers of Judah.* ²⁴ Jehoram rested with his ancestors and was buried with them in the City of David. His heir Ahaziah succeeded him.

²⁵ In the twelfth year of Jehoram ben-Ahab ruler of Israel, Ahaziah ben-Jehoram ruler of Judah began to reign. ²⁶ Ahaziah was twenty-two years old when became ruler, and he reigned in Jerusalem for one year. His mother was Athaliah, a granddaughter of Omri, ruler of Israel. ²⁷ He walked in the ways of the house of Ahab and did evil in the eyes of YHWH, as the house of Ahab did, for he was related by marriage to Ahab's family.

²⁸ Ahaziah went with Jehoram ben-Ahab to war against Hazael ruler of Aram at Ramoth Gilead. The Arameans wounded Jehoram; ²⁹ so Jehoram the ruler turned to Jezreel to recover from the wounds the Arameans had inflicted on him at Ramoth in his battle with Hazael ruler of Aram.

Then Ahaziah ben-Jehoram ruler of Judah went to Jezreel to visit Jehoram ben-Ahab, because of his wounds.

⁹:¹ The prophet Elisha summoned one of his disciples and said to him, "Tuck your cloak into your belt, take this flask of oil with you and go to Ramoth Gilead. ² When you get there, look for Jehu ben-Jehoshaphat ben-Nimshi.* Go to him, get him away from his companions, and take him into an inner room. ³ Then take the flask of oil and pour it on his head and declare, 'This is what YHWH says: I anoint you ruler over Israel.' Then open the door and run. Don't linger!"

⁴ So the young prophet went to Ramoth Gilead. ⁵ When he arrived, he found the army officers sitting together. "I have a message for you, commander," he said.

"For which of us?" asked Jehu.

"For you, commander," he replied.

⁶ Jehu got up and went into the house. Then the prophet poured the oil on Jehu's head, declaring, "This is what YHWH, the God of Israel, says: 'I anoint you ruler over YHWH's people, Israel. ⁷ You are to destroy the house of Ahab, and I will avenge the blood of my servants the prophets, as well as the blood of all

---

* Jehu's father, Jehoshaphat ben-Nimshi, is not related to Jehoshaphat the late ruler of Israel. Jehu began his career in the bodyguard of Ahab of Israel, and became a commander in Israel's army.

YHWH's servants shed by Jezebel. ⁸ The whole house of Ahab will perish. I will cut off from Ahab every last male in Israel—slave or free. ⁹ I will make the house of Ahab like the house of Jeroboam ben-Nebat and like the house of Baasha ben-Ahijah. ¹⁰ As for Jezebel, dogs will devour her on the plot of ground at Jezreel, and no one will bury her.'" Then the prophet opened the door and ran.

¹¹ When Jehu went out to the officers, one of them asked, "Is everything all right? Why did that maniac come to you?"

"You know those people and how they talk," Jehu said.

¹² "That's not true!" they cried out. "Out with it! Level with us!"

"He said, 'Thus says YHWH: 'I anoint you ruler over Israel.'" And Jehu told them everything the prophet had said.

¹³ The officers snatched up their cloaks and spread them under him on the bare steps. Then they blew the shofar and shouted, "Jehu is the ruler!"

¹⁴ So Jehu ben-Jehoshaphat ben-Nimshi started conspiring with his officers against Jehoram. (Jehoram and all Israel were defending Ramoth Gilead against Hazael ruler of Aram, ¹⁵ but Jehoram had returned to Jezreel to recover from the wounds the Arameans had inflicted on him in battle.) Jehu told them, "If you are in agreement with me, don't let anyone slip out of the city to announce the news in Jezreel." ¹⁶ Then he climbed into his chariot and drove to Jezreel, for Jehoram was resting there. Ahaziah ruler of Judah had also gone down to see Jehoram.

¹⁷ When the lookout standing on the tower of Jezreel saw Jehu's troops approaching, he called out, "I see some troops approaching!

Jehoram ordered, "Take a horse out to meet them and see if they come in peace."

¹⁸ The rider met them and asked, "The ruler wants to know—do you come in peace?"

"What business is it of yours if we come in peace?" Jehu replied. "Fall in behind me."

The lookout reported, "The messenger reached them, but he isn't returning."

¹⁹ So Jehoram sent out a second messenger. When he got there he asked, "The ruler wants to know—do you come in peace?"

Jehu replied, "What business is it of yours if we come in peace? Fall in behind me."

²⁰ The lookout reported, "The messenger has met them, but he isn't coming back, either. The chariot looks like it's being driven by Jehu ben-Nimshi—he drives like a maniac."

²¹ "Hitch up my chariot," Jehoram commanded. And when it was hitched up, Jehoram ruler of Israel and Ahaziah ruler of Judah rode out, each in his

own chariot, to meet Jehu. They met him at the plot of ground that belonged to Naboth the Jezreelite.

²² When Jehoram saw Jehu, he asked, "Have you come in peace, Jehu?"

"How can there be peace," Jehu replied, "as long as all the idolatry and witchcraft of your mother continue unabated?"

²³ Jehoram turned about and fled, screaming to Ahaziah, "It's a trap, Ahaziah!" ²⁴ Then Jehu drew his bow and arrow and shot Jehoram between the shoulders. The arrow pierced his heart and he slumped down in the chariot.

²⁵ Jehu said to Bidkar, a chariot officer, "Pick him up and throw him on the field that belonged to Naboth the Jezreelite. Remember how you and I were riding together in chariots behind Ahab when YHWH made this prophecy about him? ²⁶ 'Yesterday I saw the blood of Naboth and the blood of his children, declares YHWH, and I will surely make you pay for it on this plot of ground, declares YHWH.' Now then, pick him up and throw him on that plot, in accordance with the word of YHWH."

²⁷ When Ahaziah ruler of Judah saw what had happened, he fled up the road to Beth-Haggan. Jehu chased him, shouting, "Kill him too!" The troops wounded him in his chariot on the way up to Gur near Ibleam, but he escaped to Megiddo and died there. ²⁸ His attendants took him by chariot to Jerusalem and buried him with his ancestors in his tomb in the City of David. ²⁹ Ahaziah had became ruler of Judah in the eleventh year of Jehoram ben-Ahab.

³⁰ Then Jehu went to Jezreel. When Jezebel heard about it, she painted her eyes, arranged her hair, and looked out the window. ³¹ As Jehu entered the gate, she called out, "Have you come in peace, Zimri, you murderer of your ruler?"*

³² He looked up to her window and called out, "Who is on my side? Who?"

Two or three eunuchs came to the window and looked down at him.

³³ "Throw her down!" Jehu said. So they threw her down, and some of her blood spattered the wall and the horses as they trampled her underfoot.

³⁴ Jehu went in and ate and drank. "Take care of that cursed woman," he said, "and bury her, for she was a ruler's daughter." ³⁵ But when they went out to bury her, they found nothing except her skull, her feet and her hands.

³⁶ They went back and told Jehu, who said, "This is the word of YHWH spoken through Elijah the Tishbite: Dogs will devour Jezebel's flesh on the

---

* Like Jehu, Zimri (1 Kings 16) began as a military officer and ascended the throne of Israel by murdering the ruler and executing the rest of the ruler's family.

grounds of Jezreel. Jezebel's body will be like refuse on the ground, so that no one will be able to say, 'This is Jezebel.' "

ᏅᏒ ᏅᏒ ᏅᏒ

¹⁰·¹ Now there were in Samaria seventy sons of the house of Ahab. So Jehu wrote letters and sent them to Samaria: to the officials of Jezreel, to the elders and the guardians of Ahab's children. He said, ² "Since your ruler's sons are with you and you have chariots and horses, a fortified city and weapons, as soon as this letter reaches you ³ choose the best and most worthy of your ruler's sons and set him on your father's throne. Then fight for the ruler's house."

⁴ But they were terrified, and said, "If two rulers could not resist him, what hope is there that we can?"

⁵ So the administrators of the royal residence, the governor of the city, the elders and guardians sent this message to Jehu: "We support you and we will do anything you say. We will not appoint anyone as ruler; you do whatever you think best."

⁶ Then Jehu sent them a second letter: "If you are on my side and will obey me, take the heads of your ruler's sons and come to see me in Jezreel by this time tomorrow."

Now the sons, seventy of them, were with the leading men of the city. ⁷ When the letter arrived, the leaders took the sons and slaughtered all seventy of them. They put their heads in baskets and sent them to Jehu in Jezreel. ⁸ When the messenger arrived, he told Jehu, "They brought the heads of the sons."

Then Jehu ordered, "Put them in two piles at the entrance to the city gate until morning."

⁹ The next morning Jehu went out. He stood before all the people saying, "You are innocent. It was I who conspired against my master and killed him, but who killed all of these? ¹⁰ Know then, that not a word that YHWH spoke against the house of Ahab will fail. YHWH's promises were fulfilled through Elijah."

¹¹ So Jehu killed everyone in Jezreel who was left of the house of Ahab in Jezreel, as well as Ahab's officials, his close friends and priests, until he had left not one survivor.

¹² Jehu then set out and went towards Samaria. At Beth Eked of the Shephards, ¹³ he met some relatives of the ruler Ahaziah of Judah and asked, "Who are you?"

"We are relatives of Ahaziah, and we have come down to greet the families of the ruler and the queen mother."

[14] "Take them alive!" he ordered. So they took them alive and slaughtered them by the well of Beth Eked—forty two of them. Jehu left no survivors.

[15] After he left there, he came upon Jehonadab ben-Recab, who was on his way to meet him. Jehu greeted him and said, "Are you in accord with me, as I am with you?"

"I am," Jehonadab answered.

"If so," said Jehu, "give me your hand." So he did, and Jehu helped him up into the chariot. [16] Jehu said, "Come with me and see my zeal for YHWH." Then Jehonadab made him ride in Jehu's chariot.

[17] When Jehu came to Samaria, he killed all who were left there of Ahab's family; he destroyed them, in accordance with the word of YHWH spoken to Elijah.

[18] Then Jehu brought all the people together and said to them, "Ahab served Ba'al a little—Jehu will serve him much. [19] Now summon all the prophets of Ba'al, all his ministers and all his priests. See that no one is missing, for I am going to hold a great sacrifice for Ba'al. Anyone who fails to come will no longer live." But Jehu was acting deceptively in order to destroy the ministers of Ba'al.

[20] Jehu said, "Call an assembly in honor of Ba'al." So the people proclaimed it. [21] Then Jehu sent word throughout Israel, and all the ministers of Ba'al came—not a single one stayed away. They crowded into the Temple of Ba'al until it was full from one end to the other. [22] And Jehu said to the keeper of the wardrobe, "Bring robes for all the ministers of Ba'al." So he brought out robes for them.

[23] Then Jehu and Jehonadab ben-Recab went into the Temple of Ba'al. Jehu said to the ministers of Ba'al, "Look around to see that no servants of YHWH are here with you—only ministers of Ba'al." [24] So they went in to make sacrifices and burnt offerings.

Now Jehu had posted eighty men outside with this warning: "If one of you lets escape any I am placing in your hands, it will be your life for his life."

[25] As soon as Jehu finished making the burnt offering, he ordered the guards and officers: "Go in and kill them all! Let no one escape!" So the soldiers slew them with the sword. The guards and officers threw the bodies out and then entered the inner shine of the Temple of Ba'al. [26] They brought the sacred stone out of the Temple of Ba'al and burned it. [27] They demolished the sacred stone of Ba'al and tore down the Temple of Ba'al, and the people have used it for a latrine to this day. [28] So Jehu destroyed Ba'al worship in Israel.

²⁹ He did not, however, turn away from the sins that Jeroboam ben-Nebat had caused Israel to commit—the worship of the golden calves at Bethel and Dan.

³⁰ YHWH said to Jehu, "Because you did well in accomplishing what is right in my eyes and did to the house of Ahab all I had in mind to do, your descendants will sit on the judgment seat of Israel to the fourth generation."

³¹ Yet Jehu was not careful to keep the law of YHWH, the God of Israel, with all his heart. He did not turn away from the sins that Jeroboam had caused Israel to commit.

³² In those days YHWH began to reduce the size of Israel. Hazael overpowered the people of Israel throughout their territory ³³ east of the Jordan in all the land of Gilead (the region held by Gad, Reuben, and Manassah), from Aroer by the Arnon Gorge through Gilead to Bashan.

³⁴ The other events of Jehu's reign, all he did, and all the accomplishments, are written in *The Book of the Annals of the Rulers of Israel*.

³⁵ Jehu rested with his ancestors and was buried in Samaria. And Jehoahaz his son succeeded him as ruler. ³⁶ The time that Jehu reigned over Israel in Samaria was twenty-eight years.

11:1 When Athaliah the mother of Ahaziah saw that her son was dead, she proceeded to destroy the entire royal family. ² But Jehosheba, the daughter of Jehoram the late ruler, and sister to Ahaziah,* took Joash, Ahaziah's son and heir to the throne, and abducted him, in order to protect him from the royal family, who were about to be murdered. She hid him and his nurse in a bedroom, hiding them from Athaliah; so he remained among the living. ³ He and the nurse remained hidden in a storeroom of the Temple for six years while Athaliah ruled the land.†

⁴ In the seventh year, Jehoiada sent for the commanders of units of one hundred, the foreign-born bodyguard, and the guards, and had them brought to the Temple of YHWH. He made a covenant with them and put them under oath at the Temple of YHWH. Then he showed them Joash, the late ruler's son, ⁵ and gave them these orders: "One-third of you who are on duty on the Sabbath are to be on your guard at the royal residence. ⁶ The rest of you are to be on special duty in the Temple, one-third at the Foundation Gate and the final third at the gate behind the guards. ⁷ The two of your divisions who are going off duty that week shall keep guard over the Temple of YHWH for the ruler. ⁸ You will surround the ruler with weapons drawn, and anyone who even tries to approach the cordon will be put to death. Stay with Joash wherever he goes."

---

* Jehosheba was also the wife of Jehoida the high priest.
† Athalia was the only female ruler of Judah.

⁹ The commanders of one hundred did everything Jehoiada the priest had ordered; each took the guards assigned, the guards coming on duty on the Sabbath and the guards who went off, and they reported to Jehoiada. ¹⁰ The priest distributed to the commanders David's spears and shields, which were kept in the Temple. ¹¹ The guards, holding their weapons, took up their stations around the ruler, from corner to corner of the Temple and from north to south. ¹² Then Jehoiada brought out the ruler's young son, put the crown on him, handed him the Testimony, and anointed him ruler. The people applauded, shouting, "Long live the ruler!"

¹³ When Athaliah heard the din made by the guards and the people, she came into the Temple of YHWH where the people were gathered. ¹⁴ She found Joash the ruler standing by the pillar, as was the custom, amidst outbursts of singing and fanfares of trumpets in the ruler's honor. All the populace rejoiced and blew the trumpets. Athaliah tore her clothes, screaming, "Treason! Treason!"

¹⁵ Jehoiada the priest ordered the commanders in charge of the troops, "Bring her outside the precincts and put to death anyone who follows her." The priest continued, "She must not be put to death in the Temple of YHWH." ¹⁶ They seized her and brought her out by the entry for horses to the royal residence, and there she was put to death.

¹⁷ Jehoiada made a covenant—between YHWH on one side, and the ruler and people on the other—that they should be YHWH's people; and another covenant between the ruler and the people. ¹⁸ All the country people then went to the Temple of Ba'al and demolished it; they smashed its altars and images and killed Mattan the priest of Ba'al in front of the altars.

Then Jehoiada the priest posted guards at the Temple of YHWH. ¹⁹ He took with him the commander of the units of one hundred, the bodyguard, the guards and all the people of the land, and together they brought the ruler down from the Temple of YHWH and went to the royal residence, entering by way of the gate of the guards. The ruler then took his place on the royal judgment seat, ²⁰ and all the people of the land rejoiced. And the city was quiet, for Athaliah had been put to the sword in the royal residence. ²¹ Joash was seven years old when he was crowned ruler.

12:1 It was in the seventh year of Jehu that Joash became the ruler, and he reigned for forty years. His mother was Zibiah from Beersheba. ² Joash was just in the eyes of YHWH during all the years that he received instruction from Jehoiada. ³ The local shrines, however, were not removed and the people continued to offer sacrifices and burn incense there.

⁴ Joash said to the priests, "Collect all the money that is brought as sacred offerings to the Temple of YHWH—the money collected in the

census, the money received from personal vows and the money brought voluntarily to the Temple. ⁵ Let every priest receive the money from one of the treasurers, and let it be used to repair whatever damage is found in the Temple."

⁶ But by the twenty-third year of Joash, the priests still had not repaired the Temple. ⁷ So Joash summoned Jehoiada and the other priests and asked them, "Why are you not repairing the damages done to the Temple? Take no more from your treasurers, but hand over what you have already received for repairing the Temple." ⁸ The priests agreed that they would not collect any more money from the people and that they would not repair the Temple themselves.

⁹ Jehoiada the priest took a chest and bored a hole in its lid. He placed it beside the altar, on the right side as the Temple of YHWH is entered. The priest who guarded the entrance put into the chest all the money that was brought to the Temple of YHWH. ¹⁰ Whenever they saw that there was a large amount in the chest, the royal secretary and the high priest came, counted the money that had been brought into the Temple of YHWH and put it in bags. ¹¹ When the amount had been determined, they gave the money to the agents appointed to supervise the work of the Temple. With it they paid the workers on the Temple of YHWH—the carpenters and builders, ¹² the masons and the stonecutters. They purchased timber and dressed stone for the repair of the Temple of YHWH, and met all the other expenses of restoring the Temple.

¹³ The money brought into the Temple was not spent on making silver basins, wick trimmers, sprinkling bowls, trumpets or any other articles of gold or silver for the Temple of YHWH. ¹⁴ It was instead paid to the workers, who used it to repair the Temple. ¹⁵ The stewards of the money did not require an accounting from the agents to whom they gave the money to pay the workers, for the transactions were performed with trust. ¹⁶ The money from the guilt offerings and sin offerings was not brought into the Temple of YHWH—it belonged to the priests.

¹⁷ About this time Hazael ruler of Aram went up and attacked Gath and captured it. Then he turned to attack Jerusalem. ¹⁸ But Joash ruler of Judah took all the sacred objects dedicated by his ancestors—Jehoshapaht, Jehoram, and Ahaziah, the rulers of Judah—and the gifts he himself had dedicated and all the gold in the treasuries of the Temple of YHWH and of the royal residence, and sent them to Hazael ruler of Aram, who then withdrew from Jerusalem.

¹⁹ The other events of the reign of Joash, and all he did, are written in *The Book of the Annals of the Rulers of Judah*. ²⁰ His attendants rose up against him in a conspiracy and assassinated him in the house of Millo on the descent

of Silla. ²¹ It was his attendants Jozachar ben-Shimeath and Jehosabad ben-Shomer who struck the fatal blow. He was buried with his ancestors in the City of David. His heir Amaziah succeeded him.

¹³˸¹ In the twenty-third year of Joash ben-Ahaziah ruler of Judah, Jehoahaz ben-Jehu became ruler of Israel in Samaria, and he reigned for seventeen years. ² He did evil in the eyes of YHWH because he perpetuated the crimes that Jeroboam ben-Nebat had made Israel commit, and never departed from them. ³ YHWH was angry with Israel and repeatedly delivered them into the hands of Hazael ruler of Aram, and into the hands of Ben-Hadad ben-Hazael. ⁴ But Jehoahaz pleaded with YHWH; and YHWH listened to him after seeing the suffering that the ruler of Aram inflicted upon Israel. ⁵ So YHWH granted Israel a deliverer,* and they gained their freedom from Aram; and the Israelites lived in their homes as before. ⁶ But they did not depart from the sins that the house of Jeroboam had led Israel to commit—they even continued in those ways. And the Asherah pole continued to stand in Samaria.

⁷ Nothing was left of the army Jehoahaz except for fifty cavalry, ten chariots and ten thousand foot soldiers, for the ruler of Aram destroyed the rest and made them eat dust at threshing time. ⁸ The other events of the reign of Jehoahaz, all he did and his achievements, are all written in *The Book of the Annals of the Rulers of Israel.* ⁹ Jehoahaz rested with his ancestors and was buried in Samaria. And Jehoash his son succeeded him as ruler.

¹⁰ In the thirty-seventh year of Joash ruler of Judah, Jehoash ben-Jehoahaz became ruler of Israel in Samaria, and he reigned for sixteen years. ¹¹ He did evil in the eyes of YHWH and did not turn away from any of the crimes that Jeroboam ben-Nebat had caused Israel to commit. He did not end them.

¹² The other events of the reign of Jehoash, all he did and his achievements, including his war against Amaziah ruler of Judah, are written in *The Book of the Annals of the Rulers of Israel.* ¹³ Jehoash rested with his ancestors, and Jeroboam succeeded him on the judgment seat. Jehoash was buried in Samaria with the rulers of Israel.

¹⁴ Now Elisha was terminally ill. Jehoash ruler of Israel went down to see him and wept over the prophet. "My father! My father!" he cried "The chariot and cavalry of Israel!"

¹⁵ Elisha said, "Take a bow and some arrows," which he did. ¹⁶ "Take the bow in your hands," he said to the ruler of Israel. When the ruler took it,

---

* Most commentators believe this deliverer to be either Jehoahaz's son Jehoash, who regained all the cities that Aram had taken from his father, or Jehoahaz's grandson Jeroboam, who restored the former boundaries of Israel (14:25).

Elisha put his hands on the ruler's hands. ¹⁷ "Open the east window," he said, and the ruler opened it. "Now shoot!" Elisha ordered, and he shot. "God's arrow of victory, the victory over the Aram!" Elisha shouted. "You will completely destroy the Armeans at Aphek." ¹⁸ Then he said, "Take the arrows," and the ruler took them. Elisha told him, "Strike the ground." He struck it three times and stopped. ¹⁹ The prophet was angry with him, and said, "You should have struck the ground five or six times. Then you would have defeated the Aram and completely destroyed them. But now you will defeat them only three times."

²⁰ Then Elisha died and was buried.

Now Moabite raiders used to invade the country every spring. ²¹ Once, while some people of Israel were at a burial, they saw a band of raiders approaching quickly. So they threw the man's body into Elisha's tomb. When the body touched Elisha's bones, the man came to life and stood up on his feet.

²² Hazael ruler of Aram oppressed Israel throughout the reign of Jehoahaz. ²³ But YHWH was gracious to the people and had compassion and showed concern for them because of the covenant with Abraham, Issac, and Jacob. To this day, YHWH has been unwilling to destroy them or banish them from the divine presence.

²⁴ Hazael ruler of Aram died, and Ben-Hadad his son succeeded him as ruler. ²⁵ Then Jehoash ben-Jehoahaz recaptured from Ben-Hadad, Hazael's son, the towns that Ben-Hadad had taken in battle from his father Jehoahaz. Three times Jehoash defeated him, and so he recovered the villages of Israel.

14:1 In the second year of Jehoash ben-Jehoahaz ruler of Israel, Amaziah ben-Joash ruler of Judah began to reign. ² He was twenty-five years old when he was crowned ruler, and he reigned in Jerusalem for twenty-nine years. His mother's name was Johoaddin and she was from Jerusalem. ³ He was just in the eyes of YHWH, but not like his ancestor, David. In everything he followed the example of his father Joash. ⁴ But the local shrines were not removed. And the people continued to offer sacrifices and burn incense there.

⁵ Once the realm was firmly in his grasp, he executed the officials who had murdered his father the ruler. ⁶ But he did not put the children of the assassins to death, for he obeyed YHWH's command written in the Book of the Law of Moses: "Parents will not be put to death for their children, nor children for their parents; each of you will die for your own sins."

⁷ He defeated ten thousand Edomites in the Valley of Salt and captured Sela in battle, naming it Joktheel, the name it carries to this day. ⁸ Then

Amaziah sent messengers to Jehoash ben-Jehoahaz ben-Jehu, ruler of Israel, with the challenge, "Come, meet me face to face."

⁹ But Jehoash ruler of Israel replied to Amaziah ruler of Judah, "A thistle in Lebanon sent a message to a cedar in Lebanon, 'Give your daughter to my son in marriage.' Then a wild beast in Lebanon came along and trampled on the thistle. ¹⁰ You have indeed defeated Edom and now you are arrogant. Glory in your victory, and stay at home! Why ask for trouble and cause your own downfall and that of Judah as well?"

¹¹ Amaziah, however, would not listen, so Jehoash ruler of Israel attacked. He and Amaziah ruler of Judah faced each other at Beth Shemesh in Judah. ¹² Judah was routed by Israel, and every warrior fled home. ¹³ At Beth Shemesh, Jehoash ruler of Israel captured Amaziah ruler of Judah ben-Joash ben-Ahaziah. Then Jehoash went to Jerusalem and broke down the wall of Jerusalem from the Ephraim Gate to the Corner Gate—a section about six hundred feet long. ¹⁴ He took all the gold and silver and all the articles found in the Temple of YHWH and in the treasuries of the royal residence. He also took hostages and returned to Samaria.

¹⁵ The other events of the reign of Jehoash, what he did and his achievements, including his war against Amaziah ruler of Judah, are written in *The Book of the Annals of the Rulers of Israel*. ¹⁶ Jehoash rested with his ancestors and was buried in Samaria with the rulers of Israel. And Jeroboam his son succeeded him as ruler.

¹⁷ Amaziah ben-Joash ruler of Judah lived for fifteen years after the death of Jehoash ben-Jehoahaz ruler of Israel. ¹⁸ The other events of Amaziah's reign are written in *The Book of the Annals of the Rulers of Israel*. ¹⁹ They conspired against him in Jerusalem, and he fled to Lachish, but they sent men after him to Lachish and killed him there. ²⁰ He was brought back by horse and was buried in Jerusalem with his ancestors, in the City of David.

²¹ Then all the people of Judah took the sixteen-year-old Azariah and made him ruler in place of his father Amaziah. ²² He rebuilt Elath and restored it to Judah after Amaziah rested with his ancestors.

²³ In the fifteenth year of Amaziah ben-Joash ruler of Judah, Jeroboam ben-Jehoash ruler of Israel became ruler in Samaria and reigned for forty-one years. ²⁴ He did evil in the eyes of YHWH and did not turn away from any of the crimes of Jeroboam ben-Nebat, who had led Israel to sin. ²⁵ He restored the boundaries of Israel from Lebo Hamath to the Sea of the Arabah, in accordance with the word of YHWH, the God of Israel, spoken through his servant Jonas ben-Amittai, the prophet from Gath Hepher.

²⁶ YHWH saw how bitterly everyone in Israel, whether slave or free, was suffering. There was no one to deliver the people. ²⁷ And since YHWH had not said he would wipe out the name of Israel from under heaven, he rescued them by the hand of Jeroboam ben-Jehoash.

²⁸ As for the other events in Jeroboam's reign, all he did, and his military achievements, including how he recovered for Israel, both Damascus and Hamath, which belonged to Yaudi, they are written in *The Book of the Annals of the Rulers of Israel*. ²⁹ Jeroboam rested with his ancestors, the rulers of Israel. And Zechariah his son succeeded him as ruler.

15:1 In the twenty-seventh year of Jeroboam ruler of Israel, Azariah ben-Amaziah ruler of Judah began to reign. ² He was sixteen years old when he was crowned ruler, and he reigned in Jerusalem for fifty-two years. His mother's name was Jecoliah. She was from Jerusalem. ³ He was just in the eyes of YHWH, like his father Azariah. ⁴ The local shrines, however, were not removed; and the people continued to offer sacrifices and burn incense there. ⁵ YHWH inflicted the ruler with leprosy until the day he died, and he lived in a separate house. Jotham, the ruler's son, was in charge of the royal residence and governed the people of the land.

⁶ As for the other events of Azariah's reign, and all he did, they are written in *The Book of the Annals of the Ruler of Judah*. ⁷ Azariah rested with his ancestors and was buried near them in the City of David. And Jothan his heir succeeded him as ruler.

⁸ In the thirty-eighth year of Azariah ruler of Judah, Zechariah ben-Jeroboam became ruler of Israel in Samaria, and he reigned for six months. ⁹ Like his ancestors, he did evil in the eyes of YHWH. He did not turn away from the sins of Jeroboam ben-Nebat, who had caused Israel to do evil. ¹⁰ Shallum ben-Jabesh plotted against Zechariah. He attacked him in front of the people, assassinated him and succeeded him as ruler. ¹¹ The other events of Zechariah's reign are written in *The Book of the Annals of the Rulers of Israel*. ¹² So the word of YHWH spoken to Jehu was fulfilled: "Your descendants will sit on the judgment seat of Israel to the fourth generation."

¹³ Shallum ben-Jabesh became ruler in the thirty-ninth year of Uzziah ruler of Judah, and he reigned in Samaria for one month. ¹⁴ Then Menahem ben-Gadi went from Tirzah up to Samaria, assassinated him and succeeded him as ruler. ¹⁵ The other events of Shallum's reign, and the conspiracy he led, are written in *The Book of the Annals of the Rulers of Israel*. ¹⁶ At that time, Menahem marched from Tirzah, and attacked Tiphsah and

everyone in the city and its vicinity, because they refused to open the gates. He sacked Tipsah and ripped open all the pregnant women.

[17] In the thirty-ninth year of Azariah ruler of Judah, Menahem ben-Gadi became ruler of Israel, and he reigned in Samaria for ten years. [18] He was evil in the eyes of YHWH. During his entire reign he did not turn away from the sins that Jeroboam ben-Nabat had caused Israel to commit.

[19] Then Pul ruler of Assyria invaded the land, and Menahaem gave him one thousand talents of silver to gain his support and strengthen his own hold on the realm. [20] Menahem exacted this money from Israel. All the wealthy had to contribute fifty shekels of silver for tribute to the ruler of Assyria. So the ruler of Assyria withdrew and stayed in the land no longer.

[21] As for the other events of Menahem's reign, and all he did, they are written in *The Book of the Annals of the Rulers of Israel.* [22] Menahem rested with his ancestors. And Pekahiah his heir succeeded him as ruler.

[23] In the fiftieth year of Azariah ruler of Judah, Pekahiah ben-Menahem became ruler of Israel in Samaria, and he reigned for two years. [24] Pekahiah was evil in the eyes of YHWH. He did not turn away from the sins that Jeroboam ben-Nebat had caused Israel to commit. [25] Pekah ben-Remaaliah, one of his chief officers, conspired against him. Taking fifty Gileadites with him, he assassinated Pekaahiah, along with Argob and Arieh, in the citadel of the royal residence at Samaria. So Pekah killed Pekahiah and succeeded him as ruler.

[26] The other events of Pekahiah's reign, and all he did, they are written in *The Book of the Annals of the Rulers of Israel.*

[27] In the fifty-second year of Azariah ruler of Judah, Pekah ben-Remaliah became ruler of Israel in Samaria, and he reigned for twenty years. [28] He was evil in the eyes of YHWH. He did not turn away from the sins that Jeroboam ben-Nebat had caused Israel to commit.

[29] In the time of Pekah, King Tiglath-pileser ruler of Assyria came and took Ijon, Abel Beth Maacah, Janoah, Kedesh, and Hazor. He took Gilead and Galilee, including all the land of Naphtali, and deported all the people to Assyria. [30] Then Hoshea ben-Elah conspired against Pekah ben-Remaliah. He attacked and assassinated him, and then succeeded him as ruler in the twentieth year of Jotham ben-Uzziah. [31] As for the other events of Pekah's reign, and all he did, they are written in *The Book of the Annals of the Rulers of Israel.*

[32] In the second year of Pekah ben-Remaliah ruler of Israel, Jotham ben-Uzziah ruler of Judah began to reign. [33] He was twenty-five years old when

he became ruler, and he reigned in Jerusalem for sixteen years. His mother was Jerusha bat-Zadok. ³⁴ He was just in the eyes of YHWH, like his father Uzziah. ³⁵ The local shrines, however, were not removed. And the people continued to offer sacrifices and burn incense there. Jotham rebuilt the Upper Gate of the Temple of YHWH.

³⁶ All the other events of Jotham's reign, and what he did, are in *The Book of the Annals of the Rulers of Judah.* ³⁷ It was during his reign that YHWH began to send Rezin ruler of Aram and Pekah ben-Remaliah against Judah. ³⁸ Jotham rested with his ancestors and was buried with them in the City of David, the city of his father. And Ahaz his son succeeded him as ruler.

¹⁶:¹ In the seventh year of Pekah ben-Remaliah, Ahaz ben-Jotham became ruler of Judah. ² The twenty-year-old Ahaz reigned in Jerusalem for sixteen years. Unlike David his ancestor, he did not do what was just in the eyes of YHWH. ³ He walked in the ways of the rulers of Israel and even sacrificed his child in the fire, following the vile practices of the nations YHWH had driven out before the People of Israel. ⁴ He offered sacrifices and burned incense at the local shrines, on the hilltops and under every spreading tree.

⁵ Then Rezin ruler of Aram and Pekah ben-Remaliah ruler of Israel marched up to fight against Jerusalem and besieged Ahaz, but they could not overpower him. ⁶ At that time, Rezin ruler of Aram recovered Elath for Aram by driving out the Judeans. Edomites then moved into Elath and have lived there to this day.

⁷ Ahaz sent messengers to say to Tiglath-Pileser ruler of Assyria, "I am your servant and your vassal. Come up and save me from the ruler of Aram and from the ruler of Israel, who are attacking me." ⁸ Ahaz took all the silver and gold found in the Temple of YHWH and in the treasuries of the royal residence and sent it as a gift to the ruler of Assyria. ⁹ The ruler of Assyria complied by attacking Damascus and captured it. He deported its inhabitants to Kir and put Rezin to death.

¹⁰ Then Ahaz the ruler went to Damascus to meet Tiglath-Pileser ruler of Assyria. He saw an altar in Damascus and sent a sketch of it to Uriah the priest, with detailed plans for its construction. ¹¹ So Uriah the priest built an altar in accordance with all the plans that Ahaz the ruler had sent from Damascus and finished it before Ahaz the ruler returned. ¹² When the ruler returned from Damascus and saw the altar, he approached it and presented offerings on it. ¹³ He offered up his burnt offerings and his grain offering, poured out his drink offering, and sprinkled the blood of his fellowship offerings on the altar. ¹⁴ The bronze altar that stood before YHWH was brought from the front of the Temple—from between the new altar and the Temple of YHWH—and put on the north side of the new altar.

¹⁵ The ruler Ahaz then gave these orders to Uriah the priest: "On the large new altar, offer the morning burnt offering and the evening grain offering, the ruler's burnt offering and his grain offering, and the burnt offering of all the people of the land, and their grain offering and their drink offering. Sprinkle on the altar all the blood of the burnt offerings and sacrifices. But I will use the bronze altar for seeking guidance." ¹⁶ And Uriah the priest did just as Ahaz the ruler had ordered.

¹⁷ Ahaz the ruler took away the side panels and removed the basins from the moveable stands. He removed the Sea from the bronze bulls that supported it and set it on a stone base. ¹⁸ In deference to the ruler of Assyria, he took away the Sabbath canopy that had been built at the Temple and removed the royal entrance outside the Temple of YHWH.

¹⁹ As for the other events of the reign of Ahaz, what he did, they are written in *The Book of the Annals of the Rulers of Judah*. ²⁰ Ahaz rested with his ancestors and was buried with them in the City of David. And Hezekiah his son succeeded him as ruler.

ଔ   ଔ   ଔ

¹⁷:¹ In the twelfth year of Ahaz ruler of Judah, Hoshea ben-Elah became ruler of Israel in Samaria, and he reigned for nine years. ² He did evil in the eyes of YHWH, but not like the rulers of Israel who had preceded him.

³ Shalmaneser ruler of Assyria came up to attack Hoshea, who had been Shalmaneser's vassal and had paid him tribute. ⁴ But the ruler of Assyria discovered that Hoshea was a traitor, sending envoys to the ruler of Egypt and quitting the payment of tribute to the ruler of Assyria, as he had done annually. So Shalmaneser seized him and put him in prison. ⁵ Then the ruler of Assyria invaded the entire country, marching against Samaria, and laid siege to it for three years.

⁶ In the ninth year of Hoshea, the ruler of Assyria captured Samaria and deported the people of Israel to Assyria. He settled them in Halah, in Gozan on the Habor River and in the towns of the Medes.

⁷ All this took place because the people of Israel had sinned against YHWH their God, who had brought them up out of Egypt from under the power of Pharaoh ruler of Egypt. They worshiped other gods ⁸ and followed the practices of the nations YHWH had driven out before them, as well as the practices that the ruler of Israel introduced. ⁹ The people of Israel and the rulers they made for themselves plotted treacheries against their God. They built local shrines for themselves wherever they lived, from watchtowers to fortified cities. ¹⁰ They set up pillars and sacred poles for themselves on every high hill and under every spreading tree. ¹¹ They sacrificed there after the

manner of the nations that YHWH had expelled before them, and did evil things there, provoking the anger of YHWH. [12] They served idols, although YHWH had said to them, "This you must not do."

[13] YHWH warned Israel and Judah through all his prophets and seers: "Turn from your evil ways. Observe my commands and decrees, in accordance with the entire Law I commanded your ancestors and delivered to them through my servants and prophets." [14] But they would not listen and were as stubborn and rebellious as their ancestors had been, for they too refused to put their trust in YHWH their God. [15] They rejected YHWH's decrees and the covenant he had made with their ancestors and the warnings he had given them. They followed worthless idols and they themselves became worthless. They imitated the nations around them although YHWH had ordered them, "Do not do as they do!" They did things YHWH forbade them to do.

[16] They rejected all the commandments of YHWH their God and made idols of cast metal for themselves, two calves, and an Asherah pole. They worshiped the whole Host of Heaven, and they served Ba'al. [17] They sacrificed their sons and daughters in the fire. They practiced divination and sorcery and sold themselves to be evil in the eyes of YHWH, provoking YHWH to anger.

[18] YHWH was very angry with Israel and removed the people from the divine presence. Only the tribe of Judah was left, [19] and even the people of Judah did not keep the commands of YHWH, their God. They followed the practices Israel had introduced. [20] YHWH rejected all the people of Israel, afflicting them and giving them into the hands of plunderers, until they were removed from YHWH's presence.

[21] Once YHWH tore Israel away from the house of David, the people made Jeroboam ben-Nebat their ruler. Jeroboam seduced Israel away from following YHWH and caused the people to commit a great sin. [22] The People of Israel persisted in all the sins of Jeroboam and did not turn away from them [23] until YHWH removed them from the divine presence, as they had been warned through all YHWH's servants the prophets.

So the People of Israel were taken from their homeland into exile in Assyria, and they are still there.

[24] The ruler of Assyria brought people from Babylon, Cuthat, Avva, Hamath, and Sepharvaim and settled them in the towns of Samaria to replace the People of Israel. They took over Samaria and lived in its towns. [25] When they first lived there, they did not worship YHWH, so YHWH sent lions against them and the lions killed a number of them.

[26] It was reported to the ruler of Assyria, "The people you deported and resettled in the towns of Samaria do not know what the god of that country requires of them."

²⁷ So the ruler of Assyria gave an order: "Send back there one of the priests you took captive from Samaria who can teach the people what the god of the land requires." ²⁸ So one of the priests who had been exiled from Samaria came to live in Bethel and taught them how to worship YHWH.

²⁹ Yet each people made its own gods in the villages where it had settled, and set them up in the holy places the people of Samaria had made at the local shrines. ³⁰ The people from Babylon made Succoth Benoth, the settlers from Cuthah made Nergal, and the settlers from Hamath made Ashima. ³¹ The Avvites made Nibhaz and Tartak; and the Sheparvites burned their children in the fire as sacrifices to Adrammelech and Anammelech. ³² They worshipped YHWH, but they also appointed all sorts of their own people to officiate for them as priests in the local shrines. ³³ They worshipped YHWH, but they also worshipped their own gods in accordance with the customs of the nations from which they had been brought.

³⁴ To this day they persist in their former practices. They neither worship YHWH nor adhere to the decrees and ordinances, the laws and commands that YHWH gave the descendants of Jacob, now called Israel. ³⁵ When YHWH made a covenant with the people of Israel, he commanded them: "Do not worship any other gods or bow down to them, serve them or sacrifice to them. ³⁶ But YHWH, who brought you up out of Egypt with mighty power and outstretched arms, is the God you must worship. You are to bow down to this God, and offer sacrifices to this God. ³⁷ You must always be careful to keep the decrees and ordinances, the laws and the commands YHWH wrote for you. Do not worship other gods. ³⁸ Do not forget the covenant I made with you, and do not worship other gods. ³⁹ Rather, worship YHWH. It is this God who will deliver you from the hands of your enemies."

⁴⁰ They would not listen, though, but persisted in their former ways. ⁴¹ Even while these people worshiped YHWH, they served their idols. To this day their children and grandchildren continue to do as their mothers and fathers did.

18:1–25:30

In the third year of Hoshea ben-Elah the ruler of Israel, Hezekiah ben-Ahaz ruler of Judah began to reign. ² He was twenty-five years old when he became ruler, and he reigned in Jerusalem for twenty-nine years. His mother was Abilah bat-Zechariah.

³ He was just in the eyes of YHWH, as his father David had been. ⁴ He removed the local shrines, smashed the sacred stones and cut down the Ashererah poles. He broke into pieces the bronze snake called Nehushtan that Moses had made, to which up to that time the People of Israel had burned incense.

⁵ Hezekiah trusted in YHWH, the God of Israel. There was no one like him among all the rulers of Judah, either before or after. ⁶ He held fast to YHWH and did not cease to follow YHWH's way. He kept the commands that YHWH had given to Moses. ⁷ Because of this, YHWH was with him and he was successful in whatever he undertook. He rebelled against the ruler of Assyria and did not serve him. ⁸ From watchtower to fortified city, he defeated the Philistines, as far as Gaza and its territory.

⁹ In Hezekiah's fourth year, which was the seventh year of Hoshea ben-Elah ruler of Israel, Shalmaneser ruler of Assyria marched against Samaria and attacked it. ¹⁰ After three years, the Assyrians took it. So Samaria was captured in Hezekiah's sixth year, which was the ninth year of Hoshea ruler of Israel. ¹¹ The ruler of Assyria deported Israel to Assyria and settled the people in Halah, in Gozan on the Habor River, and in towns of the Medes. ¹² This happened because they had not obeyed YHWH their God, but violated YHWH's covenant—all that Moses, YHWH's servant, had commanded. They neither listened to the commands nor carried them out.

¹³ In the fourteenth year of Hezekiah's reign, Sennacherib ruler of Assyria attacked all the fortified cities of Judah and captured them. ¹⁴ So Hezekiah ruler of Judah sent this message to the ruler of Assyria at Lachish: "I have erred. Withdraw your troops and I will pay whatever you ask of me." The ruler of Assyria exacted from Hezekiah ruler of Judah three hundred talents of silver and thirty talents of gold. ¹⁵ So Hezekiah gave him all the silver that was found in the Temple of YHWH and in the treasuries of the royal residence.

¹⁶ At this time Hezekiah ruler of Judah stripped off the gold with which he had covered the doors and lintels of the Temple of YHWH, and gave it to the ruler of Assyria.

¹⁷ From Lachish to Hezekiah the ruler at Jerusalem the ruler of Assyria sent his supreme commander, his chief officer and his field commander with a large army. They came up to Jerusalem and stopped at the aqueduct of the Upper Pool, on the road to the Laundry Field. ¹⁸ They called for the ruler; and Eliakim ben-Hilkiah the palace administrator, Shebna the secretary, and Joah ben-Asaph the recorder went out with them.

¹⁹ The field commander said to them, "Tell Hezekiah that this is what the Great Ruler, the ruler of Assyria says: On what are you basing this confi-

dence of yours? ²⁰ You say you have strategy and military might, but your words are empty. On whom are you depending, that you rebel against me? ²¹ Look now, you are depending on Egypt, that splintering reed of a staff, that pierces the hand of anyone who leans on it! Such is Pharaoh ruler of Egypt to all who depend on him. ²² And if you say to me, 'We are depending on YHWH'—isn't this the God whose local shrines and altars Hezekiah removed, saying to Judah and Jerusalem, 'You must worship before this altar in Jerusalem?'

²³ "Come now, make a bargain with my ruler, the ruler of Assyria: I will give you two thousand horses, if you can provide riders! ²⁴ How can you repulse one officer of the least of my superior's officials, though you are depending on Egypt for chariots and cavalry? ²⁵ And have I come to attack and destroy this place without word from your God? Your God told me to march against this country and destroy it."

²⁶ Then Eliakim ben-Hilkiah, Shebna, and Joah said to the field commander, "Please speak to your attendants in Aramaic, since we understand it. Don't speak to us in Hebrew in the hearing of the people on the wall."

²⁷ But the commander replied, "Was it only to your superior and you that my superior sent me to say these things, and not to the people sitting on the wall—who, like you, will have to eat their own filth and drink their own urine?"

²⁸ Then the commander stood and called out in Hebrew: "Hear the word of the Great Ruler, the ruler of Assyria! ²⁹ This is what the ruler says: Do not let Hezekiah deceive you. He cannot deliver you from my hand. ³⁰ Do not let Hezekiah persuade you to trust in your God when he says, 'YHWH will surely deliver us—this city will not be given into the hand of the ruler of Assyria.'

³¹ "Do not listen to Hezekiah. This is what the ruler of Assyria says: Make a treaty with me and come out to me. Then all of you will eat from your own vine and fig-tree and drink water from your own well, ³² until I come and take you to a land like your own, a land of grain and new wine, a land of bread and vineyards, a land of olive trees and honey. Choose life and not death! Do not listen to Hezekiah, for he is misleading you when he says, 'YHWH will rescue us.' ³³ Has the god of any nation ever delivered the land from the hand of the ruler of Assyria? ³⁴ Where are the gods of Hamath and Arpad? Where are the gods of Sepharvaim, Hena and Ivvah? Have they rescued Samaria from my hand? ³⁵ Who of all the gods of these countries has been able to save their land from me? How then can your God deliver Jerusalem from my hand?"

³⁶ But the people remained silent and said nothing in reply, because Hezekiah commanded, "Do not answer him."

³⁷ Then Eliakim ben-Hilkiah the administrator of the royal residence, Shebna the secretary, and Joah ben-Asaph the recorder went to Hezekiah, with their clothes torn, and told him what the commander had said.

19:1 When Hezekiah the ruler heard this, he tore his clothes, put on sackcloth and entered the Temple of YHWH. ² To the prophet Isaiah ben-Amoz he sent Eliakim the royal residence administrator, Shebna the secretary and the leading priests, all wearing sackcloth ³ They told him, "This is what Hezekiah says: This day is a day of distress, rebuke and disgrace, as when children come to the point of birth and there is no strength to deliver them. ⁴ It may be that YHWH will hear all the words of the field commander, whose superior, the ruler of Assyria, has been sent to ridicule the living God, and will rebuke him for the words that YHWH your God heard. Pray therefore for the remnant that survives."

⁵ When Hezekiah the ruler's officials came to Isaiah, ⁶ he said to them, "Tell your superior, 'This is what YHWH says: Do not be afraid of what you have heard—those words with which the underlings of the ruler of Assyria blasphemed me. ⁷ Listen! I am going to put such a spirit in him that when he hears a fearful rumor, he will return to his country, where I will have him cut down with the sword.'" ⁸ When the field commander learned that the ruler of Assyria had left Lachish, he withdrew and found the ruler fighting against Libnah.

⁹ Now Sennacherib received a report that Tirhakah, the Cushite ruler of Egypt, was marching out to fight against him. So he again sent messengers to Hezekiah with this word, ¹⁰ "Say to Hezekiah ruler of Judah: Do not let the god you depend on deceive you when your god says, 'Jerusalem will not be handed over to the ruler of Assyria.' ¹¹ Surely you have heard what the rulers of Assyria did to all the countries, destroying them completely. And you will be delivered? ¹² Did the gods of the nations that were destroyed by my ancestors deliver them: the gods of Gozan, Haran, Rezeph and the people of Eden who were in Tel Assar? ¹³ Where is the ruler of Hamath, the ruler of Arpad, the ruler of the city of Sepharvaim, or of Hena or Ivvah?"

¹⁴ Hezekiah received the letter from the messengers and read it. Then he went up to the Temple of YHWH and spread it out before YHWH. ¹⁵ And Hezekiah prayed to YHWH; "YHWH, the God of Israel, enthroned between the cherubim, you alone are the God over all the realms of the earth. You made heaven and earth. ¹⁶ Lend an ear, YHWH, and listen; open your eyes, YHWH, and see; listen to the words Sennacherib sent to insult the living God."

¹⁷ "It is true, YHWH, that the Assyrian rulers laid waste these nations and their lands. ¹⁸ They threw their gods in the fire and destroyed them, for they were not gods but only wood and stone, fashioned by human hands. ¹⁹ Now,

YHWH, deliver us from his hand, so that all realms on earth may know that you alone are YHWH."

²⁰ Then Isaiah ben-Amoz sent a message to Hezekial: "This is what YHWH, the God of Israel says: I heard your prayer concerning Sennacherib ruler of Assyria. ²¹ This is the word that YHWH spoke against him:

> "The youthful Daughter of Zion
> despises you and mocks you.
> The Daughter of Jerusalem
> tosses her head as you flee.

²² Who is it you have
> insulted and blasphemed?
> Against whom have you raised your voice
> and lifted your eyes in pride?
> Against the Prophet of Israel!

²³ By your messengers
> you heaped insults on Yhwh.
> And you said, 'With my many chariots
> I have ascended the heights of the mountains,
> the utmost heights of Lebanon.
> I cut down its tallest cedars,
> the choicest of its pines.

²⁴ I dug wells in foreign lands
> and drunk the water there.
> With soles on my feet
> I dried up all the streams of Egypt.'

²⁵ Have you not heard?
> Long ago I ordained it.
> In the days of old I planned it;
> now I have brought it to pass,
> that you turned fortified cities into piles of rubble.

²⁶ Their people, drained of power,
> are dismayed and ashamed.
> They are like plants in the field,
> like tender green shoots,
> like grass spouting on the roof,
> scorched before it grows up.

²⁷ But I know where you stay
> and when you come and go
> and how you rage against me.

²⁸ Because you rage against me
> and your insolence has reached my ears,

I will put my hook in your nose
and my bit in your mouth,
and I will make you return
by the way you came.
²⁹ This will be the sign for you, Hezekiah;
This year you will eat what grows by itself,
and the second year what springs from that.
But in the third year you sow and reap,
plant vineyards and eat their fruit.
³⁰ Once more a remnant of the house of Judah
will take root below and bear fruit above.
³¹ For out of Jerusalem will come a remnant,
and out of Mount Zion a band of survivors.
The zeal of Yh wh Omnipotent
will accomplish this.
³² Therefore this is what Yh wh says about the ruler of Assyria:
He will enter this city or shoot an arrow here.
He will not come before it with shield
or build a siege ramp against it.
³³ By the way he came he will return;
he will not enter this city and save it, declares Yh wh.
³⁴ I will defend this city and save it,
for my sake and for the sake of David my servant."

³⁵ That night the angel of YHWH went out and put to death one hundred and eighty-five thousand in the Assyrian camp. When the people got up the next morning—so many dead bodies! ³⁶ So Sennacheerib ruler of Assyria broke camp and withdrew. He returned to Nineveh and stayed there.

³⁷ One day, while he worshipped in the temple of his god Nisroch, his sons Adrammelech and Sharezer cut him down with the sword, and they escaped to the land of Ararat. And Esarhaddon his son succeeded him as ruler.

^{20:1} In those days Hezekiah became ill and was at the point of death. The prophet Isaiah ben-Amoz went to him, and said, "This is what YHWH says: Put your house in order, because you are going to die. You will never recover."

² Hezekiah turned his face to the wall and prayed to YHWH, ³ "Remember, YHWH, how I walked before you faithfully and with wholehearted devotion and did what is good in your eyes." And Hezekiah wept bitter tears.

⁴ Before Isaiah left the middle court, the word of YHWH came to him: ⁵ "Go back and tell Hezekiah, the leader of my people, 'This is what YHWH, the God of your ancestor David, says: I heard your prayer and saw your tears, and I will cure you. On the third day from now you will go up to the Temple of

YHWH. ⁶ I will deliver you and this city from the hands of the ruler of Assyria. I will defend this city for my sake and for the sake of my servant David.'"

⁷ Then Isaiah said, "Prepare a poultice of figs." They followed his instructions and applied it to the boil, and he recovered.

⁸ Hezekiah asked Isaiah, "What will be the sign that YHWH will heal me and that I will go up to the Temple of YHWH on the third day from now?"

⁹ Isaiah replied, "This is YHWH's sign to you that YHWH will do to you as promised: Shall the shadow go forward ten steps, down the Stairway of Ahaz, or shall it go back ten steps?"*

¹⁰ "It is a simple matter for the shadow to go forward ten steps," said Hezekiah, "so have it go back ten steps instead."

¹¹ Then the prophet Isaiah called upon YHWH, and YHWH made the shadow go back the ten steps it had gone down on the Stairway of Ahaz.

¹² At that time Merodach-Baladan ben-Baladan ruler of Babylon sent letters and a gift, for he had heard of Hezekiah's illness. ¹³ Hezekiah received the messengers and showed them all that was in his storehouses—the silver, the gold, the spices and the fine oil—his armory and everything found among his treasures. There was nothing in his royal residence or in all of his realm that Hezekiah did not show them.

¹⁴ Then the prophet Isaiah went to Hezekiah and asked, "What did those messengers say, and where did they come from?"

"From a distant land," Hezekiah replied. "They came from Babylon."

¹⁵ And Isaiah asked, "What did they see in your royal residence?"

"They saw everything in my royal residence."

¹⁶ Then Isaiah said to Hezekiah, "Hear the word of YHWH: ¹⁷ The time will surely come when everything in your royal residence, and all that your predecessors have stored up until this day, will be carried off to Babylon. Nothing will be left, says YHWH. ¹⁸ And some of your descendants, your own flesh and blood, that are to be born to you, will be taken away, and they will become eunuchs in the royal residence of the ruler of Babylon."

¹⁹ "The word of YHWH that you spoke is good," Hekeziah replied. For he thought, "Will there not be peace and security in my lifetime?"

²⁰ As for the other events of Hezekiah's reign, all his achievements and

---

* The Hebrew word means "steps," both literally (as steps of a staircase) and figuratively (as degrees.) If the literal sense is meant, this may have indicated a stone stairway in the city named for Hezekiah's father, with the adjoining building's shadow going up or down the step. If the figurative sense is meant, many scholars feel it could indicate the degree markings on the face of a sundial; such a "Sundial of Ahaz" would likely have been on display outside the palace.

how he made the pool and the tunnel by which he brought water into the city, they are written in *The Book of the Annals of the Rulers of Judah.* 21 Hezekiah rested with his ancestors. And Manasseh his son succeeded him as ruler.

21:1 Manasseh was twelve years old when he was crowned ruler, and he reigned in Jerusalem for fifty-five years. His mother's name was Hephzibah. 2 He did evil in the eyes of YHWH, following the abominable practices of the nations that YHWH had driven out before the people of Israel. 3 He rebuilt the local shrines his predecessor had destroyed. He also erected altars to Ba'al and made an Asherah pole, as Ahab ruler of Israel had done. He prostrated himself before all the host of heaven and served them. 4 He built altars in the Temple of YHWH, of which YHWH had said, "In Jerusalem I will put my Name." 5 In both courts of the Temple of YHWH, he built altars for all the host of heaven. 6 He sacrificed his own son in the fire, practiced sorcery and divination, and consulted mediums and spiritualists. He was evil in the eyes YHWH, provoking God to anger.

7 The ruler took the carved Asherah pole he had made and put it in the Temple, of which YHWH had said to David and David's heir Solomon, "In this Temple and in Jerusalem, which I chose out of all the tribes of Israel, I will put my Name forever. 8 I will not again make the feet of the People of Israel wander from the land I gave their ancestors, if only they will be careful to do everything I commanded them and will keep the whole Law that Moses gave them." 9 But the people did not listen. Manasseh led them astray, so they did more evil than the nations that YHWH had destroyed before the People of Israel.

10 YHWH said through the prophets: 11 "Manasseh ruler of Judah committed these abominable sins. He did more evil than the Amoritres had done who preceded him and led Judah into sin with idols. 12 This, then, is what YHWH, the God of Israel, says: I am about to bring so much disaster on Jerusalem and Judah that it will ring in the ears of everyone who hears of it. 13 I will use against Jerusalem the measuring rod I used against Samaria and the plumb-line I used against the house of Ahab. I will wipe out Jerusalem the way a plate is wiped and turned upside down. 14 I will cast off what is left of my people, my own possessions, and hand them over to their enemies. They will be plundered and looted by all their foes, 15 because they did what is wrong in my eyes and provoked me to anger from the day their ancestors came up out of Egypt until this day."

16 Manasseh also shed so much innocent blood that he filled Jerusalem from end to end, besides the sins into which he led Judah by doing what is displeasing to YHWH.

¹⁷ The other events of Manassah's reign, and all he did, including the sin he committed, are written in *The Book of the Annals of the Rulers of Judah.* ¹⁸ Manassah rested with his ancestors and was buried in the royal residence garden, the garden of Uzzi. And Amon succeeded him as ruler.

¹⁹ Amon was twenty-two years old when he came to the judgment seat, and he reigned in Jerusalem for two years. His mother was Meshullemeth bat-Haruz from Jotbah. ²⁰ He did what was evil in the eyes of YHWH as his father Manasseh had done. ²¹ Following in his father's steps, he served the idols that Manassah had served and prostrated before them. ²² He abandoned YHWH, the God of our ancestors, and did not conform to YHWH's ways. ²³ Amon's officials conspired against him and assassinated him in the royal residence. ²⁴ Then the country people killed all the conspirators and made Josiah ruler in his place.

²⁵ As for the other events in Amon's reign, and what he did, they are written in *The Book of the Annals of the Rulers of Judah.* He was buried in his grave in the garden of Uzza. Josiah succeeded him as ruler.

^{22:1} Josiah was eight years old when he became ruler, and he reigned in Jerusalem for thirty-one years. His mother's name was Jedidah ben-Adaiah; she was from Bozkath. ² Josiah was just in the eyes of YHWH and walked in all the ways of his ancestor.

³ In the eighteenth year of his reign, Josiah the ruler sent his secretary, Shaphan ben-Azaliah ben-Meshullam, to the Temple of YHWH. ⁴ He said, "Go up to Hilkiah the high priest and make him gather the money that has been brought in the Temple of YHWH, which the doorkeepers collected from the people. ⁵ Make them entrust it to the agents appointed to supervise the work on the Temple. And make them pay the workers who repair the Temple of YHWH— ⁶ the carpenters, the builders and the masons. Also make them purchase timber and dressed stone for repairs on the Temple. ⁷ But they need not account for the funds entrusted to them, because they hold positions of trust."

⁸ The high priest Hilkiah said to Shaphan the secretary, "I found this Book of the Law in the Temple of YHWH."* He gave it to Shaphan, who read it. ⁹ Then Shaphan the secretary went to the ruler and reported, "Your officials have paid out the money that was in the Temple of YHWH and have entrusted it to the workers and supervisors in the Temple."

¹⁰ Then Spaphan the secretary reported to the ruler: "Hilkiah the priest gave me a book." And Shaphan read from the book in the presence of the ruler.

---

* This is almost certainly the book of *Deuteronomy;* the changes that Josiah instituted are usually referred to as the Deuteronomic Reforms. Josiah is widely considered to be the greatest ruler in Judah after David.

¹¹ When the ruler heard the words of the Book of the Law, he tore his clothes. ¹² He then gave these orders to Hilkiah the priest, Ahikam ben-Shaphan, Acbor ben-Micaiah, Shaphan the secretary, and Asaiah the ruler's attendant: ¹³ "Go and ask YHWH for me, for the people and for all Judah about the words of this book that was found. YHWH's great anger must be smouldering against us, for our ancestors did not obey the commands in this book—they have not acted in accordance with all that is written there concerning us."

¹⁴ Hilkiah the priest, Akiham, Acbor, Shaphan, and Asaiah went to speak to the prophet Huldah, who was the wife of Shallum ben-Tikvah ben-Harbas, keeper of the wardrobe. She lived in Jerusalem, in the Second District. ¹⁵ She said to them, "This is what YHWH says: 'Tell whoever sent you to me— ¹⁶ thus says YHWH—that I will bring disaster on this place and on its people, according to everything written in the book that the ruler of Judah read. ¹⁷ For they abandoned me and burned incense to other gods and provoked me to anger by all the idols made with their hands. My anger will burn against this place and will not be quenched.' ¹⁸ Tell the ruler of Judah, who sent you to ask YHWH, 'This is what YHWH, the God of Israel, says concerning the words you heard: ¹⁹ Because your heart was responsive and you humbled yourself before YHWH when you heard that I spoke against this place and its people, that you would become accursed and laid to waste, and because you tore your clothes and wept in my presence, I have heard you, declares YHWH. ²⁰ Therefore I will gather you to your ancestors and you will be buried in peace—your eyes will not see all the disaster I am to bring on this place.' "

So they took her answer back to the ruler.

23:1 Then the ruler called together all the elders of Judah and Jerusalem. ² He went up to the Temple of YHWH with the people of Judah, the inhabitants of Jerusalem, the priests and the prophets—all the people from the least to the greatest. He read in their hearing all the words of the Book of the Law that had been found in the Temple of YHWH. ³ The ruler stood by the pillar and renewed the Covenant in the presence of YHWH: to follow YHWH and keep YHWH's commands, regulations and decrees with whole heart and whole soul, confirming the terms of the Covenant in this book. Then all the people pledged themselves to the Covenant.

⁴ The ruler ordered Hilkiah the high priest, the priests who were next in rank, and the doorkeepers to remove from the Temple of YHWH all the articles made for Ba'al and Asherah and the Host of Heaven. He burned them outside Jerusalem in the fields of the Kidron Valley and took the ashes to Bethel. ⁵ He suppressed the pagan priests appointed by the rulers of Judah to burn incense on the local shrines of the towns of Judah and around Je-

rusalem—the priests who burned incense to Ba'al, to the sun and the moon, to the constellations and the planets and the Host of Heaven. 6 He took the Asherah pole from the Temple of YHWH to the Kidron Valley outside Jerusalem and burned it there. He ground it to powder and scattered it over the graves in the public cemetary. 7 He also tore down the cubicles of the male prostitutes in the Temple of YHWH and where women wove vestments in honor of Asherah.

8 Josiah brought all the priests from the town Judah and desecrated the local shrines, from Geba to Beersheba, where the priests had burned incense. He broke down the shrines to the goat gods at the entrance to the Gate of Joshua, the city governor, which is on the left side of the city gate. 9 Although the priests of the local shrines did not serve at the altar of YHWH in Jerusalem, they ate unleavened bread with the priests of their clan. 10 Josiah desecrated Topheth,* which was in the Valley of Ben-Hinnom, so that no one could sacrifice a child in the fire of Molech. 11 He removed the horses that the rulers of Judah had set up in honor of the sun at the entrance to the Temple of YHWH, beside the room of the eunuch Nathan-Melech in the colonnade; Josiah then burned the chariots dedicated to the sun.

12 He pulled down the altars the rulers of Judah had set up on the roof near the upper room of Ahaz, and the altars Manasseh had built in the two courts of the Temple of YHWH. He pounded them to dust and threw it into the Kidrow Valley. 13 Josiah destroyed the local shrines east of Jerusalem, south of the Mount of Olives, and smashed the shrines that Solomon ruler of Israel had built for Ashtoreth, the loathsome goddess of the Sidonians, and for Milcom the abominable god of the Ammonites. 14 He tore down the sacred pillars and cut down the sacred poles and filled with human bones the places where they had stood.

15 At Bethel, he dismantled the altar by the shrine made by Jeroboam ben-Nebat, who had led Israel into sin, and destroyed the shrine itself. He broke its stones in pieces, crushed them to dust, and burnt the sacred pole. 16 When Josiah saw the graves there on the hill, he sent the bones from them and burned them on the altar to desecrate it, thus fulfilling the word of YHWH announced by the prophet when Jeroboam stood by the altar at the feast. When Josiah saw the grave of the prophet of God who had come from Judah and foretold these things, 17 he asked, "What is that monument I am looking at?"

The people of the town replied, "It is the grave of the prophet of God who came from Judah and foretold all that you did to the altar at Bethel."

---

* Topheth, which means "burning place," was that part of the Hinnom Valley (in Greek, *Gehenna*, which came to personify the concept of Hell), just outside Jerusalem, where children were sacrificed to the Ammonite god Molech (also called Milcom in v. 13). "Molech" means ruler.

¹⁸ "Leave it alone," he said; "let no one disturb his bones." So they spared his bones along with the bones of the prophet who had come from Samaria. ¹⁹ Josiah also suppressed all the temples at the shrines in the towns of Samaria, which the rulers of Israel had built, provoking YHWH's anger, and Josiah did to them what he had done at Bethel. ²⁰ He slaughtered on the altars all the priests of the shrines who were there, and he burned human bones on them. Then he returned to Jerusalem.

²¹ The ruler ordered all the people to keep the Passover to YHWH, as it is written in the Book of the Law. ²² Not since the days of the judges who led Israel, nor throughout the days of the rulers of Israel and the days of rulers of Judah, had any such a Passover been observed. ²³ But in the eighteenth year of Josiah the ruler, this Passover was celebrated to YHWH in Jerusalem.

²⁴ And Josiah got rid of the mediums and the spiritualists, the household gods, the idols, and all the other abominable objects in Judah and in Jerusalem, so that he might fulfill the requirements of the Law written in the book that Hilkiah the priest had discovered in the Temple of YHWH. ²⁵ No ruler before him had turned to YHWH with all his heart and soul and strength, following the entire Law of Moses. Nor was there ever a ruler like him again.

²⁶ Yet YHWH's anger did not abate. It still burned against Judah for all the provocation Manasseh had given him. ²⁷ "I will also banish Judah from my presence," YHWH declared, "as I banished Israel. And I will reject this city of Jerusalem that I once chose, and the house where I promised that my Name should be."

²⁸ The other events and acts of Josiah's reign are recorded in *The Book of the Annals of the Rulers of Judah*. ²⁹ It was in his reign that Pharaoh Neco ruler of Egypt set out for the Euphrates River to help the ruler of Assyria. Josiah the ruler went to meet Neco, and when they met at Megiddo, Pharaoh Neco murdered him. ³⁰ Josiah's attendants brought his body from Megiddo to Jerusalem and buried him in his own grave site. Then the people of the land took Josiah's son Jehoahaz and anointed him ruler in place of Josiah.

³¹ Jehoahaz was twenty-three years old when he came to the judgment seat and he reigned in Jerusalem for three months. His mother was Hamital bat-Jeremiah of Libnah. ³² He did evil in the eyes of YHWH, as his ancestors had done. ³³ Pharaoh Neco removed him from the throne in Jerusalem, and imposed a land tax of one hundred talents of silver and one talent of gold. ³⁴ He made Josiah's son Eliakim ruler in place of Jehoahaz and changed his name to Jehoiakim. He carried Jehoiakim away to Egypt, where he lived for the rest of his life. ³⁵ Jehoiakim handed over the silver and gold to Pharaoh,

taxing the country to meet Pharaoh's demands. To pay Pharaoh he exacted it from the people, from everyone according to assessments.

³⁶ Jehoiakim was twenty-five years old when he came to the throne, and he reigned in Jerusalem for eleven years. His mother was Zebidah bat-Pedaiah of Rumah. ³⁷ He did what was evil in the eyes of YHWH as his ancestors had done.

²⁴:¹ During the reign of Jehoiakim, Nebuchadnezzar ruler of Babylon attacked, and Jehoiakim became his vassal. Three years later, however, Jehoiakim broke with him and revolted. ² YHWH sent Babylonians, Arameans, Moabites, and Ammonite raiders against Jehoiakim, sending them to destroy Judah, in accordance with the word of YHWH proclaimed by YHWH's servants the prophets. ³ All this happened to Judah in fulfillment of YHWH's purpose, to banish the people from the divine presence for the sin Manasseh had committed, ⁴ including the shedding of innocent blood. He had flooded Jerusalem with innocent blood, and YHWH would not forgive him.

⁵ The other events and acts of Jehoiakim's reign are recorded in *The Book of the Annals of the Rulers of Judah*. ⁶ He rested with his ancestors, and his son Jehoiachin succeeded him as ruler. ⁷ No more did the Egyptian ruler march out from his own country, for the ruler of Babylon stripped him of all his possessions from the Nile to the Euphrates.

⁸ Jehoiachin was eighteen years old when he was crowned ruler, and he reigned in Jerusalem for three months. His mother was Nehushta bat-Elnathan; she was from Jerusalem. ⁹ He was evil in the eyes of YHWH, as his father had been. ¹⁰ At that time the officers of Nebuchadnezzar advanced in Jerusalem and besieged it. ¹¹ Nebuchadnezzar ruler of Babylon advanced, and his troopes besieged the city. ¹² Jehoiachin ruler of Judah, his mother, his attendants, his nobles, and his officials all surrendered to them.

In the eighth year of the reign of the ruler of Babylon, he took Jehoiachin prisoner. ¹³ As YHWH had declared, Nebuchadnezzar looted all the treasures from the Temple of YHWH and from the royal residence, and took away all the gold articles Solomon ruler of Israel had made for the Temple of YHWH. ¹⁴ He carried into exile all of Jerusalem—all the officers and warriors, and all the skilled workers and artisans—a total of ten thousand. Only the poorest people of the land were left behind.

¹⁵ Nebuchadnezzar took Jehoiachin captive to Babylon. He also took from Jerusalem to Babylon the ruler's mother, his wives, his officials and the prominent citizens of the land. ¹⁶ Nebuchadnezzar deported to Babylon the entire force of seven thousand fighting troops, strong and fit for war, and a thousand skilled workers and artisans.

¹⁷ Nebuchadnezzar made Mattaniah, Jehoiachin's uncle, ruler in Jehoiachin's stead, and changed Mattaniah's name to Zedekiah. ¹⁸ Zedekiah was twenty-one years old when he was crowned ruler, and he reigned in Jerusalem for eleven years. His mother was Hamutal bat-Jeremiah; she was from Libnah. ¹⁹ He did evil in the eyes of YHWH, just as Jehoiakim had done. ²⁰ It was because of YHWH's anger that all this happened to Jerusalem and Judah, and in the end YHWH thrust them from the divine presence.

²⁵:¹ Zedekiah rebelled against the ruler of Babylon. In the ninth year of his reign, on the tenth day of the tenth month, Nebuchadnezzar moved against Jerusalem with his entire army. He laid siege and built towers against it on every side. ² The assault lasted until the eleventh year of Zedekiah the ruler.

³ In the fourth month of that year, on the ninth day of the month, the famine in the city was so severe that there was no food for the people to eat. ⁴ Then the city wall was breached, and the whole army fled that night through the gate between the two walls near the ruler's garden, even though the Babylonians were surrounding the city. They fled toward the Arabah, ⁵ but the Babylonian army pursued the ruler and captured him in the plains of Jericho. All his army was separated and scattered, ⁶ and he was held prisoner. Zedekiah was taken to the ruler of Babylon at Riblah, where sentence was pronounced: ⁷ They killed his children before his eyes. Then they put out his eyes, bound him with bronze shackles, and took him to Babylon.

⁸ On the seventh day of the ninth month, in the nineteenth year of Nebuchadnezzar ruler of Babylon, Nebuzaradan commander of the imperial guard, an official of the ruler of Babylon, came to Jerusalem. ⁹ He set fire to the Temple of YHWH, the royal residence and all the houses of Jerusalem. He burned down every important building. ¹⁰ The whole Babylonian army, under the commander of the imperial guard, broke down the walls around Jerusalem. ¹¹ Nebuzaradan the commander of the guard carried into exile the people who remained in the city, along with the rest of the populace and whoever had gone over to the ruler of Babylon. ¹² But the commander left behind some of the poorest people of the land to work the vineyards and fields.

¹³ The Babylonians broke up the bronze pillars, the movable stands and the bronze Sea that were at the Temple of YHWH and they carried the bronze to Babylon. ¹⁴ They also took away the pots, shovels, wick trimmers, dishes and all the bronze articles used in the Temple service. ¹⁵ The commander of the imperial guard took away the censers and sprinkling bowls—everything that was made of pure gold or silver.

¹⁶ The bronze from the two pillars, the Sea, and the movable stands, which Solomon had made for the Temple of YHWH, was more than could

be weighed. [17] Each pillar was twenty-seven feet high. The bronze capital on top of one pillar was four-and-a-half feet high, and was decorated with a network and pomegranates of bronze all around. The other pillar, with its network, was similar.

[18] The commander of the guard took as prisoners Seraiah, the high priest, Zephaniah the priest next in rank, and the three doorkeepers. [19] Of the remainder still in the city, he took the officer in charge of the warriors, five with right of access to the ruler who were still in the city, the adjutant-general whose duty was to muster the people for war, and sixty citizens who were still there. [20] Nebuzaradan the commander took them all and bought them to the ruler of Babylon in Riblah. [21] There at Riblah, in the land of Hamath, the ruler had them executed. So the people of Judah went into captivity, away from their land.

[22] For governor over the people left behind in Judah, Nebuchadnazzar ruler of Babylon appointed Gedaliah ben-Ahikam ben-Shaphan. [23] When all the army officers and their troops learned that the ruler of Babylon had appointed Gedaliah as governor, they came to Gedaliah at Mizpah—Ishmael ben-Nethaniah, Johanan ben-Kareah, Seriah ben-Tanhumeth the Netophathite, Jaazaniah ben-the Maacathite, and their followers. [24] Gedaliah took an oath to reassure them and their followers. "Do not be afraid of the Babylonian officials," he said. "Settle down in the land and serve the ruler of Babylon, and all will be well with you."

[25] But in the seventh month Ishmael ben-Nethaniah ben-Elishsama, who was a member of the royal house, came with ten followers and assassinated Gedaliah and the Jews and Chaldeans who were with him at Mizpah. [26] So all the people, high and low, and the captains of the armed forces, fled to Egypt for fear of the Chaldeans.

[27] In the thirty-seventh year of the exile of Jehoiachin ruler of Judah, on the twenty-seventh day of the twelfth month, in the year that Evil-merodach became ruler of Babylon, the new ruler released Jehoiachin from prison. [28] He spoke kindly to him and gave him a seat of honor higher than the other rulers who were with him in Babylon. [29] So Jehoiachin put aside his prison clothes and for the rest of his life ate regularly at the ruler's table. [30] Day by day the ruler gave Jehoiachin a regular allowance as long as he lived.

the later prophets

ísaíah

fíRst ísaíah*

1:1–12:6

$t$he vísíon of ísaíah ben-amoz con-
cerning Judah and Jerusalem during the reigns of Uzziah, Jotham, Ahaz,
and Hezekiah, rulers of Judah.

2 Hear this, you heavens! Earth, listen to me,
for it is YHWH who speaks:†

---

* The book of *Isaiah* is divided into three principal sections. While the entire book of *Isaiah* is attributed
to Isaiah ben-Amoz, the book actually contains prophetic material spanning more than two hundred
years. This first section, known as "First Isaiah," consists of the forewarnings of the prophet known
as Isaiah of Jerusalem, who preached in Judah during the eighth century B.C.E., with supplementary
material from anonymous disciples and prophets who saw themselves, or were seen by editors, as
coming out of "the Isaiah mold" (see 8:16, which mentions his followers). Isaiah of Jerusalem was
a contemporary of Amos and Hosea and watched from Jerusalem as Israel was swallowed up by
Assyria; Isaiah's name means "Yhwh is deliverance." Chapters 40-55 are known as "Second Isaiah."
This collection consists largely of salvation oracles addressing the Babylonian exile in the mid-sixth
century B.C.E. Chapters 56-66 form "Third Isaiah," prophecies to a Jewish community in late sixth
century Judah struggling to rebuild itself.

† The literary form of these lines is that of a lawsuit. God, as supreme ruler over Israel, ends the Covenant
with Israel and now stands as both plaintiff and judge against a rebellious Israel. God summons the
heavens and the earth to act as the jury in hearing Israel's violations of the covenant.

I reared children, I nurtured them,
　　but they rebelled against me.
3　The ox knows its owner,
　　the donkey knows its owner's feed trough;
　　but Israel doesn't know me;
　　my people don't understand.
4　Oh, what a sinful nation you are!
　　A people weighed down with injustice!
　　You're a gang of thugs, corrupt children
　　　who abandoned and despised me—
　　YHWH, the Holy One of Israel—
　　　and turned your backs on me!"
5　Why do you invite more punishment?
　　Why do you persist in more rebellion?
　　You have a massive head wound,
　　　your heart is completely diseased;
6　there is nothing healthy in you,
　　　from the top of your head to the sole of your foot—
　　nothing but wounds, welts, and open sores,
　　　neither dressed nor bandaged nor soothed with oil.
7　Your country lies barren,
　　　your villages are ash heaps;
　　foreigners pillage your land before your very eyes.
　　　Only foreigners can devastate a land so utterly!
8　Zion alone remains,
　　　standing like a sentinel's hut in a vineyard,
　　like a lean-to in a melon patch—
　　　like a city under siege.
9　Had YHWH Omnipotent* not left a few survivors,†
　　we should have become like Sodom,
　　　another Gomorrah.
10　Hear the word of YHWH, you rulers of "Sodom"!
　　Listen to the command of YHWH, you people of "Gomorrah":
11　"These interminable sacrifices of yours: what are they to me?"
　　says YHWH.

---

* "Omnipotent" here translates *Tsva'ot*, which means "of Hosts" or "of the Armies," and can refer to earthly armies, angelic forces, or even stars in the sky. The word is often translated "Almighty," and is a picture of universal power and authority, indicating that all created beings and forces are under God's dominion.

† The Hebrew word used here, *saîrd*, is not the usual word that Isaiah uses for "remnant," which is *she'ar*. Here, Isaiah is referring to the survivors of the invasion of 701 rather than the purified remnant. Still, this remnant was proof of God's mercy in sparing a people who deserved destruction.

"I am fed up with burnt offerings of rams and the fat of calves!
   The blood of bulls, lambs, and goats nauseates me.
12 When you came to present yourselves before me,
   who asked you to trample over my courts?*
13 Don't bring any more of your useless offerings to me—
   their incense fills me with loathing.
   New moons, Sabbaths, assemblies—
   I cannot endure another festival of injustice!
14 Your new moons and your pilgrimages
   I despise with all my soul.
   They are wearisome to me;
   I am tired of bearing them.
15 When you open up your hands in prayer,
   I turn my eyes away from you.
   You may heap prayer upon prayer, but I won't hear them—
   your hands are covered with blood!
16 Wash! Clean yourselves!
   Get your injustice out of my sight!
   Cease to do evil
17   and learn to do good!
   Search for justice
   and help the oppressed!
   Protect those who are orphaned
   and plead the case of those who are widowed!
18 "Come now! Let's look at the choices before you,"†
   says YHWH.
   "Though your sins are like scarlet,
   they can be white as snow.
   Though they are red as crimson,
   they can be like fleece.
19 If you are willing to obey,
   you will eat the best that the land has to offer—
20 but if you persist in rebellion
   the sword will consume you instead!"
   The mouth of YHWH has spoken.
21 Look how the faithful city
   has perverted itself!
   Once a place of justice where fairness dwelled,
   it is now home to murderers.

---

* This conjures the image of sacrificial livestock being paraded through the courtyard.
† God, as the divine judge, is summoning Judah to defend itself against the charges.

²² Your silver has turned to dross,
   your best wine is now diluted with water.
²³ Your rulers are now rebels,
   consorting with thieves.
All are greedy for profit
   and chase after bribes.
They deny justice to orphans,
   and cause the widowed to go begging.
²⁴ This, therefore, is the declaration of YHWH Omnipotent,
   the Strong One of Israel:
"Alas, I will pour out my rage on my enemies,
   avenge myself on my foes—
²⁵ I will turn my hand against you!
I will refine your dross with the hottest heat,
   purging all your impurities.
²⁶ I will turn your judges into what they once were
   and make your counselors like those of old.
Then you will be called
   the Home of Justice, the Faithful City.
²⁷ Justice itself will redeem Zion;
   those who return there will be a righteous people.
²⁸ Rebels and criminals together will be shattered
   and those who abandon YHWH will be lost.
²⁹ The sacred oaks that once delighted you will shame you,*
   and your garden shrines will fail you.
³⁰ You will be like an oak tree without leaves,
   like a waterless garden.
³¹ The powerful will become like a fuse,
   their handiwork like a match.
Bring them together, and they will burn,
   with no one to extinguish them."

෬ ෬ ෬

^{2:1} This is what Isaiah ben-Amoz saw concerning Judah and Jerusalem:
² In the last days, the mountain of YHWH's Temple
   will be established as the most important mountain
and raised above all other hills—
   all nations will stream toward it.

---

* The sacred oaks were places were Cannanite fertility rites were performed.

³ Many people will come and say:
"Come, let us climb YHWH's mountain
to the Temple of the God of Jacob,
that we may be instructed in God's ways
and walk in God's paths."
Instruction* will be given from Zion
and the word of YHWH from Jerusalem.
⁴ God will judge between the nations
and render decisions for many countries.†
They will beat their swords into plowshares,
and their spears into pruning hooks;‡
one nation will not raise the sword against another,
and never again will they train for war.

⁵ O house of Leah and Rachel and Jacob, come,
let us walk in the light of YHWH!
⁶ For you have abandoned your people,
O house of Leah and Rachel and Jacob!
They are full of influences from the East—
they practice divination like the Philistines
and make treaties with foreigners.§
⁷ Their land is filled with silver and gold,
and there is no end to their treasures.
Their land is full of horses,
and their chariots are innumerable.
⁸ Their land is full of idols,
and they prostrate themselves to the work of their hands.
⁹ Humankind will be brought low,
all the people will be humbled—
but do not forgive them!
¹⁰ Make them go hide in the caves
and cower in the dust
from the terror of YHWH
and the splendor of your majesty!

---

* Literally, *Torah*, the Law or Teaching, the complete revelation of God's mind and heart.
† "Judge" here means to arbitrate disputes between contending parties.
‡ A plowshare is the sharp blade of a plow that cuts the earth and creates a furrow; a pruning hook is a device that looks like a pole with a curved knife on it, used by gardeners to reach and prune the tallest trees and vines.
§ Literally, "they strike hands." Making a treaty with another nation meant accommodating their gods.

¹¹ The eyes of the arrogant will be cast down
and their pride brought low—
YHWH alone will be exalted on that Day.*
¹² YHWH Omnipotent has a Day set aside:
against the proud and lofty,
against all that is exalted—
and they will be humbled—
¹³ against all the cedars of Lebanon, tall and lofty,
and all the oaks of Bashan,†
¹⁴ against all the high mountains
and all the steep hills,
¹⁵ against every lofty tower
and every fortified wall,
¹⁶ against every ship of Tarshish
and every stately vessel.
¹⁷ The arrogance of humankind will be brought low
and their smugness humiliated,
¹⁸ and their idols will be utterly destroyed.
¹⁹ People will hide in caves in the cliffs
and holes in the ground,
hiding from terror of YHWH,
from the brilliance of God's majesty.
²⁰ On that Day the people will throw
to the rodents and the bats
their idols of silver and their idols of gold
which they made for worship.
²¹ They will flee to rocky caverns and to fissures in cliffs
from terror of YHWH,
from the brilliance of God's majesty
when God comes forth to make the earth tremble.‡
²² Stop trusting in mortals,
who have only the breath in their nostrils!
Of what value are they?

---

* This is the first of many occurrences of the phrase "On that Day" (*bayyôm hahû*) in *Isaiah*. The phrase is repeated like a mantra at the beginning or end of a particular passage to add emphasis to an overwhelming manifestation of God's power. While such passages speak to any period of God's "visitation," any time of reckoning when long-delayed justice is imparted, they have also been used by some commentators to evoke a day of apocalyptic judgment.
† Cedars are a symbol of pretentiousness and self-importance. The reference to the oaks of Bashan may refer to Canaanite fertility practices that took place in oak groves.
‡ Literally, to tremble [before God] as with terror, or to inspire with awe.

3:1 Look—the sovereign YHWH Omnipotent
   is depriving Jerusalem and Judah support* of every kind:
   all support of bread,
   all support of water.
2 "Whether warrior or soldier,
   judge or prophet,
   fortuneteller or elder,
3 military leader or dignitary or counselor,
   skilled artisan or expert magician—
4 I will appoint children as their governors,
   mere infants will rule over them."†
5 People will oppress one another,
   citizen against citizen, neighbor against neighbor.
   The young will rise up against the elderly,
   the corrupt against the honorable.
6 Family members will approach a relative and say,
   "Look, you have clothes and we don't,
   so you be our leader—
   take charge of this heap of ruins!"
7 But then the relative will protest,
   "I have no cures—
   I don't even have food or clothing at home.
   Don't make me leader of these people!"
8 Jerusalem staggers, Judah falls
   because their words and their deeds
   go against YHWH
   and defy God's glorious presence.
9 The look on their faces testifies against them.
   They parade their sins the way Sodom did.
   Woe to them!
   They brought this disaster upon themselves.
10 Tell them:
   "Blessed are the just! All will go well with you.
   You will enjoy the fruit of your deeds!
11 But woe to the unjust! All will go ill with you.
   You have earned the disaster striking you."

---

* The Hebrew *mash'en* may be best understood today as referring to the social infrastructure. The divine judgment against Judah removes the very things that hold the society together.
† Ahaz was a child when he began to rule.

¹² Oh, my people!
  You are oppressed by the young
  and ruled by the inexperienced!
  Oh, my people!
  Your leaders lead you astray
  and erase the paths you should follow.
¹³ YHWH takes the bench
  to pass sentence on the people.
¹⁴ YHWH calls to judgment
  the elders and the leaders of the people:
  "You are the perpetrators who destroy my vineyard!
  What you've plundered from the poor is still in your house!
¹⁵ Why do you crush my people,
  and grind the faces of the poor into the ground?"
  demands YHWH Omnipotent.
¹⁶ Because the wealthy of Jerusalem are haughty,*
  striding along with outstretched necks and wanton glances,
  with mincing gait and ankles tinkling with bracelets,
¹⁷ YHWH will afflict their heads with scabs
  and make their hair fall out.
¹⁸ In that Day, YHWH will take away the tinkling ankle jewelry,
  the tiaras and the moon-shaped necklaces,†
¹⁹   the pendants, bracelets, and scarves,
²⁰   the headdresses, armlets, and sashes,
  the talismans and amulets,
²¹   the signet rings and nose rings,
²²   the festal robes, mantles, cloaks, and purses,
²³   the lace gowns, linen garments, turbans, and veils.
²⁴ In the place of perfume: stench.
  In the place of sashes: ropes.
  In the place of a fine coiffure: a shaved head.
  In the place of beauty: a brand.‡

---

* The original text reads, "Because the daughters of Zion are haughty...." For centuries, this passage has been used as a tool for the vilification of women. Commentators have seen it as everything from a caution against immodest dress to a warning that women should not be in positions of leadership, whereas it is really a rebuke against the oppression of poor people. Luxury had become great during Uzziah's prosperous reign, and in that era, women were used as trophies to display their husbands' and fathers' wealth—ostentatious materialism gotten at the expense of the poor. As always, the Hebrew Scriptures sees one of the greatest injustices as neglect of the underclass while a wealthy minority prospers.
† Symbols of Goddess worship.
‡ A brand or primitive tattoo was used upon slaves to indicate ownership.

²⁵ Your soldiers will fall by the sword,
your warriors will fall in battle.
²⁶ The gates of Zion will mourn and lament,
and you will sit on the ground in despair, desolate and alone.
4:1 In that Day, seven widowed women
will take hold of one man* and say,
"We'll eat our own bread and wear our own clothes;
just let us be called by your name so we won't be disgraced."

² In that Day, the Branch† of YHWH
will be beautiful and glorious
and the fruit of the earth will be
the pride and grandeur of Israel's survivors.
³ Those who are left in Zion and remain in Jerusalem
will be called holy, chosen for survival in Jerusalem.
⁴ When God washes away the filth of Jerusalem's people
and cleanses Jerusalem of its bloodshed
by a wind of judgment,
a wind of destruction,
⁵ YHWH will create over the whole site of Mount Zion
and on those assembled there
a cloud of smoke by day
and a bright flame of fire by night.
And the glory of God
will be an awning over all,
⁶ a tent to give daily shade from the heat,
a refuge and cover from the storm and the rain.‡

5:1 Let me now sing of my friend—
it is a love song about a vineyard.§
My friend had a vineyard
on a fertile hillside.

---

* In other words, so many men will die in battle that women will greatly outnumber men.
† *Semah*, "branch," may refer to a national liberator from the line of David, or to the purified remnant that will escape the impending judgment. A third possible meaning may be based on a parallelism in Hebrew poetry that matches "branch" with "fruit of the earth." In this case, the phrase would refer to a renewal of nature and the establishment of a future ideal Judah.
‡ The images used here are the ways that God was present to the people during the forty years in the desert.
§ This stanza, through verse 7, echoes the form of a popular ballad that may have been sung at vintage festivals. While the ballad begins on a happy note, in this case a hard truth is revealed at the end: despite all the care given to the vineyard, the only grapes it yields are rotten.

2   My friend dug the soil, cleared the stones,
     and planted the choicest vines;
   then within it built a watchtower,
     and constructed a winepress.
   My friend anticipated the crop of grapes,
     but what it yielded was rotten grapes.*

3   "Now, inhabitants of Jerusalem and people of Judah—
     judge between me and my vineyard:

4   What more could I have done for my vineyard
     that I haven't done?
   Why, when I looked for the crop of grapes
     did it bring forth bad fruit?

5   Now I will let you know
     what I mean to do to my vineyard:
   take away its hedge, give it over to grazing,
     break through its wall, let it be trampled!

6   I will let it go to wilderness;
     it will not be pruned or hoed,
   but overgrown with thorns and briars.
   I will command the clouds
     not to send rain upon it."

7   The vineyard of the YHWH Omnipotent is the house of Israel
     and the people of Judah are God's cherished vine.
   YHWH looked for justice, but found bloodshed;
     for righteousness, but found only a cry of suffering.†

8   Woe to you who add house to house
     and join field to field
   until no space is left
     and you are left alone in the countryside.‡

9   YHWH Omnipotent made this solemn oath
     in my hearing:
   "Many houses lie in ruins,
     large and beautiful houses with no one living in them.

---

* Or, possibly, "wild grapes," indicating either the people's their refusal to be "domesticated" and obedient, or their straying after pagan gods.

† Here there are several plays on words in Hebrew that escape translation: "YHWH looked for justice (*mishpat*), but found bloodshed (*mishpah*); for righteousness (*shedaqâ*), but found only a cry of suffering (*sheaqa*—literally, "outcry"). *Mishpat* is the revealed will of God concerning the sum total of a person's duties—to God, to others, and to self. *Shedaqâ* is the correlate with *mishpat* and means whatever actions flow from the divine will.

‡ This refers to practices of land-grabbing by the wealthy.

¹⁰ A ten-acre vineyard will yield only six gallons of wine;
   ten bushels of seed will produce only one bushel of grain."
¹¹ Those who rise early to chase after alcohol—
   what unfortunate people they are!*
   They stay up late at night
   until they're inflamed with wine.
¹² They have harps and lyres at their banquets,
   tambourines and flutes—and wine!
   But they have no regard for what YHWH does,
   no respect for the work of God's hands.
¹³ "This is why my people will go into exile—
   because they don't understand
   that their multitudes are starving
   and their masses are collapsing from thirst.
¹⁴ Therefore the grave licks its chops
   and opens its mouth wide beyond measure—
   and down goes that multitude, those masses,
   that jubilation, that revelry!"
¹⁵ Humanity will bow down
   and humankind will be humbled,
   and the arrogant will be forced
   to lower their insolent gaze.
¹⁶ But YHWH Omnipotent will triumph through justice,
   and reveal holiness through righteousness.
¹⁷ Then the sheep will graze as if in the pasture;
   fatlings and kids will feed among the ruins.

¹⁸ Woe to you who drag corruption along
   like a sheep on a tether and a bridle on a heifer!
¹⁹ Woe to you who say, "Hurry up, God, work fast,
   let's see these plans of yours, Holy One of Israel!
   Fulfill your designs quickly
   if you want us to pay attention to you!"
²⁰ Woe to you who call evil good and good evil,
   who exchange darkness for light and light for darkness,
   bitter for sweet and sweet for bitter!
²¹ Woe to you who are wise in your own sight
   and believe in your own shrewdness.

---

* This line translates the single word "Oy!" Often translated "woe" or "alas," it is literally "oh" or "ah,"
and is an expression of deep grief, pity, or the apprehension that evil is about to befall someone; it
was also used in funeral laments, and may be translated, "they are as good as dead."

22 Woe to you heroes—at drinking wine!
   You champions—at mixing strong drinks!
23 You who will acquit the guilty for a bribe
   and deny the innocent of their rights!
24 As tongues of fire lick the stubble
   and chaff withers in the fire,
   so your roots will rot
   and your blossoms will crumble into dust;
   for you rejected the Instruction of YHWH Omnipotent,
   and despised the word of the Holy One of Israel!

25 This is why YHWH, afire with wrath against the people,
   stretches out a mighty arm to strike them down:
   the mountains quake,
   and corpses litter the streets.
   Even now God's anger has not abated,
   even now God's arm remains outstretched!
26 YHWH will send a signal to a nation far away,
   a call for those at the ends of the earth!
   Here they come,
   with lightning speed!*
27 None of them shows weariness, none stumbles,
   none either slumbers or sleeps.
   None of them has a loosened belt,
   none has a broken sandal strap.
28 Their arrows are sharpened
   and their bows are strung.
   The hooves of their horses clatter like stones,
   the wheels of their chariots whirl like tornadoes.
29 They roar like a lion,
   they roar like a lioness!
   They growl as they seize their prey,
   carrying it off beyond rescue.
30 Their victory roar
   is like the roar of the sea.
   All who view the land can see darkness closing in,
   the gathering clouds overcoming the light.

---

* This refers to the invasion by Assyria. There is a constant theme in prophetic literature that God operates through history, even using other nations to execute judgment over Israel.

⁶·¹ In the year of the death of Uzziah, ruler of Judah, I saw YHWH seated on a high and lofty judgment seat, in a robe whose train filled the Temple. ² Seraphs* were stationed above; each of them had six wings: with two they covered their faces, with two they covered their feet,† and with two they flew.

³ They would cry out to one another, "Holy! Holy! Holy is YHWH Omnipotent! All the earth is filled with God's glory!" ⁴ The doorposts and thresholds quaked at the sound of their shouting, and the Temple kept filling with smoke.

⁵ Then I said, "Woe is me, I am doomed! I have unclean lips, and I live among a people of unclean lips! And my eyes have seen the Ruler, YHWH Omnipotent!"‡

⁶ Then one of the seraphs flew to me, holding an ember which it had taken with tongs from the altar. ⁷ The seraph touched my mouth with the ember. "See," it said, "now that this has touched your lips, your corruption is removed, and your sin is pardoned."

⁸ Then I heard the voice of the Holy One saying, "Whom shall I send? Who will go for us?"

"Here I am," I said, "send me!"

⁹ And God said:

"Go, and say to this people:
'Hear continually, but never comprehend!
See continually, but never perceive!'
¹⁰ Dull the minds§ of this people,
stop their ears,
shut their eyes—
otherwise they might see with their eyes,
hear with their ears,
understand with their minds,
and then turn back and be healed!"

---

* Literally, "burning ones," generally depicted as fiery beings surrounded by serpentine flashes of lightning. In the book of *Numbers*, the poisonous snakes, or "fiery serpents," were also called seraphs. Two close linguistic cognates for "seraph" are Sharrapu, the Babylonian fire-god; and serefs, Egyptian griffins that stood guard over the graves of royalty, huge figures with the body of a lion and the head of an eagle.

† A common biblical euphemism for the genitals.

‡ Isaiah's lips are "unclean" because he is human and thus sinful, and unworthy to praise God. His words also echoe the experience of Moses, who was told, "You cannot see my face, for no one can see me and live."

§ Other translations, "heart." In Hebrew the heart, in addition to being the seat of emotion and courage, was where thought, knowledge, reflection, and will came from.

¹¹ Then I asked, "How long, O God?"
And God said:
  "Until cities lie wasted and deserted,
    houses are empty,
    and the land is utterly desolate.
¹² YHWH will drive the people far away,
    and there will be a vast emptiness in all the land.
¹³ But one-tenth will remain,
    and will repent.
  Like a terebinth* or an oak
    that burns to the ground in a fire,
    then is cut down, leaving only its stump—
    in that stump is the holy seed!"

      ଔ ଔ ଔ

^{7:1} In the reign of Ahaz ben-Jotham ben-Uzziah, ruler of Judah, the city of Jerusalem was attacked by Rezin, ruler of Syria, and Pekah ben-Remaliah, ruler of Israel.† But they were not able to conquer it. ² When word came to the House of David‡ that Syria had allied itself with Ephraim, the heart of Ahaz and the people shook, as the trees of the forest shake in the wind.

³ YHWH said to Isaiah: "Go with your son Shear-jashub,§ and meet Ahaz at the end of the conduit of the upper pool on the Fuller's Field road, ⁴ and say, 'Take care to remain calm and do not fear; do not be intimidated by Rezin and Syria, or by ben-Remaliah—they're just two smoldering sticks of firewood— ⁵ or because Syria and Ephraim and ben-Remaliah have plotted to ruin you, saying, ⁶ "We will invade Judah and terrorize it and seize it for ourselves, and set up ben-Tabeel as its ruler." '

⁷ "Thus says YHWH: This will not stand, it will not be!

---

* A small Mediterranean tree (*Pistacia terebinthus*) that is a source of tanning material and turpentine; it is a relative of the pistachio tree.
† The land of Israel was divided into two realms after Solomon's death 192 years earlier: Israel (also called Ephraim), with Samaria as its capital, in the north, and Judah in the south, having Jerusalem as its capital. This attack against Jerusalem was occasioned by Ahaz' refusal to enter into an alliance with Ephraim and Syria against Sargon, ruler of the Assyrian empire. Sargon conquered the northern realm thirteen years after this prophecy; by the time the "sixty-five years" of verse 9 had passed, the vast majority of its people would be in exile.
‡ This includes Ahaz and his family, as well as the royal court; in the next chapter, when the House of David is being addressed, it is likely that the prophecy is taking place at the court of Ahaz.
§ "A Remnant Shall Return." As is typical in Isaiah, the name signifies both a threat and a promise: as a threat, it may mean that there will be only a few survivors if Ahaz pursues his alliance with Assyria; as a promise, it may mean that a faithful remnant will rebuild Judah if Ahaz is wise enough to believe in God and stay politically neutral.

⁸ "The capital of Syria is Damascus; the chief of Damascus is Rezin. ⁹ The capital of Ephraim is Samaria; the chief of Samaria is ben-Remaliah. But within sixty-five years, Ephraim will be crushed, and no longer a nation. If you do not stand by me, you will not stand at all."

¹⁰ Once more YHWH spoke to Ahaz and said, ¹¹ "Ask for a sign from YHWH your God; let it be deep as the netherworld, or high as the sky!"

¹² But Ahaz answered, "I will not ask! I will not put YHWH to a test!"

¹³ Then Isaiah said, "Listen, O House of David! Is it not enough for you to weary those around you, must you also weary my God? ¹⁴ Therefore, the Holy One will give you a sign: This young woman* will become pregnant and will give birth. You will name the child Immanu-El.† ¹⁵ This child will be living on curds and honey by the time it knows how to refuse evil and do good.‡ ¹⁶ But before that time—before the child knows how to refuse evil and do good—the land of the two rulers you dread will be laid waste.

¹⁷ "However, YHWH will bring upon you, your people, and your ancestral house a time unlike any since Ephraim seceded from Judah—it will be the time of the ruler of Assyria! ¹⁸ On that Day, YHWH will whistle for 'mosquitoes' from the delta of the Egyptian Nile and 'bees' from the land of Assyria. ¹⁹ They will all come and settle in the steep ravines and in the crevices in the rocks, on all the thorn bushes and at the watering holes. ²⁰ In those times YHWH will shave the hair of your head, your groin, and your entire body with a razor hired from beyond the River—the ruler of Assyria.§

---

* Isaiah was likely indicating a young woman at the court of Ahaz who was present during the prophecy, and it is she who is being addressed in latter part of the verse ("You will name..."). The Hebrew word *almah* simply means an unmarried adolescent female, or a woman of marriageable age; a different word, *bethulah*, is the technical term for a virgin. A growing number of scholars feel that this young woman here and the prophet in 8:3 are the same person, and that the child she conceives with Isaiah, whom he names Maher-shalal-hash-baz, is the same child whom she will call Immanuel.

† Immanuel is commonly translated "God with us," though the little preposition *im* can also mean "among" or even "against." Again, the name is both a threat and a promise: as a threat, it may mean that God is against us, and will destroy us if we invite Assyria into Judah; as a promise, it may mean that God is on our side and will save us if we avoid getting mixed up with Assyria or with Israel and Damascus.

‡ That is, by the time the infant is a young child. The "curds and honey" mentioned here and in verse 22 have a layered meaning: While they echo the promise of a prosperous and pleasurable homeland "flowing with milk and honey," the reference to "curds," a staple food of the Bedouins, signifies that while Assyria will conquer Israel, the population of Judah will also be decimated, and they will be forced into a nomadic existence.

§ After a debilitating seige on Jerusalem by Israel, and in the hope of staving off further attacks from the northern Israelites and Syria, Ahaz makes an alliance with Tiglath-Pileser III, ruler of Assyria (the "hired razor"), who was creating a massive empire. While this alliance effectively destroyed the northern realm, Ahaz and Judah became vassals of Assyria, and Ahaz was compelled to acknowledge the Assyrian gods as his own. This era was remembered as one of the worst times of apostasy from God in the southern realm. Shaving the body of all hair is a symbol of abject shame.

²¹ In those days you will keep only a single cow and two goats, ²² yet milk will be so abundant that everyone will have curds to eat*—indeed, all who remain in the land will eat curds and honey. ²³ In those days all the places where there once were a thousand vines worth a thousand silver shekels, there will only be briars and thorns. ²⁴ Hunters will go there with bow and arrow, for the land will be covered with briars and thorns. ²⁵ Even the hills you once cultivated with a hoe will not be accessible because of the briars and thorns. They will become places where cattle and sheep are turned loose to graze."

8:1 YHWH told me, "Take a large scroll and write on it in common script: 'For Maher-shalal-hash-baz.'† ² Then call in Uriah the priest and Zechariah ben-Jeberekiah as my witnesses of record."

³ Then I had relations with the prophet, and she gave birth to a child. Then God said to me, "Name the child Maher-shalal-hash-baz. ⁴ For before the child can say, 'Mama,' or 'Papa,' the wealth of Damascus and the spoil of Samaria will be carried away by the ruler of Assyria."

⁵ YHWH spoke to me again and said, ⁶ "Because this people refused the tranquilly flowing waters of Shiloah and tremble with fear over Rezin ben-Remaliah, ⁷ YHWH will bring up against them the mighty floodwater of the Euphrates—the ruler of Assyria in majesty and power. The river will rise above its channels and overflow its banks.‡ ⁸ It will sweep on into Judah as a flood, swirling over it, passing through it and reaching up to its neck. Its outspread wings will cover the breadth of your land, Immanu-El.

⁹   "Band together, you nations, for you will be shattered.
    Listen, all you distant countries:
    gird yourselves, and be shattered anyway;
    come up with a plan, and it will be thwarted!
¹⁰   Devise a strategy, but do so in vain;
    give your orders, but they won't be carried out—
    for God is with us!"§

---

* In other words, so many people will be killed in battle and the population will be so sparse that even a few animals will produce enough cheese to feed everyone.

† "Speeds the Spoil, Hastens the Prey." As a threat, the name may mean that if Judah joins Israel and Damascus against Assyria, the superior power—Assyria—will make haste to conquer Judah as soon as it is finished with the other allies. As a promise, the name may mean that a neutral Judah will be freed from the strong-arming threats of Israel and Damascus because their rebellion against Assyria will be crushed quickly.

‡ In other words, since Judah wouldn't trust God to protect them, but resorted to an alliance with Tiglath-Pileser, the Assyrians will flood into their land and overwhelm them.

§ This could also be translated, "give your orders, but they won't be carried out, Immanu-El!"

¹¹ YHWH took me by the hand and warned me not to behave like these people, said,

¹² "Do not call 'conspiracy' what these people call conspiracy,
    don't fear what they fear, or dread what they dread.
¹³ It is YHWH Omnipotent whom you are to hold sacred
    and who must be the object of your fear and awe.
¹⁴ God will become a snare*
    to both houses of Israel—
a stone that causes people to stumble,
    a rock that makes them fall—
a trap and a snare
    for the inhabitants of Jerusalem.
¹⁵ Many will stumble and be broken;
    they will be caught in the snare and captured.
¹⁶ Now, tie up the scroll of this testimony,
    and seal this intruction in the heart of my disciples."

¹⁷ I will wait patiently for YHWH, whose face is hidden from the house of Leah and Rachel and Jacob. I will put my trust in God. ¹⁸ I and the children YHWH has given me to be signs and object lessons in Israel, sent by YHWH Omnipotent who dwells on Mount Zion.

¹⁹ "When people tell you,
'Seek guidance from mediums and spiritualists
    who whisper and mutter incantations!
A nation must surely consult its gods
    and its dead on behalf of the living!'
²⁰ then cling to this instruction,
    this testimony!
For on those who tell you such things,
    the light has not yet dawned.
²¹ Despondency and starvation will overtake them,
    and they will be anxious and fearful.
When they look up,
    they will rage against their ruler and their God.
²² When they look down,
    they will find only inescapable distress and gloom.
And they will be thrust
    into total darkness.

---

* The traditional text has "sanctuary," but this is likely a scribal error; "snare," in Hebrew, has a very similar spelling.

9:1 "But there will be no more gloom
for the land that was in anguish!
In the past God humbled
the land of Zebulun, the land of Naphtali;*
but in the future God will bring glory
to this Road to the Sea,
this Land Beyond the Jordan,
this Galilee of the Nations.
2 The people walking in darkness
are seeing a brilliant light—
upon those who dwell in a land of deep shadows
light is shining!
3 God, you have made the nation greater—
you have brought them abundant joy!
They celebrate in your presence
as with the harvest celebrations,
or as warriors celebrate when dividing spoils.
4 For the yoke that burdened them,
the weight on their shoulders,
the rod of their oppressors—
you have shattered it, as you did at the defeat of Midian.
5 For every boot that tramped in battle,
every cloak that was dragged through blood,
is now used as fuel for the fire.
6 For a child is born to us,
an heir is given us,
upon whose shoulders
dominion will rest.
This One shall be called
Wonderful Counselor,† the Strength of God,‡
Eternal Protector,§ Champion of Peace.**

---

* Galilee, or *ha-Galil* ("the circle"), as it was known, was an international crossroads. Surrounded by Gentile nations, it was home to several Israelite tribes, including Naphtali to the north (next to the Sea of Galilee, on the northwest side), and Zebulun to the south (further west, near the Mediterranean); together they comprise Upper and Lower Galilee. The great caravans of the world passed though Galilee. The Road to the Sea led from Damascus through Galilee down to Egypt and to Africa; the Road to the East led through Galilee as well.
† Or "wise guide," though the phrase could also indicate an extraordinary military strategist.
‡ Literally, "strong god," or "god-hero."
§ Literally, "parent forever," though the context emphasizes a parent's protective role.
** Some scholars believe that these six verses are excerpted from a longer ceremonial piece celebrating a royal ascension. In this passage, God's promise of an eternal dynasty with David was reaffirmed and the hopes were raised of the idealic ruler of the future. The passage focuses not on one particular member of the Davidic line, but on the ideal ruler.

⁷ This dominion, and this peace,
    will grow without end,
with David's throne and realm
    sustained with justice and fairness,
    now and forever.
The zeal of YHWH Omnipotent
    will accomplish it!"

ᘓ   ᘓ   ᘓ

⁸ The Sovereign One has sent a message
    against the house of Leah and Rachel and Jacob;
it fell upon Israel
⁹   and all the people knew it was from God—
Ephraim and the inhabitants of Samaria.
    But proudly and arrogantly they said,
¹⁰ 'The bricks may have fallen,
    but we will build with dressed stones;
the sycamores have been cut down,
    but we will replant with cedars.'
¹¹ So YHWH is raising up adversaries against them
    and stirring up their old enemies—
¹² Syrians to the east and the Philistines to the west
    consume Israel in one gulp.
Even so, God's anger has not abated;
    God's hand is still ready to strike!

¹³ But the people did not turn to the One who struck them,
    nor prayed to YHWH Omnipotent.
¹⁴ So YHWH cut off from Israel
    both head and tail,
palm-frond and reed—
    all in a single day!
¹⁵ The elders and the prominent citizens
    are the head;
the prophet who teaches lies
    is the tail.
¹⁶ Those who lead these people
    lead them astray,
and those who are led
    get swallowed up.

¹⁷ That is why the Sovereign One
   is showing no mercy to the young,
   no compassion for the orphans, widows and widowers.
   For everyone is hypocritical and cruel,
   everyone speaks of vile things.
   Even so, God's anger has not abated;
   God's hand is still ready to strike!

¹⁸ Corruption burns the land like a fire—
   it consumes thorns and briars,
   it sets forest thickets blazing
   and swirling upward in a column of smoke.
¹⁹ The fury of YHWH Omnipotent
   sets the land ablaze.
   The people are fuel for the fire,
   with no compassion for those closest to them.
²⁰ They devour everything they can find to their right,
   yet they are still hungry.
   They turn to the left and eat what is there,
   but they are still not satisfied.
   They even resort to eating
   the flesh of their own arm!
²¹ Manasseh feeds on Ephraim
   and Ephraim on Manasseh,
   and together they turn against Judah.
   Even so, God's anger has not abated;
   God's hand is still ready to strike!

10:1 Woe to you who make unjust policies
   and draft oppressive legislation,
² who deprive the powerless of justice
   and rob poor people—my people—of their rights,
   who prey upon the widowed
   and rob orphans.
³ What will you do on that Day of reckoning
   when disaster comes from far away?
   To whom will you flee for aid,
   and where will you bury your wealth?
⁴ How will you avoid crouching among the captives
   or falling among the casualties?
   Even so, God's anger has not abated;
   God's hand is still ready to strike!

⁵ Woe to you, Assyria, the tool of my anger,
the staff I brandished in my fury!
⁶ I sent you against a corrupt nation
and I ordered you against a people under my wrath,
to pillage and plunder freely
and to trample them down like mud in the streets.
⁷ But you did not intend to do this;
your heart did not plan it so.
No, your heart's desire was to destroy everything,
to go on endlessly cutting nations to pieces.
⁸ The ruler of Assyria boasted,
"All of my commanders are rulers in their own right!
⁹ Hasn't Calneh suffered the fate of Carchemish?
Is not Hamath like Arpad, Samaria like Damascus?*
¹⁰ I have overcome empires full of false gods,
who had more idols than even Jerusalem and Samaria.
¹¹ And now, what I did to Samaria and its worthless gods,
I will do also to Jerusalem and its idols!"

¹² Once the Holy One has finished punishing Mount Zion and Jerusalem, God will punish the arrogant boasting and the haughty pride of Assyria's ruler, ¹³ who said,

"By my own power I have done this,
and by my own wisdom—that's how smart I am.
I have pushed back the frontiers of nations
and plundered their treasures.
I have brought their inhabitants down to the dust
with heroic strength.
¹⁴ My hand has seized the people's riches
as if they were in a bird's nest.
As people pick up abandoned eggs,
I have picked up the whole earth,
with not a wing flapping,
not a beak opening, not a peep."
¹⁵ Does the axe claim more credit than the chopper,
or the saw more strength than the woodcutter?
Can the staff take the walker in hand,
or the club wield itself against what is not made of wood?

---

* All of these are city-states that were conquered by Assyria over a span of twenty-three years.

¹⁶ Therefore the Sovereign YHWH Omnipotent,
   will send a wasting disease to your warriors;
   beneath your bounty, a flame will be kindled
   into a consuming fire.
¹⁷ The Light of Israel will become a fire,
   their Holy One a flame—
   and God will burn and devour in a single day
   the ruler's thorns and briars.
¹⁸ YHWH will destroy—body and soul—
   the glory of the ruler's forests and fertile land;
   they will waste away
   like the victim of a dreaded sickness.
¹⁹ The remaining trees of the ruler's forest
   will be so few a child could reckon the number.

²⁰ On that Day the remnant of Israel, the survivors of the house of Leah and Rachel and Jacob, will no longer rely on the ruler who struck them down but will truly rely on YHWH, the Holy One of Israel. ²¹ A remnant will return, a remnant of Leah and Rachel and Jacob, to the Mighty God. ²² Israel, although your people may be as many as the sands of the sea, only a remnant of them will return. Overwhelming and righteous destruction has been decreed. ²³ The Sovereign YHWH Omnipotent will carry out the destruction decreed upon our whole land.

²⁴ Therefore, this is what the Sovereign YHWH Omnipotent says: "My people in Zion, do not fear the Assyrians, even though they beat you with their rods and raise their staffs against you as the Egyptians did. ²⁵ For in a very short time my wrath will end and my anger will be directed to their destruction.

²⁶ YHWH Omnipotent will lash them with a whip—
   remember Midian at the rock of Oreb?
   And YHWH will raise a staff over the waters—
   remember Egypt?
²⁷ On that Day their burdens will be lifted from your shoulders;
   their yoke will be lifted from your neck.
²⁸ An invader from Rimmon reaches Aiath,
   passes through Migron,
   and stores supplies at Michmash.
²⁹ The invader passes through Maabarah
   and camps for the night at Geba.
   Ramah is terrified,
   Gibeah of Saul flees.

³⁰ Bat-Gallim, cry out loud!
     Laishah, hear her!
     Anathoth, answer her!
³¹ Madmenah runs away;
     the inhabitants of Gebim flee.
³² Today the invader will reach Nob,
     and give the signal to attack Mount Zion,
     the hill of Jerusalem.

³³ But Sovereign YHWH Omnipotent
     will shatter the trees with a terrifying power!
   See how the tallest are cut off,
     the loftiest brought down!
³⁴ The forest thickets will fall beneath the axe.
     The majestic trees of Lebanon will collapse.
^{11:1} Then a shoot will sprout from the stump of Jesse;
     from Jesse's roots, a branch will blossom:*
² The Spirit of YHWH will rest on you—
     a spirit of wisdom and understanding,
     a spirit of counsel and strength,
     a spirit of knowledge and reverence for YHWH.
³ You will delight in obeying YHWH,
     and you won't judge by appearances,
     or make decisions by hearsay.
⁴ You will treat poor people with fairness
     and will uphold the rights of the land's downtrodden.
   With a single word you will strike down tyrants;
     with your decrees you will execute evil people.
⁵ Justice will be the belt around this your waist—
     faithfulness will gird you up.
⁶ Then the wolf will dwell with the lamb,
     and the leopard will lie down with the young goat;
   the calf and the lion cub will graze together,
     and a little child will lead them.
⁷ The cow will feed with the bear;
     their young will lie down together.
   The lion will eat hay like the ox.
⁸ The baby will play next to the den of the cobra,
     and the toddler will dance over the viper's nest.

---

* Jesse is the progenitor of the Davidic lineage, suggesting that a new "David," not simply another failed descendant of David, will come into power.

⁹   There will be no harm, no destruction
      anywhere in my holy mountain;*
   for as water fills the sea,
      so the land will be filled with knowledge of YHWH.

¹⁰ On that Day, the Root of Jesse will serve as a symbol to the peoples of the world—nations will flock to you, and your home will be a place of honor. ¹¹ On that Day, YHWH will once more raise a hand to recover the remnant of what is left of the people, and gather them back from Assyria, Egypt, Pathros,† Ethiopia, Elam, Shinar, Hamath, and the islands of the sea.

¹²   YHWH will hoist a banner for the nations
      and will assemble the outcasts of Israel.
   God will bring back the scattered people of Judah
      from the four corners of the earth.
¹³   The jealousy of Ephraim will cease,
      and Judah's enemies will be cut down.
   Ephraim will not be jealous of Judah
      and Judah will not be hostile toward Ephraim.
¹⁴   They will swoop down on the Philistines' western flank
      and together plunder the tribes of the east:
   Edom and Moab will be in their grasp
      and Ammon will submit to them.
¹⁵   YHWH will dry up the gulf of the Sea of Egypt;
      with a scorching wind God will sweep over the Euphrates
   and break it into seven streams
      so that people can cross on foot.
¹⁶   There will be a highway leading out of Assyria
      for the remnant of the people that is left,
   just as there was for Israel
      when it came up out of Egypt.

12:1 On that Day, Israel will say:
   "I praise you, YHWH!
      Yes, you were angry with me,
   but your anger has abated
      and now you are a comfort to me.
²   You are my deliverer, O God!
      I trust you and am no longer afraid of you—

---

* Mount Zion, as the seat of power, is here emblematic of the entire country.
† Upper Egypt.

you are my strength and my refuge.
  You are my deliverer."
3 With joy you will draw water
  from the wells of salvation.
4 And on that Day you will say:
"Give thanks to YHWH,
  invoke God's holy Name!
Make known among all the people what YHWH has done.
  Proclaim that God's Name is exalted.
5 Sing praises to YHWH, for God has triumphed.
  Let this be known throughout the world!
6 Cry out, shout aloud, you who dwell in Zion,
  for the Holy One of Israel dwells among us in majesty!"

13:1–23:18*

*A*n oracle; the vision that Isaiah ben-Amoz saw concerning Babylon:

2 "On a bare hill raise a banner,
  sound the call to them.
Signal them to come
  to the gates of the nobles.
3 I myself issue the order
  to my sacred warriors.
I summon my troops to serve my anger—
  those who rejoice in my triumph."
4 Listen! A noise on the mountains,
  a sound made by a multitude.
It is the din of dominions,
  of nations coming together.
It is YHWH Omnipotent,
  mustering the army for battle.
5 They come from distant lands,
  from the ends of the heavens—
YHWH and the weapons of judgment,
  coming to destroy the whole earth.

---

* Chapters 13-23 contain a set of oracles against foreign nations.

isaiah 13

⁶   Wail, for the day of YHWH comes!
      Destruction is coming from El Shaddai—the Breasted God!
⁷   At this, all hands go limp—
      people's hearts fail them.
⁸   Terror seizes them;
      pain and agony grips them.
    They writhe like a woman in labor,
      they look at each other, faces flushed with fear.
⁹   Look! The Day of YHWH comes—
      a cruel day, with wrath and fierce anger—
    to desolate the land,
      and destroy the criminals in it.
¹⁰   The stars in heaven and their constellations
      will not show their light;
    the sun will be dark as soon as it rises,
      and the moon will not reflect its light.
¹¹   "I will punish the world for its injustice
      and ciminals for their crimes.
    I will put an end to the pride of oppressors,
      and humble the arrogance of tyrants.
¹²   I will make mortals scarcer than fine gold,
      rarer than the gold of Ophir.
¹³   Thus I will make the heavens tremble,
      and the earth will shake to its foundations
    at the wrath of YHWH Omnipotent,
      in the Day of my burning anger.
¹⁴   Like a startled gazelle,
      like sheep without a shepherd,
    all will return to their own people;
      all will flee to their own lands.
¹⁵   Whoever is caught will be run through,
      captives will fall by the sword.
¹⁶   Their infants will be dashed on rocks
      before their eyes.
    Their houses will be looted
      and their inhabitants debased.
¹⁷   Look, I am inciting the Medes against them—
      they have no regard for silver
      and do not delight in gold.
¹⁸   Their bow slaughters the young;
      they take no mercy on infants,
      they do not view children with pity.

¹⁹ Babylon, the jewel of nations,
   the glory of Chaldean pride,
will be overthrown
   as I overthrew Sodom and Gomorrah.
²⁰ No one will live or be born there
   for many generations.
Bedouins will not pitch their tents there;
   shepherds will not feed their flocks there.
²¹ Only wild animals of the desert will rest there:
   owls will fill its houses,
ostriches will make a home there,
   and wild goats will leap about.
²² Hyenas will howl in its mansions,
   wolves in its luxurious homes.
Its time is close at hand,
   its days are numbered."

14:1 But YHWH will have compassion on Leah and Rachel and Jacob, and will again choose Israel and will restore them in their own land. Foreigners will join them and attach themselves to the house of Leah and Rachel and Jacob. ² Nations will bring Israel back to its homeland, and once they are settled, the family of Jacob will make them their servants, women and men alike. Israel will capture those who captured them, and rule those who ruled them.

³ Once YHWH gives you relief from your suffering and turmoil and cruel bondage, ⁴ you will take up this taunt against the ruler of Babylon:*

How the oppressor has met its end!
   What an end to its arrogance!
⁵ YHWH has broken the staff of the unjust
   and the scepter of tyrants,
⁶ who angrily struck down the peoples
   with unceasing blows,
who furiously trod down nations
   with relentless persecution.
⁷ Now the whole earth is at rest and at peace,
   singing for joy!
⁸ Even the pine trees and the cedars of Lebanon
   rejoice at your fate, saying,
"Since you were laid low,
   no lumberjack comes to cut us down!"

---

* The following verses are a mocking dirge about the death of the ruler of Babylon. The mix of solemn beauty and biting sarcasm makes it one of the great pieces of Hebrew literature.

⁹ Below, the land of the dead is all abuzz
   ready to greet you when you arrive!
   It rouses ghosts to welcome you,
   all the former leaders of the world—
   those who ruled over the nations
   rise from their places of honor to greet you.
¹⁰ They all speak up and say to you,
   "Now you are brought low, as we were—
   now you are like us!"
¹¹ All your pomp has been cast down to Sheol
   along with the noise of your harps!
   Maggots thrive beneath you,
   and worms cover you!
¹² How you have fallen from heaven,
   Morning Star, Child of the Dawn!*
   How is it that you are now eating the dirt,
   you who made other nations fall prostrate before you?
¹³ You once thought to yourself, "I will scale the heavens,
   to set up my judgment seat above God's stars!
   I will sit on the Assembly Mount,
   on the heights of Mount Zaphon!
¹⁴ I will ascend to the tops of the clouds.
   I will make myself like the Most High!"†
¹⁵ But now you are brought down to Sheol,
   to the very bottom of the Pit.
¹⁶ Those who see you stare at you!
   They ponder your fate—
   "Is this the same person who shook the earth,
   who made nations quake,
¹⁷ who turned the world into a desert,
   who overturned its cities,
   and would not release its captives?"
¹⁸ All the rulers of the nations lie in state,
   each in their own tomb.
¹⁹ But you have been discarded without a burial,
   like loathsome carrion.

---

* The ruler is likened to a mythological figure from the Canaanite religion, Helel ben-Shahar. Shahar was the Canaanite god of dawn. Many older versions translate "Morning Star, Child of the Dawn" as "Lucifer," which means "light-bearer." Originally, "Lucifer" was was not an epithet for the devil at all, but was the common Roman name for the planet Venus.
† This passage borrows heavily from Canaanite myth, comparing the pride of the ruler to a minor Canaanite deity who tried to become head of the pantheon.

Like a corpse trampled underfoot
  you lie under a pile of the slain,
under those pierced by a sword,
  thrown into a stony ditch.
²⁰ You will not be buried with the other rulers,
  for you ruined your land
  and brought death to your people.
The offspring of the unjust
  will leave no name behind them.
²¹ Prepare a place to execute their descendants
  for the sins of their ancestors!
Never again must they be allowed rise up,
  to vanquish the earth
  or cover the land with their cities.
²² "I will rise up against them,"
  declares YHWH Omnipotent.
"I will destroy what remains of Babylon—
  its name, its descendants, its posterity.
²³ And I will make it a vast swamp,
  and give it over to the water birds.
I will sweep through it with the broom of destruction."*
  This is the word of YHWH Omnipotent.

²⁴ YHWH Omnipotent has sworn this oath:
"Surely, as I planned so it shall be,
  and as I decided so it shall happen.
²⁵ I will crush Assyria in my land,
  and on my mountain trample them underfoot;
their yoke will be removed from my people,
  their burden will be removed from their shoulders."†
²⁶ This is the plan governing the whole world,
  this is the hand stretched out over all the nations.
²⁷ For YHWH Omnipotent has decided,
  and who can frustrate it?
The hand of God is stretched out,
  and who can turn it back?

---

* With the breakdown of social infrastructure, and in particular, the irrigation system, Babylon would become a wasteland.
† The Assyrian ruler Sennacherib had overreached and would not take Jerusalem in this campaign. Hezekiah put up a resistance, of which Isaiah approved. The verse that follows contrasts God's sovereignty with Assyria's plan of world domination.

௰ ௰ ௰

²⁸ This oracle came the year Ahaz the ruler died:

²⁹ Do not rejoice, all you Philistines,
   now that the rod that chastised you is broken—
   for from the root of the snake will spring up a viper,
   and its fruit will be a flying venomous serpent!
³⁰ The poorest of the poor will find green pastures,
   and those in need will lie down in a safe place.
   But I will destroy your root with famine,
   and kill off your remnant.
³¹ Wail, O city gate! Howl, O city!
   Melt with fear, all you Philistines!
   For a formidable foe is coming out of the north,
   with not even one deserter in its ranks.
³² What answers will be given to the envoys of that nation?
   "YHWH established Zion
   and God's afflicted people will find refuge there."

௰ ௰ ௰

15:1 An oracle concerning Moab:

   On the night Ar is laid waste, Moab is doomed.
   On the night Kir is laid waste, Moab is doomed.*
² The people of Dibon go up to the shrines to weep.
   Moab wails over Nebo and over Medeba.
   People shave their heads;
   every beard is cut off.
³ They wear sackcloth in the streets,
   they cry out on the roofs.
   In the public squares they weep and wail;
   tears stream down their faces.
⁴ Heshbon and Elealeh howl—
   their voices are heard all the way to Jahaz.
   Moab's finest warriors hear it, and tremble;
   their courage melts away.
⁵ My heart groans for Moab,
   its refugees have reached Zoar,
   as far as Eglath Shelishiyah.

---

* Kir was a fortress in Moab, located on the main route between Egypt and Mesopotamia, east of the
Jordan. Because of its strength and strategic importance, it was the object of every attack on Moab.

Ascending to Luhith, they continue to weep.
On the way to Horonaim they cry, "Disaster!"
⁶ The waters of Nimrim are dried up
and the grass is withered, the vegetation dead;
there is not a green thing anywhere.
⁷ So the people transport what little wealth they acquired
across the River of the Willows.
⁸ Their distress cries echo along the frontiers of Moab,
their wailing reaches as far as Eglaim and Beer-elim.
⁹ The waters of Dibon run with blood,
yet more is in store for Dibon:
a lion to pounce on anyone who flees Moab,
and on any of its survivors.
¹⁶:¹ The rulers of the land receive lambs as tribute,
from Sela, across the desert,
to the mountain of the daughter of Zion.
² Flying to and fro like befuddled birds,
the Moabites at the fords of the Arnon say,
³ "Help us make a decision!
Give us advice!
Make your shadow shield us at high noon
as if it were night!
Shield the refugees!
Protect the fugitives!
⁴ Let the exiles from Moab find a home with you
and shelter them from the destroyers!"
When the oppressor has left and the despoiling is over
and the invader has vanished from the land,
⁵ a trustworthy judgment seat
will be set up in David's tent.
On it will preside a true judge,
one who cares for justice and pursues right.
⁶ We have heard of Moab's pride—an extreme pride—
heard of its arrogance, its conceit, its insolence.
But its boastings are false!
⁷ So let the Moabites wail for Moab!
Let them mourn for the raisin cakes of Kir-hareseth*
in their utter bewilderment.
⁸ For the fields of Heshbon wither—
the vines of Sibmah as well.

---

* These were used in ceremonies dedicated to the Canaanite goddess Asherah.

The rulers of the nations trampled the choicest vines,
　vines which once reached as far as Jazer,
trailed out through the desert,
　and spread their branches across the sea.
⁹ I will weep for Sibmah's vines as I weep for Jazer.
　I will drench you with tears, O Heshbon and Elealeh;
for the shouts of joy over your ripened fruit
　and your harvests have been silenced.
¹⁰ Joy and celebration are taken away from the orchards.
　No one sings in the vineyards; no shouts of joy are raised.
There is no treading out of wine at the presses,
　for I have silenced the celebrating of the harvesters.
¹¹ Consequently, my heart throbs like a harp for Moab,
　my soul aches for Kir-hareseth.
¹² Though the Moabites come to worship at the shrines,
　they only wear themselves out.
Though they flock to their sanctuaries to pray,
　it avails them nothing.

¹³ Such was the word of YHWH already spoken about Moab. ¹⁴ But now YHWH says, "Within three years—as a bonded worker would count them—Moab's splendor and all its many people will be despised, and its survivors will be few and feeble."*

ଔ　ଔ　ଔ

¹⁷:¹ An oracle concerning Damascus:

"Damascus will cease to be a city;
　it will become a heap of ruins.
² 　Her towns will be deserted for all time.
Flocks will graze and take their rest there
　and no one will disturb them.
³ Ephraim will lose its defenses,
　and Damascus its sovereignty
The remnant of Aram†
　will share the fate of Israel's glory,"
declares YHWH Omnipotent.

---

* Three years was the legal time limit on bonded servitude in Deuteronomy 15:18. The same three-year limit on bonded servitude is given in the Code of Hammurabi. The years were to be counted precisely, so as not to violate the law.
† The biblical name for ancient Syria.

⁴ On that Day the glory of Jacob will be brought low,
      and the fat of its flesh will grow lean—
⁵ as when the reaper hugs an armful of standing corn
      and slices off its ears,
   or when they glean the ears in the Valley of Rephaim,
      and only gleanings are left;
⁶ or the way it is when an olive tree is beaten
      and only two or three berries are left hanging
      from the topmost branch,
   with four or five on the other branches of the tree."
   This is the word of YHWH, the God of Israel.
⁷ On that Day all will look to their Creator,
      and their eyes will turn to the Holy One of Israel.
⁸ They will no longer be interested in their altars,
      their own handiwork;
   or in objects their hands have made—
      the sacred poles and incense pillars.*
⁹ On that Day your fortified cities
      will be like the deserted places of the Hivites and the Amorites,
      which they fled when Israel approached.
¹⁰ All will be desolation
      because you have forgotten God, your Liberator.
   You have not remembered your Rock, your fortress.
   Therefore, although you set out the finest of seedlings
      and plant exotic vine sprigs,†
¹¹ and though you make them grow the same day you plant them,
      and get your seedlings to flower the very next morning,
   your harvest will disappear—
      in a day of disease and desperate pain.
¹² Listen! It is the thunder of vast forces,
      thundering like the roar of the sea!
   Listen! It is the roar of nations,
      a roaring like the roaring of mighty waters!
¹³ Although nations roar like the roar of surging waters,
      when God rebukes them they flee far away,
   driven before the wind like chaff on the hills,
      like whirling dust before a rainstorm.

---

* The sacred poles were set up in shrines dedicated to the goddess Asherah.
† This refers to the gardens set up to honor the Canaanite god of vegetation, Tammuz, whose annual
   dying and rising was celebrated in cultic festivals.

¹⁴ In the evening, sudden terror!
   Before the morning, everything they have is lost!
   This is the fate of those who loot us,
   the lot of those who plunder us.

ଓ   ଓ   ଓ

¹⁸ᐟ¹ Woe to the land of whirring insects
   along the rivers of Cush,*
² which sends envoys in reed boats over the water!
   Go, swift messengers, to a tall people of bronze skin,
   a people dreaded far and near,
   whose land is parted by rivers.†
³ All you people of the world,
   you who live on the earth,
   you will see a signal flag raised on the mountains,
   you will hear the sound of the shofar.
⁴ These are the words YHWH said to me:
   "Quietly, I will look down from my dwelling place
   like shimmering heat in the summer sunshine,
   or like harvest time when the dew is heavy.
⁵ For, before the harvest, after blossom time,
   when the former flowers are now ripening grapes,
   I will cut off the shoots with pruning hooks,
   and trim the spreading branches.
⁶ They will all be left
   to the mountain-dwelling birds of prey,
   and to the animals of the earth.
   The birds of prey will feed on them all summer long
   and the animals of the earth all winter long."

⁷ In those days gifts will be brought to YHWH Omnipotent from a tall people of bronze skin, a people dreaded far and near, a people strong and aggressive whose land is parted by rivers. They will bring it to the place where the name of YHWH Omnipotent dwells, to Mount Zion.

ଓ   ଓ   ଓ

---

* Present-day Ethiopia.
† The occasion for this oracle may be the arrival of the ambassador from Ethiopian-ruled Egypt, who tried to convince Hezekiah to join in the revolt against Assyria. The oracle is Isaiah's message for the ambassador to take back to Egypt.

^{19:1} An oracle concerning Egypt:*

Take notice! YHWH, riding a swift cloud, comes to Egypt.
The idols of Egypt tremble in God's presence,
and the Egyptians' hearts melt within them.

² "I will stir Egyptian against Egyptian,†
and they will fight one against the other,
neighbor against neighbor,
city against city,
domain against domain.

³ The Egyptians will be disheartened
and I will confound their plans.
They will consult their idols and their spiritist mediums,
their magicians and sorcerers,

⁴ but I will turn Egypt over to a harsh sovereign:
a fierce ruler will govern them,"‡
says YHWH Omnipotent.

⁵ The waters of the Nile will dry up
and the river bed will be parched and dry.

⁶ The canals will stink.
The branches of the Nile will dwindle and dry up;
reeds and rushes will wither away.

⁷ The water lilies along the Nile
and everything sown along it will wither and die.
All will blow away and disappear.

⁸ Those who fish for a living will groan.
Those who cast with hooks in the Nile will mourn
and those who fish with nets will lament.§

⁹ Those who make linen from combed flax will despair,
and the weavers of cotton will go hungry.

¹⁰ The weavers will be dejected,
and all the wage earners will grieve.

¹¹ The officials of Zoan are complete fools;
the wisest counselors of Pharaoh give stupid advice.
How can they say to Pharaoh, "I am a sage,
a descendant of ancient rulers"?

---

* Many scholars consider this "Oracle of Egypt" to be post-exilic.
† This may refer to the breakdown in the social order before the Ethiopian Dynasty took control.
‡ Probably an Assyrian ruler, but this may refer to Piankhi, the Ethiopian ruler.
§ The Nile was, and is, the source of livelihood in Egypt. In fact, a good harvest depended on the regular flooding of the river. Without the river, the desert would take over the land and the powers of death would have won.

¹² Where are your wise women and men?
  Let them come forward,
  Let them explain to you
    what YHWH Omnipotent has planned against Egypt.
¹³ The officials of Zoan are fools;
    the leaders of Memphis are deluded;
    the elders of their clans have led Egypt astray.
¹⁴ YHWH has infused them with a spirit of blindness
    that distorts their judgment;
  they have Egypt staggering in all it does,
    like a drunkard reeling in vomit.
¹⁵ Neither head nor tail, palm branch nor reed,
    will be able to do anything for Egypt.

¹⁶ On that Day, the Egyptians will be like the weak-willed. They will tremble with fear at the outstretched arm YHWH Omnipotent raises against them. ¹⁷ And the land of Judah will humiliate the Egyptians. The very mention of its name will sow confusion because of the plans that YHWH Omnipotent has prepared for them.

¹⁸ On that Day, there will be five cities in Egypt speaking the language of Canaan and swearing allegiance to YHWH Omnipotent, and one of them will be called Heliopolis—the City of the Sun.

¹⁹ On that Day, there will be an altar to YHWH in the heart of Egypt, with a sacred pillar set up to YHWH at its frontier. ²⁰ It will serve as a sign and a reminder of YHWH Omnipotent in Egypt. When they cry out to YHWH because of their oppressors, God will send them a Liberator, a defender who will rescue them. ²¹ So YHWH will be made known in Egypt, and in that day they will acknowledge the Holy One. They will offer sacrifices and burnt offerings. They will make vows to YHWH and keep them. ²² Though YHWH has struck Egypt with a plague, they will be healed. They will turn to YHWH, who will listen to their supplications and heal them.

²³ On that Day, there will be a highway between Egypt and Assyria. Assyria will have access to Egypt, and Egypt will have access to Assyria. And Egyptians and Assryians will worship together. ²⁴ On that Day, Israel will come together with Egypt and Assyria, and the three will be a blessing on the earth. ²⁵ YHWH Omnipotent will bless them, saying, "Blessed be Egypt my people, Assyria my handiwork, and Israel my heritage!"

ଓ   ଓ   ଓ

20:1 In the year that Sargon, ruler of Assyria, sent his general to Ashdod to attack it and capture it, ² YHWH spoke through Isaiah ben-Amoz and said,

"Remove the sackcloth from your body and your sandals from your feet." Isaiah did so and went about naked and barefoot.

³ Then YHWH said, "Just as Isaiah went about naked and barefoot for three years as a sign and a portent against Egypt and Ethiopia, ⁴ so will the ruler of Assyria lead away the Egyptians and the Ethiopians as exiles, both the young and the old, the naked and the barefoot, with bare buttocks*—the shame of Egypt. ⁵ All will be dismayed; their trust in Cush and their pride in Egypt will be filled with fear and put to shame. ⁶ In that day the people who live along the coast will say, "See what has happened to those in whom we put our trust and to whom we fled for aid and safety from the ruler of Assyria! Now, how are we going to escape?"

ଔ   ଔ   ଔ

²¹·¹ An oracle concerning the Desert by the Sea:†

Like whirlwinds sweeping through the Negev,
   an invader comes from the desert,
   from a land of terror.
² A grim vision is revealed to me:
   the traitor betrayed, the spoiler despoiled.
Advance, Elam! Up, Media, to the seige!
   I will put an end to all the groaning that Babylon has caused!
³ At this vision my body writhes in pain,
   pangs seize me like a woman in labor;
   I am staggered by what I see.
⁴ My heart skips a beat, I tremble with fear;
   the evening I longed for has become a horror.
⁵ They prepare the table,
   they spread the tablecloth,
  they eat, they drink.‡
   Up, commanders, and oil your shields!
⁶ For this is what YHWH said to me:

---

* An idiom roughly equivalent to our phrase "butt-naked."
† "The Desert by the Sea" most likely refers to the area around the Persian Gulf, the region of Babylon. In 722 B.C.E. a Chaldean chieftan from that region named Marduk-apal-iddina (called Merodach-Baladan in 39:1) revolted against Assyria, captured Babylon with the help of Elam, and was crowned ruler. Hezekiah, the ruler of Judah, hoped that Marduk-apal-iddina would be able to break the strength of the Assyrian Empire. Isaiah is warning them that this will not happen; for the better part of the next century, Bablylonian rulers (often supported by Elam) alternated with Assyrian rulers.
‡ That is, they are preoccupied with comfort and utterly unprepared for the battle to come.

"Go, post lookouts;
    have them report whatever they see.
7 Whether they see chariots with a team of horses—
    or riders on donkeys, or riders on camels—
  have them pay attention,
    careful attention!"
8 Now the sentinel calls:
  "I stand on the watchtower all day long,
    I am at my post throughout the night!
9 Look, here they come!
    Riders, a pair of horses!"
  Then the sentinel shouts:
  "Fallen, fallen is Babylon!
    All the images of its gods
    lie shattered on the ground!"
10 My downtrodden people, once crushed on the threshing floor, what I
heard from the YHWH Omnipotent, the God of Israel, I announce to you.

℞ ℞ ℞

11 An oracle concerning Dumah:*

  Someone calls to me from Seir,
  "Sentinel, what is left of the night?
  Sentinel, what is left of the night?"
12 The sentinel reports:
  "Morning comes,
    but then the night.
  If you're trying to ask something,
    then come back and ask it!"†

℞ ℞ ℞

13 An oracle concerning Arabia:

  In the scrub of the desert plain
    you will lodge, you Dedanite caravans.

---

* A nomadic tribe, descendants of Ishmael, who may have settled in the territory of Seir, also known
  as Edom. Many scholars see a linguistic connection between Edom, Dumah, and Idumea (as the
  region was known later). "Dumah" means "silence."
† The question, "What is left of the night?" is code for "Will there soon be an end to these difficult
  times?" The sentinel—that is, the prophet—seems to be giving a sarcastic retort, but is actually
  answering, "There will be some relief ('the morning'), but it will be short-lived ('the night')."

¹⁴ Bring water to these thirsty people,
and meet the fugitives with bread,
O inhabitants of the land of Tema!
¹⁵ For they fled from the sword,
the drawn sword,
from the bent bow,
and from the heat of battle.

¹⁶ This is what YHWH says to me: "Within one year, according to the years of a hired worker, all the glory of Kedar will come to an end. ¹⁷ And the remaining bows of Kedar's archers will be few.* YHWH, the God of Israel, has spoken."

ଓ ଓ ଓ

^{22:1} An oracle concerning the Valley of Vision.†

What troubles you now,
that all of you have gone up to the rooftops,
² O town full of commotion,
O city of tumult and revelry?
Your slain were not dispatched by the sword,
nor did they die battle—
³ all your leaders simply ran away,
fleeing to a distant place!
Your strongest troops were captured together,
without a single arrow's having been shot!
⁴ So I said, "Don't look at me!
Let me weep in private!
Don't try to console me
over the destruction of my people!"‡
⁵ For YHWH Omnipotent has planned a day
of tumult and trampling and terror in the Valley of Vision,

---

* Dedan and Kedar were wealthy semi-nomadic merchant tribes whose settlements were in southern and northern Arabia, respectively. Tema was an oasis in northwest Arabia.
† The Valley of Vision is a euphemism for Jerusalem, probably because it was often the center of the prophetic message. However, Jerusalem rests on four hills or mounts, and is surrounded by deep valleys or ravines (the Hinnom Valley on the east, the Kidron Valley on the west) and beyond them, other hills, which made Jerusalem nearly unassailable except from the north. If "mountain" stands for strength, "valley" speaks of Jerusalem's vulnerability. This oracle was probably written at the time of the attack on Jerusalem in 701 (from the north), during Assyrian ruler Sennacherib's first campaign against the Babylonians.
‡ Literally, "the daughter of my people," with "daughter" used as a metaphor for the prophet's emotional bond with Israel, as well as their vulnerability and weakness against Assyria.

a day of battering down walls
and crying out to the mountains.
6 For though Elam takes up the quiver with charioteers and horses,
and Kir readies the shield,*
7 though your choicest valleys are full of chariots,
and cavalry are posted at the city gates,
8 Judah's defenses are truly stripped away!
On that Day, you checked the weapons
that had been stored in the House of the Forest;
9 you saw how many breaks there were
in the walls of the City of David;
and you stored water in the Lower Pool.†
10 Then you surveyed the houses of Jerusalem,
tearing some down to repair and fortify the wall,
11 and between the two walls
you constructed a reservoir for the water of the Old Pool.‡
But for all this, you did not call upon the One who made it,
or consider the One who constructed it long ago!
12 On that Day, the Sovereign YHWH Omnipotent
called for weeping and the beating of breast in mourning,
for shaving the head and dressing in sackcloth.
13 Instead, there was joy and merrymaking,
the killing of cattle and slaughtering of sheep,
the eating of meat and drinking of wine!
"Let us eat and drink," you said,
"For tomorrow we die!"
14 YHWH Omnipotent whispered these words to me:
"This sin cannot be atoned for,"
says the Sovereign YHWH Omnipotent,
"not until the day you die."

ൟ   ൟ   ൟ

15 This is what the Sovereign YHWH Omnipotent says:

"Go! Go to this official named Shebna, the palace governor, and say,
16 'What are you doing here, and who gave you permission to cut out a tomb
here for yourself? Why should you hew a tomb in an eminent place, and

---

* Elam and Kir were both allies of Babylon in its war with Assyria.
† In case the war cut off their access to outside water sources.
‡ This is probably a reference to the Siloam Aqueduct, which Hezekiah constructed to bring water
from the Spring of Gihon into Jerusalem.

carve for yourself a resting place in a rock? ¹⁷ YHWH is about to shake you out, as a coat is shaken to rid it of lice. ¹⁸ God will roll you up tightly and throw you like a ball into a land of vast expanses, and there you will die, you and the chariots you glory in, you who bring disgrace on the entire palace! ¹⁹ I will remove you from your office and pull you down from your station.

²⁰ 'The day you are demoted, I will summon my faithful one Eliakim ben-Hilkiah. ²¹ I will clothe Eliakim with your robe and gird him with your sash and entrust him with your authority! He will care for the inhabitants of Jerusalem, and for the house of Judah. ²² I will place the key of the House of David on his shoulder.* When he opens, no one will shut. When he shuts, no one will open. ²³ I will fix him like a peg securely fastened to the wall, to be a place of honor for his family. ²⁴ On Eliakim will hang all the glory of his family: its offshoots and its offspring—all the lesser vessels, the bowls and all the jars—will hang from this peg.

²⁵ 'But a day will come,' declares YHWH Omnipotent, 'when even the peg securely fastened to the wall will give way; it will be sheared off and will fall, and the load hanging on it will be cut down.'"

YHWH has spoken.

ের্ত্র   ের্ত্র   ের্ত্র

²³⁻¹ An oracle concerning Tyre:†

Wail, you ships of Tarshish!
　Your fortress is now in ruins.
You will get the news
　while returning from Cyprus.
²　Lament, you island people, you merchants of Sidon!
　Your agents crossed the great sea
³　buying the grain of Shihor,
　the harvest of the Nile;
　you were the merchant of the nations.

---

* This may be an actual key worn by the palace governor or administrator (second in authority only to the ruler), or some official insignia; or it may be symbolic of the administrator's ability to grant access to the ruler—or block it. In chapter 36, Shebna is listed as the secretary of state, and Eliakim is indeed the palace governor.
† Tyre, an ancient Phonecian trading port, was actually made up of two distinct cities: a mainland city and an island city. The policy of the city had been to pay tribute to Assyria. When Sennacherib came to power, many regions in the area joined in a rebellion against the high tribute prices that had been demanded, and Hezekiah unwisely led the revolt. Sennacherib marched from the north into Palestine intent on devastating cities that had rebelled and attacked Tyre and other coastal cities, which quickly fell. The defeat of Tyre caused many of the city-states as far away as Moab and Ammon to promptly reassert their allegiance to Assyria.

⁴   Shame on you, Sidon, fortress of the sea!
    For the sea has spoken:*
    "I have neither gone into labor nor given birth,
    I have raised neither young women nor young men."
⁵   When the report reaches Egypt,
    its people will be anguished over the fate of Tyre.
⁶   Sail to Tarshish!†
    Howl, you dwellers on the seacoast!
⁷   Is this your city of revelry, this ancient city,
    the founder of colonies in far-off places?
⁸   Whose plan was it to attack Tyre,
    whose honored traders and celebrated merchants
    were renowned throughout the earth?
⁹   YHWH Omnipotent planned it—
    to prick the pride of the celebrated,
    to humble the renowned of the earth!
¹⁰ Go back to farming, people of Tarshish,
    the way they do in the Nile region;
    for Tyre, your marketplace, is no more.
¹¹ YHWH stretched out a hand over the sea,
    and made the empires tremble;
    for YHWH ordered the fortresses of Phoenicia
    to be destroyed!
¹² God said, "No more revelry for you,
    O piteously oppressed Sidon!
    Though you make your escape to Cyprus,
    even there you will find no respite."
¹³ Look at the Chaldeans—no longer a people!‡
    Assyria gave their land to the desert animals!
    They built siege towers, tore down its buildings,
    and turned it into a ruin.
¹⁴ Wail, you ships of Tarshish!
    Your fortress is now destroyed!

¹⁵ From that time, Tyre will be forgotten for seventy years, the span of a
ruler's life. However, at the end of those seventy years, its plight will be like

---

* Tyre and Sidon, being coastal cities, are metaphorically children of the sea; the image of a childless
sea foretells a time when those cities are completely depopulated.
† Another wealthy trading port, though biblical scholars disagree widely on where Tarshish was
located. Most authors are divided between Spain, Greece, and Phoenicia, but the context clearly
implies that Tarshish, Tyre, and Sidon were all coastal cities in the same general area.
‡ That is, the Babylonians. This refers to Assyria's defeat of Babylonia and the deportation of 200,000
of its people in 702, the year before this oracle was written.

that of the profligate in the song:

¹⁶ "Take up the harp, stroll through the streets,
you forgotten slattern;
strum the strings sweetly, sing your old songs,
in hopes that you will be remembered."

¹⁷ At the end of seventy years, YHWH will visit Tyre, and it will return once again to trade, to debauch itself with all the rulers on the face of the earth. ¹⁸ But this time its merchandise and its profits will be set apart for YHWH. They will not be stored or hoarded, but its merchandise will supply abundant food and fine clothing for those who live in the presence of YHWH.

24:1–27:13*

Look! YHWH is going to lay waste the earth and devastate it;
God will turn the earth upside down and scatter its inhabitants!
² The same fate awaits both priest and laity,
both overseer and bonded worker,
both employer and worker,
both buyer and seller,
both lender and borrower,
both creditor and debtor.
³ The earth will be empty, plundered, and stripped bare,
for YHWH has spoken.
⁴ The earth dries up and withers, the world languishes and withers.
The most exalted people of the earth simply fade away.
⁵ The earth lies polluted by its inhabitants,
for they disobeyed the Law, violated its statutes,
and broke the everlasting Covenant.
⁶ Consequently, a curse fell over the face of the earth.†
Its people must bear the consequences of their guilt.

---

* Chapters 24-27 are known as the Isaiah Apocalypse. These chapters, written at least one hundred years after Isaiah of Jerusalem lived, contain apocalyptic themes popular in later Hebrew writings, but it is difficult to set these oracles in a particular historical context. Older material from Isaiah of Jerusalem may have been rewritten to encompass the apocalyptic themes.

† Covenants or treaties in the Middle East often had curses or punishments attached to them which would apply if the treaty was violated, much as modern contracts have clauses explaining the penalties if the contract is broken. Covenants between human beings and God or gods often included a threatened loss of crops or outright agricultural devastation.

For this reason earth's inhabitants are consumed by fire
and few of them remain.

7 The wine dries up, the vines wilt,
and all the revelers sorrowfully groan.

8 The merry beat of tambourines falls silent,
the merrymakers are stilled,
and the joyful harp is stilled.

9 They drink wine, but there is no singing;
beer is bitter to the imbiber.

10 The shattered city lies in chaos;
the entryway of every house is barred.

11 In the street the cries are for more wine;
all joy turns to gloom.

12 The city is nothing but rubble,
and the city gates have been battered to pieces.

13 As it will be in the land,*
so it will be among the nations—
as when the olive tree has been beaten and stripped of its fruit,
or like the leftovers at the end of the grape harvest.

14 They lift up their voices, singing for joy,
acclaiming in the west the majesty of YHWH.

15 Therefore let YHWH be glorified in the east,
and exalt the name of YHWH, the God of Israel,
in the coastlands and on the islands of the sea.

16 We heard them sing songs of praise from the ends of the earth:
"Glory to the Just One!"
But I say, "I'm wasting away, I'm wasting away! Woe is me!
They betray! Deceivers betray with treachery!"

17 Terror and pit and snare are upon you,
inhabitants of the earth!

18 Those who run away at the sound of terror
will fall into the pit;
those who climb out of the pit
will be trapped by the snare.
The floodgates of heaven are opened,
and the foundations of the earth shake.

19 The earth is broken in pieces;
the earth is split in two;
the earth quakes violently.

---

* I.e., Judah.

²⁰ The earth staggers like a drunk;
it sways like a hut;
its sins lie heavy on it,
and it falls, and will never rise again.
²¹ On that Day YHWH will punish
the powers in the heavens above,*
and the earthly rulers on earth.
²² All of them will be herded together like prisoners in a dungeon,
shut up in a jail and punished over many years.
²³ The moon will be humiliated,
and the sun hides its face in shame,
compared to the glory in which YHWH Omnipotent will reign
on Mount Zion and in Jerusalem, and before its elders.

^{25·1} YHWH, you are my God—
I exalt you! I praise your Name!
For you do marvelous things,
planned long ago with steadfast faithfulness.
² You turned cities into dump heaps,
fortified cities into rubble;
strongholds of foreigners are no more,
never to be rebuilt.
³ It is for this reason
that the powerful honor you,
and cities of ruthless people fear you.
⁴ Yet you are a refuge to poor people
refuge to the needy in their distress,
shelter in the storm,
shade from the heat—
for the breath of the ruthless
is like an ice storm ⁵ or a scorching drought.
You subdue the roar of the enemy,
and the mantra of tyrants is stilled.
⁶ On this mountain,
YHWH Omnipotent will prepare for all peoples
a banquet of rich food,
a banquet of fine wines,
food rich and succulent,
and fine, aged wines.

---

* Possibly the sun, moon, and stars, which are always affected in apocalyptic literature (stars fall, moon turns to blood, etc.); or spiritual powers such as the angelic court.

⁷ On this mountain,
   God will remove the mourning veil covering all peoples,
   the shroud covering all nations,
⁸   destroying all death forever.
   God will wipe away
     the tears from every cheek,
   and will take away the shame
     of God's people on earth, wherever they live.
   YHWH has spoken.
⁹ On that Day it will be said,
   "This is our God,
     this is the One for whose liberation we waited,
   YHWH is the One in whom we had hoped!
   We rejoice exultantly in our deliverance,
¹⁰   for the hand of YHWH rests on this mountain!"
   But Moab will be trampled down
     like straw trampled in the manure.
¹¹ They will spread out their arms in it,
     like a swimmer trying to swim—
   but God will bring down their pride
     despite the skill of their hands!
   Your high-walled fortresses?
     God will bring them down,
   raze them to the ground,
     grind them into dust.
²⁶:¹ On that Day
     this song will be sung throughout Judah:
   "We have a strong city,
     and Liberation will be its walls and ramparts!
² Open the gates! Let the upright nation enter,
     a nation that remains faithful.
³ A nation of firm purpose* you keep in peace and security
     because it trusts in you.
⁴ Trust in YHWH forever!
     For you, YHWH, are an eternal Rock.
⁵ You humble those in high places,
     and bring down their lofty citadel;
   you bring it down, and raze it to the ground,
     flinging it down in the dust.

---

* Unwavering faith in God's vindication.

⁶ It is trampled underfoot by the oppressed,
  by the feet of the poor and needy.
⁷ The path of justice is straight, O Upright One,
  because you smooth the way for the just.
⁸ We have waited in hope on your road, YHWH,
  for your judgments to be handed down;
  your Name, your reputation,
  is all that our souls desire.
⁹ My soul yearns for you in the night,
  and my spirit within me keeps vigil.
¹⁰ If favor is shown to evildoers,
  they do not learn the meaning of justice.
  Even in a land where equity is paramount,
  they deal in corruption,
  they fail to see God's majesty.
¹¹ YHWH, your hand is raised, poised to act,
  but they do not see it.
  Shame them by letting them witness
  your zeal for your people!
  May the fire reserved for your enemies
  consume them!
¹² YHWH, you make us whole,*
  because you have requited our wrongs.
¹³ YHWH, our God,
  powers others than you have ruled over us,
  but we praise only your Name.
¹⁴ These dead do not live again,
  their departed spirits will not rise.
  For you punished them and brought them down,
  you wiped out all memory of them.
¹⁵ You enlarged our nation, YHWH—
  you enlarged our nation and revealed your glory.
  you extended all the frontiers of the country.
¹⁶ YHWH, we searched for you even in our distress;
  we could barely whisper a prayer
  because your chastening was upon us.
¹⁷ As when a pregnant woman nears the time to give birth,
  and writhes and cries out in her labor pains,
  so were we, YHWH, in your presence.

---

* The Hebrew is *shalom*, which is usually translated "peace," but has a larger meaning. In the context of this passage, it means that God's just punishment brings wholeness to Israel.

¹⁸ We conceived, we writhed in pain,
   but we gave birth to nothing but wind.
We could not bring liberation to the earth,
   we could not bring humankind to birth.
¹⁹ But your dead will live, their corpses will rise!
   Arise and sing, you who lie in the dust!
You will be covered in the dew of the morning's first light,
   and the earth will give birth to her departed spirits.
²⁰ Come, my people, enter your chambers,
   and shut the doors behind you;
hide yourselves for a little while
   until the wrath is past—
²¹ for YHWH is coming down from heaven
   to punish the earthlings for their sins.
The earth will reveal the blood spilled on it
   and hide those murdered no more.
^{27:1} On that Day, YHWH will take up
   a fierce and massive and powerful sword
and pursue Leviathan the elusive serpent,
   Leviathan the coiled serpent—
   and God will slay the dragon of the deep.
² On that Day you will sing
   about a delightful vineyard!
³ I, YHWH, am its keeper.
   I water it continually.
I guard it night and day
   so that no harm may come to it.
⁴ This is not anger—
   but if I were given briars and thorns,
   I would march against them in battle and burn them up.
⁵ So let my vineyard cling to me for protection,
   and let them make peace with me,
   let them make peace with me!
⁶ In days to come, the children of Leah and Rachel and Jacob
   will take root
and Israel will grow and blossom
   and fill all the earth with fruit.
⁷ Have they been struck down
   as YHWH stuck down their enemies?
Have they been slaughtered
   as YHWH slaughtered their enemies?

8 God's quarrel with Jerusalem ends
by driving Jerusalem into exile,
carrying them off by a cruel blast
as fierce as a stormwind from the east.
9 It is there that Jacob's wrong is atoned for,
here is the ransom for his sin:
God treats all the altar stones
like clumps of chalk that are ground to powder—
no Asherah poles or incense altars are left standing.
10 The fortified city lies desolate,
abandoned, forsaken like the desert;
the calves graze there,
and there they take their rest,
there they strip bare what few branches remain.
11 When the boughs dry up and snap off,
the wood gatherers take them for fires.
For this is a nation without understanding;
so their Maker has no compassion on them,
and their Creator shows them no favor.

12 On that Day, YHWH will begin "beating the tree" from the flowing Euphrates to the River of Egypt, and you Israelites will be gathered up one by one. 13 And on that Day, a great shofar will be blown, and those lost in the land of Assyria, and those driven out of the land of Egypt, will come and worship YHWH on the holy mountain of Jerusalem.

28:1–35:10*

*W*oe to that garland, the pride of Ephraim's drunkards,
the fading flower of its glorious beauty,†
sitting on the heads of those bloated with rich food,
crowning those passed out with wine.
2 You see, the Sovereign YHWH
has someone mighty and strong in mind—
someone like a driving rain,
a powerful hailstorm, a destructive wind,

---

* This section comprises a set of prophetic oracles datable to 715-701 B.C.E. concerning Judah and foreign policy; chapters 34 and 35 appear to be post-exilic additions.
† The "garland" is Samaria, capital of the northern realm, also called Ephraim.

a flooding downpour, a powerful torrent—
    someone who will hurl that crown to the ground.
3   That wreath, the pride of Ephraim's drunkards,
    will be trampled to the ground.
4   The fading power of its glorious beauty,
    set on the heads of those bloated with rich food,
    will be like a ripe fig—
    it gets picked and eaten the minute someone sees it.
5   On that Day, YHWH Omnipotent will be a garland of glory,
    a diadem of beauty for the remnant.
6   YHWH will be the spirit of justice to the one sitting in judgment,
    a reservoir of strength to those repelling the foe at the gate.
7   These also lose their way through wine;
    they stagger, smelling of strong drink:
    even priests and prophets reel from hard liquor,
    confused by wine, staggering from beer,
    blurred in vision, stumbling in judgment.
8   Tables are covered with filthy vomit;
    nothing is clean.
9   "Who does this prophet think we are," they ask,
    "teaching us knowledge and interpreting his message like this?
    Does he think we're babies just weaned from milk?
    Children just taken from the breast?
    It's all,
10   *'Mumble after mumble,*
        whisper after whisper;
        here again, there again.'*
11   When he talks to us, it's as though he's stammering,
    or speaking in a foreign language!"
12   So when the prophet told them,
    "This is the place to rest;
    let the weary rest here," and
    "This is the place of security,"
    nobody listens.†

---

* The Hebrew is deliberately monosyllabic sing-song: *Sav lasav, sav lasav, kav lakav, kav lakav, ze'er sham, ze'er sham.* It is certainly an attempt to mock Isaiah's preaching. It may represent the impression those who don't heed Isaiah's words have of his preaching—all incoherent ramblings. Or it could be translated, "Do this, do that, rule upon rule upon rule, a little here, a little there"—indicating that the priests feel that Isaiah's insistance upon obeying God is authoritarian and repressive.
† The prophet is warning the people to trust in God's protection and avoid political entanglements with other nations in an attempt to bolster national security.

13 So let the word of YHWH be,
   'Mumble after mumble,
   whisper after whisper;
   here again, there again.'
   As soon as they march forth, they will fall backward,
      and become ensnared, broken, and conquered.
14 Now, listen to the word of YHWH,
      you scoffers who rule this people in Jerusalem!
15 You boast, "We entered into a covenant with death,
      we made an agreement with the grave.
   If an overwhelming plague passes through,
      it will not even touch us;
   for we have made lies our refuge,
      and falsehood are our hiding place!"
16 Now, listen to the word of YHWH:
   "I am laying a stone in Zion, a block of granite,
      a precious cornerstone, a solid foundation.
   Those who put their trust in it
      will never be disappointed.
17 I will make justice the measuring line,
      and integrity the plumb line.
   Hailstones will sweep away your refuge of lies,
      and flood waters will carry away your hiding place.
18 Then your covenant with death will be annulled,
      and your agreement with the grave will be broken;
   when an overwhelming plague passes through,
      it will completely trample you.
19 As often as it sweeps by, it will take you away;
      morning after morning, by day and by night,
      it will sweep through."
   Once you understand this message,
      you will be consumed with terror.*
20 The bed is too short for you to sleep in,
      the blanket too narrow to wrap around you.†
21 YHWH will rise up again, as on Mount Perazim,
      and will rage again, as in the Valley of Gibeon,‡
   to do the work of the Most High—a strange work, indeed!—
      and to perform God's deeds—quite foreign deeds!

---

* Or possibly, "Only fear will make you understand this message."
† In other words, their feelings of rest and security will prove empty and disappointing.
‡ Sites of victories over the Philistines in the days of David, and over the Cananites during the time of Joshua.

²² Halt your arrogance,
   or your chains will get heavier!
The Soverign One, YHWH Omnipotent, told me
   of the destruction decreed against the whole land.
²³ Listen! Hear my voice!
   Pay attention to what I say.
²⁴ When plowing,
   does the farmer plow continuously
   breaking down and harrowing the soil?
²⁵ Doesn't the farmer instead
   scatter dill seed and cumin seed on level ground,
   and plant wheat in a row, barley in a strip,
   and grain along the edges?
²⁶ Doesn't YHWH instruct
   and train the farmer properly?
²⁷ Caraway isn't threshed with a sledge hammer,
   a wagonwheel isn't rolled over cumin!
Caraway is beaten out with a rod,
   cumin with a stick.
²⁸ Grain must be ground to make bread,
   but it cannot be threshed forever.
Horses and wagons drive over the grain,
   but that doesn't grind it into flour.
²⁹ All of this also comes from YHWH Omnipotent,
   magnificent in counsel, wonderful in wisdom.

ଓ   ଓ   ଓ

²⁹:¹ Woe to you Ariel, Ariel,*
   the city where David settled!
When another year has come and gone,
   with its full cycle of festivals celebrated,
² I will besiege you, Ariel!
   You will mourn and lament,
   and Jerusalem will be like an altar hearth before me.
³ And like David, I will encamp against it;
   I will circle you with towers
   and set my siegeworks against you.

---

* The name Ariel usually means "lioness of God," from the words 'ari and el. Here, however, it derives
from 'ara, "to burn," and means "altar hearth," the top of the altar with horns at its four corners
where offerings are burned. It is also possible to connect the name Ariel to the Akkadian word
arallu, the name for both the netherworld and the world mountain.

⁴ Once brought low,
  you will speak from deep in the ground,
and your speech, like a ghost's,
  will sound muffled by dry earth.
⁵ Yet your many enemies will be like fine dust,
  the ruthless hordes like blown chaff.
Suddenly, in an instant,
⁶   YHWH Omnipotent will appear
with thunder and earthquake and a mighty din,
  with wind storms, tornadoes,
  and the flames of a devouring fire.
⁷ Then the hordes of all the nations
  warring against Ariel,
all those who attack it with their siegeworks,
  all those who hem it in,
will fade as in a dream,
  a vision at night,
⁸ as when hungry people dream of eating,
  but wake up still hungry;
as when thirsty people dream of drinking,
  but wake up still thirsty.
So will it be with the hordes of all the nations
  that fight against Mount Zion.
⁹ You will be stunned and amazed,
  blinded and unseeing.
You'll act drunk, but not from wine,
  stagger, but not from drinking.
¹⁰ For YHWH has poured on you a spirit of lethargy.
  God has sealed your eyes, you prophets!
  God has veiled your heads, you seers!

¹¹ For you, this whole vision is nothing but words sealed in a scroll. If you give the scroll to someone, and say to that person, "Please read this," the other says, "I can't, it is sealed." ¹² Or if you give it to another to read, the person says, "I can't. I don't know how to read."

¹³ YHWH says:

"These people come near me with their mouth
  and honor me with their lips,
  but their hearts are far from me.
Their worship of me is made up only
  of rules taught by mortals.

14 Therefore, once more I will shock this people,
    adding shock to shock;
    the wisdom of the wise will perish,
    the intelligence of the intelligentsia will vanish.
15 Woe to those who seek to hide their plans
    too deep for YHWH to see,
    who work in darkness and think,
    'Who sees us? Who will know?'
16 You turn things upside down!
    Will the potter be thought of as the clay?
    Will the object that is made say to the artisan,
    'You didn't make me'?
    Can the pot say to the potter,
    'You know nothing'?
17 In a short time, a very short time,
    Lebanon will be changed into an orchard,
    and fertile land will be turned into a forest.*
18 On that Day,
    the deaf will be able to hear the words read to them;
    after a life of shadow and darkness,
    the eyes of the blind will see.
19 The lowly will again rejoice in YHWH,
    and those who are poor will exult in the Holy One of Israel.
20 For tyrants will be no more,
    mockers will vanish,
    and those disposed to do evil will be destroyed—
21 liars who incriminate others,
    'loophole experts' who try to trip up arbitrators;
    and those who defraud others
    and leave the innocent with empty claims.
22 Therefore YHWH, Sarah's and Abraham's redeemer,
    says this to the house of Leah and Rachel and Jacob:
    No longer will the Israelites be ashamed,
    nor will their faces show embarrassment,
23 for they will see what my hands have done in their midst,
    and they will keep my name holy.
    They will sanctify the Holy One of Leah and Rachel and Jacob,
    and stand in awe of the God of Israel.

---

* This indicates a complete reversal of the status quo: the renowned forests of Lebanon, a symbol of the powerful, will become a common orchard, while the orchard, a symbol of the oppressed and lowly, will grow into a mighty forest.

²⁴ Wayward spirits will learn wisdom,
and grumblers will accept instruction."

^{30:1} "Woe to obstinate children," declares YHWH,
"to those who carry out plans I did not make,
forming alliances, but not by my Spirit,
adding sin to sin;
² who set out for Egypt
without consulting me
to take refuge under the protection of the Pharaoh,
and to seek shelter in Egypt's shadow!*
³ But the protection of the Pharaoh will bring shame onto you.
Egypt's shade will bring you disgrace.
⁴ Though their officials are at Zoan
and their envoys reach Hanes,
⁵ everyone comes to shame
through a people useless to them,
who bring neither help nor advantage,
only shame and disgrace."

ଔ   ଔ   ଔ

⁶ An oracle concerning the animals of the Negev:

Through a land of hardship and distress,
of lioness and roaring lion,
of viper and darting snakes,
they haul their wealth
on the back of a donkey
and their treasures
on the hump of a camel
to that unprofitable nation,
⁷ Egypt, whose help is worthless and futile.
Therefore I name Egypt
"Rahab the Do-Nothing."†

---

* This was likely the summer of 714 B.C.E., when Hezekiah formed a coalition with Babylonia and Egypt against Assyria; under Sennacherib, Assyria attacked Jerusalem thirteen years later.
† Rahab was the name for a monster of chaos which Isaiah depicts as opposing YHWH, who imposes order on the chaos. In this passage, Egypt is accused of being an agent of chaos, doing nothing to maintain the Divine Order.

⁸ Go now, write it on a tablet before them,
    inscribe it in a notebook,
so that it may be an everlasting witness
    for the days to come.
⁹ These rebellious and deceitful people
    are like children unwilling to listen
to God's instruction.
¹⁰ They say to their seers,
    "Stop seeing visions!"
and to their prophets,
    "Stop producing true visions for us!
Tell us pleasant things!
    Prophesy illusions!
¹¹ Turn aside, leave the true path,
    and stop confronting us with the Holy One of Israel!"
¹² Therefore this is what the Holy One of Israel says:
    "Since you have rejected my message,
relying on oppression and depending on deceit,
¹³ this sin will become your downfall—
    like a break in a high wall, cracking and bulging,
that collapses without warning, in an instant.
¹⁴ You'll be like pottery breaking into pieces,
    shattering so mercilessly that among its pieces
not a shard remains to take coals from a hearth
    or to scoop water from a cistern."
¹⁵ This is what YHWH, the Holy One of Israel, says:
    "If you had repented and waited patiently,
you'd have been saved;
    if you had been quiet and trusted me,
you'd have found strength.*
But you refused, ¹⁶ saying,
    "No! We will flee on horses!"
—so you will flee indeed!
and, "We will ride on swift horses!"
    —so your pursuers will be swift!
¹⁷ One thousand will flee at the threat of one;
    and at the threat of five, you will all flee,
until you are as isolated
    as a flagstaff on top of a mountain,
a banner on a hill."

---

* Traditionally, "In returning and rest you are saved; in quietness and trust is your strength."

18   Yet YHWH longs to be gracious to you.
       God rises to show you compassion,
       for YHWH is a God of justice.
     Blessed are those who wait for
       the God of justice!
19   O people of Zion, residents of Jerusalem,
       weep no more.
     At the sound of your cry
       YHWH will indeed be gracious to you;
       hearing it, God will answer you.
20   Though YHWH may give you the bread of adversity
       and the water of affliction,
     yet your Teacher will not hide from you anymore;
       your eyes will see your Teacher.
21   And when you turn to the right
       and when you turn to the left,
     your ears will hear a voice behind you saying,
       "This is the way—walk in it."
22   Then you will defile your silver-plated idols
       and your goldplated images.
     You will scatter them like filthy rags;
       you will say to them, "Away with you!"
23   YHWH will give you rain
       for the seed you sow in the ground,
     and the food that comes from the land
       will be rich and plentiful.
     In that Day your cattle
       will graze in broad meadows
24   and the oxen and donkeys that till the soil
       will eat silage that has been winnowed with shovel and fork.*
25   Streams of water will flow
       down every lofty mountain and high hill
     on the day of massacre
       when fortresses fall.
26   The moon will shine like the sun,
       and the sunlight will be seven times brighter than normal,
       like the light of seven full days,
     on the Day that YHWH binds up the bruises of the chosen people
       and heals the wounds inflicted on them.

---

* In other words, crops will be so plentiful that even beasts of burden will have choice food to eat.

²⁷ Look, the Name of YHWH
   comes from a distant place,
burning with divine anger
   and covered with thick billowing smoke!
God's lips are full of wrath
   and God's tongue is a consuming fire.
²⁸ God's breath is a rushing torrent,
   rising up to the neck.
YHWH sifts the nations
   in the sieve that separates worthless chaff,
and places the bit of God's bridle
   in the jaws of the nations.
²⁹ And you will sing
   as on the night you celebrate a holy festival;
your hearts will rejoice
   as when the people set out to the sound of the flute
to go up God's mountain,
   to worship the Rock of Israel.
³⁰ And YHWH's majestic voice will be heard
   and YHWH's mighty arm will be seen
in furious anger and a flame of devouring fire,
   with cloudbursts, tornadoes, and hailstones.
³¹ The Assyrians will be terror-stricken at YHWH's voice,
   when God's rod strikes.
³² And with every stroke of the staff of punishment
   with which YHWH will beat the Assyrians,
God's people will rejoice with music and song,
   and will dance* as God fights the enemy.
³³ Tophetht was prepared long ago,
   and made ready for the ruler.
Its fire pit was constructed wide and deep
   with an abundance of fire and wood.
The breath of YHWH, like a stream of burning sulfur,
   sets it ablaze.

31:1 Woe to those who go down to Egypt for help,
   who put their hopes in horses

---

* Others, "with weapons of brandishing." A slight emendation of the received Hebrew text yields our translation, "will dance," which pairs nicely with the previous line's "music and song."
† Topheth, which means "burning place," was that part of the Hinnom Valley (in Greek, Gehenna, which came to personify the concept of Hell), just outside Jerusalem, where children were sacrificed to the Ammonite god Molech. "Molech" means ruler.

and rely on Egypt's many chariots and strong cavalry
but refuse to seek help from YHWH.
2 YHWH also is wise, yet brings disaster,
and does not go back on a word, once given;
God will rise against the House of Evildoers,
and against all of their allies who work their villainy.
3 The Egyptians are mortals, not gods,
their horses are flesh, not spirit.
When YHWH raises a mighty arm,
helpers stumble, and the helped fall down;
both are lost.
4 This is what YHWH says to me:
"A lion or a cub growls over its prey—
and though a group of shepherds tries to rout them,
the lions aren't frightened by their shouts
or disturbed by their clamor.
So YHWH Omnipotent will come down
to do battle on the heights of Mount Zion!
5 Like the birds hovering overhead,
so YHWH Omnipotent will protect Jerusalem;
YHWH will protect it and defend it,
will spare it and will rescue it.
6 Turn back to the One
you so deeply betrayed, people of Israel!
7 For on that Day all of you will throw away
your idols of silver and your idols of gold,
which your hands have made—to your guilt.
8 Then the Assyrians will fall by a sword
not made by mortal hand;
and a sword—not a human one—
will devour them.
They will flee from the sword,
and their young people will be subjected to forced labor.
9 In their terror they will abandon their stronghold,
and their panic-stricken leaders will desert their standards.
It is YHWH who speaks, whose fire is in Zion,
whose furnace is in Jerusalem!

32:1 Watch: a ruler will reign with integrity,
and officials will rule with fairness.*

---

* This passage looks forward to an idyllic messianic era.

2   They will all be like a shelter from the wind,
     a place of refuge from the storm;
   like streams of water in a dry place,
     like the shade of a high cliff in a parched land.
3   Then the eyes of the seeing will no longer be blind,
     and the ears of the hearing will listen.
4   The minds of the rash will know and understand,
     and the stammerer will speak fluently and plainly.
5   No longer will the villain be called noble
     nor will the liar be highly regarded!
6   But today, villains speak villany,
     plotting evil in their hearts;
   all their exploits are godless,
     and misrepresent who YHWH is;
   they steal from the starving,
     and withhold water from the thirsty.
7   As for liars—
     their evil deeds are legend!
   They devise evil plots to deceive the poor and ruin their lives,
     and deny justice to the needy.
8   But truly noble people form noble designs,
     and they bear themselves nobly.
9   Rise up, complacent ones, and hear my words!
     Self-important children, listen to what I have to say!
10   In a little more than a year, presumptuous ones,
     you will be troubled:
   for the vintage will fail,
     and there will be no fruit harvest.
11   Tremble, men and women of ease,
     and shudder, you complacent ones!
   Strip yourselves naked
     and wrap up in sackcloth!
12   Beat your breasts for the pleasant fields,
     for the fruitful vine,
13   for the soil of my people, where thorns and briars thrive,
     for all the happy houses, for the festive city—
14   because the palace will be abandoned,
     the bustling city deserted;
   citadel and watchtower will be ruins forevermore;
     a delightful place for wild asses, a pasture for flocks,

---

* Echoing the prophecy in 29:19.

15 until the Spirit from on high
   is lavished on us.
   Then the desert will turn into an orchard,
   and the orchard is abundant as a forest.*
16 Justice will dwell in that desert,
   and integrity will live in this orchard.
17 It is justice that will bring us peace—
   only justice will produce quietness and lasting security.
18 My people will abide in a peaceful environment,
   with secure dwellings, quiet places for rest—
19 even if a hailstorm should lay low the forest
   and level the city completely!
20 How blessed you will be,
   sowing your seeds along the streams,
   your cattle and donkeys ranging free!

33:1 Woe to you, you destroyer,
   you who have not been destroyed!
   Woe to you, you traitor,
   you who were never betrayed!
   Once your ravaging is over,
   you will be ravaged.
   Once your plundering is over,
   you will be plundered.
2 YHWH, have mercy on us!
   We hope in you!
   Be our strong arm every morning,
   be our deliverance in times of trouble!
3 At the crack of thunder people flee,
   nations scatter at your roar.
4 They plundered for spoil
   like caterpillers stripping the vegetation;
   they devour it
   like a swarm of locusts.
5 Yet YHWH dwells on high
   and fills Zion with justice and integrity.
6 YHWH will be your life-long stability,
   providing an abundance of
   salvation, wisdom, and knowledge—
   the treasure that comes from revering YHWH.

⁷   Listen, Ariel* laments in the streets,
        envoys of Shalom weep bitterly.
⁸   Roads are deserted,
        no one travels them.
    The treaty is broken,
        its witnesses despised.
    Trust and respect
        fade away.
⁹   The land mourns; it wastes away;
        ashamed, Lebanon withers away;
    Sharon is a desert,
        Bashan and Carmel drop their leaves.
¹⁰ "Now is the time for me to rise," says YHWH,
        "I will lift myself up, now I will be exalted!
¹¹ You conceive chaff and give birth to stubble;
        my breath will consume you like fire!
¹² The nations will be piles of white ash,
        like thorns cut down ready to burn.
¹³ Hear, distant people, what I have done;
        those of you near-by, acknowledge my power!"
¹⁴ Zion's sinners are terrified,
        trembling grips the godless:
    "Who among us
        can survive the consuming fire?
    Who among us can endure
        everlasting flames?"
¹⁵ Those who walk with integrity
        and speak the truth,
    who reject profit from extortion,
        and do not take bribes,
    who stop their ears to murder plots
        and shut their eyes against evil—
¹⁶ these people will thrive on the heights,
        their refuge a fortress of rocks,
        their food and water assured.
¹⁷ Your eyes will view the ruler in full regalia,
        they will view a land stretching far away.

---

* The meaning of the word is uncertain. If the received Hebrew is correct, it could mean (as discussed above in 29:2) "altar hearth," which would refer to the sacrificial altar—and, by extension, Jerusalem itself. With a different vowel pointing, it could mean "valiant warrior" (with "envoys of Shalom" then translated as "peace envoys") to indicate that hawks and doves alike are in mourning. Or it could be the name Ariel as an epithet for Jerusalem, as is Shalom (Jerusalem means "teaching of peace.")

¹⁸ You will murmer in awe:
"Who could count all this money?
Who could have weighed all this tribute?
Who could inventory everything in these towers?"

¹⁹ No longer will you see these arrogant people,
whose language was so obscure,
whose stammering tongue you could not comprehend.

²⁰ Look upon Zion, the city of our appointed festivals!
Your eyes will see Jerusalem,
a quiet, secure home,
an immovable tent,
all its pegs eternally in place,
with ropes that never fray.

²¹ For there, YHWH the majestic will be like
a place of broad rivers and streams for us,
where no galley rows,
where passes no mighty ship.

²² YHWH is our judge,
YHWH is our lawgiver,
YHWH is our ruler—
the One who frees us!

²³ Though now our rigging is slack,
our mast is not secure,
and we can't spread our sails,
on that Day, there will be so much prey and plunder
that all will have a share,
and even the slow and infirm will carry off the spoil.

²⁴ No one who lives in Zion will say, "I am sick."
The sins of all who dwell there will be forgiven.

34:1 Approach, you nations, and pay attention!
Let the earth and all who inhabit it listen!
Let the world and all that it yields hear me!

² You see, YHWH is enraged with all nations,
and furious with all their armies.
God has doomed them
and will give them over for slaughter.

³ Their slain will be thrown into the streets,
and the stench of their corpses will rise;
the mountains will flow with their blood.

⁴ All the stars of heaven will dissolve
and the skies will roll up like a scroll;

the stars will fall like leaves falling from the vine,
   or fruit dropping from a fig tree.
5 When my sword has drunk its fill in the heavens,
   see how it descends on Edom,
   upon a people I doomed to judgment!
6 YHWH has a sword sated with blood,
   it is gorged with fat,
with the blood of goats and lambs,
   and the fat of ram's kidneys.
For YHWH is holding a sacrifice in Bozrah,
   a great slaughter in Edom.
7 Wild oxen will be slaughtered along with them.
   as will yearling steers and mighty bulls.
Their land will be soaked in blood
   and their soil enriched with fat.
8 For YHWH has a day of vengeance,
   a year of vindication, to uphold Zion's cause.
9 Edom's streams will be turned into pitch,
   its soil into sulfur;
its land will become burning tar,
10   never to be quenched, day or night;
   smoke rising from it eternally.
Generation after generation it will lie waste,
   and it will be impassable forever.
11 The jackdaw and the desert owl
   will possess it;
the great owl and the raven
   will nest there.
YHWH will stretch out over Edom
   the measuring line of chaos
   and the plumb line of desolation.
12 Its nobles will have nothing there
   to call it a realm,
all its governors
   will melt away.
13 Thorns will grow over its citadels,
   nettles and thistles over its fortresses.
It will become the lair of wolves,
   the haunt of owls.
14 Wildcats will meet with jackals;
   hairy goats will call to one another,

as the night creatures gather
   to find themselves a place to rest.*
15 There will the owl nest and lay her eggs,
   she will hatch the owlets,
caring for them under the shadow of her wings;
   there, too, the vultures will gather,
   each one with its mate.
16 Look in the Book of YHWH and read it:
   not one of these will be missing,
   none will lack its mate,
for YHWH has personally ordered it,
   and God's spirit has gathered them together.
17 It is God who allots each its place,
   God's hand that portions out their territory;
they will possess it forever,
   generation after generation they will live in it.

35:1 Let the desert and the wilderness exult!
   Let the Arabah rejoice and bloom like the crocus!
2 Let it blossom profusely,
   let it rejoice and sing for joy!
The glory of Lebanon is bestowed on it,
   the splendor of Carmel and Sharon.
They will see the glory of YHWH,
   the splendor of our God.
3 Strengthen all weary hands,
   steady all trembling knees.
4 Say to all those of faint heart:
   "Take courage! Do not be afraid!
Look, YHWH is coming,
   vindication is coming,
the recompense of God—
   God is coming to save you!"
5 Then the eyes of the blind will be opened,
   the ears of the deaf will be unsealed.
6 Then those who cannot walk will leap like deer
   and the tongues of those who cannot speak will sing for joy.
Waters will break forth in the wilderness,
   and there will be streams in the desert.

---

* "Hairy goats" may refer to satyrs or male goatlike demons; similarly, "night creatures" may refer
to the "Lilith," a female night demon—or may simply be the tiny screech owl.

⁷ The scorched earth will become a lake;
   the parched land, springs of water.
   The lairs where jackals used to dwell
   will become thickets of reed and papyrus.
⁸ And through it will run a highway,
   a road called the Sacred Path.
   The unclean may not travel by it,
   but it will be for God's people alone;
   and no traveler—not even fools—
   will go astray.
⁹ No lions will be there,
   nor will any fierce beast roam about it,
   but the redeemed will walk there—
¹⁰   for those whom YHWH has ransomed will return.
   They will enter Zion shouting for joy,
   with everlasting joy on their faces;
   joy and gladness will go with them,
   and sorrow and lament will flee away.

36:1–39:8*

In the fourteenth year of the reign of Hezekiah the ruler, Sennacherib the ruler of Assyria came up against all the fortified cities of Judah and captured them. ² Sennacherib sent his field commander from Lachish to Jerusalem to attack Hezekiah with a large army. When the commander took up a position at the aqueduct of the Upper Pool, on the road to the Fuller's field, ³ Eliakim ben-Hilkiah, the palace governor, Shebna, the secretary of state,† and Joah ben-Asaph, the recording secretary, went out to meet the commander.

⁴ The commander said to them, "Tell Hezekiah that this is the message of the Great Ruler, the Ruler of Assyria: 'What are you basing your boldness on, that you would rebel against me? ⁵ Do you think that mere words are strategy and military strength? Who are you allied with? ⁶ It couldn't possibly be Egypt, that broken reed of a staff, which pierces the hand and wounds whoever leans on it! This is what Pharaoh, ruler of Egypt, amounts to for those allied with him. ⁷ And if you were to say, "We depend on YHWH, our God"—isn't that the one whose shrines and altars Hezekiah has suppressed, telling Judah and Jerusalem they must worship before this altar alone?'*

---

* These three chapters are an historical appendix dealing with Hezekiah and the Assyrian crisis.

† Hebrew *saphar*, usually translated "scribe," an official whose duties ranged from that of chief comptroller to chief legal counsel. Note that Shebna used to be the palace governor (chapter 22) but was demoted because of overweaning ambition.

⁸ "Come now, make a deal with Sennacherib my ruler, and I will give you 2,000 horses—if you can find riders to put on them! ⁹ How could you refuse such an offer, even to the deputy of one of Sennacherib's lowest subjects, and rely instead on Egypt for chariots and horses? ¹⁰ Do you think I attacked this land and destroyed it without the consent of YHWH? No, it was YHWH who said to me, 'Go up and destroy this land'!"

¹¹ Then Eliakim, Shebna, and Joah said to the commander, "Please speak to us in Aramaic, since we understand it. Don't speak Hebrew to us within earshot of the people on the city wall."

¹² The commander replied, "Was it only to your ruler and you that Sennacherib sent me to say these things? Isn't this message particularly pertinent to those defending the wall, who will have to eat their own dung and drink their own urine with you?"

¹³ Then the commander stepped back and shouted in Hebrew, "Hear the message of the Great Ruler, the Ruler of Assyria! ¹⁴ These are his words: 'Don't be deceived by Hezekiah, who is powerless to save you. ¹⁵ Don't let him persuade you to rely on YHWH, and tell you that YHWH will most certainly save you and that this city will never be surrendered to the ruler of Assyria.' ¹⁶ Don't listen to Hezekiah, for this is what the ruler of Assyria says: 'Make your peace with me, and surrender! Then each and every one of you will eat from your own vine and fig tree and drink from your own cistern, ¹⁷ until I come and take you to a land like this one—a land of grain and new wine, a land of bread and vineyards. ¹⁸ Do not let Hezekiah mislead you by saying, 'YHWH will deliver us.' Has the god of any nation saved the land from the hand of the ruler of Assyria? ¹⁹ Where are the gods of Hamath and Arpad? Where are the gods of Sepharvaim? Have they rescued Samaria from me? ²⁰ Who are all the gods of these countries that have been able to save their land from me? How then can YHWH save Jerusalem from my hand?"

²¹ But the people remained silent and did not reply, for Hezekiah had sent down orders not to reply. ²² Eliakim ben-Hilkiah, the palace governor, Shebna, the secretary of state, and Joah ben-Asaph, the recording secretary, returned to Hezekiah with their clothes torn as a sign of grief, and reported the words of the commander.

37:1 When Hezekiah the ruler heard the report, he tore his clothes, dressed in sackcloth and entered the house of YHWH. ² The ruler sent Eliakim, the palace governor, Shebna, the secretary of state, and the senior priests—all

---

* 2 Chronicles 30-31 tells of a campaign in which Hezekiah had all the local shrines, incense altars, sacred pillars, and other places of worship throughout Judah destroyed, and centralized all worship of Yhwh at the altar in Jerusalem. These reforms were apparently twofold: they weeded out the worship of other gods and goddesses, which had gotten mixed with the worship of Yhwh; and created a new order through reforms which placed Hezekiah in complete control of the economy, food supplies, and other materials necessary for a revolt against Assyria.

clothed in sackcloth—to the prophet Isaiah ben-Amoz, [3] to convey this message from Hezekiah:

"This is what Hezekiah says: 'This day is a day of distress, rebuke and disgrace. We are like the woman who hasn't the strength to give birth to the child she carries. [4] It may be that YHWH your God will hear the words of the field commander, whom the ruler of Assyria sent to mock the living God, and will refute those mocking words. Offer your prayers for the remnant that remains.'"

[5] When the ruler's officials came to Isaiah, [6] they were given this message for Hezekiah: "This is the word of YHWH: 'Do not panic at what you heard when the Assyrian's minions blasphemed me. [7] I will delude him with a rumor, and he will return home. And there I will make him fall by the sword.'"

[8] Meanwhile, when the commander returned to camp, he learned that Sennacherib had moved on from Lachish and was attacking Libnah. [9] But when the ruler of Assyria learned that Tirhakah, ruler of Ethiopia, was on the way to attack him, Sennacherib once more sent messengers to Hezekiah of Judah [10] to say to him, "How can you be deluded by YHWH into believing the promise that Jerusalem will not fall into the hands of the ruler of Assyria? [11] You yourself must have learned what the rulers of Assyria have done to other countries—they totally destroyed them! Then how can you escape? [12] Did their gods save the countries my predecessors destroyed—Gozan, Haran, Rezeph, and the people of Eden living in Telassar? [13] Where are the rulers of Lahir, Sehparvaim, Hena and Ivvah?"

[14] Hezekiah received the letter from the messengers, and, having read it, went up to the Temple and spread it out before YHWH [15] and prayed, [16] "YHWH Omnipotent, God of Israel, enthroned on the cherubim, you alone are God of all the nations of the world. You made heaven and earth. [17] Incline your ear, YHWH, and listen! Open your eyes, YHWH, and see! Hear all the words of Sennacherib sent to mock the living God! [18] YHWH, it's true—the rulers of Assyria have lain waste all the other nations, [19] and consigned their gods to the flames. They destroyed them, for they were not gods, but the handiwork of mortals, merely wood and stone. [20] Now, YHWH our God, save us from Sennacherib's power, so that all the nations of the earth may know that you alone, YHWH, are God."

[21] Isaiah ben-Amoz sent Hezekiah this message: "This is the word of YHWH, the God of Israel: I have heard your prayer to me concerning Sennacherib ruler of Assyria, [22] and this is the word YHWH spoke against him:

> The young daughter Zion
> despises you and mocks you!
> The daughter of Jerusalem
> tosses her head as you flee!*

---

* In other words, Judah at its most vulnerable is able to rout the Assyrians.

²³ Who is it
    you mocked and blasphemed?
Against whom have your raised your voice
    and lifted your insolent eyes?
    —The Holy One of Israel!
²⁴ You sent your minions to mock YHWH;
    you said, "With my many chariots
I ascended the mountain heights,
    I have gone to the far reaches of Lebanon.
I felled its tallest cedars,
    its finest pines;
I reached the highest peaks,
    its densest forest.
²⁵ I dug wells in foreign lands
    and drank distant water,
and with the sole of my foot
    I dried all the streams of Egypt!"
²⁶ Have you not heard?
    Long ago I planned for it,
from days of old I designed it,
    and now I carry it out:
your purpose was to bring down fortified cities
    in heaps of ruins.
²⁷ Now their powerless people
    are confused and ashamed.
They, like plants in a field,
    like tender green shoots,
    like sprouts of grass on the roof,
    are singed before growing up.
²⁸ But I know where you dwell
    and when you come and go
    and how often you rage against me—
²⁹ and because you rage against me
    and because your insolence
    has reached my ears,
I will put my hook in your nose
    and my bit in your mouth
and I will make you return
    by the way you came!

³⁰ "This will be the sign for you, Hezekiah: This year, you will eat what grows by itself, and the second year, what springs from that; then in the

third year, you will sow, reap, plant vineyards, and eat their fruit. ³¹ The surviving remnant of the house of Judah will bring new roots from below ground and bear fruit above ground.

³² "For a remnant will come out of Jerusalem
and survivors from Mount Zion.
The zeal of YHWH Omnipotent
will accomplish this.
³³ Therefore, this is the word of YHWH about the ruler of Assyria:
The enemy will not enter this city
or shoot an arrow there;
They will not approach it with a shield
or build up a siege ramp against it.
³⁴ They will return by the same road they came by;
they will not enter this city.
This is the word of YHWH.
³⁵ I will defend this city to deliver it for my own sake
and for the sake my obedient one David."

³⁶ The angel of YHWH went out and struck down 185,000 troops in the Assyrian camp; when morning came they all lay there dead. ³⁷ Sennacherib, ruler of Assyria, broke camp and marched away to Ninevah for an extended stay.

³⁸ One day, while Sennacherib was worshipping in the temple of the god Nisroch, his sons Adrammelech and Sharezer assassinated him, and fled to the land of Ararat. Sennacherib's son Esar-haddon became the new ruler.

38:1 In those days, when Hezekiah fell ill and was at the point of death, the prophet Isaiah ben-Amoz came and said, "Thus says YHWH: Put your affairs in order, for you are going to die; you will not recover."

Then Hezekiah turned his face to the wall and prayed to YHWH, "Remember, I beg you, YHWH, how faithfully and how wholeheartedly I have behaved in your presence and done what is right in your sight." Then Hezekiah wept bitterly.

⁴ Then the word of God came to Isaiah and said, ⁵ "Go, tell Hezekiah: I have heard your prayer and seen your tears. I will add fifteen years to your life. ⁶ I will rescue you and this city from the hand of the ruler of Assyria. I will be a shield to this city."

²¹ Isaiah then ordered a poultice of figs to be taken and applied to the skin eruption, that he might recover. ²² Then Hezekiah asked, "What is the sign telling me that I will go up to the Temple of YHWH?"*

---

* Veses 21 and 22, which are often placed at the end of the chapter, maintain the sequence of events and could logically be placed here.

⁷ Isaiah answered, "This will be the sign for you from God that what was promised will be done. ⁸ Watch: I will make the shadow on the stairway, cast by the setting sun, go back up ten steps on the Stairway of Ahaz." And the sun's shadow went back the ten steps on the stairway on which it had gone down.

⁹ A poem written by Hezekiah, the ruler of Judah, after recovering from an illness:

10   I said, "In the prime of my life I must depart;
       in the middle of my days I am consigned to the gates of Sheol;
       I have been called away for the rest of my days."
11   I said, "I will no longer see YHWH in the land of the living.
       I will no longer look upon mortals
       or be with those dwelling on the earth.
12   Like a nomad's tent
       my dwelling has been pulled down
       and taken away from me.
       You rolled up my life,
       like weavers when they cut the last thread from the loom.
       Day and night
       you make an end of me.
13   I am racked with pain all night long.
       all my bones are broken, as if by a lion;
       Day and night
       you make an end of me.
14   Like a swallow or a dove,
       I twitter, I moan.
       My eyes grew dim
       as I look to the skies.
       Sovereign One, I am overwhelmed!
       Be my security.
15   But what can I say?
       God promised me,
       and God brought it to pass.
       Sleep has abandoned me
       because of the bitterness of my soul.
16   Despite all these things, Sovereign One,
       my soul is revived;
       you have restored me to health;
       and brought me back to life.

¹⁷ I now see that it was good for me to suffer;
and your love saved me from
the pit of destruction.
You have turned your back
on all my sins.
¹⁸ For Sheol cannot be grateful to you,
death cannot praise you to the heights;
those who fall down to the Pit
cannot hope for your faithfulness.
¹⁹ The living, the living, are grateful to you,
as am I all this day;
parents make known to their children
your faithfulness.
²⁰ YHWH has saved me,
and we will sing and make music
all the days of our lives
in the Temple of YHWH.

^{39:1} At that time Merodach-baladan ben-Baladad, the ruler of Babylon,* sent envoys carrying letters and a gift to Hezekiah, for Merodach-baladan learned of his illness and recovery. ² Hezekiah welcomed them and gave them a tour of his treasury—the silver, the gold, the spices, the precious oils, the whole armory and storehouses. There was nothing in the ruler's residence or in the realm that Hezekiah did not show them.

³ Then the prophet Isaiah came to Hezekiah the ruler and said, "What did the envoys say? Where were they from?"

Hezekiah replied, "They came to me from a far country, from Babylon."

⁴ The prophet asked, "What did they see in your residence?"

Hezekiah answered, "They saw everything I have in the house. There was nothing in the storehouses that I did not show them."

⁵ Then Isaiah said to Hezekiah, "Hear the word of YHWH Omnipotent: ⁶ Days are coming when everything in your residence, everything your ancestors passed on to you up to this very day, will be carried off to Babylon. Nothing will be left, says YHWH. ⁷ Some of your own heirs born to you will be taken away; they will be made eunuchs in the residence of the ruler of Babylon."

⁸ Then Hezekiah said to Isaiah, "The word of YHWH that you spoke is good." For Hezekiah was thinking that peace and security would last during his lifetime.

---

* That is, "New Babylonia," or Chaldea.

seconò ísaíah

"**C**onsole my people, give them comfort,"
says your God.†

2 "Speak tenderly to Jerusalem's heart,
and tell it
that its time of service is ended,
that its iniquity is atoned for,
that it has received from YHWH's hand
double punishment for all its sins."

3 A voice cries out,
"Clear a path through the wilderness for YHWH!
Make a straight road through the desert for our God!

4 Let every valley be filled in,
every mountain and hill be laid low;
let every cliff become a plain,
and the ridges become a valley!

5 Then the glory of YHWH will be revealed,
and all humankind will see it."
The mouth of YHWH has spoken!

6 A voice commands, "Cry out!"
and I answer, "What will I say?"
—"All flesh is grass
and its beauty is like the wildflowers:

7 the grass withers
and the flower wilts
when the breath of YHWH blows on them.
How the people are like grass!

8 Grass withers, and flowers wilt,
but the promise of our God will stand forever."

9 Go up on a high mountain,
you who bring good news to Zion!

---

* Chapter 40 begins "Second Isaiah," a series of poems proclaiming that a new day is coming, a time of liberation. This theme was appropriated by the writers of the Christian scriptures to express their own sense that the Reign of God was at hand.

† The first poem of Second Isaiah begins with a dialogue. Some commentators see it as God speaking to the assembly of the heavenly Council; others hear God a prophet's calling. In either case, God is ordering that Jerusalem be comforted for the trials it has suffered, proclaiming pardon for the people of Israel, release from their guilt, and announcing the return of the exiles from Babylon.

Shout with a loud voice,
you who bring good news to Jerusalem!
Shout without fear,
and say to the towns of Judah
"Here is your God!"
¹⁰ YHWH, O Sovereign One,
you come with power,
and rule with a strong arm!
You bring your reward with you,
and your reparation* comes before you.
¹¹ Like a shepherd you feed your flock,
gathering the lambs and holding them close,
and leading mother ewes with gentleness.

¹² Who else measures the waters of the sea
in a hollowed hand,
and by the breadth of a hand
marks off the heavens?†
Who else holds the dust of the earth
in a basket,
or weighs mountains on a scale
and hills on a balance?
¹³ Who has directed the Spirit of YHWH,
or has instructed God like a counselor?
¹⁴ To whom does YHWH go to for enlightenment?
Who taught God the rules of life?
Who taught YHWH knowledge,
and showed God the way of understanding?
¹⁵ Surely, the nations are like a drop in a bucket to YHWH,
like dust on the scales;
to God, entire islands weigh no more
than a fleck of dust.
¹⁶ Not even Lebanon has enough firewood
for a sacrificial fire large enough for God,
nor does it have enough animals
for an adequate burnt offering.

---

* The Hebrew is the common word for the wages of a laborer, but has numerous contextual shadings, like payback or harsh punishment, or reparation or compensation after hardship. We favor the latter reading, since it neatly parallels the sentiments expressed in verse 2.

† The writer is making a subtle echo of Genesis 1:6, where God "separated water from water" on the second day of creation. In Hebrew, "waters" is *mayim*, and "heavens" or "sky" is *shamayim*—literally, the "waters up there."

¹⁷ All the nations are as nothing before God;
 they are reckoned as less than nothing,
 like primeval chaos.
¹⁸ To whom, then, will you compare God?
 What likeness will suffice?
¹⁹ A carefully crafted idol
 overlaid with gold by a metalsmith
 with a silver chain,
²⁰ sitting on a base of precious mulberry wood—
 carefully selected because it does not decay—
 so that the idol is firm and won't topple?
²¹ Did you not know?
 Have you not heard?
Was it not told to you from the beginning?
 Have you not understood since the earth was founded?
²² YHWH sits above the vaulted roof of the world,
 and its inhabitants look like grasshoppers!
God stretches out the skies like a curtain,
 and spreads them out like a tent for mortals to live under!
²³ God reduces the privileged to nothing
 and throws the rulers of the earth into chaos.*
²⁴ No sooner are they planted,
 no sooner are they sown,
 no sooner do they take root on earth,
than God blows on them and they wither,
 and a stormwind sweeps them away like chaff.
²⁵ "To whom can you liken me?
 Who is my equal?" says the Holy One.
²⁶ Lift up your eyes and ask yourself
 who made these stars,
if not the One who drills them like an army,
 calling each by name?
Because God is so great in strength,
 so mighty in power,
 not a single one is missing.
²⁷ How can you say,
 tribe of Leah and Rachel and Jacob,
"My destiny is hidden from YHWH,
 my rights are ignored by my God?"

---

* Here and in verse 17, the writer uses the word *tohu*, which was first used in Genesis 1 to describe the state of the earth before the Spirit begins her creative work.

²⁸ Do you not know? Have you not heard?
YHWH is the everlasting God,
the Creator of the ends of the earth.
This God does not faint or grow weary;
with a depth of understanding that is unsearchable.
²⁹ God gives strength to the weary,
and empowers the powerless.
³⁰ Young women may grow tired and weary,
young men may stumble and fall,
³¹ but those who wait* for YHWH
find a renewed power:
they soar on eagles' wings,
they run and don't get weary,
they walk and never tire.

^{41.1} "Be silent before me, you coastlands!
You nations—rest up, and get ready!
Then come forward and state your case:
let us come together as litigants.
² Who has raised up a Victor from the east?†
Who has called someone to stand up in righteousness?
Who turns nations into his subjects
and overthrows their rulers—
reducing them to dust with that sword,
like wind-blown chaff with that bow,
³ putting them to flight
and passing on unscathed,
moving so quickly
that his feet barely touch the road?
⁴ Who did this?
Who accomplished it?

---

* To "wait" for God is to cultivate an attitude of hope and patient expectation—the very definition of faith. Usually the Hebrew verb means a waiting for God to act, to bring vindication or to rescue the people from oppression; here, however, it is more akin to the Taoist concept of *wu wei*, or non-action: by waiting for God's empowerment instead of relying on one's own resources, one receives an inexhaustible supply of strength.

† The "Victor from the east" referred to in these poems is Cyrus the Great, the famous Persian ruler whose chain of victories brought hope of liberation to those in exile in Babylon. Second Isaiah challenges the other nations to prove that their gods were powerful enough to call Cyrus from the east to liberate the captive nations. Through the medium of a trial, Second Isaiah proves that YHWH alone was powerful enough to call Cyrus, and that Cyrus was doing the will of God. The Greek author Xenophon wrote that "Cyrus received from nature a figure of remarkable beauty, and a heart full of humanity; he was very zealous for science, and so impassioned for honor that he endured all works and exposed himself to all dangers."

Who has called forth each generation
   from the very beginning?
I, YHWH, was with that first generation,
   and I will with be the last!
5   The remotest islands have seen these works,
      and they are afraid;
   the ends of the earth tremble
      as they come before the bench.
6   Each helps the other as they come forward;
      'Have courage,' they tell one another.
7   Yes, the artisan encourages the metalsmith
      and the carpenter encourages the blacksmith,
   making sure their 'god' is welded together properly,
      and nailing it down so that it won't topple over!
8   But you, Israel, my subjects,
      Leah, Rachel, and Jacob, the ones I chose,
      descendants of Abraham, my friend—
9   I am bringing you back from the ends of the earth,
      I summon you from its farthest corners;
   I call you as my own:
      I choose you, and will not reject you:
10   Fear not, for I am with you,
      do not be afraid, for I am your God.
   I will strengthen you, I will help you,
      and I will uphold you with my strong right hand.
11   And all who defy you
      will be confounded and put to shame.
   All who oppose you
      will be as nothing, never to be seen again.
12   Though you look for your enemies,
      you will not find them
   Those who wage war against you
      will be as nothing—nothing at all.
13   I am YHWH, your God!
      I have taken your right hand in mine.*
14   Don't be afraid, tribe of Leah and Rachel and Jacob, poor worms!
      Don't be afraid, Israel, puny mite!†

---

* The right hand was the place of honor and strength. To sit at God's right hand is to be especially honored; but to have the positions reversed, and have God willingly be at one's right hand, is astounding—it is God saying, in effect, "Whatever you want, whatever you need, I will do it."
† The prophet points out that even though Israel is weak and insignificant in the eyes of many larger and more powerful nations, Israel is still loved deeply and faithfully by YHWH.

I will help you—it is YHWH who speaks—
the Holy One of Israel is your Redeemer.*
15 See, I will turn you into a threshing sledge,
sharp, new, and double-edged,
to thresh the mountains and crush them,
and turn the hills to chaff.
16 You will winnow them,
and the wind will blow them away,
the stormwind will scatter them.
But you yourself will rejoice in YHWH,
and glory in the Holy One of Israel.
17 The poor and the needy seek water but find none;
their tongues are parched with thirst.
But I, YHWH, will answer them myself!
I, the God of Israel, will not abandon them.
18 I will make rivers run on barren heights,
and fountains bubble up in the valleys;
I will turn the wilderness into a lake,
and dry ground into a spring.
19 I will put cedar trees in the wilderness,
acacias, myrtles, and olives.
In the desert I will plant the cypress,
the elm, and the evergreen side by side,
20 so that all may see and know,
all may observe and understand
that the hand of YHWH has done this,
that the Holy One of Israel has created it.

21 "So defend yourself," says YHWH.
"State your case," says the Ruler of Leah, Rachel, and Jacob.
22 "Bring in your 'gods'
to predict what is going to happen.
Let them interpret the meaning of past events
so that we can ponder them;
or let them predict the future for us!
23 You idols—foretell what is yet to come,
and convince us that you are gods!

---

* "Redeemer" refers to the duty of the next of kin to obtain justice for a family member who was
treated unjustly. If someone was forced to sell land to pay debts, for example, the redeemer, or
goel, bought back the land to keep it in the family. The redeemer was both liberator and avenger.
On another, higher level, God was seen as the Redeemer who brings justice to the weak and
oppressed.

At the least do *something*, good or bad—
    anything that will strike us with awe and terror!
²⁴ You can't! You really are less than nothing,
    and your works are worthless!
That's why choosing you
    is such an abomination!
²⁵ I sent for someone from the north,*
    and he is on his way—
someone from the east
    who calls on my Name,
someone who marches against rulers
    as if they were potters treading clay.
²⁶ Who declared it initially, so that we might know,
    foretold it, so that we could say 'It came true'?
Not one of you idols declared it,
    not one of you foretold it—
no one has heard you
    utter a single word!
²⁷ I was the first to say to Zion, 'Here they come!'
    I sent Jerusalem a messenger with the good news.
²⁸ But I look around and see no one—
    no one among these 'gods' to give counsel,
    no one to answer my questions.
²⁹ They are a delusion!
    Their works amount to nothing,
    their statues are just wind and chaos."

        ଔ   ଔ   ଔ

⁴²⁻¹ "Here is my Servant,† whom I uphold
    my chosen one, in whom I delight!
I have endowed you with my Spirit
    that you may bring true justice to the nations.
² You do not cry out or raise your voice,
    or make yourself heard in the street.

---

* Cyrus.
† 42:1-9 is the first of the four passages identified as "Servant Songs" in *Isaiah*. Read out of context, the passages have been interpreted as speaking about an individual, a messianic figure. But taken in context (as verses 6 and 19 make clear), the passages are about the people of Israel as a whole, called to teach and enlighten, to be examples of justice and faith, and even to serve the world through suffering.

³ So gentle that you do not break a bruised reed,
    or quench a wavering flame,
    faithfully you will bring forth true justice.
⁴ You will neither waver nor be crushed
    until justice is established on earth,
    for the islands await your teaching!
⁵ Thus says YHWH,
    who created the heavens and spread them out,
  who gave shape to the earth and what it produces,
    who gave life to its peoples and spirit to its inhabitants:
⁶ I, YHWH, have called you to serve the cause of right;
    I have taken you by the hand, and I watch over you.
  I have appointed you to be a covenant people,
    a light to the nations:
⁷ to open the eyes of the blind,
    to free captives from prison,
    and those who sit in darkness from the dungeon.
⁸ I am YHWH! This is my Name!
    I will not yield my glory to another god
    or my praise to idols!
⁹ See how former predictions have come true.
    And now I declare new things!
  Before they spring forth,
    I tell them to you."

ભ ભ ભ

¹⁰ Sing YHWH a new song,
    sing God's praise to the ends of the earth!
  Let the sea and all that fills it sing God's praise,
    the islands and all who inhabit them!
¹¹ Let the desert and its settlements rejoice,
    and the encampments where Keder lives rejoice.
  Let the people of Sela sing for joy,
    let them shout from the mountain tops!
¹² Let them give glory to YHWH,
    and declare God's praise in the coastlands!
¹³ For YHWH will go forth as a hero,
    with a fury like that of a warrior—
  with a shout, YHWH raises this battle cry,
    and leads the charge against the foe:

¹⁴ "For a long time I held my peace,
   restrained myself and held myself in check.
But now I groan as if giving birth,
   gasping and panting!
¹⁵ I will lay waste the mountains and hills,
   and dry up all their greenery.
I will turn the rivers into wildernesses,
   drying every pool.
¹⁶ Those who are blind, I will lead by a route they don't know,
   and guide them by unfamiliar paths.
I will turn the darkness before them into light
   and straighten out their twisting roads.
These things I will do,
   and I will not abandon them.
¹⁷ But the rest—
   those who put their trust into carved idols,
who say to carved idols, 'You are our gods,'
   they will be routed and completely put to shame!
¹⁸ Listen closely, you who are deaf,
   look and see, you who are blind:
¹⁹ No one is as blind as my Servant,
   none so deaf as my messenger!
Who is as blind as my Chosen,
   as deaf as the Servant of YHWH?
²⁰ You saw many things, but did not observe them;
   your ears were open, but you paid no attention;
²¹ It pleased YHWH—for the sake of integrity—
   to make divine law great and glorious.
²² But this is a people plundered and looted,
   all of them hidden away in dungeons,
   or forgotten in prisons.
They were carried off as spoil
   without hope of ransom.
They became plunder,
   with no one to say, 'Give them back!'
²³ Who among you will listen to all this?
   Who will will pay attention, and heed it in the future?
²⁴ Who handed my people over for plunder,
   or Israel for spoil?
Wasn't it I, YHWH,
   against whom they sinned?

They refused to follow my ways,
    refused to obey my laws.
25 So I poured out my blazing anger on them,
    the violence of war.
It enveloped them in flames,
    yet they did not understand;
it consumed them,
    and still they didn't take it seriously!
43:1 But now, Leah and Rachel and Jacob,
    hear the word of YHWH—
the One who created you,
    the One who fashioned you, Israel:
Do not be afraid, for I have redeemed you;
    I have called you by name; you are mine.
2 When you pass through the seas, I will be with you;
    when you pass over the rivers, you will not drown.
Walk through fire, and you will not be singed;
    walk through flames and you will not be burned.
3 I am YHWH, your God,
    the Holy One of Israel, your deliverer.
I give Egypt as ransom for you,
    Nubia and Seba in exchange for you.
4 You are more precious to me than Assyria;
    you are honored, and I love you.
I will give people in exchange for you,
    whole nations in exchange for your life.
5 Have no fear, for I am with you;
    I will bring your descendants from the east
    and gather them from the west.
6 To the north I will say, 'Give them up!'
    and to the south, 'Do not hold them back!
Bring my daughters and sons from afar,
    return them from the ends of the earth—
7 everyone who is called by my Name,
    whom I created for my glory,
    whom I formed and made!
8 Bring forth this people—
    a people who have eyes but cannot see,
    a people who have ears but cannot hear!'
9 All the nations gather together
    and the peoples assemble.

Who among them foretold this
and revealed to us the former things?
Let them present their witnesses to verify their words,
that the jury might say, 'It is true.'

¹⁰ You are *my* witnesses, says YHWH,
my chosen Servant,
so that you may know and believe me
and understand who I am.
Before me no god existed,
nor will there be one after me.

¹¹ Who am I? I am YHWH,
and there is no Liberator except me.

¹² It was I who made it known;
I who declared it and saved you;
It was I who was in your midst, and not some foreign god,
and you are my witnesses—it is YHWH who speaks—
that I am God.

¹³ I am God from all eternity,
and no one can take you out of my hand.
What I do,
no one can undo!"

¹⁴ These are the words of YHWH, your Redeemer,
the Holy One of Israel:
"For your sakes I will send an army to Babylon
and make all the Chaldeans fugitives
in their ships of which they are so proud.*

¹⁵ I am YHWH, your Holy One,
Israel's Creator, your Ruler."

¹⁶ Thus says YHWH,
who made a road through the sea,
a path in the mighty waters,

¹⁷ who led chariots and warriors to their doom,
a mighty army fallen, never to rise again,
snuffed out and extinguished like a wick:

¹⁸ "Forget the events of the past,
ignore the things of long ago!

¹⁹ Look, I am doing something new!
Now it springs forth—can't you see it?

---

* The original Hebrew text had no vowels; they were added later by scribes, as an aid to pronunciation. With a slightly different vowel pointing, this phrase becomes, "and turn their joyful shouts into dirges."

I'm making a road in the desert
and setting rivers to flow in the wasteland.
20 Wild beasts will honor me—
the jackals and the ostriches—
for I will put water in the desert
and rivers in the wasteland
for my chosen people to drink,
21 these people whom I formed for myself
so that they might declare my praise.
22 Yet you did not call upon me, O Leah and Rachel and Jacob!
You grew weary of me, O Israel!
23 You didn't bring me your lambs for burnt offerings,
nor honored me with your sacrifices.
Did I burden you with requests for offerings?
Did I weary you with demands for frankincense?
24 You didn't buy me any fragrant calamus reeds with your money,
or sate me with the fat of your sacrifices.
Instead, you burdened me with your sins,
and wearied me with your crimes!
25 Who am I? I'm the one who wipes out your offenses!
For my own sake, I do not remember your wrongs.
26 So order me to appear, and let us argue the matter together!
Make your case, and prove your innocence!
27 Your earliest ancestor sinned,
and your priests and prophets rebelled against me.
28 So I profaned the dignitaries of your temple,
put the people under a solemn curse,*
and made a laugingstock out of Israel.
44:1 "But now listen, O Leah and Rachel and Jacob, my Servant!
Listen, O Israel, whom I chose!
2 Thus says YHWH, your maker, your helper,
who formed you in the womb:
Have no fear, O Leah and Rachel and Jacob, my Servant!
Don't be afraid, Upright One, whom I chose!
For I will pour down rain on parched ground,
showers on dry soil—
I will pour my spirit on your descendants
and my blessings on your offspring!

---

* This is the concept of *cherem*, the utter and irrevocable devotion of things, individuals, or entire peoples over to God—which usually entailed their complete destruction.

⁴ They will spring up like grass in a spring meadow,
   like poplar trees by flowing streams.
⁵ This one will say, 'I belong to YHWH,'
   that one will adopt the name of Leah or Rachel or Jacob,
   others will write 'This belongs to YHWH' on their hand
   and adopt the name of Israel."

⁶ This is what YHWH says —
   Israel's Ruler and Redeemer, YHWH Omnipotent:
   "I am the first and I am the last;
   apart from me there is no God.
⁷ Who is like me?
   Let them declare their proof
   and set it out before me:
   let them predict things to come long before they happen,
   let them announce future events!
⁸ Have courage! Don't be afraid!
   Didn't I proclaim and foretell this long ago?
   You are my witnesses!
   Is there any god apart from me?
   Is there any other Rock?
   I know of none!
⁹ Idol crafters are less than nothing;
   their cherished images profit no one.
   Their witnesses are blind;
   their ignorance magnifies their foolishness.
¹⁰ Who would make a god or cast a metal image
   unless there was profit in it?
¹¹ Watch how all the devotees of this 'god' will be put to shame —
   after all, its artisans are just human beings!
   Let them all assemble,
   let them come together and take a stand,
   and there they will be terrified and disgraced.
¹² The blacksmith fashions the image,
   working it over the coals,
   shaping it with a hammer —
   forging it with a strong arm.
   Should blacksmiths become hungry,
   their strength fails, like that of any other human;*

---

* "Like any other human" is supplied for clarity. The prophet is saying that these idols are made not only by human beings, but by frail and fallible humans at that; how then can their creations be imbued with any godlike power?

should they get thirsty,
they feel faint, like any other human.
¹³ Woodworkers draw a careful line
and mark out the design with a scriber;
they plane the wood and measure it with calipers,
and carve it into the shape of a human being—
and a beautiful human being at that!—
destined to be set up in a shrine.
¹⁴ Before that, they cut down a tree—
a cedar or a cypress or an oak—
which they have raised for themselves
among the trees of the forest.
Or they plant a stout fir,
and wait while the rain nourishes it.
¹⁵ Some of this wood becomes fuel for our fires:
with some of it they warm the room,
and with some of it they bake the bread.
But with some of it they make a god,
to be worshipped!
People take this wood and turn into an idol,
then bow down before it!
¹⁶ Half of the wood they burn in a hearth,
where they roast the meat and eat it with satisfaction.
They warm themselves and say,
'How nice and warm to sit and watch this fire!'
¹⁷ With the rest of the wood, they make a god,
an image to be prostrated before,
prayed to and petitioned:
'Save me, for you are my god!'
¹⁸ People like this
neither know nor understand.
like their idols, they have eyes but cannot see,
they have minds but cannot think.
¹⁹ People like this
do not reason;
they have neither the imagination
nor the common sense to say,
'I have burned half of my wood,
and used its embers to bake bread
and to roast meat to eat;

should I really make the rest into something abhorrent,
    and bow down to a block of wood?'
20 They feed on ashes
    with a deluded mind leading them astray;
and they cannot save themselves or even say,
    'Isn't this thing in my hand just a fraud?'
21 Remember all this, my people,
    for you are my Servant;
I formed you, and you are my Servant—
    O Israel, do not forget me!
22 I swept away your faults like a cloud,
    your sins like the morning mist.
Return to me,
    for I redeemed you!"

23 Sing for joy, O heavens, for YHWH has done it!
    Shout out, O earth below!
Break out in song, O mountains,
    all you forests, and all you trees—
for YHWH has redeemed Leah and Rachel and Jacob,
    and will be glorified in Israel!
24 Thus says YHWH, your Redeemer,
    who formed you in the womb:
"I am the God who created all things,
    I alone stretched out the heavens,
    I alone fashioned the earth.
25 I foil the signs of false prophets
    and make fools of fortunetellers;
it is I who overturns wise counsel,
    and makes their wisdom seem foolish.
26 I confirm the word of my prophets,
    I fulfill the predictions of my messengers—
I say of Jerusalem, 'It will be inhabited';
    of the towns of Judah, 'They will be rebuilt,'
    and of their ruins, 'I will restore them.'
27 I say to deep waters, 'Be dry!'
    I will dry up all your rivers.
28 I say to Cyrus, 'You will be my shepherd,
    and you will carry out my plans,

so that Jerusalem may be rebuilt,
and the foundation of the Temple restored.'

45:1 "Thus says YHWH to the Anointed One,* Cyrus,
whom I have taken by the right hand,
for whom I have subdued nations,
stripped the loins of monarchs,†
and thrown open all doors
so that even the town gates cannot be shut:
² I will go before you and level the mountains;
I will shatter the bronze doors
and cut through the bars of iron.
³ I will give you the hidden treasures,
and hoards from secret places,
so that you may know that I am YHWH,
Israel's God, who calls you by name.
⁴ For the sake of Leah and Rachel and Jacob, my Servant,
and for the sake of Israel, my chosen one,
I called you by name, conferring on you an honored title,
even though you do not know me.
⁵ I am YHWH, and there is no other;
there is no God besides me.
It is I who arm you,
though you know me not,
⁶ that nations may know
from the rising to the setting of the sun
that there is no one besides me.
I am YHWH, there is no other.
⁷ I form light and create darkness.
I make peace and create evil.‡
It is I, YHWH,
who do all these things.
⁸ Let justice descend, O heavens, like dew from above,
and let the clouds rain down righteousness!

---

* "Anointed One" is the English translation of *mashiach*, that is, "messiah." Pouring oil on an individual's head showed that a leader had received God's personal help, guidance, or commissioning. In Israel, high priests, prophets, and rulers were anointed; in Babylonia and Assyria, brides, freed slaves, priests, and people involved in certain property transactions were anointed as well. Here the Persian ruler Cyrus is called God's anointed one, or messiah, because he responds to God's call to allow Jews exiled in Babylonia to return to their homeland.
† A euphemism for military disarmament.
‡ "Peace," or *shalom*, can also be translated "well-being"; and "evil," or *ra*, can also be translated "calamity."

Let the earth open, and let salvation blossom!
   Let justice spring up with it!
   I, YHWH, have created this!
9   Will the pot quarrel with the potter,
       or the earthen vessels with the hand that shapes it?
   Will the clay ask the potter, 'What are you doing?'
       or 'Where is your skill?'
10   Will a child say to one parent, 'What are you begetting?'
       or to the other, 'What are you giving birth to?'
11   Thus says YHWH,
       the Holy One of Israel, our Maker:
   Will you question about my children,
       or instruct me about my handiwork?
12   I made the earth and created humankind upon it—
       those were *my* hands that stretched the sky,
       and I marshaled their starry hosts!
13   I have stirred up Cyrus to restore justice;
       I will make his way smooth.
   Cyrus is the person who will rebuild my city
       and set my exiles free,
   but not for a price or a reward,"
       says YHWH Almighty.
14   These are the words of YHWH:
   "Laborers of Egypt and merchants of Ethiopia
       and tall Sabeans will come to you and be yours;
   they will walk behind you,
       coming over to you as if they were given in tribute.
   They will bow down to you
       and plead with you, saying,
   'Surely God is with you, and there is no other;
       there is no other God.
15   Truly you have a secret God—
       the God of Israel is a Liberator!'

16   All the makers of idols are confounded
       and brought to shame:
       they all slink off, humiliated.
17   But Israel has been delivered by YHWH,
       a deliverance for all time to come;
       they will never be confused or ashamed.
18   Thus says YHWH, Creator of the heavens,
       the God who designed and made the earth,

who established it firmly,
  and did not create it to be a desolation,*
  but rather a place to be lived in:
"I am YHWH, and there are no others like me.
¹⁹ I have not spoken in secrets,
  in a land of darkness;
I did not say to Jacob's descendants,
  'You will find me in chaos.'
I, YHWH, speak the truth.
  I declare what is right.
²⁰ Gather yourselves together,
  assemble and draw near, you survivors of the nations!
They ignorantly carry about their wooden idols,
  and continue to pray to a god that cannot save.
²¹ I challenge them to declare and present their case—
  let them take the stand!
Who announced this from the beginning,
  and foretold it from long ago?
  Was it not I, YHWH?
There is no other God but me,
  a just and saving God—
  there is none but me.
²² Turn to me and be saved, all of you—
  even those at the ends of the earth,
for I am God;
  there is no other!†
²³ By my own self I swear;
  I never go back on my word,
  for it is the truth when I say that
before me every knee will bend,
  and by me every tongue will swear—
all will say, 'From YHWH alone
  comes victory and strength.' "

---

* Here and in verse 19 are more references to Genesis 1. There the earth, before God's creative work, is *tohu va-bohu*, desolation (or chaos) and emptiness; here, God says it was not created to be *tohu*—but was intended as our home.

† For Second Isaiah, Israel is a light to all nations and a servant of God's purposes. Israel's chosenness means that through Israel all the world will be blessed; as Rabbi Louis Jacobs puts it, "The world owes to Israel the idea of the one God of righteousness and holiness. This is how God became known to humankind." For the first time, God is seen as Redeemer (*go'el*) not only of Israel, but also of all of humankind. Second Isaiah issues an invitation to all the people's of the earth to acknowledge the sovereignty of God.

All who were angry with YHWH
will stand there ashamed.
25 In YHWH,
all generations of Israel
will find justice and vindication.

ᬒ ᬒ ᬒ

46:1 Bel is crouching;
Nebo is stooping.*
Their images,
once carried among your possessions,
are now loaded on beasts of burden,
and weigh down the weary animals.
2 They stoop and crouch together,
these gods who cannot bring even bundles to safety
and they themselves go off into captivity.

3 "Listen to me, house of Leah, Rachel, and Jacob,
and the remnant of the house of Israel:
I carried you from your conception,
I supported you from your birth;
4 and even when you are old, I am with you,
and when your hair turns gray I will carry you still.
I created you and I will carry you;
I will sustain you and I will save you.

5 "To whom will you liken me? Who is my equal?
To whom will you compare me? Who is like me?
6 Some pour out gold from their bags,
weigh out silver on the scales;
then hire a goldsmith to craft a god,
before which they fall down and worship.
7 They lift it onto their shoulders to carry;
they set it up in its place.
There it stands, immobile,
unable to answer those crying out,
unable to save them from their troubles.

---

* Bel is the Babylonian counterpart of the Phoenician god Ba'al, the storm/sky god; Nebo is the Babylonian deity Nabu, god of the scribal arts.

8   Remember this, fix it in your mind,
        take it to heart, you rebellious ones:
9   remember what happened of long ago.
     For I am God—there is no other;
        I am God—there is no one like me.
10   From the beginning I reveal the outcome;
        from ancient days I foretell what is still to come.
     I say, 'My purpose will be fulfilled,
        I will bring about everything I have planned.'
11   I call forth a bird of prey from the east—
        from far away a person to carry out my plan.
     No sooner said than done,
        no sooner planned than carried out.
12   Listen to me, you hard-hearted,
        you who are far from deliverance:
13   I am bringing justice close, it is not far off;
        I bring liberation, and it will not be delayed.
     I will bring liberation to Zion,
        I will adorn Israel with my beauty."

47:1 "Come down and squat in the dust,
        'Fair Child' Babylon!
     Sit on the ground, not on your throne,
        'Fair Child' Chaldea!
     You will no longer be called
        tender and delicate.*
2   Take the millstone,
        grind the meal!
     Undo your hair,
        remove your fine clothes!
     Bare your legs,
        cross the water!†

---

* This "dirge" over Babylon is filled with biting sarcasm and mockery. The people of Babylon blithely go about their business unaware that the die has already been cast against them. The Assyrians will soon conquer them and bring them under complete subjugation. The prophet sees Cyrus as the instrument of God's wrath against Babylon the same way that God used Babylon to punish a rebellious Israel. Through Cyrus, Babylon will meet the same fate that Jerusalem had suffered—a city conquered, its people sent into exile.

† The meaning of this verse is given extra emphasis in Hebrew, where the very sound of the words evoke a millstone grinding wheat. Grinding meal was extremely difficult labor done only by animals, slaves, or prisoners; a delinquent was said to be "worthy of the mill." The second phrase indicates the exposed and disheveled state of captives and mourners; the third depicts people who must hike up their garments so high that they expose themselves as they cross the rivers—specifically, the rivers that lie between Judah and Persia, where the Chaldeans would be taken as captives.

3   Uncover yourself
          so that your shame will be exposed.
      I will take vengeance!
          I will spare no one!"
4   Our Redeemer—whose name is the YHWH Omnipotent,
          the Holy One of Israel—says this:
5   "Sit in silence and go into the darkness,
          'Fair Child' Chaldea,
      for you will never again be called
          the sovereign of many nations.
6   I was angry with my people,
          and I profaned my heritage;
      I surrendered them into your hands
          and you showed them no mercy—
      even on the aged
          you laid a crushing yoke.
7   You said, 'I will be a sovereign forever!'
          You didn't think about your deeds
          and gave no thought to their outcome.
8   Now listen to this,
          spoiled lover of pleasure!
      While reigning securely you say,
          'Me, me, me! No one else matters!
      I will never be without a spouse,
          never suffer the loss of children!'
9   Yet in the blink of an eye,
          both of these will come upon you in full measure:
      in a single day you'll lose
          your children and your spouse—
      despite your many incantations,
          despite your many spells.
10   Secure in your depravity, you mused,
          'No one can see me.'
      Your wisdom and your knowledge
          led you astray;
      and in your heart of hearts you said,
          'Me, me, me! No one else matters!'
11   So grave misfortune will come upon you,
          and you will not know how to conjure it away;
      disaster will fall upon you
          which you cannot avert;

unforeseen ruin
    will quickly overtake you.
¹² Keep working your spells and all your incantations
    that you have practiced since childhood!
  Maybe they will work!
  Maybe they will scare away misfortune!
¹³ Alas, all your counsellors' advice
    has come to naught.
  Your astrologers, your stargazers,
    your sages who, at each new moon,
  foretell what will happen to you next—
    let them stand up and save you now!
¹⁴ Look at them, they're like stubble, consumed in the fire—
    they cannot save themselves from the flames.
  Here there are no coals for warmth,
    here there is no comforting fire to gaze into!
¹⁵ See what profit they have brought you,
    these merchants you have dealt with all your life!*
  They all go off, each in a separate direction,
    each powerless to save you."

⁴⁸˙¹ Hear these words, O house of Leah, Rachel, and Jacob,
    you who go by the name Israel,
  who came from the line of Judah—
  you who swear by the Name of YHWH,
    and invoke the God of Israel,
    but do neither in truth or with integrity!
² You who call yourselves citizens of the holy city,
    and depend upon the God of Israel,
  hear the One whose name
    is YHWH Omnipotent:
³ "The former things I declared long ago,
    I revealed it with my own mouth;
  then suddenly I acted,
    and it was done.

---

* Babylon's cultivation of the mystical arts—the practice of magic, the use of herbs, the study of astrology, etc.—was renowned throughout the world, as was its affluent merchant class. Here the prophet speaks about magicians in one breath and merchants in the next, as if the two are inextricably linked—but neither riches nor magic is able to save Babylon from the coming disaster.

4   For I knew how stubborn you were:
        the tendons in your neck were iron,
        your forehead was like bronze.*
5   That's why I told you these things long ago,
        and stated them to you before they happened,
    so that you couldn't say,
        'My idols did these things,
    my wooden image,
        my metal god ordained them.'
6   You heard these things;
        think hard on it and admit their truth.
    From this time on I will tell of new things,
        hidden things you did not know before now.
7   They are being created now,
        not in the past.
    Before today you've never heard of them,
        so you can't say, 'Oh, I already knew all this.'
8   You've never heard these things,
        you've never known them,
        no word of them reached your ears in the past.
    For I know how treacherous you are;
        you've been known as a rebel from your birth.
9   For the sake of my own Name's sake
        I was patient;
    rather then destroy you, I restrained myself,
        so as not to cut you off completely.
10 Instead, I have refined you—
        though not in fire, as silver is.
    I have tempered you
        in the furnace of affliction.
11 For my own sake, for my own sake,
        I do this.
    How can I let my Name be defamed,
        or yield my glory to a lesser god?
12 Children of Leah, Rachel, and Jacob, listen to me!
        Listen, Israel, whom I called!
    I am the One;
        I am the first, and I am the last.

---

* To be "stiff-necked" is to be obstinate and inflexible, as if one can't turn one's head from side to
  side—rather like a donkey resisting a change in direction. A "forehead of bronze" means that one's
  thinking is similarly inflexible and unyielding.

¹³ My hand set the foundation of the earth,
   my right hand spread out the heavens;
when I summon them,
   they stand at attention.
¹⁴ Assemble, all of you, and listen!
   Which of your idols declared these things?
YHWH's friend will do my pleasure against Babylon,
   and be my arm against the Chaldeans.
¹⁵ I, yes, I myself have spoken,
   yes, I summoned Cyrus,
I brought him, and he will triumph.
¹⁶ Come close, and listen to this—
   from the very first, I spoke nothing in secret,
and when it is fulfilled, I am there:
'And now, Exalted YHWH has sent me,
   endowed with God's Spirit!' " *
¹⁷ Thus says YHWH, your Redeemer,
   the Holy One of Israel:
"I, YHWH, teach you what is good for you,
   I lead you on the road you should go.
¹⁸ If only you would pay attention to my commandments,
   your peace would have been like a river,
   your integrity like the waves of a sea.
¹⁹ Your children would have been like the sand,
   your descendants as numerous as its grains.
Never would your name have been cut off
   or blotted out before me.
²⁰ Leave Babylon, flee from the Chaldeans!
   Declare this with shouts of joy, proclaim it,
   and send it forth to the ends of the earth!
Shout, 'YHWH has redeemed us,
   the children of Leah, Rachel, and Jacob!
²¹ We did not thirst when we were led through the desert—
   water sprang out of the rocks for us,
   YHWH split the rock and the water gushed out!' " †

---

* The speaker is Cyrus. Throughout "Second Isaiah," particularly in Cyrus's speeches or the servant songs, the phrase 'Adonai YHWH is used repeatedly. We hear in this construction a form of address that a diplomat or visiting dignitary might use, like "your esteemed royal highness." 'Adonai, usually translated "Lord" in other versions and "Sovereign" throughout The Inclusive Hebrew Scriptures, is here rendered "Exalted," to echo the speech of a ruler praising a foreign but sovereign God.
† The inclusion of verse 22 here ("There is no peace," says YHWH, "for the corrupt!") is almost certainly a scribal error; the same verse appears verbatim at the end of chapter 57, where it fits beautifully in context, whereas here it is a non sequitur.

Íslanòs, listen to me!
Pay attention, distant peoples!
YHWH called me before I was born,
and named me from my mother's womb.*
2 God made my mouth a sharp sword,
and hid me in the shadow of the hand of the Most High.
The Almighty made me into a sharpened arrow,
and concealed me in God's quiver.
3 The Holy One said to me,
"You are my Servant, Israel,
in whom I will be glorified."
4 I had been thinking, "I have toiled in vain,
I have exhausted myself for nothing!"—
yet all the while my cause was with YHWH,
and my reward was with my God.
5 Thus says YHWH,
who formed me in the womb to be God's Servant,
who destined me to bring back the children of Jacob
and gather again the people of Israel:
6 "It is not enough for you to do my bidding,
to restore the tribes of Leah, Rachel, and Jacob
and bring back the survivors of Israel;
I will make you the light of the nations,
so that my salvation may reach to the ends of the earth."

7 Thus says YHWH,
the Redeemer of Israel, the Holy One,
to the one deeply despised,
the one abhorred by nations,
the one enslaved by despots:
"Rulers will stand when you walk in the room
and court officials will pay homage
because of YHWH, who is faithful,
because of the Holy One of Israel, who chose you."

---

* 49:1-6 is the second of the Servant Songs in Second Isaiah. The identification of Israel, the nation, as the suffering servant is made explicit in 49:3. In this song, God makes explicit also that the servant brings God's liberation to all the earth (49:6).

8   Thus says YHWH:
     "At the time of my favor I will answer you,
         on the day of salvation I will help you.
     I will keep you,
         and appoint you to be a covenant people.
     I will restore the land
         and assign you the properties that have lain waste.
9   I will say to the prisoners, 'Come out!'
         and to those who are in darkness, 'Show yourselves!'
     Congested roadways will become
         places where they can safely graze,
     and barren heights will become
         lush pastureland for them.
10   They will never hunger or thirst,
         and scorching wind and sun will never plague them;
     for the One who has compassion on them
         will lead and guide them to springs of water.
11   I will make roads through all the mountains,
         and my highways will be raised up,
12   because they are on their way from afar,
         some from the north or the west,
         others from the land of Aswan.*
13   Shout for joy, you heavens! Exalt, you earth!
         You mountains, break into happy cries!
     For YHWH consoles the people
         and takes pity on those who are afflicted.
14   But Zion said,
         'YHWH has abandoned me,
         Adonai has forgotten me.'
15   Does a woman forget her baby at the breast,
         or fail to cherish the child of her womb?
     Yet even if these forget,
         I will never forget you.
16   Look and see:
         I have inscribed you on the palms of my hands;
         your walls are forever before me.
17   Your children hurry back,
         while those those who laid you waste are leaving.

_____

* The Babylonian empire extended as far north as modern Turkey, as far west as modern Iran, and
  as far south as the Aswan region in southern Egypt.

¹⁸ Raise your gaze and view the horizon—
they're all gathering, they're all coming home.
As I live—I, YHWH, swear it—
you will wear your children like ornaments,
and adorn yourself like a bride or groom.
¹⁹ Though you were ruined and desolate
and your land laid waste,
your land will soon be too small for its inhabitants,
and those who ruined you will be far away.
²⁰ The children you thought you had lost
will say in your hearing,
'We need more room to live in,
this place is to small for us!'
²¹ Then you will say in your heart of hearts,
'Who gave birth to these for me? I was bereaved and barren.
Who raised them, when I was in exile?
I was by myself—where did they come from?' "

²² Thus says YHWH, the Sovereign One:
"I will send a message to the nations
and hoist my signal to the peoples,
and they will bring your daughters and sons,
holding them in their arms,
carrying them on their shoulders.
²³ Rulers will become their foster parents,
nursing and nurturing them.
They will fall prostrate before you,
foreheads touching the ground,
licking the dust from your feet.
Then you will know that I am YHWH;
those who hope in me are never disappointed."

²⁴ Can booty be snatched from the looter, you ask,
or captives liberated from the tyrant?
²⁵ Thus says YHWH:
"Captives will indeed be liberated from the tyrants,
and booty will be snatched from the looters!
For I will fight with those who fight with you
and I will save your children.
²⁶ I will make your oppressors eat their own flesh;
they will be drunk on their own blood as on new wine.

Then all humankind will know
that I am YHWH your Liberator and your Redeemer,
the Mighty One of Leah and Rachel and Jacob."

50:1 Thus says YHWH:
"Where is your parents' writ of divorce,
with which I put them away?
Or to which of my creditors did I sell you?
No! You were sold for your own depravity,
and your parents were put away
because of your own corruption!
2   Why did no one welcome me when I came?
Why did no one answer when I called?
Is my arm too short to redeem?
Am I powerless to rescue?
With a simple rebuke I can dry up the sea
and turn the rivers into a desert,
their fish stinking without water,
dying of thirst.
3   I can clothe the heavens in mourning,
and make sackcloth its covering!"

4   Exalted YHWH* has given me
a skilled and well-trained tongue,
so that I can sustain the weary
with a timely word.
God awakens me morning after morning—
wakens my ear, to listen like a student.
5   Exalted YHWH opened my ears
and I have obeyed,
I did not turn away.
6   I offered my back to those beating me,
offered my cheeks to those who would humiliate me.†
I did not hide my face from insults
or spitting.
7   Because Exalted YHWH helps me,
insults cannot wound me,

---

* 50:4-11 is the third Servant Song. This song details the suffering that the servant will bear, knowing
that God has chosen the servant to walk the path that will end in vindication and exaltation. The song
makes clear that it is through the suffering of God's servant that the reign of God comes to be.
† Literally, "my cheeks to those who make bald," that is, to those who would pull out the beard, an
act regarded throughout the Middle East as one of extreme violation and debasement.

for I have set my face like flint,
  because I know I will not be put to shame.
8 My vindicator
    is at my side.
  Who would dare accuse me?
    Let us confront each other!
  Who are my adversaries?
    Let them accuse me!
9 It is Exalted YHWH who helps me.
    Who will judge me guilty?
  All of them will wear out like a piece of clothing;
    moths will devour them.
10 Who among you reveres YHWH,
    and obeys the word of God's Servant?
  You who walk in the dark,
    who have no light,
  trust in God's Name
    and rely on my God!
11 But all of you who set wildfires,
    you who equip yourselves flaming arrows,
  walk in the flames of your own fires,
    and feel the arrows you set blazing!
  This is what you will receive from my hand:
    you will lie down in torment.

51:1 Listen closely to what I say,
    you who pursue justice,
    you who seek YHWH,
  consider the rock from which you were hewn,
    the quarry from which you were cut:
2 Look to Abraham, your father,
    and Sarah, your mother who bore you.
  They were but one couple when I called them,
    but I blessed them and made them many.
3 Indeed, YHWH will comfort Zion,
    will give comfort to all its ruins—
  will turn its desert into an Eden,
    its desert will be like the garden of YHWH.
  Joy and happiness will be found there,
    thanksgiving and the sound of music.
4 "Hear me, my people!
    Listen to me, my nation!

For Instruction* comes from me,
 and my justice will be a beacon to the peoples.
5 My vindication draws near,
 my deliverance approaches;
 my arm will bring justice to the people
 and the islands will put their hope in me.
 They will put their future in my hands.
6 Lift your eyes and look up to the heavens,
 then look to the earth below:
 for the heavens will vanish like smoke;
 the earth will wear out like a coat,
 and those who live on it will die like flies.
 But my liberation will last forever,
 my vindication will never fail.
7 Listen to me, my people, you who love justice
 and hold my teachings in your heart:
 Do not fear the insults of others,
 don't be alarmed when they curse you.
8 For the moth will chew them like a coat,
 the worm will swallow them like wool,
 but my liberation will last forever,
 my vindication from generation to generation."

ଔ   ଔ   ଔ

9 Wake up! Wake up!†
 Clothe yourself in strength, O arm of YHWH!
 Rise up, as in former days,
 as in times long past!
 Didn't you hack Rahab‡ to pieces
 and run through the dragon?
10 Didn't you dry up the sea,
 the waters of the great deep?
 Didn't you make the bottom of the sea a road
 for the redeemed to pass through?

---

* *Torah*, or the Law.
† This section, 51:9 through 52:6, consists of three "songs," each of which begins with the phrase, "Wake up! Wake up!" and ends with God promising liberation and restoration. The first urges God to rise up and take action; the second mourns a Jerusalem that has been long trampled and oppressed; the third addresses a revived Zion and invites it to celebrate God's deliverance.
‡ As in Psalm 87 and earlier in Isaiah, Rahab is again used as a symbolic name for Egypt; here it may also refer to the Egyptian army that was destroyed during the exodus at the Sea of Reeds.

11 "The ransomed of YHWH will return," God replies,
   "entering Zion with triumphant shouts,
   crowned with everlasting joy.
They will be filled with joy and gladness;
   sorrow and sighing will melt away.
12 I, I am your Comforter;
   why, then, should you fear mortals who will die,
   who must perish like grass?
13 Why did you forget YHWH your Maker,
   who stretched out the heavens
   and laid the foundations of the earth?
You were fearful daily, continuously,
   afraid of the fury of your oppressors
bent on your destruction.
   But where is your oppressor's fury now?
14 Those who have been bowed down in chains
   will soon be set free.
They will not.be cut down and slain,
   nor will they lack bread.
15 I am YHWH, your God,
   who so stirred up the waves that they roared.
   YHWH Omnipotent is my name,
16 I have put my words in your mouth,
   and hid you in the shadow of my hand—
I, who set the heavens in their place,
   who laid the foundations of the earth,
   who say to Zion, 'You are my people.' "

17 Wake up! Wake up!
   Get up, Jerusalem,
you who drank from YHWH's hand
   the cup of divine wrath,
you who drained to its dregs
   the cup of stupor!
18 There is no one to guide you
   among all the children you bore;
among all the offspring she reared
   there is not one to take you by the hand.
19 A double portion of calamity came down upon you—
   who will console you?
Havoc, ruin, famine, the sword—
   who will comfort you?

²⁰ Your children lie in a stupor at every street intersection,
   like antelope entrapped in a net;
glutted on YHWH's wrath,
   the rebuke of your God.
²¹ Therefore, pay attention to this
   you who are wounded,
   you who are drunk, but not with wine:
²² Thus says your Sovereign, YHWH, your God,
   who pleads the cause of the people:
"Herewith I take out of your hand
   the cup of reeling, the chalice of my wrath.
   You will never drink from it again.
²³ I will put it into the hands of your tormentors
   who have said to you,
'Prostrate yourself,
   so that we may walk over you!'
so you offered your bodies to be like the ground,
   to become a street for them to walk on."

^{52:1} Wake up! Wake up!
   Get up, Zion, and clothe yourself with strength!
Dress up in your splendid garments,
   Jerusalem, you holy city!
The uninitiated and the unclean*
   will never again enter you!
² Arise, captive Jerusalem, and shake off the dust!
   Untie the ropes around your neck, captive child of Zion!
³ For this is what YHWH says:
"You were sold for nothing
   and you will be redeemed without money."
⁴ For thus says Exalted YHWH:
"First there was Egypt,
   where my people went down to sojourn,
and later on, Assyria—
   and their lives were robbed!
⁵ And now what do I discover here, with Babylon?" asks YHWH.
"My people are carried off without cause,
   their oppressors mock them," says YHWH,
   "and daily, continuously, my Name is reviled.

---

* The "uninitiated" are those outside of the Covenant between Israel and God; the "unclean" are Israelites who break the ceremonial purity code.

6 Therefore my people will know my Name;
    therefore in that day they will know
that I am the one who foretold it.
    Yes, I am the one!"

ଊ   ଊ   ଊ

7 How welcome upon the mountains
    are the feet of one who brings good news—
who announces peace,
    and brings news of happy things,
and proclaims deliverance,
    saying to Zion, "Your God reigns!"
8 Listen! Those who keep watch raise a cry,
    together they shout for joy—
for they see with their own eyes
    YHWH's restoration of Zion!*
9 Break out together in song,
    O ruins of Jerusalem!
For YHWH comforts the people,
    and redeems Jerusalem.†
10 YHWH bares a holy arm
    in the sight of all the nations;
all the ends of the earth will behold
    the salvation of our God!

11 Depart! Depart! Leave that place!
    Touch nothing that is unclean!
Put Babylon behind you; keep yourself pure,
    you who carry of YHWH's vessels!
12 But you will not come out in a hurry
    or flee like fugitives;‡
for YHWH will go before you—
    your rearguard will be Israel's God.

---

* Or "YHWH's return to Zion."

† I.e., serves as a *go'el*, or kinsperson who takes on the obligation to free family members from servitude, ensure the continuance of the family name (and the family's title to their land), and provide for their economic support. Here God is promising to protect the people and restore them to their rightful place.

‡ As was the case during the exodus from Egypt.

¹³ "You will prosper, my Servant,
   you will be raised up and highly exalted.*
¹⁴ Even as the crowds were appalled after seeing you—
   you were so disfigured as to no longer look human—
¹⁵ so will the crowds be shocked at you,†
   and rulers will stand speechless before you;
   for they will see something never told
   and witness something never heard:
^{53:1} 'Who would have believed
   what we have just heard?
When was the arm of YHWH
   revealed in you?‡
² You grew up like a sapling before us,
   like a root in parched soil!
You had no stately form or majesty to make us look at you,
   there was no beauty to attract us.
³ You were rejected and despised by all;
   you know suffering intimately,§
   and you are acquainted with sickness.
When we saw you, we turned our faces away;
   we despised you and did not value you.
⁴ Yet you bore our illnesses
   and carried our suffering.

---

* 52:13 to 53:12 is the last of the Servant Songs in *Isaiah*. In its historical context this passage refers to the exiled nation of Israel. Biblical scholars also think that early Christian writers, seeking to understand their experience of Jesus' life and their continuing experience of Jesus after his death, found in the Servant Song passages a way to explain Jesus' life, death, and resurrection. For this reason, the evangelists' descriptions of Jesus echo the events described in this and the other Servant Songs in Isaiah. In this part of the last Servant Song, the theme is the reversal of Israel's humiliation at the hands of foreign conquerors and the elevation of Israel to its appropriate position in God's world order.

† The Hebrew word, *nazah*, is a homonym and has two unrelated meanings: to leap, startle, or shock; and to spurt (as with blood) or sprinkle (as with water, blood, or oil in ceremonial settings). While the image could be of the Servant "sprinkling" the nations to cleanse them spiritually, our translation neatly fits the parallelism of the previous verse and the context of the current verse.

‡ Literally, "And the arm of YHWH, upon whom was she revealed?"

§ This phrase has frequently been rendered as "man of sorrows" and the title applied to Jesus. However, the phrase as used in Isaiah was applied to the nation of Israel, whose suffering suggested that God had despised and rejected the people. In this and the following passages, Israel's suffering is understood as vicarious suffering, meant to restore all the world's peoples to God. What makes this sacrifice different from animal sacrifice is the lack of any magical qualities, any suggestion that the sacrifice controls the actions of God. Instead, the sacrifice is initiated by God, springing from God's love and tenderness for God's people. Israel, as the suffering Servant of God, takes on the guilt of the people of the world. The sacrifice of the Israelites is offered by God to the people of the earth as a way to overcome their guilt and to live under the reign of God. The historical context exists alongside the knowledge that the early Christian writers used Isaiah's words to describe their experience of the life, death, and resurrection of Jesus.

We thought you were being punished,
struck down by God, and brought low—
5 but it was for our offenses that you were pierced,
for our sins that you were crushed;
upon you lies a chastening that brings us wholeness,*
and through your wounds we are healed.
6 All of us, like sheep, have gone astray;
each of us goes our own way.
But YHWH has laid upon you
the guilt of us all.'
7 Though treated harshly, you bore it humbly
and never opened your mouth.
Like a lamb being led to slaughter, or a sheep before shearers,
you were silent and never opened your mouth.
8 Seized by force and condemned, you were taken away;
who would ever have foreseen your destiny?
You were taken from the land of the living
through the sin of my people, who deserved the punishment.
9 You were buried with evildoers
and entombed with the rich,
though you had done no wrong,
and deceit was not found in your mouth.
10 But YHWH chose to crush and afflict you;
if you make yourself a reparation offering†
you will see your descendants,
you will prolong your days,
and the will of YHWH will prevail through you.
11 Through your suffering,
you will see contentment and light.
By your knowledge, my Righteous One, my Servant,
you will justify many by taking their guilt upon yourself.

---

* The Hebrew word used here is *shalom*, often translated "peace," though the concept includes complete well-being—physical, emotional, and spiritual—and emphasizes the health and wholeness of one's relationships. In modern Hebrew, the common phrase for "How are you?" is *"Ma shalom cha?"* or "How is your peace? How are your relationships?"

† The phrase is ambiguous, mainly because of the word *nephesh*, which literally means "soul"; it most frequently is used figuratively to mean oneself, but it can also mean one's actual physical life. The Hebrew could therefore mean "if you give your life as a reparation (or atonement) offering," or it could mean "if you yourself make a reparation offering" as prescribed in the Torah, the way lepers and others who had been ill for a long time would offer a reparation offering in order to be declared ritually pure and thus again participate in the full worship of the Temple. Here the Servant is depicted as being fully restored after an illness; seeing one's children and grandchildren and living a long life are signs of God's restoration, as in the case of Job.

¹² Therefore, I will grant you a reward among the great,
and you will divide the spoils with the mighty;
for you exposed yourself to death itself,
and allowed yourself to be counted among criminals,
while you bore the guilt of many
and interceded for sinners."

⁵⁴:¹ "Shout for joy,
O childless woman!
Break out in jubilant song,
you who have not given birth!
For more numerous are the children of one who is single
than the children of the married woman," says YHWH.
² "Enlarge your tent,
stretch out your hangings,
lengthen your ropes
and strengthen your stakes!
³ For you will spread abroad,
to the right and to the left;
your descendants will take possession of the nations
and resettle the abandoned cities!
⁴ Fear not! You will not be put to shame.
Do not cower! You will not be disgraced.
You will forget the shame of your youth
and the disgrace of the past will be forgotten.
⁵ For now your Creator will be your spouse,
whose name is YHWH Omnipotent.
Your Redeemer is the Holy One of Israel,
who is called 'the God of all the earth.'
⁶ For YHWH calls you back—
like a grieving spouse abandoned by a mate,
a couple who married too young,
who part impetuously and then regret it,"
says your God.
⁷ "I did abandon you for a brief moment,
but with much tenderness I will take you back.
⁸ In an outburst of anger, I hid my face momentarily;
but with everlasting love I will gather you,"
says YHWH, your Redeemer.
⁹ "I am now as I was in the days of Noah
when I swore that Noah's waters
should never flood the earth again.

So now I swear not to be angry with you,
    or to make threats against you.
10 For the mountains may disappear
    and the hills may depart,
but my love will never leave you
    nor my covenant of peace be shaken,"
    says YHWH, who has mercy on you.
11 "O afflicted one, storm-battered and without consolation,
    I will lay your pavements in turquoise,
    and your foundations in sapphires.
12 I will make your battlements of rubies,
    your gates of crystal,
    and all your walls of precious stones.
13 Your children will all be taught by YHWH;
    the prosperity of your children will be great.
14 In justice you will be established,
    far from the fear of oppression,
    where destruction cannot come near you.
15 If anyone attacks you, it will not be my doing;
    whoever attacks you will fall before you.
16 You see, it is I who created the blacksmith
    who fans the coals in the fire,
    and forges a weapon fit for its purpose.
And it is I who created the destroyer
    to wreak havoc.
17 The weapon has not been forged
    that will prevail against you;
    and you will refute every tongue accusing you.
This is the heritage of the Servants of YHWH,
    and their vindication from me,"
    says YHWH.
55:1 "All you who are thirsty,
    come to the water!
You who have no money,
    come, buy food and eat!
Come, buy wine and milk.
    without money, without price!
2 Why spend your money for what is not bread,
    your wages for what fails to satisfy?
Heed me, and you will eat well,
    you will delight in rich fare;

³ bend your ear and come to me,
   listen, that you may have life:
   I will make an everlasting Covenant with you—
      in fulfillment of the blessings promised to David.
⁴ See, I have made of you to be a witness to the peoples,
   a leader and commander of the nations.
⁵ See, you will summon nations you never knew,
   and nations that never knew you will come hurrying to you—
   for the sake of YHWH, the Holy One of Israel,
      who will glorify you.
⁶ Seek me, YHWH, while I may still be found,
   call upon me while I am near!
⁷ Let the corrupt abandon their ways,
   the evil their thoughts.
   Let them return to YHWH, and I will have mercy on them;
   return to God, for I will freely pardon.
⁸ For my thoughts are not your thoughts,
   nor are your ways, my ways," says YHWH.
⁹ As high as the heavens are above the earth,
   so high are my ways above your ways
   and my thoughts above your thoughts.
¹⁰ For just as from the heavens
   the rain and snow come down
and do not return there
   till they have watered the earth,
making it fertile and fruitful,
   giving seed to the sower and bread for food,
¹¹ so will my word be
   that goes forth from my mouth:
it will not return to me empty,
   but will carry out my will,
   achieving the end for which I sent it.
¹² And you will go out joyfully,
   and be led out in peace;
the mountains and hills before you
   will break into cries of joy,
and all the trees in the countryside
   will clap their hands.
¹³ The cypress will grow in place of the thorn bush,
   the myrtle will replace the briers;
and they will stand as a memorial to YHWH,
   an everlasting sign never to be destroyed."

***t*hus** says YHWH:
"Do what is right!
  Work for justice!
For my liberation is about to come,
  and my justice is about to be revealed."
2 Happy is the person who does this,
  and happy is the person who holds to it—
who observes the Sabbath and does not profane it,
  and keeps one's hands from evil deeds.
3 Foreigners who would follow YHWH should not say,
  "YHWH will surely exclude me from this people."
Nor should the eunuch say,
  "And I am a dried-up tree."
4 For thus says YHWH:
"To the eunuchs who keep my Sabbath,
  who choose that which pleases me
  and hold fast to my Covenant—
5 to them I will create within my Temple and its walls a memorial,
  and a name better than that of daughters and sons.
I will give them an everlasting name
  that will not be excised.
6 And the foreigners who join themselves to me,
    ministering to me,
  loving the name of YHWH and worshiping me—
    all who observe the Sabbath and do not profane it,
    and cling to my Covenant—
7 these I will bring to my holy mountain
    and make them joyful in my house of prayer.
Their burnt offerings and their sacrifices
    will be acceptable on my altar,
for my house will be called a house of prayer
    for all peoples!"*

---

* Eunuchs and foreigners are symbolic of outsiders and outcasts. The gay and lesbian community
has taken the promises in these verses to be emblematic of the idea that they, too, are welcome in
the "kindom" of God.

8   Thus says the Sovereign YHWH,
         who gathers the diaspora of Israel:
     "There are others I will gather
         besides those already gathered:
9   all you wild animals of the plains and the forests,
         come and eat your fill!
10   Our sentinels are blind,*
         they are beyond knowing;
     they are watchdogs who don't bark,
         silent, slumbering, at ease.
11   But these dogs have a good appetite,
         they never get enough.
     They are like foolish shepherds,
         all going their own ways,
         all intent on their own needs.
12   'Come,' they say, 'it's time for our wine!
     And 'Let's drink our fill of the hard stuff!
     And tomorrow will be like today,
         and maybe even better!' "

57:1 "People of integrity perish, and no one cares;
         devout women and men are taken away.
      But what they don't realize is that
         the people of integrity are taken away to be spared from evil!
2   And they find peace—
         they will rest on their deathbed,
         all who walked uprightly.
3   But as for you—
         come closer, you heirs of necromancers,
         you children of perverts and reprobates!
4   Who is it that you mock?
         Against whom do you sneer and stick out your tongue?
      Aren't you the spawn of sin,
         the offspring of lies?
5   You burn with lust under the oak trees,†
         under the trees of the forest—

---

* These are Israel's spiritual leaders—prophets and priests who have strayed from the covenant.
† The prophet is referring to pagan fertility rites. Other practices borrowed from Babylon's religious life are reflected in the following verses.

sacrificing your children in the rivers,
        under overhanging cliffs.
6   The smooth stones in the rivers—your idols—
        are your inheritance, your lot;
     you pour out drink offerings to them,
        and then give them grain offerings.
     Should I be appeased in light of this?
7   You made your bed on a lofty, a high hill
        and there you went up to sacrifice.
8   You hung your pagan symbols on your doorpost
        and, forsaking me, you turned down the sheets,
        inviting new lovers into your bed;
     you made your covenant with them,
        for you loved their bed,
        you loved to gaze upon their nakedness.*
9   Off you journeyed to Molech with oil,
        with your many ointments and perfumes; †
     you sent envoys to far away places,
        even down to Sheol itself!
10   All this travel wearied you,
        but you didn't say, "This is hopeless!"
     You rekindled your desires
        at the expense of your anxieties.
11   Who is it you fear so much
        that you lead a life of falsehood?
     Did you ever remember me
        or give me any thought?
     Didn't I look away, keep my silence,
        so you would feel no fear of me?
12   I will expose your 'justice' and your works—
        deeds that did not benefit you!
13   When you cry out for help,
        let your pantheon of idols redeem you!
     The wind will blow them away,
        a breath will sweep them off.
     But whoever takes refuge in me will possess the land,
        and inherit my holy mountain.

---

* Sexual profligacy is here used as a symbol for the worship of other gods, as is the travel metaphor
  in the next verses.
† Molech was the Cannanite god of the underworld, to whom first-born male children were sacrificed;
  it is also a play on words, since the Hebrew *melech* means "ruler," and oil was used to anoint a new
  ruler for service, as was ointment or perfume.

¹⁴ It is destined to be said,
        'Rebuild! Rebuild! Open up the road!
    Remove the wreckage
        blocking the way of my people!'
¹⁵ For thus says the High and Exalted One,
        whose home is eternal, whose Name is holy:
    I dwell in a high and holy place
        with those who are humbled and broken in spirit,
    so I can revive the spirit of you who are dejected,
        revive the heart of you who are contrite.
¹⁶ I will not accuse you forever,
        nor will I always be angry—
    for then your spirit would grow faint before me,
        your breath which I created.
¹⁷ I was enraged by your sinful greed.
        I punished you and withdrew my favor,
        but you maintained your willful ways.
¹⁸ I know your ways—and I will heal you.
        I will lead you and comfort you,
    you and those among you who mourn,
¹⁹   bringing praise to your lips.
    I will bring peace, peace,
        to those far and near," says YHWH,
        "and I will heal them.
²⁰ But those who do evil are like the churning sea
        that cannot quiet itself;
        its waters toss up silt and sand.
²¹   There is no peace," says YHWH,
        for the corrupt."

⁵⁸:¹ "Shout for all you are worth,
        raise your voice like a trumpet!
    Proclaim to the people their faults,
        tell the house of Leah and Rachel and Jacob their sins!
²   They seek me daily,
        they long to know my ways,
    like a nation that wants to act with integrity
        and not ignore the Law of its God.
    They ask me for laws that are just,
        they long for God to draw near.
³   Yet they say, 'Why should we fast
        if you never see it?

Why do penance
   if you never notice?'
Because when you fast, it's business as usual,
   and you oppress all your workers!
4 Because when you fast, you quarrel and fight
   and strike the poor with your fist!
Fasting like yours today
   will never make your voice heard on high!
5 Is that the sort of fast that pleases me—
   a day when people humiliate themselves,
hanging their heads like a reed,
   lying down on sackcloth and ashes?
Is that what you call fasting,
   a day acceptable to YHWH?
6 On the contrary!
   This is the sort of fast that pleases me:
Remove the chains of injustice!
   Undo the ropes of the yoke!*
Let those who are oppressed go free,
   and break every yoke you encounter!
7 Share your bread with those who are hungry,
   and shelter homeless poor people!
Clothe those who are naked,
   and don't hide from the needs of your own flesh and blood!
8 Do this, and your light will shine like the dawn—
   and your healing will break forth like lightning!
Your integrity will go before you,
   and the glory of YHWH will be your rearguard.
9 Cry, and YHWH will answer;
   call, and God will say, 'I am here'—
provided you remove from your midst
   all oppression, finger-pointing, and malicious talk!
10 If you give yourself to the hungry
   and satisfy the needs of the afflicted,
then your light will rise in the darkness,
   and your shadows will become like noon.
11 YHWH will always guide you,
   giving relief in desert places.

---

* A yoke, the heavy wooden crossbars that encircle the necks of a pair of oxen or other draft animals
working together, is a symbol of subjugation and bondage; here it implies the burden that the working
poor face—never making enough money to be able to change their situation for the better.

God will give strength to your bones
and you will be like a watered garden,
like a spring of water
whose waters never run dry.
¹² You will rebuild the ancient ruins,
and build upon age-old foundations.
You will be called Repairer of Broken Walls,
and Restorer of Ruined Neighborhoods.*
¹³ If you refrain from trampling the Sabbath
and doing business on the holy day,
if you call the Sabbath delightful
and the day sacred to YHWH honorable,
if you honor it by not pursuing your own ways,
seeking your own pleasure,
or speaking your own words,
¹⁴ then will you find your happiness in YHWH,
and I will lead you triumphant
over the heights of the land.
I will feed you on the heritage
of Leah and Rachel and Jacob, your ancestors!"
The mouth of YHWH has spoken.

ଔ ଔ ଔ

59:1 Surely YHWH's arm is not too short to save us,
nor God's ear too dull to hear us!
² But it is your iniquities
that have separated you from your God—
your sins have hidden the Holy One's face from you
so God could not hear from you.
³ Your hands are stained with blood
and your fingers with crime.
Your lips speak lies,
your tongue utters treachery.
⁴ You have no desire for truth in your courts,
and none of you testifies truthfully.
You rely on empty pleas and lies,
you conceive oppression and give birth to sin.

---

* Many cities in the ancient world were walled and gated for protection of the inhabitants from outside threats; a breach in the wall was a threat to everyone's security. To be called a repairer of broken walls and a restorer of ruined neighborhoods (or "ruined streets in which to dwell") is to be dedicated to reclaiming a community's safety and dignity from those who would steal and destroy it.

5   You hatch adder's eggs
      and weave spider's webs.
    Those who eat their eggs will die
      because what is hatched is a viper.
6   Your spider webs are useless as clothing—
      no one can use them to cover themselves.
    Your works are deeds of iniquity,
      you commit acts of violence.
7   Your feet rush into crime,
      and quickly they shed innocent blood.
    You have nothing but harmful ideas,
      leaving a trail of havoc and ruin.
8   You don't know the way of peace;
      your paths are not paths to justice.
    Your roads are crooked roads,
      and those who walk them never know peace.
9   This is why justice avoids us
      and deliverance never reaches us!
    We look for the light but see only darkness;
      we wait for brightness but walk in deep shadows.
10 We grope like the blind along a wall,
      feeling our way like blind people;
    we stumble at noon as if it were midnight,
      we stumble among the healthy as if we were dead.
11 We all growl like bears,
      we mourn like turtle doves.
    We search for justice to no avail;
      for deliverance, but it is too far away.
12 Our transgressions against God are too many,
      our sins witness it.
    We feel our transgressions daily,
      they never leave us:
13 rebelling and denying YHWH,
      and refusing to follow our God,
    fomenting oppression and revolt,
      uttering lies we have conceived in our hearts.
14 Justice is shuffled aside,
      and integrity stands a long way off;
    truth stumbles in the streets,
      and honesty is consigned to the alleys.
15 Truth is nowhere to be found,
      and those who shun evil are mugged in the street.

YHWH looks on with displeasure,
    for there is no justice.
16 The Holy One saw that aid was not forthcoming,
    and was appalled that no one intervened;
so God's own might brought about victory
    supported by the divine hunger for justice.
17 Wearing the breastplate of integrity
    and the helmet of liberation,
YHWH wears the clothing of vengeance
    and is wrapped in zeal like a cloak.
18 They will pay according to their deeds:
    wrath in payment to adversaries,
    retribution in payment to foes.
The coastlands will get their due;
19   those in the west will fear the name of YHWH
    and those in the east, God's glory;
for God will come
    like a flood-swollen river
    driven forward by the Spirit of YHWH.*
20 "The Redeemer will come to Zion,
    to those of Leah, Rachel, and Jacob
who repent of their rebellion,"
    says YHWH.

21 "This, for my part, is the covenant I make with them: my Spirit will be upon you, and my words, which I have put in your mouth, will not depart from your mouth or the mouths of your children or the mouths of your children's children," says YHWH, "now and for all time."

60:1 "Arise, shine, for your light has come!
    the glory of YHWH is rising upon you!
2 Though darkness still covers the earth
    and dense clouds enshroud the nations,
upon you YHWH now dawns,
    and God's glory will be seen among you!
3 The nations will come to your light
    and the leaders to your bright dawn!
4 Lift up your eyes, and look around:
    they're all gathering and coming to you—

---

* In Hebrew, the noun *ruach* is translated variously as "spirit," "breath," or "wind," so here the river could be driven forward by a powerful wind from God. But since the Redeemer or *go'el* in the next verse is the manifestation of this "flood-swollen river," it is likely that it is God's feminine presence, the Spirit, that is driving the Redeemer to rise up.

your daughters and your sons
  journey from afar, escorted in safety;
5 you'll see them and beam with joy,
  your heart will swell with pride.
The riches of the sea will flow to you,
  and the wealth of the nations will come to you—
6 camel caravans will cover your roads,
  the dromedaries of Midian and Ephah;
everyone in Sheba will come,
  bringing gold and incense
  and singing the praise of YHWH.
7 All the flocks of Kedar will be gathered to you,
  the rams of Nebaioth will serve you:*
they will be acceptable offerings on my altar
  to glorify the splendor of my Temple.
8 Who are these who float aloft like clouds,
  like doves to their roosts?
9 They are vessels assembling along the coasts,
  with ships from Tarshish leading the way,
to bring your children from far away,
  carrying their silver and gold,
to the honor of YHWH your God,
  the Holy One of Israel,
  who graced you with splendor.
10 Foreigners will rebuild your walls,
  and their rulers will serve you;
though in my anger I struck you down,
  I will restore you in my favor, and have compassion on you.
11 Your gates will be open night and day—
  they will never be shut—
inviting the wealth of the nations
  with their rulers being led in procession.†
12 All nations and realms not serving you will perish;
  they will be utterly destroyed.
13 The glory of Lebanon will come to you,
  with cypress, pine, and fir
to adorn my holy sanctuary,
  to honor the place where I stand.

---

* Kedar and Nebaioth were nomadic Bedouin tribes.
† This phrase may include the image of the foreign rulers being brought in as prisoners, as tribute to
  the victorious YHWH.

¹⁴ The descendants of your oppressors
   will approach you, bending low;
all who despised you
   will bow down at your feet.
They will call you "City of YHWH,
   Zion of the Holy One of Israel."
¹⁵ Once you were hated and neglected,
   with no visitors passing through;
but I will make you acclaimed forever
   and a source of everlasting joy.
¹⁶ You will suckle the milk of nations,
   and be nursed at the breasts of foreign rulers.
Then you will learn that I, YHWH, am your Deliverer.
   Your Redeemer is the Mighty One of Leah, Rachel, and Jacob.
¹⁷ Rather than bronze, I will bring you gold.
   Rather than iron, I will bring you silver;
bronze in exchange for wood
   and iron in exchange for stone.
I will appoint peace to govern you
   and integrity to counsel you.
¹⁸ Never again will the sounds of violence
   be heard in your land;
never again will there be devastation and destruction
   within your frontiers;
and you will name your walls Liberation
   and your gates Praise.
¹⁹ Never again will the sun light your day
   never again will the brightness of the moon light your night.
For YHWH will be your everlasting light;
   your God will be your glory.
²⁰ Never again will your sun set,
   never again will the moon withdraw;
YHWH will be your everlasting light,
   and your days of mourning will end.
²¹ All your people will love justice;
   they will possess the land forever.
They are the shoots I planted,
   the work of my hands for my glory.
²² The least of them will become a clan
   and the smallest a mighty nation;
At its appointed time, I, YHWH,
   will bring all this to pass."

61:1 "The Spirit of Exalted YHWH is upon me,
for YHWH has anointed me:
God has sent me to bring good news to those who are poor;
to heal broken hearts;
to proclaim release to those held captive
and liberation to those in prison;
2 to announce a year of favor from YHWH,
and the day of God's vindication;
to comfort all who mourn,
3 to provide for those who grieve in Zion—
to give them a wreath of flowers instead of ashes,
the oil of gladness instead of tears,
a cloak of praise instead of despair./
They will be known as trees of integrity,
planted by YHWH to display God's glory.
4 They will restore the ancient ruins,
and rebuild sites long devastated;
they will repair the ruined cities,
neglected for generations.
5 Strangers will tend your flocks;
foreigners will till your fields and dress your vineyards;
6 but you will be called priests of YHWH
and ministers of our God;
you will enjoy the richness of nations,
and inherit their wealth.
7 'Because your shame was double—
insults and abuses were your lot—
now you will receive a double share in your land,
and everlasting joy will be yours.
8 For I, YHWH, love justice;
I hate robbery and sin.
So I will faithfully compensate you,
and I will make an everlasting covenant with you.
9 Your descendants will be renowned among the nations;
and your offspring among the people;
all who see you will acknowledge
that you are a people blessed by YHWH.'
10 I will joyfully exult in YHWH,
who is the joy of my soul!

My God clothed me with a robe of deliverance
and wrapped me in a mantle of justice,
the way a bridegroom puts on a turban
and a bride bedecks herself with jewels.
¹¹ For as the earth brings forth its shoots,
and a garden brings its seeds to blossom,
so Exalted YHWH makes justice sprout,
and praise spring up before all nations.
⁶²:¹ For Zion's sake, I will not be silent;
for the sake of Jerusalem, I will not rest—
not until her integrity shines like the dawn,
her deliverance like a flaming torch.
² The nations will see your vindication,
and the rulers your splendor;
you will have a new name
that YHWH's mouth will bestow.
³ You will be a garland of beauty in YHWH's hands,
a solemn crown worn by your God.
⁴ Never again will you be called Forsaken.
Never again will your land be called Desolate.
But you will be called My Delight Is in Her,
and your land will be called Married.
For YHWH will take delight in you
and your land will be joined with God in wedlock.
⁵ For just as a young couple marry,
you will be forever married to this land;
as a newly married couple rejoice over each other,
so will YHWH rejoice over you.
⁶ I have posted sentinels upon your walls, Jerusalem;
all day, all night, they will endlessly cry,
'You who call on God's name, do not rest,
⁷ and do not let God rest
until the Almighty establishes Jerusalem
and makes it renowned throughout the world!'
⁸ YHWH swore this
with a raised hand and a mighty arm:
'Never again will I give your grain
to feed your enemies;
never again will foreigners drink your wine
for which you toiled;
⁹ but its harvesters
will eat it and praise YHWH;

and those who gather the grapes
    will drink the wine in the courts of my sanctuary.'
10 Pass through, pass through the gates!
    Prepare the way for the people!
Repair! Repair the roads!
    Remove the boulders! Raise a banner for the nation!
11 This is YHWH's proclamation to the ends of the earth—
    Say this to Zion, your beloved:
'Look, your Deliverer comes
    with a sure reward and abundant recompense
12 called the Holy People,
    and the Redeemed of YHWH.
You yourself will be named Sought After,
    and A City Not Forsaken.' "

               CR CR CR

63:1 Who is this coming from Edom,
    from Bozrah in crimson stained garments?
Who is this so splendidly attired,
    striding along in magnificent strength?
"It is I, proclaiming justice,
    empowement, and liberation!"
2 Why are your robes red,
    like the clothes of one treading grapes in the wine press?"
3 "I have trodden the wine press alone,
    for none of my people was with me.
I trod them in my anger
    and trampled them in my fury;
their blood splashed on my garments
    and stained my clothes.
4 For the day of my vengeance was in my heart,
    and the year when I redeem had come.
5 I looked, but there was no one to help me;
    I watched, but no one would support me.
So my own right arm brought deliverance,
    my rage alone sustained me.
6 I trampled my people in my wrath,
    I crushed them in my anger;
    and I drained their blood onto the ground."

⁷ I will tell you of YHWH's unfailing love,
　　and sing the praises of YHWH
for all that YHWH did for us—
　　the many good things done for the house of Israel,
　　which God did with motherly compassion*
　　and many kindnesses.
⁸ For YHWH said, "Truly these are my people,
　　children who will not be false to me"—
and so God became their Liberator.
⁹ In all their distress, O God, you were distressed,
　　and the angel of your Presence saved them;
you redeemed them out of deep love
　　and profound mercy;
you lifted them up and carried them
　　from time immemorial.
¹⁰ But they rebelled
　　and it grieved your holy Spirit.
Then you became their foe;
　　you alone fought against them.
¹¹ Then they recalled the days of old,
　　the days of Moses and the people of Israel:
"Where is the One who brought us up out of the sea
　　with the shepherds of our flock?
Where is the One
　　who put the holy Spirit among us,
¹² whose glorious arm led them at Moses' right hand,
　　who divided the waters before us
　　and gained everlasting renown,
¹³ who led us without stumbling through the depths
　　like a sure-footed horse in open country?
¹⁴ Like cattle descending into the valley,
　　the Spirit of YHWH gave us a place to rest."
Thus you led your people
　　and made for yourself a glorious name.
¹⁵ Now look down from heaven,
　　and see us from your holy and glorious dwelling place!
Where is your zeal, your strength,
　　your burning love and motherly compassion?

---

* The Hebrew word *racham*, usually rendered simply "compassion," is derived from the word for womb; *racham* is essentially "womb-love."

Why do you hold them back from us?

16 For you are our mother and father!
Abraham may not know us
and Israel may not acknowledge us,
but you, YHWH, are our mother and father;
"Our Redeemer Forever" is your name.

17 YHWH, why do you let us wander from your ways
and let our hearts grow too hard to revere you?
Return to us for the sake of your children,
the tribes of your heritage!

18 Your holy people possessed your sanctuary for a little while;
but now our enemies have trampled down your holy place.

19 Too long we have been
like those people whom you do not rule,
like those not called by your Name.

64:1 Oh, that you would rend the heavens and come down,
that the mountains would shake before you!

2 As fire kindles the brushwood
and the fire makes water boil,
make your Name known to your adversaries,
and let the nations tremble before you!

3 When you did awesome things
that we could not have expected,
you came down,
and the mountains quaked in your presence!

4 From ages past no ear has ever heard,
no eye has ever seen any God but you
intervening for those who wait for you!

5 Oh, that you would find us doing right,
that we would be mindful of you in our ways!
You are angry because we are sinful;
we sinned for so long—how can we be saved?

6 All of us became unclean and soiled,
even our good deeds are polluted.
We have all withered like leaves,
and our guilt carries us away like the wind.

7 No one calls upon your Name,
there is none who clings to you,
for you hid your face from us
and delivered us into the hands of our sins

⁸ Yet you are our mother and father, YHWH;
   we are the clay and you are the potter,
   we are all the work of your hands.
⁹ Don't let your anger go beyond measure, O God,
   don't remember our sins forever,
   for we are all your people.
¹⁰ Your holy cities have become a desert;
   even Zion is deserted, and Jerusalem is desolate.
¹¹ Our holy and glorious Temple
      in which our ancestors praised you
   has been burned to the ground,
      and all that we cherished is now ruins.
¹² After all this, O God,
      can you go unmoved,
   oppressing us beyond measure
      with your silence?
⁶⁵:¹ "I was ready to respond,
      but no one asked;
   ready to be discovered,
      but no one hunted for me.
   I said, 'Here I am, here I am!'
      to a nation that did not call on my Name.
² I held out my hand for a whole day
      to a rebellious people,
   who went the way of all flesh
      by following their own whims;
³ a people who continually provoke me to my face,
      offering sacrifices in gardens,
      burning incense on brick altars;
⁴ who lounge in tombs
      and keep nightlong vigils in secret,
   who eat the flesh of swine
      with a broth made of unclean meat.
⁵ 'Don't come any closer,' they tell people,
      'for I am too holy for you.'
   People like this are a smoldering fire,
      smoke in my nostrils daily!
⁶ Look, I have your inscribed record before me;
      I will not be silent.
   And I will pay them back
      once I settle my accounts with them,

7   for their sins and the sins of their ancestors,"
        says YHWH,
    "for offering sacrifices on the mountains
        and defiling me on the hills.
    I will measure into their laps
        full payment for their former iniquities."
8   Thus says YHWH:
    "Just as there is juice in a cluster of grapes,
        and the gardener says, 'Don't destroy it,
        there is a blessing in it,'
    so will I act for the sake of you who serve me;
        I will not destroy the whole nation.
9   I will give descendants to Leah and Rachel and Jacob
        and to Judah heirs who will dwell on my mountains;
    my chosen ones will occupy the land,
        and those who serve me will dwell there.
10 Flocks will range in Sharon,
        cattle will pasture in the Valley of Achor,
        for my people who sought me out.
11 But you who abandon YHWH,
        who forget my holy mountain,
    who spread a table for the god of Fortune
        and fill cups of wine for Destiny,
12 I will destine you to the sword
        and all of you will fall slaughtered;
    for when I called, you did not answer,
        when I spoke, you did not listen;
    you did what was evil to me,
        and chose to displease me."
13 Therefore, these are the words of the Sovereign YHWH:
    "You will witness my servants eating
        while you will go hungry;
    you will witness my servants drinking
        while you will go thirsty;
    you will witness my servants rejoicing
        while you will be shamed;
14 you will witness my servants singing with a glad heart,
        while you will cry out with an aching heart
        and wail from anguish of spirit.
15 Your name will be used by my chosen ones as a curse,
        and Sovereign YHWH will put you to death;
        but my servants will receive a new name.

¹⁶ Then those invoking a blessing in the land
     will bless by the power of God's faithfulness;
 and those invoking an oath in the land
     will swear by the power of God's faithfulness.
 The former troubles are to be forgotten,
     and they will be hidden from my eyes.
¹⁷ For I am about to create
     new heavens and a new earth!
 The things of the past
     will not be remembered or come to mind!
¹⁸ Be glad and rejoice forever and ever in what I create,
     because I now create Jerusalem to be a joy
     and its people to be a delight!
¹⁹ I will rejoice in Jerusalem,
     and delight in my people;
 no more shall the sound of weeping be heard in it
     or the cry of distress.
²⁰ No longer will there be in it an infant who lives but a few days,
     or old people who do not live out their days.
 They die as mere youths who reach but a hundred years,
     and those who fall short of a hundred will be thought accursed.
²¹ At last they will live in the houses they build,
     and eat the fruit of the vineyard they plant.
²² They will not build for another to inhabit;
     they will not plant for another to eat.
 For the days of my people will be like the days of a tree,
     and my chosen ones will enjoy the fruit of their labors.
²³ They will not labor in vain
     or bear children doomed to die;
 for they and their descendants
     are a people blessed by God.
²⁴ Even before they call upon me, I will answer;
     and while they speak, I will hear.
²⁵ The wolf and the lamb will feed side by side;
     the lion will eat straw like an ox.
 Serpents will be content to crawl on the ground;
     they will not injure or destroy in all my holy mountain,"
 says YHWH.

^{66:1} Thus says YHWH:
     "The heavens are my judgment seat,
     the earth is my footstool.

Where is the house you will build for me?
Where will my resting place be?
2 Wasn't all of this made by my hand?
Doesn't all of this belong to me?"
says YHWH.
"The one I esteem
is humble and contrite in spirit;
and reveres my word.
3 Slaughtering an ox is like murdering a person;
sacrificing a lamb is like breaking a dog's neck;
presenting a grain offering is like offering swine's blood;
burning incense is like worshipping an idol.
Since people have adopted these practices,
and delight in these abominations,
4 I will choose to mock them
and bring upon them what they dread;
for when I called, no one responded,
when I spoke, no one listened.
They did what was evil in my sight
and chose what displeased me.
5 Hear the Word of YHWH
you who revere God's word!
Your own people, who are hostile to you
and reject you for my Name's sake,
mock you and say, "Let YHWH be manifest in glory!
Let us see your joy!"
But they will be put to shame.
6 That roaring noise from the city,
the thunder you hear in the Temple,
is the voice of God punishing the evildoers
for their blasphemy.
7 Without labor pains Zion gives birth,
and bears an heir before any contractions begin!*
8 Has anyone ever heard of such a thing?
Has anyone ever witnessed such a thing?
Can a nation be born in one day,
a country brought to birth in a moment?
Yet Zion, as soon as she was in labor
has delivered heirs!

---

* An effortless childbirth is used as a symbol for the joyful re-creation of the people of God.

⁹ Shall I open the womb and not deliver?" says YHWH.
"Shall I, the deliverer, close the womb?" says YHWH.
¹⁰ "Rejoice with Jerusalem and be glad because of her,
all you who love her;
Exult, exult with her,
all you who were mourning over her!
¹¹ Oh, that you may suckle fully
of the milk of her comfort,
that you may nurse with delight
at her abundant breasts!"
¹² For thus says YHWH:
"I will spread peace over her like a river,
and the wealth of the nations like an overflowing torrent.
As nurslings, you will be carried in her arms,
and fondled in her lap;
as a mother comforts her child
¹³ so will I comfort you;
in Jerusalem you will find your comfort."
¹⁴ When you see this, your heart will rejoice,
and your bodies will flourish like the grass.
God's faithful ones
will see the power of YHWH,
but God's enemies
will know heaven's wrath.
¹⁵ For YHWH will come with fire,
in chariots like a whirlwind,
in a furious avenging anger,
chastising with a flaming fire.
¹⁶ For with fire and the sword
YHWH will bring judgment upon all humankind;
and many will be slain by YHWH.
¹⁷ Those who purify and sanctify themselves for garden rituals
and follow the rites of Achad,*
eating the flesh of swine, rats, and vermin,
they will come to an end together,"
say YHWH.

¹⁸ "For I know their works and their thoughts. I am coming to gather the nations of every language. They will come to witness my glory. ¹⁹ I will give

---

* *Achad*, or "The Only One," refers to the Syrian/Babylonian god Adad (whose name also means "One"), the triune Mesopotamian storm god identified with the Canaanite Hadad, the Egyptian Rimmon, and the Phoenician Ba'al/Bel. Other translators render this phrase "following one in the center."

them a sign and send some of their survivors to the nations: to Tarshish, Put, and Lud—famous as archers—Tubal, and Javan,* to the distant coastlands that have never heard of me or seen my glory. And they will declare my glory among the nations. ²⁰ As an offering to YHWH, they will bring all of your sisters and brothers on horses and in chariots, in carts, upon mules and camels, from all the nations to my holy mountain in Jerusalem," says YHWH, "like Israelites bringing oblations in clean vessels to the Temple of YHWH. ²¹ And some of them I will make priests and Levites,"says YHWH.

²² "For as the new heavens and the new earth,
    which I am making, will endure before me,"
declares YHWH,
    "so will your progeny and your name endure.
Month after month, at the new moon,
    week after week on the Sabbath,
all humankind will bow down before me,"
    says YHWH.
²⁴ "And they will step outside
    to view the corpses of those who rebelled against me,
where the devouring worm never dies
    and the fire is never quenched.†
All peoples will look upon them with horror."

---

* Ancient peoples representing modern Spain, Libya, Lydia in Asia Minor, northern Europe, and Greece.
† A reference to the Hinnom Valley ("Gehenna") outside Jerusalem, which was used as the town dump; a fire was kept burning perpetually to consume the refuse. The location is also the notorious site where children were sacrificed to Molech, "the detestable god of the Ammonites" spoken of in 57:9.

jeremiah

1:1–29:38

the words* of jeremiah ben-hilkiah,
a member of the priestly family in Anathoth in the land of Benjamin. ² The
word of YHWH came to Jeremiah during the thirteenth year of the reign
of Josiah ben-Amon, the ruler of Judah, ³ continued through the reign of
Jehoiakim, and ended during the the eleventh year of the reign of Josiah's
son Zedekiah when, in the fifth month, the inhabitants of Jerusalem went
into exile.

⁴ Now the word of YHWH came to me and said:
⁵ "Before I formed you in the womb, I chose you.
Before you were born, I dedicated you.
I appointed you as a prophet to the nations."
⁶ I said, "But Sovereign YHWH!
I don't know how to speak! I'm too young!"

---

* The Hebrew *dibrê* also means "actions" and "events."

7 But YHWH said,
"Do not say, 'I am too young.'
Now, go wherever I send you.
And say whatever I command you.
8 Do not fear anyone,
for I am with you to protect you.
It is YHWH who speaks."
9 Then YHWH touched my mouth and said to me,
10 "Look, I am putting my words in your mouth.
This day I appoint you
over nations and territories,
to uproot and to tear down,
to destroy and to overthrow,
to build and to plant."

11 The word of YHWH came to me saying, "Jeremiah, what do you see?"
"I see a branch of an almond tree," I replied.

12 Then YHWH said to me, "That is so. It means that I am watching* to see
that my word is fulfilled."

13 The word of YHWH came to me a second time: "What do you see?"
And I said, "I see a boiling cauldron whose face is from the north."

14 Then YHWH replied:
"Disaster is coming from the north
against all who dwell in the land.
15 For now I am summoning all the clans
from the northern realm, says YHWH.
Each clan will set up a judgment seat
before the gates of Jerusalem;†
they will surround its walls
and lay siege to every city in Judah.
16 I will argue my case against my people for all their wrongdoing:
for abandoning me,
for burning incense to other gods,
for worshiping idols they themselves crafted.
17 So now, Jeremiah, brace yourself for action.
Stand up and tell them all I command you.

---

* This is a play on words in Hebrew that does not translate into English: the word for almond tree is *shaqed*, which is a homonym of the word for "watching."

† Commentators are divided over whether the passage refers to the invaders' setting up their thrones—that is, their rulers' command posts—as part of the siege against the city, or to the establishment of their rulers after victory in preparation for passing judgment on their defeated enemies in the city. The question, then, is whether these judgment seats are before the gates outside the wall, or inside.

Do not break down in their presence,
    lest in their presence I break you down.
18 Look—today I make you a fortified city,
    a pillar of iron and a wall of bronze,
    so you may confront this whole land:
    the royalty of Judah and the officials,
    its priests and its people.
19 They will assault you
    but will never conquer you,
    for I am with you to deliver you—
    it is YHWH who speaks."

2:1 The word of YHWH came to me, and said,
2 "Go! Proclaim this in the hearing of Jerusalem!
    Thus says YHWH:
    I remember the devotion of your youth,
    how you loved me as a spouse,
    how you accompanied me in the desert,
    through an unsown land.
3 Israel was consecrated to YHWH,
    the firstfruits of God's harvest.
    All who devoured it were punished,
    and disaster overtook them.
    Thus says YHWH.
4 Hear the word of YHWH, House of Jacob,
    all you tribes of the house of Israel!
5 Thus says YHWH:
    What fault did your ancestors find in me,
    to make them wander so far astray?
    They pursued hollow idols
    and became hollow themselves.
6 They did not ask, 'Where is YHWH,
    who brought us up out from Egypt
    and led us through the desert,
    a barren and desolate country,
    a land of drought and darkness,
    a land no one passes through,
    a land where no one dwells?'
7 I brought you into a land of plenty
    to eat its fruits and other good things.
    But once you entered my land you defiled it
    and made my heritage an abomination.

⁸ The priests never asked themselves, 'Where is YHWH?'
The administrators of the law ignored me.
The shepherds of the people rebelled against me.
The prophets prophesied in the name of Ba'al
and pursued the Worthless One.*

⁹ So once more I accuse you, says YHWH—
I accuse you and your children's children!

¹⁰ Cross over to the coasts of Cyprus and look closely,
send envoys to Kedar and examine carefully.
See if there has ever been
anything like this:

¹¹ Has a people ever changed its gods,
even though they aren't gods at all?
But my people exchanged their Glory
for Worthlessness.

¹² Be appalled, O heavens, at this,
be shocked and stupefied!
says YHWH.

¹³ For my people committed two sins:
they abandoned me,
the fountain of living water;
and they dug deep cisterns for themselves,
broken cisterns that hold no water.

¹⁴ Are the people of Israel bonded servants, born to live in bondage?
Then why are they now plunder?

¹⁵ The lions roared against them,
roared mightily,
and made their land a desolation,
their cities burned and empty.

¹⁶ The people of Noph and Tahpanhes†
will smash the crown of your head.

¹⁷ This is the price you have paid
for abandoning YHWH, your God,
who led you the whole way!

¹⁸ What do you gain now by going to Egypt
to drink the water of the Nile?
What good is it now to go to Assyria
to drink the water of the Euphrates?

---

* This is a pun: "Worthless One," *ya'al*, rhymes with Ba'al.
† Two cities in Egypt. Noph, also known as Memphis, was the ancient capital of Egypt; and Tahpanhes was a wealthy trading port located on Lake Menzaleh north of Cairo and west of modern Port Said. Together they represent the twin threats of political and economic power.

19 It is your own wrongdoing that punishes you;
   your own apostasies that convict you.
   See for yourself how bitter it is, how evil it is,
   that you abandon YHWH, your God;
   that there is no awe for me in you,
   says YHWH Omnipotent.
20 A long time ago you broke your yoke and burst your bonds,
   and said, 'I will not serve you.'
   On every high hill and under every green tree
   you sprawl out wantonly.*
21 Yet I planted you, a choice vine, a proven strain,
   How then did you degenerate into an alien vine?
22 Though you scrub yourself with lye
   and use up all the soap,
   the stain of your guilt is still before me,
   says YHWH.
23 How can you say, 'I am not defiled,
   I have not pursued the Ba'als'?
   Look at your conduct in the Valley!†
   Acknowledge what you did—
   acting like a lust-filled camel racing here and there,
24 like a wild donkey rushing off to the wilderness,
   eagerly sniffing at the wind,
   unrestrained, wild and beyond corralling.
   Is someone looking for you? Do not doubt
   that they'll find you easily whenever you're in heat!
25 Stop running! Your feet will soon be bare‡
   and your throat raw and dry.
   But you say, 'It's no use!
   I am in love with these strangers, and I follow them.'
26 Just as thieves are ashamed once caught,
   so the house of Israel is ashamed—
   they, their rulers, their officials,
   their priests and their prophets.
27 They say to a tree, 'You are my father,'
   or to a stone, 'You are my mother.'
   They showed me their backs,
   not their faces.

---

* The Hebrew word *zanah* denotes any illicit sexual activity, ranging from adultery to prostitution.
† This refers to the Valley of Hinnom, where children were sacrificed to Ba'al and Molech.
‡ Because their shoes will have worn out in pursuit of other gods, the "strangers" mentioned in the second half of the verse.

Yet whenever they're in trouble,
they say, 'Come! Rescue us!'
28 Where are the gods then
that you crafted for yourselves?
Call on them to save you, if they can,
in your time of need.
For you have as many gods
as you have towns, Judah!
29 Why do you accuse me?*
Every one of you is a rebel, says YHWH.
30 I struck your people in vain—
they refused to be disciplined.
With your own sword you devoured your prophets
like a ravenous lion.
31 You of this generation:
listen to the word of YHWH!
Have I been a desert to Israel,
a wilderness of deepest darkness?
Why do my people say, 'We broke away;
we will come to you no more'?
32 Can the young girl forget her jewelry
or a bride her finery?
Yet my people have forgotten me
for days without number.
33 You excel at finding lovers—
you could teach professionals how to get clients!
34 Yes, there is blood on your garments—
the lifeblood of the innocent poor,
though you did not catch them
breaking into your home.
Yet in spite of this
35   you say, 'I am innocent,
turn your anger away from me!'
So I will bring judgment against you for saying,
'I have not sinned.'
36 How you demean yourselves
by changing your allegiances!
Egypt will disappoint you
just as you were disappointed by Assyria.

---

* That is, of abandoning Israel to the northern invaders. God replies that they are being treated with
absolute justice.

³⁷ You will come away from there
   holding your head in your hands,
 for YHWH rejected those you trusted
   and you will gain nothing from them.
^{3:1} A couple divorces and one of them remarries.
   Can they still have relations with each other?
 Wouldn't that defile the land?
 You have been promiscuous with many lovers,
   and yet you would come back to me? says YHWH.
² Look up to the barren heights and behold.
   Where have they not lain with you?
 You scoured the side roads for lovers,
   like a nomad in the desert.
 You polluted the countryside
   with your lust and your vices.
³ So the showers have been withheld
   and the spring rain did not come.
 Yet you are conspicuous in your wantonness
   and refuse to blush with shame.
⁴ But even now you call out to me,
   'God, I am your child!
 You've been my companion
   even from my youth.
⁵ Will you be angry with me forever?
   Will you be indignant to the end?'
 This is how you talk.
 But then you commit all the evil things you do."

⁶ In the reign of Josiah the ruler, YHWH said to me, "Have you seen what the faithless People of Israel did? Have you seen how they went up every hill and under every spreading tree, and committed adultery? ⁷ I thought that after all this they would return to me, but they did not. And their treacherous sibling Judah witnessed it. ⁸ Judah saw that because of faithless Israel's adulteries, I rejected the people with a writ of divorce and sent them away. Yet I also witnessed Judah's brazen acts of faithlessness. ⁹ Judah defiled the land with its casual idolatry and its adulterous worship of wood and stone. ¹⁰ And after all that, unfaithful Judah did not return to me with all its heart; it only pretended to," says YHWH.

¹¹ YHWH said to me, "Apostate Israel is less guilty than the faithless Judah. ¹² Go, and proclaim this message toward the north, and say:

'Return, faithless Israel, says YHWH,
  and I will not let my anger fall on you.
I am merciful, says YHWH;
  I will not be angry with you forever.
13 Just admit that you are guilty:
  that you rebelled against YHWH God;
  that you were promiscuous with foreign gods
    under every spreading tree;
  that you disobey all my commands,
    says YHWH.
14 Return, rebellious children! says YHWH
    for I am your Sovereign;
  I will take you—one from each town,
    two from each tribe—and bring you to Zion.
15 I will appoint over you shepherds
    after my own heart,
  and they will feed you on knowledge
    and understanding.
16 When you multiply and become fruitful in the land, says YHWH,
    no one will ever again say,
  "Where is the Ark of the Covenant of YHWH?"
  They will no longer think of it, or remember it,
    or miss it, or make another.'*

17 "When that time comes, Jerusalem will be called Throne of God. All the nations will gather there in the Name of YHWH and they will no longer follow the dictates of their own stubborn hearts. 18 In those days, the house of Judah will join the house of Israel, and together they will come from the land of the north to the land that I gave your ancestors for a heritage.

19 "I thought to myself,
  'How I would love to adopt you as my own child,
    giving you spacious land,
    a heritage more beautiful than that of any other nation!'
  And I hoped you would call me 'Abba,'
    and never cease to follow me.
20 But like a faithless spouse
    who abandons the conjugal bed,
  you have abandoned me, house of Israel,
    says YHWH.

---

* In other words, God will be so obviously present among the people that there will be no need for a special place where God's *shekinah* (or presence) would appear.

21 A cry is heard on the bare heights—
    the weeping and the pleading of Israel's people.
They have perverted their ways
    and have forgotten YHWH, their God.
22 Return, you faithless people,
    I will heal your apostasy:
'Here we are, we come to you,
    for you are YHWH, our God!
23 Surely the idolatrous orgies on the mountains
    and in the hills was a mere aberration.
Surely the salvation of Israel
    is in YHWH, our God!
24 From our youth, Ba'al has devoured
    the fruits of our parents' labors,
their flocks and herds,
    their daughters and sons.
25 Let us lie down in our shame,
    let confusion be our blanket.
We sinned against YHWH, our God,
    we and our parents alike.
From the time when we were young until this day
    we disobeyed YHWH our God!'
4:1 If you return, Israel, says YHWH,
    if you return to me,
if you remove your odious idols out of my sight
    and stray no more,
2 and if in truth, justice, and integrity
    you swear, 'As YHWH lives!'
then the nations will pray to be blessed like you,
    and they will glory in you.
3 These are the words of God
    to the people of Judah and Jerusalem:
Plow your fallow ground
    and do not sow among thorns.
4 Dedicate yourselves completely to YHWH,
    remove the hardness of your hearts,
you citizens of Judah and inhabitants of Jerusalem;
    or the flame of my wrath will burn
    without end because of the evil of your ways.
5 Declare this throughout Judah,
    proclaim it in Jerusalem!

Blow the shofar throughout the land!
    Shout it out, and say,
'Everyone! Assemble your defenses!
    Return to the fortified cities!'
6 Raise the signal to return to Zion!
    Flee to safety immediately!
For I am bringing disaster from the north,
    with great destruction."

7 A lion has come out of its lair,
    the destroyer of nations has set out.
It has left its place
    to lay waste your land
and destroy your cities
    and their inhabitants.
8 So dress yourself in sackcloth,
    lament and wail,
for the fierce anger of YHWH
    has not left us.
9 "In that day," says YHWH,
    "the courage of the ruler
    and the ruler's council will fail,
priests will be horrified,
    prophets will be appalled."

10 I said, "Ah, Sovereign YHWH, how completely you tricked this people and Jerusalem when you said, 'There will be peace,' when there was a sword at our throats!"

11 "At that time," says YHWH, "this people and Jerusalem will be told: A scorching wind from the barren heights in the desert sweeps down on my people—not to winnow or to cleanse, 12 for it is too strong for that. Now I announce my judgment against my people."

13 Behold! The enemy advances like clouds,
    their chariots move like a desert storm;
    their horses are swifter than eagles.
Trouble approaches!
    We are lost!
14 Jerusalem, wash the evil from your heart.
    You may yet be saved.
How long will you harbor within you
    your evil schemes?

¹⁵ For a voice comes out of Dan
  and announces disaster from Mount Ephraim.
¹⁶ Tell the nations, proclaim it to Jerusalem:
  Invaders approach from a distant country;
  chanting a war cry against the cities of Judah.
¹⁷ They surround it like troops guarding a field—
  "Because Jerusalem rebelled against me,"
  says YHWH.
¹⁸ "Your own ways, your own deeds
  brought this down upon you—
this is your bitter doom!
  How it must pierce your heart!"

¹⁹ Oh, my pain, my pain,
  I writhe in pain!
How my heart throbs!
  I cannot keep silent.
I hear the trumpet sound—
  the sound of battle.
²⁰ Disaster dogs disaster!
  The whole land lies in ruin.
My tents are destroyed in a moment,
  my shelter in an instant.
²¹ How long must I view the battle flag
  and hear the sound of trumpets?
²² "My people are fools—
  they don't even know me," says YHWH.
"They are spoiled children—
  they do not understand.
They are clever only in crime—
  they know nothing of goodness!"
²³ I looked at the earth—
  it was chaos and emptiness.*
I looked to the heavens—
  their light was gone.
²⁴ I looked to the mountains—
  they quaked,
  and the hills swayed back and forth.

---

* Literally, *tohu va-bohu* and usually translated "formless and void," the words used to describe the primordial earth in Genesis before God's spirit began her creative work.

²⁵ I looked—
   I saw no one. Nothing!
   All the birds had flown away.
²⁶ I looked—
   the fertile land was desert.
   All its towns laid waste before YHWH,
   before God's fierce wrath.
²⁷ Thus says YHWH: "The whole land will be desolate,
   but I will not completely destroy it.
²⁸ So the earth mourns
   and the heavens above turn black.
   For I made known my intentions.
   I made up my mind. I will not turn back."
²⁹ At the sound of cavalry and archers
   every city takes to flight.
   The people hide in the bush, climb into the hills.
   Their cities lie abandoned, uninhabited.
³⁰ And you,
   you who are doomed to defeat:
   Why do you dress yourself in scarlet
   and wear gold rings and bracelets?
   Why do you shade your eyes with paint?
   It's all in vain!
   Your lovers despise you.
   They seek your life.
³¹ I hear a sound of a woman in labor,
   a piercing cry of the first birth.
   It is Zion who gasps for breath,
   stretching out its hands.
   "Why me?" it cries. "I am so tired,
   so tired of all this slaughter!"

^{5.1} "Tour the streets of Jerusalem," says YHWH.
   "Look around and take note, search its squares.
   If you can find one just person seeking the truth,
   then I will forgive the city.
² Although they say, 'As YHWH lives,'
   in truth, they really don't believe it."

³ YHWH, your eyes seek integrity.
   But when you struck these people, they felt no pain.

You crushed them, but they refused to be admonished.
They made their faces harder than flint and refused to repent.
4   Then I said to myself,
"I've been preaching to the poor—
they don't know any better.
They don't know the way of YHWH,
or what God requires of them.
5   I will go to the people in power
and speak with them.
They will know the way of YHWH,
and learn my ordinances."
But they too broke free of God's yoke,
released themselves from their bonds.
6   Therefore a lion from the bush will attack them;
a wolf from the plains will destroy them;
a leopard will prowl about their villages
and rip apart anyone who ventures out.
For their sins are many
and their backsliding beyond numbers.

7   "Why should I forgive you?
Your children abandoned me
and swore by gods who are not gods.
I satisfied all their needs,
yet they were unfaithful
and frequented other gods.
8   They were like well-fed and lusty stallions and mares,
neighing after one another in their desire.
9   Shouldn't I punish them for this?"
says YHWH.
"Shouldn't I avenge myself
on a people such as this?
10   Go through their vineyards and ruin them,
but don't destroy them completely.
Strip off the branches,
for these people do not belong to YHWH.
11   The house of Israel and the house of Judah
have been completely unfaithful to me,"
says YHWH.
12   "They denied me and said,
'YHWH does not matter.

No harm will come to us.
We'll feel neither sword nor famine.
13 The prophets are only full of wind,*
the word is not in them,
so let their prophecies fall upon themselves.'
14 Therefore," says YHWH Omnipotent,
"because they talk this way,
I will make my word a fire in your mouth,
that will enflame this people like firewood.
15 Israel, I bring against you a distant nation,
an ancient and enduring nation,
whose language you do not know,
whose language you cannot understand.
16 They are mighty warriors
whose quivers are an open tomb.
17 They will devour
your harvests and your food,
your daughters and your sons,
your flocks and your herds,
your vines and your fig trees.
They will destroy with the sword
your walled cities in which you trust.

18 "But even in those days," says YHWH, "I will not completely bring you to an end. 19 When they ask, 'Why has YHWH God done all this to us?' tell them, 'Just as you abandoned me and served foreign gods in your land, so you will serve strangers in a land that is not yours.'

20 "Announce this to the people of Jacob,
proclaim it in Judah:
21 Listen, you foolish and senseless people:
you have eyes and see nothing;
you have ears and hear nothing.
22 Have you no fear of me?" says YHWH.
"Will you not tremble before me,
the One who places the sand as a boundary of the sea,
a perpetual barrier which cannot be bypassed?
Though the waves toss, they cannot prevail,
though they roar, they cannot pass over it.
23 But these people have obstinate and rebellious hearts.
They turned aside and strayed apart.

---

* A pun. Wind is *ruach*, which also means spirit; and the prophets spoke by the Spirit of God. Here, however, the people claim that the prophets are speaking lies, or full of wind, not spirit.

²⁴ They don't say in their hearts,
'Let us revere YHWH our God,
who gives us the seasonal rain
in the autumn and in the spring,
and keeps for us
the weeks appointed for the harvest.'
²⁵ Your iniquities upset nature's order of things;
your sins deprived you of its bounty.
²⁶ For there are criminals among my people
who lie in ambush like hunters waiting for birds,
who prey on their own people.
²⁷ Their homes are as full of fraud,
as a cage is full of birds.
Eventually they become wealthy and powerful
²⁸ and have grown fat and sleek.
There is no end to their evil deeds.
They do not judge with justice the cause of the orphan,
nor do they defend the cause of the poor.
²⁹ Will I not punish these people for this?"
asks YHWH.
"Will I not exact vengeance
on people such as this?
³⁰ An appalling and terrible thing
has happened in the land:
³¹ prophets who prophesy falsehoods,
priests who rule by their own authority—
and my people love it this way.
But what will you do in the long run?"

^{6:1} Flee for safety, tribe of Benjamin,
from the midst of Jerusalem!
Blow the trumpet in Tekoa,
and raise a warning flag on Beth-hakkerem!
For disaster looms out of the north—
an immense calamity.
² Zion, delightful and lovely—
your end is near.
³ Shepherds with their flocks
will come against you.
They will pitch their tents around you,
each grazing their piece of pasture.

4   Prepare for battle against Zion:
         "Arise! We attack at noon!"
     Woe to us! For daylight declines,
         and evening shadows lengthen!
5   "Arise, troops! We attack at night,
         and destroy your palaces!"
6   For thus says YHWH Omnipotent:
         "Cut down its trees!
     Set up a seige ramp against Jerusalem!
     This city must be punished.
     Only oppression is found in its walls.
7   As a well pours out its water,
         so you pour out your corruption.
     The sound of violence and destruction
         echoes in your streets.
     Sickness and wounds
         are ever before me.
8   Be warned, Jerusalem,
         or I will abandon you.
     I will leave you desolate,
         a land without inhabitants."

9   YHWH Omnipotent said to me,
     "Glean, as a vine is gleaned,
         the remnant of Israel.
     One last time, like the vintner,
         pass your hand over each branch."
10   But to whom will I talk and give a warning,
         that they will hear?
     Their ears are covered over—
         they cannot listen!
     The word of YHWH is to them
         an object of scorn—
         they take no pleasure in it.
11   But I am full of YHWH's wrath.
         I weary of holding it in.
     "Pour it out on the children of the streets,
         on the young in their gatherings.
     Husband and wife will be caught in it,
         and the elderly, weighed down with age.
12   Their houses will be turned over to others—
         their fields and households together—

when I stretch out my hand
    against the inhabitants of the land.
13 From the least to the greatest,
    all are greedy for ill-won gain.
From prophet to priest—
    all are frauds.
14 Carelessly they treated the wound of my people,
    saying 'Peace, Peace,' when there is no peace!
15 They should all be ashamed
    of their loathsome conduct.
But they have no shame—
    they forgot how to blush.
Therefore, they will fall among the fallen.
    They will trip up when the time comes to punish them,"
says YHWH.

16 Thus says YHWH:
"Stand at the crossroads and look.
    Ask about the ancient paths.
Ask what the good way is, and walk that way.
    Then you will find peace within yourselves.
But the people say,
    'We will not walk it.'
17 I also appointed sentinels for you:
    'Listen for the sound of the trumpet.'
But you said,
    'We will not listen.'
18 Therefore, hear this, you nations,
    and understand, you witnesses,
    what will happen to such obstinate people!
19 Hear this, earth:
    I am about to bring disaster upon my people—
    the fruit of their own schemes.
For they did not heed my words;
    they rejected my Instruction.
20 What good is it to me
    if frankincense is brought from Sheba
    or sweet cane from a distant land,
when your sacrifices are not acceptable,
    not pleasing to me?
21 Therefore, says YHWH,
    I will place stumbling blocks before this people,

parents and children will stumble over them,
neighbors and friends will perish."

²² Thus says YHWH:
"Look, an army comes from a northern land;
a great nation stirs itself from the far corners of the earth.
²³ These warriors take up the bow and the javelin.
They are cruel, merciless.
Their sound is like the roar of the sea.
they move on horses,
equipped like warriors in battle,
against you, Zion."
²⁴ Early reports of them come to us
and our hands go limp.
Agony grips us,
like pangs of women in labor.
²⁵ Don't go out into the open.
don't travel on the road.
For the enemy, with sword in hand,
spreads terror in all directions.
²⁶ O my people, put on sackcloth
and roll in ashes!
Wail bitterly as if mourning for an only child.
For suddenly the Destroyer is upon us.
²⁷ "Jeremiah, I appointed you to be an assayer,
a refiner of my people:
you are to know and test their ways.
²⁸ They are stubborn, rebellious—
mischief-makers, corrupt to a person.
²⁹ The bellows blow,
the fires flare.
Lead, copper, iron—vainly the refiner refines,
but the impurities are not removed.
³⁰ Call them Rejected Silver,
for YHWH has rejected them."

7:1 The word came to Jeremiah from YHWH and said, ² "Stand at the gate of the Temple of YHWH and there proclaim this message: 'Listen to the word of YHWH, all you people of Judah who enter through these gates to worship YHWH! ³ YHWH Omnipotent, the God of Israel, says this: Reform your behavior and your actions, and I will let you live here in this place. ⁴ Put no trust in such deceitful words as, "This is the Temple of YHWH! The Temple of YHWH! The Temple of YHWH!" ⁵ But if you do reform your behavior and your actions—if you treat one another with justice, ⁶ if you do not exploit the immigrant, the orphan, or the widowed, if you no longer shed innocent blood in this place, or follow other gods to your own ruin— ⁷ then here in this place I will allow you to stay, in this land I gave your ancestors for all time.

⁸ " 'But here you are, putting your trust in lies to your own detriment. ⁹ Do you really think you can steal, murder, commit adultery, lie, and worship Ba'al and other gods you do not even know, ¹⁰ and then come here and stand before me in the Temple and say, "We are saved!"—only to go back and repeat all these evils? ¹¹ This Temple that bears my Name—do you take for a den of thieves? Yet I have seen all these things going on! It is YHWH who speaks.

¹² " 'Go now to my place in Shiloh where I first gave my Name a home, and see what I did to it because of the depravity of the people Israel! ¹³ You committed all these sins—it is YHWH who speaks—and refused to listen when I spoke to you again and again. And when I called you, you did not answer. ¹⁴ So I will do to this house that bears my Name—the house you trust in, the house I gave to you and to your ancestors—what I did to Shiloh. ¹⁵ I will drive you out of my sight, just as I drove out all your relatives, all the descendants of Ephraim.'

¹⁶ "As for you, Jeremiah, you must not intercede for this people, or raise either pleas or prayers on their behalf. Do not plead for them, for if you do, I will not hear you. ¹⁷ Can't you see what they are doing in the towns of Judah and in the streets of Jerusalem? ¹⁸ The children gather the wood, the fathers light the fire, the women knead the dough, to make cakes for the Queen of Heaven.* Then, to grieve me, they pour out drink offerings to other gods. ¹⁹ But is it I who grieves? says YHWH. No. It is they, themselves who are wounded, to their own harm. ²⁰ Therefore, this is what the Sovereign YHWH says: my anger and my wrath will be poured out on this place, over people and beasts, trees of the forests, fruit of the orchards. It will burn and not be extinguished."

²¹ Thus says YHWH Omnipotent, the God of Israel:

"Add your burnt offerings to your sacrifices and eat the meat. ²² For when I brought your ancestors up out of the land of Egypt, I did not give them orders about burnt offerings and sacrifices alone. ²³ I also gave them this command: 'Obey me, and I will be your God and you will be my people. Walk in my ways so that it may go well with you.' ²⁴ But they did not listen;

---

* This is the Canaanite goddess Astarte, known to the Hebrews as Ashtoreth and to the Mesopotamians as Ishtar. She is mentioned again in Jeremiah 44:17-19, 25.

they did not pay attention. They walked in the hardness of their own evil hearts and turned their backs on me, instead of turning their faces toward me! ²⁵ From the day their ancestors came up out of Egypt until today, I have sent them all my faithful prophets. Every day I got up early and sent them out. ²⁶ Yet they have not listened to me or heeded me. They have stiffened their necks and behaved worse than their ancestors. ²⁷ When you speak all these words to them, they will not listen to you either. When you call to them, they will not answer. ²⁸ So tell them this: 'This is the nation that does not listen to the voice of YHWH its God, or take correction. Faithfulness has disappeared. Truth itself is banished from their speech.

²⁹ " 'Jerusalem, cut off your hair and throw it away.
Raise a lament from the barren heights.
For YHWH has rejected and abandoned
the generation that provoked God's wrath.'

³⁰ "Yes, the children of Judah did what displeases me—it is your God who speaks. They set up their abominations in the Temple that bears my Name, defiling it. ³¹ And they built the shrines of Topheth in the Valley of Ben Hinnom to sacrifice their children by fire. This I never commanded, nor did I even contemplate it.

³² "Therefore, the time is coming, says YHWH, when it will no longer be called Topheth, or the Valley of Ben-Hinnom, but it will be called the Valley of Slaughter. For they will bury their dead in Topheth until there is no more room. ³³ At that time the dead bodies will become carrion for the birds of prey and for the wild animals, with no one to chase them away. ³⁴ And I will silence the shouts of rejoicing and mirth, the voices of bride and bridegroom in the towns of Judah and in the streets of Jerusalem, for the whole land will become a desert.

8:1 "When that time comes, says YHWH, the bones of the rulers of Judah and of the officials, of the priests and prophets, and of the inhabitants of Jerusalem, will be taken from their tombs. ² They will be spread out before the sun, the moon, and all the host of heaven, which they loved and served, followed, consulted, and worshiped. They will not be gathered and reburied. Instead, they will remain where they are on the ground like dung. ³ In all the places I will drive the remnant of this defiled family, they will prefer death to life, says YHWH Omnipotent. ⁴ You are to say to them, 'YHWH says this:

When you fall, you cannot stand again.
If you go astray can you ever find your way back?
⁵ Why does this people persist in apostasy—
in perpetual apostasy?
They have clung to lies
and refused to return.

6   I listened closely,
        but they do not speak the truth.
    They don't repent of their sins—not one of them!—
        saying, "What have I done!"
    They pursue their own course
        like a horse charging into battle.
7   Even the stork that flies above
        knows the time to migrate.
    So too, the turtledove, swallow, and crane
        move on at the right time;
    but my people pay no attention
        to YHWH's Law.
8   How dare you say, "We are wise,"
        and "the Law of YHWH is on our side,"
    when the lying pens of scribes
        have falsified the texts?
9   The wise will be put to shame,
        caught out, dismayed.
    Since they rejected the word of YHWH,
        what is it in them that can be called wise?
10 Therefore I will give their spouses to others,
        the fields to other conquerors,
    because from the least to the greatest,
        all are greedy for gain;
    from prophet to priest
        everyone deals in fraud.
11 They dress my people's wound carelessly,
        saying, "Peace, Peace," knowing that there is no peace.
12 Are they ashamed of their loathsome conduct?
        No, they feel no shame; they don't even know how to blush.
    So they will fall among the fallen.
        They will be overthrown when I come to punish them,
        says YHWH.
13 I say to myself, I will gather in the harvest,
        says YHWH.
    But there are no grapes on the vine,
        no figs on the fig tree.
    Even the leaves are withered,
        and what I gave them will be taken from them.' "

14 Why do we sit here idle?
        Come together, and take action!

Let us go into the fortified cities
    and perish there.
For YHWH God
    doomed us to perish,
gave us poisoned water to drink,
    because we sinned against YHWH.

15 We were hoping for peace,
    but no good came of it—
for a time of healing,
    but there was only terror.

16 The snorting of the horses
    is heard from Dan.
The sound of the stallion's neighing
    shakes the ground.
They come to devour the land
    and all that fills it,
the city and those who live in it.

17 "Take note, I am releasing vipers among you,
    adders that refused to be charmed—
and they do bite!"
    says YHWH.

18 Joy abandons me.
    There is no cure for my grief.
My heart is sick.

19 Hear the cry of distress of my people
    from a distant land:
"Is YHWH not in Zion?
    Is its ruler not there anymore?"
And YHWH replies,
    "Why do they provoke me
with their carved images,
    with their useless foreign gods?"

20 The harvest is past, summer is ended
    and we are not saved.

21 I am devastated, for my people are devastated.
    I mourn. Terror grips me.

22 Is there no balm in Gilead?
    Is there no physician there?
Why then has the health of my people
    not been attended to?

9:1 Oh, that my head were a spring of water
    and my eyes a fountain of tears,

so that I might weep day and night
for the slain of my people!
² Oh, that I had a lodging place,
a desert shelter for nomads!
Then I could leave my people—
go away from them.
For they are all adulterers,
a band of outlaws.
³ "They bend their tongues like bows
and shoot lies in a land.
They hold the truth hostage.
They move from crime to crime,
caring for nothing and not for me,
says YHWH.
⁴ Beware of your neighbors.
put no trust in any of your kin.
All your relatives are liars.
All your friends are slanderers.
⁵ They all deceive their neighbors;
no one speaks the truth.
Their tongues are accustomed to lying,
and tire themselves with sinning.
⁶ Wrong builds upon wrong, treachery upon treachery;
and they refuse to acknowledge me, says YHWH.
⁷ This, then, is what YHWH Omnipotent has to say:
I will now refine them and test them,
for what else can I do with such troublemakers?
⁸ Their tongues are deadly weapons,
they spit deceit through their mouths.
They have friendly words for neighbors
while secretly planning ambushes.
⁹ Will I not punish them for these things?
says YHWH.
Will I not exact vengeance
on such a people?
¹⁰ I will wail and weep for the mountains,
and lament for the desert pastures.
They are desolate and untraveled,
and lowing cattle are not heard.
The birds of the air have fled,
and even the animals are gone.

¹¹ I will turn Jerusalem into a pile of ruins,
   a lair for jackals.
I will make the towns of Judah
   an uninhabited waste."

¹² I asked, "Who is wise enough to understand this? And who has been commanded by YHWH to explain it? Why is the land desolate, turned into an arid and untraveled waste?"

¹³ YHWH replied, "It is because they abandoned the Law that I set before them. They neither obeyed me nor followed my Law. ¹⁴ Instead, they stubbornly followed the fancies of their own hearts and worshipped the Ba'als, as their ancestors taught them. ¹⁵ Therefore, these are the words of YHWH Omnipotent, the God of Israel: I will feed this people wormwood* and give them poisoned water to drink. ¹⁶ I will scatter them among the nations that neither they nor their ancestors knew. I will harass them with the sword until I have made an end to them. ¹⁷ Thus says YHWH Omnipotent:

You there! Call together the mourners!
   Send for the most skilled among them.
¹⁸ Have them come quickly to wail over us
   until our eyes overflow with tears
   and our eyelids are wet with weeping.
¹⁹ The sound of weeping resounds throughout Zion:
   'How we are ruined!
How great is our shame!
   We must abandon our land!
   Our homes are in ruins.'
²⁰ Listen, People of Israel, to the words of YHWH,
   and let your ears receive this word—
Teach your children the lament,
   teach your neighbors this dirge:
²¹ 'Death has entered through our windows,
   and made its way into our citadels.
It cut off the children from the streets
   and the youth in the public squares.'
²² Thus says YHWH:
Corpses will lie like dung
   in an open field,

---

* *Artemisia absinthium*, remarkable for its extreme bitterness, is symbolic of affliction, remorse, and punitive suffering. Wormwood was used medicinally (most frequently as a vermifuge, hence the name) from the most ancient times, and was venerated as a gift from the Goddess. The "poisoned water" is similarly euphemistic for bitterness.

like sheaves of grain behind the reaper
with no one to gather it.
23 Thus says YHWH:
Let not the wise boast of their wisdom
or the strong boast of their strength,
or the rich boast of their wealth,
24 but let them boast about this:
that they understand me and know me,
that I am YHWH,
who acts on the earth
with unfailing love, justice, and integrity,
for in these I take delight, says YHWH.
25 The time is coming, says YHWH,
when I will punish all who keep the Covenant in name only.*
26 Egypt, Judah, Edom, the Ammonites, Moab,
and all who well on the fringes of the desert—
the men of these nations are uncircumcised,
but the house of Israel is uncircumcised in heart!"

10:1 Listen, Israel! Listen to these words
that YHWH spoke against you:
2 "Don't adopt the ways of the nations.
Don't be terrified at heavenly signs—
let the nations be terrified of them.
3 For the carved idols of the nations are frauds:
a tree in a forest is cut down
and worked with a chisel
by the hands of an artisan.
4 Workers adorn it with silver and gold decorations
and fasten it down with hammer and nails,
to keep it from tottering.
5 Their idols are as silent
as scarecrows in a melon patch.
Because they cannot walk
they are carried about.
Don't fear them,
for they can do no harm
nor can they do good."

---

* Literally, "circumcised in the flesh only" or "circumcised and yet uncircumcised."

⁶ No one is like you, YHWH!
    You are great, and great is your mighty Name.
⁷ Who would not revere you, O ruler of nations?
    This is your due.
    Where among the wise of the nations,
        and among all their rulers,
        can any be found like you?
⁸ One and all, they are stupid and foolish,
        being guided by blocks of wood,
⁹ overlaid with silver brought from Tarshish,
        and gold from Ophir,
    the work of artisans and goldsmiths,
        'gods' dressed in blue and purple cloth
        woven by skilled workers.
¹⁰ But YHWH is the God of truth;
        a living God, an everlasting ruler
    whose wrath quakes the earth,
        whose fury the nations cannot endure.
¹¹ Tell them this:
    The gods who did not create heaven and earth
        will perish from the earth and from under the heavens.
¹² The earth was created through God's power.
        God's wisdom fixed the earth in place
    and God's knowledge unfurled the skies.
¹³ The waters in the heavens roar when God thunders.
        God raises clouds from the ends of the earth,
    sending lightning with the rain and bringing out
        the wind from its storehouses.
¹⁴ All the people are crude and deluded.
        All the goldsmiths are shamed by their idols.
    Their castings are fakes
        that do not breathe.
¹⁵ They are worthless, objects of mockery.
        They will perish on their day of reckoning.
¹⁶ The Portion of Jacob* is not like this.
        Jacob's God created the universe,
    and the People of Israel are the treasured possession
        of YHWH Omnipotent.

---

* "Portion" here denotes territorial allotment or inheritance; it means that for all the emphasis on the Land, Israel's true home is God.

¹⁷ Pack your belongings! Flee the country!
   You are living under a siege. ·
¹⁸ For thus says YHWH:
   "This time I will throw out the inhabitants of the land,
   and they will desperately search me out."
¹⁹ I suffer the agony
   of an open wound!
   We used to think, "This is only an illness,
   and we can bear it"—
²⁰ but now my tent is wrecked,
   and my tent ropes are frayed.
   My children left;
   they have gone away.
   No one is left to pitch my tent again,
   no one to set up my shelter.
²¹ The dull shepherds
   do not seek YHWH.
   So they have not prospered
   and their flock is scattered.
²² News! A rumor is making the rounds;
   a mighty uproar comes from the land of the north.
   They will desolate the cities of Judah,
   turning them into lairs for jackals.
²³ YHWH, I know that my life is not my own.
   I am powerless to direct my own steps.
²⁴ Reprimand me, YHWH—
   but with justice, not wrath,
   or you will reduce me to nothing.
²⁵ Pour out your wrath on the nations
   that refuse to acknowledge you;
   on tribes that do not call on you by name.
   For they have devoured Jacob,
   devoured Jacob completely,
   and destroyed his homeland.

11:1 The word that came to Jeremiah from YHWH: ² "Listen to the words of this covenant, and relate them to the inhabitants of Judah and the citizens of Jerusalem. ³ Tell them that this is the word of YHWH, the God of Israel. May any who do not heed the words of this covenant be cursed, ⁴ just as I commanded when I brought them up out of the land of Egypt, from that iron-smelting furnace, and said, 'Obey me, and do everything I command you, and you will be my people and I will be your God. ⁵ Then I will fulfill the oath I swore to your ancestors: to give them a land flowing with milk and honey—the land you occupy today.' "

I replied, "Amen, YHWH."

6 Then YHWH said to me, "Proclaim all this in the towns of Judah and in the streets of Jerusalem: 'Hear the terms of this covenant and obey it. 7 From the time I brought your ancestors up from Egypt until today, I warned them again and again, and said, Obey me. 8 But they did not obey me. They paid no attention to me, and all of them followed the prompting of their own stubborn and sinful hearts. So I brought on them all the curses of this covenant, which they had been commanded to follow but did not keep.' "

9 Then YHWH said to me: "There is a conspiracy among the people of Judah and the citizens of Jerusalem. 10 They reverted to the sins of their ancestors, who refused to listen to my words. They followed other gods and served them. Both the house of Israel and the house of Judah broke the covenant I made with their ancestors. 11 These, then, are the words of YHWH: I am about to bring upon them a disaster from which they cannot escape. They may plead with me for help, but I will not listen. 12 Then the cities of Judah and the inhabitants of Jerusalem can go and cry for help to the gods to whom they burn incense. But these will be of no help at all to them in the time of their anguish.

13 For you have as many gods
 as you have towns, O Judah.
You built as many incense altars to Ba'al
 as Jerusalem has streets.

14 "You Jeremiah, must neither intercede for this people, nor raise either plea or prayer on their behalf, for I will not listen when they call to me in the time of their distress.

15 What are you, my beloved, doing in my house?
 You are playing the hypocrite!
Can vows and consecrated meat
 avert your punishment,
when you engage in your wrongdoing
 only to rejoice?
16 YHWH called you a spreading olive tree
 studded with beautiful fruit.
But with the roar of a mighty storm
 it will be set afire
 and its branches will be broken.

17 "I, YHWH Omnipotent, who planted you, have decreed disaster for you because of the evil which the house of Israel and the house of Judah did, provoking my wrath by burning sacrifices to Ba'al."

¹⁸ Then YHWH warned me, and I knew. God opened my eyes to their deeds. ¹⁹ I had been like a gentle lamb led to the slaughter. I did not realize they plotted against me, saying, "Let us destroy the tree and its fruit. Let us cut him off from the land of the living, that his name be remembered no more."

²⁰ But you, YHWH Omnipotent, who judge justly
and test the heart and mind,
let me witness your vengeance upon them,
for my cause is committed to you.

²¹ "Therefore, thus says YHWH concerning the conspirators in Anathoth who seek your life, who threatened, 'Prophesy no more in the Name of God or we will kill you'—²² these are YHWH's words: I am about to punish them. Their young will die by the sword, their daughters and sons by famine. ²³ Not one of them will survive. For in the year of reckoning for them I will bring disaster upon the people of Anathoth."

12:1 Right is on your side, YHWH,
even when I argue with you.
Yet I would plead my case with you about your justice:
Why does the way of the evildoer prosper?
Why do the treacherous thrive?
² You planted them
and their roots go down deep.
They flourish and bear fruit.
You are forever on their lips
yet so far from their hearts.
³ But you know me, YHWH, you see me.
you probe my heart, which is in your hands.
Drag them away like sheep to be butchered!
Set them apart for the day of slaughter!
⁴ How much longer must our land lay parched
and the grass in the fields wither?
No birds or animals remain in it,
for its people are corrupt,
saying, "God can't see what we do."
⁵ "But if you raced on foot with mortals
and they wore you out," YHWH replies,
"how can you now compete with horses?*
If you stumbled in open country,
how will you manage in the thickets along the Jordan?

---

* In other words, if you were shocked at the betrayal by the conspirators from Ananathoth, how much worse when you feel the hatred of the whole nation?

jeremiah 12

⁶ Your sisters and brothers, your kin—
even they betrayed you.
They raised a cry against you.
Don't trust them even when
they speak well of you.
⁷ I will abandon the house of Israel," says YHWH.
"I will turn my back on my heritage.
I will give my beloved
into the hands of their enemies."
⁸ My own people turned against me
like lions in the bush
They roar against me,
and so I now hate them.
⁹ Or is my heritage like a hyena's den,
or like a speckled bird of prey?
Come, gather round, all you wild beasts;
come, flock to the feast!
¹⁰ A gang of shepherds ravaged my vineyard
and overran my portion of land.
They turned my portion of land
into a deserted wilderness.
¹¹ They turned it into a desolate place.
Desolate, it cries out to me in mourning.
The whole country is desolate
because no one has a heart for the land.
¹² Plunderers swarmed over
the open spaces of the wilderness.
YHWH's sword devours the land
from one end to the other.
There is no peace for any living thing.
¹³ Farmers sow wheat and reap thistles.
Their sifting gleans no grain.
The failed harvest distresses them,
for the fierce anger of YHWH is upon them.

¹⁴ Thus says YHWH: "As for all who laid their hands on the heritage I gave my people Israel, I will uproot them from their own land—and I will also uproot Judah from among them. ¹⁵ But once I uproot them, I will pity them and restore them to their holdings and their land. ¹⁶ If they will learn the ways of my people and swear by my Name and say 'As YHWH lives,' just as they had earlier taught my people to swear by Ba'al, then they will establish

their families among my people. ¹⁷ But I will uproot and destroy any nation that will not listen to me."

13¹ YHWH said to me: "Buy yourself a linen loincloth. Wear it around your loins, and never wash it."

² I bought the loincloth, as YHWH commanded, and put it on.

³ A second time the word of YHWH came to me, ⁴ "Take the loincloth that you bought and are wearing, and go now to the Euphrates. There hide it in a cleft of a rock."

⁵ So I went and hid it near the Euphrates, as YHWH commanded.

⁶ Much later, YHWH said to me, "Go now to the Euphrates and fetch the loincloth I ordered you to hide there."

⁷ So I returned to the Euphrates, and I searched, and I found the place where it was hidden. The loincloth had rotted; it was good for nothing.

⁸ Then the message of YHWH came to me:

⁹ "Thus says YHWH: Thus also will I allow the pride of Judah and the great pride of Jerusalem to rot. ¹⁰ This depraved people who refuse to listen to my words, who walk in the stubbornness of their hearts, and follow other gods to serve and adore them, will become like this loincloth—good for nothing. ¹¹ For just as a loincloth clings to a person's body, so I had intended the whole house of Judah to cling to me—it is YHWH who speaks—to be my people, my glory, my honor, and my boast. But they did not listen.

¹² "Tell the people: 'These are the words of YHWH, the God of Israel: Wine jars should be filled with wine.' If they reply that they know that wine jars should be filled with wine, ¹³ then you are to say to them, 'Thus says YHWH: I will fill all the inhabitants of the land with wine until they are drunk—rulers who sit on David's judgment seat, the priests, the prophets, and all the inhabitants of Jerusalem. ¹⁴ I will smash them one against the other, parents and children together, says YHWH. I will allow no pity or mercy or compassion to keep me from destroying them.'

¹⁵   "Pay attention: Don't be too proud to listen,
        for it is YHWH who speaks.
¹⁶   Give glory to YHWH your God
        before darkness falls,
    before your feet stumble
        on the darkening hillside,
    before God turns the light you seek
        into deep gloom and thick darkness.
¹⁷   But if you will not listen,
        I will secretly weep because of your pride."

My eyes will weep bitter tears
running down my cheeks
for YHWH's flock carried off into exile.

¹⁸ YHWH said, "Say to the ruler and the queen mother,*
'Come down from your judgment seats,
for your symbol of power will fall to the ground.
¹⁹ The towns of the Negev are besieged
with no one to relieve them.
All of Judah is swept away into exile,
swept away completely.
²⁰ Lift up your eyes and see
the migrants from the north.
Where is the flock once entrusted to you,
the flock of which you were so proud?
²¹ What will you say when they are set up over you,
whom you prepared to be your allies?
Will you not writhe in pain
like the pain of a mother
giving birth to a child?
²² And if you ask yourself,
"Why is this happening to me?"
it is because of your manifold sins
that your clothing is stripped off and you are violated.
²³ Can Ethiopians change the color of their skin,
or leopards their spots?
And you, can you do what is right
after a lifetime of wrongdoing?
²⁴ I will scatter you like chaff
driven by the desert wind.
²⁵ This is your lot,
the portion I measured our for you, says YHWH,
because you forgot me
and relied on false gods.
²⁶ So I myself ripped off your clothing
and laid bare your shame:
²⁷ your adulteries, your lustful neighing,
your unbridled depravity.

---

* At this period in Israel's history, the queen was not the wife of the ruler, but the dowager, the widow of the previous ruler and the mother of the present one. Her status and power, and the age of the present ruler, might allow her to act as co-regent. Though it is the ruler being addressed, it is clear from the later verses in this chapter that the whole people are included in the judgment.

I witnessed your abominations*
from the hills to the open fields.
Woe to you, O Jerusalem!
How long will it be till you are pure once more?' "

14:1 This is YHWH's message that came to Jeremiah about the droughts:

2　Judah is in mourning,
the villages languish.
Citizens sit on the ground mourning—
a cry goes up from Jerusalem.
3　Nobles send their peons for water.
They go to the wells and find nothing,
returning empty handed.
Disappointment and shame are their lot,
they cover their heads.
4　Because the ground is cracked for lack of rain in the land,
the farmers' hopes are dashed.
They uncover their heads in grief.
5　The doe in the field
abandons her newborn fawn
because there is no grass.
6　Wild donkeys standing on the bare heights
gasp for air like jackals.
Their eyes grow dim
for lack of pasture.
7　Yes, our sins testify against us.
Have mercy, YHWH, for your Name's sake!
For our apostasies are plentiful
and we have wronged you.
8　Hope of Israel,
our Liberator in time of need,
why be like a stranger in the land,
like a traveler turning in for the night?
9　Must you be like one who is stunned,
or like warriors suddenly powerless to save themselves?
You are in our midst, YHWH,
and we bear your Name.
Do not abandon us!

---

* The word here denotes the worship of idols, and the ritual sexual practices that accompanied the worship.

¹⁰ YHWH says of this people: "They love to wander. They stray from my ways. They wander where they will. Therefore, YHWH will not accept them, but will remember their wrongdoing and punish them for their sins."

¹¹ YHWH also said this to me: "Don't pray for the benefit of this people. ¹² Though they fast, I refuse to hear their cry. If they offer burnt offerings and grain offerings, I will not accept them. Instead, I will wipe them out with the sword, famine, and plague."

¹³ But I said, "Ah, Sovereign YHWH! Their prophets keep saying to them, 'You will not see the sword or suffer famine. Indeed, I will give you lasting peace in this place.'"

¹⁴ Then YHWH said to me, "The prophets are speaking lies in my Name. I did not send them. I gave them no orders. I never spoke to them. They are prophesying false visions, hollow predictions, and the delusions of their own minds. ¹⁵ Thus says YHWH concerning the prophets who speak in my Name: I did not send them, yet they say, 'Sword and famine will not visit this land.' So it will be by sword and famine that those prophets will meet their end! ¹⁶ And the people to whom they prophesy will be thrown out into the streets of Jerusalem, victims of the sword and famine: they, their spouses, their daughters and sons. And there will be no one to bury them. I will pour down upon them the disaster they have earned. ¹⁷ Say this to them:

'Tears flood my eyes,
    day and night, unceasingly,
for a crushing blow falls on the most vulnerable of my people,
    a brutal injury.
¹⁸ If I go into the countryside,
    there lie bodies killed by the sword.
If I go into the city,
    I see people sick with hunger.
Even prophets and priests
    wander about an unfamiliar land.
¹⁹ Have you rejected Judah altogether?
    Does your very soul loathe Zion?
Why have you struck us down
    without hope of cure?
We were hoping for peace, to no avail.
    For a time of healing, but in its place came terror.
²⁰ YHWH, we confess our transgressions
    and our ancestors' guilt:
    we sinned against you.

²¹ For your Name's sake, do not reject us.
    Do not disgrace the judgment seat of your glory.
    Remember us!
    Don't break your covenant with us!
²² Can the worthless idols of the nations make it rain?
    Can the skies grant showers?
    No, only you can, YHWH!
    You are our hope,
        for it is you who did all these things.' "

15:1 YHWH continued, "Even if Moses and Samuel stood before me, I would not be moved to pity this people. Send them away; out of my sight. Let them go! ² And if they should ask, 'Where are we to go?' say to them, 'Thus says YHWH:

    Those destined for death—to death!
    Those destined for the sword—to the sword!
    Those destined to starvation—to starvation!
    Those destined for captivity—to captivity!'

³ "I consign four kinds of destroyers for them, says YHWH: the sword to kill, dogs to drag away, and birds of prey and wild animals to devour and destroy. ⁴ I will make them objects of horror to all the nations of the earth, because of the crimes committed in Jerusalem by Manasseh ben-Hezekiah, ruler of Judah.

⁵ "Who is there to pity you, Jerusalem?
    Who is there to grieve for you?
    Who will pause to ask how you are?
⁶ You rejected me, says YHWH,
        you turned your back on me.
    So I stretched out my hand over you to destroy you—
        I can no longer show mercy.
⁷ I will winnow the people with a winnowing fork
        at the city gates of the land.
    I will bring bereavement and destruction on my people,
        because they refuse to forsake their ways.
⁸ I will make more widows and widowers of them
        than the sands of the sea.
    At noon, I will release a plunderer
        against the parents of their young.
    With sudden swiftness I will bring
        down upon them anguish and terror.

9 The parents of seven will grow faint
and breathe their last.*
Their sun will set while it is still light.
They will be disgraced and humiliated.
And I will give the rest of them
to the sword of their enemies.
10 They'll say, 'Woe to me, my parents, that you gave me birth,
a sign of strife and contention to all the land!
I neither borrow nor lend,
yet everyone curses me.'
11 But YHWH says:
It is I who send you away—
for your own good!
It is I who make your enemies attack you,
in times of disaster and in times of distress.
12 Can common iron
break northern steel?†
13 I will hand your wealth and your treasures
over as plunder, without charge,
because of all your sins throughout your country.
14 I will make you slaves of your enemies
in a country you do not know.
My wrath will kindle a fire
that will consume you."

15 YHWH, remember me!
Remember me and help me!
Avenge me on my persecutors.
You are slow to anger—do not take me away.
For I suffer insults for your sake.
16 When your words came, I devoured them.
Your word was my delight
and the joy of my heart.
For I was called by your Name,
YHWH God Omnipotent.

---

* In other words, parents—even those with many children—will receive news that all their children have been killed, and they will die from the shock.
† Literally, "Can iron break northern iron and (or mixed with) bronze?" Common iron was rather weak; better iron came from the north, and it was frequently combined with bronze to make a stronger metal not unlike steel. So God is asking whether the people of Israel really think they can stand against the powerful enemy from the north who is about to overrun the country.

¹⁷ I took no pleasure in sitting with merrymakers;
with your hand on me I sat alone,
choking with the indignation you filled me with.
¹⁸ Why is my pain ongoing,
my wound incurable, refusing to heal?
Why, you're like a spring that dries up when it's needed most,
like waters that can't be relied upon!
¹⁹ Then YHWH answered me:
"If you repent,*
I will return you to my service.
If you extract the valuable from the worthless,
you will be my mouthpiece.
Let them come back to you,
but you must not go back to them.
²⁰ I will make you a bronze wall
fortified against this people.
They will fight against you
but they will not overcome you.
For I am with you,
to save you and deliver you—
it is YHWH who speaks.
²¹ I will free you from the hand of the evildoer,
and rescue you from the clutches of the violent."

16:1 Then the Word of YHWH came to me: ² "You must neither marry nor have children in this place. ³ For thus says YHWH concerning the children born in this place, and the mothers and fathers who conceive them in this land: ⁴ They will succumb to deadly diseases. They will be neither mourned nor buried but will be like dung spread over the ground. They will perish by the sword and by famine, and their corpses will become food for the birds and the animals.

⁵ "For thus says YHWH: Do not enter a house that is in mourning. Do not go to mourn the dead or to bring comfort to the living, says YHWH, for I have withdrawn from this people my blessing, my love, and my mercy. ⁶ Both high and low will die in this land. But there must be no burials. No one is to mourn, nor are any to gash themselves or shave their heads for the dead. ⁷ No one must offer food to comfort those mourning for the dead—not even for a mother or a father—nor may anyone offer a cup of consolation for them.

---

* Jeremiah is being called to repentance from thinking that God is unreliable—an accusation that is tantamount to apostasy, since it is the very accusation that Israel levelled against God in times past.

⁸ "Do not enter a house where there is feasting and sit down to eat and drink. ⁹ For this is what YHWH Omnipotent, the God of Israel, has to say: Before your eyes and in your days I will silence every sound of joy and gladness, the voices of bride and bridegroom.

¹⁰ "When you inform these people about all this and they ask you, 'Why has YHWH decreed this great disaster that is to come upon us? What is our crime? What sin have we committed against YHWH, our God?' ¹¹ say to them, 'It is because your ancestors abandoned me—it is YHWH who speaks—and followed alien gods, serving and worshiping them. They abandoned me and did not keep the Law. ¹² And you have behaved even worse than your ancestors, for here you are, every one of you, following your stubborn evil will, refusing to listen to me! ¹³ So I will throw you out of this land into a land unknown either to you or to your ancestors. In that land you will serve other gods day and night, for I will show you no favor.'

¹⁴ "Therefore the time is coming, says YHWH, when people will no longer swear, 'As YHWH lives, who brought us up out of Egypt,' ¹⁵ but will say, 'As YHWH lives, who brought the Israelites back from the land of the north and out of all the countries to which we were banished.' For I will restore them to the land I gave their ancestors.

¹⁶ "But now I will send for many fishermen and women, says YHWH, and they will fish for the people. And afterwards I will send for many hunters, and they will hunt for the people from every mountain and hill and from the crevices in the rocks. ¹⁷ For my eyes are on all their ways, which are not hidden from me. Nor are their sins concealed from my sight. ¹⁸ I will repay them double for their corruption and their evil deeds. For they have defiled my land with corpses of their vile idols."

¹⁹   YHWH, my strength and my stronghold,
        my refuge in troubled times—
    the nations will come to you
        from the ends of the earth and say,
    "Our ancestors inherited false gods,
        worthless and empty idols.
²⁰ For if human beings can make their own gods
        then they are not gods!"
²¹ "This time," says YHWH, "I will teach them:
    I will teach them once more
    my power and my might
        and they will learn that my Name is YHWH.
17:1 Judah's sin is engraved with an iron stylus,
        written with a fine point

on the tablet of their hearts
and on the horns of their altars
2   as a testimony against them.
Their altars and their Asherah poles *
stand beneath every spreading tree
on the heights ³ and in the hills
in the mountain country.
Because of your sin throughout your country,
I will hand your wealth and treasures as plunder,
along with all your shrines.
4   You will lose the inheritance I gave you
through your own fault.
I will enslave you to your enemies
in a land you do not know.
For you have inflamed my wrath,
and it will burn eternally."

5   "Cursed are those who trust in human ways," says YHWH,
"who rely on things of the flesh,
whose hearts turn away from YHWH.
6   They are like stunted vegetation in the desert
with no hope in the future.
It stands in stony wastes in the desert,
an uninhabited land of salt.
7   Blessed are those who put their trust in God,
with God for their hope.
8   They are like a tree planted by the river
that thrusts its roots toward the stream.
When the heat comes it feels no heat,
its leaves stay green.
It is untroubled in a year of drought,
and never ceases to bear fruit.
9   The human heart is more deceitful than
than anything else,
and desperately sick—who can understand it?
10   I, YHWH, search into the heart,
I probe the mind,
to give to all people
what their actions and conduct deserve.

---

* Wooden monuments and sacred groves dedicated the fertility goddess Asherah, also known as Astarte.

11 Like the partridge hatching the eggs it did not lay,
    so are all who gain wealth unjustly.
It will leave them in mid-life,
    and at the end of their life
    they will prove themselves the fool."

12 You are the Throne of Glory,
    exalted from the beginning,
    where our sanctuary is found!
13 You are the Hope of Israel, YHWH!
    All who abandon you will be shamed.
Whoever turns from you
    will be uprooted from the land,
for abandoning YHWH,
    the spring of living water.
14 Heal me, YHWH, and I will be healed.
    Save me, and I will be saved,
    you whom I praise.
15 They say to me, "Where is the promise of YHWH?
    Let it come to pass now!"
16 It is not the prospect of disaster
    that forces me to call to you.
I did not wish for this day of despair.
    You are fully aware of what passes my lips.
17 Do not become a terror to me.
    You are my refuge in the day of disaster.
18 May my persecutors be foiled, not I!
    May they be terrified, not I!
Bring upon them the terrible day!
    Destroy them, destroy them twice over!

19 YHWH replied to me: "Go! Stand at the Benjamin Gate, through which the rulers of Judah go in and out. And stand at all the other gates of Jerusalem. 20 Say to all who will listen: 'Hear the word of our God, rulers of Judah, and all the people of Judah and all who come through these gates. 21 This is what YHWH says: Do not risk your life by carrying a load on the Sabbath or bringing it through the gates of Jerusalem. 22 Do not bring a load out of your homes or do any work on the Sabbath. Keep the Sabbath day holy, as I commanded your ancestors. 23 Yet they did not listen or pay attention. They were stubborn and would not listen or respond to discipline. 24 But if you are careful to obey me, declares YHWH, and do not carry loads through the gates of this city on the Sabbath, but keep the Sabbath day

holy by resting on that day, ²⁵ then the rulers who sit on David's judgment seat will come through the gates of this city with their officials, riding on horses and in chariots, accompanied by the people of Judah and Jerusalem, and this city will be inhabited forever. ²⁶ People will come from the towns of Judah and the villages around Jerusalem, from the territory of Benjamin and the western foothills, from the hill country and the Negev, bringing to the Temple of YHWH burnt offerings and sacrifices, grain offerings, incense, and thank offerings. ²⁷ But if you do not obey me and keep my Sabbath day holy by refraining from carrying any load as you come through the gates of Jerusalem on the Sabbath day, then I will enkindle my unquenchable fire in the gates of Jerusalem that will consume its fortresses.' "

18:1 This word came to Jeremiah from YHWH: ² "Get up and make your way down to the potter's house. I will give you my message there."

³ So I went down to the potter's house, and there the potter was working at the wheel. ⁴ Whenever the object of clay that the potter was making turned out badly, the potter tried again, making of the clay another object, of whatever sort the potter pleased.

⁵ Then the word of YHWH came to me: ⁶ "House of Israel, can I not do to you what this potter does?—it is YHWH who speaks. Indeed, like clay in the hand of the potter, so are you in my hand, house of Israel. ⁷ At any moment I may announce that a nation or a dominion is to be uprooted, pulled down or destroyed. ⁸ But if the nation I threatened abandons its depraved ways, I will change my mind and not inflict on it the disaster I planned. ⁹ At another moment I may announce that I will build up a nation or establish one. ¹⁰ But if it does something displeasing to me, refusing to listen to my voice, then I will reconsider the good I had intended to do for it."

¹¹ Then YHWH said, "Now tell the people of Judah and the inhabitants of Jerusalem: 'Thus says YHWH: Beware! I am preparing a disaster for you and devising a plan against you. Turn away from your evil life, each one of you, give up your evil ways, amend your conduct.' ¹² But they will answer, 'What is the use of talking? We will not amend our ways—each will follow the whims of our own corrupted hearts.' ¹³ This is what YHWH says in reply:

"Inquire among the nations:
    Has anyone ever heard the like of this?
Israel the Pure
    has committed a deed most horrible.
¹⁴   Do the snows of Lebanon ever melt from its lofty crags?
    Do the mountain streams ever dry up?
¹⁵   No! But my people forgot me.
    They burn their incense to worthless idols,

which makes them stumble in their ancient ways
    and they take to side streets and unmarked roads.
16 They turn their land into a waste,
    an object of derision.
All who pass by
    shake their heads in horror.
17 I will scatter them before the enemy
    like the eastern wind.
I will show them not my face, but my back
    in the hour of their ruin."

CR   CR   CR

18 The people of Judah and the citizens of Jerusalem said, "Let us devise a plot against Jeremiah. His absence will not mean the loss of instruction from the priests, or of counsel from the wise, or of messages from the prophets. So let us destroy him by his own tongue. Let us carefully note every word Jeremiah speaks."

19 Jeremiah prayed,

"Hear me, O God,
    and listen to what my adversaries are saying.
Must good be repaid with evil?
    They are digging a pit for me.
20 Remember that I stood before you
    to speak on their behalf,
    so that you would turn your wrath from them.
21 So abandon their children to famine;
    leave them to the mercy of the sword.
May their spouses be childless and widows!
May their widowers die of plague,
    their youth cut down in combat!
22 Let cries be heard from their houses
    when you bring marauders suddenly upon them!
For they dug a pit to entrap me
    and set snares for my feet.
23 But you, YHWH,
    know all their murderous plots against me.
Do not forgive their iniquity
    or wipe their sin from your sight.
Make them stumble before you.
    Judge them in the moment of your wrath."

¹⁹⁺¹ YHWH said this: "Go to the potter and buy an earthenware jar. Take some of the elders and some of the priests with you. ² Then go out to the valley of Ben-hinnon, near the entrance of the Potsherd Gate. There proclaim what I tell you. ³ Say: 'Hear the word of YHWH, rulers of Judah and inhabitants of Jerusalem. These are the words of YHWH Omnipotent, the God of Israel: I am going to bring such ruin upon on you that it will ring in the ears of everyone who hears it. ⁴ For they abandoned me, and made this a place for alien gods. They offered sacrifices in it to gods that neither they nor their ancestors, nor the rulers of Judah, had ever known. And they filled this place with the blood of the innocent. ⁵ They constructed the high places of Ba'al to sacrifice their children by fire there. But I never ordered or decreed that—it never entered my mind!

⁶ " 'So beware! The days are coming, says YHWH, when people will no longer call this place Topheth or Valley of Ben-hinnon; they'll call it Valley of Slaughter.*⁷ I will void the plans of Judah and Jerusalem in this place. I will make the people fall by the sword before their enemies, and by the hands of those who seek their lives. And I will give their corpses over to the birds and animals to devour. ⁸ I will turn this city into a scene of abject horror—a site so desolate that passers-by will shake their heads, whistling in amazement. ⁹ I will make people eat the flesh of their daughters and sons, and they will eat one another's flesh during the stress of the siege laid down upon them by their enemies who seek their life.' "

¹⁰ "Then you are to break this jug in front of the group with you, ¹¹ saying to them: 'These are the words of YHWH Omnipotent: I will smash this nation and this city just as a potter's jar is smashed and cannot be repaired. They will bury their dead in Topheth until there is no more room. ¹² This is what I will do to this place and to those who dwell here, says YHWH. I will make this city like Topheth. ¹³ And like the altars of Topheth, the residences of Jerusalem and those of the rulers of Judah will be defiled—all the houses where they burned incense on roofs to all the Host of Heaven and poured drink offerings to other gods.' "

¹⁴ When Jeremiah returned from Topheth, where YHWH had sent him to prophesy, and stood in the court of the Temple of YHWH, he said to all the people: ¹⁵ "These are the words of YHWH Omnipotent, the God of Israel: 'I am about to bring on this city and on the villages surrounding it, all the disaster I threatened them with, for they have grown stiff-necked and would not listen to my words.' "

---

* Topheth, which means "burning place," was that part of the Hinnom Valley (in Greek, Gehenna, which came to personify the concept of Hell), just outside Jerusalem, where children were sacrificed to the Ammonite god Molech.

²⁰·¹ Now the priest Pashhur ben-Immer, the chief officer of the Temple of YHWH, heard Jeremiah prophesying these things. ² He had him flogged and put into the stocks at the Upper Benjamin Gate, the gate leading into the Temple of YHWH.

³ The next morning, when Pashhur had him taken out of the stocks, Jeremiah said to the chief officer: "YHWH says your name is no longer Pashhur, 'Freedom,' but Magor-missabib, 'Terror on Every Side.' ⁴ For these are the words of YHWH: I will make you a terror to yourself and to all your friends. They will fall by the sword of the enemy before your very eyes. I will hand over all Judah to the ruler of Babylon, who will deport them to Babylon and put them to the sword. ⁵ And I will hand over to their enemies the city's store of wealth, its riches, and all the treasures of Judah's rulers. They will commandeer it and cart it off to Babylon. ⁶ You, Pashhur, and all your household will go into exile in Babylon. You will die and be buried there, you and all your friends to whom you prophesied lies."

⁷ You fooled me, YHWH, and I let myself be fooled.
    You were too strong for me, and you triumphed.
All day long, I am an object of laughter.
    Everyone mocks me.
⁸ Whenever I speak, I must cry out,
    proclaiming violence and desolation.
The word of YHWH has brought me
    derision and reproach all day long.
⁹ I say to myself, "I will not mention God,
    nor will I speak in the Name of YHWH any more."
But then it becomes like fire burning in my heart,
    imprisoned in my bones.
I grow weary holding it in,
    I cannot endure it.
¹⁰ Yes, I hear the whispering of many,
    "Terror all around!
Denounce him!
    Let us denounce Jeremiah!"
All who were my friends
    are watching for any misstep.
They say, "Perhaps he will trip up,
    then we can get the better of him
    and take our vengeance on him."
¹¹ But YHWH is with me, like a mighty champion.
    My persecutors will trip up,
    they will not triumph.

They will be put to utter shame,
to lasting, unforgettable disgrace.
12 YHWH Omnipotent, you who test the just,
who probe both mind and heart,
let me witness the vengeance you take on them,
for to you I have entrusted my cause.
13 Sing to YHWH, praise to YHWH,
for God has rescued the life of the poor
from the power of the corrupt!
14 Cursed be the day I was born!
May the day my mother bore me not be blessed!
15 A curse on whoever brought word to my father,
"A child is born to you, an heir,"
and gladdened my father's heart.
16 May that messenger fare like the cities
that YHWH overthrew without mercy!
May that messenger hear screams in the morning
and battle cries at high noon!
17 For death did not claim me before birth
and my mother did not become my grave—
her womb enlarged forever.
18 Why did I come forth from the womb
to see only toil and sorrow,
to spend my days in shame?

21:1 This message came to Jeremiah from YHWH when Zedekiah the ruler sent Pashhur ben-Malkijah and the priest Zephaniah ben-Maaseiah to Jeremiah and said, 2 "Please consult YHWH for us, for Nebuchadnezzar ruler of Babylon makes war on us. Perhaps YHWH will work a miracle on our behalf, so that Nebuchadnezzar will lift the siege."

3 But Jeremiah said to them, "Tell Zedekiah 4 that these are the words of YHWH, the God of Israel: 'I will turn your own weapons against you—the very ones in your hands that you are using to fight the ruler of Babylon and the Chaldeans who are outside the wall besieging you. 5 I myself will fight against you with an outstretched hand and a mighty arm in anger, fury and a burning rage. 6 I will strike down those living in this city, human and animal alike. They will die of a horrible plague. 7 After that, YHWH declares, Zedekiah the ruler of Judah, his officials, and all who survive after the sword, the plague, and the famine, I will deliver to Nebuchadnezzar ruler of Babylon and to their enemies who seek their lives. The enemy will strike them down with the sword, showing no pity, mercy or compassion.'

⁸ "And to the people you are to say: 'YHWH says this: I offer you now a choice between a way of life and a way of death. ⁹ Whoever remains in the city will die by the sword, famine or plague. But whoever goes out and surrenders to the Chaldeans besieging you will survive. You will escape with your life. ¹⁰ I set my face against this city determined to do it harm, not good, says YHWH. It will be handed over to the Babylonian ruler, who will burn it to the ground.'

¹¹   "Listen to the word of YHWH,
          house of the ruler of Judah!
¹²   Hear the word of YHWH,
          house of David!
      Administer justice every morning,
          rescue the victim from the hands of the oppressor,
      or the fire of my fury will blaze up
          with an unquenchable flame
      because of your evil deeds.
¹³   My quarrel with you,
          you valley dwellers,
      you rocks on the plain,
          is that you said,
      'Who can come down against us?
          Who can penetrate our refuge?'
¹⁴   I will punish as your deeds deserve,
          says YHWH,
      I will set fire to your woodlands
          that will consume all around you."

22:1 Thus says YHWH: "Go down to the house of Judah's ruler with this message: ² 'Ruler of Judah, who sit on David's judgment seat—hear this word from YHWH. It is for you, your attendants, and your people who pass through these gates. ³ YHWH God says: Act with justice and integrity: rescue the victim from the oppressor; do not oppress or mistreat resident aliens or the orphaned or widowed, and don't shed innocent blood in this place. ⁴ If you carry out these commands, the rulers who will sit on David's judgment seat will come through the gates of this house riding in chariots and on horses—they, their attendants and their people. ⁵ But I solemnly swear, says YHWH, that if you do not carry out these commands, this house will become a ruin.

⁶   "For thus says YHWH about the house of the rulers of Judah:
      Though you are like Gilead to me,
          like the summit of Lebanon,
      I swear I will turn you into a desert,
          a land of uninhabited towns.

⁷ I will send destroyers against you
   armed with their weapons.
   They will cut down your choicest cedars
   and use them for kindling.

⁸ "Travelers from many nations will pass by this city and will ask one another, 'Why has YHWH done such a thing to this great city?' ⁹ The answer is that they abandoned their covenant with YHWH by worshiping other gods and serving them.

¹⁰ Neither weep for the dead
   nor lament their loss.
   Weep rather for the exiled
   who will never return,
   never again behold the land of their birth."

¹¹ Thus says YHWH concerning Shallum ben-Josiah, ruler of Judah, who succeeded his father Josiah as ruler and was forced to leave this place: "He will never return. ¹² Josiah will die in the land of his exile. He will never see this country again.

¹³ "Woe to the ruler who builds a house without integrity
   and its upper rooms with injustice,
   enslaving the citizenry,
   not paying for their labor!
¹⁴ Woe to the ruler who says,
   'I will build myself a spacious house
   with airy upper rooms,
   and numerous open windows,
   cedar paneling painted in vermillion.'
¹⁵ Do you outrival other rulers
   because you panel in cedar?
   Did not your predecessor, like you,
   eat and drink?
   He practiced justice and integrity
   and all went well for him.
¹⁶ He defended the cause of the poor and needy,
   and all went well for him.
   Is that not what it means to know me?·
   says YHWH.
¹⁷ But your eyes, your heart,
   are set only on dishonest gain,
   on shedding innocent blood,
   on oppression and tyranny."

18 Thus says YHWH
concerning Jehoiakim ben-Josiah, ruler of Judah:
"Mourners will not say, 'Alas, dear one, my friend'
or 'Alas, my ruler; alas, my leader.'
19 You will be buried like a dead donkey,
dragged off and flung out
beyond the gates of the Jerusalem.
20 Go up to Lebanon and scream,
let your voice be heard in Bashan,
cry out from Abarim,
for all your allies are crushed.
21 I spoke to you in your secure days,
but you said, 'I will not listen.'
You were this way since your youth.
You never obeyed me.
22 A wind will carry away all your shepherds,
and your allies will go into captivity.
Then you will be humiliated and shamed
for all your evil you have done.
23 You inhabitants of Lebanon
who dwell among the cedars:
How you will groan when pains overtake you,
like labor pangs!"

24 To Jehoiachin ben-Jehoiakim ruler of Judah, YHWH says, "As I live, even if you were a signet ring on my right hand, I would still tear you off. 25 I will hand you over to those who seek your life, into the hands of those you fear, into the hands of Nebuchadnezzar ruler of Babylon and into the hands of the Chaldeans. 26 I will thrust you and the mother who bore you into another country than that of your birth, and there you will die. 27 You will never return to the land you long for.

28 "Is this Jehoiachin, then, a despised,
broken pot, something no one wants?
Why else are he and his children thrown out,
cast out into a country they do not know?
29 O land, land, land!
Hear the word of YHWH!
30 Thus says YHWH:
List Jehoiachin as childless,
as one who in a lifetime will not prosper,
as one who will not leave prosperous offspring,
or sit on David's judgment seat or rule anymore."

23:1 "Woe to the shepherds who are destroying and scattering the sheep in my pasture!" declares YHWH. **2** "Thus says YHWH, the God of Israel, concerning the shepherds who are tending my people: You have scattered my flock and driven them away, and you have not attended to them. Behold, I am about to attend to you for the evil of your deeds, declares YHWH. **3** Then I myself will gather the remnant of my flock out of all the countries where I have dispersed them, and will bring them back to their own pasture, and they will be fruitful and multiply. **4** I will also raise up shepherds who will look after them and pasture them. They will no longer be afraid or terrified nor will any be missing, declares YHWH.

5 Behold, the days are coming, declares YHWH,
    when I will raise up for the house of David a righteous branch,
    who will reign as a true ruler and act wisely,
        and do what is just and right in the land.
6 In those days, Judah will be saved,
        and Israel will dwell securely.
    This is the Name on which they will call:
        'YHWH, Our Justice.'

7 Therefore, the days are coming, says YHWH, when people will no longer say, 'As YHWH lives, who brought us up out of the land of Egypt,' **8** but rather, 'As YHWH lives, who brought the Israelites back from the land of the north'—and from all the countries to which I dispersed them, to live on their own soil."

9 On the prophets:
    My heart is broken inside me.
        All my bones tremble.
    I am like a drunk,
        like someone overcome with wine.
    It is because of YHWH
        and because of God's holy words.
10 For the land is full of adulterers
        and because of them the soil lies parched
        and the pastures in the desert are dried up.
    The prophets follow an evil path,
        and use their power unjustly.
11 "Yes, both the prophets and the priests are godless.
        I have witnessed their sinfulness even in my Temple," says YHWH.
12 "So their path will prove to be
        a treacherous journey for them,
    a pitfall into which they will be driven
        and fall headfirst.

For I will visit them with disaster
in their year of reckoning, says YHWH.
13 I witnessed the most repulsive thing
among the prophets of Samaria:
They prophesied by Ba'al
and led my people Israel astray.
14 And among the prophets of Jerusalem
I see something just as loathsome:
adulterers and hypocrites.
They encourage the hands of the corrupt
so that no one repents from sinning.
They are all like Sodom to me,
the people of Jerusalem are like Gomorrah."
15 Thus says YHWH Omnipotent, therefore, about the prophets:
"I will make them eat wormwood
and drink poisoned water.
For the prophets of Jerusalem spread godlessness
throughout the land.
16 Thus says YHWH:
Do not listen to what the prophets prophesy to you.
They only fill you with false hope.
They recite visions of their flights of fancy,
not what comes from the mouth of YHWH.
17 They continue to say to those who despise me,
'You will prosper in your ways.'
And the obstinate they encourage with,
'No harm will come your way.'
18 But who among them stood in the council of YHWH
in order to see and hear God's word?
Who among them listened and heard my word?
19 Beware! The storm of YHWH will burst forth in wrath
like a desert storm cascading on the heads of all these evildoers.
20 YHWH's anger will not turn back
until the divine purpose has been fully accomplished.
You will clearly understand this
in days to come.
21 I did not send these prophets,
yet they run off at the mouth.
I did not speak to them,
yet they prophesy.
22 But had they stood in my council,
they would have proclaimed my word to my people

to turn them from their evil ways
and from their evil deeds.
²³ Am I a God only when I am nearby, says YHWH,
and not a God when far away?
²⁴ Can anyone so hide in secret places
where I cannot find them? says YHWH.
Do I not fill both heaven and earth?
says YHWH.

²⁵ "I heard what these prophets say—the ones who speak lies in my Name:
'I had a dream!' they say, 'I had a dream!' ²⁶ How long will these lying
prophets maintain these fictions in their hearts—these delusions of their
own minds? ²⁷ They think the dreams they tell one another will make my
people forget my Name, just as their ancestors forgot my Name and could
only remember Ba'al. ²⁸ Let the prophet who has a dream tell it. But let the
one who has my word speak it faithfully. What do straw and grain have in
common? It is YHWH who speaks. ²⁹ Is not my word like fire, says YHWH,
and like the hammer that smashes the rock into pieces?

³⁰ "Therefore, thus says YHWH: I oppose those prophets, imposters who
steal words from one another—words presumed to be mine. ³¹ Thus says
YHWH: I oppose those prophets who concoct words of their own and then
say, 'Thus says YHWH.' ³² I oppose those prophets who prophesy false
dreams, says YHWH, who recount them in order to lead my people astray
by their lies and their recklessness. Yet I neither sent them nor appointed
them. They bring my people no good at all.

³³ "When any of these people, or a prophet or a priest, asks you, 'What is
the sad burden of YHWH?' say to them, 'Sad burden? You are the sad burden! Yes, you! And I mean to be rid of you, says YHWH.' ³⁴ And if a prophet
or a priest or any others mentions 'the sad burden,' I will punish them and
their household. ³⁵ This is the form of words you will use in speaking among
yourselves: 'What answer has YHWH given?' or 'What has YHWH said?'
³⁶ You must never again mention 'the sad burden of YHWH.' For how can
YHWH's word be a sad burden to anyone? But you distort the words of the
living God, YHWH Omnipotent. ³⁷ This is the form of words you will use in
speaking to a prophet: 'What answer has YHWH given you?' or 'What did
YHWH say to you?' ³⁸ But to any of you who do say 'the sad burden of our
God,' thus says YHWH: Because you say 'the sad burden of our God,' even
though I send word to you not to say it, ³⁹ I myself will put you out of my
mind and cast you out of my presence along with the city I gave you and
your ancestors. ⁴⁰ I will inflict you with endless shame, endless and unforgettable disgrace."

24:1 After Jehoiachin ben-Jehoiakim ruler of Judah, as well as the officials, the craft workers, and the artisans of Judah, were carried off into exile from Jerusalem to Babylon by Nebuchadnezzar, ruler of Babylon, YHWH showed me two baskets of figs placed before the Temple of YHWH. 2 One basket held excellent figs, like the figs that ripen first. The other basket held bad figs, so bad they were inedible.

3 Then YHWH asked me, "What do you see, Jeremiah?"

I answered, "Figs. The good figs are very good and the bad figs are very bad, so bad they are inedible."

4 Then the word of YHWH came to me: 5 "This what YHWH, the God of Israel, says: Like the good figs, I regard as good the exiles of Judah whom I sent away from here to the land of the Chaldeans. 6 I will look after their welfare and restore them to this land. I will build them up and not tear them down. I will plant them and not uproot them. 7 I will give them the heart to know me, for I am YHWH. They will be my people and I will be their God, for they will return to me with a full heart.

8 "But like the bad figs that are so bad that they are inedible, I will deal with Zedekiah, ruler of Judah, his officials, and the survivors from Jerusalem, both those who remain in this land and those who settled in Egypt. 9 I will make them repugnant and offensive to all the realms of the earth—shameful, a byword and a laughingstock, and cursed in every place I will have driven them. 10 And I will send sword, famine, and disease upon them until they are utterly wiped out from the land I gave to them and their ancestors."

25:1 This word came to Jeremiah concerning all the people of Judah in the fourth year of Jehoiakim ben-Josiah, ruler of Judah, which coincided with the first year of Nebuchadnezzar ruler of Babylon. 2 Jeremiah the prophet proclaimed it to all the people of Judah and all the citizens of Jerusalem:

3 For twenty-three years, from the thirteenth year of Josiah ben-Amon, ruler of Judah, up to the present, the word of YHWH has come to me, and I spoke persistently to you, but you did not listen.

4 And though YHWH sent you prophets, God's servants, you neither listened to them, nor showed a will to listen. 5 YHWH promised that if every one of you turned away from your corrupt ways and evil conduct, you would dwell forever on the soil given to your ancestors long ago: 6 "You must not follow alien gods, neither serving them nor worshiping them. You must refrain from provoking my anger by the things you make. And then I will not harm you. 7 But you did not listen to me, says YHWH; you provoked me to anger with your idols made by your hands and brought harm upon yourselves.

⁸ "Therefore these are the words of YHWH: Because you did not heed my words, ⁹ I will summon all the tribes of the north, says YHWH, and I will send for my instrument, Nebuchadnezzar, ruler of Babylon. And I will bring him against this land and its inhabitants and all its neighboring nations. I will exterminate them and make them an object of horror, scorn and everlasting disgrace. ¹⁰ I will silence every sound of joy and rejoicing, the voice of the bride and the voice of the bridegroom, even the sound of the millstone. The light of every lamp will remain unlit.

¹¹ "For seventy years this whole land will remain a ruin and a waste, while its inhabitants languish in slavery under the ruler of Babylon. ¹² When seventy years have passed, I will punish the ruler of Babylon and his people, says YHWH, for all their iniquities, and turn the land of the Chaldeans into a desert forever. ¹³ I will bring down upon that land all the words I spoke against it and everything I write in this book, which Jeremiah prophesied against all the nations. ¹⁴ For mighty nations and powerful rulers will enslave them, and thus I will repay them according to their deeds and the work of their hands."

¹⁵ These were the words that YHWH, the God of Israel, said to me: "Accept from my hand this cup of wrath, and make all the nations to whom I send you drink it. ¹⁶ Once they drink it, they will stagger and go out of their minds because of the sword I am sending among them."

¹⁷ So I accepted the cup from YHWH's hand and made all the nations drink it, all the peoples to whom YHWH sent me: ¹⁸ Jerusalem and the villages of Judah, as well as their rulers and officials, to make them a ruin and an object of horror, scorn, and everlasting disgrace, as they still are; ¹⁹ Pharaoh, ruler of Egypt, his officials, officers, all the Egyptians, and ²⁰ all the foreigners there; all the rulers of Uz; all the rulers of the Philistines—all those of Ashkelon, Gaza, Ekron, and the remnant at Ashdod; ²¹ Edom, Moab, and the Ammonites, ²² all the rulers of Tyre, Sidon, and the coastlands across the sea; ²³ Dedan, Tema, Buz, and all who live along the fringes of the desert; ²⁴ all the Arabian rulers living in the desert; ²⁵ all the rulers of Zimri, Elam, and all the Medes; ²⁶ all the rulers of the north, neighbors or distant from each other—all the rulers on the face of the earth. Last of all the ruler of Sheshach* will have to drink it too.

²⁷ Then God said to me, "Tell the people that YHWH, the God of Israel, says this: 'Drink, get drunk and vomit, fall down and get up no more because of the sword I am sending among you.' ²⁸ And if they refuse to accept the cup from your hand to drink, say to them: 'Thus says YHWH Omnipotent: You must drink it! ²⁹ See, I begin by bringing disaster on the city bearing my

---

* *Sheshach* is a cryptogram for Babylon.

Name; and you think you are going to be exempt? No, you will not be, for I summon a sword against all the inhabitants of the earth, declares YHWH Omnipotent.' ³⁰ Now prophesy to them and tell them all I have said."

YHWH will roar from on high,
thundering from God's holy dwelling place.
Roaring mightily against the promised land,
God roars mightily against the faithful,
shouting like those treading grapes,
against all the inhabitants of the earth.
³¹ The roar reaches to the ends of the earth,
for God brings charges against the nations.
God accuses all humankind
and hands the evildoer over to the sword.
³² Thus says YHWH Omnipotent:
"See! Disaster spreads from nation to nations,
and a great storm is rising from
the ends of the earth."

³³ In those days the people slain by YHWH will extend from one end of the earth to the other. They will be neither mourned nor buried. They will be like dung spread on the soil.

³⁴ Wail, shepherds, weep!
Roll in the ashes, you leaders of the flock.
For your time to be slaughtered has arrived.
You will die like fine rams.
³⁵ Shepherds will have no sanctuary to flee to,
their leaders no place to hide.
³⁶ Listen! Hear the cry of the shepherds,
the wailing of the leaders of the flock,
for YHWH destroys their pasture land.
³⁷ The pleasant meadows will be laid to waste
because of the fierce wrath of YHWH.
³⁸ Like a lion abandoning its lair
they flee from the wasted land
under the sword of oppression
and YHWH's fierce anger.

ᘓ   ᘓ   ᘓ

²⁶:¹ In the beginning of the reign of Jehoiakim ben-Josiah, ruler of Judah, this word came from YHWH: ² "Thus says YHWH: Stand in the court of the

Temple of YHWH and speak to the people of all the villages of Judah who come to worship in the Temple of God. Whatever I command you, tell them, and omit nothing. ³ Perhaps they will listen and turn back from their ways, so that I may repent of the evil I have planned to inflict upon them for their evil deeds. ⁴ Say to them, 'It is your God who speaks: If you will not listen to me or live according to the Law I placed before you, ⁵ and if you will not listen to the words of my faithful prophets—I constantly send them to you, though you do not obey them!— ⁶ I will treat this house like Shiloh, and make this the city that all the nations of the earth will name when they wish a curse upon one another.' "

⁷ Now the priests, the prophets, and the all the people heard Jeremiah speak these words in the Temple of YHWH. ⁸ When Jeremiah finished speaking all that YHWH had ordered him to speak to all the people, the priests, the prophets, and the people laid hold of him and said, "You must die! ⁹ Why have you prophesied in the Name of God that this Temple will be like Shiloh, and this city will be desolate and deserted?" And all the people gathered around Jeremiah in the Temple of YHWH.

¹⁰ When the officials of Judah heard what was happening, they left their offices and went up to the Temple of YHWH and took their places at the entrance of the New Gate. ¹¹ Then the priests and the prophets said to the officials and all the people, "Jeremiah deserves to die! He has prophesied against this city, as you have heard with your own ears!"

¹² But Jeremiah replied to the people: "YHWH alone sent me to say all the things you have heard against this Temple and this city. ¹³ So now reform your behavior and your actions, and listen to the voice of YHWH your God. If you do, YHWH will relent and not bring down on you the disaster that is planned for you. ¹⁴ As for myself, I am in your hands. Do with me as you think is good and right. ¹⁵ But mark well: If you put me to death, it is innocent blood you bring upon yourselves, on this city, and on its citizens. For in truth it was YHWH who sent me to you, to speak all these things for you to hear."

¹⁶ The officials and the people then said to the priests and the prophets, "Jeremiah does not deserve to die. He spoke to us in the Name of YHWH."

¹⁷ Some of the elders of the land stood up and said to the gathered crowd, ¹⁸ "In the time of Hezekiah the ruler of Judah, Micah of Moresheth prophesied and said to all the people of Judah, 'These are the words of YHWH Omnipotent: Zion will become a ploughed field, Jerusalem a pile of ruins, and the Temple hill a wooded mound.' ¹⁹ Did Hezekiah the ruler and all Judah put him to death? Didn't Hezekiah show reverence for YHWH and seek God's favor, and did not YHWH choose not to bring about the disaster pronounced against them? But here we are about to bring disaster upon ourselves!"

²⁰ There was another who prophesied in the Name of YHWH: Uriah ben-Shemaiah, from Kiriath-jearim. He prophesied the same things against this city and this land that Jeremiah did. ²¹ When Jehoiakim and his officer and officials heard this, the ruler sought to put him to death. Uriah heard of it and fled to Egypt. ²² But Jehoiakim the ruler sent Elnathan ben-Acbor to Egypt, along with some others, ²³ and brought Uriah back from Egypt to Jehoiakim. The ruler had Uriah put to the sword and his body was thrown into the common burial ground. ²⁴ But Ahikim ben-Shaphan protected Jeremiah, so that he was not handed over to the people for execution.

²⁷⁻¹ At the beginning of the reign of Zedekiah the ruler ben-Josiah of Judah, this word from YHWH came to Jeremiah. ² This is what YHWH said to me: "Make a yoke of ropes and crossbars and put it on your neck. ³ Then send word to the rulers of Edom, Moab, Ammon, Tyre and Sidon through their envoys who came to Zedekiah ruler of Jerusalem, ⁴ and give them this message for their superiors: 'These are the words of YHWH Omnipotent, the God of Israel.' Say to your superiors: ⁵ 'It was I who with my mighty power and outstretched arm created the earth, along with its people and its animals. And I give it to whomever I please. ⁶ For now I gave all these lands to Nebuchadnezzar ruler of Babylon, my instrument, and I also made all the creatures of the wild subject to him. ⁷ All the nations will serve him, his heir, and his grandchildren until the time of his own land's destiny comes. Mighty nations and rulers will be his subjects. ⁸ Any nation or realm that will not serve Nebuchadnezzar ruler of Babylon or submit to his yoke I will punish with the sword, famine, and diseases, says YHWH, until I have completed its destruction at his hand. ⁹ So you are not to listen to your prophets, your diviners, your dreamers, your soothsayers, or your sorcerers who say to you, "You will not serve the ruler of Babylon." ¹⁰ They prophesy lies to you. If you listen, you will be carried far away from your native land. I will banish you and you will perish. ¹¹ But any nation that will submit to the yoke of the ruler of Babylon and serve him I will leave on its own land, says YHWH. Its people will cultivate it and live on it.' "

¹² I spoke to Zedekiah the ruler of Judah in the same way: "Submit your necks to the yoke of the ruler of Babylon. Serve him and the Chaldeans and you will survive. ¹³ Why should you and your people die by the sword, famine, and disease as YHWH spoke concerning any nation that chooses not to serve the ruler of Babylon? ¹⁴ Do not listen to the prophets who tell you not to serve the ruler of Babylon, for they prophesy lies to you. ¹⁵ "I did not send them," says YHWH, "and they are prophesying falsely in my Name. For this I will expel you and you will die, you and your prophets who prophesy to you."

¹⁶ Then I spoke to the priests and to all the people, and said, "Thus says YHWH: Do not heed the words of your prophets who prophesy to you and say, 'The vessels from the Temple of YHWH will soon be returned from Babylon,' for they prophesy a lie to you. ¹⁷ Do not listen to them. Subject yourselves the ruler of Babylon and live. Why should this city become a ruin? ¹⁸ If they are really prophets, and if the word of YHWH is with them, let them plead with God that the vessels remaining in the Temple of YHWH and in the residence of the ruler and in Jerusalem not be taken to Babylon. ¹⁹ For this is what YHWH says about the pillars, the Sea, the movable stand and the other furnishings left in the city, ²⁰ which Nebuchadnezzar ruler of Babylon did not remove when he deported Jeconiah ben-Jehoiakim, ruler of Judah, from Jerusalem to Babylon, together with all the officials of Judah and Jerusalem. ²¹ These are the words of YHWH Omnipotent, the God of Israel, about the things left in the Temple and the residence of the ruler of Judah and in Jerusalem. ²² They will be taken to Babylon and there they will remain until the day I come for them, says YHWH. Then I will return them and restore them to this place."

28.1 In the beginning of the reign of Zedekiah, ruler of Judah, in the fifth month of the fourth year, the prophet Hananiah ben-Azzur of Gibeon spoke to Jeremiah in the Temple, in the presence of the priests and all the people. ² He said, "YHWH, the God of Israel, says this: I will break the yoke of the ruler of Babylon. ³ Within two years I will bring back all the vessels of the Temple of YHWH which Nebuchadnezzar ruler of Babylon took. ⁴ And I will also bring back Jeconiah ben-Jehoiakim, ruler of Judah, and all the exiles of Judah who have gone to Babylon—it is YHWH who speaks. Yes, I am going to break the yoke of the ruler of Babylon!"

⁵ Jeremiah the prophet then answered the prophet Hananiah in front of the priests and all the people there in the Temple of YHWH. ⁶ "Amen!" he said. "May YHWH do so! May YHWH fulfill the words you have prophesied, and return to us from Babylon the vessels of the Temple of YHWH and all the exiles. ⁷ But listen carefully to what I'm about to say to you and all the people: ⁸ From of old, the prophets who preceded you and me prophesied war, famine, and plague for many countries and great empires. ⁹ But the prophet who prophesies peace will be recognized as having been sent by YHWH only when the prophesied words come true."

¹⁰ The prophet Hananiah then took the yoke off the neck of the prophet Jeremiah and broke it. ¹¹ In front of all the people, Hananiah said, "YHWH says this: This is how, in two years' time, I will break the yoke of Nebuchadnezzar, ruler of Babylon, and take it off the necks of all the nations." At this, the prophet Jeremiah went away.

¹² Some time after the prophet Hananiah broke the yoke from off the neck of the prophet Jeremiah, the word of YHWH came to Jeremiah and said, ¹³ "Go! Tell Hananiah this: 'It is YHWH who speaks: By breaking a wooden yoke, you forge an iron yoke. ¹⁴ For thus says YHWH Omnipotent, the God of Israel: A yoke of iron I now place on the necks of the nations serving Nebuchadnezzar, ruler of Babylon, and they will serve the ruler. Even the beasts of the field will serve the ruler of Babylon.'"

¹⁵ To the prophet Hananiah the prophet Jeremiah said, "Hear this, Hananiah: YHWH has not sent you. You have raised false expectations in this people. ¹⁶ For this, says YHWH, I will wipe you off the face of the earth. This very year you will die, because you have preached rebellion against YHWH."

¹⁷ That same year, in the seventh month, Hananiah the prophet died.

²⁹·¹ Jeremiah sent a letter from Jerusalem to Babylon to the surviving elders among the exiles, to the priests, the prophets, and all the other people Nebuchadnezzar had deported. ² This happened after Jehoiachin, together with the queen mother, the officials, the other leaders of Judah and Jerusalem, and the craftworkers and artisans departed from Jerusalem. ³ Jeremiah entrusted the letter to Elasah ben-Shaphan and to Gemariah ben-Hilkiah, whom Zedekiah ruler of Judah sent to Nebuchadnezzar ruler of Babylon. The letter read:

⁴ "Thus says YHWH Omnipotent, the God of Israel, to all the exiles I deported from Jerusalem to Babylon: ⁵ Build houses to live in. Plant gardens and eat what they grow. ⁶ Marry and raise daughters and sons. Find wives for your sons and husbands for your daughters, that they may bear daughters and sons. Multiply while you are there. Do not decrease. ⁷ Rather, seek the peace and the prosperity of the city to which I exiled you. Pray to YHWH for it, for if it prospers, you will prosper. ⁸ This is what YHWH, the God of Israel, says: Do not let the diviners and prophets among you deceive you. Don't listen to the dreams they dream, ⁹ for they lie when they prophesy in my Name. I did not send them, declares YHWH.

¹⁰ "Thus says YHWH: Only when the seventy years granted to Babylon are over will I visit you and fulfill my promise to bring you back to this place. ¹¹ I alone know my purpose for you, says YHWH, my purpose for your prosperity and my purpose not to harm you, my purpose to give you hope with a future in it. ¹² At that time you will call upon me and come and pray to me, and I will listen to you. ¹³ You will seek me and find me when you seek me wholeheartedly. ¹⁴ I will let you find me, says YHWH, and I will restore your fortunes. And I will gather you from all the nations and all the places to which I banished you, says YHWH, and restore you to the place from which I carried you into exile.

¹⁵ "You might be tempted to believe that YHWH has raised up prophets for you in Babylon. ¹⁶ Thus says YHWH concerning the ruler who sits on the judgment seat of David and all the people dwelling in this city, your fellow citizens who did not go with you into exile— ¹⁷ thus says YHWH Omnipotent: I will loose upon them the sword, famine, and plague, and I will make them like figs so rotten they are inedible. ¹⁸ I will pursue them with the sword, famine and plague, and will make them repugnant to all the realms of the earth, to be an object of cursing and horror, of derision and reproach, among all the nations where I will exile them. ¹⁹ For they did not listen to my words, says YHWH, when time and again I sent my servants the prophets.

²⁰ "Therefore, hear the word of YHWH, all you exiles whom I sent from Jerusalem to Babylon. ²¹ This is what YHWH, the God of Israel, has to say about Ahab ben-Kolaiah and Zedekiah ben-Maaseiah, who are prophesying lies to you in my Name: I will hand them over to Nebuchadnezzar ruler of Babylon, who will put them to death before your eyes. ²² And because of them this curse will be invoked by all the exiles of Judah in Babylon. They will say: 'May God treat you like Ahab and Zedekiah, whom the ruler of Babylon roasted alive!' ²³ For their conduct in Israel was an outrage. They committed adultery with their neighbor's wives. They prophesied in my Name without my authority, and what they prophesied was false. I know this and I can testify to it, says YHWH.

²⁴ "Also tell Shemaiah of Nehelam that ²⁵ YHWH, the God of Israel, says this: You sent letters in your own name to all the people in Jerusalem, to Zephaniah ben-Maaseiah the priest, and to all the other priests. You told Zephaniah, ²⁶ 'God appointed you priest in place of Jehoiada the priest, and as an official in charge of the Temple of YHWH, you have the duty to put any lunatic posing as a prophet into the stocks and the iron collar. ²⁷ Why, then, have you not restrained Jeremiah of Anathoth, who poses as a prophet to you? ²⁸ He sent to us a message in Babylon, and said, "Your exile in Babylon will be a long exile. Build houses to live in. Plant gardens and eat what they grow."' ²⁹ But when Zephaniah the priest read your letter to Jeremiah the prophet, ³⁰ this word of YHWH came to Jeremiah: ³¹ 'Send this message to all the exiles: This is what YHWH says about Shemaiah the Nehelamite—because Shemaiah prophesied to you, even though I did not send him, and has led you into believing a lie, ³² this is what YHWH says: I will most certainly punish Shemaiah the Nehelemite and his descendants. There will be no one living among this people to see the good I will do to my people, says YHWH, for he spoke rebellion against me.'"

$\mathcal{t}$he word of YHWH came to Jeremiah and said, ² "Thus says YHWH, the God of Israel: Write in a book all the words I dictate to you. ³ For the time is coming, says YHWH, when I will restore the fortunes of my people, Judah and Israel, says YHWH, and I will bring them back to take possession of the land I gave their ancestors."

⁴ These are the words YHWH spoke about Judah and Israel:

⁵ "Thus says YHWH:
I have heard a cry of panic,
of terror, not of peace.
⁶ Ask now, and see:
Can a man bear children?
Why then do I see every male gripping his loins
like a woman in labor?
Why has every face turned deadly pale?
⁷ Alas! That will be a terrible day!
There will be no other like it.
A time of anguish for Jacob,
who will succeed in the end.

⁸ "On that day, says YHWH Omnipotent, I will break the yoke from the neck of the people, and rip off their bonds. Strangers will no longer reduce them to servitude. ⁹ They will serve YHWH their God and David their ruler, whom I will raise up for them.

¹⁰ "But do not fear, my servant Jacob,
do not be dismayed, O Israel.
Thus says YHWH.
For I will rescue you from distant lands,
your descendants from lands of exile.
Jacob will return to quiet and ease,
with no one to provoke fear again.
¹¹ For I am with you, and I will rescue you.
Thus says YHWH.
I will destroy all the nations
among whom I scattered you.
But I will not destroy you.
I will punish you only as you deserve.
I will not let you go wholly unpunished.

¹² For thus says YHWH:
   your disease is incurable,
   your injury beyond healing.
¹³ There is no one to tend your wound.
   No medicine can make you whole again.
¹⁴ All your lovers have forgotten you;
   they care nothing for you.
   Yes, I struck you down like a foe,
   punished you like an enemy.
   For your guilt is immense;
   your sins are so many.
¹⁵ Why complain so over your wounds?
   Your disease is incurable.
   It was because your guilt was so great and your sins so many
   that I did all this to you.
¹⁶ But all who devour you will be devoured.
   All your foes will be exiled.
   The plunderers will be plundered
   and your oppressors will be oppressed.
¹⁷ Though you are labeled an outcast
   and no one cares for you, says YHWH,
   I will restore you to health
   and heal your wounds.
¹⁸ Thus says YHWH:
   I will return the fortunes of Jacob's tents
   and show mercy on all his dwellings.
   The city will be rebuilt upon its ruins
   and the citadel on its proper site.
¹⁹ Out of them will come the songs of thanksgiving
   and the sounds of merriment.
   I will multiply them—
   their numbers will not decrease.
   I will honor them,
   and they will not be belittled.
²⁰ Their children will live as in former times,
   their community established before me.
   I will punish all their oppressors.
²¹ Their leader will be one of their own;
   their ruler will come from among them.
   I will draw their leader near;
   the leader will be dear to me.

Thus says YHWH:

22 You will be my people
and I will be your God.
23 Watch! The storm of YHWH
will burst out in wrath,
like a sweeping desert storm
coming on the heads of evildoers.
24 The unbridled wrath of YHWH will not relent
until the intentions of God's heart are fully realized.
In days to come
you will understand.

31:1 "When that time comes, says YHWH, I will be the God of all the tribes of Israel. And they will be my people.

2 "Thus says YHWH:
The people who survive the sword
will find forgiveness in the desert.
I will come to give rest to Israel.
3 They'll say, 'YHWH appeared to us in the past, and said,
"In everlasting love I conceived you."'
And now I will continue
to show my love for you.
4 I will build you up again,
and you will stand firm, Beloved Israel.
You will take up your tambourines once more
and go forth with the crowd of merrymakers.
5 Once again you will plant vineyards
on Samaria's mountainsides.
The planters will plant
and will enjoy the fruit.
6 For the day will come when sentinels
will cry out on Ephraim's hills,
'Come, let us go up to Zion,
to YHWH.'
7 For thus says YHWH:
Sing aloud with joy for Jacob!
Hail the Head of Nations!
Make your praises heard, and say,
'YHWH, save your people, Israel's remnant!'
8 For I will bring them from the lands of the north
and gather them from the ends of the earth—

the blind and the lame
   will be among them,
along with expectant mothers and women in labor.
   They will return in vast numbers.
⁹ They will return weeping and praying.
   I will guide them in my mercy.
I will lead them beside streams of water,
   along level ground where they will not stumble.
For I am forever a mother and father to Israel,
   and Ephraim is my firstborn."

¹⁰ Hear the word of YHWH, you nations,
   proclaim it on faraway shores:
"The one who scattered Israel will gather it in,
   and watch over it as shepherds watch their flocks."
¹¹ For YHWH ransomed Jacob
   and delivered the people from a foe stronger than they.
¹² When the people arrive they will shout for joy on Zion's heights,
   radiant over God's goodness—
over the grain, wine and oil,
   over the young of the flocks and herds.
They will flourish like well watered gardens,
   and sorrow will be no more.
¹³ Then the young women will dance with joy,
   and the young men and the elderly will make merry.
"I will turn their mourning into joy;
   I will comfort them, exchanging gladness for sorrow.
¹⁴ I will satisfy the priests with the fat of the land,
   and my people their fill of the bounty," says YHWH.

¹⁵ Thus says YHWH:
"A voice is heard in Ramah,
   mourning and bitter weeping.
Rachel, weeping for her children,
   refuses to be comforted,
   for her children are no more."
¹⁶ Thus says YHWH:
"Stop your weeping,
   shed no more tears.
Your hardships will be atoned for,"
   says YHWH,

"and they will return
from the land of the enemy.
17 There is hope for your future,"
says YHWH.
18 "For I plainly heard Ephraim pleading,
'You rebuked me and I have been rebuked,
like a wild calf that has not been broken.
Take me back! Let me return!
For you are YHWH, my God.
19 Yes, I strayed off. Now I am contrite.
Now that I understand, I beat my breast.
I am ashamed and humiliated
for I bear the disgrace of my youth.'
20 Is not my child Ephraim dear to me?
Is not Ephraim the child in whom I delight?
As often as I have spoken against my child,
I think of Ephraim with tenderness.
My heart yearns for him;
surely I will have mercy on Ephraim, says YHWH.
21 Set up the road signs! Build landmarks!
Make sure of the highway, the road ahead!
Return, Beloved Israel!
Return to your villages and cities!
22 How long will you stray, faithless child?
For YHWH has created something new in the world:
Woman will encircle man.*
23 Thus says YHWH Omnipotent, the God of Israel:
Once again these words will be heard
in the land of Judah and in its villages,
when I restore their fortunes:
'May God bless you,
abode of integrity, holy mountain!'
24 Judah and all its villages,
the farmers and their shepherds,
will dwell there together.

---

* The Hebrew reads *neqebâ tesôbeb gaber* and is usually translated "a woman will encompass (or surround) a man." The meaning of the verb is uncertain, and has sparked heated debate. Some believe Jeremiah means that Israel will be so secure after the restoration that not only will women no longer need the protection of men, they will actually become men's protectors. However, to be parallel with the first part of the verse, the verb more likely means "encircle" in the sense of courtship: that so eager will Israel be to renew its relationship with God that the "wife" who broke faith (Israel) will now court her "husband" (God).

²⁵ I will give drink to the thirsty,
and satisfy all who languish."
²⁶ At this I woke up and looked around.
My sleep had been pleasant.

²⁷ "The days are surely coming, says YHWH, when I will sow Israel and Judah with the seed of people and the seed of livestock. ²⁸ And just as I watched over them to uproot, to tear down, and to overthrow, to destroy and to bring disaster, so I will watch over them to build up and to plant, says YHWH. ²⁹ In those days people will no longer say, 'The parents ate sour grapes, but it is the children's teeth that are set on edge.' ³⁰ Rather, all will die for their own sins. And only the teeth of those who eat sour grapes will be set on edge.*

³¹ "Behold, the days are coming, says YHWH, when I will establish a new covenant with the house of Israel and the house of Judah. ³² It will not be like the covenant I made with their ancestors when I took them by the hand to bring them up out of the land of Egypt—a covenant they broke, though I was their spouse, says YHWH. ³³ But this is the covenant I will make with the house of Israel after those days, says YHWH: I will put my Law in their minds and on their hearts. I will be their God, and they will be my people.

³⁴ "No longer will they need to teach one another or remind one another to listen to YHWH. All of them, high and low alike, will listen to me, says YHWH, for I will forgive their misdeeds and will remember their sins no more.

³⁵ "Thus says YHWH,
who gives the light of the sun by day
and the fixed order of the moon
and the stars for light by night,
who stirs up the sea to make its waves roar,
whose Name is YHWH:
³⁶ If I ever annulled the order of all things—
thus says YHWH—
only then would the House of Israel
cease to be a nation in my presence forever.
³⁷ Thus says YHWH:
If the heavens above could be measured,
and the foundations of the earth below could be fathomed,
only then would I reject all the descendants of Israel
because of all they have done.

---

* The old proverb says that children get blamed for their parents' wrongdoing. But when Israel is restored, says Jeremiah, all people will be responsible for their own actions alone.

Thus says YHWH.

[38] "The days are coming, says YHWH, when this city will be rebuilt for me from the tower of Hanamel to the Corner Gate. [39] The measuring line will stretch from there straight to the hill of Gareb and then turn to Goah. [40] The whole valley where dead bodies and ashes are thrown, and all the terraces out to the Kidron Valley on the east as far as the corner of the Horse Gate, will be holy to YHWH. The city will never again be uprooted and demolished."

ଓ   ଓ   ଓ

[32.1] The word that came to Jeremiah from YHWH in the tenth year of Zedekiah ruler of Judah, which was also the eighteenth year of Nebuchadnezzar.

[2] At that time the army of the ruler of Babylon was besieging Jerusalem, and the prophet Jeremiah was imprisoned in the court of the guardhouse attached to the residence of the ruler of Jerusalem. [3] Zedekiah the ruler imprisoned him after demanding, "How dare you prophesy the way you do? You say: 'These are the words of YHWH: I will surrender this city into the hands of the ruler of Babylon, who will capture it. [4] Zedekiah the ruler will not evade the hands of the Chaldeans, and will certainly be placed in the custody of the ruler of Babylon. He will speak with the ruler of Babylon face to face and view the ruler with his own eyes. [5] Nebuchadnezzar will take Zedekiah to Babylon, where he will remain until I attend to him, declares YHWH. If you fight against the Chaldeans, you will not win.'"

[6] The word of YHWH came to me* and said, [7] "Hanamel, the son of your uncle Shallum, will come to you and say, 'Buy my field in Anathtoth. As next of kin you have the right of redemption to purchase it.'' [8] And just as YHWH foretold, my cousin Hanamel came to me in the court of the guardhouse and said, "Buy my field at Anatoth in Benjamin. You have the right of redemption to purchase it as next of kin. So why not purchase it?" I knew that this was the word of YHWH.

[9] So I bought the field in Anathoth from my cousin Hanamel, and weighed out the money—seventeen shekels of silver. [10] I signed the deed and sealed it, had it witnessed and then weighed out the money on a scale. [11] I took the copies of the deed of purchase—both the sealed copy containing the terms and conditions and the unsealed copy—[12] and gave them to Baruch ben-Neriah

---

* The text here inserts "said Jeremiah," to cue the reader that it is no longer Zedekiah speaking. In English, however, this suggests that the two are speaking in dialog, whereas what follows is apparently Jeremiah's discourse to his disciples from prison.

ben-Mahseiah in the presence of my cousin Hanamel and of the witnesses who had signed the deed and all the people of Judah who happened to be in the court of the guardhouse. [13] I gave Baruch these instructions in their presence: [14] "Thus says YHWH Omnipotent, the God of Israel: Take these deeds, both this sealed deed of purchase and the unsealed deed of purchase, and put them in a clay jar so that they may be preserved for a very long time. [15] For this is what YHWH Omnipotent, the God of Israel, says: Houses, fields and vineyards will once again be purchased in this land."

[16] After I gave the deed of purchase to Baruch ben-Neriah, I said this to YHWH:

[17] "Sovereign YHWH, by your great power and your outstretched hand you made the heavens and the earth. Nothing is impossible to you. [18] You show constant love to the thousandth generation, but punish children for the sins of their parents. Great and Almighty God whose Name is YHWH Omnipotent, [19] wonderful are your purposes and mighty are your deeds. Your eyes can see all the ways of mortals. You judge everyone according to conduct and deed. [20] You worked miraculous signs and wonders in Egypt and do the same to this day in Israel and among all people; your renown continues to this day. [21] You brought your people up out of Egypt with signs and wonders, with a strong hand and an outstretched arm, and with great terror. [22] Then you gave them this land you had sworn to give to their ancestors, a land flowing with milk and honey. [23] In due course they came in and took possession of it. But they did not obey you or follow your Law. They did not do what you had commanded them to do. So you brought all this disaster upon them.

[24] "See how the siege ramps are erected to take the city. The city, faced with sword, famine and plague, is now at the mercy of the Chaldeans attacking it. What you predicted is now a fact, as you can now see. [25] And even though the city will fall into the hands of the Chaldeans, yet you, Sovereign YHWH, said to me, 'Buy the field for money and have the transaction witnessed.'"

[26] Then the word of YHWH came to Jeremiah: [27] "I am YHWH, the God of all living creatures. Is anything impossible to me? [28] Therefore, thus says YHWH: I am going to give this city into the hands of the Chaldeans and into the hands of Nebuchadnezzar of Babylon, who will capture it. [29] The Chaldeans attacking this city will take it and set it on fire. They will burn it down along with the houses upon whose roofs offerings were made to Ba'al and libations were poured out to other gods, provoking my wrath.

[30] "For the people of Israel and the people of Judah did nothing but evil in my sight from the time of their youth. Indeed, the people of Israel did nothing but provoke my anger by their idolatry, says YHWH. [31] For this city has so inflamed my anger and my fury from the time it was built until to-

day, that I must remove it from my sight. [32] The people of Israel and Judah provoked me by all the evil they did—they, their rulers and officials, their priests and prophets, the people of Judah and the residents of Jerusalem. [33] They turned their backs on me, not their faces. Though I persistently instructed them, they refused to listen or respond to discipline. [34] They defiled my Temple by setting up their abominations and idols. [35] They built shrines of Ba'al in the Valley of Ben-hinnom. There they sacrificed their children to Molech. I never commanded them to do such a thing; it never entered my mind that they would carry out such an abomination and bring such great guilt upon Judah.

[36] "You are saying about this city, 'By the sword, by famine, and by plague it will be handed into the hands of the ruler of Babylon';* but this is what YHWH the God of Israel says: [37] Surely I will gather them from all the lands to which I banished them while in my furious anger and great wrath. I will bring them back to this place and allow them to live in security. [38] They will be my people, and I will be their God. [39] I will give them a singleness of heart and one way of life that they may worship me at all times, for their own good and for the good of their children after them. [40] I will make an everlasting covenant with them. And I will never cease in my effort for their good. I will put an awe of me into their hearts, so that they will never turn from me. [41] I will rejoice in doing good for them, and I will plant them firmly in this land in faithfulness, with all my heart and all my soul. [42] Thus says YHWH: Just as I brought this great disaster down upon this people, so will I bring upon them all the good fortune I now promise them. [43] Fields will be purchased in this land of which you say, 'It is a wasteland, without people or animals. It has been given over to the Chaldeans.' [44] Fields will be purchased, deeds will be signed, sealed, and witnessed in the land of Benjamin, in the places around Jerusalem, in the cities of Judah, of the hill country, of the Shephelah and of the Negev. For I will restore their fortunes, says YHWH."

[33:1] The word came to Jeremiah a second time while he was still imprisoned in the court of the guardhouse.

[2] "Thus says YHWH who created the earth, God who formed it and established it, whose Name is YHWH. [3] Call to me and I will answer you and tell you great and wondrous things of which you are still unaware.

[4] "For this is what YHWH, the God of Israel, says about the houses of this city and the houses of the rulers of Judah which are torn down, about the siege works and the sword [5] and the Chaldean attackers who leave the

---

* YHWH here seems to be implying that Jeremiah is not speaking God's words or is telling only part of the story, when in fact this prophecy was part of YHWH's message to Jeremiah in 14:12.

houses filled with corpses: I struck them down in anger and rage, and hid my face from this city for all the evil done there.

⁶ "Yet I will bring recovery and healing. I will heal Judah and Israel and I will let them enjoy enduring peace and security. ⁷ I will restore the fortunes of Judah and the fortunes of Israel, and rebuild them as once they were. ⁸ I will cleanse them of all their sins against me, and I will forgive all the guilt of their sins of rebellion against me. ⁹ And this city will bring praise to my Name—praise and glory before all the nations of the world that hear of all the good things I do for it. They will be filled with awe and wonder at the abundant prosperity and peace I provide for it.

¹⁰ "Thus says YHWH: you say of this place, 'It lies in ruins, lacking both people or animals throughout the towns of Judah and the streets of Jerusalem. All of it is a wasteland inhabited by neither people nor animals.' ¹¹ Yet in this place there will be heard once more the sounds of joy and gladness, the voices of bride and bridegroom. Here too will be heard the shouting of voices, 'Praise YHWH Omnipotent, for our God is a good God, whose love endures forever,' as they offer praise and thanksgiving in the Temple. For I will restore the fortunes of this land as they were before, says YHWH.

¹² "Thus says YHWH: In this place and in all its towns, now ruined and sheltering neither people nor animals, once again there will be pastures for the shepherds to rest their flocks. ¹³ In the towns of the hill country, of the Shephelal and of the Negev, in the land of Benjamin, in the places surrounding Jerusalem, and in the towns of Judah, flocks will once again pass under the hand of the shepherd who counts them, says YHWH.

¹⁴ "The days are surely coming, says YHWH, when I will bestow on Israel and Judah all the blessings I promised them. ¹⁵ In those days and at that time I will raise up a righteous branch from the line of David, who will bring justice and integrity to the land. ¹⁶ In those days Judah will be safe and Jerusalem will be secure. They will call the land, 'YHWH is our Justice.'

¹⁷ "For thus says YHWH: David will never lack a successor on the judgment seat of Israel. ¹⁸ Nor will there ever be lacking a levitical priest to present whole offerings, to burn grain offerings and to make other offerings every day."

¹⁹ The word of YHWH came to Jeremiah and said, ²⁰ "Thus says YHWH: It would be as unthinkable to annul the covenant I made with the day and with the night, to make them fall out of their proper order, ²¹ as to annul my covenant with my servant David, so that he would have none of his line to sit on the judgment seat. And it would be unthinkable to annul my covenant with the levitical priests who minister to me. ²² Just as the stars of the sky cannot be counted and the sands of the sea cannot be measured,

so I will increase the offspring of my servant David, and the Levites who minister to me."

²³ The word of YHWH came to Jeremiah and said, ²⁴ "Have you heard what these people say? 'YHWH chose two families* and eventually rejected them.' They hold my people in such contempt that they no longer consider them as a nation! ²⁵ Thus says YHWH: As certain as I established my covenant with day and night—the very laws of heaven and earth—²⁶ so too I would never reject the descendants of Leah, Rachel, and Jacob, and of my servant David. I will never fail to choose a descendant of David as ruler over the descendants of Sarah and Abraham, Rebecca and Issac, and Leah and Rachel and Jacob. I will restore their fortunes and I will have mercy on them."

34:1 The word that came to Jeremiah from YHWH, when Nebuchadnezzar the ruler of Babylon, his army, all the realms and all the subjects of his empire were at war with Jerusalem and its surrounding villages:

² "Thus says YHWH, the God of Israel: Go and speak to Zedekiah ruler of Judah, and say, 'Thus says YHWH: I will turn this city over to the ruler of Babylon, who will burn it to the ground. ³ You yourself will not escape—your capture is certain and you will be handed over to him. You will see the ruler of Babylon eye to eye, you will speak with him face to face, and you will be sent to Babylon. ⁴ Yet hear the word of YHWH, Zedekiah, ruler of Judah! This is God's word: You will not die by the sword. ⁵ You will die in peace. And just as people made funeral fires in honor of your ancestors who preceded you, so will a funeral fire be built in your honor and the lament will be sounded, "Alas, Ruler!" I myself make this promise, says YHWH.' "

⁶ Then the prophet Jeremiah spoke all these words to Zedekiah the ruler of Judah, in Jerusalem, ⁷ when the army of the ruler of Babylon was fighting against Jerusalem and all the villages of Judah that were left, Lachish and Azekah—for these were the only fortified villages that remained.

⁸ This is the word that came to Jeremiah from YHWH, after Zedekiah the ruler made a covenant with the people, proclaiming liberty to all people in Jerusalem. ⁹ All were to set free any Hebrews in bondage, female and male, so that no Jew should oppress another.* ¹⁰ And they obeyed, all the officials,

---

* It is likely that Israel and Judah are the two families in view here, since together they form the single nation spoken of in the next sentence. Some scholars, however, identify the two families as those of David and Levi, since they are mentioned in previous verses; others see them as the descendants of Jacob and David, both of them mentioned in verse 26.

military officers, and residents, entering into an agreement that they would set free their bonded workers, female and male, and never return them to bondage. ¹¹ Later, however, the covenanters changed their minds and took back the bonded workers they had set free and put them into bondage again.

¹² YHWH said to Jeremiah, ¹³ "This is what YHWH, the God of Israel, says: I made a Covenant with your ancestors when I brought you out of Egypt, out of the land of bondage. I said: ¹⁴ 'Every seventh year you must free any Hebrews who sold themselves to you. After they serve their six years, you must let them go free.' But your ancestors did not listen to me or obey me.

¹⁵ "You repented recently and did what is just in my sight: You proclaimed liberty to one another, and you made a covenant with me in the Temple that bears my Name. ¹⁶ But then you turned around and profaned my Name. Each of you forced all the people you had freed, female and male, to become your bonded workers again.

¹⁷ "Therefore, thus says YHWH: You did not obey me by granting liberty to your neighbors and friends. Now I am going to grant you liberty, says YHWH—liberty to die by the sword, by pestilence, and by plague. I will make you appalling to all the realms of the earth. ¹⁸ And to whoever broke my covenant and did not keep the terms of the covenant made before me, I will treat you like the calf that was cut in two so that all could pass between the halves.† ¹⁹ The leaders of Judah and Jerusalem, all the officials, the priests, and all the people of the land who walked between the two halves of the calf, ²⁰ I will hand over to their enemies who seek their lives. Their corpses will become food for the birds of the air and the wild animals of the earth. ²¹ And as for Zedekiah ruler of Judah and his officials, I will hand them over to their enemies who seek their lives—to the army of the ruler of Babylon, which is now raising the siege. ²² I will give the command, says YHWH, and bring the Babylonians back to this city. They will attack it, capture it, and burn it to the ground. I will lay waste the towns of Judah so that no one can dwell there."

³⁵:¹ The word that came to Jeremiah from YHWH during the reign of Jehoiakim the ruler ben-Josiah of Judah: ² "Go to the Rechabite family and

---

* The use of "Hebrew" and "Jew" in the text is deliberate on Jeremiah's part. "Hebrew" is used to distinguish the people of Israel from foreigners; the word *'ibriy* means "one from beyond" or "from the other side" (possibly the other side of the Euphrates, but if the name is Canaanite in origin, it may mean the other side of the Jordan); here it indicates that everyone of Jewish descent—either from Judah in the south, or refugees from what used to be Israel in the north—would be freed, but not foreign-born slaves. "Jew," *yehudiy*, means "from the family of Judah" and in *Jeremiah* more specifically describes the people of the southern tribes.

† Genesis 15 introduces this common Near Eastern practice of cutting up a calf and solemnly walking between the halves in order to ratify a covenant or treaty. It involved swearing an oath by invoking the name of the god, and pronouncing self-maledictory curses on themselves should they fail to keep the covenant—essentially saying, "May we have a fate like this calf if we break the agreement."

invite them to come to one of the rooms of the Temple of YHWH and give them wine to drink."

³ So I took Jaazaniah ben-Jeremiah ben-Habaziniah and his off-spring—the whole Rechabite community— ⁴ and I brought them into the Temple of YHWH , into the room of the heirs of Hanan ben-Igdaliah, a man of God, which was near the officials' rooms, above the room of Maaseiah ben-Shallum, keeper of the threshold. ⁵ Then I set before the Rechabites cups and pitchers full of wine. I invited them to have some wine. ⁶ But they replied: "We will not drink your wine, for our ancestor, Jonadab ben-Rechab commanded us: 'Neither you nor your descendants must ever drink wine. ⁷ Nor must you ever build houses, sow seed or plant vineyards. You must never have any of these things. You must live in tents. Then you will live a long time in the land where you are nomads.' ⁸ We have obeyed everything our ancestor Jonadab ben-Rechab commanded us. Neither we nor our spouses nor our daughters and sons have ever drunk wine ⁹ or built houses to live in or had vineyards, fields or crops. ¹⁰ We have lived in tents and have fully obeyed and observed everything our ancestor Jonadab commanded us. ¹¹ But when Nebuchadnezzar the ruler of Babylon invaded our land, we said, 'Let us go to Jerusalem to escape the Babylonian and Aramaean armies.' So we have remained in Jerusalem."

¹² The word of YHWH came to Jeremiah, and said: ¹³ "This is what YHWH Omnipotent, the God of Israel, says: Go! Proclaim this to the people of Judah and the people of Jerusalem, 'Will you never learn your lesson and obey my words?' says YHWH. ¹⁴ Jonadab ben-Rechab ordered his offspring not to drink wine and this command has been carried out. To this day they do not drink wine, for they obey the command of their ancestor. But I spoke to you again and again, and you have not obeyed me. ¹⁵ Again and again I sent you my servants the prophets. They told you, 'Each of you must turn from your sinful ways and amend what you do. Do not follow other gods to serve them, and then you will live in the land I gave to you and to your ancestors.' But you neither listened to me nor obeyed me. ¹⁶ The descendants of Jonadab ben-Rechab carried out the command their ancestors gave them, but these people have not obeyed me.

¹⁷ "Therefore, this is what YHWH, God Omnipotent, the God of Israel, says: Listen! I am going to bring on Judah and on everyone living in Jerusalem every disaster I pronounced against them. I spoke to them, but they did not listen. I called to them, but they did not answer."

¹⁸ Then Jeremiah said to the family of the Rechabites: "This is what YHWH Omnipotent, the God of Israel, says: 'You obeyed the command of your ancestor Jonadab and have followed all his instructions and have done ev-

erything he commanded. ¹⁹ Therefore, this is what YHWH Omnipotent, the God of Israel says: Jonadab ben-Rechab will never fail to have a descendant stand before me.' "

³⁶:¹ In the fourth year of Jehoiakim ben-Josiah of Judah, this word came to Jeremiah from YHWH: ² "Take a scroll and write on it all the words I spoke to you about Jerusalem, Judah, and all the nations from the day I first spoke to you during the reign of Josiah down to today. ³ Perhaps when the house of Judah hears of all the disasters I intend to inflict on its people, all of them will turn from the sinful ways, so that I may forgive their iniquity and their sin."

⁴ So Jeremiah called Baruch ben-Neriah, and while Jeremiah dictated, Barach wrote down on a scroll all the words YHWH spoke to him. ⁵ Then Jeremiah instructed Baruch: "Since I am prohibited from entering the Temple of YHWH,* ⁶ I want you to go there on a fast day and read aloud to the people all the words of YHWH from the scroll you wrote as I dictated. Read them also to all the people of Judah who come in from the towns. ⁷ Perhaps they will offer their prayers to YHWH and all of them will turn from their evil ways, for great is the anger and wrath with which YHWH threatens this people." ⁸ And Baruch ben-Neriah did all that Jeremiah had ordered about reading from the scroll the words of YHWH in the Temple of YHWH.

⁹ In the fifth year of Jehoiakim ben-Josiah the ruler of Judah, in the ninth month, all the people of Jerusalem and all the people who came in from the towns of Judah proclaimed a fast before YHWH. ¹⁰ Then in the Temple of YHWH Baruch read aloud to all the people Jeremiah's words from the scroll. Baruch read them from the room of Gemariah, son of the adjutant general Shaphan, which was in the upper court at the entrance of the New Gate of YHWH's Temple.

¹¹ When Micaiah ben-Gemariah ben-Shaphan heard all God's words from the scroll, ¹² he went down to the house of the ruler and entered the secretary's room. All the officials were meeting there: Elishama the scribe, Delaiah ben-Shemaiah, Elnathan ben-Achbor, Gemariah ben-Shaphan, Zedekiah ben-Hananiah, and all the other officials.

¹³ After Micaiah told them everything he had heard Baruch read to the people from the scroll, ¹⁴ all the officials sent Jehudi ben-Nethaniah ben-Shelemiah ben-Cushi to say to Baruch, "Bring the scroll from which you read to the people and follow me."

---

* While it is never made explicit in the text, some commentators believe that Jeremiah's banning from the Temple was for the scathing sermons he had delivered there earlier (see chapters 7 and 26).

When Baruch ben-Neriah appeared before them with the scroll, ¹⁵ they said, "Take a seat and read it to us," which he did. ¹⁶ When they heard what was written down, they turned to one another in alarm, and said to Baruch, "We certainly must report this to the ruler."

¹⁷ Then they asked Baruch how he had come to write all this. ¹⁸ He explained, "Jeremiah dictated every word of it to me, and I wrote it down with ink on a scroll." ¹⁹ And the officials said to him, "You and Jeremiah must go into hiding so that no one can know where you are."

²⁰ Once they deposited the scroll in the room of Elishama the chief adviser, they went to the court and reported the whole affair to the ruler. ²¹ Then the ruler sent Jehudi to fetch the scroll from the room of Elishama the chief adviser, who read it aloud in the presence of the ruler and the officials attending him. ²² Since it was the ninth month of the year, the ruler was sitting in his winter apartments before a brazier with a fire in it. ²³ Each time Jehudi read three or four columns of the scroll, the ruler cut them off with a pen knife and threw them into the brazier. He continued to do this until the entire scroll was burned up in the brazier. ²⁴ Neither the ruler nor any of his attendants showed any signs of alarm, nor did they tear their clothes.* ²⁵ Elnathan, Delaiah and Gemariah urged the ruler not to destroy the scroll, but he would not listen to them. ²⁶ Instead, the ruler commanded his son Jerahmeel, along with Seraiah ben-Azeiel and Shelemiah ben-Abdeel, to arrest Baruch the scribe and Jeremiah the prophet. But YHWH had hidden them.

²⁷ After the ruler burned the scroll containing the words that Jeremiah had dictated to Baruch, the word of YHWH came to Jeremiah: ²⁸ "Take another scroll and write down all the words that were on the first scroll, which Jehoiakim ruler of Judah burned up. ²⁹ And tell Jehoiakim ruler of Judah, 'This is what YHWH says: You burned the first scroll and said, "Why did you write on it that the ruler of Babylon would certainly come and destroy this land and cut both people and animals from it?"'

³⁰ "Therefore, this is what YHWH says about Jehoiakim ruler of Judah: He will have no one to sit on the judgment seat of David. His body will be thrown out and exposed to the heat by day and the cold at night. ³¹ I will punish him, his children and his officials for their corruption. I will bring down on them, the people living in Jerusalem, and the people of Judah every disaster I pronounced against them, because they did not listen."

³² So Jeremiah took another scroll and gave it to the scribe Baruch ben-Neriah, and as Jeremiah dictated, Baruch wrote down all the words of the

---

* A common sign of grief or outrage.

scroll that Jehoiakim ruler of Judah had burned in the brazier. And many similar words were added to them.

37:1 Zedekiah ben-Josiah was made ruler of Judah by Nebuchadnezzar ruler of Babylon. He reigned in place of Jehoiachin ben-Jehoiakim. 2 But neither Zedekiah nor his attendants nor the people of the land paid any attention to the words of their God spoken through the prophet Jeremiah.

3 But Zedekiah the ruler sent Jehucal ben-Shelemiah with the priest Zephaniah ben-Maaseiah to Jeremiah the prophet with this message: "Please pray to YHWH our God for us."

4 At the time Jeremiah was free to move among the people, for he had not yet been imprisoned. 5 Meanwhile, Pharaoh's army had marched out of Egypt, and when the Babylonians besieging Jerusalem learned about the Egyptians, they withdrew from Jerusalem.

6 Then the word of YHWH came to Jeremiah the prophet: 7 "Thus says YHWH, the God of Israel: Tell the ruler of Judah, who sent you to consult me, that this army of Pharaoh's that marched out to come to your aid will retreat to its own land—to Egypt— 8 and the Babylonians will return to the attack on this city. They will capture it and burn it to the ground.

9 "Thus says YHWH: Do not lie to yourself that the Babylonians will leave. They will not. 10 Even if you defeated the whole Babylonian army attacking you, and the only troops left were the wounded in their tents, the wounded would regroup and burn down this city."

11 After the Babylonian army withdrew from Jerusalem because of Pharaoh's army, 12 Jeremiah made plans to leave the city and go to the territory of Benjamin to take possession of his property there. 13 But when he reached the Benjamin Gate, a captain of the guard named Irijah ben-Shelemiah ben-Hananiah arrested him, and said, "You are deserting to the Babylonians."

14 "That is not true," Jeremiah said, "I am not deserting to the Babylonians."

But Irijah, refusing to listen, took Jeremiah to the officials. 15 They were furious with Jeremiah, and had him beaten and imprisoned in the house of Jonathan the scribe—it had been turned into a prison. 16 Jeremiah was thrown into a pit-cell in the dungeon, where he remained for many days.

17 Zedekiah the ruler had Jeremiah brought before him in the ruler's residence. "Is there any word from YHWH?" asked Zedekiah.

"Yes, there is," replied the prophet; "you will be handed over to the ruler of Babylon." 18 Jeremiah then asked, "What crime did I commit against you, your officials or your people, that you would have me thrown into prison?

[19] Where are your prophets who prophesied to you, 'The ruler of Babylon will not attack you or this land'? [20] But now please hear me, sovereign ruler. Be good enough to hear my plea, and do not send me back to the house of Jonathan the scribe, for I will die there."

[21] Zedekiah the ruler then gave orders for Jeremiah to be confined in the courtyard of the guard and given a daily ration of one loaf of bread from the Street of the Bakers as long as there was bread in the city. So Jeremiah remained in the courtyard of the guard.

[38:1] But Shephatiah ben-Mattan, Gedaliah ben-Pashhur, Jucal ben-Shelemiah and Pashhur ben-Malchiah heard what Jeremiah was telling the people: [2] "Thus says YHWH: All who stay in the city will die by the sword, by pestilence or by plague. But all who go over to the Babylonians will live. You will escape with your life. You will live. [3] Thus says YHWH: This city is certain to fall into the hands of the army of the ruler of Babylon and be captured."

[4] Then the officials said to the ruler, "The prophet must be put to death. His words are demoralizing the soldiers left in the city, as well as the populace. He is seeking not what is best for them, but what is worst."

[5] "Do as you wish," Zedekiah answered. "I can't do anything to stop you."

[6] So they took Jeremiah and put him into the cistern in the courtyard of the guard, letting him down with ropes. The cistern held no water, only mud, and Jeremiah sank into the mud.

[7] But when Ebed-melech the Ethiopian, a eunuch in the ruler's house, learned that Jeremiah had been imprisoned in the cistern, [8] he went to the ruler, who was sitting at the Benjamin Gate. [9] "Your majesty," he said, "these officials are acting viciously in their treatment of Jeremiah. They threw him into a cistern where he will starve to death, for there is no more bread in the city."

[10] The ruler instructed Ebed-melech the Ethopian to take thirty attendants and pull him out of the cistern before he died.* [11] So Ebed-melech took the thirty attendants and went to a room in the house of the ruler. They took some old rags and worn clothes from the room and let them down with ropes to Jeremiah in the cistern. [12] Ebed-melech the Ethiopian said to Jeremiah, "Put these old rags and worn-out clothes under your arms to pad the ropes." Jeremiah did as instructed, [13] and he was pulled up with ropes and lifted out of the cistern. And Jeremiah remained in the courtyard of the guard.

[14] Then Zedekiah the ruler sent for the prophet Jeremiah and had him brought to the third entrance of the Temple of YHWH. "I am going to ask you something," the ruler said to Jeremiah. "Do not hide anything from me."

---

* Some translations give the number as three rather than thirty, under the assumption that the text has a scribal error; but we believe that the Hebrew is correct, and that it is likely the larger number was needed to protect Jeremiah and Ebed-melech from any counter-measures from the officials.

¹⁵ Jeremiah said to Zedekiah, "If I give you an answer, won't you kill me? Even if I did counsel you, you wouldn't listen to me."

¹⁶ Then Zedekiah the ruler secretly swore an oath to Jeremiah, "As YHWH lives, who gave us our lives, I will not put you to death or hand you over to these men who seek your life."

¹⁷ Then Jeremiah said to Zedekiah, "Thus says YHWH, the God Omnipotent, the God of Israel: Only if you surrender to the officers of the ruler of Babylon will you live and this city will not be burned to the ground. You and your family will survive. ¹⁸ If, however, you do not surrender to the officers of the ruler of Babylon, the city will be turned over the Babylonians and they will burn it down to the ground. And you yourself will not escape from their hands."

¹⁹ Zedekiah the ruler said to Jeremiah, "I fear the people of Judah who deserted to the Babylonians, for I might be handed over to them and they would abuse me."

²⁰ Jeremiah replied, "They will not hand you over. Obey YHWH by doing what I tell you. Then it will go well with you and your life will be spared. ²¹ But if you refuse to surrender, this is what YHWH revealed to me: ²² All the women left in the house of the ruler of Judah will be brought out to the officials of the ruler of Babylon. Those women will say to you:

'Those who claimed to be your friends
  misled you and conquered you.
Now that your feet are stuck in the mud,
  they have turned and abandoned you.'

²³ "Then all the women and the children will be led out to the Babylonians and you yourself will not escape. You will seized by the ruler of the Babylonians and this city will be burned to the ground."

²⁴ Then Zedekiah said to Jeremiah, "Don't let anyone know of this conversation, or you may die. ²⁵ If the officials get word that I talked with you, and they come to you and say, 'Tell us what you said to the ruler, and what the ruler said to you—don't hide anything, or we will kill you,' ²⁶ then tell them, 'I was pleading with the ruler not to send me back to Jonathans's house to die there.'"

²⁷ The officials came and questioned Jeremiah, and he told them what the ruler had told him what to say. So they chose not to question him further, because no one had overheard the conversation with the ruler. ²⁸ Jeremiah remained in the courtyard of the guard until the day Jerusalem was captured.

³⁹·¹ In the ninth year of Zedekiah ruler of Judah, in the tenth month, Nebuchadnezzar ruler of Babylon marched with his whole army against

Jerusalem and besieged it. ² On the ninth day of the fourth month of the eleventh year of Zedekiah's reign, the city wall was breached. ³ With Jerusalem captured, all the officials of the ruler of Babylon came and took their quarters at the Middle Gate: Nergal-Sharezer of Samgar, Nebo-Sarsekim, a ranking officer, and Nergalsarezer, the commander of the frontier troops, and all the officials of the ruler of Babylon. ⁴ When Zedekiah ruler of Judah saw them, he and his armed escort fled. They left the city after dark by way of the ruler's garden, through the gate between the two walls, and headed toward the Jordan Valley.

⁵ But the Babylonian army, in pursuit, overtook Zedekiah on the plains of Jericho. The captors took the ruler to Nebuchadnezzar ruler of Babylon at Riblah in the land of Hamath, where they sentenced him. ⁶ The ruler of Babylon had Zedekiah's heirs executed before his eyes and killed all of Zedekiah's officials. ⁷ Then he blinded Zedekiah, had him bound with bronze shackles, and took him to Babylon.

⁸ The Babylonians burned the ruler's residence and the houses of the people. Then they tore down the walls of Jerusalem. ⁹ Then Nebuzaradan, the captain of the guard, deported to Babylon those remaining in the city, along with the remaining artisans, and the deserters who swore allegiance to Babylon.* ¹⁰ He left behind only the poorest people, who possessed nothing at all, leaving to them the vineyards and the fields.

¹¹ Nebuchadnezzar the ruler of Babylon gave these orders concerning Jeremiah to Nebuzaradan commander of the guard: ¹² "Take custody of him and take good care of him. Let no harm come to him, and do for him whatever he asks." ¹³ So Nebuzaradan the captain of the guard sent Nebushazban the eunuch, Nergalsarezer the commander of the frontier troops, and all the chief officers of the ruler of Babylon ¹⁴ to fetch Jeremiah from the courtyard of the guard. They handed him over to Ahikam ben-Shaphan to take him back to his home. So he remained among his own.

¹⁵ While Jeremiah was imprisoned, the word of YHWH came to him in the courtyard of the guard: ¹⁶ "Go! Tell Ebed-Melech the Ethiopian: 'Thus says YHWH Omnipotent, the God of Israel: I will fulfill my words against this city, prophesying ruin, not prosperity. At that time my words will be fulfilled before your eyes. ¹⁷ But I will rescue you on that day, says YHWH, and you will not be handed over to those you fear. ¹⁸ I will save you. And you will not fall by the sword. You will escape with your life, for you put your trust in me, says YHWH.' "

---

* It is common in populations that face occupation or deportation for a portion of the people to change allegiances and defect to the other side of the conflict. Here the deserters are also being taken to Babylon, but there they will be treated more humanely than the other prisoners and exiles.

⁴⁰:¹ A message came from YHWH concerning Jeremiah.

Nebuzaradan commander of the guard had taken him in chains to Ramah together with the other captives from Jerusalem and Judah who were being deported to Babylon. ² When the commander caught up to Jeremiah, he said, "YHWH your God decreed this disaster, ³ and now YHWH brought it about, and did what had been prophesied, for all of you sinned against YHWH and disobeyed God's voice. Consequently all these events occurred. ⁴ But as for you, Jeremiah, I am removing the chains from your wrists. Come with me to Babylon, and I will look after you. On the other hand, if you care not to come with me, very well. The whole land lies before you. Go wherever you consider it good and right to go. ⁵ If you remain, you can always return to Gedaliah ben-Ahikim ben-Shaphan, whom the ruler of Babylon appointed governor of the towns of Judah, and stay with him among the people. Or go wherever you consider it good and right for you to go."

Then the commander gave Jeremiah provisions and a gift and let him go. ⁶ So Jeremiah returned to Gedaliah ben-Ahikam at Mizpah, and stayed with him among the people who remained behind in the land.

⁷ When the defeated leaders and their troops who were dispersed in open country learned that the ruler of Babylon had appointed Gedaliah ben-Ahikim as governor over the land and put him in charge of the children, women and men who were the poorest in the land and had not been taken off into exile to Babylon, ⁸ they went to Gelaliah at Mizpah—Ishmael ben-Nethaniah, brothers Johanan and Jonathan ben-Kareah, Seraiah ben-Tanhumeth, the heirs of Ephai the Netophathite, and Jaazaniah ben-Maacathite and their followers. ⁹ Gedaliah ben-Ahikim ben-Shaphan took an oath to reassure them and their followers: "Don't be afraid to serve the Babylonians," he said. "Settle down in the land, serve the ruler of Babylon and all will go well with you. ¹⁰ I will stay at Mizpah to represent you to the Babylonians who come to us, but you are to harvest the wine, summer fruit and oil, and store them in your vessels. Then settle down in the towns you occupy."

¹¹When all the Judeans in Moab, Ammon, Edom, and all the other countries heard that the Babylonian ruler had left a remnant in Judah and appointed Gedaliah ben-Aikam ben-Shaphan as governor over them, ¹² they all came back to the land of Judah, to Gedaliah at Mizhah, from all the countries to which they had dispersed. And they harvested an abundance of wine and summer fruit.

¹³ Johanan ben-Kareah and all the captains of the armed bands in open country came to Gedaliah at Mizpah ¹⁴ and said, "Do you realize that Baalis, the ruler of the Ammonites, has sent Ishmael ben-Nethaniah to assassinate you?" But Gedaliah ben-Ahikam did not believe it.

¹⁵ Then Johanan ben-Kareah spoke privately with Gedaliah in Mizpah, "Let me go, unbeknown to anyone else, and kill Ishmael ben-Nethaniah. Why should he assassinate you and cause all the people of Judah who are gathering around you to be scattered and the remnant of Judah to be lost?"

¹⁶ But Gedaliah ben-Ahikam said to Johanan ben-Kareah, "Don't do such a thing! What you say about Ishmael is a lie!"

41:1 Yet in the seventh month, Ishmael ben-Nethaniah ben-Elishama, who was related to the deceased ruler and had been one the ruler's officers, came with ten companions to Gedaliah ben-Ahikam at Mizpah. While they were eating together there, ² Ishmael ben-Nethaniah rose and assassinated Gedaliah ben-Ahikam ben-Shaphan, whom the Babylonian ruler had appointed governor of the land. ³ Ishmael also murdered all the people of Judah who were with Gedaliah at Mizpah, as well as the Babylonian soldiers stationed there.

⁴ The next day, before anyone learned of it, ⁵ eighty people came from Shechem, Shiloh, and Samaria, bringing grain offerings and incense with them to the Temple of YHWH. They had shaved their heads, torn their clothes, and cut themselves. ⁶ Ishmael ben-Nethaniah went out from Mizpah to meet them, weeping as he went, and when he met them, said, "Come to Gedaliah ben-Ahikam." ⁷ When they entered the city, Ishmael ben-Nethaniah and his companions started killing them and threw their bodies into a cistern. ⁸ But ten of them said to Ishmael, "Don't kill us! We have wheat, barley, oil, and honey, hidden in a field." So he let them alone and did not murder them with the others.

⁹ The cistern into which he threw the bodies of those he killed was the large one which Asa the ruler had dug when he was threatened by Baasha ruler of Israel, and this Ishmael ben-Nethanial filled with the murdered. ¹⁰ Then Ishmael rounded up the rest of the people in Mizpah: the ruler's daughters along with the others who were left behind, over whom Nebuzaradan commander of the guard had appointed Gedaliah ben-Ahikam governor. It was with these people that Ishmael set out to cross over to the Ammonites.

¹¹ When Johanan ben-Kareah and all the captains of the armed bands heard of the crimes committed by Ishmael ben-Nethaniah, ¹² they mustered their followers and set out to attack him. They caught up with him near the great pool of Gibeon. ¹³ At the sight of Johanan ben-Kareah, all the leaders and the forces with them, all the people with Ishmael were beside themselves with joy. ¹⁴ All the people whom Ishmael had led away from Mizpah turned around and went over to Johanan ben-Kareah. ¹⁵ But Ishmael ben-Nethaniah escaped from Johanan with eight of his followers and fled to the Ammonites.

¹⁶ Then Johanan ben-Kareah and all the captains who were with him led away all the survivors from Mizpah whom he had rescued from Ishmael ben-Nethaniah after the assassination of Gelaliah ben-Ahikam: the women, the children, the court officials, and the soldiers he had brought from Gibeon. ¹⁷ And they set out, stopping at Geruth Kimham near Bethlehem on the way to Egypt ¹⁸ to escape the Babylonians. For they feared the Babylonians because of Ishmael ben-Nethaniah, who had murdered Gedaliah ben-Ahikam, governor of the land who had been appointed by the ruler of Babylon.

⁴²:¹ Then all the captains of the armed bands, Johanan ben-Kareah and Azariah ben-Hoshaiah and all the people, the least to the greatest, approached ² Jeremiah saying, "Please listen to our request. Pray to YHWH for this entire remnant. For as you now see, though we were once many, now that there are few of us left. ³ Pray that YHWH will tell us what we should do and where we should go."

⁴ Jeremiah replied, "I hear what you say. Yes, I will pray to YHWH your God as you request. I will tell you everything YHWH your God says and will keep nothing back from you."

⁵ Then they said to Jeremiah, "May YHWH be a faithful and true witness against us if we do not do exactly what YHWH sends you to tell us. ⁶ Whether it is favorable to us or not, we will obey YHWH to whom we send you, so that it will go well for us, for we will obey YHWH."

⁷ Ten days later the word of YHWH came to Jeremiah. ⁸ So he called together Johanan ben-Jareah and all the captains of the armed bands who were with him and all the people from the least to the greatest. ⁹ He said to them, "This is what YHWH the God of Israel to whom you sent me to present your petition, says: ¹⁰ 'If you remain in this land, I will build you up and not tear you down. I will plant you and not uproot you, for I have grieved over the disaster I inflicted on you. ¹¹ Do not be afraid of the ruler of Babylon, whom you now fear, says YHWH, for I am with you to rescue you and to liberate you from his power. ¹² I will show you compassion so that he too will have compassion on you, and will let you remain in this land. ¹³ But if you say, "We will not stay in this land," and so disobey YHWH, ¹⁴ and if you say, "No, we will go down and live in Egypt, where we will not see war or hear the trumpet or hunger for bread,"¹⁵ then hear the word of YHWH, remnant of Judah—thus says YHWH Omnipotent, the God of Israel: If you are determined to go down to Egypt and settle there, ¹⁶ then the sword you fear will overtake you there, there in the land of Egypt. The famine you dread will follow you down into Egypt and there you will die. ¹⁷ All who insist on going down to settle in Egypt will die by the sword, by famine and by the plague. Not one of you will survive or escape the disaster I will bring on

you. ¹⁸ Just as my anger and my wrath have been poured out on those living in Jerusalem, says YHWH Omnipotent, the God of Israel, so will my wrath be poured out on you when you go down to Egypt. You will be an object of curses and horror, of condemnation and of reproach. You will never see this place again.'

¹⁹ "Remnant of Judah, YHWH has spoken to you. Don't go down to Egypt. Be sure of this: I warn you solemnly ²⁰ that if you do, you made a fatal mistake when you sent me to YHWH and said, 'Pray to YHWH for us and tell us everything YHWH says and we will do it.' ²¹ I have told you today, but you still have not obeyed YHWH in all God sent me to tell you. ²² So now, be sure of this: if you persist, you will die by the sword, by famine, and by plague in the place where you want to go to settle."

⁴³:¹ When Jeremiah finished telling the people all that YHWH their God had sent to say, ² Azariah ben-Hoshaiah and Johanan ben-Kareach and their companion had the boldness to say to Jeremiah, "You are a liar! YHWH our God did not send you to say, 'You must not go down to Egypt and settle there.' ³ Baruch ben-Neriah is manipulating you against us in order to put us under the power of the Babylonians, to be murdered or exiled to Babylon." ⁴ So Johanan ben-Kareah and all the leaders of the armed bands disobeyed YHWH's command to stay in the land of Judah. ⁵ Instead, Johanan ben-Kareah and the leaders of the armed bands led away the remnant who had come back to live in the land of Judah from all the nations where they had been scattered. ⁶ They also led away all the children, women, and men as well as the ruler's daughters whom Nebuzaradan, the commander of the guard, had left behind with Gedaliah ben-Ahikam ben-Shaphan, Jeremiah the prophet, and Baruch ben-Neriah. ⁷ So they entered Egypt in disobedience to YHWH and went as far as Tahpanhes.

⁸ In Tahpanhes the word of YHWH came to Jeremiah: ⁹ "With the people of Judah watching, take some large stones and set them in the clay in the pavement at the entrance of Pharaoh's residence in Tahpanhes, ¹⁰ and say to them, 'Thus says YHWH Omnipotent, the God of Israel: I will send for my servant Nebucadnezzar the ruler of Babylon, who will place his judgment seat on these stones I set here, and spread his canopy over them. ¹¹ He will come and ravage Egypt,

> bringing plague to those destined for the plague,
> captivity to those destined for captivity,
> and the sword for those destined for the sword.

¹² " 'The ruler of Babylon will set fire to the temples of the gods of Egypt, and burn the buildings and carry the gods away into captivity. He will pick clean the land of Egypt as shepherds pick their cloaks clean of vermin.

And the ruler will leave there unscathed. ¹³ Nebuchadnezzar will break the obelisks of the Temple of the Sun* in the land of Egypt, and burn down the temples of the gods of Egypt.'"

⁴⁴:¹ The word that came to Jeremiah for all the people of Judah living in the land of Egypt—at Middol, at Tahpanhes, at Memphis—in the region of Pathros: "Thus says YHWH Omnipotent, the God of Israel: You yourselves saw all the destruction I brought on Jerusalem and on the towns of Judah. Look at them now, desolate and uninhabited, ³ because of the evil they had perpetrated, provoking me to anger by burning incense and by worshipping other gods that neither they nor you nor your ancestors knew. ⁴ Again and again I sent my servants the prophets to you, and said, 'Don't do these repugnant things that I hate.' ⁵ But your ancestors did not listen; they did not pay attention. Instead, they perpetuated their evil ways by offering incense to other gods. ⁶ So I poured out my anger and wrath and swept like a blaze of fire through the towns of Judah and the streets of Jerusalem until they were reduced to the waste they are to this day. ⁷ Now, thus says YHWH, the God Omnipotent, the God of Israel: Why are you doing such a great harm to yourselves, so that every man and woman, every child and infant, is cut off from Judah, yourselves without a remnant? ⁸ Why do you so provoke me to anger by what you do with your hands, making offerings to other gods in that place where you settled? You will destroy yourselves and become an object of ridicule and reproach among the nations of the earth. ⁹ Have you forgotten the evils committed by your ancestors and by the rulers of Judah and the atrocities committed by the women and men in the land of Judah and in the streets of Jerusalem? ¹⁰ To this day you have shown neither contrition nor fear, nor have you walked in my law and my statutes I set before you and before your ancestors.

¹¹ "Therefore, thus says YHWH Omnipotent, the God of Israel: I have resolved to bring disaster on you and to destroy all Judah. ¹² I will remove the remnant of Judah who are determined to settle in Egypt. They will all perish in Egypt. They will fall by the sword or die from famine. They will become an object of cursing and horror, of derision and ridicule. ¹³ I will punish those dwelling in Egypt like those dwelling in Jerusalem, with the sword, with famine, with the plague. ¹⁴ None of the remnant of Judah who went to live in Egypt will escape or survive to return to the land of Judah, to which they long to return to live. None will return except for a few fugitives."

¹⁵ A large assembly of the people (all the women who were burning incense to other gods, together with their husbands—indeed, all of the Jews living in Pathros in the land of Egypt) answered Jeremiah, ¹⁶ "We are not

---

* This temple was located in Heliopolis, now a suburb of Cairo. The city was famous for its conical pillars dedicated to Amon-Ra, the sun god (Heliopolis means "city of the sun").

going to listen to the message you delivered to us in the name of YHWH! [17] On the contrary, we will do everything we set out to do: we will burn incense to the Queen of Heaven and pour out drink offerings to her, just as our ancestors did and just as our rulers and our officials did in our towns and in the streets of Jerusalem. At that time we had plenty of food, we were prosperous and there were no misfortunes. [18] But since we stopped burning incense to the Queen of Heaven and pouring out drink offerings to her, we have lacked everything and have perished by the sword and by famine."

[19] The women added, "When we burned incense to the Queen of Heaven and poured out drink offerings to her, don't you think our husbands knew that we were pouring out drink offerings to her, that we offered cakes marked with her image?"*

[20] Then Jeremiah said to all the people, both the women and the men who had answered him, [21] "Don't you think that YHWH remembers and keeps thinking about the way you burned incense in the towns of Judah and in the streets of Jerusalem, you and your ancestors, your rulers and your officials, the people of the land? [22] When YHWH could no longer endure your evil deeds and the abominable things you did, your land was turned into a desolate waste without inhabitants, as it remains today. [23] Because you burned incense and sinned against YHWH, because you have not obeyed YHWH or followed God's laws, decrees, or teachings, this disaster came upon you, and it is still upon you today."

[24] To all the gathered assembly, especially to the women, Jeremiah declared, "Hear the word of YHWH, all you people of Judah in the land of Egypt! [25] Thus says YHWH Omnipotent, the God of Israel: You and your spouses have shown by your actions what you promised when you said, 'We will certainly carry out the vows we made to burn incense and pour out libations to the Queen of Heaven.' Go right ahead, do what you promised! Keep your vows! [26] But hear the word of YHWH, all you people of Judah who live in the land of Egypt: I swear by my great Name, says YHWH, that my Name will no longer be pronounced on the lips of any of the people of Judah in the land of Egypt: they will not swear, 'As YHWH lives.' [27] I will watch over you to bring you evil and not good, and all the people of Judah dwelling in Egypt will meet their doom by the sword and by plague until no one is left. [28] It will be at that time that any survivors remaining to dwell in Egypt will know whose word prevails—mine or theirs.

---

* This scene is interesting on two accounts: it is the women who are leading the worship of a female deity, Ashtaroth/Astarte/Ishtar, with the consent and even participation of their husbands; and they are interpreting the disasters that befell them in Judah not as judgment for forsaking the worship of YHWH, but as misfortune because they had forsaken the more ancient worship of the Queen of Heaven.

²⁹ "This is the sign I will give you, says YHWH, to punish you in this place, so that you may know that my threats of harm against you will surely prevail. ³⁰ Thus says YHWH: I will give Pharaoh Hophra, ruler of Egypt, into the hands of his enemies who seek his life, just as I gave Zedekiah the ruler of Judah into the hands of Nebuchadnezzar ruler of Babylon, the enemy who sought his life."

45:1 The word that the prophet Jeremiah dictated to Baruch ben-Neriah, who wrote it down on a scroll, in the fourth year of Jehoiakim ben-Josiah ruler of Judah: ² "This is what YHWH, the God of Israel, says to you, Baruch: ³ You said, 'Woe is me! For YHWH has added grief to my trails. I wore myself out with my labors and can find no rest.' " ⁴ This is what you will say to Baruch: "Thus says YHWH: What I built I demolish. What I plant I uproot. So it will be with the whole world. ⁵ You seek great things for yourself. Stop seeking. I am about to bring disaster upon humankind, says YHWH, but wherever you go I will let you escape with your life."

Ꮗ   Ꮗ   Ꮪ

46:1 This is the word of YHWH that came to the prophet Jeremiah about the nations:

² Concerning Egypt:

About the army of Pharaoh Neco ruler of Egypt, which suffered defeat at Carchemish on the Euphrates River at the hand of Nebuchadnezzar ruler of Babylon, in the fourth year of Jehoiakim ben-Josiah ruler of Judah:

³   "Take up buckler and shield
       and move out to battle!
⁴   Harness the horses,
       mount the steeds!
     Helmeted, take your positions!
       Polish your spears!
       Put on your coat of mail!
⁵   What is this I see?
       They are retreating,
       they fall back in headlong flight.
     They dare not even glance back.
       Terror is everywhere, says YHWH.
⁶   The swiftest cannot flee,
       nor can the bravest save themselves.

They stumble and fall in the north
   by the River Euphrates.
7 Who is this rising like the Nile;
   like rivers in spring flood?
8 Egypt rises like the Nile,
   like rivers in spring flood.
'I will rise and flood the earth,' says Egypt;
   'I will destroy cities
   and their inhabitants.'
9 Charge forward, you horses!
   Drive swiftly, charioteers!
Advance, warriors,
   Cushites and Putites with shields;
   Lydians with bows at the ready!
10 But this is the day of YHWH Omnipotent,
   a day of vengeance, vengeance on God's foes.
The devouring sword seeks satisfaction;
   its thirst for blood to be quenched.
For Sovereign YHWH Omnipotent
   has a sacrifice to offer
   in the land of the north, by the Euphrates.
11 Go up to Gilead in search of balm,
   you innocent people of Egypt!
You search for new medicines in vain,
   since nothing can rescue you.
12 The nations learned of your shame;
   your cries echoing over the earth.
Warrior stumbled over warrior
   and both collapsed together."

13 This is the word that YHWH spoke to Jeremiah the prophet about the advance of Nebuchadnezzar the ruler of Babylon to attack the land of Egypt:
14 "Announce this in Egypt, proclaim it in Migdal;
   proclaim it in Memphis and Tahpanhes,
saying, 'Stand by,' and 'at the ready.'
   For the sword devours all around you.
15 Why did Apis flee? Why didn't your bull-god stand fast?
   Because YHWH thrust it down!
16 Egypt's rabble stumbles, it totters.
   One said to another,
'Get up, let us return to our own,
   to our native land, away from the oppressors' sword.'

17 Rename the ruler of Egypt
    'Pharoah Loud-Mouth Who Missed His Chance.'
18 As surely as I live, says the Sovereign One,
    whose name is YHWH Omnipotent,
someone will come who is like a Tabor among the mountains,
    a Carmel high above the sea.
19 Pack up for exile,
    you who dwell in Egypt,
for Memphis is to be laid waste
    lying in ruins without life.
20 Egypt was a prime heifer
    and a gadfly from the north slaughtered it.
21 The mercenaries were like fattened calves.
They turned their heels and ran away—
    they did not stand their ground,
for their day of disaster, the day of reckoning is upon them.
22 Egypt hisses like a cornered snake;
    the enemy comes in force
to fall on it like woodcutters with axes.
23 They will chop down its forest, says YHWH,
    dense though it may be,
more numerous than locusts,
    beyond being counted.
24 The Egyptians will be put to shame,
    enslaved by the people of the north.

25 "YHWH Omnipotent, the God of Israel, says: I am about to exact punishment upon Amon god of Thebes, on Pharoah, on Egypt and its gods and its rulers and on those who put their trust in Pharaoh. 26 I will hand them over to those seeking their lives, to Nebuchadnezzar ruler of Babylon and his officers. But in later days Egypt will be inhabited again as in the past, says YHWH.

27 "But as for you, fear not, servant Jacob,
    do not be dismayed, Israel,
for I will bring you back from far away,
    and your children from the land of their exile.
Once more Jacob will live in peace and security,
    with no one to fear.
28 Don't fear, my Servant Jacob,
    for I am with you, says YHWH.
I will put an end to all the nations
    among whom I scatter you;
but I will not destroy you;

I will discipline you,
    but only as you deserve;
I will not let you go
    entirely unpunished."

⁴⁷·¹ This is the word of YHWH that came to the prophet Jeremiah concerning the Philistines before Pharaoh attacked Gaza:

²   Thus says YHWH:
"See how waters are rising from the north
    and swelling into a torrent,
overflowing the country and everything in it,
    the towns and their residents.
The people will cry out.
The inhabitants of the land will wail
³   at the thundering hooves of galloping steeds,
    at the clatter of chariots
    and the rumbling of their wheels.
Parents do not turn back for their own children,
    so feeble are their hands.
⁴   For the day has come
    to destroy all the Philistines;
Tyre and Sidon will be destroyed
    to their last defender.
Yes, YHWH is destroying the Philistines,
    the remnant of the island of Caphtor.
⁵   Gaza will shave its head in mourning,
    Ashkalon is silenced.
O remnant of their power,
    how long will you gash yourselves and wail?
⁶   'Sword of YHWH!' you cry,
    'how much longer before you tire?
Return to your scabbard,
    halt, be still!'
⁷   But how can it be still when YHWH
    gives it a task to complete
against Ashkelon and against the sea coast?
    These are the tasks assigned to it.'"

⁴⁸·¹ Concerning Moab:

Thus says YHWH Omnipotent,
    the God of Israel:

"Woe to Nebo!
It is laid waste!
Kiriathaim is shamed,
now that it is has been captured.
Within its citadels,
all is confusion and alarm:
2   It is no longer the boast of Moab!
Its downfall was plotted at Heshbon,
'Come, let us put an end to that nation.'
And you who inhabit Madhmen will also perish,
pursued by the sword.
3   Listen! A cry emanates from Horonaim,
'Disaster and utter havoc!'
4   'Moab is detroyed,'
its little ones cry out.
5   For at the ascent to Luhith
the people go up weeping bitterly;
and at the descent of Horonaim
they heard the cry of anguish,
6   'Flee! Run for your lives!
Scramble like wild asses in the desert!'
7   Because you put your trust in your citadels
you too will be captured,
and Chemosh will go into exile
with its priests and officials.
8   The destroyer will descend on every town—
none will escape.
The valley will be laid waste
and the upland plundered, says YHWH.
9   Build a tomb for Moab
for it is totally destroyed;
its towns are ruined,
and no one lives in them.
10 A curse on all
who slack in YHWH's work!
A curse on all
who withhold their swords from bloodshed!
11 Moab has been at ease since childhood,
settled like wine on its dregs;
not emptied from vessel to vessel,
not driven into exile;

so its flavor remains unaltered
its aroma unchanged.

¹² "Therefore, the days are coming, says YHWH, when I will send Moab decanters to decant itself; I will empty its vessels and smash its jars. ¹³ Then Moab will be ashamed of Chemosh just as the house of Israel was ashamed of Bethel, in whom it put its trust.

¹⁴ "How can you say, 'We are warriors,
valiant in battle'?
¹⁵ The destroyer of Moab and its towns
has launched an attack;
the flower of its youth
will go down to be slaughtered,
says the Ruler, whose name is YHWH Omnipotent.
¹⁶ The fall of Moab is at hand,
its doom will happen quickly.
¹⁷ Mourn for it, you who live near it,
all you who know its fame;
say, 'Now the mighty scepter is broken,
the splendid staff.'
¹⁸ Come down from your glory
and squat on the parched ground,
natives of Dibon;
for the spoiler of Moab
advanced against you
and destroyed your stronghold.
¹⁹ Stand by the road and watch,
you who live in Aroer;
ask the men fleeing
and the woman escaping,
'What has happened?'
²⁰ Moab is disgraced, it is shattered.
Wail! Cry out!
Announce by the Arnon River
that Moab is no more.

²¹ "Judgment came to the plateau—to Holon, Jahzah, and Mephaath; ²² to Dibon, Nebo, and Beth Diblathaim, ²³ to Kiriathaim, Beth Gamul, and Beth Meon, ²⁴ to Kerioth and Bozrah—to all the towns of Moab, far and near.

²⁵ "Moab's horn is cut off,
its arm is broken, says YHWH.

²⁶ "Make Moab drunk—it has defied YHWH. Let Moab wallow in its vomit; in its turn a subject for derision. ²⁷ Wasn't Israel a subject for derision to you? Yet was it ever in league with thieves, that every time you spoke of it you shook your head?

²⁸ "Inhabitants of Moab, abandon the towns,
    take up residence among the rocks.
Learn from the dove that makes its nest
    in the rock face of a narrow cleft.
²⁹ We heard of the pride of Moab—
    for it is very proud indeed—
of its loftiness, its pride, its arrogance,
    and its haughty heart.
³⁰ I know of its insolence, says YHWH;
    its boasting is false; its deeds are false.
³¹ Therefore I wail over Moab;
    I cry out for all Moab;
    I mourn for the people of Kir-heres.
³² More than for Jazer I weep for you,
    O vine of Sibmah.
Your branches spread as far as the sea;
    they reached as far as the sea of Jazer.
The destroyer ravaged
    your ripened fruit and grapes.
³³ Joy and gladness are long gone
    from the fertile land of Moab.
I stopped the flow of wine from the presses.
    No one treads the grapes with shouts of joy;
    the shouting now is not for joy.

³⁴ "The sound of a cry rises from Heshbon to Elealeh and Jahaz; from Zoar as far as Horonaim and Eglath Shelishiyah, the waters of Nimrim are dried up forever. ³⁵ In Moab I will put an end to whoever makes offerings at the high places, and to whoever burns incense to other gods, says YHWH. ³⁶ Therefore my heart moans for Moab like a flute, and my heart moans like a flute for the people of Kir-heres; for the wealth they gained is gone.

³⁷ "For every head is shaved, every beard is cut off; on all hands, gashes; sackcloth on the loins. ³⁸ On all the housetops of Moab and in the city squares there is nothing but lamentation; for I broke Moab like an abandoned vessel, says YHWH. ³⁹ How broken it is! How its people lament! Moab turns its back in shame! And it has become an object of derision and horror to all its neighbors.

⁴⁰ "For thus says YHWH:
Look! An eagle swooping down
spreads its wings over Moab.
⁴¹ Towns will be captured,
strongholds seized.
At that time the hearts of Moab's warriors
will be like the hearts of people in travail.
⁴² Moab will be finished as a people
because it defied YHWH.
⁴³ Terror, the pit, the snare—
these are your future, inhabitants of Moab!
Thus says YHWH.
⁴⁴ All who flee from the terror
will fall into the pit;
and everyone who climbs out of the pit,
will be caught up into the snare;
for I will bring upon Moab
the era of its punishment, says YHWH.
⁴⁵ In the shadow of Heshbon,
fugitives pause, exhausted;
for a fire has blazed forth from Heshbon,
a blaze from the house of Sihon,
consuming the braggarts of Moab
from forehead to crown.
⁴⁶ Woe to you, Moab!
The people of Chemosh vanished.
For your daughters are now in captivity,
your sons in exile.
⁴⁷ Yet in days to come I will restore
the fortunes of Moab, says YHWH."

Here ends the judgment on Moab.

^{49:1} Concerning the Ammonites:

Thus says YHWH:
"Has Israel no offspring,
no heirs?
Why then has Milcom
inherited the land of Gad,
and why have Milcom's people
settled in its towns?

2   But the days are coming, says YHWH,
         when I will sound the battle cry
         against Rabbah of the Ammonites;
      it will become a deserted ruin,
         with its surrounding villages burned down;
         and Israel will expel those who expelled them, says YHWH.
3   Wail, Heshbon, for Ai is laid waste!
         Cry out, children of Rabbah!
      Dress in sackcloth, lament,
         with gashes on your bodies.
      Milcom is destined for exile
         with his priests and officials.
4   Why do you boast in your strength,
         you renegade people who trust in arms,
         saying, 'Who will dare attack us?'
5   Beware, for I will bring terror upon you
         from every side, says YHWH Omnipotent;
      for all of you will be scattered,
         with no one to gather the fugitives.
6   Yet later I will restore
         the fortunes of the Ammonites, says YHWH."

7 Concerning Edom:

         Thus says YHWH Omnipotent:
         "Is there no longer wisdom in Teman?
      Has counsel perished from the prudent?
         Has their wisdom vanished?
8   Flee, turn back, take refuge in deep caves,
         inhabitants of Dedan;
      for I will bring destruction on Esau
         on the day I punish it.
9   If grape pickers came to you
         would they not leave a few grapes?
      When robbers come in the night
         even they steal only what they want.
10   It is I who am despoiling Esau.
         I uncovered its hiding places,
         and it is unable to to conceal itself.
      Esau's progeny is destroyed,
         together with its family and its neighbors;
         Esau is no more.

¹¹   But leave your orphans with me,
     I will keep them alive;
      your widows will be safe with me.

¹² "For thus says YHWH: Those of you who were not destined to drink the cup must drink it nonetheless; you will not go unpunished. You will not escape. You must drink it. ¹³ For I swear, says YHWH, that Bozrah will become an object of horror and ridicule, a waste, a curse; all its towns will be perpetual wastes."

¹⁴   As an emissary was going among the nations, saying,
     "Assemble yourselves to attack Esau,
     and rise up for battle,"
   I heard this message from YHWH:
¹⁵ "Now I will make you the smallest of nations;
     despised among humankind.
¹⁶ Though you inspire terror,
     your pride of heart has deceived you,
   you who live in the clefts of the rocks,
     who occupy the tops of the hill.
   Though you nest as high as the eagle
     I will bring you down from there, says YHWH.

¹⁷ "Edom will become an object of horror; all the passersby will be appalled and hiss at the sight of its destruction. ¹⁸ Just as when Sodom and Gomorrah and their neighbors were destroyed, says YHWH, so no one will dwell there, nor will anyone settle there. ¹⁹ Like a lion moving up from Jordon's thickets to a perennial pasture, I will pounce and chase Edom from its land. And I will appoint over it whomever I choose. For who is like me? Who can summon me? What shepherds can stand their ground before me? ²⁰ Hear, then, what YHWH plans against Edom and has in mind for the people of Teman: The young of the flock will be dragged off and their pasture will be destroyed. ²¹ The earth will tremble at the sound of the collapse. The sound of anguish will echo off the Sea of Reeds.

²²   "Look! An eagle will soar swoop down,
     spreading its wings over Bozrah.
   At that time the hearts of Edom's warriors
     will be like the hearts of people in travail."

²³ Concerning Damascus:

   "Hamath and Arpad are confused,
     for they received news of disaster;

they melt in fear, roiling like the sea
    that cannot be quieted.
²⁴ Enfeebled Damascus turns to flee
    when panic sets in;
anguish and sorrow seize it
    like people in the grip of travail.
²⁵ How can this renowned city be abandoned,
    this delightful city?
²⁶ Surely its youth will be cut down in its squares,
    and all its defenders will perish,
    says YHWH Omnipotent.
²⁷ And I will set afire the walls of Damascus,
    which will consume Ben-hadad's fortresses."

²⁸ Concerning Kedar and the realms of Hazor which Nebuchadnezzar ruler of Babylon defeated:

Thus says YHWH:
"Take up arms! Move out against Kedar!
    Destroy the people dwelling in the eastern deserts.
²⁹ Confiscate their tents and their flocks,
    their fabrics, all their goods and their camels;
Let the cry ring out, 'Terror on every side!'
³⁰ Flee, make your escape,
    take refuge in the remotest of places,
    you people of Hazor, says YHWH,
for Nebuchadnezzar ruler of Babylon
    has plotted against you
    and devised plans against you.
³¹ Rise up, march on a nation at ease,
    living securely, says YHWH,
that has no gates and no barriers,
    a people in solitary ease.
³² Their camels will be taken as booty,
    their large herds as plunder.
I will scatter them to the winds,
    to roam the fringes of the desert;
and I will bring disaster down on them
    from every side, says YHWH.
³³ Hazor will become a lain of jackals,
    an everlasting waste;

no one will live there,
no one will dwell there."

³⁴ The word of YHWH that came to the prophet Jeremiah concerning Elam, at the onset of the reign of Zedekiah the ruler of Judah.

³⁵ Thus says YHWH Omnipotent: "I will break the bow of Elam, the mainstay of its people's might. ³⁶ I will bring upon them the four winds from the four corners of heaven. And I will scatter them to all these four winds, and there will be no nations to which the Elamites have not been driven for refuge.

³⁷ "I will make the Elamites tremble before their foes, before the enemy determined to kill them. I will bring disaster down upon them with my own fierce anger. I will pursue them with the sword until all are destroyed. ³⁸ I will set up my judgment seat in Elam, and destroy its ruler and officials, says YHWH.

³⁹ "Yet in days to come I will restore the fortunes of Elam, says YHWH."

ҩ   ҩ   ҩ

⁵⁰⁻¹ This is the word YHWH spoke through the prophet Jeremiah concerning Babylon and the land of Babylonia:

² "Publish it among the nations, proclaim it;
    make no secret of it!
Babylon is captured,
    Bel is shamed and Marduk terrified.
Its images are put to shame,
    its idols disgraced.
³ A nation from the north will attack
    and lay it waste.
No one will survive in it;
    both animals and people will flee.

⁴ "In those days, at that time, says YHWH, the people of Israel and people of Judah will come, and together they will seek out YHWH their God, weeping as they go. ⁵ They will ask the way to Zion, though they will already be facing the right direction. 'Come,' they will say, 'let us join ourselves to YHWH by an everlasting covenant never to be forgotten!'

⁶ "My people have been lost sheep. Their shepherds led them astray and let them roam the mountains. They wandered from mountain to mountain, forgetful of their fold. ⁷ All who came upon them devoured them, and their enemies said, 'Don't blame us. It all happened because they sinned against YHWH, their true fold, the hope of their ancestors.'

⁸ "Flee from Babylon, leave the land of Babylonia, and become like the goats that lead the flock. ⁹ For I will stir up an alliance of mighty nations against Babylon. They will come from the land of the north, drawing up battle formations against it; from there it will be captured. Theirs will be like the arrows of skilled warriors who never return empty-handed. ¹⁰ Babylonia will be plundered; and all who plunder it will have their fill, says YHWH.

¹¹ "For you rejoiced, Babylon, you danced—
   you who plundered my possession!
   You played like a heifer in the tender grass,
      you neighed like a stallion.
¹² Now your motherland* is thoroughly shamed,
      she who gave you life is disgraced.
   Look at her, the least of nations,
      a parched and barren wilderness.
¹³ Because of YHWH's wrath,
      she will now be unoccupied, uninhabited,
      and totally desolate.
   Passersby will be appalled at the Great City
      and hiss because of her wounds.
¹⁴ Take up your positions around Babylon,
      bend the bow and shoot at it—
   spare no arrows,
      for Babylon sinned against YHWH.
¹⁵ Raise a shout against it from all sides, saying,
      'It has surrendered, its bulwarks breached,
      its walls torn down.'
   For this is YHWH's vengeance:
      take vengeance on it,
      do to it what it has done to others.
¹⁶ Deprive Babylon of the sower,
      and of the reaper at harvest time.
   Because of the oppressor's sword,
      let all return to their people,
      let all return to their homeland.

¹⁷ "Israel is a scattered flock that lions chased away. The first to devour it was the ruler of Assyria; the last to crush its bones was Nebuchadnezzar ruler of Babylon. ¹⁸ Therefore, thus says YHWH Omnipotent, the God of Israel: I am about to punish the ruler of Babylon and his land, as I punished the ruler of Assyria. ¹⁹ And I will restore Israel to its own pasture, to graze on Carmel

---

* Babylonia is the motherland; Babylon is its capitol and its seat of power.

and Bashan; on Ephraim's hills and in Gilead it will eat its fill. ²⁰ In those days and at that time, says YHWH, searchers will seek out Israel's iniquity, but none will be found. For I will forgive the remnant I spared.

²¹ "Attack the land of Merathaim
and all who dwell in Pekod;
and destroy them, says YHWH,
do all I commanded you to do.
²² The sound of war reverberates
throughout the land
and there is great destruction!
²³ How broken and shattered
is the hammer of the whole world!
How desolate Babylon is
among the nations!
²⁴ I set a trap for you, Babylon,
and you were caught before you knew it.
You were discovered and seized
for challenging YHWH.
²⁵ YHWH opened the armory
and took out the weapon of wrath;
for YHWH Omnipotent has work to do
in the land of Babylon.
²⁶ Come against it from every quarter,
throw open its granaries,
pile up the plunder like mounds of grain;
put it under the sacred ban*
until nothing is left.
²⁷ Kill all the bulls,†
lead them down to the slaughter.
Woe to them! For their day has come,
the time of their punishment.

²⁸ "Listen! Fugitives and refugees from the land of Babylon come to declare in Zion the vengeance of YHWH, vengeance for God's Temple.

²⁹ "Summon archers against Babylon, all who bend the bow. Encamp around it; let no one escape. Repay it according to its deeds. Do to it just as it did to others—for it arrogantly defied YHWH, the Holy One of Israel.

---

* This is the concept of *cherem*, the complete and irrevocable giving of something to God, generally translated as "sacred ban" or "divine curse." It usually entailed the annihilation of whatever (or whomever) was thus devoted—theoretically to be consumed by God's glory.

† The royal heirs and the city officials.

³⁰ Therefore, its youth will fall in its squares, and all its soldiers will be destroyed on that day, says YHWH.

> ³¹ "I oppose you, arrogant one, says YHWH Omnipotent;
> for your day has come,
> the day I will punish you.
> ³² The arrogant will stumble and fall,
> with no one to raise the fallen.
> And I will kindle a fire in its towns
> that will consume all its surroundings.

³³ "Thus says YHWH Omnipotent: The people of Israel are oppressed, and the people of Judah as well. All their captors hold them fast and refuse to release them. ³⁴ Their Redeemer is strong: YHWH Omnipotent is my name. I will plead their cause, so that I may give rest to the earth, and unrest to the inhabitants of Babylon.

> ³⁵ "A sword hangs over the Babylonians, says YHWH,
> and over the inhabitants of Babylon,
> and its officials and its sages!
> ³⁶ A sword hangs over its false prophets!
> They will turn into fools.
> A sword hangs over its warriors, who despair;
> They are to be filled with terror.
> ³⁷ A sword hangs over its horses
> and its chariots,
> and over the mixed rabble in its midst,
> who scramble to disguise themselves.
> A sword hangs over its treasures,
> which will be plundered.
> ³⁸ A sword hangs over its water,
> and it will dry up;
> for it is a land of idols—
> the people boast about their idols.

³⁹ "Therefore wild animals will dwell there with hyenas and ostriches. The land will never again be peopled; it will be uninhabited for all generations. ⁴⁰ Just as when God overthrew Sodom and Gomorrah and their neighboring cities, says YHWH, so no one will live there, nor will anyone settle here.

> ⁴¹ "Look! An army comes from the north,
> a great nation and many rulers are rousing themselves
> from the farthest corners of the earth.*

---

* This is the empire of the Medes and Persians, together with the vassal kings who provided forces for its army.

⁴² Armed with bow and spear,
    they are cruel and ruthless;
astride their mounts
    they sound like the roaring of the sea;
they come in battle formation
    to attack you, Babylon!
⁴³ The ruler of Babylon hears news of them,
    and his arms hang limp;
he is seized in anguish,
    and his agony is like that of a woman in labor.

⁴⁴ "Like a lion moving up from Jordan's thickets to a perennial pasture, I will pounce and chase its people away and appoint whomever I choose. For who is like me? Who can summon me? What shepherds can stand their ground before me?

⁴⁵ "Therefore hear the plan YHWH made for Babylon, and what God has purposed against the land of the Babylonians: The young of the flock will be dragged off and their pasture destroyed. ⁴⁶ And at the sound of Babylon's capture the earth will tremble; its cry will resound throughout the nations.

51:1 "Thus says YHWH: I will stir up
    a destructive wind against Babylon
    and the inhabitants of Leb-qamai;
² and I will send foreigners to Babylon
    to winnow it and leave the country bare.
For they will assault it from every side
    on the day of its disaster.
³ Don't allow the archer to string the bow
    or put on a coat of mail!
Don't spare Babylon's youth!
    Obliterate its army!
⁴ Let them fall in battle in Babylon,
    slain in its streets.
⁵ Israel and Judah have not been abandoned
    by their God, YHWH Omnipotent;
though their land is filled with guilt
    before the Holy One of Israel."

⁶ Abandon Babylon, run for your life,
    every one of you!
Do not perish for its guilt,
    for this is YHWH's day of vengeance.

7 Babylon was a gold cup in God's hand;
　　it made the whole world drunk.
　The nations drank its wine
　　which turned them mad.
8 Then suddenly Babylon fell, shattered;
　　Wail for it!
　Bring balm for its wound;
　　maybe it can be healed.
9 We would have healed Babylon,
　　but it could not be healed.
　Let us leave it and return to our own ways,
　　for her doom reaches to the heavens,
　　it rises up to the clouds.
10 YHWH vindicated us;
　　come, let us proclaim in Zion
　　what YHWH our God did.

11 Sharpen the arrows, fill the quivers! YHWH roused the spirit of the rulers of the Medes, for YHWH had a plan for destroying Babylon. YHWH will take vengeance, vengeance for God's Temple.

12 Lift up a banner opposite the walls of Babylon!
　　Mount a strong defense! Reinforce the guard!
　Station the watchers! Prepare for an ambush!
　　For YHWH made a plan
　　and treated the people of Babylon as promised.
13 You who dwell beside mighty waters,
　　rich in treasures, your end is near,
　　the thread of your life is now snipped.
14 YHWH Omnipotent swore,
　　"Surely I will fill you with troops
　who will swarm like locusts;
　　who will shout triumphantly over you."
15 It was God's power that made the earth;
　　who established the world by divine wisdom;
　　and by divine understanding unfurled the skies.
16 When God thunders
　　the waters in the heavens roar;
　God makes clouds rise
　　from the ends of the earth,
　and opens rifts for the rain
　　and releases the wind from its storehouse.

¹⁷ At this the people are stupefied and ignorant;
goldsmiths are shamed by their idols.
Their images are delusions,
and there is no breath in them.
¹⁸ They are worthless, objects of mockery,
that perish when their judgment comes.
¹⁹ YHWH, the Portion of Jacob,
is not like these,
for YHWH forms everything;
and Israel is the tribe of YHWH's heritage—
YHWH Omnipotent is that name!

²⁰ You are my mace, YHWH,
my war weapon.
With you I subdue nations,
with you I overcome realms.
²¹ With you I separate horse from rider,
with you I separate chariot and charioteer.
²² With you I shatter wives and husbands,
with you I shatter old people and children,
with you I shatter young women and young men.
²³ With you I shatter the shepherd and the flock,
with you I shatter the farmer and the livestock,
with you I shatter governors and officials.

²⁴ "I will repay Babylon and all who live in Babylonia
for all the wrong they did in Zion, says YHWH.
²⁵ My quarrel is with you, destroying mountain,
you who destroy the entire world, says YHWH.
I will stretch out my hand against you,
roll you down from the cliff
and turn you into a burned-out mountain.
²⁶ No stone taken from you
will be used for a cornerstone,
nor any stone for a foundation,
for you will be desolate forever, says YHWH."

²⁷ Lift up a banner in the earth!
Blow the trumpet among the nations!
Prepare them for battle against Babylon,
summon the rulers of Ararat, Minni, and Askenaz.

Appoint a commander against the enemy;
    bring up the cavalry, bristling like locusts.

28 Prepare the nations for war against it: the rulers of Medes, with their governors and deputies, and all the countries under their domination.

29 The earth quakes and writhes,
    for YHWH's plans against Babylon stand:
  to lay waste the land of Babylon
    into an unpopulated wilderness.
30 The Babylonian warriors stopped fighting,
    yet they remain in their strongholds;
  their strength has failed,
    they are like people in travail;
  Babylon's buildings are afire,
    the bars of its gates are shattered.
31 Couriers dash to meet couriers,
    messengers to meet messengers,
  to announce to the ruler of Babylon
    that the city is taken,
32 the river crossings seized, the marshes afire
    and the garrison panic-stricken.
33 For thus says YHWH Omnipotent,
    the God of Israel:
  "Babylon is like the threshing floor
    when it is trampled;
    harvest time will be here very soon now."

34 Nebuchadnezzar the ruler has crushed me;
    thrown me into confusion
    and made me into an empty jar.
  He has swallowed me like a serpent
    and filled his belly with my delicacies,
    and then spewed me out.
35 Every citizen of Zion will say,
    "May its violence to me, all my suffering,
    be avenged on Babylon."
  Jerusalem will say,
    "May my blood be avenged
    on the inhabitants of Babylon."
36 Therefore thus says YHWH:
  "I will defend your cause
    and take vengeance for you.

I will dry up the sea
and make its fountains dry;
37 and Babylon will become
of ruins a heap, a den of jackels,
an object of horror and derision,
a place where none want to live.
38 All its people roam like young lions,
they growl like cubs.
39 But while they are inflamed,
I will set out a feast for them
and make them drunk till they are merry,
and let them sleep a perpetual sleep
and never wake, says YHWH.
40 I will bring them down like lambs to the slaughter,
like rams and goats.
41 Sheshak is captured,
the pride of the world taken.
What a horror Babylon has become
among the nations!
42 The sea will rise over Babylon,
and waves will cover it.
43 Its towns will be desolate,
a dry and desert wilderness,
a land without people,
through which none dare travel.
44 I will punish Bel in Babylon
and make it vomit what it has swallowed.
The nations will no longer pay homage to it.
And the wall of Babylon will fall.
45 Leave this place, you people! Run for your lives!
Flee from the fierce anger of YHWH."

46 But do not be fainthearted. Do not be fearful as rumor follows rumor.
One rumor is in favor one year and another is in favor next year. Violence
rules on this earth and one tyrant cancels out another.

47 "Therefore the days are coming
when I will punish Babylon's idols;
its whole land will be a disgrace
and its slain will all lie fallen within it.
48 Then heaven and earth and all within them
will shout for joy over Babylon,
for out of the north marauders will attack, says YHWH.

⁴⁹ Babylon in its turn must fall
　　because of Israel's slain,
　as the slain of all the world
　　fell because of Babylon.
⁵⁰ Leave and don't linger,
　　you who escaped the sword!
　Remember YHWH in a distant land
　　and think of Jerusalem."
⁵¹ We are shamed, having heard the insults;
　　dishonor covers our face:
　aliens have entered into
　　the holy places of YHWH's house.
⁵² "But days are coming, says YHWH,
　　when I will punish its idols;
　and throughout the land
　　the groans of the wounded are heard.
⁵³ Even if Babylon reaches the sky
　　and fortifies its lofty citadel,
　my destroyers would still fall on it
　　at my command, says YHWH."

⁵⁴ Listen to the shouting from Babylon,
　　sounds of immense destruction from it.
⁵⁵ The advancing wave booms and roars
　　like mighty oceans,
　for YHWH despoils Babylon
　　and will silence the din of the city.
⁵⁶ A destroyer has come against Babylon;
　　its warriors are captives, their bows broken;
　but YHWH, a God of retribution, repays in full.
⁵⁷ "I will make its officials and sages drunk,
　　its governors, its deputies, and its warriors;
　they will sleep a perpetual sleep and never wake,"
　　says the Ruler, whose name is YHWH Omnipotent.
⁵⁸ Thus says YHWH Omnipotent:
　"Babylon's thick wall will be torn down
　　and its high gate set afire;
　the exhausting labor of the peoples is useless;
　　and the labor of nations is only fuel for the fire."

⁵⁹ This is the order that the prophet Jeremiah gave Seraiah ben-Neriah
ben-Mahseiah, when he went with Zedekiah ruler of Judah to Babylon, in

the fourth year of his reign. Seraiah was the quartermaster. ⁶⁰ Jeremiah wrote in a scroll all about the disasters that would come upon Babylon—all that were recorded concerning Babylon.

⁶¹ And Jeremiah said to Seraiah, "When you come to Babylon, see that you read aloud what is written on the scroll. ⁶² Then say, 'YHWH, you yourself threatened to destroy this place so that neither people nor animals will ever live in this desolate place again.' ⁶³ When you finish reading this scroll, tie a stone to it and throw it into the middle of the Euphrates, ⁶⁴ saying, 'So will Babylon sink, never to rise again after the disaster I am going to bring upon it.'"

The words of Jeremiah end here.

Zedekiah, twenty-two years old when he became the ruler, reigned in Jerusalem for eleven years.* Zedekiah's mother, Hamutal from Libnah, was Jeremiah's daughter. ² The ruler did what was evil in the sight of YHWH, just as Jehoiakim had done. ³ Indeed, Jerusalem and Judah so angered YHWH that in the end God banished them from the divine presence.

Now Zedekiah rebelled against the ruler of Babylon. ⁴ So in the ninth year of Zedekiah's reign, on the tenth day of the tenth month, Nebuchadnezzar ruler of Babylon marched against Jerusalem with a whole army. They camped outside the city and built siegeworks against it on every side. ⁵ The siege lasted until the eleventh year of Zedekiah the ruler. ⁶ The famine was so severe that by the ninth day of the fourth month there was no food left for the people to eat. ⁷ On that day, the city wall was breached, and all the defending troops fled; though the Babylonians surrounded Jerusalem, the defenders left the city at night through the gate between the two walls near the ruler's garden. They retreated toward the Arabah, ⁸ but the Babylonian soldiers pursued the ruler, and overtook Zedekiah on the plains of Jericho. Now separated from him, all his troops scattered, ⁹ and he was captured.

Zedekiah was taken to the ruler of Babylon at Riglah in the land of Hamath, where sentence was passed on him. ¹⁰ The ruler of Babylon had

---

* This last chapter is a later addition, though chronologically it belongs considerably earlier in the book, and much of the material repeats the text of chapter 39.

Zedekiah's heirs slain before his eyes, and put to death all the officers of Judah at Riblah. ¹¹ Then he had Zedekiah bound with bronze shackles, had his eyes put out, and took him to Babylon. He was imprisoned there till the day he died.

¹² On the tenth day of the fifth month, in the nineteenth year of Nebuchadnezzar ruler of Babylon, Nebuzaradan commander of the guard came to Jerusalem, ¹³ and set fire to the Temple and the ruler's residence as well as to all the houses in the city. Every important building was burned to the ground. ¹⁴ The entire Babylonian army under the commander of the guard pulled down all the walls surrounding Jerusalem. ¹⁵ Nebuzardan the commander of the guard carried off into exile whoever was left in the city, and whoever had deserted to the ruler of Babylon, together with the rest of the artisans. ¹⁶ But Nebuzaradan the commander of the guard left some of the poorest people of the land to work the vineyards and the fields.

¹⁷ The Babylonians broke up the bronze pillars, the movable stands and the bronze Sea in the Temple of YHWH and carried off all the metal to Babylon. ¹⁸ They took away the pots, shovels, snuffers, basins, ladles, and all the vessels of bronze used in the Temple service. ¹⁹ The commander of the guard also took away the small bowls, the fire pans, the basins, the pots, the lampstands, the spoons, and the gold and silver libation bowls. ²⁰ The two pillars, the Sea and the twelve bronze bulls that supported it, and the movable stands that Solomon the ruler had made for the Temple of YHWH, contained bronze that was beyond weighing. ²¹ Each of the pillars was 27 feet high and 18 feet in circumference; the hollow pillars were four fingers thick. ²² The bronze capital on top of one of the pillars was nearly 8 feet high and was decorated with a network of pomegranates all around. The other pillar was similar, and also had pomegranates. ²³ There were 96 pomegranates on the sides; in all, there were 100 pomegranates above the surrounding network.

²⁴ The commander of the guard took as prisoners Seraiah the chief priest, Zephaniah the deputy chief priest, and the three doorkeepers. ²⁵ Of those still in the city he took the officer in charge of the defending soldiers, and the seven members of the ruler's council. He also took the adjutant general responsible for military conscription and sixty citizens of distinction who remained in the city. ²⁶ All of these Nebuzaradan commander of the guard brought to the ruler of Babylon at Riblah. ²⁷ There the ruler of Babylon had them flogged and executed at Riblah in the land of Hamath.

So Judah went into exile, away from its own land. ²⁸ These were the people deported by Nebuchadnezzar: in the seventh year of his reign, 3,023 people of Judah; ²⁹ in Nebuchadnezzar's eighteenth year, 832 people from Jerusalem;

[30] in Nebuchadnezzar's twenty-third year, 745 people of Judah taken into exile by Nebuzaradan, commander of the guard. There were 4,600 people in all.

[31] In the thirty-seventh year of the exile of Jehoiachin ruler of Judah, on the twenty-fifth day of the twelfth month, Evil-Merodach, in the first year of his elevation to the throne of Babylon, released Jehoiachin ruler of Judah from prison. [32] Evil-Merodach treated him kindly and gave him a seat of honor higher than the seats of other rulers who were exiled in Babylon. [33] So Jehoiachin set aside his prison garb and lived as a pensioner of the ruler for the rest of his life. [34] For his daily needs the ruler of Babylon gave Jehoiachin a regular allowance till the day of his death.

ezekiel

When i was thirty years old and
living among the exiles by the Kebar River, on the fifth day of the fourth
month, the heavens opened and I had visions of God.* ² On the fifth day of
the month—it was the fifth year of exile for Jehoiachin the ruler— ³ the word
of YHWH came to the priest Ezekiel ben-Buzi, in the land of the Chaldeans
by the Kebar River.† It was there that YHWH's hand rested on me.

⁴ In my vision I saw a vast desert storm, a whirlwind coming down from
the north—a huge cloud surrounded by a brilliant light, with fire flashing out of it. The center of the cloud—the center of the fire—looked like

---

* The Talmud says, in one famous passage, "The story of creation should not be expounded before two
persons, nor the chapter on the Chariot before even one, unless that person is a sage and already has
an independent understanding of the matter." This vision has stood as the central image of Jewish
mysticism for a good twenty-one centuries; "merkabah mysticism" (which relates to the throne of
God and the Chariot, or merkabah, that bears it) found its greatest voice during the Middle Ages
and strongly influenced the development of the Kabbalah. Biblical scholars have long felt that this
chapter is among the most difficult to translate in the entire Bible; the text abounds in obscurities
and apparent confusion.
† The Kebar "River" was the Nari Kabari, or Great Canal, an irrigation canal that left the Euphrates
above Babylon and flowed southeast before rejoining the Euphrates.

electricity.* ⁵ Within the fire I saw what looked like four living creatures† in human form. ⁶ Each had four faces and four wings. ⁷ Their legs stood together rigidly as if they had a single straight leg, the bottom of which was rounded like a single calf's foot, and the legs gleamed like glowing bronze. ⁸ They had human hands under their wings on all four sides. And all four figures had faces and wings, ⁹ and the wings touched one another. They did not turn when they moved—each went straight ahead, any direction that it faced.

¹⁰ Each of the four had a human face, a lion's face to the right, a bull's face to the left, and an eagle's face— ¹¹ thus were their faces.‡ Two of their four wings spread upward and touched the wings of the figure on either side of them, and two of their wings covered their bodies. ¹² They moved straight ahead, any direction they faced; whichever way the wind blew, they went, without turning as they moved. ¹³ In the midst of these living creatures was a fiery glow like burning coals, or like torches moving back and forth between them—it was a bright fire, and lightning flashed forth from it. ¹⁴ The creatures sped to and fro like thunderbolts.§

¹⁵ As I looked at the living creatures, I saw four wheels on the ground, one beside each creature. ¹⁶ The wheels glistened as if made of chrysolite. Each of the four identical wheels held a second wheel intersecting it at right angles, ¹⁷ giving the wheel the ability to move in any of the four directions that the creatures faced without turning as they moved. ¹⁸ The wheels were enormous, and they were terrifying because the rims were covered all over with eyes.

¹⁹ When the living creatures moved, the wheels beside them moved; and when the living creatures lifted from the ground, the wheels lifted. ²⁰ Wherever the wind moved, they would move, and the wheels moved as well,

---

* The Hebrew word is *hashmal*, which is the modern Hebrew word for electricity. The ancient Hebrew word, however, may refer to an amber-colored alloy of silver and gold called electrum, known for its high reflectability; or it could refer to amber, the resin gum of prehistoric pine trees, known from antiquity to have electrical properties when rubbed—indeed, the word "electricity" is derived from the *elektron*, the Greek word for amber. The Jewish mystical tradition found hashmal a powerful concept. A passage in the Talmud says that *hashmal* may be interpreted as "speech without sound" or "speaking silence," or may be viewed as a sort of acronym for the phrase "living creatures speaking fire" in Hebrew. Another passage cites the story of a child "who was reading at the home of a teacher, and suddenly apprehended what *hashmal* was, whereupon a fire went forth from *hashmal* and consumed the child" as the reason some rabbis sought to conceal or suppress the book of *Ezekiel*.

† If Ezekiel's description of the living creatures seems confusing to us, it may be because the vision was confusing to him. Though the term "living creatures" is feminine in the Hebrew, Ezekiel frequently employs masculine suffixes and verb agreements; this may indicate the difficulty Ezekiel had in describing the creatures' androgyny—or even what they looked like. They clearly resemble Assyrian or Akkadian winged sphinxes in many details: most had a human head or torso, the wings of an eagle, the forelegs of a lion, and the hindquarters of a bull.

‡ The number four—four faces, four wings, four creatures—symbolizes the four directions, that is, the omnipresence of divinity in the world and nature. These four may represent the four main "tribes" of land creatures: humankind, birds, wild animals, and domestic animals.

§ Or possibly, "kept disappearing and reappearing like lightning flashes."

because the spirit of the living creatures was in the wheels.* ²¹ When the beings moved, the wheels moved; when they stopped, the wheels stopped. And when they rose from the ground, the wheels rose up as well, for the spirit of the living creatures was in the wheels.

²² Over the heads of the living creatures was something like an expanse† that glistened like a sheet of ice. ²³ Under this vault-like structure their wings spread out toward one another and each had a pair of wings covering its body. ²⁴ When the creatures moved, their wings made a noise like the roar of rushing waters, like the voice of the Breasted God,‡ like the din of a moving army,§ ²⁵ and a Voice came from above the expanse over their heads. When they stood still, they lowered their wings.

²⁶ Above the vault over their heads there appeared what looked a judgment seat of sapphire, and high above on the judgment seat sat a figure in the likeness of a human being. ²⁷ From the waist up, the figure looked like electricity, like metal glowing in a furnace; and from the waist down, it looked like fire surrounded by a brilliant light. ²⁸ The radiance was like the appearance of a rainbow in the clouds on a rainy day. It looked like the appearance of the Glory of YHWH. When I saw it, I fell on my face, and heard a Voice speaking to me.

2:1 The Voice said, "Mere mortal,** stand up, and I will speak with you!" ² As it spoke, spirit entered me and raised me onto my feet, and I heard these words:

³ "Mere mortal, I am sending you to the Israelites, to a rebellious nation that revolted against me; they and their ancestors have been rebelling against me to this very day. ⁴ The people to whom I send you are defiant and stubborn. You are to say to them, 'Thus says Sovereign YHWH!' ⁵ And whether they listen or they don't—for they are a rebellious house—they will know that a prophet has come among them. ⁶ And you, mere mortal, fear neither them nor their words. Don't be afraid even if they resist and reject

---

* In Hebrew, *ruach* means wind, spirit, or even breath; it is the animating and life-giving principle, the creative and healing activity of God that bridges the gap between the divine and the human; it is both kinetic energy and the spark of life.

† This is the same word as in Genesis 1:6, where God created an expanse in the heavens to separate "the water above" from "the water below."

‡ The name *El Shaddai* is usually translated "the Almighty," under the assumption that it derives either from the word *shadad*, which means "burly" or "powerful," or from *shadah*, which means "mountain," making the name mean "God of the mountains." There is growing opinion, however, that Shaddai may derive from the word *shad* or "breast"—thus El Shaddai may be a feminine image of God meaning "the Breasted God." Then again, since mountains are frequently shaped like breasts, these two interpretations are not mutually exclusive.

§ The Hebrew text here repeats the end of the next verse, most likely through a scribal error.

** The phrase *ben-Adam*, which means "offspring of Adam" or "child of humanity," occurs over ninety times in the text. The term is used to contrast the mortality of the prophet with the immortal grandeur of God.

you, and you find yourself among briers and thorns and living among scorpions. Don't be afraid of what they say; don't be terrified by them, for they are a rebellious house. [7] You must speak my words to them, whether they listen or, in their rebelliousness, refuse to listen. [8] But you, mere mortal, heed what I say to you and don't rebel like them. Open your mouth and eat what I feed you."

[9] Then I looked and I saw a hand stretched to me, holding a scroll. [10] The scroll, unrolled for me so that I would see the writing front and back, held words of lament, mourning and woe.

[3:1] Then the Voice said to me, "Mere mortal, eat what is before you. Eat this scroll and then go and speak to to the House of Israel."

[2] So I opened my mouth and was given the scroll to eat, [3] as the Voice said, "Mere mortal, eat this scroll I hand you and fill your stomach with it." I swallowed it, and it tasted as sweet as honey in my mouth.

[4] The Voice said to me, "Mere mortal, go to the Israelites and declare my words to them. [5] I am sending you not to a people of obscure speech and difficult language, but to the House of Israel. [6] I send you not to big nations that speak a foreign and difficult tongue, whose words you cannot understand—though if I were to send you to them, they would listen to you! [7] But the House of Israel is unwilling to listen to you because its people are unwilling to listen to me, for the whole House of Israel is hard-headed and obstinate. [8] But I will make you as hard-headed and obstinate as they are! [9] I will give you a resolve that is as hard as a diamond, for a diamond is harder than flint. Don't fear them. Don't be terrified by them; for they are a rebellious house.

[10] "Mere mortal, listen carefully to all that I say to you. Take it to heart. [11] Now go to your exiled sisters and brothers and say to them, 'Thus says Sovereign YHWH!'—whether they listen or choose not to listen."

[12] Then the spirit lifted me up, and I heard behind me a sound of a powerful earthquake as the Glory of YHWH rose from its place— [13] it was the sound of the living creatures' wings brushing against one another, and the sound of the wheels alongside them, that made the loud rumbling. [14] The wind lifted me up and carried me away, bitter in the fury of my spirit, with the hand of YHWH heavily upon me. [15] I came to the exiles living on the ancient flood plain by the Kebar River. And I sat there among them, stunned, for seven days.

[16] After seven days the word of YHWH came to me: [17] "Mere mortal, I appointed you to be a sentinel to the Israelites; you are to pass to them the warnings you receive from me. [18] If I pronounce a death sentence on evil-

doers, and you do not warn or dissuade them to forsake evil and make a new start—thus saving their lives—the evildoers will die for their sins, but I will hold you accountable for their deaths. ¹⁹ But if you warn evildoers but they do not listen and change their ways, they will die for their sins, and you will have saved yourself. ²⁰ Again, if good people abandon justice and commit iniquity, and I place stumbling blocks before them, they will die. If you do not warn them, they will die for their sins and their former good deeds will not be considered—and I will hold you accountable for their deaths. ²¹ But if you warn the just ones not to sin, and they obey, then they will have saved their lives because they heeded your warnings, and you will have saved your own life."

²² The hand of YHWH was upon me there, and God said to me, "Get up and go out to the valley, and there I will speak to you."

²³ I got up and went out into the valley. And there stood the Glory of YHWH, like the Glory I had seen by the Kebar River, and I prostrated myself before it. ²⁴ Then spirit entered me and set me upon my feet. YHWH said to me, "Go, shut yourself in your house. ²⁵ As for you, mere mortal, ropes have been put upon you; they will bind you and keep you from going among the people. ²⁶ And I will make your tongue stick to the roof of your mouth. Speechless, you will be unable to censure them, for they are a rebellious house.* ²⁷ But when I have something to say to you, I will open your mouth, and you will tell them, 'Thus says Sovereign YHWH.' Whoever will listen, let them listen; and whoever will not listen, let them not listen. For they are a rebellious house.

ল্য   ল্য   ল্য

4:1 "Mere mortal, take a clay tablet and lay it in front of you. Draw a picture of Jerusalem on it. ² Portray it as embattled: place war machines and palisades and ramps against its walls and war camps all around it. Put battering rams on every side. ³ Then take an iron pan and position it as if it were an iron wall between you and the city; turn your face toward it. It will be the besieged and you the besieger. This is to be a sign to the House of Israel.

⁴ "Then lie on your left side and take on the weight of Israel's punishment. For as long as you lie on your left side you will bear its punishment. ⁵ I appoint you to do this for 390 days—one day for each year of their guilt. So for 390 days you will bear the sin of the House of Israel. ⁶ Once you complete

---

* In other words, by preventing Ezekiel from preaching, God is keeping him from warning the people and saving them from punishment.

ezekiel 4

this, lie down on your right side and bear the sin of Judah. I appoint you to do this for forty days—one day for each year of their guilt.* ⁷ Then set your face toward the siege of Jerusalem and with a bared arm prophesy against it. ⁸ Now you can understand why I tie you with ropes so that you cannot turn from one side to the other until you have finished the days of your seige.

⁹ "Take wheat, barley, beans, lentils, millet, and spelt. Store them in a single container and use the mixture for making bread. Eat it during the 390 days you lie in your side. ¹⁰ Your daily ration, eaten at a set time, is eight ounces. ¹¹ Your daily ration of drinking water, one pint, is to be drunk at a set time. ¹² Eat your bread like a barley cake, which you have baked in the sight of the people using human excrement as fuel. ¹³ Do it this way," YHWH continued, "because this is the way the Israelites will eat their bread—unclean—when I exile them among the nations."

¹⁴ Then I protested, "But Sovereign YHWH, I have never defiled myself! Never in my whole life did I eat anything that died a natural death or mauled by wild animals!"

¹⁵ And God said to me, "Very well. I will allow you to use cow dung rather than human dung when baking your bread."

¹⁶ Then God said to me, "Mere mortal, I will cut short the supply of bread in Jerusalem. People will anxiously weigh out the bread they eat and, with dismay, measure out the water they drink. ¹⁷ But their food and water will dwindle until they stare at one another in horror because they are wasting away—all because of their sin.

5:1 "Mere mortal, take a sharp sword and, using it like a razor, shave your head and your chin. Then take a set of scales and divide the hair into three piles. ² Once the seige ends, burn one-third of the hair in a fire in the center of the city; take another third and go through the city, cutting it into bits with the sword; and scatter the final third to the wind—for I will pursue the people with a sword in my hand! ³ Then take a few strands of your hair

---

* These numbers are both symbolic and literal. When added together, the 390 and 40 years total 430, the exact number of years that Israel had sojourned in Egypt; Hosea made the connection explicit when he spoke of the Assyrian captivity as being "a return to Egypt," and Ezekiel's symbolic bondage for these fourteen months underscores the symbol even further: the nation's rebellion against God, say the prophets, always leads to captivity and bondage. The 390 years of Israel's guilt began in 979 B.C.E., when Jeroboam erected the altar to the golden calves (prompting the nation's division into northern and southern realms), and ended with the seige of Jerusalem in 589. The 40 years of Judah's guilt are likely the period from the broken treaty during the thirteenth year of Josiah's reign in 627 to the fall of Jerusalem in 587—the period during which Jeremiah was prophesying. Despite the sweeping national reforms instituted by Josiah in 622, Jeremiah believed that the reforms were largely superficial and created a false sense of security, since they were based on the outward performance of religious rites unaccompanied by genuine inward transformation.

and wrap them in the folds of your robe. ⁴ Finally, take a few strands and throw them into a fire and burn them up; for a fire will spread from there to the whole House of Israel.*

⁵ "For thus says Sovereign YHWH: This is Jerusalem, which I placed in the middle of the nations, surrounded by foreign countries. But it rebelled against my decrees and my statutes even more than the surrounding countries. ⁶ For it rejected my decrees and refused to keep my statutes. ⁷ You are more insubordinate than the nations surrounding you, says YHWH, and have neither followed my laws nor kept my decrees, nor even followed the statutes of the nations surrounding you. ⁸ Therefore, says YHWH, I myself will challenge you! I will punish you in full view of the nations. ⁹ And because of all your abominations, I will do something I never did before, and the like of which I will never do again. ¹⁰ Parents will eat their children, and children will eat their parents in your midst, Jerusalem. I will punish you, and I will scatter your survivors to the four winds. ¹¹ As I live, says Sovereign YHWH, because you defiled my Temple with your vile idols and detestable practices, I in turn will cut you down† without pity—no one will be spared. ¹² One-third of you will die of pestilence or famine; one-third will fall by the sword in the countries surrounding you; and one-third I will scatter to the winds and will pursue with a drawn sword.

¹³ "I will be appeased only when my wrath is spent and my fury ceases. And you will know that I, YHWH, spoke in my jealousy, when I spent my fury on you. ¹⁴ I will have reduced you to ruins and made you an object of mockery to the nations surrounding you and to all who pass by. ¹⁵ You will become an object of contempt and shame, an object lesson of horror to the nations surrounding you, once I pass sentence on you and punish you in anger and fury. I, YHWH, have spoken.

¹⁶ "When I release my deadly arrows of starvation against you, I will shoot to kill. I will send one famine after another on you and cut off your supply of bread. ¹⁷ Against you I intend to send famine and wild animals to rob you of your children. Pestilence and bloodshed will surge through you, and I will bring the sword against you. I, YHWH, have spoken."

6:1 The word of YHWH came to me: ² "Mere mortal, look toward the mountains of Israel and prophesy against them. ³ Say, 'Mountains of Israel, hear

---

* The hair is a sign of dignity, and because it grows faster than any other part of the body, is also a special sign of God's life-giving presence. The act of shaving here is symbolic of God's action in destroying Judah. The reference to the few strands in the prophet's robe is symbolic of the remnant who would be salvaged from captivity.

† Some Hebrew manuscripts have "will withdraw," which could indicate that God's protective presence will be removed so that Chaldea is able to destroy Jerusalem without mercy.

the word of Sovereign YHWH! This is what Sovereign YHWH says to the mountains and the hills, to the ravines and the valleys: I myself will bring a sword against you, and I will destroy your shrines. ⁴ Your altars will be wiped out, your incense altars broken down, and I will slay your people in front of your idols. ⁵ I will pile the corpses of the Israelites before their idols and scatter their bones among the ruins of your altars. ⁶ Wherever you dwell, your towns will be laid waste and your shrines smashed; your altars will be destroyed and laid waste; your idols abolished and smashed; your incense altars torn down; and the gods you created wiped out. ⁷ Your people will fall slain in your midst, and then you will know that I am YHWH.'

⁸ "But I will spare a remnant. Some of you will escape the sword among the nations and be scattered among their lands. ⁹ There in exile among the nations, those who escape will remember me, and know that I am broken-hearted over their wanton and wayward hearts which strayed from me, hurt by their adulterous eyes which lusted after their idols. They will hate themselves for the evil they have done and for all their detestable practices. ¹⁰ And they will understand that it was not without good reason that I, YHWH, brought this disaster on them."

¹¹ Thus says Sovereign YHWH: "Beat your hands together and stamp your feet and cry out, 'Woe is me, for all the vile abominations of the House of Israel! For we will fall by the sword, by pestilance and by plague!' ¹² Those in distant places will die by pestilence and those nearby will die by the sword. Any who survive or are spared will die of famine. Thus will I spend my rage upon them. ¹³ You will know that I am YHWH when your slain fall among the idols around the altars, on every high hill and mountaintop, under every spreading tree or leafy oak—places where you offered fragrant incense to your idols. ¹⁴ And I will stretch out my hand against you and make the land a desolate waste, more desolate than the desert of Riblah.* Then you will know that I am YHWH."

7:1 The word of YHWH came to me: ² "Mere mortal, Sovereign YHWH says this to the land of Israel:

'The end is coming
to the four corners of the earth.
³ Now the end is upon you
and I will unleash my anger on you.
I will judge you according to your conduct
and repay you for all your detestable practices.

---

* The town of Riblah (the Hebrew text has "Diblah," but this is a scribal error) was located on the extreme northern border of Israel, where Nebuchadnezzar had his headquarters during his campaign against Jerusalem.

4   I will neither show mercy
      nor spare you.
    I will punish you for your conduct
      and the abominations in your midst.
    Then you will know
      that I am in your midst.
5   Thus says YHWH:
      disasters approach, one after another.
6   The end has come!
    The end has come!
    It has roused itself against you.
    It has come!
7   Doom is coming upon you,
      dweller in the land.
    The time has come, the day is near—
      a day of panic, not of rejoicing.
8   Soon now I will pour out
      my wrath on you;
      let my anger spend itself.
    I will judge you by your ways
      and punish you for your abominations.
9   Neither will I look on you with mercy
      nor will I spare you;
    I will make you suffer for your ways
      and your detestable practices in your midst.
    Then you will know it is I, YHWH,
      who struck you.
10   The day approachs;
      doom has burst forth;
    the rod has budded
      arrogance has blossomed!
11   Violence leads to flagrant abuses.
      None will be left, none of that crowd.
    No wealth,
      nothing of value.
12   The time is near,
      the day has arrived.
    Let neither buyer rejoice nor seller regret,
      for anger reigns against all equally.

13 " /Sellers will not recover what they sold in their lifetime, for the vision concerning their whole crowd will not be revoked. And their sinfulness

ensures them a short lifetime. ¹⁴ The trumpet sounds for battle, but none go into battle, for my wrath is upon the whole multitude of them.

¹⁵ " 'Outside is the sword, inside are pestilence and famine. Those out in the open will die by the sword; those in the city will die by famine and pestilence. ¹⁶ Any who survive will be found in the mountains, cooing like valley doves, all moaning over their evil deeds. ¹⁷ All hands will grow weak; all knees turn to water. ¹⁸ They will dress up in sackcloth, but be clothed in terror. Shame will cover their faces and heads will be shaved bald. ¹⁹ They will fling their silver into the streets and treat gold as so much filth. Their silver and gold will not save them on the day of YHWH's fury. Their hunger will not be satisfied nor their bellies filled. For their evil deeds will be their downfall. ²⁰ They prided themselves on their beautiful jewelry—with which they fashioned their abominable idols; therefore, I will make them look upon it as something unclean. ²¹ I will hand it over as plunder to foreigners and booty to the evildoers of the world, who will profane it.

²² " 'I will turn my face from them while they desecrate my treasured place. Thieves will enter it and desecrate it. ²³ Prepare chains, for the land is full of bloodshed and the city is full of violence. ²⁴ I will allow the most corrupt of the nations to possess their homes. I will put an end to the pride of the mighty; and their sanctuaries will be defiled. ²⁵ Once terror reigns, they will seek peace—to no avail. ²⁶ Calamity upon calamity will rule, and rumor upon rumor. They will seek a vision from the prophet; but neither teaching of the law from the priest nor counsel from the elder is to be given. ²⁷ The ruler will mourn; officials will be wrapped in despair; and the hands of the rural folk will tremble. I will treat them as they deserve and I will judge them by their conduct. Then they will learn that I am YHWH.' "

આ   આ   આ

8:1 On the fifth day of the sixth month in the sixth year of Jehoiachin's exile, as I sat at home visiting with the elders of Judah, I suddenly felt the power of Sovereign YHWH come over me. ² I saw what looked like a human figure; from the waist down it seemed to be nothing but fire, and from there up it glittered like polished brass. ³ The figure stretched out what appeared to be a hand and, taking me by the hair on my head, lifted me up between heaven and earth. And in visions from God, a spirit took me to Jerusalem, to the entrance to the north gate of the inner court, where stood the Idol of Jealousy.

⁴ And there before me was the Glory of the God of Israel, the same vision I had seen in the valley. ⁵ Then God said to me: "Mere mortal, look to the north." So I looked, and in the entrance north of the altar gate stood the Idol

of Jealousy. ⁶ And once more God addressed me: "Mere mortal, do you see what they are doing? These utterly detestable things the House of Israel is doing here will drive me from my sanctuary! And you will see even more detestable things!"

⁷ Then the spirit brought me to the entrance to the court. I looked, and I saw a hole in the wall. ⁸ "Dig through the wall, mere mortal," it instructed me. I did as I was instructed, and after making an opening, was told, ⁹ "Go in and see the vile abominations they practice there." ¹⁰ I went in and saw portrayed on the wall all kinds of creeping things, loathsome animals and all the idols of the House of Israel. ¹¹ Standing before them were seventy elders of Israel, with Jaazaniah ben-Shaphan in the middle; each held a censer from which rose fragrant incense smoke. ¹² The spirit said to me, "Mere mortal, see what the elders of Israel do in the dark, all at shrines of their own carved idols? They believe that YHWH doesn't see them; that YHWH has abandoned the country." ¹³ The spirit also said to me, "You will see even more of the detestable things they practice."

¹⁴ Then I was brought to the entrance of the north gate of the Temple where people were sitting there weeping for Tammuz.* ¹⁵ I was told, "See this, mere mortal? You will see even more of the detestable things they practice."

¹⁶ And I was then brought into the inner court of the Temple. There, at the entrance of the Temple, between the porch and the altar, stood about twenty-five people with their backs to the Temple; they faced east and prostrated themselves to the rising sun. ¹⁷ Then God said to me, "Have you seen enough, mere mortal? Is it such a trivial thing that they do here? Must they also fill the country with violence and continually provoke my anger? Look, they are putting the branch to their nose! ¹⁸ I will not look on them with pity and spare them. Even if they shout in my ears, I will not spare them."

9:1 Then a loud voice rang out in my ears: "Here they come, those nominated to punish the city, each carrying a weapon of destruction." ² I saw six warriors approach from the direction of the upper gate, which faces north, each carrying a weapon of destruction. With them was a scribe clothed in linen and carrying a writing case. They entered and stood beside the bronze altar.

³ Then the Glory of the God of Israel rose from above the cherubim† where it rested and moved to the threshold of the Temple. Then God called to the scribe clothed in linen carrying a writing kit ⁴ and said, "Go throughout

---

* Tammuz was the Babylonian god of vegetation; his Sumerian name was Dumuzi.
† The cherubim or *kerubim* were fearsome mythic creatures, great winged sphynxes or griffins— essentially the four living creatures of chapter 1 in iconic representation. The reference here is to the bronze cherubim that were attached to the cover of the Ark of the Covenant as it sat in the inner sanctuary of the Temple; the *shekinah*, or Presence of YHWH, would rest above it.

the city of Jerusalem and mark the forehead of everyone who laments and grieves over all the vile things being done in it."

⁵ To the others, I heard YHWH say, "Follow the scribe through the city and strike; show neither mercy nor compassion. ⁶ Execute the elderly, young women and men, mothers and children, but don't touch any who have the mark. Begin at my sanctuary." So they began with the elders standing in front of the Temple.

⁷ "Defile the Temple," God said. "Fill the court with corpses, and move out." So they went out and began executing throughout the city. ⁸ While they were executing I was left alone. And I prostrated myself, crying out, "O Sovereign YHWH! Are you going to destroy the entire remnant of Israel in this outpouring of your rage on Jerusalem?"

⁹ And God answered, "The iniquity of Israel and Judah is beyond measure. The countryside is filled with bloodshed and the city is filled with injustice. They say, 'YHWH abandoned the land; YHWH does not see.' ¹⁰ I will neither look down on them with pity nor spare them. And I will bring down upon their heads what they did."

¹¹ Then the scribe clothed in linen and carrying a writing case brought word, saying, "I have done what you commanded."

10:1 I looked and I saw a judgment seat of sapphires above the expanse over the heads of the cherubim. ² God said to the scribe clothed in linen, "Go in among the wheels under the cherubim. Fill your hands with burning coals from among the cherubim and scatter them over the city." I watched as the scribe went in.

³ The cherubim stood at the right side of the Temple as the scribe entered, and a cloud filled the court. ⁴ Then the Glory of YHWH rose from above the cherubim and moved to the threshold of the Temple. The cloud filled the Temple, and the court was full of the radiance of the Glory of YHWH. ⁵ The noise of the wings of the cherubim could be heard as far away as the outer court; it sounded like the voice of the Breasted God.

⁶ When YHWH commanded the scribe in linen, "Take fire among the wheels, from among the cherubim," the scribe went in and stood beside a wheel. ⁷ Then one of the cherubim reached a hand into the fire among them, and took some of the coals and put them in the hands of the scribe in linen, who took it and went away. ⁸ Under the wings of the cherubim could be seen what looked like human hands.

⁹ I looked and saw four wheels beside the cherubim, one wheel beside each creature. The wheels sparkled like chrysolite, ¹⁰ and all four were alike. Each was like a wheel intersecting another wheel at right angles. ¹¹ As they moved they went in any one of the four directions the cherubim faced, always going straight ahead. The cherubim went in whatever direction the

head was facing, without turning as they went. ¹² Their entire bodies—their backs, hands, and wings—as well as the wheels were completely covered with eyes. ¹³ I heard the wheels being called "the whirling wheels." ¹⁴ Each of the cherubim had four faces: One face was that of a cherub; another, that of a human being; another, that of a lion; and another, that of an eagle.*

¹⁵ Then the cherubim rose upward from the ground. These were the same living creatures I had seen at the Kebar River. ¹⁶ When the cherubim moved, the wheels beside them moved. And when the cherubim spread their wings to rise from the ground, the wheels did not leave their sides. ¹⁷ When the cherubim stood still, the wheels also stood still. And when the cherubim rose, the wheels rose with them, for the spirit of the creatures was in the wheels.

¹⁸ Then the Glory of YHWH departed from the threshold of the Temple and hovered above the cherubim. ¹⁹ They spread their wings and raised themselves from the ground. I watched them move with the wheels beside them. They stopped at the entrance to the east gate of the Temple. And the Glory of YHWH of Israel was above them.

²⁰ These were the living creatures that I had seen beneath YHWH of Israel by the Kebar River, and I then knew that they were cherubim. ²¹ Each had four faces and four wings, and under their wings was what looked like human hands. ²² Their faces were like those I had seen in my vision by the Kebar River. Each one moved straight forward.

11:1 Then the spirit lifted me up and brought me to the gate of the Temple facing east. There at the entrance to the gate stood twenty-five prominent citizens. Among them I saw Jaazaniah ben-Azzur, and Pelatiah ben-Benaiah, officials of the people. ² YHWH said to me, "Mere mortal, these are the people who concoct evil schemes and spread bad advice in the city.† ³ They say, 'Isn't it about the time to build houses? This city is a cooking pot, and we are the meat!' ⁴ Therefore, prophesy against them—prophesy, mere mortal!"

⁵ Then the Spirit of God fell on me, and told me what to say. This is what YHWH told me to say: "Thus says YHWH: I know what you've been saying, House of Israel, and I know what you have in mind. ⁶ You killed many people in this city and filled its streets with corpses. ⁷ Now, thus says Sovereign YHWH: It is the bodies of your victims that are the meat, in this cooking-pot of a city. But I will drive you out of the city. ⁸ You fear the sword, so the

---

* This description may be a scribal error; whereas here one face is described as being that of a cherub, in the first chapter the corresponding face was that of a bull; indeed, the Egyptian, Assyrian, and Babylonian versions of the cherubim (Hebrew: *kerubim*) generally had a bull's body, a lion's paws and tail, an eagle's wings, and a human head.

† This refers to the pro-Egyptian rulers who were the moving power in the revolt against Babylon.

sword is what I will bring against you, declares Sovereign YHWH. ⁹ I will drive you out of the city and hand you over to foreigners. I will bring you to justice. ¹⁰ You will fall by the sword, and the sword brings my judgment against you at the frontier of Israel. Then you will know that I am YHWH. ¹¹ This city will not be your cooking pot, nor will you be inside it long enough to become meat—I will bring judgment against you at the border of Israel. ¹² And you will know that I am YHWH, for you did not follow my decrees or keep my statutes. Instead, you have adopted the practices of the nations around you."

¹³ Now as I was prophesying, Pelatiah ben-Benaiah dropped dead. And I threw myself on the ground, crying out in a loud voice, "Sovereign YHWH! Will you completely destroy the remnant of Israel?"

¹⁴ Then the word of YHWH came to me: ¹⁵ "Mere mortal, your own kin, this whole people of Israel, all of them, are the ones the inhabitants of Jerusalem are talking about when they say, 'They are separated from YHWH; this land has been given over to us as our possession.' ¹⁶ Now say, 'Thus says Sovereign YHWH: Although I sent them away among the nations and scattered them among the countries, yet for a little while I was a sanctuary for them in the places where they were exiled.'

¹⁷ "Then, say: 'This is what Sovereign YHWH says: I will gather you from among the nations and bring you back from the countries where you were scattered, and I will return to you the land of Israel again. ¹⁸ When you return you will get rid of the vile idols and abominable practices. ¹⁹ And I will give you singleness of heart and put a new spirit in you. I will remove the heart of stone from your bodies and give you a heart of flesh. ²⁰ Then you will follow my decrees and carefully keep my laws. You will be my people, and I will be your God. ²¹ But those of you whose hearts are set on vile and abominable practices will be answerable for all that you did. This is the word of Sovereign YHWH.'"

²² Then the cherubim lifted their wings, with their wheels beside them and the Glory of the God of Israel above them. ²³ The Glory of YHWH rose up and left the city, and halted on the mountain to its east.

²⁴ The Spirit lifted me up and brought me back to the exiles in Babylon. Everything had happened in a vision given by the Spirit of God. Then the vision I saw left me. And I told the exiles all the things that YHWH had shown me.

ଔ   ଔ   ଔ

12:1 The word of YHWH came to me: ² "Mere mortal, you are living among a rebellious people. They have eyes to see but see nothing; they have ears to hear but hear nothing. ³ They are a rebellious people. So, mere mortal, pack your belongings for exile, and set off by day as they watch. Then go to another place in their sight. Perhaps they will acknowledge that they are a rebellious people. ⁴ Again: pack your belongings for exile. Then in the evening set off as if going into exile. ⁵ As they watch, dig a hole in the wall and go out through it. ⁶ Then shoulder your belongings as they watch, and move out into the dark with your face covered so that you cannot see the land. For I am making you a sign for the House of Israel."

⁷ So I did as commanded. During the day I brought out my belongings and packed for exile. Then in the evening I dug a hole in the wall with my own hands, shouldered my belongings, and carried them out into the dark as the people watched. ⁸ In the morning the word of YHWH came to me: ⁹ "Mere mortal, did the Israelites, that rebellious people, ask you what you are doing? ¹⁰ Say to them, 'Thus says YHWH: This oracle concerns the ruler and all the people of Jerusalem.' ¹¹ Say to them: 'I am a sign to warn you; what I did will be done to you. You will go into exile as prisoners. ¹² As dusk approaches, your ruler will shoulder a pack and exit through a hole in the wall; and the ruler's face will be covered so that he can avoid seeing the country. ¹³ I will spread my net over the ruler, who will be caught in my trap. And I will bring him to Babylon, the land of the Chaldeans. ¹⁴ I will scatter to the four winds all the ruler's attendants—the bodyguards, the troops. And I will pursue them with a drawn sword. ¹⁵ And they will know that I am YHWH, once I have dispersed them among the nations and scattered them over the earth. ¹⁶ But I will leave a remnant, survivors of sword, famine and plague, to acknowledge all their abominations to the peoples among whom they will go, so that these too may learn that I am YHWH.' "

¹⁷ This word of YHWH came to me: ¹⁸ "Mere mortal, tremble as you eat your bread, shudder with fear as you drink your water. ¹⁹ Say to the people: 'Thus says Sovereign YHWH to the people living in Jerusalem and in the land of Israel: You will anxiously eat your bread and drink your water in fear. For your land will be stripped of everything because of the violence of those dwelling there. ²⁰ The inhabited towns too will be laid waste and the land devastated. Then you will know that I am YHWH.' "

²¹ The word of YHWH came to me: ²² "Mere mortal, what is this proverb you have in the land of Israel?—'Days pass by and visions fade.' ²³ Now, say to the people: 'Thus says Sovereign YHWH: I will put an end to this proverb, and you will use it no more in Israel. Instead, you will say, "Days draw near when every vision becomes reality." ²⁴ There will be no more false visions, no more flattering divinations among the Israelites, ²⁵ for I, YHWH, will say

what I will, and it will be fulfilled without delay. For in your days, rebellious house, I will fulfill whatever I say, declares Sovereign YHWH.' "

²⁶ The word of YHWH came to me: ²⁷ "Mere mortal, the House of Israel is saying, 'The visions the prophets see will be fulfilled many years from now—they prophesy for the distant future.' ²⁸ Now, say to them, 'Thus says YHWH: None of my words will be delayed any longer; whatever I say will be fulfilled, declares Sovereign YHWH.' "

13:1 The word of YHWH came to me, saying: ² "Mere mortal, prophesy against the Israelite prophets now prophesying. Say to those prophesying out of their own thoughts or fancies: 'Hear the word of YHWH! ³ Thus says YHWH: Woe to the foolish prophets who follow their own spirit, and see nothing! ⁴ Your prophets, Israel, are like foxes among the ruins. ⁵ You have not moved into the breach to repair the smashed wall around the House of Israel, so that it may hold steady in the battle on the day of YHWH. ⁶ Theirs is a false vision; their soothsaying is a lie. They claim, "It is the word of YHWH," when it is not YHWH who sent them; yet they expect God to fulfill their words. ⁷ Can you deny that yours are empty visions, that you speak prophesies that are lies when you say, "It is YHWH who speaks," when I myself have not spoken?

⁸ " 'So this is what Sovereign YHWH says: Because you spoke lies and your visions are fabrications, I have turned against you, says Sovereign YHWH. ⁹ My hand will be raised against the prophets who see false visions and speak lying divinations. They will not belong to the council of my people. Their names will not be entered in the register of the House of Israel, and they will not enter the land of Israel. Then you will know that I am Sovereign YHWH.

¹⁰ " 'They deserve this because they misled my people by saying that all is well when all is not well. It is as if my people built an unstable wall and these prophets used whitewash on it, not plaster.* ¹¹ Tell these whitewashers that it will collapse, for it will rain torrents, and I will send hailstones and unleash a great wind. ¹² When the wall crumbles, people will ask, "What happened to all the whitewash you used?"

¹³ " 'So thus says Sovereign YHWH: In my wrath I will unleash a great wind, rain will come in torrents, and I will send down hailstones in destructive fury. ¹⁴ I will tear down the wall you painted with whitewash and I will level it to the ground so that its foundation will be laid bare. When it falls, you will perish with it. Then you will know that I am YHWH. ¹⁵ I will spend

---

* Mud walls required a hard, water-resistant coating in order to support them during the rainy season. Whitewash would offer only the appearance of security until the rains came.

my fury on the wall and on those who whitewashed it, and I will say to you, "The wall is no more and those who whitewashed it are no more—¹⁶ those prophets of Israel who prophesied about Jerusalem and had visions of peace for it when there was no peace," says Sovereign YHWH.'

¹⁷ "Now, mere mortal, turn your face against those soothsayers among your people whose prophesies come from their own flights of fancy. Prophesy against them, ¹⁸ saying: 'Thus says Sovereign YHWH: Woe to you, who sew magic charms on people's wrists and provide people of all ages with magic veils! Will you ensnare the lives of my people while preserving your own? ¹⁹ You have blasphemed me before my people for a few handfuls of barley and scraps of bread. By lying to my people, who love to listen to lies, you killed those who should not have died, and spared those who should not have lived.

²⁰ " 'Thus says Sovereign YHWH: I stand against your magic charms that you use to ensnare people like birds. I will free the people you snare like birds. ²¹ I will rip off your veils; and I will rescue my people from your clutches, for they will not longer fall prey to your power. Then you will know that I am YHWH. ²² Because you disheartened the just of heart with your lies—when I had caused them no grief—and because you encouraged the corrupt not to turn from their sinful ways and so save their lives, ²³ therefore you will no longer see false visions or practice divination. I will save my people from your hands. And then you will know that I am YHWH.' "

14:1 As I sat at home visiting with some of the elders of Israel, ² this word of YHWH came to me: ³ "Mere mortal, these people have enshrined their own idols in their hearts. And they are obsessed with the sinful things that caused their downfall. Am I to be consulted by people like them? ⁴ So speak to them, and say: 'Thus says Sovereign YHWH: All members of the House of Israel who have enshrined idols in their hearts, or who are obsessed with the sinful things that caused your downfall and yet come looking for the prophet—I, YHWH, will answer them, despite their gross idolatry, ⁵ in order to recapture the hearts of the people of Israel, who deserted me for their idols.'

⁶ "Therefore, say to the House of Israel, 'Thus says Sovereign YHWH: Repent! Turn away from your idols, turn your backs from your abominable practices. ⁷ All who renounce me by enshrining their own idols in their hearts—whether Israelites or resident aliens—and who cling to the cause of their sins, and then come looking for the prophet to consult me, they will get this answer from me, YHWH: ⁸ that I will set my face against you, and make you an example and a byword; I will cut you off from my people, you will know that I am YHWH.'

⁹ "If a prophet is seduced into delivering a prophecy to such a reprobate, it is I, YHWH, who deceived that prophet. I will stretch out my hand against such prophets and rid them from my people Israel. ¹⁰ Both are to be punished—the prophets and the people who consulted them are guilty. ¹¹ Never again will the people of Israel stray from me, nor will they defile themselves with their sins. They will be my people and I will be their God, says Sovereign YHWH."

¹² The word of YHWH came to me: ¹³ "Mere mortal, when a country sins against me by unfaithfulness and I stretch out my hand against it to cut off its supply of bread, and send famine upon it and kill its citizens and its animals, ¹⁴ even if such noteworthy people as Noah, Daniel,* and Job were there, they could save only themselves because of their integrity, says Sovereign YHWH.

¹⁵ "Or if I were to send wild animals into that country to destroy its people, and it becomes so desolated that travelers avoid it because of the wild animals, ¹⁶ and if these three noteworthy figures were there, as I live, says Sovereign YHWH, they could not save their own daughters and sons. They alone would be saved, but the country would be desolate.

¹⁷ "Or if I were to bring the sword against that country, and say, 'Let the sword slash throughout the land,' and I kill its people and its animals, ¹⁸ as I live, says Sovereign YHWH, they could not save their own daughters and sons. They alone would be saved. ¹⁹ Or if I send a plague into that country and pour out my fury on it through bloodshed, destroying the people and their animals, ²⁰ and if Noah, Daniel, and Job were there, as I live, they could not save their own daughters and sons. They could save only themselves because of their integrity, says Sovereign YHWH.

²¹ "For thus says Sovereign YHWH: How much worse will it be when I send my four deadly judgments against Jerusalem—the sword, famine, wild animals, and the plague—to kill its people and its animals! ²² Yet there will be survivors. Daughters and sons will be brought out of it. They will come to you, and when you witness their conduct, their actions, you will be consoled for the disaster I inflicted on Jerusalem, despite all I did to it. ²³ They will console you when you witness their conduct and their actions. And you will know that it was not without cause that I did what I did, says Sovereign YHWH."

---

* The Daniel referred to here is not the same one as in the book of *Daniel*. This Daniel is probably a popular figure known from antiquity; the reference may be to Danel of the ancient Canaanite city Ugarit, who was a judge of great integrity and was known for his effectiveness in calling upon divine intervention.

^{15:1} The word of YHWH came to me:

2   "Mere mortal, how is the wood of the vine
        superior to other wood?
     How is it superior to a tree branch
        in the forest?
3   Is its wood useful?
     Can pegs for hanging things be made from it?
4   When used for fuel
        and its two ends burn up
     with the middle charred,
        is it fit for any use at all?
5   When whole it was used for nothing.
     Now, how much less useful
        is the charred middle!

6 "Therefore says Sovereign YHWH: Like the wood of the vine among the trees of the forest, which I give to the fire for fuel, so will I give up the citizens of Jerusalem. 7 I will set my face against them. Although they survived the fire, the fire is yet to consume them. And you will know that I am YHWH, when I set my face against them. 8 And I will make the country desolate for they were unfaithful, says Sovereign YHWH."

^{16:1} The word of YHWH came to me: 2 "Mere mortal, confront Jerusalem with her detestable practices 3 and say, 'Thus says Sovereign YHWH to Jerusalem: Your ancestry and your birth were in the land of the Canaanites; your father was an Amorite and your mother was a Hittite. 4 At your birth, your umbilical cord wasn't cut, nor were you washed in water to clean you off, nor rubbed with salt and wrapped in swaddling clothes. 5 No one looked on you with pity or was compassionate enough to do any of these things. You were thrown out on the bare ground on the day you were born. 6 I came along and saw you kicking about in your blood, and as you lay there in your blood I said to you, "Live!" 7 I helped you grow up like a plant in the field. You grew up and came to full womanhood with firm breasts. Your hair had grown long, yet you were naked and bare. 8 Later, as I passed by, I noticed you were old enough for love. I spread a corner of my cloak over you, covering your nakedness. I gave you a solemn oath and entered into a covenant with you, declares Sovereign YHWH, and you became mine. 9 I bathed you with water, washed the blood from you and anointed you with oil. 10 I gave you brocaded robes and sandals of fine leather. I dressed you in a linen headband and a silk cloak. 11 I adorned you with jewelry—bracelets on your wrists, a chain around your neck, 12 a ring in your nose, earrings on your ears, and a beautiful diadem on your head. 13 So you were adorned

with gold and silver, clothed in fine linen and brocade. For food you had fine flour, honey, and olive oil. You became a great beauty and rose to be a ruler. ¹⁴ And your fame spread among the nations because of your beauty, for the splendor I gave you made your beauty perfect, says Sovereign YHWH.

¹⁵ " 'Then you became infatuated with your own beauty, and you exploited your fame; you compromised your integrity and took up with every passerby. ¹⁶ You used the cloth of your garments to decorate your shrines in gaudy colors. It was there that you lost your birthright. ¹⁷ You took the fine jewelry I gave you, and made idols which compromised you futher. ¹⁸ You covered the idols with your brocaded robes, and offered up my oil and my incense to them. ¹⁹ The food I provided you—the fine flour, the oil, and the honey—you set before them as an offering of soothing odor, says Sovereign YHWH.

²⁰ " 'Then you took the daughters and sons whom we had parented and sacrificed them as food to the idols. Wasn't your infidelity compromising enough? ²¹ You slaughtered my children and sacrificed them to idols. ²² In all your detestable practices and abominations you did not remember the days of your youth, when you were naked, kicking helplessly in your blood.

²³ " 'Woe to you! Woe to you! says Sovereign YHWH. After all the evil you did, ²⁴ you built yourself a shrine and set it on a mound, and did this in every square ²⁵ and at the head of every street. You made your beauty into something detestable, and you would spread your legs for anyone passing by, so debauched were you. ²⁶ You seduced the Egyptians, your lustful neighbors, and became even more promiscuous just to make me angry. ²⁷ So now I have stretched out my hand against you and cut off your food supply. And I gave you up to the will of those who hate you—to Philistine women, who were shocked by your lewd behavior.* ²⁸ You had relations with the Assyrians because you were not satisfied; but when you were done, were still were unsatisfied. ²⁹ You sold yourself in Chaldea, that land of merchants, yet even with this you were not satisfied.

³⁰ " 'How sick was your heart, says Sovereign YHWH, for you to do all these things, the actions of a profligate? ³¹ When you built your shrine at the beginning of every street and set your mound in every square, it wasn't prostitution, for you didn't take money. ³² No, you were an adulterer who would rather sleep with a stranger than with a spouse! ³³ And while prostitutes accept gifts, you gave your lovers gifts—to bribe them to come to you from every direction just to sleep with you.† ³⁴ So you're the opposite of a

---

* The people of the region of Philistia in the coastal region of southern Palestine took on the religious practices of other Canaanite peoples, which included highly sexualized religious rites. To say that the Philistine women were shocked at Israel's lewd behavior is rather like saying, "It's enough to make a prostitute blush."

† Biblical language often employs sexual imagery as a metaphor for idolatry and apostasy; God is consistently depicted in the Prophets as a passionate lover who longs for intimate relationship with the people—indeed, the Hebrew word for "to know" is also the word for "to have sex with."

prostitute: no one solicited you for sexual favors, and you paid them instead of their paying you, and that is a big difference.

35 " 'Therefore, you idolater, hear the word of the YHWH! 36 Thus says Sovereign YHWH: Because your lewdness was so brazen, and because you offered your body to your lovers and to all your detestable idols—just as you offered the blood of your children to those idols— 37 therefore I will gather all your lovers with whom you took your pleasure, those you truly loved and those you hated. I will gather them against you from every direction, and expose you for all to see. 38 Thus I will judge you the way adulterers or killers are judged: I will bring on you my bloody wrath and passion. 39 I hand you over to your lovers, and they will tear down your shrines, demolish your mounds, strip you of your clothing, take away your jewels, and leave you naked and bare. 40 They will incite a crowd against you and they will stone you and cut you to pieces with their swords. 41 They will burn your houses with fire and punish you in the sight of many women. Then I will stop your promiscuity, and you will no longer pay your lovers. 42 When I have vented my rage, and my passion has been exhausted, I will be pacified and no longer angry. 43 Because you have not remembered the days of your youth but have provoked me by doing all these things, I will bring your own conduct upon you, says Sovereign YHWH, so that you will continue your promiscuity on top of all your other abominations.

44 " 'Everyone who quotes proverbs will quote this proverb concerning you: "Like mother, like daughter." 45 You're your mother's daughter! She too hated her husband and children. Your mother was a Hittite and your father an Amorite.*

" 'You're the sister of your sisters, too, who hated their husbands and children. 46 Your older sister is Samaria, who lives to your north with her daughters; and your younger sister is Sodom, who lives to your south with her daughters. 47 You haven't merely followed their ways or participated in their idolatries; you've acted even more debauched than they. 48 As I live, says Sovereign YHWH, your sister Sodom and her daughters have not done as you and your daughters have done! 49 This was the guilt of your sister Sodom: she and her daughters were arrogant; they had abundant food and not a care in the world, but she refused to help the poor and needy. 50 In their arrogance, they did abominable things before me, so when I saw it, I swept them away. 51 Nor did Samaria commit half of your sins; you committed far more abominations than she. Beside all the abominations you committed, your sisters look righteous! 52 You bear the disgrace for making your sisters' judgment lighter. Because of your sins, in which you acted more abominably than they

---

* Both were tribal people who lived in the land of Canaan; they were perpetually at war before Joshua's campaign to take the land.

did, they are more righteous than you. You should indeed be ashamed and stand in disgrace for making your sisters appear righteous!

⁵³ " 'Nevertheless, I will restore their captivity—the captivity of Sodom and her daughters, the captivity of Samaria and her daughters, and your own captivity as well. ⁵⁴ Thus you will bear your humiliation and feel ashamed for behaving in such a way that they could look virtuous compared to you. ⁵⁵ Your sisters, Sodom with her daughters and Samaria with her daughters, will return to their former state, and you with your daughters will also return to your former state. ⁵⁶ Just as you never spoke the name "Sodom" when you were well off, ⁵⁷ before your wickedness was uncovered, so now you have become a byword for the women of Aram and surrounding territories, and for the Philistine women—those surrounding you who despise you. ⁵⁸ You have borne the just punishment of your lewdness and abominations, says YHWH. ⁵⁹ For thus says Sovereign YHWH: I will do with you as you have done, you who spat on your oath to me by breaking the Covenant.

⁶⁰ " 'Nevertheless, I will remember my Covenant that I made with you in the days of your youth, and I will establish an everlasting covenant with you. ⁶¹ You'll remember your ways and be ashamed when I take your older and younger sisters and give them to you as daughters, though they are not part of your covenant. ⁶² It is with you that I will establish my covenant, and you will know that I am YHWH. ⁶³ When I have forgiven you for all that you have done, you will remember and be ashamed, and never again open your mouth because of your humiliation, says Sovereign YHWH.' "

17:1 The word of YHWH came to me: ² "Mere mortal, propose a riddle and set forth this allegory to the House of Israel. ³ 'Thus says YHWH:

> A great eagle
>> with broad wings and long pinions,
> in full plumage of varied colors,
>> came to the Lebanon.
> Landing atop a cedar, ⁴ it broke off
>> the topmost shoot,
> carrying it away to a land of merchants,
>> and planted it in a city of traders.
> ⁵ Then the eagle carried off a seedling vine
>> and planted it in rich soil;
> like a willow planted by abundant water,
> ⁶ it sprouted and became a vine,
> speading out low to the ground
>> with branches turned back to the stem,
>> its roots deep in the rich loam.

And it became a vine
with branches and rich foliage.
⁷ Along came a second great eagle
with broad wings and full plumage.
And now the vine twisted its roots toward the eagle;
and reached its branches toward it
so that eagle might water it.
From the soil where it was planted
⁸ it was transplanted to rich soil near abundant water,
so that it might grow branches and bear fruit
and become a noble vine.'
⁹ Say: 'Thus says Sovereign YHWH:
Will it prosper?
Won't it be uprooted,
stripped of its fruit, so that it withers?
All its new growth will wither.
It will not take a strong arm or many hands
to pull it up by the roots.
¹⁰ Will it thrive if it is transplanted?
Won't it shrivel up
when the east wind blows—
wither away in the soil that nurtured it?' "

¹¹ Then the word of YHWH came to me: ¹² "Say to this rebellious house: 'Don't you understand what all this means? The ruler of Babylon went to Jerusalem, carried off its ruler and all its officials, and took them back with him to Babylon. ¹³ He took an offspring of the ruler and made a treaty with him, putting him under oath. Then the ruler of Babylon carried off the chief officials of the land. ¹⁴ Brought down like this, hardly able to rise, the country will survive only by keeping its treaty. ¹⁵ But the ruler rebelled against Babylon by sending envoys to Egypt for horses and a large army. Will that succeed? Will he go unpunished for such boldness? Will he break the treaty and escape?

¹⁶ " 'As I live, says Sovereign YHWH, I swear he will die in Babylon, in the land of the ruler with whom he had made the treaty he broke. ¹⁷ Pharaoh, his mighty army and hordes of troops, will not help in the war, when siege ramps are thrown up and towers are built to destroy multitudes. ¹⁸ The offspring violated a treaty to which he was bound and ignored an oath. He did all this and will not go unpunished.

¹⁹ " 'Sovereign YHWH says: As I live, the offspring of the ruler made light of an oath sworn in my name and violated the covenant made with me. ²⁰ I will spread my net and he will be caught in my snare. I will bring him to

Babylon and punish him there for being unfaithful to me. ²¹ All his retreating troops will fall by the sword, with the survivors scattered to the winds. Then you will know that I, YHWH, have spoken.

²² " 'This is what Sovereign YHWH says: I myself will take a shoot from the top of a cedar and plant it. I will break off a tender sprig from its topmost shoots and plant it on a lofty and high mountain. ²³ I will plant it on the mountain heights of Israel. It will grow branches, bear fruit and become a splendid cedar. All kinds of birds will nest in it. They will find shelter in the shade of its branches. ²⁴ All the trees of the countryside will know that I am YHWH who stunt tall trees and make low trees grow. I dry up the green tree and I make the dry tree flourish. I, YHWH have spoken, and I will do it.' "

¹⁸:¹ The word of YHWH came to me: ² "What do you mean by repeating this proverb about the land of Israel:

'Parents eat sour grapes
and their children's teeth
are set on edge'?

³ "As I live, says Sovereign YHWH, you will no longer quote this proverb in Israel. ⁴ For every living soul belongs to me—the parents as well as the child; both alike belong to me. It is only the person who sins who will die. ⁵ If people are just and do what is lawful and what is right— ⁶ if they never feast at mountain shrines or raise their eyes to the idols of the House of Israel; never seduce another's spouse or have sex during menstruation;*⁷ never oppress others, but return debtors' collateral once loans are repaid, and never take anything through fraud; always clothe the naked and feed the hungry; ⁸ never charge interest on loans; abstain from evil, and execute true justice between one person and another; ⁹ and conform to my statutes and keep my laws—then they are indeed righteous, and they will surely live, says Sovereign YHWH.

¹⁰ "But if the offspring of the just engage in violence and bloodshed, who turn their backs on these laws and statutes, ¹¹ even though their parents were faithful—if they feast at mountain shrines; seduce others's spouses; ¹² oppress the poor and needy and take things through fraud; fail to return debtors' collateral once loans are repaid; raise their eyes to idols and partici-

---

* In the religious life of Israel, the loss of blood through menstruation or childbirth, like the discharge of semen, indicated a loss of life force and, therefore, unworthiness before God. At the start of her period, a woman was to separate herself from the wider community for seven days; any man having sex with her also became ceremonially unclean for seven days. Atonement sacrifices were offered after a woman's menstrual cycle, as they were for a wide variety of situations after ritual purity had been restored (such as when a house had been cleaned of mildew). "Righteousness" is here depicted as being a matter not only of social justice, but also of religious observance and ceremonial purity.

pate in detestable rites; [13] or lend for profit or charge interest—such as these must not live. They must die because they commit all these abominations, and their blood will be on their own heads. [14] But suppose these sinful offspring have children who don't do all these things— [15] they don't feast at mountain shrines or raise their eyes to the idols of the House of Israel; never seduce others' spouses; [16] never wrong others, but return debtors' collateral once loans are repaid, and never take anything through fraud; always clothe the naked and feed the hungry; [17] abstain from evil, not lending for profit or charging interest, and respecting my statutes and laws—such as these are not to die for the wrongdoings of their parents. They will live.

[18] "If the parents were guilty of oppression and fraud, lived a life of wrongdoing in the community, and died because of their iniquities, [19] you might wonder, 'Why does the offspring not share in the guilt of the parent?' It is because the just children always did what was just and right and carefully obeyed God's laws. They will live. [20] It is only sinners who will die. A child is not responsible for the evil of the parent. Nor is a parent for the child's. The just will have their own integrity noted on their accounts, and the evildoers their own corruption. [21] If the evildoers renounce all their corrupt ways and keep all my laws, doing what is just and right, they will live. They will not die. [22] None of their prior offenses will be held against them. For their righteous conduct, they will live. [23] Do I desire the death of the sinner? says Sovereign YHWH. Isn't it my desire that sinners turn from their ways and live

sam
goo
bec
25
unj
tak
sin
thei
wrc
it is
30
wa)
cor
sel\
tak
19

'What a lioness your mother was
among the lions!

[handwritten note: As I live says our God / if people; never 7-9]

She lay down among her young,
  rearing her cubs.
3 She favored one of her cubs
  and it became a strong lion.
It learned to tear its prey;
  it devoured human flesh.
4 The nations learned of it
  and trapped it in a pit.
They led it away with hooks
  to the land of Egypt.
5 When the lioness witnessed her hopes dashed,
  her expectations lost,
she took another cub
  and made it into a strong lion.
6 It prowled among the other lions,
  for it was now a strong lion.
It learned to tear its prey
  and to devour human flesh.
7 It broke down the strongholds of its enemy,
  and destroyed their towns.
The country and its people were terrified
  by the sound of its roaring.
8 Then the nations marched out against it
  from the surrounding provinces;
they spread their net;
  and it was caught in their pit.
9 With hooks they put it in a cage,
  and brought it to the ruler of Babylon;
they put it into custody
  and its roar ceased to be heard
  on the mountains of Israel.
10 Your mother was a vine in a vineyard
  planted by the waterside;
she was fruitful and filled with branches
  from the abundant water.
11 Her branches were strong,
  fit for sovereign rule;
she spread far and wide,
  finding her way among the foliage;
conspicuous for her size,
  for her many branches.

¹² But she was uprooted furiously
and thrown to the ground.
The east wind shriveled her up,
she was stripped of her fruit.
Her strong branches dried up
and fire consumed them.
¹³ Now she is planted in a wilderness,
a dry and thirsty land.
¹⁴ Fire spread from one of her branches
and consumed her fruit.
No strong branch remains
fit for sovereign rule.' "

ଔ   ଔ   ଔ

^{20:1} On the tenth day of the fifth month in the seventh year of Jehoiachin's exile, some of the elders of Israel came to consult YHWH, and sat down before me. ² And the word of YHWH came to me: ³ "Mere mortal, speak to the elders of Israel and say to them, 'Thus says Sovereign YHWH: Why do you come? Why do you seek me? As I live, you will not find me, says Sovereign YHWH.'

⁴ "Will you judge them, mere mortal, will you judge them? Then confront them with the abominations of their ancestors, ⁵ by saying to them, 'Thus says Sovereign YHWH: On the day I chose Israel, I swore with uplifted hands to the descendants of the house of Jacob and revealed myself to them in Egypt. With uplifted hands I said to them, "I am YHWH your God." ⁶ On that day I swore to them that I would bring them up out of the land of Egypt into a land I had searched out for them, a land flowing with milk and honey, the most beautiful of all lands. ⁷ I told every one of them to cast off the vile images they had set their eyes on, and not defile themselves with idols from Egypt. I am YHWH their God. ⁸ But they rebelled against me. They would not listen to me; and they did not rid themselves of the vile images they had set their eyes on, nor did they throw away the idols of Egypt. So I said I would pour out my wrath on them and spend my rage against them in the land of Egypt. ⁹ But then I acted out of respect for my Name, so that it would not be profaned in the sight of the nations among whom Israel dwelled: I revealed myself to them by bringing them up out of Egypt. ¹⁰ So I led them out of Egypt and brought them into the desert. ¹¹ I gave them my decrees and revealed to them my laws, for the people who obey them will have life through them. ¹² And I gave them my Sabbaths to serve as a sign between us, so that they would know that I, YHWH, sanctify

them. ¹³ But the Israelites rebelled against me in the desert; they did not conform to my statutes, they rejected my laws—even though it is by keeping them that people have life—and they totally desecrated my Sabbaths. I then resolved to pour my wrath on them in the desert to destroy them. ¹⁴ But then I acted out of respect for my Name, so that it would not be profaned in the sight of the nations who had witnessed me bringing them up out of Egypt. ¹⁵ In the desert, however, I swore to them with uplifted hands that I would not bring them into the land I had given them, a land flowing with milk and honey, the fairest of all lands, ¹⁶ for they rejected my laws, did not conform to my statutes and desecrated my Sabbaths. For their hearts were dedicated to idols. ¹⁷ But I looked on them with pity and did not destroy them or put an end to them in the desert. ¹⁸ I warned their children in the desert not to conform to the rules and practices of their ancestors, nor to defile themselves with idols. ¹⁹ "I am YHWH your God," I said to them. "You must conform to my statutes, observe my laws and act according to them. ²⁰ You must keep my Sabbaths holy, and they will become a sign between us; so you will know I am YHWH your God." ²¹ But those children rebelled against me. They did not conform to my statutes or observe my laws, even though obeying them would give them life. And they desecrated my Sabbaths. Again I resolved to pour out my wrath and vent my anger on them in the desert. ²² But I restrained my hand out of respect for my Name, so that it would not be profaned in the sight of the nations who had witnessed me bringing them up out from Egypt. ²³ While in the desert, though, I swore to them with uplifted hand that I would disperse them among the nations and scatter them over the earth ²⁴ because they had disobeyed my laws, rejected my statutes, desecrated my Sabbaths, and were concerned only for the idols of their ancestors. ²⁵ I even gave them over to statutes that were not good and laws that could not give them life. ²⁶ I let them become defiled through their sacrifices—making their own firstborn children pass through the fire—hoping that it might fill them with revulsion so that they would understand that I am YHWH.'

²⁷ "Therefore, mere mortal, speak to the people of Israel and say to them, 'This is what Sovereign YHWH says: Once more your ancestors blasphemed me by being unfaithful to me. ²⁸ I brought them into the land I had promised them, but any time they saw a high hill or a leafy tree, they sacrificed to other gods there, making offerings that provoked me to anger; they presented their fragrant incense and poured out their drink offerings. ²⁹ So I asked them, "What is this high place you go to?" They called it Bamah—"High Place"—which is still its name today.'

³⁰ "Therefore say to the House of Israel: 'Thus says Sovereign YHWH: Will you defile yourselves the way your ancestors did, and lust after their detestable practices? ³¹ When you offer your sacrifices—the sacrifice of your

children in the fire—you continue to defile yourselves, and you still have all your idols to this day! Will you seek me, House of Israel? As surely as I live, says Sovereign YHWH, you will not find me!

³² " 'What you're thinking—that you can be like the nations, like the families of the lands, and worship wood and stone—will never happen. ³³ As I live, says Sovereign YHWH, I will rule you with a strong hand, with my arm outstretched and my wrath poured out! ³⁴ I will bring you from the nations and gather you from the countries to which you were scattered—with a mighty hand, an arm outstretched, and wrath outpoured. ³⁵ I will bring you into the desert of the nations and there, face to face, I will execute judgment on you. ³⁶ As I judged your ancestors in the desert of the land of Egypt, so will I judge you now, says Sovereign YHWH. ³⁷ I will make you pass under my staff,* counting you as you enter, and bring you into the bond of the covenant. ³⁸ I will purge you of those who revolt and rebel against me. I will take them out of the land they live in now, but they will not set foot back in the land of Israel. And you will know that I am YHWH.

³⁹ " 'As for you, House of Israel, thus says Sovereign YHWH: Go ahead and serve your idols from now on, every one of you, if you won't listen to me. But you will not profane my holy Name with your sacrifices and your idols. ⁴⁰ For on my holy mountain, the lofty mountain of Israel, says Sovereign YHWH, there in the land, the entire House of Israel will serve me. There I will accept its people. There I will require their gifts and their choicest offerings, and all else they consecrate to me. ⁴¹ I will accept you when you make offerings with your soothing odor, after I have brought you from the nations and gather you from the countries where you have been scattered. ⁴² When I bring you into the land of Israel, the land I swore with a raised hand to give to your ancestors, then you will know that I am YHWH. ⁴³ There you will remember your conduct and all the acts by which you defiled yourselves, and you will loathe yourselves for all your corruption. ⁴⁴ You will know that I am YHWH, when I deal with you for my Name's sake and not according to your evil ways or your corrupt practices, House of Israel, says Sovereign YHWH.' "

21:1 The word of YHWH came to me: ² "Mere mortal, set your face toward Teman, preach against the Darom, and prophesy against the brushland in the Negev;† ³ say to the brushland of the Negev, 'Hear the word of YHWH:

---

* The image is of a shepherd counting the sheep as they enter the fold, but the Hebrew root of the phrase "pass under" is the same as in the phrase, "pass through the fire," as if some of the sheep would be sacrificed as the children were.

† These three place names are all synonyms for "south": Teman means the region on the right (travelers oriented themselves by facing east); Darom means the region of brightness (the coveted "southern exposure"); and Negev means the region of dryness (the desert was located there). Judah and Jerusalem are south from Israel, and since they are the subject of Ezekiel's prophecy, he faced south, even though he was in Babylon and Jerusalem was some 540 miles to the west.

YHWH says, I will kindle a fire in you, and it will devour all your trees, both green and dry. The blazing flame will not be quenched, and every face from south to north will be scorched by it. ⁴ Everyone will see that I, YHWH, kindled it. It will not be extinguished.'"

⁵ Then I said, "Ah, Sovereign YHWH! People are saying of me, 'Why does he always talk in parables?'"

⁶ So the word of YHWH came to me: ⁷ "Mere mortal, set your face against Jerusalem and preach against its sanctuaries. Prophesy against the land of Israel, ⁸ saying to it, 'Thus says YHWH: I am coming against you, with my sword drawn from its sheath, and I will cut off from you both the just and the sinner. ⁹ Because I intend to cut off from you both the just and the sinner, my sword will be drawn from its sheath against everyone from the Negev northward. ¹⁰ Then humankind will know that I, YHWH, have drawn my sword from its scabbard. It will not be sheathed again.' ¹¹ Then groan, mere mortal, groan before the people with a broken heart and bitter grief. ¹² And when they ask, 'Why all this groaning?' tell them, 'Because of the news I just received. Hearts will melt and hands will go limp; there will be troubled spirits, trembling knees will be as weak as water.' It is coming! It surely will happen, says Sovereign YHWH."

¹³ Again the word of YHWH came to me: ¹⁴ "Mere mortal, prophesy and say, 'Thus says YHWH:

> A sword, a sword
>   is sharpened and polished,
> ¹⁵ sharpened to kill and kill again,
>   polished to flash like lightning!
> But how can you celebrate,
>   you who dispised the rod,
>   rejected all discipline?
> ¹⁶ The sword, highly polished,
>   is grasped with the hand,
> sharpened and polished
>   for the hand of the slayer.
> ¹⁷ Yes, shout and howl, mere mortal;
>   for it is meant for my people,
> for the rulers of Israel,
>   subjects of the sword,
> slain with the people—
>   beat your breast, Israel!
> ¹⁸ The sword has been tested;
>   how can it not come to pass

since it scorns even the scepter?
says Sovereign YHWH.'
19 And you, mere mortal, prophesy;
strike your hands together.
Let the sword fall twice, thrice—
it is a killing sword,
a sword for great slaughter,
closing in on the people everywhere.
20 Hearts will melt
and many will fall
for I stationed the sword of slaughter
at every gate.
Yes! It is made to flash brilliantly,
and polished to kill.
21 It slashes to the right,
then strikes to the left,
wherever the blade is directed.
22 I as well will strike my hands together
and assuage my anger upon you.
I, YHWH, have spoken."

23 The word of YHWH came to me: 24 "Mere mortal, mark out two roads for the sword of the ruler of Babylon to take, both starting from the same country. Then make a signpost for the place where the roads fork. 25 Mark one road for the sword to come to the Ammonite city of Rabbah, and one to Judah and fortified Jerusalem. 26 For the ruler of Babylon will stop at the fork, the junction of the two roads, to seek an omen. He will cast lots with arrows, consult household gods, and inspect the livers of animals. 27 The arrow marked 'Jerusalem' will fall to his right, telling the ruler to set up battering rams against the gates, build a ramp, and erect siegeworks. 28 The city's inhabitants will think this omen is false because they swore oaths,* but when they are taken captive, they will remember their guilt. 29 Therefore, says Sovereign YHWH: 'Because you exposed your guilt by your open rebellion, revealing your sins in everything you do—because you did this, you will be captured. 30 As for you, corrupt ruler of Israel, your fate has overtaken you; your time of punishment is at hand. 31 Thus says Sovereign YHWH: Remove your diadem, take off your crown! Nothing will remain as it was: the lowly will be exalted and the exalted will be brought low. 32 A ruin! A ruin! I will make it an utter ruin! It will not be restored until the rightful ruler comes, and I will install that person.' "

---

* This refers to the events recounted in 17:13-18, where Zedekiah swears allegiance to Nebuchadnezzar, then breaks his treaty by trying to get Egypt's assistance in the war against Babylon.

³³ "Mere mortal, prophesy this: 'Thus says Sovereign YHWH about the Ammonites with their insults:

> A sword, a sword! Drawn for slaughter,
>   polished to destroy, flashing like lightning!
> ³⁴ Your false visions, your lying divinations
>   will be laid on the necks of evildoers
>   whose day has come, who will be slain;
>   whose fate will come to them
>   in their hour of final punishment.
> ³⁵ Return your sword to its sheath!
>   I will judge you where you were born,
>   in the land of your origin.
> ³⁶ I will pour out my wrath on you
>   I will pour out my fury on you.
>   I will turn you over to barbarians,
>   skilled in destruction.
> ³⁷ You will be fuel for the fire,
>   your blood will be shed in your land,
>   and never more remembered;
>   for I, YHWH, have spoken.' "

^{22:1} The word of YHWH came to me: ² "You, mere mortal—will you judge? Will you judge this murderous city and bring charges against it, and then confront it with all its abominable deeds? ³ Then say, 'Thus says Sovereign YHWH: You are a city bringing doom on itself! You shed blood in your midst and defile yourself by making idols. ⁴ You are guilty of the blood you shed and are defiled by the idols you made. You have brought your own days to a close; the end of your years has arrived. Therefore I will make you an object of scorn to the nations and a laughingstock to all the countries. ⁵ Folk nearby and folk far away will mock you, the infamous city, driven by turmoil. ⁶ In you, the rulers of Israel used their power to shed blood. ⁷ In you, mothers and fathers are treated contemptuously, foreigners are oppressed, and the orphan and the elderly are mistreated. ⁸ You despised what I hold sacred and desecrated my Sabbaths. ⁹ In you, Jerusalem, perjurers slander so they can shed blood; and dwelling in you are those who eat at the mountain shrines and act lewdly. ¹⁰ In you are people who have sex with their parents, and who have sex with women during their period, when they are ceremonially unclean. ¹¹ In you adulterers thrive, defile their children's spouses, and have sex with their own siblings. ¹² In you people accept bribes to shed blood, charge usurious interest rates, and get rich by defrauding your neighbors and extorting money from them. And you have forgotten me, says Sovereign YHWH. ¹³ See, I strike with my clenched fist at your

dishonest gains and the bloodshed within your walls. ¹⁴ Will your strength and your courage endure on the day I deal with you? I, YHWH, have spoken, and I will act. ¹⁵ I will disperse you among the nations and scatter you throughout the lands. I will burn the uncleanness out of you. ¹⁶ Once you are defiled in the eyes of the nations, you will know that I am YHWH.'"

¹⁷ The word of YHWH came to me: ¹⁸ "Mere mortal, the House of Israel has become slag to me. They are nothing but silver, bronze, tin, iron, and lead—but in a crucible furnace, the dross will turn to silver!* ¹⁹ Therefore, says Sovereign YHWH, 'Since all of you have become slag, I will gather you into Jerusalem; ²⁰ as silver, bronze, tin, iron, and lead are gathered into a crucible furnace to be melted with a fiery blast, so will I gather you in my fierce anger and throw you into the fire† to melt you. ²¹ I will gather and I will fan the fire of my wrath until you are melted. ²² As silver is melted in a crucible furnace, so will you be melted inside the city, and you will know that I, YHWH, have poured out my wrath on you.'"

²³ Again the word of YHWH came to me: ²⁴ "Mere mortal, say to the land, 'You are a land without rain or showers in the day of my wrath. ²⁵ Your prophets are a gang of thugs, a pride of lions tearing apart its prey. They devour people—first making widows and widowers of them, then stealing their jewelry and precious treasures. ²⁶ Your priests do violence to my Law and profane my holy things: they do not distinguish between the holy and the mundane, do not teach the difference between unclean and clean, and shut their eyes to the keeping of my Sabbaths. This profanes me among them. ²⁷ Your officials are wolves tearing apart their prey. They shed blood and kill people to make unjust gains, ²⁸ then your prophets whitewash those deeds with false visions and lying divinations, saying "Thus says Sovereign YHWH" when YHWH has said no such thing. ²⁹ The people of the land practice extortion and robbery. They oppress the poor and the needy and mistreat resident aliens by denying them justice.‡ ³⁰ I looked for a person among them who would build up the wall and stand before me in the gap on behalf of the land so that I would not have to destroy it, but I found no one. ³¹ So I will pour out my fury on the people and consume them with my fiery anger, bringing down on their own heads all they have done, says Sovereign YHWH.'"

²³:¹ The word of YHWH came to me and said, ² "Mere mortal, there were once two siblings, children of the same mother. ³ When they were in Egypt,

---

* Slag (also called dross or scoria) is the scum or waste product that floats to the surface of water when ores and metals are processed. A crucible furnace is a smelting oven with a large ceramic bowl inside of it to catch or retain the molten product.
† Or "into Jerusalem"; the Hebrew phrase ends with "will throw you" or "will put you," leaving the reader to decide where the people will be put.
‡ Or possibly, "without redress."

they were promiscuous; they were promiscuous while they were yet children. It was in Egypt that they first knew physical pleasure, and there that they became sexually aware, though they were still virgins. ⁴ The elder was named Oholah; the younger, Oholibah.* Oholah is Samaria, and Oholibah is Jerusalem.

"They belonged to me, and they had many daughters and sons. ⁵ But though they swore allegiance to me, Oholah became promiscuous, and lusted for new lovers—the Assyrians, ⁶ because they dressed in purple, had power and authority, were young and desirable, and were skilled in warfare. ⁷ Oholah became allied with Assyria's best warriors, and wallowed in the idol-worship of Assyria, ⁸ continuing a licentiousness begun in Egypt, taking lovers even as a youth, and being debauched over and over again.

⁹ "That is why I have given Oholah—that is, Samaria—over to the Assyrians, since they had been so much in love. ¹⁰ But the Assyrians stripped Oholah naked, seized its daughters and sons, and finally put Oholah to the sword. Oholah became notorious for the punishment done to it.

¹¹ "Oholah's sibling Oholibah witnessed all of this, but was even more depraved, indulging in a promiscuity even worse than Oholah's. ¹² Oholibah also fell in love with its neighboring Assyrians, because they dressed in purple, had power and authority, were young and desirable, and were skilled in warfare. ¹³ Then I saw that Oholibah had become defiled—that both of these siblings had gone down the same path. ¹⁴ Oholibah became more promiscuous than ever: no sooner had Oholibah seen the vermillion-colored wall carvings of the Chaldeans, ¹⁵ depicting people with sashes around their waists and turbans on their heads, regal and noble Babylonians, the original inhabitants of Chaldea, ¹⁶ than Oholibah fell in love with Chaldea at first sight and sent messengers to form an alliance. ¹⁷ The Babylonians came to Oholibah and they became lovers, defiling Oholibah all the more. ¹⁸ Having been disgraced, Oholibah—that is, Jerusalem—broke the alliance

---

* Oholah means "her own tent" or "tent-woman," that is, a worshiper at a tent shrine. Oholibah means "my tent (or Tabernacle) is in her." Exekiel is contrasting the so-called synchretistic worship of YHWH in Samaria—the old northern realm of Israel—with the more legitimate worship in Jerusalem. In 721 B.C.E., 27,290 people from the ten northern tribes, mainly from the middle and upper classes, were deported to distant parts of the Assyrian empire. Assyria then resettled Israel with captives from other conquered territories, and these intermarried with the Jews left in the land, most of them poor people. When the Jewish exiles returned, they said that the people who had remained behind were no longer Jews, claiming that they had mingled the worship of YHWH with "heathen" religious and cultural traditions, and so barred them from rebuilding the Jerusalem Temple. This enraged the Samaritans, who said that they were keeping the one true faith because they followed the Torah alone; they rejected the Prophets and the Writings—indeed, all Jewish literature written after the Torah—believing that the Judeans had been led astray. (In fact, the Samaritans claimed to have the only authentic copy of the Torah; it is their copy that was used in creating the Septuagint, the Greek translation of the Hebrew scriptures.) So they went back to Samaria and built a rival temple on Mount Gerizim, and the bitter antagonism between the two groups continued for centuries. Today there are about 650 Samaritans left in Israel, all living near Mount Gerizim.

ezekiel 23

and withdrew its affection from Chaldea. ¹⁹ Oholibah had flaunted its promiscuity, exposing itself until I withdrew my affection from Oholibah just as I had from Oholah.

²⁰ "But then, Oholibah, you became even more wanton, lusting after paramours who had penises like donkeys and ejaculated like stallions; ²¹ you yearned for the debauchery of your youth, when the Egyptians fondled your young breasts and played with your nipples. ²² So now, Oholibah, Sovereign YHWH says this: I will set against you all your lovers from whom you have withdrawn your affection, and will let them attack you from all directions— ²³ Babylonians and Chaldeans, warriors from Pekod and Shoa and Koa, together with those young and desirable Assyrians dressed in purple, with their power and authority and their skill in warfare. ²⁴ They will attack you with fleets of wheeled chariots and a host of troops; they will set themselves against you on all sides with bucklers, shields, and helmets. I will let them carry out my punishment—they will punish you as you see fit. ²⁵ I will direct my passion against you, and they will handle you with fury, cutting off noses and ears. Your survivors will fall by the sword, and they will take away your daughters and sons; anything left behind will be destroyed by fire. ²⁶ They will strip you of your clothes and take away your beautiful jewels. ²⁷ I will put an end to your wantonness and promiscuity in the land of Egypt, and you will no longer yearn for Egypt or even remember it. ²⁸ For thus says Soverign YHWH: I am going to deliver you into the hands of those you hate, into the hands of people from whom you turned in disgust. ²⁹ They will treat you with scorn, and they will take away everything you have worked for, and leave you naked and bare; your naked promiscuity will be exposed. ³⁰ These things shall be done to you for your debauchery with the nations, for defiling yourself with their fetishes. ³¹ You walked Oholah's path; so I will put the same cup in your hand.

³² "Thus says Sovereign YHWH:
    You shall drink from that cup,
        a cup deep and wide;
        it will cause derision and scorn.
    Because it holds so much,
³³   you will be filled with drunkenness and woe.
    The cup of desolation and horror,
        the cup of your sibling Samaria—
³⁴ you will drink it, down to its dregs,
        then you'll shatter the cup
        and lacerate yourself with the shards.
    For I have spoken,
        says Sovereign YHWH.

³⁵ "I promise you, says Sovereign YHWH, that because you have forgotten me and turned your back on me, you must bear the consequences of your promiscuity."

³⁶ Then YHWH said to me: "Mere mortal, are you ready to judge Oholah and Oholibah? Then charge them with their abominations. ³⁷ For they have committed adultery, and blood is on their hands; they have committed adultery with their idols, and have even sacrificed the children they bore to me, offering them to their gods as food. ³⁸ At the same time, they also defiled my Holy Place and profaned my Sabbaths. ³⁹ The very day that they slaughtered their children to their idols, they entered my Holy Place to desecrate it. They did that in my own Temple! ⁴⁰ Moreover, they called for foreigners to come; they sent a messenger and the strangers came. Oholibah, you bathed and groomed yourself and dressed in your finest clothes, ⁴¹ then reclined on a stately couch before a table spread for a feast—on which you placed my incense and my oil. ⁴² A great crowd, shouting and carefree and drunk, arrived from the desert; and they put bracelets on your arms and splendid beautiful crowns on your head. ⁴³ Then I said, 'Oholibah, you're worn out from all your adultery, and now you're going to have sex with these strangers. You're no better than a prostitute, ⁴⁴ and these are your clients! You'll go with anyone you find attractive, Oholah and Oholibah!'

⁴⁵ "But righteous people will punish them as adulterers and murderers, for they have worshiped other gods, and they have blood on their hands. ⁴⁶ For thus says Sovereign YHWH: Summon an assembly against them, and deliver them over to terror and plunder. ⁴⁷ Let the assembly stone them and cut them down with swords; let the assembly kill their daughters and sons, and burn down their homes. ⁴⁸ I will put an end to idolatry in the land; and all will hear my warning not to imitate your promiscuity. ⁴⁹ You will be punished for your wantonness, and you will suffer the penalty for your sinful idolatry. And you will know that I am Sovereign YHWH."

ೞ ೞ ೞ

24:1 On the tenth day of the tenth month in the ninth year, the word of YHWH came to me: ² "Mere mortal, write down this date, this very date, for the ruler of Babylon has laid siege to Jerusalem this very day.* ³ Sing a derisive song to this rebellious house. Say to it:

" 'Thus says Sovereign YHWH:

> Put the pot on the fire, put it on,
>   and pour water into it.

---

* In our calendar it would be January 15, 588 B.C.E.

ezekiel 24   550

4   Put cuts of meat in as well,
      leg and shoulder, the best cuts.
    Fill it with choice bones.
5   Take the pick of the flock.
      Pile firewood underneath;
    simmer the stew
      and boil the bones.
6   Thus says YHWH:
    Woe to the bloodstained city,
      that rusty cooking pot
      whose rust will never be scoured away;
    empty it piece by piece
      without stopping to choose
      which stays and which goes.
7   The city has blood in its midst,
      and it is poured out on the bare rock;
    the blood is not poured on the ground
      where the dust would cover it up.
8   I spilled its blood on the naked rock
      to make sure it couldn't be covered;
    it fuels my wrath
      so I can take my revenge.
9   Therefore, thus says Sovereign YHWH:
    Woe to this bloody city!
      I will pile the firewood high!
10 I'll heap on the fuel, kindle the fire,
      boil the meat well, mix in the spices,
      and let the bones burn,
11 then set the empty pot on the coals
      and heat it until it glows red hot;
    the heat will melt away its impurities
      and burn away its rust.
12 It frustrates all effort to clean it,
      its coat of rust won't come off,
      not even by fire.
13 When I tried to cleanse you
      of your filty lewdness,
    you refused to be cleansed
      of your impurities;
    you will not be clean again
      until my fury at you subsides.

¹⁴ " 'I, YHWH, have spoken; the time is at hand. I will act. I will not hold back; I will not refrain; I will not relent. I will judge you by your ways and by what you did in the past, says Sovereign YHWH.' "

¹⁵ The word of YHWH came to me: ¹⁶ "Mere mortal, I am about to take away your heart's desire with a disease. Don't weep or mourn or shed a single tear. ¹⁷ Sigh silently; don't mourn the dead. Bind up your turban, put on your sandals, and show no signs of mourning. Do not cover your face with a veil, and don't eat the bread of mourning."*

¹⁸ So the next morning I preached to the people as usual; that night, my wife died. And on the next morning I got up and did what as I had been commanded. ¹⁹ The people asked me what was the significance of my actions for them. ²⁰ I said to them: "The word of YHWH told me ²¹ to say to the House of Israel, 'Thus says YHWH: I am about to desecrate my sanctuary, which has been the pride of your power, the delight of your eyes, the object of your affections. The daughters and sons you left behind will fall by the sword. ²² And you are to do as Ezekiel did: You will not cover your face with a veil or eat the food of mourners. ²³ You will keep your head covered and your sandals on your feet. You will not mourn or weep; but you will waste away because of your sins, and you will groan to one another. ²⁴ Ezekiel will be a sign to warn you. You will do just as he did. When this happens, you will know that I am Sovereign YHWH.'

²⁵ "And you, mere mortal, on the day I take away their stronghold, their joy and their glory, the delight of their eyes, their heart's desire—their daughers and sons as well— ²⁶ on that day a fugitive will come to tell you the news. ²⁷ At that time your mouth will be opened and you will speak with the fugitive and will no longer be silent. So you will be a sign to them, and they will know that I am YHWH."

25:1–48:35

The word of YHWH came to me:

² "Mere mortal, set your face against the Ammonites and prophesy against them. ³ Say to them, 'Hear the word of YHWH: Because you shouted "Hur-

---

* This is food from friends to comfort and sustain someone who has been recently bereaved.

rah!" when my Holy Place was desecrated and when the land of Israel was laid waste and when the people of Judah went into exile, ⁴ I am handing you over to the children of the east.* They will set up their encampments among you and pitch their tents in your midst. They will eat your fruit and drink your milk. ⁵ I will turn Rabbah into a camel pasture and Ammon into a sheepfold. Then you will know that I am YHWH. ⁶ For thus says Sovereign YHWH: Because you clapped your hands and stamped your feet, rejoicing with all the malice of your heart against the land of Israel, ⁷ I will stretch out my hand over you and give you up as plunder for the nations. I will cut you off from other peoples and wipe you out as a country. And you will know that I am YHWH.' "

⁸ Thus says Sovereign YHWH: "Because Moab and Seir said that the House of Judah is like all the other nations, ⁹ I will expose the flank of Moab, beginning with its frontier towns—Beth Jeshimoth, Baal Meon, and Kiria-thaim—the glory of your land. ¹⁰ I will give both Moab and the Ammonites to the children of the east, so that all memory of the Ammonites will be blotted out among the nations. ¹¹ And so I will bring down my judgment on Moab. Then they will know that I am YHWH."

¹² Thus says Sovereign YHWH: "Because Edom took revenge on Judah and in so doing incurred lasting guilt, ¹³ I will stretch out my hand over Edom, says YHWH God, and destroy both the people and the animals in it. I will lay waste the land from Teman as far as Dedan, and their people will fall by the sword. ¹⁴ I will take vengeance on Edom through my people the Israelites. And they will deal with Edom as my anger and wrath dictate. Edom will experience my vengeance, says Sovereign YHWH."

¹⁵ Thus says Sovereign YHWH: "Because the Philistines resorted to revenge so heartily, and with age-old hostility sought to destroy Judah, ¹⁶ I will stretch out my hand over the Philistines, says Sovereign YHWH. I will wipe out the Kerethites and destroy the rest of the seacoast. ¹⁷ I will perform frightful acts of vengeance on them and punish them in my wrath. Then they will know that I am Sovereign YHWH, when I take vengeance on them."

ᘓ ᘓ ᘓ

---

* These are the Bedouins, nomadic shepherd tribes whose ancient nickname was "the children of the east"; they had formed part of Nebuchadnezzar's army. After the Chaldeans desolated the country, Bedouins came and, with the consent of the Chaldeans, took possession of the land for themselves.

26:1 In the eleventh year, on the first day of the month, the word of YHWH came to me: 2 "Mere mortal, because Tyre said of Jerusalem, 'Aha, what had been the gateway to the nations is broken, and now its gates lie open to me; I will prosper now that the land is in ruins,' 3 Sovereign YHWH says this:

> I stand against you, Tyre!
> I will raise up against many nations,
> as the sea raises up its waves.
> 4 They will destroy the walls of Tyre
> and overthrow its towers.
> I will scrape away its soil
> and leave it a bare rock.
> 5 It will become a tiny island
> where fishnets hang to dry.
> I have spoken it,
> says Sovereign YHWH.
> It will become plunder for nations;
> 6 its settlements on the mainland
> ravaged by the sword.
> Then its people will know that I am YHWH.
> 7 For thus says Sovereign YHWH:
> From the north I will bring Nebuchadnezzar,
> ruler of Babylon, ruler of rulers;
> he will come with horses, chariots, cavalry,
> and a massive infantry force.
> 8 He will put to the sword
> your settlements on the mainland.
> He will set up siege works,
> siege ramps up to your walls;
> and raise a roof of shields against you.
> 9 Nebuchadnezzar will launch battering rams
> against your walls
> and chop down your towers with axes.
> 10 His hosts of horses
> will cover you with dust.
> The thunder of horses and chariot wheels
> will shake your walls
> when he enters your gates
> like the invaders of a breached city.
> 11 Horse's hooves will trample your streets
> as the city is put to the sword,
> and bring to the ground
> your strong pillars.

¹² Your wealth will turn into spoil,
       your merchandise will become plunder.
   Your walls will be leveled,
       your fine houses destroyed.
   Your stones, timbers and rubble
       will be thrown into the sea.
¹³ I will silence the music of your songs,
       and the sound of your harps will cease.
¹⁴ I will build you into a bare rock;
       a place to spread fishnets to dry.
   You will never be rebuilt.
       For I have spoken, says Sovereign YHWH.' "

¹⁵ Thus says Sovereign YHWH to Tyre: "How the coastlands will shake at the sound of your downfall, as the wounded groan and the slaughter goes on in your midst. ¹⁶ Then the rulers will step down from their judgment seats; they'll remove their robes and lay aside their brocaded garments. They will clothe themselves in terror and sit on the ground, trembling every moment, aghast at their fate. ¹⁷ They will take up this dirge over you:

   'How you are destroyed,
       swept from the seas, city of renown!
   You were a power on the seas
       you and your inhabitants;
       but you terrorized all who lived there.
¹⁸ Now the coastlands tremble
       on the day of your surrender;
   the islands of the sea
       are appalled at your demise.'

¹⁹ "For thus says Sovereign YHWH: When I make you into a city laid waste, like cities never inhabited, when I bring the ocean depths over you and its vast waters cover you, ²⁰ then I will thrust you down to the netherworld with those who descend into the Pit, and you will not return or take your place in the land of the living. ²¹ I will bring you to a horrible end and you will be no more. You will be sought, but you will never be found again," says Sovereign YHWH.

²⁷:¹ The word of YHWH came to me: ² "Mere mortal, raise a lament over Tyre ³ and say to it, 'You sit enthroned at the gateway to the sea, and you carried the trade of the nations to distant coasts and islands. To you Sovereign YHWH says this:

Tyre, you say,
"I am a beautiful ship."

4 Your domain was the high seas,
and perfectly your builders created you.
5 They made all the planking
out of fir from Mount Hermon;
they took cedar from Lebanon
to make your mast.
6 Your oars came from Bashan;
your decks, inlaid with ivory,
were cypress from the coasts of Cyprus.
7 Fine embroidered linen from Egypt
served as your sail and your flag;
your blue and purple awnings
were from Elishah's coasts.*
8 Sidonese and Arvadian sailors
served as your oarers;
your own sailors, Trye,
were aboard to handle the sailing.
9 Your skilled sailors from Gebal were aboard
to serve as shipwrights to caulk the seams.
All ships at sea and their sailors
came alongside to trade for your wares.
10 Persians, Lydians, and Putans
served as soldiers in your army.
They honored you by hanging
their shields and helmets on your walls.
11 Arvadians and Helechians
guarded your walls on every side;
Gammadians were posted
on your towers;
they hung their shields on your walls
making your beauty perfect.

12 " 'Tarshish did business with you because of your great wealth of goods: silver, iron, tin and lead they exchanged for your wares. 13 Javan, Tubal and Meshech traded with you, offering indentured workers and bronze utensils as your imports. 14 Traders from Togarmah offered horses and mules as your

---

* In Genesis, Elishah was one of the descendants of Javan, whose territory was Greece; his decendants settled in the Greek colonies—in this case, southern Italy or Sicily. Other places named in this section are Mediterranean coastal cities and regions in Africa, Europe, and Asia. Here Ezekiel likens Tyre to a trading ship; the shipwreck is a metaphor for the attack on it by the Chaldeans under Nebuchadnezzar.

imports, cavalry horses and mules as your wares. ¹⁵ Rhodians did business with you. Many islands were customers. They paid you with ivory tusks and ebony. ¹⁶ Edom did business with you for your range of products. They traded turquoise, purple fabric, embroidered work, fine linen, coral, and rubies for your wares, ¹⁷ and both Judah and Israel traded with you. For your merchandise they exchanged wheat from Minnith, cakes, honey, oil, and balm. ¹⁸ For your range of products and great wealth of goods, Damascus did business with you in wine from Helbon and white wool, ¹⁹ Vedan and Javan from Uzal traded for your wares; they trafficked with you in polished iron, cassia, and calamus. ²⁰ Dedan traded with you in coarse woolens for saddle cloths. ²¹ Arabia and all the rulers of Kedar traded with you. They were sources of your commerce in lambs, rams, and goats. ²² In exchange for your products, merchants from Sheba and Raamah traded with you, offering all the choicest spices, every kind of precious stone, and gold. ²³ Haran, Kanneh, and Eden, merchants from Sheba, Asshur, and Chlimad, traded with you. ²⁴ They were your dealers in choice items: violet cloths and brocades, stores of colored fabric rolled up and tied with cords.

²⁵ " 'Ships of Tarshish carried your wares;
      you were filled with heavy cargo on the high seas.
²⁶   Your oarers took you out
        into the open water;
      but an east wind wrecked you
        far out to sea.
²⁷   Your wealth, your merchandise, and your wares;
        your mariners, your sailors, your shipwrights,
      your merchants and your soldiers
        and everyone else on board
      were thrown into the sea
        on the day of your shipwreck.
²⁸   The shorelands will shake
        when your sailors cry out.
²⁹   All the oarers
        will abandon their ships;
      the mariners and the sailors
        will watch from the shore.
³⁰   They will loudly mourn your fate
        and cry bitterly over you;
      they will throw dirt over their heads
        and roll in ashes.
³¹   They will shave their heads over your distress
        and put on sackcloth.

They will weep for you with anguish
and with bitter mourning.
³² They will wail and mourn
and take up a lament over you:
"Who was ever destroyed like Tyre
in the middle of the sea?"
³³ When your merchandise went to sea
you pleased nation after nation;
you pleased ruler after ruler
with your great wealth and your wares.
³⁴ Now you lie shattered by the sea
in the watery deep;
your wares and your your crews
went down with you.
³⁵ All living along the coastlands
are appalled at your fate;
their rulers shudder with horror,
their features wasted with fear.
³⁶ The merchants among the nations
gasp at the sight of you;
destruction came to you,
and you will be no more.' "

28:1 The word of YHWH came to me: ² "Mere mortal, say to the ruler of Tyre, 'Thus says YHWH:

Because of your proud heart, you say,
"I am a god,
I sit on the judgment seat of a god
in the heart of the seas."
But you are a mortal, not a god,
though you consider yourself to be like one.
³ Are you wiser than Daniel?
Are any sages wiser than you?
⁴ By your wisdom and understanding
you amassed great wealth,
adding gold and silver
to your treasuries.
⁵ Your treasuries grew
through your trading skills;
and as your wealth grew
your pride grew, too.

⁶ Therefore, thus says Sovereign YHWH:
Because you consider yourself wise,
as wise as a god,
⁷ I will bring foreigners against you,
the most ruthless of nations;
they will draw their swords against
your beauty and wisdom
and defile your shining splendor.
⁸ They will thrust you down to the Pit,
to a violent end on the high seas.
⁹ Will you then say, "I am a god"
in the presence of your murderers?
You'll be nothing but a mortal, not a god,
in the hands of those who will strike you down.
¹⁰ You will die the death of the abased,*
by the hands of foreigners.
I have spoken,
says Sovereign YHWH.' "

¹¹ This word of YHWH came to me: ¹² "Mere mortal, take up a lament for
the ruler of Tyre, saying, 'This is what Sovereign YHWH says:

You were the model of perfection
full of wisdom and perfect in beauty.
¹³ You were in Eden, God's garden;
every precious gem adorned you:
ruby, topaz, emerald, chrysolite, onyx,
jasper, sapphire, turquoise and beryl.
Your gold, so beautifully crafted,
was ready for you the day you were created.
¹⁴ I created you as a towering cherub
with outstretched wings, a guardian;
you were on God's holy mountain
and walked among fiery stones.
¹⁵ You were blameless in your ways
from the day you were created—
until iniquity found you.
¹⁶ Your commerce grew as great
as your temptation to violence,
which filled your heart with sin.

---

* "The abased" is literally "the uncircumcised," but where in other books the term is roughly equivalent
to "heathens," throughout Ezekiel it is used as a term of great reproach and terrible ignominy.

So I threw you down, disgraced,
from the mount of God,
and destroyed you, a guardian cherub,
from among the fiery stones.
17 Your beauty led to your arrogance;
you corrupted your wisdom
for the sake of your splendor.
I flung you to the ground,
and made a spectacle of you before rulers.
18 You defiled your sanctuaries
with your sins and dishonest trade.
I kindled a fire in your midst
and it has consumed you.
I reduced you to ashes on the earth
for all to see.
19 All the nations who knew you
were appalled at your fate;
yours was a horrible end,
and you will be no more.' "

20 The word of YHWH came to me: 21 "Mere mortal, set your face toward Sidon,* and prophesy against it, 22 saying, 'Thus says Sovereign YHWH:

I stand against you, Sidon,
and I will show my glory in your midst.
People will know that I am Sovereign YHWH
when I punish you and manifest my holiness in you.
23 I will send the plague to you
and make blood flow in your streets.
Beseiged on every side by the sword,
the slain will fall within your walls.
Then people will know
that I am Sovereign YHWH.

24 " 'No longer will the House of Israel suffer from pricking briers and sharp thorns—the neighboring countries who despise them. Then they will know that I am Sovereign YHWH.

25 " 'Thus says Sovereign YHWH: When I gather my people, the Israelites, from the nations to which they were scattered, I will manifest my holiness among them in the sight of the nations. Then they will dwell in their own land, which I gave to my servant Jacob. 26 They will live there in security, building

---

* Tyre's sister-city.

houses and planting vineyards, when I punish their neighbors who treated them with contempt. And they will know that I am YHWH their God.' "

☙ ☙ ☙

29:1 On the twelfth day of the tenth month in the tenth year, the word of YHWH came to me: 2 "Mere mortal, set your face against Pharaoh ruler of Egypt and prophesy against him and against all Egypt. 3 Speak to the ruler, saying, 'Thus says Sovereign YHWH:

I stand against you, Pharaoh,
  ruler of Egypt;
You are the great monster*
  that lurks among the streams of the Nile.
You say, "The Nile is mine.
  It was made for me."
4 But I will hook you by the jaws
  and make the fish in in its streams
  cling to your scales.
Then I will haul you out of the streams
  with its fish clinging to your scales.
5 I will hurl you into the desert;
  you and your fish will land on open ground
  with none to bury you.
I will give you as food
  to the animals of the earth
  and the birds of the air.
6 Then all the inhabitants of Egypt
  will know that I am YHWH.
The support you gave to the Israelites
  was no better than a staff made of reed.†
7 When they grasped you,
  you splintered in their hands
  and sliced up their palms;
when they leaned on you,
  you broke and made their limbs give way.

8 " 'Therefore, thus says Sovereign YHWH: I will bring a sword against you and destroy your people and your animals. 9 Egypt will turn into a desolate

---

* The Hebrew word is *tannin*, which describes any large reptile from great serpents to dragons, and here refers to the Nile crocodile.
† Israel sought Egypt's help against the Babylonian invasion, but Egypt's support was half-hearted at best.

wasteland, and your people will know that I am Sovereign YHWH. Because you said, "The Nile is mine, it was I who made it," ¹⁰ I stand against you and against your waterways. I will make Egypt desolate from Migdol to Syene, as far as the border of Ethiopia. ¹¹ No human foot will pass through it. No animal foot will pass through it. It will be uninhabited for forty years. ¹² I will make Egypt the most desolate of desolate lands, its cities the most derelict of derelict cities. For forty years they will lie derelict, and I will scatter the Egyptians among the nations, dispersing them among the countries. ¹³ And at the end of forty years, says Sovereign YHWH, I will gather the Egyptians from among the peoples among whom they were scattered. ¹⁴ I will restore the fortunes of Egypt, and return them to the land of Pathros, the land of their origin.* And there they will be a lowly realm. ¹⁵ It will be the lowliest of realms and will never again exalt itself above other nations. I will make it so weak that it will never again rule over other nations. ¹⁶ The Egyptians will never again be a source of confidence for the people of Israel. But it will be a reminder of their weakness in turning to it for help. They will know that I am Sovereign YHWH.' "

¹⁷ On the first day of the first month in the twenty-seventh year, the word of YHWH came to me: ¹⁸ "Mere mortal, Nebuchadnezzar ruler of Babylon kept his army in the field against Tyre so long that everyone's head was rubbed bare and every shoulder rubbed raw. Yet the ruler and his army gained nothing from their campaign against Tyre. ¹⁹ Therefore thus says Sovereign YHWH: I will give the land of Egypt to Nebuchadnezzar ruler of Babylon. And he will carry off its wealth, despoil it, and plunder it, and that will serve as pay for his army. ²⁰ I give him the land of Egypt in payment for his services, for he was acting on my behalf, says Sovereign YHWH. ²¹ On that day I will assist Israel in renewing its strength, and restore to you the power to speak among them, and they will know that I am YHWH."

30:1 The word of YHWH came to me: ² "Mere mortal, prophesy, saying, 'Thus says YHWH:

Wail!
Rue the day!

---

* Ancient Egyptians considered themselves to be "the People of Two Lands": Lower Egypt, encompassing the lowlands of the Nile Delta region (which Egyptians called *Kemet*, "the black land," after its dark, rich soil), and Upper Egypt (*Deshret*, "the red land," referring to the desert sand), which extends to the highlands at the southern border. The ancient capital city of Memphis, just north of modern Cairo, is essentially where the two regions met. The Hebrew scriptures call Lower Egypt *Mazor* ("the fortified land") and Upper Egypt *Pathros* (after the Egyptian Pa-to-Res, or "land of the south"), though the Hebrews referred to the whole land as *Mizraim*, "the two Mazors"; today, Egyptians call their country Misr.

3   For a day is near,
        the day of YHWH is near!
     It will be a cloudy day,
        a time of doom for the nations.
4   A sword will come down on Egypt
        and there will be anguish in Ethiopia;
     when the slain fall in Egypt,
        its wealth will be carried off
        and its foundations destroyed.
5   Ethiopia, Put, Lud, all of Arabia,
        Libya, and the inhabitants of the allied countries
        will fall by the sword along with Egypt.
6   For thus says YHWH:
     The supporters of Egypt will fall,
        and its proud strength will fail.
     From Migdol to Aswan
        they will fall by the sword,
        says Sovereign YHWH.
7   They will be desolated
        along with other desolated countries,
     and its cities
        will lie among other ruined cities.
8   When I set fire to Egypt
        and all its helpers are shattered,
     then they will know
        that I am YHWH.
9   On that day,
        messengers whom I have dispatched
     will set out for Ethopia
        to shake it out of its complacency.
     Anguish will overtake it in Egypt's day of doom;
        for such a day is at hand.
10   Thus says Sovereign YHWH:
        I will put an end to the hordes of Egypt,
     by the hand of Nebuchadnezzar
        ruler of Babylon.
11   He and his people with him,
        the most ruthless of nations,
        will be brought in to destroy the land.
     They will draw their swords against Egypt.
        and fill the land with the slain.

¹² I will dry up the streams of the Nile
and sell the land into the hands of evil people.
I will bring desolation to its land
and everything in it
by the hands of foreigners;
I, YHWH, have spoken.
¹³ Thus says Sovereign YHWH:
I will destroy the idols
and put an end to the idols in Memphis.
No longer will there be a ruler in Egypt,
and I will spread fear throughout the land.
¹⁴ I will desolate Pathros,
set fire to Zoan,
and punish Thebes.
¹⁵ I will pour my wrath on Pelusium,
the stronghold of Egypt,
and cut off the hordes of Thebes.
¹⁶ I will set fire to Egypt;
Pelusium will writhe in agony.
Thebes will fall after being stormed,
and Memphis will be racked with anguish.
¹⁷ The youth of Heliopolis and Bubastis
will fall by the sword
and the cities, too,
will fall into captivity.
¹⁸ That day at Tahpanhes will be dark
when I smash the yoke of Egypt;
there its proud might will come to an end;
it will lie under cloud cover
and its towns will go into captivity.
¹⁹ Such will be the punishment I give Egypt,
and they will know that I am YHWH.' "

²⁰ On the seventh day of the first month in the eleventh year, the word of YHWH came to me: ²¹ "Mere mortal, I broke the arm of Pharoah, the ruler of Egypt. And it has not been bound up and put in a splint to become strong enough to hold a sword. ²² Therefore thus says Sovereign YHWH: I am going to deal with Pharoah, the ruler of Egypt; I will break both his arms, the sound one and the broken one, to make the sword fall from his hands. ²³ I will scatter the Egyptians among the nations and disperse them throughout the earth. ²⁴ I will strengthen the arms of the ruler of Babylon and put my

sword in his hand. I will break Pharoah's arm and he will lie wounded and groaning before me. ²⁵ I will give strength to the arms of the ruler of Babylon, but the arms of Pharoah will fall limp. Then Egypt will know that I am YHWH, when I put my sword in the hands of the ruler of Babylon which he brandishes against Egypt. ²⁶ Then I will disperse the Egyptians among the nations and scatter them throughout the countries. Then they will know that I am YHWH."

31:1 On the first day of the third month in the eleventh year, the word of YHWH came to me: ² "Mere mortal, say to Pharaoh ruler of Egypt and to all his subjects:

'To whom will I compare you
in your greatness?
³   Look to Assyria,
once a Lebanon cedar
with handsome branches
overshadowing the forest,
towering aloft,
its top among the clouds.
⁴   Springs nourished it,
and deep waters made it grow tall;
their streams flowed around its base,
sending their channels
to all the trees in the countryside.
⁵   So it towered high above
every other tree of the field.
Its boughs grew larger
and its branches extended out,
nourished by an abundance of water.
⁶   All the birds of the air
nested in its boughs;
under its branches wild animals
gave birth to their young.
All the great nations
thrived in its shade.
⁷   It was majestic in its beauty
with its spreading boughs,
its roots reaching deeply
into an abundance of water.
⁸   No cedars of God's garden could equal it;
no cypress could compare to its boughs;

no plane tree had such branches;
no tree in God's garden rivaled its beauty.
⁹   I made it beautiful,
made its mass of spreading boughs
the envy of every tree in Eden,
God's garden.

¹⁰ " 'Therefore, thus says Sovereign YHWH: Because it towered high with its top among the clouds, so proud of its height, ¹¹ I gave it into the hands of the ruler of the nations, to do with it as its sinful ways deserve. ¹² Foreigners, the most ruthless of nations, cut it down and left it lying there. Its branches fell on the mountains and in all the valleys. Its boughs lie broken in all the streams of the land. And all the peoples of the earth went away from its shade and abandoned it. ¹³ The birds settled on its fallen trunk, and all the animals of the fields took shelter in its branches. ¹⁴ Never again will the well-watered trees soar so high or push their tops through the clouds. Nor will the strongest of them, even the well-watered among them, attain their full height. For all have been given over to death, to the world below, to share the fate of all humankind and go down into the Pit. ¹⁵ Thus says Sovereign YHWH: On the day it went down to Sheol, I closed the Deep over it and covered it. I restrained the rivers so that their mighty waters were checked. I made Lebanon mourn over it, and all the trees of the fields wilted in sympathy. ¹⁶ I made nations shake at the sound of its downfall, when I brought it down to Sheol with those who go down into the Pit. From this all the trees of Eden, the choicest and the finest of Lebanon, all the well-watered trees, drew comfort in the netherworld. ¹⁷ Those who lived in its shade, its allies among the nations, had also gone down to Sheol, joining those slain by the sword. ¹⁸ Which of the trees of Eden are equal to you in splendor and majesty? Yet, you too, will be brought down with the trees of Eden to the world down under. You will rest with those slain by the sword, with the abased. So it will be with Pharaoh and all his subjects, says Sovereign YHWH.' "

32:1 On the first day of the twelfth month in twelfth year, the word of YHWH came to me: ² "Mere mortal, raise a lament over Pharaoh, the ruler of Egypt, saying:

You are a lion among the nations;
you are like a sea monster
thrashing about in your waters,
disturbing the water with your feet
and muddying the rivers.
³   Thus says Sovereign YHWH:

When many nations are assembled
 I will cast my net over you,
and you will be hauled ashore
 in its netting.
⁴ I will drag you ashore
 and drop you in an open field,
and all the birds of the air
 will flock on you;
and the wild animals of the world
 will gorge themselves on you.
⁵ I will scatter your flesh on the mountains,
 and fill the valleys with your carcass.
⁶ I will drench the land up to the ridges
 with your flowing blood,
and your flesh
 will fill the ravines.
⁷ When I snuff you out,
 I will blacken the heavens and darken its stars.
I will cover the sun with a cloud,
 and the moon will give no light.
⁸ I will darken above you
 the shining lights of heaven
and bring darkness over your land,
 says Sovereign YHWH.
⁹ I will cause multitudes
 to be scandalized at you,
when I bring your destruction among the nations,
 to countries you have never known.
¹⁰ I will cause many to be shocked at you,
 their rulers shuddering at your fate
when I brandish my sword
 before them.
On the day of your downfall
 all will tremble for their own lives.
¹¹ For thus says Sovereign YHWH:
The sword of the ruler of Babylon
 will descend upon you.
¹² I will cause your armies to fall
 by the swords of warriors,
all of them most terrible
 among the nations.

They will bring down the pride of Egypt,
and all its warriors will perish.
¹³ I will destroy its livestock
from beside abundant waters.
No hoof—nor any human foot—will ever
churn them up again.
¹⁴ Then I will let its waters settle
and let its streams run like oil,
says Sovereign YHWH.
¹⁵ When I desolate the land of Egypt,
when the land is emptied of everything,
when I strike down all signs of life,
then Egypt will know that I am Sovereign YHWH.
¹⁶ This is the lamentation to be chanted.
The women of the nations will chant it.
They will chant it over Egypt
and all its former armies, says Sovereign YHWH.

¹⁷ On the fifteenth day of the first month in the twelfth year, the word of YHWH came to me: ¹⁸ "Mere mortal, raise a lament, you and the women of the nations, over Egypt's armies and leaders. I will consign them to the netherworld, in the company of those to descend into the abyss. ¹⁹ Say to them, 'Are you more favored than others? Go down now and be laid among the abased.' ²⁰ They will fall among those killed by the sword. Egypt has been handed over to the sword. Let it be dragged off with all its armies. ²¹ From the grave the mighty leaders will say of Egypt and its allies, 'They came down and they lie with the abased, with those killed by the sword.' ²² Assyria is there with its entire army. Egypt is surrounded by graves of its slain, all of whom fell by the sword. ²³ Their graves are set in the deepest depths of the abyss, with its slain buried around it, all victims of the sword, who once spread terror in the land of the living. ²⁴ Elam is there, with all its armies surrounding its grave. All of them are slain, fallen by the sword; who having spread terror in the land of the living, went down abased to the world below. They bear their shame with the dwellers below. ²⁵ A bed is made for Egypt among the slain, with all its armies lying around its grave. All of them are abased, killed by the sword. Because their terror spread to the land of the living, they bear their shame with those who go down to the netherworld. They rest among the slain. ²⁶ Meshech and Tubal are there, with all their armies around their graves; all of them abased, killed by the sword because they had spread their terror in the land of the living. ²⁷ Nor do they lie beside the fallen heroes of the nations, who went down to Sheol with their battle gear, with their swords

beneath their heads and their shields under their bones*—for the terror of the warriors was upon the land of the living. ²⁸ Pharaoh, you too will be lie broken, dead in the company of the abased with those slain by the sword. ²⁹ Edom is there, its rulers and its officials; despite their power they lie with others killed by the sword. They lie with the abased, with those who go down to the grave. ³⁰ All the rulers of the north and all the Sidonians are there; they went down with the slain disgraced despite the terror of their power. They lie abased with those killed by the sword and share the shame with those who go down into the grave. ³¹ When Pharaoh sees them, he will be consoled for all his warriors who were killed by the sword, says Sovereign YHWH. Though I had Pharaoh spread terror in the land of the living, he and his masses of troops will be laid among the abased with those killed by the sword. This is the word of Sovereign YHWH."

33:1 The word of YHWH came to me: ² "Mere mortal, speak to your people, saying, 'If I bring the sword to a land, and the people of that land take one of their number to serve as their sentinel, ³ when the sentinel sees the sword coming against the land, a shofar will blow to warn the people. ⁴ If its hearers do not heed the warning and are overtaken by the sword, their blood will be on their own heads. ⁵ They heard the shofar but did not heed the warning, so they are responsible for their own deaths; had they responded to the warning, they would have saved their lives. ⁶ But if the sentinel sees the sword coming and does not blow the shofar, and the people are not warned, and the sword comes and takes the lives of any of them, they die because of their sins, but I will hold the sentinel accountable for their deaths.'

⁷ "Now you, mere mortal, I make you the sentinel for the House of Israel. Whenever you hear a word from my mouth, you must give my warning. ⁸ If I say to evildoers, 'You will surely die,' and you do not warn them to turn from their ways, the evildoers will die because of their sin, but I will hold you responsible for their deaths. ⁹ But if you warn evildoers to turn from their sin, they will die for their sins, but you will have saved your life.

¹⁰ "Now then, mere mortal, say to the House of Israel, 'You've been saying things like this, complaining, "We are burdened by our sins and our offenses, and we waste away because of them. How can we survive?"' ¹¹ Say to them, 'As I live, says Sovereign YHWH, I take no pleasure in the death of sinners—I prefer that they turn from their ways and live. Turn back! Turn back from your evil ways! Why should you die, House of Israel?'

¹² "Therefore, mere mortal, say to your Israelite sisters and brothers, 'When good people disobey, their previous integrity will not save them; and when

---

* This was a standard burial arrangement for warriors.

evildoers repent, their previous sinfulness will not make them fall. ¹³ If I tell the just that they will surely live, but then they trust that their previous record will save them even when they do evil, none of their just works will be remembered. They will die for the evil they committed. ¹⁴ And if I say to sinners, "You will surely die," and they turn away from their sins and do what is just and right—¹⁵ if they restore what they took in pledge for a loan, return what they stole, follow the decrees that give life and turn from evil, they will surely live, they will not die. ¹⁶ None of the sins they committed will be remembered against them. If they do what is just and right, they will surely live.'

¹⁷ "But your Israelite sisters and brothers say, 'The way of God is not just,' when it is their own way that is not just. ¹⁸ A just person who turns from being just and does something evil will die for it. ¹⁹ But if sinners turn away from their sin and do what is just and right, they will live by doing so. ²⁰ You say, 'The way of YHWH is not just,' but I will judge each one of you according to your own ways."

℘ ℘ ℘

²¹ On the fifth day of the twelfth month, in the twelfth year of our captivity, the refugees from Jerusalem came to me and reported that the city had fallen. ²² Now the evening before the fugitives arrived, the hand of YHWH came upon me; but God opened my mouth just before the fugitives arrived in the morning, and I was silent no longer.

²³ It was then that the word of YHWH said to me, ²⁴ "Mere mortal, the people living in the ruins back in Israel are saying, 'When Abraham took possession of the land he was but one person. But we are many; surely, then, the land has been granted to us as our possession.' ²⁵ So say to them, 'Thus says Sovereign YHWH: You eat meat with the blood still in it, you worship idols, you shed blood, and yet you expect to take possession of the land? ²⁶ You depend on your swords, you commit abominations, you defile one another's spouses, and yet you expect to take possession of the land?' ²⁷ Tell them, 'Thus says Sovereign YHWH: As I live, the people living back among the ruins will fall by the sword, while those out in open country I will give to the wild beasts to be devoured. And whoever is holed up in strongholds and caves will die of a plague. ²⁸ And I will make the land a place of desolation and waste, and its proud strength will end; the mountains of Israel will become so desolate that people will fear to cross them. ²⁹ When I make the land a desolate waste because of all the detestable things the people did, then they will know that I am the YHWH.'

³⁰ "As for you, mere mortal, the people here will gather in groups and talk of you by the walls and in the doorways of houses, and say to one

another, 'Let us go to hear what the message from YHWH is.' ³¹ They will gather round you, as they usually do, sitting before you to listen to your words—but they don't practice them. They say they're devoted to you, but their hearts pursue nothing but dishonest gain. ³² To them you are no more than a singer of love songs who has a wonderful voice and plays music well. They will listen to what you say, but they will do nothing about it. ³³ When it all comes true—and it will indeed come true—then they will know that a prophet had been among them."

෬ ෬ ෬

³⁴:¹ The word of YHWH came to me: ² "Mere mortal, prophesy against the shepherds of Israel: prophesy, saying to them: 'You shepherds, thus says the word of YHWH: Woe to you shepherds of Israel who take care only of yourselves. Shouldn't you be taking care of the flock? ³ You drink its milk, wear its wool, and slaughter the fat ones, but you to not take care of the flock. ⁴ You have not strengthened the weak, healed the sick, or treated the wounded; you have not brought back the strayers, or sought the lost; but you have ruled them with harshness and brutality. ⁵ They scattered because there was no shepherd, and once scattered they became food for all the wild animals. ⁶ My sheep wandered over all the mountains and on every high hill. My sheep are scattered throughout the world, with no one to ask about them or search for them.

⁷ " 'Therefore, you shepherds, hear the word of YHWH: ⁸ As I live, says Sovereign YHWH, because my flock lacks a shepherd, it has been looted and is now the prey of wild animals. And because my shepherds did not search for my scattered flock, caring for themselves rather than for my flock, ⁹ hear the word of YHWH, you shepherds: ¹⁰ Thus says Sovereign YHWH, I am going to deal with the shepherds, and I will hold them accountable for my flock. I will remove them from tending my flock so that the shepherds can no longer feed themselves. I will rescue my flock from their mouths, for it will no longer be food for them. ¹¹ For thus says Sovereign YHWH: I myself will search for my sheep; I will seek them out. ¹² As shepherds seek out their flocks when their flocks are scattered in every direction, so I will search for my sheep and rescue them, no matter where they scattered on that day of full clouds and thick darkness. ¹³ I will bring them out from the countries and bring them into their own land. And I will feed them on the mountains of Israel, by its streams and wherever there is a settlement. ¹⁴ I will feed them on good pasture land, and the mountain heights of Israel will be their grazing ground. ¹⁵ I myself will tend my flock and have it lie down, thus says Sovereign YHWH. ¹⁶ I will seek out the lost, I will return the

strayed, I will bind up the injured, and I will strengthen the weak, and I will watch over the fat and the sleek. I will be a true shepherd to them.

17 " 'As for you, my flock, thus says Sovereign YHWH: I will judge between one sheep and another, between rams and goats. 18 Isn't it enough for you to feed on the good pasture, that you must trample over the rest of the pasture? Isn't it enough that you have all the clear drinking water, that you must also muddy the rest with your feet? 19 My flock must graze on what you have trampled underfoot and drink what you have muddied. 20 Therefore, thus says YHWH to you: I myself will judge between the fat sheep and the lean sheep, 21 for you shove aside the weak with flank and shoulder; you butt them with your horns until they are scattered in every direction.

22 " 'I will save my flock and they will be ravaged no longer. I will judge between one sheep and another. 23 I will set up over them one shepherd to care for them: my servant David.* He will care for them and be their shepherd. 24 And I, YHWH, will be their God, and my servant David will be their leader. I, YHWH, have spoken. 25 I will make a covenant of peace with my sheep and banish wild animals from the land, so that my people can live in the open pastures and sleep safely in the forests. 26 I will bless them and the region surrounding my hill. And I will send down seasonal rains, showers of blessings. 27 The trees of the field will yield their fruit, and the earth will yield its crop. The people will be secure in their land. And when I break the bars of their yoke and rescue them from the hands of their slaveholders, they will know that I am YHWH. 28 They will no longer be plundered by the nations, nor will the wild animals devour them. They will live secure, free from terror. 29 I will provide for them a land renowned for its crops, and they will never again be victimized by famine in the land, nor bear the scorn of the nations. 30 Then they will know that I, YHWH, am their God, and that they, the House of Israel, are my people, says Sovereign YHWH. 31 You are my sheep, the flock that I tend, and I am your God, says Sovereign YHWH.' "

35:1 The word of YHWH came to me: 2 "Mere mortal, set your face against Mount Seir, prophesying against it, and say to it, 'Thus says Sovereign YHWH:

3   I will deal with you, Mount Seir;
     I stretch out my hand against you
     and reduce you to a desolate waste.
4   I will leave your towns in ruins
     and you will become a desolation.

---

* That is, someone of David's lineage.

Then you will know
that I am YHWH,
5 because you nurtured an ancient enmity
and handed over the Israelites
to the sword in the hour of their doom,
the hour of their final punishment.
6 Therefore, as I live, says Sovereign YHWH,
I will make bloodshed your destiny,
and bloodshed will pursue you;
you are certainly guilty of blood,
and boodshed will pursue you.
7 I will turn the hill country of Seir
into a desolate waste
which travelers will avoid.
8 I will fill your mountains with the slain;
those killed by the sword
will fall in your hills, valleys, and ravines.
9 I will desolate you for all time;
your towns will be uninhabited.
Then you will know that I am YHWH.

10 " 'Because you said, "These two nations and countries will be ours and we will capture them," even though, I, YHWH, was there, 11 therefore, as surely as I live, says Sovereign YHWH, I will treat you with the anger and envy that you showed me because of your enmity against them. And I will make myself known among you by the way I judge you. 12 You will know that I, YHWH, heard all the blasphemous things you said against the mountains of Israel. You said, "They are laid waste; they are given to us to devour." 13 You boasted against me, saying outrageous things. I myself heard you. 14 Thus says Sovereign YHWH: I will make you so desolate that the whole world will rejoice. 15 I will treat you as you treated my very own possession, Israel, when you gloated over its desolation. You will be desolate, Mount Seir, and all of Edom, all of it. Then you will know that I am YHWH.' "

36:1 "Mere mortal, prophesy to the mountains of Israel and say, 'Mountains of Israel, hear the word of YHWH! 2 Thus says Sovereign YHWH: Your ememy has boasted over you, saying, "Aha, now the ancient heights are ours!" ' 3 So prophesy, saying: 'Thus says YHWH: Because they made you desolate, and crushed from all sides so that you became the possession of the rest of the nations, and the object of people's malicious talk and slander, 4 therefore, mountains of Israel, hear the word of Sovereign YHWH: Thus says Sovereign YHWH to the mountains and the hills, the waterways and valleys and desolate wastes, and the deserted towns that are a source of plunder, that have become objects of derision for neighboring nations. ⁵ Therefore, thus says Sovereign YHWH: I speak out of my hot jealously against the rest of the nations, and against all of Edom, who with heartfelt joy and utter contempt possessed my land, especially my pastures, to plunder it.'

⁶ "Therefore prophesy this about the the land of Israel—say to the mountains and the hills, the waterways and the valleys, 'Thus says Sovereign YHWH: I said what was on my mind in jealous anger because you had to endure the ridicule of the nations. ⁷ Therefore, thus says Sovereign YHWH, I swear with uplifted hand that your neighboring nations will in turn be ridiculed. ⁸ But you, mountains of Israel, will grow branches and bear fruit for my people Israel; for their homecoming is near. ⁹ I am concerned about you and will look on you with favor; and you will be tilled and sown. ¹⁰ I will multiply many people on you—the entire House of Israel. The towns will be reinhabited and the ruins rebuilt. ¹¹ I will increase your populations, both human and animal. And they will be fruitful and multiply. I will settle people among you as in the past and make you prosper, even more than before. Then you will know that I am YHWH. ¹² I will make my people Israel walk on you and possess you, so that you will become their inheritance; I will never again bereave them of their children. ¹³ Thus says Sovereign YHWH: It is said that you are a land that devours human beings and deprives your nation of children; ¹⁴ but you will no longer devour human beings and deprive your nation of children, says Sovereign YHWH. ¹⁵ No longer will I let you be insulted by the nations, no longer will you bear disgrace from the peoples—nor will you cause your nation to stumble any longer,* says Sovereign YHWH.' "

¹⁶ Again the word of YHWH came to me: ¹⁷ "Mere mortal, when the House of Israel lived on its own soil, they defiled it by their conduct and their actions. Their conduct before me was like someone living in ceremonial defilement. ¹⁸ So I poured out my wrath on them because they had shed blood in the land and defiled it with idols. ¹⁹ I dispersed them among the nations, and they were scattered throughout the countries. I judged them according to their conduct and their actions. ²⁰ And every time they came into another country, they profaned my holy Name, for it was said of them, 'These are YHWH's people, yet they had to leave God's land.' ²¹ But because I had concern for my holy Name, which the House of Israel had profaned among the nations where it was exiled, ²² say to the House of Israel, 'Thus says Sovereign YHWH: It is not for your sake, House of Israel, that I do what I am about to do, but for the sake of my Name, which you profaned among

---

* This promise, spoken to the mountains of Israel, refers to the hilltop shrines to other gods that, in prophetic language, "caused the people to stumble."

the nations where you were exiled. ²³ I will show the holiness of my great Name, which was profaned among the nations, the Name you profaned among them. Then the nations will know that I am YHWH, says Sovereign YHWH, when through you I show myself holy in their eyes.

²⁴ " 'For I will bring you back from the nations, and gather you from every land, and bring you into your own land. ²⁵ I will sprinkle pure water over you, and you will be purified from everything that defiles you. I will purify you from the taint of all your idols. ²⁶ I will give you a new heart and put a new spirit within you. I will remove the heart of stone from your body and give you a heart of flesh. ²⁷ I will put my Spirit within you and make you conform to my statutes. And you will faithfully observe my laws. ²⁸ Then you will dwell in the land I gave to your ancestors. You will be my people and I will be your God. ²⁹ And after I have saved you from all that defiles you, I will command the grain to be abundant; I will not bring a famine upon you. ³⁰ I will make the trees bear fruit abundantly and make the soil yield large crops, so that famine will never again disgrace you among the nations.

³¹ " 'Then you will recall your sinful ways and your evil deeds, and you will loathe yourselves for your detestable practices and your abominations. ³² I assure you that it is not for your sake that I do this, says Sovereign YHWH. Let it be known to yourselves. Be ashamed and dismayed for what you did, House of Israel. ³³ Thus says Sovereign YHWH: On the day I cleanse you from your iniquities, I will resettle the towns and the ruins will be rebuilt. ³⁴ The desolate land will be tilled, no longer the eyesore of desolation for all passersby to see. ³⁵ And they will say, "What once was desolate land has now become like the garden of Eden. And the waste, the desolation, and the ruined towns are now inhabited and fortified." ³⁶ Then the nations surrounding you will know that I, YHWH, rebuilt the ruined places and replanted the land laid waste. Then they will know that I, YHWH, have spoken, and I will do it.' "

³⁷ Thus says Sovereign YHWH: "Once again I will let the people of the House of Israel ask me to do this for them: to increase their population like a flock. ³⁸ Like the flock for sacrifices, like the flock at Jerusalem during the festivals, so will the ruined towns be filled with flocks of people."

○३   ○३   ○३

37:1 The hand of YHWH was upon me, and it carried me away by the Spirit of YHWH and set me down in a valley—a valley full of bones. ² God made me walk up and down among them. And I saw that there was a vast number of bones lying there in the valley, and they were very dry. ³ God asked me, "Mere mortal, can these bones live?"

I answered, "Only you know that, Sovereign YHWH."

⁴ And God said, "Prophesy to these bones, and say to them: 'Dry bones, hear the word of YHWH! ⁵ Sovereign YHWH says to these bones: I am going to breathe life into you. ⁶ I will fasten sinews on you, clothe you with flesh, cover you with skin, and give you breath. And you will live; and you will know that I am Sovereign YHWH.'"

⁷ So I prophesied as I was commanded, and as I prophesied, suddenly there was a noise, a rattling, and all the bones came together, bone to matching bone. ⁸ As I watched, sinews appeared on them, flesh clothed them, and skin covered them. But there was no breath in them.

⁹ Then God said to me, "Prophesy to the wind;* prophesy, mere mortal, and say to it: 'Thus says Sovereign YHWH: Approach from the four winds, Breath, and breathe on these slain, that they may live.'"

¹⁰ I prophesied as I was commanded, and breath came into them; they came alive, and stood up on their feet—a vast multitude.

¹¹ Then God said to me, "Mere mortal, these bones are the whole House of Israel. The people keep saying, 'Our bones are dry, our hope is gone, and we are doomed.' ¹² Prophesy, therefore, and say to them, 'Thus says Sovereign YHWH: I am going to open your graves and raise you up from the dead, my people. I will return you to the land of Israel. ¹³ When I open your graves and raise you up, you, my people, will know that I am YHWH. ¹⁴ Then I will put my Spirit into you and you will return to life, and I will settle you back on your own land. Then you will know that I, YHWH, have spoken and made all this happen, says Sovereign YHWH.'"

¹⁵ The word of YHWH came to me: ¹⁶ "Mere mortal, take a branch and write on it, 'Judah and the Israelites loyal to them.' Then take a second branch and write on it, 'Joseph—the branch of Ephraim—and all the Israelites loyal to them.' ¹⁷ Hold them together in your hand so they form a single branch. ¹⁸ When the Israelites ask you to tell them what this means, ¹⁹ say to them: 'Thus says Sovereign YHWH: I will take the branch of Joseph, which belongs to Ephraim and the other tribes of Israel, and join it to the branch of Judah, making them one branch; and they will be one branch in my hand.' ²⁰ When you hold up the branches which you have inscribed for all to see, ²¹ say to them: 'Thus says Sovereign YHWH: I will take the Israelites from their places of exile among the nations. I will gather them from every quarter of the globe and restore them to their own land. ²² I will make them into a single nation in the land, on the mountains of Israel. There will be one ruler over

---

* Recall that the Hebrew word for breath, *ruach*, is the same word used for wind and spirit (or Spirit), so this phrase could be translated, "Prophesy to the breath."

all of them and they will never again be two nations, or divided into two realms. ²³ They will never again defile themselves with idols, their detestable practices, and all their acts of disloyalty. I will save them from their apostasies into which they fell, and I will cleanse them. Then they will be my people and I will be their God. ²⁴ My servant David will be their ruler over them, and they all will have one shepherd. They will obey my laws and carefully follow my decrees. ²⁵ They will live in the land I gave my servants Jacob, Leah, and Rachel—the land of your ancestors. They and their children and their grandchildren will live there forever. And my servant David will be their leader for all time. ²⁶ I will make a covenant of peace with them; it will be an everlasting covenant with them. And I will bless them and multiply them. And I will set my Holy Place among them forever. ²⁷ My Presence will rest upon them, and I will be their God, and they will be my people. ²⁸ And when my Holy Place is in their midst forever, the nations will know that I, YHWH, have made Israel sacred.' "

CR CR CR

³⁸:¹ The word of YHWH came to me: ² "Mere mortal, set your face toward Gog in the land of Magog, the chief ruler of Meshech and Tubal.* Prophesy against him and say, ³ 'Thus says Sovereign YHWH: I will deal with you, Gog, chief ruler of Meshech and Tubal. ⁴ I will turn you around, put hooks into your jaws, and you and your troops I will drag along, all your horses and fully equipped cavalry, a great company, all of them with shield and buckler, armed with swords. ⁵ Persia, Ethiopia, and Put, all armed with shields and helmets; ⁶ Gomer and all its battalions; Beth-Togarmah from the remote

---

* Chapters 38 and 39 have been fodder for endless eschatological theories, and the sweeping perspective of the prophecy and its future setting have prompted some interpreters to read it as a vision about the end-time battle of Armageddon. Some translations render "chief ruler of Meshech and Tubal" as "ruler of Rosh, Meshech, and Tubal," with commentators even associating Rosh with Russia, Meshech with Moscow, and Tubal with Tiblisi or Tobolsk—an interpretation that gained popularity during the Cold War. But Rosh simply means "head or chief," and Meshech and Tubal were descendants of Noah said to have settled in the area around the Black and Caspian Seas, where the Moshi (or Mushki) and Tubalu (or Tibareni) peoples lived in Ezekiel's day. Historically, most of Israel's invaders have come from the north; Meshech and Tubal are simply the furthest north that Israel could conceive, and so they took on an apocalyptic tone. Indeed, as scholar Barry Bandstra has pointed out, this Gog of the land of Magog "is evil incarnate, a caricature of all Israel's enemies combined"; the writer of the New Testament book of Revelation affirms this interpretation, calling Gog and Magog "the nations in the four quarters of the earth" who gather for war against the faithful. Even so, Gog, Magog, and the rest have entered into various Hebrew, Arabic, and Christian mythologies. In the Middle Ages it was believed that Gog and Magog were nations that had been confined behind mountains by Alexander the Great, who used 6,000 bronze- and ironworkers to build a gate to hold them back; and the Encyclopaedia Britannica notes that "an independent legend of Gog and Magog surrounds the two colossal wooden effigies in the Guildhall in London. They are thought to represent survivors of a race of giants destroyed by Brutus the Trojan, legendary founder of London."

north, with its troops—many nations will be with you. ⁷ Be ready, well prepared, you and all the nations with you; hold yourself at my disposal. ⁸ It will be a long time before you are called to arms, but in the distant future you, Gog, will march against a land restored from the ravages of war—a land whose people have been gathered from many nations. You will come to the mountains of Israel, which had long laid desolate, and march against a people who, having returned from exile, are now living in security. ⁹ You and all the armies of many nations will go up, advancing like a tornado, like a cloud covering the land. ¹⁰ Sovereign YHWH says: At that time evil thoughts will come to your mind and you will hatch a scheme. ¹¹ You will say, "Let us attack this land of unprotected villages. Let us attack this peaceful and unsuspecting people, dwelling peacefully without walls and without gates. ¹² I will plunder and loot and raise my hand against the resettled ruins, against these people gathered from the nations. They are rich in livestock and goods, dwelling at the very center of the world." ¹³ Sheba and Dedan and the merchants of Tarshish and all its villages will say to you, "Did you come to plunder? Have you gathered your multitude to carry off spoil, to carry off silver and gold, cattle and goods, and much booty?"'

¹⁴ "Therefore, mere mortal, prophesy to Gog and say, 'Thus says Sovereign YHWH: On that day, you will notice that my people Israel are living securely, ¹⁵ and come with many nations from your place out of the remotest part of the north, you and the multitudes with you—all of them on horseback—a great multitude, a large army. ¹⁶ You will advance against my people Israel like a cloud covering the land. This will happen on that distant day: I will bring you to my land so that the nations will know me; before their eyes, Gog, I will manifest my holiness through you! ¹⁷ Thus says Sovereign YHWH: It was you I spoke of in the past through my servants the prophets of Israel, who prophesied for years, foretelling your invasion.'

¹⁸ "On that day, when Gog comes against the land of Israel, says Sovereign YHWH, my wrath will boil over. ¹⁹ I swear in my jealousy and in my blazing wrath that there will then be an enormous earthquake in the land of Israel. ²⁰ The fish of the sea, the birds of the air, the animals of the fields, every creature moving on the ground, and all the people on the face of the earth will tremble before me. Mountains will be thrown down, cliffs will crumble, and every wall will collapse to the ground. ²¹ I will confront Gog with every form of terror, says Sovereign YHWH, and his followers will turn their swords against one another. ²² I will punish Gog with plague and bloodshed, and send torrential rains, hailstones, fire and brimstone against him and his multitudes, and the many nations with him. ²³ I intend to display my greatness and holiness, and I will make myself known in the sight of many nations. Then they will know that I am Sovereign YHWH.

³⁹:¹ "And you, mere mortal, prophesy against Gog, saying: 'Thus says YHWH: I stand against you, Gog, ruler of Meshech and Tubal. ² I will turn you around and lead you on. I will bring you from the far north and send you against the mountains of Israel. ³ Then I will knock the bow from your left hand and dash the arrows from your right hand. ⁴ On the mountains of Israel you will be killed, you and your multitudes, and the nations with you. I will make you into food for all the birds and the wild animals. ⁵ You will fall in open country, for I have spoken, says Sovereign YHWH. ⁶ I will send fire upon Magog and those living undisturbed in the coastland. And they will know that I am Sovereign YHWH.'

⁷ "I will make my holy Name known* to my people Israel; and I will no longer allow my holy Name to be profaned. The nations will learn that I, YHWH, am the Holy One of Israel. ⁸ All this is coming! It is YHWH your God who speaks. This is the day of which I spoke. ⁹ Then those living in the towns of Israel will go out and make bonfires, and will feed the fires with weapons: bucklers and shields, bows and arrows, javelins and clubs. For seven years they will use them as firewood. ¹⁰ They will have no need to gather wood from the fields or chop down trees from the forests. For they will use the weapons for fuel. And they will plunder their plunderers, and loot their looters, says Sovereign YHWH.

¹¹ "On that day I will bury Gog in Israel, in the Valley of the Travelers east of the sea. It will be blocked off to travelers, for Gog and his multitude will be buried there. It will be called the Valley of Gog's Multitude. ¹² It will take the Israelites seven months to bury the invaders and purify the land. ¹³ And all the people will share in the burying. And it will bring honor to them on the day I show my glory, says Sovereign YHWH. ¹⁴ Workers will be appointed to permanent positions, moving through the country in search of bodies of the dead, in order to cleanse the land. They will carry out their search for seven months. ¹⁵ As the searchers move through the land, anyone who sees a human bone is to mark the spot with a sign. The workers will then bury it in the Valley of Gog's Multitude. ¹⁶ And this will be the end of that multitude, and the land will be purified.

¹⁷ "And you, mere mortal, call out to all the birds and all the wild animals, and say, 'Thus says Sovereign YHWH: Assemble and gather, come from all around to the sacrifice I am preparing for you on the mountains of Israel. There you will eat flesh and drink blood. ¹⁸ You will eat the flesh of mighty warriors and drink the blood of rulers of the earth as if they were all rams and lambs, goats and fattened bulls from Basham. ¹⁹ You will feed full of fat and drink yourselves drunk with blood at this sacrifice I am preparing

---

* While the Hebrew verb *yada* means "to know" in the everyday sense, it also means "to experience" or "to know intimately." Here it means that Israel will once again be in intimate relationship with God.

for you. ²⁰ You will glut yourselves at my table on horses and chargers, on heroes and common troops, says Sovereign YHWH.'

²¹ "I will display my glory among the nations, and all the nations will see the punishment I inflict and feel the hand I lay upon them. ²² From that day forward the House of Israel will know that I am YHWH their God. ²³ And the nations will know that the House of Israel went into exile only for its people's iniquity, for being unfaithful to me. So I hid my face from them and handed them over to their enemies, and they all fell by the sword. ²⁴ I dealt with them according to their defilement and their offenses, and hid my face from them. ²⁵ But now Sovereign YHWH says this: Now I will restore the fortunes of Jacob, and have mercy on the whole House of Israel. And I will be jealous for my holy Hame. ²⁶ When the people reside once more in their homeland undisturbed and free from terror, they will forget their shame and all the treachery they practiced against me. ²⁷ When I return them from the nations and gather them from the lands of their enemies, I will make them exemplify my holiness for all the nations to see. ²⁸ After having sent them into exile among the nations, when I gather them together again in their own land and leave none of them behind, then they will know that I am YHWH their God. ²⁹ I will no longer hide my face from them, for I will pour out my Spirit on the House of Israel, says Sovereign YHWH."

ଔ ଔ ଔ

⁴⁰:¹ At the beginning of the year, on the tenth day of the month, in the twenty-fifth year of our exile—that is, fourteen years after the city fell—on that very day the hand of YHWH came upon me and took me to Jerusalem. ² In a vision from God I was brought to the land of Israel and set atop a very high mountain; to the south stood the outline of a city. ³ When God brought me there, a figure stood there, whose appearance was like bronze. The figure stood at the gate holding a linen cord and a measuring rod. ⁴ The figure—my guide—said to me, "Mere mortal, look closely and listen carefully, concentrate on all that I show you. This is why you are here. Tell the House of Israel everything you see."

⁵ Around the outside of the Temple area ran a wall on every side. My guide held a measuring rod, a reed six cubits long—reckoned by the long cubit, that is, one cubit plus a handbreadth;* when the guide measured the wall, it was one rod deep and one rod high.

---

* The long cubit therefore measured twenty-one or twenty-two inches, so the measuring rod was between ten-and-a-half and eleven feet long. While in this translation we normally convert cubits to feet and inches, some of the measurements in this section have particular symbolism, so we have kept them as they are in the text.

⁶ The guide went up to the gatehouse that faced eastward and climbed its steps, then measured the threshold of the gate. It was one rod wide—the first threshold was one rod wide. ⁷ Then came a series of guardrooms, alcoves one rod wide and one rod deep, with a partition five cubits long between them; then finally the second threshold of the gate, at the vestibule immediately in front of the gate, which was also one rod wide. ⁸ The gate vestibule that faced inward was one rod deep; ⁹ my guide's measurement of the vestibule, including its posts, came to eight cubits, because its posts were two cubits wide. The vestibule of the gate was at its inner end. ¹⁰ The guards' alcoves—there were three on each side of the east gate building—were all of the same size, as were the posts on either side. ¹¹ The guide measured the opening of the gate, and it was ten cubits wide; the gate itself measured thirteen cubits across. ¹² Barrier walls one cubit thick surrounded the alcoves on all sides; the alcoves were six cubits square. ¹³ Their openings faced each other directly across the gateway passage, so that the guide's measurement from the back of one alcove to the back of another marked a width of twenty-five cubits. ¹⁴ The guide measured the posts as sixty cubits tall, as were the doors to the gates that were connected to the posts on each side of the court. ¹⁵ The distance from the front of the outer gate to the front of the inner vestibule of the gate was fifty cubits. ¹⁶ The alcoves of the guards on both sides of the gateway passage had shuttered windows; the vestibules also had windows on both sides. The posts that supported the alcoves and the vestibule were adorned with palms.

¹⁷ Then the guide took me into the outer court of the Temple, where there were chambers and a pavement laid down for the court. There were thirty chambers, and they faced the pavement. ¹⁸ The pavements flanked the gates; the depth of the lower pavements paralleled that of the gates. ¹⁹ Then the guide measured the width of the lower court, from in front of the inner gateway to in front of the outer gateway, and it measured 100 cubits.

As with the east gate, so with the north: ²⁰ The guide measured the gate of the outer court that faced north—its length and width, ²¹ its three alcoves on either side of the passage, its posts, and its vestibule—and it was fifty cubits long and twenty-five cubits wide, just like the first gate. ²² The windows, the vestibule, and even the palm trees of the north gate were the same as for the east gate. From the outside, seven steps led to the gateway passage, and its vestibule was directly ahead. ²³ Like the passage to the east gate, the north gateway passage ended with a gate leading into the inner court; and the guide's measurement of the distance from gate to gate was 100 cubits.

²⁴ Then the guide took me to the south side of the Temple area. There was also a gatehouse on the south side, and for its posts and vestibule my guide got the same measurements as before. ²⁵ The gateway and the vestibule had windows just like the others, fifty cubits long and twenty-five cubits wide. ²⁶ Seven steps

led up to it, with a vestibule straight ahead; its posts were decorated on both sides with palm trees. ²⁷ The inner court also had a gate toward the south; and the court measured 100 cubits from the outer south gate to the inner gate.

²⁸ The guide next took me into the inner court through its south gate. The guide's measurement of this inner gate yielded the same figures as before. ²⁹ Its guards' alcoves, the posts, and the vestibule had the same measurements, and the gateway and its vestibule had windows on both sides; it was fifty cubits long and twenty-five cubits wide. ³⁰ There were vestibules on both sides, each twenty-five cubits long and five cubits wide. ³¹ Here, however, the vestibule faced the outer court. Its posts were decorated with palms, and its staircase consisted of eight steps.* ³² Then the guide took me to the eastern side of the inner court. The gate passageway there yielded the same measurements; ³³ its guards' alcoves, posts, and vestibule all measured the same as before. The gateway and its vestibule had windows on both sides; the vestibule was fifty cubits long and twenty-five cubits wide, ³⁴ and its vestibule faced the outer court. Its posts were decorated with palm trees, and its staircase had eight steps.

³⁵ Then the guide took me to the north gate, and found its measurements to be identical, ³⁶ with the same alcoves, posts, vestibule, windows on both sides, and a length of fifty cubits and a width of twenty-five cubits. ³⁷ Its posts also faced the outer court, its posts were also decorated palm trees, and its staircase also had eight steps.

³⁸ In front of that inner gate was a chamber where the burnt offering would be washed before being sacrificed. ³⁹ And inside the vestibule of the gate, there were two tables on each side where the burnt offering, and the sin offering, and the guilt offering would be slaughtered. ⁴⁰ There were four more tables outside, two on each end of the vestibule as one approaches the north gate. ⁴¹ So there were four tables on either flank of the gate—eight tables in all—at which the sacrifices were to be slaughtered.

⁴² Four of the tables were for the burnt offering, and they were of hewn stone, a cubit and a half long, a cubit and a half wide, and one cubit high, on which were laid the tools used to slaughter the burnt offerings and sacrifices. ⁴³ Shelves, one handbreadth wide,† were attached all around the inside; and the animal to be sacrificed was laid on the tables.

⁴⁴ There were two chambers for singers‡ in the inner court; one was beside the north gate, facing south, and the other beside the south gate,

---

* Seven steps led up to the outer gateway passages, but eight led up to the inner gateway. Seven is the number of fulfillment; eight is the number of the new covenant.
† Or possibly, "Double hooks, one handbreadth long."
‡ The Septuagint omits "for singers." If "singers" is not a scribal error—and it may be, since there are no other references to them in Ezekiel—then they are probably the Levite singers or cantors who sing praises and prayers in the course of their liturgies.

facing north. ⁴⁵ "The chamber that faces south," the guide explained, "is for the priests who perform the general Temple duties, ⁴⁶ while the chamber that faces north is for the priests who serve at the altar—the descendants of Zadok, who alone of the Levites may approach YHWH in the course of their service." ⁴⁷ The guide then measured the court: it was 100 cubits long and 100 cubits broad—a perfect square.* And in front of the Temple stood the altar. ⁴⁸ The guide took me into the portico of the Temple and measured it. Each of the posts that supported the portico was five cubits thick. The width of the gate was three cubits on each side.† ⁴⁹ The portico was twenty cubits wide and eleven cubits deep, and steps led up to it. Columns stood next to the posts on either side.

41:1 The guide then led me into the Temple hall, and measured the side pillars. They were six cubits wide on each side. ² The entrance was ten cubits wide, and each of the walls flanking the entrance was five cubits wide. Next the guide measured the depth and width of the hall, which was forty cubits by twenty. ³ Then, in the inner sanctuary, the guide measured the posts on either side of the entrance, two cubits deep; the entrance itself, six cubits across; and the width of the wall on either side of the entrance, seven cubits. ⁴ The sanctuary itself measured twenty cubits square. And the guide said to me, "This is the Most Holy Place."

⁵ Then the guide measured the wall of the Temple. It was six cubits thick on each side, and on all sides of the Temple were side chambers measuring four cubits wide. ⁶ The side chambers were arranged one above the other in three stories, thirty in each story. All around were projections in the Temple wall to serve as posts for the side chambers; this way, the chambers would not be fastened to the Temple wall. ⁷ Each new story was slightly wider than the one above it, to provide walkways by which one could enter the chambers; these walkways gave access from the bottom story to the top by way of the middle story. ⁸ I saw that the Temple was surrounded by a raised pavement, a platform that served as the foundation for the side chambers; its elevation was a rod's length, or six cubits. ⁹ The outer wall of the side chamber was five cubits thick, and the open area between the side chambers ¹⁰ and the chambers of the court measured twenty cubits all around the Temple. ¹¹ The side chambers, which faced the open area, had two entrances, one on the north side and one on the south; the wall surrounding the open space was five cubits wide all around. ¹² A building that faced the open space at the Temple's western end was seventy cubits deep, its walls were five cubits thick on every side, and it was ninety cubits wide.

---

* The perfect square of 1,000 square cubits is a symbol of absolute perfection.
† This may be a scribal error; some translations emend the text to read, "The width of the gate-opening was fourteen cubits, and the flanking wall of the gate was three cubits on either side." In the next verse, the Septuagint indicates that ten steps led up to the portico.

ezekiel 41

¹³ The guide measured the total depth of the Temple at 100 cubits; the depth of the vacant space and of the building, walls included, also came to 100 cubits. ¹⁴ The front side of the Temple, like the vacant space on the east, was 100 cubits wide. ¹⁵ The guide measured the width of the structure facing the vacant space in the rear, including the galleries on either side: 100 cubits.

The Temple hall, the inner sanctuary, and the portico next to the court, ¹⁶ together with their thresholds, framed windows, and the galleries around all three of them, were completely overlaid with wood paneling. There was paneling from the floor to the windows and window frames, ¹⁷ extending above the openings, both in the inner Temple and outside. And all over the wall, both in the inner and in the outer, were carvings ¹⁸ of cherubim and palm trees, with one palm tree between every two cherubim. Each cherub had two faces: ¹⁹ a human face looking toward the palm tree on one side of it, and a lion's that faced the palm tree on the other side. This was repeated all over the Temple; ²⁰ the cherubim and the palm trees were carved on the wall from the floor to above the openings.

The Temple hall ²¹ had four doorposts; and before the Holy Place was something that looked like ²² a wooden altar three cubits high and two cubits long; its corners, base, and sides were made of wood. And the guide said to me, "This is the table that stands before YHWH." ²³ The Temple hall had a double door, and the Holy Place also had ²⁴ a double door, and each door had two swinging leaves: two for the one door and two for the other. ²⁵ Cherubim and palm trees were carved on the doors of the hall, the way they were carved on the walls. There was a wooden lattice outside in front of the portico. ²⁶ And there were framed windows and palm trees on the walls of the portico on either side of the entrance, as well as on the Temple's side chambers and on the latticework.

⁴²:¹ Then the guide led me into the outer court, toward the north, and we came to the rooms opposite the Temple courtyard and opposite the outer wall on the north side. ² The building—its door faced north—was 100 cubits long and and fifty cubits wide. ³ Three parallel tiers of rooms stood twenty cubits from the inner court and the pavement of the outer court. ⁴ In front of the rooms, to the inside, was a passageway ten cubits wide and 100 cubits long. Their doors faced to the north. ⁵ Now the upper rooms were narrower than the middle and bottom tiers because the corridors took up what would normally be room space. ⁶ And because the building was not built with posts as were the buildings in the outer court, the upper stories were set back from the first floor.

⁷ An outer wall ran parallel to the rooms and to the outer court; it ran in front of them for fifty cubits. ⁸ While the row of rooms on the side next to

the outer court was fifty cubits long, the row of rooms on the side closest to the sanctuary was 100 cubits long. ⁹ Below the rooms was an entrance from the east, leading in from the outer court. ¹⁰ On the south side along the length of the wall of the outer court, adjoining the Temple courtyard and opposite the outer wall, were rooms ¹¹ with a passageway in front of them. These were similar to the rooms on the north side: the same length and width, the same exits and dimensions. Similar to the doorways on the north ¹² were the doorways of the rooms on the south. A doorway at the entrance to the passageway that ran parallel to the wall running eastward gave access to the rooms.

¹³ Then my guide said to me, "The north and south rooms facing the Temple courtyard are the rooms for the priests, where the priests who approach YHWH eat the most holy offerings. Here they will keep the most holy offerings—the grain offerings, the sin offerings, and the guilt offerings—for it is a holy place. ¹⁴ Once the priests enter the holy precincts they will not go into the outer court until they leave behind the vestments in which they minister, for they are holy. They must dress in other clothes before going to the places assigned to the people."

¹⁵ When my guide finished measuring the interior of the Temple area, I was led out to the gateway facing east, where measurements of the whole area took place. ¹⁶ The guide measured the east side with the measuring rod; it was 500 cubits; ¹⁷ the north side measured 500 cubits; ¹⁸ the south side measured 500 cubits; ¹⁹ and the west side measured 500 cubits. ²⁰ So all four sides of the area were measured. It had a wall around it which was 500 cubits long and 500 cubits wide, to separate the sacred from the profane.*

43:1 Then my guide led me to the gate that faced east, ² and there I saw the Glory of the God of Israel coming from the east. The sound was like the roar of rushing waters, and the earth glowed with God's glory. ³ The vision was like the vision I had received when God came to destroy the city, and like the vision I had by the Kebar River. I fell on my face before it.

⁴ The Glory of YHWH entered the Temple through the gate that faced east. ⁵ Then the Spirit lifted me up and brought me into the inner court. And the Presence of YHWH filled the Temple. ⁶ I heard someone speaking to me from

---

* "Profane," while it has come to mean irreverent or vulgar, actually used to mean "uninitiated" or simply secular. It comes from the Latin pro fanum, literally, "in front of (or just outside the doors of) the temple." The 500 cubits are comprised of 100, which symbolizes perfection, multiplied by five, which symbolizes both humanity—five senses, five fingers, five toes, five members (arms, legs, and head)—and divine Law (the five books of the Torah). The Temple of Ezekiel's vision, then, is symbolic of humankind and God in perfect relationship.

the Temple, though my guide was still standing beside me. ⁷ The voice said to me, "Mere mortal, this is the place for my judgment seat, the place for the soles of my feet. Here I will dwell among the Children of Israel forever. Never again will the House of Israel defile my holy Name—neither the people nor their leaders—with their wanton apostasy and their idolatry of dead leaders. ⁸ When they placed their threshold next to my threshold and their doorposts next to my doorposts, with only a wall between them,* they defiled my holy Name with their abominations. And in my rage, I destroyed them. ⁹ Now they must put away their their wanton idolatry and their idolatry of their dead leaders, and I will dwell among them forever.

¹⁰ "Tell the Israelites, mere mortal, about this Temple so that they will be ashamed of their abominable behavior. ¹¹ Let them consider the form and the design of the Temple, its layout, its exits and its entrances, all the particulars of its elevation and plan. Make a sketch for them to view, so that they may keep it in mind and eventually carry it out. ¹² This is the law of the Temple: All the area surrounding the Temple on top of the mountain is most holy. This is the law of the Temple.

¹³ "These are the dimensions of the altar in long cubits—a long cubit being a cubit plus the width of a hand: Its trough is one cubit deep and one cubit wide, with a rim of one span† around the edge. And this is the height of the altar: ¹⁴ from the trough on the ground to its lower ledge is two cubits, and from the lower to the upper ledge is four cubits; each ledge is one cubit wide. ¹⁵ The hearth of the altar is four cubits high, and extending from the top of the hearth are the four horns of the altar. ¹⁶ The hearth is square: twelve cubits long and twelve cubits wide. ¹⁷ The upper ledge is also a square, fourteen cubits long and fourteen wide, with a half-cubit rim around it and a one-cubit trough all around. The steps of the altar face to the east."

¹⁸ Then my guide said to me: "Mere mortal, thus says Sovereign YHWH: 'These are the statutes for the altar once it is set up for sacrificing burnt offerings and sprinkling blood on the altar when it is built: ¹⁹ Give a young bull as a sin offering to the priests, the Levites of the family of Zadok, who draw near me to minister to me, says Sovereign YHWH. ²⁰ Take some of its blood and put it on the four horns of the altar, the four corners of the ledge and all around the rim, and so purify the altar and atone for it. ²¹ Then take the the bull chosen for the sin offering and burn it in the designated place of the Temple, outside the sanctuary. ²² On the second day you will offer a male goat without blemish for a sin offering, to purify the altar as was done

---

* The "thresholds" and "doorposts" are symbolic language for worship (of YHWH as opposed to other gods) and law (following the Torah as opposed to disobedience); placing them side by side with only a wall between them speaks to the people's attempts to legitimize and publicly justify their apostasy.

† A span was the width of a hand with the fingers spread out; standardized as three handbreadths, or about nine inches.

with the bull. ²³ When you have finished the purification you are to offer a young bull and a ram from the flock, both without blemishes. ²⁴ Offer them before YHWH; the priests must sprinkle them with salt and sacrifice them as a burnt offering to YHWH. ²⁵ For seven days you are to offer a goat as a daily purification offering, as well as a young bull, and a ram from the flock without blemish. ²⁶ For seven days the priests are to atone for the altar and cleanse it, and so consecrate it. ²⁷ And once these days have run their course, from the eighth day on, the priests will offer your whole offerings and your shared offerings, and I will accept you, says Sovereign YHWH.' "

44:¹ Then my guide brought me back to the outer gate of the sanctuary, the one facing east. It was shut. ² YHWH said to me, "This gate will remain shut. It must not be opened. No one may enter through it. It is to remain shut because YHWH, the God of Israel, has entered through it. ³ The leader of the people* is the only one who may sit inside the gateway to eat in the presence of YHWH. The leader is to enter through the portico of the gateway and leave the same way."

⁴ And my guide brought me by way of the north gate to the front of the Temple. I looked and saw the glory of YHWH filling the Temple of YHWH. I fell on my face. ⁵ And YHWH said to me, "Mere mortal, take careful note, and listen closely to all I say to you, to all the rules and regulations for the Temple of YHWH. Give careful attention to who may enter the Temple and all who must be excluded from the sanctuary. ⁶ Say to that rebellious house, the House of Israel:

" 'Thus says Sovereign YHWH: House of Israel, let there be an end to all your abominations! ⁷ You have put foreigners, the rebellious of heart and uncircumcised of body, in charge my sanctuary, thus profaning my Temple; when they offer me food, fat, and blood, they are breaking my Covenant. Such are your abominable practices. ⁸ Instead of carrying out your duty to my holy things yourself, you put others in charge of my sanctuary. ⁹ Thus says Sovereign YHWH: No foreigners, uninitiated in heart and body, are to enter my sanctuary. ¹⁰ Though the Levites must bear the consequences of their iniquity, for they deserted me for their idols when Israel went astray, ¹¹ they are still allowed to minister in my sanctuary by taking charge of the gates of the Temple and serving in it. They may slaughter the burnt offerings and sacrifices for the people and stand before the people to serve

---

* Most translations render the Hebrew *nasi* as "the Prince," and in fact the word has numerous meanings, all of which are related to some leadership role. *Nasi* can mean head of a tribe, or leader of a community, or head of a country. In modern Hebrew, *nasi* is the word for president, whether of a country or a corporation. In these chapters, the *nasi* is the Davidic figure of the promised messianic era prophesied earlier in 34:24 and 37:25—essentially the renewal of the Davidic dynasty, which had been dormant since its last ruler, Zedekiah. The word *nasi* or "leader" is used instead of *melech* or "ruler," because in the messianic era, YHWH will be the people's only Ruler.

them. ¹² But because they served the Israelites in the presence of their idols, and caused people to participate in sinful acts, I have sworn with uplifted hand, says Sovereign YHWH, that they will bear the consequences of their sin. ¹³ They are not to approach me to serve me as priests or come near any of my holy or most holy things. They will bear the shame of the detestable practices they committed, ¹⁴ though I will still appoint them to their duties in the Temple and all the work to be done there.

¹⁵ " 'Only the levitical priests of the family of Zadok, who faithfully carried out the duties of my sanctuary when the Israelites went astray, may approach me and administer to me. They will stand before me to offer me the fat and the blood, says Sovereign YHWH. ¹⁶ They alone are to enter my sanctuary and they alone will approach my table to minister before me and carry out my service. ¹⁷ Whenever they enter the gates of the inner court, they are to wear linen clothes. They must not wear anything woolen while ministering at the gates of the inner court or inside the Temple. ¹⁸ They are to wear linen turbans and linen undergarments on their loins. They must not wear anything that makes them sweat. ¹⁹ Before going out into the inner court they are to remove the clothes they wore while ministering and leave them in the rooms of the sanctuary, dressing in other garments. In that way they will not consecrate the people by means of their clothes. ²⁰ They must neither shave their heads nor let their hair grow long; they must keep their hair trimmed. ²¹ Priests must not drink wine when they enter the inner court. ²² They will marry neither widows nor divorced women, only Israelite virgins; they may, however, marry widows of priests. ²³ They will teach my people the difference between the sacred and the profane, and show them how to distinguish between the clean and the unclean. ²⁴ In the case of controversy, the priests are to serve as judges and will base their decisions on my ordinances. They will keep my laws and and my statutes regarding my appointed festivals, and they will keep my Sabbaths holy. ²⁵ They must not defile themselves by approaching a dead person; but if the dead person was a parent, a daughter or a son, an unmarried sister or a brother, then the priest may defile himself. ²⁶ After the priest has been ritually purified, he must wait seven days. ²⁷ On the day the priest returns to the inner court of the sanctuary to minister, he must make a sin offering for himself, says Sovereign YHWH. ²⁸ I am to be the only inheritance the priests will have. You are to give them no possessions in Israel. I will be their possession. ²⁹ They will eat the grain offerings, the sin offerings, and the guilt offerings. Everything in Israel devoted to YHWH is to be theirs. ³⁰ The best of all the firstfruits and of all your special gifts will belong to the priests. By giving them the first portion of your ground meal, you will bring a blessing on your household. ³¹ The priests must not eat anything, whether bird or animal, that is found dead or torn by wild animals.

45:1 " 'When you apportion the land by lot among the tribes, you are to set aside for YHWH a portion of the land as a sacred tract, 25,000 cubits long and 20,000 cubits wide;* the entire area will be sacred. ² Of this, a square plot, 500 cubits long and 500 cubits wide, must be devoted to the sanctuary, with fifty cubits of open land around it. ³ In the sacred tract, where the sanctuary will be located, measure off as most holy a section 25,000 cubits long and 10,000 cubits wide. ⁴ This will be the sacred portion of the land for the priests who serve in the sanctuary and approach to minister to YHWH. It will be a place for the homes and pasture land for their livestock. ⁵ There will be another strip of land 25,000 cubits long and 10,000 wide to be set aside for the Levites, who serve in the Temple, as their property for towns to live in. ⁶ You are to allot to the city an area 5,000 cubits wide and 25,000 cubits long, adjoining the sacred tract. It will be the property of the whole House of Israel. ⁷ The leader of the people will have the land bordering each side of the area formed by the sacred tract and the property of the ciy. It will extend westward from its west side and eastward from its east side, running lengthwise from the western to the eastern border parallel to one of the tribal portions. ⁸ This land will be the portion of the leaders in Israel.

" 'And my leaders will no longer oppress my people but will allow the House of Israel to possess the land according to its tribes. ⁹ Thus says Sovereign YHWH: You have gone far enough, you leaders of Israel! Set aside your violence and oppression and do what is just and right. Stop evicting people from their land, says Sovereign YHWH. ¹⁰ Your scales must be honest; with an honest dry measure, the ephah, and an honest liquid measure, the bath. ¹¹ The ephah and the bath are to be the same size, the ephah containing one-tenth of a homer, and the bath also containing one-tenth of a homer. The homer is to be the standard measure for both.† ¹² The shekel must be equal to twenty gerahs, and your mina must be equal to sixty shekels.

¹³ " 'These are the contributions you are to make: for every homer of wheat or barley you harvest, give one-sixth of an ephah of those grains as an offering. ¹⁴ For the portion of olive oil, measured by the bath, offer one-tenth of a bath for each cor of oil that you produce—one cor equals ten baths, which equal one homer. ¹⁵ And for every 200 sheep in Israel's pastures, offer one sheep. All these gifts are to be used as offerings—grain offerings, burnt offerings, and communion offerings, to atone for the people, says Sovereign YHWH. ¹⁶ All the people of the land will be bound to this offering for the leader of Israel. ¹⁷ It will be the duty of the leader of Israel to provide the burnt offerings, the grain offerings, and the drink offerings on the feasts,

---

* The total area would be about fifty-five square miles.
† As a dry measure, the homer contained about five bushels; as a liquid measure, it contained about fifty-five gallons.

ezekiel 45

new moons, and Sabbaths—on all festivals of the House of Israel. The leader will personally offer the sin offerings, grain offerings, burnt offerings, and communion offerings to atone for the House of Israel.

¹⁸ " 'Thus says Sovereign YHWH: On the first day of the first month you will use an unblemished young bull as a sacrifice to purify the sanctuary. ¹⁹ The priest will take some of the blood of the sin offering and put it on the doorposts of the Temple, on the four corners of the upper ledge of the altar and on the gateposts of the inner court. ²⁰ You are to do the same on the seventh day of the month for anyone who sins unintentionally or through ignorance; this way you will atone for the Temple.

²¹ " 'On the fourteenth day of the first month you will observe the feast of the Passover. You will eat unleavened bread for seven days. ²² On that day the leader will offer—on the leader's own behalf, and on behalf of all the people of the land—a bull as a sin offering. ²³ And on each of the seven days of the festival, the leader will offer the following to YHWH: seven bulls and seven rams without blemish, as burnt offerings; one goat, as a sin offering; ²⁴ and one ephah of grain for each bull and ram and one hin of oil for each ephah of grain, as grain offerings. ²⁵ The same service must be followed on the feast that falls on the fifteenth day of the seventh month,* the leader making the same sin offerings, the same burnt offerings, and the same grain offerings and offerings of oil, for all seven days of the festival.

^{46:1} " 'Thus says YHWH: The east gate of the inner court will remain closed throughout the six working days. It is to be opened only on the Sabbath and at new moon. ² The leader of the people will enter from the outside through the portico of the gateway and stand at the gatepost. Then, while the priests sacrifice the leader's burnt and fellowship offerings, the leader will worship at the threshold of the gateway and leave. But the gate will not be closed until evening.

³ " 'On Sabbaths and new moons the people of the land will bow down in worship in the presence of YHWH at the entrance to the gateway. ⁴ The burnt offering to YHWH that the leader brings on the Sabbath is to be six male lambs and one ram, all without blemish. ⁵ The accompanying grain offering is to be one ephah for the ram; the grain offering with the lambs is to be as much as the leader wishes, along with a hin of oil for each ephah. ⁶ On the day of the new moon the leader is to offer a young bull, six lambs, and one ram, all without blemish. ⁷ The accompanying grain offering is to be one ephah for each bull and ram; the grain offering with the lambs is to be as much as the leader wishes, along with a hin of oil for each ephah.

---

* The Feast of Tabernacles.

⁸ " 'When entering, the leader is to go through the portico of the gateway and exit the same way. ⁹ When the people of the land come before YHWH at the appointed feasts, whoever enters through the north gate to worship is to exit through the south gate; and whoever enters through the south gate is to exit through the north gate. No one is allowed to exit through the gate entered; each is to through the opposite gate. ¹⁰ The leader will be among the rest, going in when they go in and going out when they go out. ¹¹ At the festivals and the appointed feasts, the grain offering is to be an ephah with each bull, an ephah with each ram, and as much as the worshiper pleases with the lambs, along with a hin of oil for each ephah. ¹² When the leader makes a free will offering to YHWH—it can be a free will offering or a communion offering—the gate facing to the east is to be opened for the leader, who will make the burnt offering or the communion offering as on the Sabbath. Then the leader will leave, and once the leader has gone, the gate will be closed.

¹³ " 'Each day the leader must provide a yearling lamb without blemish as a burnt offering to YHWH; it must be provided every single day. ¹⁴ In addition, every morning the leader must provide, as a gift to YHWH, an offering of one-sixth of an ephah of grain along with one-third of a hin of oil to moisten the flour; this is a lasting ordinance. ¹⁵ So the lamb, and the grain offering, and the oil must be offered daily, every morning, as a regular burnt offering.

¹⁶ " 'Thus says Sovereign YHWH: If the leader makes a bequest to an heir, it will also belong to the heir's descendants. It belongs to them by inheritance. ¹⁷ If, on the other hand, the bequest is for one of the officials, it will belong to the official only until the year of liberation, when it will revert to the leader. The leader's inheritance belongs to the heirs; only the heirs. ¹⁸ The leader must not seize any part of the people's inheritance by eviction. The leader is to give the heirs their inheritance only from what belongs to the leader. In this way all of my people will keep their own property.' "

¹⁹ Then my guide brought me through the entrance at the side of the gate to the rooms facing north, the rooms set aside for the priests, and pointed to a place on their west side, ²⁰ saying, "This is the place where the priests will cook the guilt offering and the sin offering; and where they will bake the grain offering, to avoid bringing them out into the outer court at the risk of consecrating the people."

²¹ Then my guide led me out into the outer court and brought me to the four corners of the court; and I saw at each corner another court. ²² These four courts were vaulted and had the same dimensions: forty cubits long and forty cubits wide. ²³ Around the inside of each of the four courts stood a stone ledge with fireplaces constructed all around under the ledge. ²⁴ My guide said, "There are the kitchens where the Temple ministers cook the sacrifices of the people."

47:1 Then my guide brought me back to the portico of the Temple, and I saw water flowing out from beneath the foundation of the Temple toward the east, for the façade of the Temple was toward the east. The water ran along the southern side of the Temple to the right of the altar. 2 My guide then took me outside by the north gate, and around to the outer gate facing the east, where I saw a thin stream of water on the southern side. 3 After that, my guide took me to the east with a measuring rod and measured off 1,000 cubits. I then had to wade through ankle-deep water. 4 My guide next measured off another 1,000 cubits and once again I waded through the water, which was now knee-deep. Again my guide measured off 1,000 cubits and had me wade into water up to my waist. 5 Then my guide measured off a final 1,000 cubits. But now there was a river too deep for me to wade. The water was so deep that it could be crossed only by swimming.

6 My guide then said, "Note well what you see, mere mortal," and brought me to the edge of the river, where I sat. 7 I noticed many trees along the bank of the river on both sides. 8 My guide then said, "The water flows into lands to the east and down to the Arabah. It will empty into the sea whose waters are salt and it will be made fresh. 9 Every living creature that wanders upon the face of the earth will be drawn to the river and will find refreshment there. There will be an abundance of fish, for wherever these waters flow and everything they touch will be renewed. 10 Anglers from En-gedi to En-eglaim will stand along the banks casting their nets. The fish will be rich in variety, like the fish of the Great Sea. 11 The swamps and marshes, however, will not be made fresh: they will be left for salt.

12 "Fruit trees of every kind will grow along both banks of the river. Their leaves will never whither and their fruit will never fail. They will produce fresh fruit, for they will be nourished by the waters flowing from the sanctuary. Their fruit will be food, and their leaves will be medicine."

13 Thus says Sovereign YHWH: "These are the boundaries within which you will allot the land among the twelve tribes of Israel (giving Joseph two portions).* 14 You are all to have a similar portion of this land, which I swore with upraised hand to give your ancestors and now give to you as your inheritance. 15 The boundary to the north will stretch from the Great Sea in the direction of Hethlon, past Labo of Hamath, to Zedad, 16 Berothah, and Sibraim, along the frontiers of Hamath and Damascus, to Hazar-enon, which is on the border of the Hauran. 17 So the border will extend from the

---

* When Jacob disinherited his firstborn, Reuben, his youngest son Joseph was given the birthright. The birthright holder received a double portion of the inheritance; authority over other family members and control over the family's land and holdings; and, usually, the blessing, which conferred a "favored covenant-relationship" with God.

sea to Hazar-enon, with the frontier of Hamath and Damascus to the north. This is the northern boundary.

¹⁸ "The eastern boundary is to stretch between the Hauran—toward Damascus, with Gilead on the one side and the land of Israel on the other. The Jordan will form the boundary down to the eastern sea as far as Tamar. This is the eastern boundary.

¹⁹ "The southern boundary will stretch from Tamar to the waters of Meribath-kadesh. Your region will reach to the Wadi of Egypt, and on to the Great Sea. This is the southern boundary.

²⁰ "The western boundary is the Great Sea, which forms the boundary up to a point parallel to Labo of Hamath. This is the western boundary.

²¹ "You will distribute this land among the tribes of Israel. ²² You are to assign it by lot as an inheritance for yourselves and for the resident aliens living among you who have children with you. They are to be treated as natural-born Israelites and have a share among the tribes of Israel. ²³ You will give resident aliens an allotment in whichever of the tribes of Israel they are a resident. Thus says Sovereign YHWH.

⁴⁸:¹ "These are the tribes' territories: Dan will be in the far north near Hamath, stretching from just before Hethlon through Labo of Hamath and up to Hazar-enon, on the northern border with Damascus; its territory extends from the eastern to the western boundary. ² Asher will be on the borders of Dan, from the eastern to the western boundary. ³ Naphtali will be on the border of Asher, from the eastern to the western boundary. ⁴ Manasseh will be on the border of Naphtali, from the eastern to the western boundary. ⁵ Ephraim will be on the border of Manasseh, from the eastern to the western boundary. ⁶ Reuben will be on the border of Ephraim, from the eastern to the western boundary. ⁷ Judah will be on the border of Reuben, from the eastern to the western boundary.

⁸ "On the border of Judah, there will be a portion that you are to set apart from the eastern to the western boundary, 25,000 cubits from north to south, and as wide as one of the tribal portions from the eastern to the western boundary. In the center of the tract will be the sanctuary.

⁹ "The portion that you set aside for YHWH is to be 25,000 cubits across by 20,000 north and south. ¹⁰ Within this holy land, the priests will have 25,000 cubits on the north, 10,000 on the west, 10,000 on the east, and 25,000 on the south. The sanctuary of YHWH will be in its center. ¹¹ The consecrated priests of the family of Zadok, who kept my charge and did not abandon me with the Israelites as the Levites did, ¹² are to have within this tract of land their own reserved domain, next to the territory of the Levites. ¹³ The Levites will have a portion bordering that of the priests, 25,000 cubits by 10,000. The entire tract will be 25,000 cubits across and 20,000 north and

south. ¹⁴ The Levites may not sell or exchange any part of this land, for it is the best land and must never be given away, for it is sacred to YHWH.

¹⁵ "The remaining area, 5,000 cubits along the 25,000-cubit border, is common land, assigned to the City for dwellings and pasture. The City will be at its center. ¹⁶ These are the dimensions of the City: the north side, 4,500 cubits; the south side, 4,500 cubits; the east side, 4,500 cubits; and the west side, 4,500 cubits. ¹⁷ The common land of the City will extend north 250 cubits, south 250 cubits, east 250 cubits, and west 250 cubits. ¹⁸ The remaining area bordering the reserved land is to be 10,000 cubits to the east and 10,000 to the west. Its produce will provide food for the workers of the City.

¹⁹ "The workers in the City will come from all the tribes of Israel. ²⁰ The entire tract will be 25,000 by 25,000 cubits; you are to set apart the sacred tract together with the City property as a perfect square.

²¹ "The remainder will belong to the leader: the area on both sides of the reserved portion and the City property, extending along the 25,000-cubit line eastward to the eastern boundary, and westward along the 25,000-cubit line to the western boundary, a territory parallel with the tribal portions for the leader. The reserved land and the sanctuary of the Temple will be in the middle.

²² "Thus, except for the property of the Levites and the City property, which lie in the midst of the leader's property, the territory between the portion of Judah and that of Benjamin will belong to the leader.

²³ "These are allotments for the remaining tribes: Benjamin will be from the eastern to the western boundary. ²⁴ Simeon will be on the border of Benjamin, from the eastern to the western boundary. ²⁵ Issachar will be on the border of Simeon, from the eastern to the western boundary. ²⁶ Zebulun will be on the border of Issachar, from the eastern to the western boundary. ²⁷ Gad will be on the border of Zebulun, from the eastern to the western boundary. ²⁸ The southern boundary will be the southern border of Gad, running from Tamar to the waters of Meribath-kadesh, and from there to the Wadi and on to the Great Sea. ²⁹ Thus the land is to be allotted among the tribes of Israel, and these are their portions, says YHWH.

³⁰ "These are the gates of the City, named after the tribes of Israel. There will be three gates on the north side, measuring 4,500 cubits: ³¹ Reuben's Gate, Judah's Gate, and Levi's Gate. ³² On the east side, measuring 4,500 cubits, are these three gates: Joseph's Gate, Benjamin's Gate, and Dan's Gate. ³³ On the south side, measuring 4,500 cubits, are these three gates: Simeon's Gate, Issachar's Gate, and Zebulun's Gate. ³⁴ And on the west side, measuring 4,500 cubits, are these three gates: Gad's Gate, Asher's Gate, and Naphtali's Gate. ³⁵ The perimeter of the City is 18,000 cubits.

"From then and for all time, the name of the City will be 'YHWH Is There.'"

the twelve

hosea

*t*he *wor*d o*f* *y*hwh came *t*o hosea

ben-Beeri during the reigns of Uzziah, Jotham, Ahaz, and Hezekiah in Judah, and of Jeroboam ben-Joash in Israel.*

2 When YHWH first spoke to Hosea, YHWH said: "Go! Marry a prostitute and beget children of prostitution! For the land is guilty of the most hideous kind of prostitution by forsaking YHWH."

---

* Saul, David, and Solomon ruled over all twelve tribes of Israel. When Solomon died the country split in two: the northern half consisted of ten tribes and was called "Israel," "Ephraim," or "Samaria." The southern half consisted of the tribes of Judah and Benjamin, and was ruled over by Solomon's heirs. It is referred to as "Judah," "Jerusalem," or "Zion." Hosea preached in the northern half during the final decades of its decline, following the death of Jeroboam II. He spoke within a deflated and directionless political climate—the result of a generation of political leaders whose main interests were in consolidating personal power and maintaining positions of authority at the expense of all others. For this generation, God had become the rewarder and guarantor of personal advantage. The differences between the worship of God and the rites of Ba'al had been obscured to such a degree that God was prayed to as a Ba'al-like figure who could be manipulated. The prophet uses "shock methods" to wake the people from their syncretic slumber.

³ So Hosea married Gomer bat-Diblaim,* who conceived and bore a son. ⁴ Then God said to Hosea, "Name him Jezreel, for soon I will take my revenge on the house of Jeru for the slaughter at Jezreel, and I will destroy the dominion of Israel. ⁵ On that day, I will smash Israel's bow in the valley of Jezreel."†

⁶ Then Gomer conceived again and bore a daughter. God said to Hosea, "Name her Lo-ruhamah—'No Compassion'—for I will no longer hold dear the house of Israel,‡ nor will I forgive them. ⁷ But I will hold dear the house of Judah and will rescue them—not by the bow or by the sword or by battle or by horses or riders, but by YHWH their God."

⁸ Once Gomer had weaned Lo-ruhamah, she conceived again, and bore another son. ⁹ God said:

"Name him Lo-ammi—'Not my People'—for you are *not* my people and I will *not* be your God.**

2:1 "Yet the people of Israel will be as numerous as the sands of the seashore that can neither be measured nor counted.†† And one day, instead of it being said of them 'You are not my people,' it will be said, 'You are the children of the living God.' ² At that time, the children of Judah and the children of Israel will be reunited and they will choose a single leader, and they will arise from the land, for great will be the Day of Jezreel. ³ Then you will call your brothers, 'Ammi'—'My people'—and your sisters, Ruhamah—'My Dear.'

---

* There is some speculation that Gomer may have been the name of a priestess of Ba'al. If this were true, it would add extra shock value to the text, given that Hosea was a rabid critic of Ba'al worship. Other Biblical scholars believe that Gomer and her children were fictional characters created to illustrate a point. The cold tone of the first part of Hosea echoes the coldness that has come into the relationship between God and God's chosen child, Israel. Gomer, a prostitute, stands for Israel, worshiping first one god then another. The contemptuous names given to Gomer's children illustrate how far the relationship between Israel and God has deteriorated.

† The name "Jezreel" refers to the valley or broad plain between the mountains of Samaria in the south and the Galilee heights in the north; and while it has a different etymology, in Hebrew the name is a close homonym for Israel, thus associating God's vengeance on the one with future judgment on the other. The massacre refers to the overthrow of the Omrid dynasty in II Kings 9-10—the dynasty ruled by Ahab and Jezabel. The massacre was decreed by the prophet Elisha in II Kings 9:7. This event, which from the point of view of Elisha was justified punishment for the idolatrous Omrids, is now interpreted by Hosea as an act of selfish murder. "Smashing the bow" probably refers to the Assyrian invasion in 733.

‡ *Lo-ruhama* is usually translated "she is not pitied." A closer translation might be "she who no longer has the love of her parent." The Hebrew stem connotes parental love. We have chosen the English word "dear" because it comes closest to expressing that kind of parental affection, and its subsequent withdrawal, than the more traditional translation.

** The name *Lo-ammi*—"You are not my people"—indicates that the covenant God made with Moses ("I will be with you") is at an end. God has disowned Israel. But as the next verse indicates, the promise is still alive, if Israel would but turn back to God.

†† The verse numbering of many English translations has chapter 1 continuing for two more verses, with chapter 2 beginning with our verse 3. This continues through the end of chapter 2.

⁴ "But accuse your mother—accuse her!*:
   She is not my spouse, nor am I hers!
   Let her wipe her depravity from her face
   and her unfaithfulness from between her breasts.
⁵ Otherwise, I will strip her naked
   and make her as bare as the day she was born.
   I will turn her into a desert—
   shrivel her up like a dry land and slay her with thirst.
⁶ I will show no mercy toward her children,
   for they are the children of depravity!
⁷ Their mother has been faithless
   and has conceived them in shame.
   She said, 'I will seek out lovers who will provide me
   with bread and water, wool and flax, oil and drink.'
⁸ So, I will obstruct her way with thorn bushes—
   impede her so she will not find her way.
⁹ She will chase after lovers but will never catch them,
   seek them but never find them.
   She'll even say, 'I will return to my first love,
   for I was better off then than I am now'"—
¹⁰ But since she has never acknowledged that
   I was the one who gave her grain and wine and oil,
   or that it was me who covered her with silver and gold—
   which she then sacrificed to Ba'al—
¹¹ now I will take it all away:
   my grain as it ripens, my new wine when it is ready;
   my wool and flax, given to cover her nakedness.
¹² I will reveal her lewdness to her lovers—
   none of them will rescue her from my hand.
¹³ I will bring an end to all her celebrations—
   her yearly festivals, her new moons, her Sabbaths—
   all her solemn feasts.
¹⁴ I will destroy her vines and fig trees,
   which she called 'gifts from my lovers.'
   I will turn them into brushwood
   and the animals of the field will feast upon them.
¹⁵ I will punish her for all the times she burned incense to Ba'al,
   adorning herself with rings and jewels
   and slinking out to meet with her lovers,
   forgetting all about me,"
   says YHWH.

---

* The sisters and brothers are the Southern Realm of Judah; the mother is Israel. The Hebrew *rîb*, which we have translated "accuse," connotes a formal, juridical indictment.

¹⁶ "After that, however, I will woo her;
I will lead her into the desert,
speaking tenderly to her heart.
¹⁷ There I will return her vineyards,
and change a valley of trouble* into a door of hope.
There she will sing as she did when she was young—
as she did at the time when she came out of Egypt.
¹⁸ On that day," says YHWH,
"you will call me Ishi—'My Spouse,'
and will no longer call me Ba'ali—'My Superior.'
¹⁹ For I will take away the names of the Ba'als[†] from her lips
and she will no longer pray to those names.
²⁰ On that day will I make a covenant for them
with the beasts of the field and with the birds of air,
and with the creeping things that move about the earth.
I will smash the bow and sword
and abolish war from the land,
so that all may sleep in safety.
²¹ I will bind myself to you in love[‡] forever—
yes, I will swear myself to you in rightness and justice,
in tender love and in deep compassion.
²² I will swear myself to you in love and faithfulness,
and then you will truly know YHWH.**
²³ On that day, I will speak aloud,"
says YHWH.
"I will speak out to the heavens
and they will speak out to the earth.
²⁴ The earth will speak out to the corn and the new wine and the oil,
and they will speak out to Jezreel.
²⁵ I will plant her in the earth for myself
and I will cherish the one I called 'No Compassion';
I will say to Lo-ammi, 'You are my people,'
and they will say, 'You are my God.' "

---

* Literally, "the Vally of Achor," where Achan and his family were stoned.
† Ba'als are images of the god Ba'al, or are the various forms in which Ba'al is worshiped. In addition, local Canaanite gods were known colloquially as the "ba'als" of their respective districts.
‡ Traditionally, "betroth you to me."
** The relationship of God to Israel is one of love, but Israel's proper response is "knowledge" (yd')—though the Hebrew word connotes experience rather than simple recognition or acknowledgment. This may be because the Hebrew word for love has erotic connotations that would tend to confuse worship of God with the erotic rites of the Ba'al worshipers. Hosea's concern throughout the book is to distinguish the worship of God from the cult of Ba'al.

³:¹ Then YHWH God told me, "Go! Make love to your spouse, even though she is loved by another and has been unfaithful. Love her the same way YHWH loves Israel, even though they worship other gods and love the raisin cakes."*

² So I ransomed her for six ounces of silver† and ten bushels of barley. ³ I said to her, "You will stay with me for many days. You must not be unfaithful or be intimate with any other, and I will do the same." ⁴ For the people of Israel will live many days with neither a sovereign nor tribal leaders, with neither sacrifices nor sacred pillars, with neither an ephod nor household idols.‡ ⁵ Afterward, the Children of Israel will return and seek YHWH their God and David their sovereign.** They will stand in awe at YHWH and all God's bounty in those final days.

4:1–14:9

Listen to the words of YHWH, Children of Israel! YHWH accuses all you who live in the land:

"There is no fidelity or kindness,
no knowledge of God,
throughout the land.††
² There is only cursing, lying, murder, and infidelity—
these things run rampant throughout the land,
and mayhem begets mayhem.
³ The land is in mourning because of this,
and all who live in it are languishing,
along with the beasts of the field,
the birds of the air, and the fish of the sea.

---

* These were cakes used in ceremonies dedicated to the Canaanite fertility goddess, Asherah.
† Half the price of a bondservant.
‡ The prophet is describing a period without any religious ceremony of any kind, neither the worship dictated by the Torah being practiced in the South, nor the idolatrous customs borrowed from the surrounding peoples being practiced in the North.
** That is, a ruler from the line of David.
†† Fidelity (*'emet*) and kindness (*chesed*) are virtues appropriate to covenant relationships. Knowledge of God—both the acknowledgment of God's presence in daily life, and the direct experience of God—is a concrete expression of these values. The list of sins that follows contains specific violations of the Commandments that refer to the unjust practices of debt-foreclosure, land-grabbing, and court corruption committed by the leaders of Israel.

⁴   But let no one blame another;
      let no one accuse another—
      it is with you priests that I have my quarrel!
⁵   You stagger about during the day,
      and your prophets stagger with you come nightfall—
      and you have destroyed your own people.*
⁶   My people are destroyed
      because you do not acknowledge me.
      And because you do not acknowledge me,
      I will reject you as my priests.
      Because you disregard the Law of God,
      I will disregard your children.
⁷   The more your priests were admired,†
      the more they sinned against me—
      they exchanged my glory
      for something scandalous.
⁸   They feed on the unjust deeds of my people
      and revel in their corruption.
⁹   So, this is the way it is:
      like people, like priest.
      I will punish both of them for their ways
      and repay them for their actions.
¹⁰ They will eat, but will never be filled;
      they will engage in licentious idolatry, but never be satisfied,
      because they have abandoned YHWH
      to give themselves
¹¹ to licentious idolatry and new wine,
      which takes away the heart of my people.
¹² They ask their idols for advice
      and are answered by a block of wood.
      For the spirit of idolatry leads them astray
      and they are unfaithful to their God.
¹³ They sacrifice on the tops of the mountains,
      and burn incense in the hills,
      under oaks and poplars and elms,
      where the shade is pleasant.

---

* The original Hebrew text had no vowels; small marks, called vowel points, were added at a later date. The standard Hebrew text reads, "so I will destroy your mother"; our rendering, from using different vowel points, is supported by several medieval Hebrew manuscripts and reflected in Jerome's Vulgate.
† Or possibly, "the more they increased in numbers."

This is how your children become idolaters
and their spouses become faithless.
14 But I will not punish your children
when they take part in temple rites,*
or their spouses when they are unfaithful.
For the parents themselves consort with idolaters
and offer sacrifice with sacred prostitutes
in these same temple rites!
A people without understanding
will come to ruin!†

15 "Though you, Israel, are unfaithful,
don't let Judah share your blame.
Don't go to Gilgal or Beth Aven,‡
nor swear, 'As YHWH lives!'
16 For Israel is as stiff-necked as an obstinate heifer.
How, then, can YHWH shepherd them
like sheep in a pasture?§
17 Ephráim has made an alliance with idols—
and so will be ignored.
18 When their drink is gone,
they give themselves to decadent orgies.
Their protectors love these shameful ways.
19 A storm wind will carry them off in its wings,**
and their sacrifices will bring them nothing but shame.

5:1 "Listen, you priests!
Now hear this, Israel!
Pay attention, Royal House,
for the judgment is against you.
You have been a trap at Mizpah
and a net spread out on Tabor.††

* This refers to the fertility rites of the Cannanite religion in which ritual intercourse symbolized the
conjoining of Ba'al and Astarte.
† In the ancient world, the heart, not the brain, was considered to be the organ of thought as well as
the center of a person. The meaning of "understanding" is to take the Torah to heart—to make it
the very center of our lives. In this sense, a people without heart—a people who do not make the
Torah the very center of their lives—will surely come to ruin.
‡ Beth Aven means "House of Corruption," and is a derogatory name for Beth El (or Bethel), which
means "House of God." Both Gilgal and Beth El were ancient sites originally sacred to YHWH but
which had become centers of pagan worship after Jeroboam I.
§ Or possibly, "Soon YHWH will put them out to pasture," with the same connotation that our idiom
holds.
** A prophecy, perhaps, of the fall of Israel in 721 B.C.E. and the subsequent Assyrian captivity.
†† Mountains in the east and west of Israel where pagan altars had been erected.

² The traitors are deep in blood—
I will rebuke them all.
³ I know all about Ephraim,
and Israel is not hidden from me.
Ephraim has become depraved
and Israel has become corrupt.
⁴ Their ways will not let them return to their God.
A spirit of depravity is in their heart
and they no longer know YHWH.
⁵ The arrogance of Israel testifies against them—
all of Israel, and even Ephraim, staggers in their guilt.
Judah staggers with them as well.
⁶ They go out to their flocks and herds*
to seek YHWH,
but do not find God there,
for God has abandoned them.
⁷ They have been unfaithful to YHWH
and have given birth to children of their unfaithfulness.
Now their New Moon festivals will be their undoing
and will devour their fields.

⁸ "Sound the shofar in Gibeah, and the horn in Ramah!
Sound the battle cry at Beth Aven—'Lead on, Benjamin!'
⁹ Ephraim will be razed on the day of judgment among the tribes.†
I say this for certain to the tribes of Israel.
¹⁰ The leaders of Judah
are like those who move others' boundary stones—
I will pour out my anger on them
like torrents of a great flood.‡

---

* That is, to offer sacrifice.
† *yôm tôkehâ*, or day of judgment, here connotes remedial action rather than vindictive punishment.
‡ This passage refers to what is sometimes called the Syro-Ephraimite War. What happened is part of a convoluted chain of events: The assassination of Zechariah ended the Jehu dynasty and Israel began to come apart; then Menahem tried to secure rulership over Israel by making an enormous payment of tribute to Assyria, paid for by a tax levied on tens of thousands of Israelite landholders. This helped to spur an anti-Assyrian reaction led by Pekah, who formed an alliance with Rezon of Damascus. Israel and Damascus tried to strong-arm Ahaz of Judah into joining them, which provoked Judah's attack on Israel. Ahaz appealed to Assyria for assistance and the pressure on Judah was lifted when Assyria attacked Damascus and Israel, annexing most of the northern provinces. This left a weakened government in Israel and a territory that was limited to the mountains of Samaria. Hosea sees Judah's action as a violation of the covenant and likens it to a landowner moving a neighbor's boundary stone, which is condemned in Deut. 27:17.

¹¹ Ephraim is put down, broken in judgment,
   because they willingly followed human commandments.*
¹² So now I will be like a hungry moth to Ephraim,
   like the worms that cause wood rot to Judah.
¹³ When Ephraim saw this sickness,
   and Judah saw these wounds,
Ephraim sought the aid of Assyria,
   and sent to their Great Ruler† for help.
But that Ruler will not be able to heal you,
   or cure your sores.
¹⁴ For I will be like a lion to Ephraim,
   and like a young lion to the house of Judah.
I will rip them apart and then go away.
   I will carry them off and no one will rescue them.
¹⁵ Then I will go back to my lair
   until they acknowledge their guilt and seek my face.
In their suffering
   they will make haste to seek me:
⁶·¹ 'Come! Let us return to YHWH—
   the One who has torn us asunder
   will make us whole;
the One who struck us down
   will bind our wounds.
² In two days, God will bring us back to life
   and on the third day God will restore us
   so we will live in the presence of the Most High.
³ Let us come to know YHWH intimately,
   and pursue that knowledge zealously.
And as sure as the sun rises in the morning,
   God will come,
and will return to us like the rains of winter,
   like the rains of spring that water the earth.' ‡

---

* "Human commandments" translates the word *tsaw*, which is only used here and in Isaiah, where it is a drunken slur. This may refer to Jeroboam's command to worship his golden calf. Others feel the Hebrew word was a scribal error, and translate it "a lie," "futility," "idols," or even "filth."
† A common epithet given to Assyrian rulers.
‡ The prophet is mimicking words of false repentance on the part of Israel. There are allusions to idolatrous beliefs and practices throughout these passages: the reference to two days...third day may refer to the cult of dying and rising fertility gods, since the exhortation to repentance in verse 3 is replete with imagery that would be appropriate to one of the fertility gods of the region. God is still seen by the Israelites as a Ba'al-like figure whose favors can be curried.

4 "Oh, Ephraim, what am I going to do with you?
And Judah, what am I going to do with you?
Your devotion is like the morning fog,
like the dew of the morning that vanishes!
5 So I hack them to pieces through my prophets
and slay them with the words of my mouth.
My judgments flash
like lightning before you.
6 For I desire kindness toward others, not sacrifice,
acknowledgement of God, not burnt offerings.
7 But like their first parents,* they have broken the Covenant—
they have betrayed me.
8 Giliad has become a city of evildoers,
full of bloody footprints.
9 Gangs of priests,
like marauders waiting to ambush travelers,
are murderers on the road to Shechem,†
committing hideous crimes.
10 I have seen such terrible things
in the House of Israel:
Ephraim is given to licentiousness
and Israel is corrupt.
11 And for you, Judah,
a harvest is in store for you as well,
when I have restored the fortunes of my people.
7:1 But each time I want to heal Israel,
the offense of Ephraim is exposed,
as are the crimes of Samaria.
They deal in deceit,
they are thieves who break into houses and gangs of brigands
who roam the streets.
2 They never consider that I remember
all the evil they commit.
They are swallowed up in corruption,
yet their deeds stare me in the face.
3 They entertain the ruler with their corrupt deeds
and the leaders with their lies.
4 They are all adulterers,
burning like an oven

---

* The Hebrew reads "like Adam."
† Shechem was the first capital of the Northern Realm. The priests, by enticing the people away from the true worship of YHWH, are being likened to murderers.

whose fire the baker does not tend
from the time the dough is kneaded until it rises.
5 At the Ruler's Day celebrations,
    their leaders become intoxicated with wine
    and join hands with the traitors.
6 They enflame the oven of their hearts
    while they lie in wait, scheming.
Their 'baker' sleeps all night,
    and in the morning, their oven flares up like an inferno.
7 Everyone is as hot as an oven,
    and they burn up their governors.
All of their rulers have fallen—
    and none of them call on me.
8 Ephraim has mixed in with the nations—
    Ephraim is an unturned cake,*
9 Strangers have eaten away their strength,
    but they do not recognize this—
their hair is turning gray,
    but they pay no attention.
10 Israel's arrogance testifies against them,
    but despite it all they do not come back to YHWH their God,
    nor do they seek the presence of God, despite everything.
11 Ephraim is like a dove, silly and senseless,
    crying out first to Egypt and then going to Assyria.
12 But even as they are going,
    I will cast my net over them,
I will capture them like the birds of the air.
    When I hear them roosting,
    I will punish them.
13 Woe to them!†
    They have abandoned me!
They will be destroyed
    for their treacherous acts.
I yearn to set them free,
    but they continue to slander me.

---

* Continuing the oven metaphor, Israel has intermingled with the nations like flour and water; now
   it's a pancake that didn't get turned over in time, and is ruined—scorched on one side, dried out on
   the other.
† "Woe" or "alas" translates the Hebrew (and Yiddish) word *Oy!*
‡ Like many agricultural fertility gods, Ba'al would die in the fall and rise again at the beginning of
   spring. Canaanite priests would cut themselves and pour some of their blood onto the ground to
   resurrect Ba'al and thus ensure the fertility of the crops during the next growing season.

¹⁴ They do not cry to me from their hearts,
   but instead howl in their beds.
   They gash themselves for grain and new wine,‡
   and continue to rebel against me.
¹⁵ Even though I was the one who trained them,
   and gave strength to their arms,
   they plot evil against me.
¹⁶ If they return, they won't be useful—
   they are like a defective bow.*
   Their leaders will be slain by the sword
   because of their disrespectful words.
   Because of this, they will be a laughingstock
   throughout the land of Egypt.

8:1 "Put the shofar to your lips!
   A vulture circles over YHWH's Temple
   because the people have broken my Covenant
   and gone against my Law.
² Israel cries out,
   'But God, we know you!'
³ Yet Israel has rejected what is good,
   and their enemy will hound them.
⁴ They have enthroned rulers without my permission
   and have chosen leaders not of my choice.
   They make idols for themselves out of silver and gold—
   which will be their downfall.
⁵ Hear this, Samaria:
   Cast away your calf idol!†
   How my anger burns against them!
   How long can they remain defiled?
⁶ This calf—the product of the hands of an artisan—
   is not God, it is of Israel.
   It will be smashed to bits.

---

* In verse 15, God is the one who trains the warriors for battle; in verse 16, God is the archer, and the nation is a bow—but one that is warped and will no longer shoot straight and thus cannot be trusted. The first line of the verse is difficult; other versions have "They return, but not upward," or "they return, but not to the Most High."

† When Israel split into two realms, Jeroboam I feared that his northern contingent would revolt and shift their loyalty to the southern ruler if they continued to offer sacrifices at the temple in Jerusalem, the southern capital. So he established two shrines, at Beth El and at Dan, and set up a golden calf at each of them, encouraging the people to worship the calves instead of YHWH. Ba'al was represented by a bull, and his consort Astarte or Ashtoreth, "the Queen of Heaven," was depicted as a cow.

‡ That is, the surrounding nations.

7 They have sown the wind—
  so they will reap the whirlwind.
There is no bud upon the stalk,
  so there will be no flour.
Even if it produced grain,
  strangers would devour it.‡
8 Israel has been devoured.
  Now they will dwell among the nations
  like a thing without value.
9 For they have turned to Assyria
  like a wild donkey drifting on its own.
Ephraim has sold itself to lovers.
10 Even though they have sold themselves to the nations,
  I will draw them together now.
They will languish for a time,
  oppressed by a mighty ruler.
11 Though many altars were built in Ephraim for sin offerings,
  the altars themselves are occasions for sin.

12 "I have written many profound Teachings,
  but they are treated as something alien.
13 When they offer me sacrifices,
  it is just flesh for them to eat—
YHWH has not accepted them!
  I will remember their corrupt deeds
and punish their unjust deeds.
  And they will return to Egypt.
14 For Israel has forgotten its Creator
  and builds citadels instead,
while Judah keeps on building fortified cities.
  So I will send a firestorm to their cities
  that will devour their citadels!"

9:1 "Listen, Israel: Do not rejoice,
  do not celebrate like the other nations!*
For you have betrayed your God
  with your unfaithfulness;
you lie on your back and happily collect your wages—
  on the very floors where you thresh your grain!

---

* With agricultural fertility cult festivals.

² Neither the threshing floor nor the winepress will feed the people—
the new wine will fail them.
³ They will not dwell in the land of YHWH.
Ephraim will return to Egypt
and will eat unclean food in Assyria.
⁴ They will not make drink offerings to YHWH,
nor will any sacrifice be pleasing to God.
Their sacrifices will become like the bread of mourners—
anyone who eats them will be unclean.
Their food will be for them alone;
it will not enter the Temple of YHWH.
⁵ What are you going to do on the days of the Solemn Feast?
On the festival days of YHWH?
⁶ Even if they escape destruction,
Egypt will conquer them
and Memphis will bury them.
Their treasure troves of silver will be covered with nettles
and thorns will fill their tabernacle.
⁷ The days of chastisement are coming,
the days of retribution are at hand—
let Israel know it!
Because your offenses are so many,
and your enmity so great,
the prophet is considered to be an idiot,
and spiritual people are thought crazy.
⁸ The prophet—on God's behalf—
is meant to watch over Ephraim,
yet snares await the prophet on the road
and enmity fills the Temple of God.
⁹ They have become mired in corruption,
as in the days of Gibeah.*
But God will remember their corrupt ways
and punish them for their evil deeds.

¹⁰ "When I found Israel,
it was like finding a grape vine in the desert;
when I saw your ancestors,
it was like seeing the first fruits on a fig tree.

---

* The reference to Gibeah may refer to the selection of Saul as ruler of Israel and implies that there
has been a long line of corrupt rulers who brought about the weakening of Israel.

But when they came to Ba'al of Peor,
    they consecrated themselves to Bosheth,*
and became as vile as the thing they loved.
11 The glory† of Ephraim will fly away like a bird—
    no births, no pregnancies, no conceptions.
12 Even if they were to have children,
    I will bereave them of every last one!
Woe to them when I abandon them!
13 I saw Ephraim, as I saw Tyre—
    planted in a pleasant place.
But even Ephraim
    will lead their children to slaughter."

14 Give them, YHWH!
    —"Give them what?"
Give them bodies that cannot produce children
    and homes that cannot sustain them!

15 "All their corruption began at Gilgal,
    and there I came to hate them.
I will drive them out of my Temple
    for the hideous things they do.
I will no longer love or accept them;
    all their leaders are apostates.
16 Ephraim is blighted,
    their root has dried up,
and they yield no fruit.
And even if they do give birth,
    I will slay their beloved children."

17 My God will reject them
    because they have not obeyed.
They will become drifters
    among the nations.

10:1 Israel was a fertile vine
    that yielded abundant fruit.
The more its fruit increased,
    the more altars they built;

---

* Bosheth means "shame," and is often used as a denigrating substitute for the name Ba'al. A number of individuals whose names had "Ba'al" in them were changed to "Besheth" or "Bosheth"—for example, Jerubbaal and Meribbaal, who were later called Jerubbesheth and Mephibosheth.
† Their children.

the more the land prospered,
the more sacred pillars they erected.

2   Their heart is deceitful,
and now they must bear their guilt.
YHWH will destroy their altars
and knock down their sacred pillars.

3   Then they will say, "We have no ruler
because we did not have reverence for YHWH.
But even if we had a ruler,
what good would it do us?

4   All they've ever done is make empty promises,
solemnized contracts with false oaths,
and now litigation springs up
like poisonous weeds in a plowed field!"

5   The people of Samaria tremble with fear
because the calf of Beth Aven is gone.
Its people mourn for it,
its idolatrous priests cry out over it,
because its glory has been taken away.

6   Even the calf* will be taken to Assyria
as tribute to the Great Ruler.
Ephraim will bow its head in shame
and Israel will be embarrassed
by their own carved images.

7   Samaria's ruler will be carried off
like a leaf on the water.

8   The high places of Aven will be destroyed—
these are the crimes of Israel.
Thorns and thistles
will engulf their altars.
Then they will say to the mountains, "Hide us!"
and to the hills, "Fall on us!"

9   You have sinned, Israel,
more than in the days of Gibeah,
and you continue to do so.
Did not war overtake
the children of injustice in Gibeah?

---

* That is, in addition to the people.

¹⁰ "I disciplined those licentious people;
nations were gathered against them
and they were put in bondage
for their two crimes.*
¹¹ Ephraim is a well-trained calf
who loves to thresh,†
so now I will put a yoke around its fair neck.
I will drive Ephraim, Judah will plow,
and Jacob will break up the ground!
¹² Sow justice for yourselves,
reap the fruit of unfailing love,
and break up your unplowed ground.
Now is the time to seek YHWH
until the rains of justice fall upon you.
¹³ But you have sown injustice,
you have reaped evil,
and you have eaten the fruit of lies.
Because you have depended on your own strength
and your many warriors,
¹⁴ the roar of battle will rise against your people
and all your citadels will be destroyed,
just as Shalman destroyed Beth Arbel in battle,
when parents were thrown against the rocks
with their children.
¹⁵ So this will happen to you, Beth El,
because your crimes are many.
When that day comes,
the ruler of Israel will be completely destroyed.

11:1 "When Israel was a youth,
I loved it dearly,
and out of Egypt
I called my child.
² But the more I called them,
the further they turned from me,
making sacrifices to the Ba'als
and burning incense to carved images.

---

* The two crimes are likely the grisly rape and murder of the woman in Judges 19, and the establishment of the monarchy against God's wishes.

† The people have become like the object of their worship. In this section the prophet is employing more fertility cult language—threshing, plowing, sowing, and reaping. The reference to threshing may echo the reference to licentiousness in chapter 9.

hosea 11

³ I taught Ephraim to walk,
   taking them by the arm—
but they don't acknowledge that I was the one
   who made them whole.
⁴ I led them on a leash of human kindness—
   with bonds of caring.
I removed the yoke from their necks
   and stooped to feed them.
⁵ Now they will return to Egypt
   and Assyria will rule over them
because they refuse to return to me.
⁶ Swords will flash in their villages,
   destroying their gates
and devouring them because of their plans.
⁷ My people are determined to turn away from me!
   Even though they cry out to the heights,*
   they will not be lifted up.

⁸ "How can I abandon you, Ephraim?
   How can I hand you over, Israel?
How can I make you like Admah?
   How can I treat you like Zeboiim?†
My heart is aching within me;
   I am burning with compassion!
⁹ No, I can't do it! I cannot act on my righteous anger!
   I will not turn around and destroy Ephraim!
For I am God—no mere mortal—
   the Holy One who walks among you!
¹⁰ They will follow YHWH,
   who will roar like a lion!
When they hear that great roar,
   the children of God will return from the west, trembling.
¹¹ They will come out of Egypt trembling like sparrows,
   from Assyria, like doves.
I will resettle them
   in their own homes," says YHWH.‡

---

* Either to the mountains, where they worshipped Ba'al, or the heavens.
† Admah and Zeboiim were two of the Cities of the Plain destroyed along with Sodom and Gomorrah.
‡ Many English versions continue chapter 11 through the next verse, so there is a one-verse discrepancy through the end of chapter 12.

¹²:¹ Ephraim surrounds me with lies,
  the house of Israel with deceit.
  And Judah continues to wander restlessly with El
  and transfers its loyalty to the "holy ones."*
² Ephraim feeds on wind
  and follows the east wind all day,
  multiplying their lies and treachery.
  They make a treaty with Assyria
  while they send tributes of olive oil to Egypt.
³ YHWH accuses Judah
  and will punish Jacob for what was done.
⁴ In the womb, Jacob grabbed Esau's foot;†
  as an adult, Jacob wrestled with God.
⁵ Jacob fought the angel—and won.
  Then Jacob wept and begged for a favor.
  Jacob found God at Beth El,
  and spoke to the Most High there—
⁶ YHWH God Omnipotent,‡
  YHWH is the name of renown!
⁷ Now return to your God!
  Walk in kindness and justice,
  and place unswerving trust in your God.

⁸ Ephraim is like a merchant using dishonest scales,
  a cheater who loves to defraud others!
⁹ Ephraim says, "I have found wealth!
  I have accumulated a fortune!
  With all of my money, they will not find in me
  any iniquity that is actually a sin!"§

¹⁰ "I am YHWH,
  your God since the land of Egypt.

---

* The "holy ones" are the *qedeshem*, or male temple prostitutes. The last line of the verse is difficult, and many different translations are possible. It could read, "But Judah still walks with God and is faithful to the Holy One," but the word "walks" literally means to roam or wander restlessly, not to stand firm; "God" is not the usual plural *Elohim*, but is the singular *El*, which is the name of the chief Canaanite god and was often identified with Ba'al; and "the Holy One" is plural—and even if it were a "plural of majesty," it is never used as a plural when its antecedent, God/god, is singular.

† Jacob's name means "heel-grabber" or, figuratively, deceiver.

‡ "Omnipotent" here translates *Sabaoth*, which means "of hosts" or "of the armies," and can refer to earthly armies, angelic forces, or even stars in the sky. It is often translated "Almighty."

§ This phrase echoes the refrain of corporate criminals being questioned about duplicitous business activities: "We are guilty of no wrongdoing."

I will make you live in tents again
as you did during the time of your solemn feasts.
¹¹ I have spoken through the prophets
and given them many visions
and told you parables through them.
¹² Is there corruption in Gilead?
They will come to nothing!
Do they sacrifice bulls in Gilead?
Their altars will become piles of stone in plowed fields.
¹³ Jacob fled into the land of Aram;
Israel toiled for a spouse and tended sheep to pay the dowry.
¹⁴ Through a prophet, YHWH brought Israel out of Egypt;
through a prophet, God cared for them.
¹⁵ But Ephraim gave bitter offense
so YHWH will leave their bloodguilt upon them
and will repay them for their contempt.
13:1 When Ephraim spoke, the other tribes trembled—
so exalted were they throughout Israel.
But they were guilty of Ba'al worship,
so they died.
² Now they sin more and more.
They continue to make idols of silver and gold,
skillfully shaping images,
all of them the work of artisans.
It is said of them,
'They sacrifice humans
but kiss calves!'
³ So they will be like the morning fog,
like the first dew that quickly disappears,
like the chaff that the wind blows around the threshing floor,
like smoke escaping from a window.
⁴ For I, YHWH have been your God
ever since the land of Egypt.
You will know no God but me,
have no Liberator except me!
⁵ I took care of you in the desert,
that place of sweltering heat.
⁶ I let them graze in pastureland
until they were satisfied.
But when they became complacent,
they forgot me.

7 So now I will pounce upon them like a lion;
    like a leopard I will lurk beside the road.
8 Like a bear robbed of her cubs,
    I will attack them and tear them asunder;
  I will devour them like a lion;
    a wild animal will rip them apart.
9 You are destroyed, Israel,
    because you are against me,
    against your only help.
10 Where now is your ruler
    who will rescue you?
  Where are your town chieftains
    to whom you said, "Give me a ruler and leaders"?
11 I once gave you a ruler in my anger,
    now I'll take one away in my wrath.
12 The guilt of Ephraim has been catalogued,
    all their wrongdoing has been recorded.
13 The birth pangs come for them,
    but they are children without sense—
  though it is time,
    they refuse to be born!
14 So will *I* ransom them from the power of Sheol?
    Will *I* redeem them from death? No!
  Bring on your plagues, Death!
    Bring on your destruction, Sheol!*
    Compassion will be hidden from my thoughts!
15 Even though they thrive like a reed plant,
    a scorching east wind will come,
    a wind from YHWH blowing in from the desert.
  Their springs will fail
    and their wells will dry up.
  Their treasuries will be plundered
    of all their possessions.
16 Samaria will be held guilty
    because they have rebelled against their God.
  They will fall by the sword,
    their infants will be flung against a rock
    and pregnant women will be cut to pieces."

---

* The Hebrew reads, "Where are your plagues, Death? Where is your destruction, Sheol?" but the context here indicates that "where" means "show them forth."

14:1 Listen, Israel:
　　Come back to YHWH, your God.
　　Your corruption has been your downfall!
2　Take words with you and turn to YHWH.
　　Say to God,
　　"Free us from our wrongdoing and accept our prayer
　　Instead of bulls, we offer you our lips.
3　Assyria cannot set us free.
　　We will not ride on their horses.
　　We will never again say 'Our God'
　　　to something our hands have made,
　　for it is only from you
　　　that the orphaned find mercy."

4　"I will heal their rebelliousness
　　and love them freely,
　　　for my anger against them has subsided.
5　I will be as the morning dew for Israel
　　and they will bloom like the lily.
　　Their roots will spread
　　　like the cedars of Lebanon.
6　Their branches will stretch forth.
　　　They will be as beautiful as the olive tree
　　　and their fragrance like the Lebanon cedar.
7　People will once again find comfort in their shade.
　　　They will be as abundant as the grain.
　　They will be as fruitful as a grapevine
　　　and they will be as renowned as the wine of Lebanon.
8　What more does Ephraim need with idols?
　　　I will answer you and watch over you.
　　I am like a luxuriant cypress,
　　　and all your fruit comes from me."

9　Those who are wise
　　will take these things to heart.
　　Those who are prudent
　　　will learn these things well.
　　YHWH's roads are smooth.
　　　Those who are just are able to walk on them,
　　　But the corrupt simply stumble and fall.

joel

This is the word of yhwh that was
given to Joel ben-Pethuel.*

2 Listen to this, you Elders,
      pay attention, all you inhabitants of the land!
   Has anything like this ever happened in your day,
      or in the days of your ancestors?

3 Tell your children all about it,
      and let your children tell their children,
      and let one generation pass it on to the next.
4 What the bark-stripping locust left,
      the locust swarm devoured.
   What the locust swarm left,
      the winged locust ate;

---

* Joel means "YHWH is God" and Pethuel means "vision of God."

and what the winged locust left,
    the scavenger locust finished off.*

5 Wake up, you drunkards, and weep!
    Wail, all you guzzlers of wine!
Mourn for the new wine,
    for the locusts have snatched it from your lips!
6 Vast and countless,
    a horde has invaded my land!
Flashing like the teeth of a lion,
    like the fangs of a lioness,
7 they have destroyed my vineyards
    and splintered my fig trees;
they have stripped them, and sheared off their bark—
    their branches have turned white.

8 Grieve like a young bride dressed in sackcloth
    wailing over her betrothed!
9 The grain offering and the drink offering
    are cut off from YHWH's Temple.
The priests—those who minister to YHWH—
    are in mourning.
10 The pastures are desolate
    and the land mourns,
for the grain has been destroyed,
    the new wine has dried up,
    and the olive oil is but a trickle.
11 The farmers despair and the vinedressers wail
    over the wheat and barley,
    for the field's harvest has been lost.
12 The vines wither,
    the fig trees fail.

---

* A plague of locusts and a severe drought had devastated the country's agrarian economy and consequently every important aspect of commercial, religious, and national life as well. Four different words for "locust" are used in this verse, *gazam*, *'arbeh*, *yeleq*, and *hasil*. Whether these words represent different life-stages of the locusts, or are synonyms meant to underscore the severity of damage caused by the relentless waves of locust invasion, is not entirely certain. *Gazam* means "cutter," and likely describes the ravenous early nymph that strips the bark from the trees. *'Arbeh* is the common word for locust, and may describe the adult locust swarm; they have been known to travel 1,500 miles, and are able to fly for seventeen hours at a time. A single swarm may contain up to ten billion locusts, cover a hundred square miles, and be so dense as to blot out the sun. *Yeleq* is likely the late nymph stage, when the locust molts its hornlike sheath and unfurls its wings. And *Hasil* means to "finish off," so it probably describes scavenger locusts.

Pomegranate, palm, apple—every tree in the land—
have dried up, and our joy has dried up as well.

¹³ Mourn, you priests! Put on sackcloth and wail!
Weep, you ministers of the altar!
Come—spend the night in sackcloth,
you ministers of my God,
for the Temple of your God
has been deprived of grain and drink offerings!
¹⁴ Order a fast!
Proclaim a solemn assembly!
You Elders: Call the multitude
to the Temple of YHWH your God.
Cry out to YHWH and say,
¹⁵ "Agh, the Day!* The Day of YHWH is coming!
It will arrive as a great upheaval from the Breasted One!†
¹⁶ Our food supply has been cut off as we watched;
joy and gladness are gone from the Temple of our God."

¹⁷ Seeds shrivel under clods of dirt,
and granaries stand desolate.
Barns are torn down for lack of use—
no more harvests!
¹⁸ How the animals moan!
The cattle wander aimlessly for lack of pastures.
Even the flocks of sheep are suffering.
¹⁹ I cry to you, YHWH:
Fires devoured the pastures on the wilderness
and the trees in the fields have gone up in flames!
²⁰ Even the wild animals cry to you
for the streams have dried up,
and fires have destroyed the wilderness pastures.

---

* "Agh!" is actually a transliterated and accurate rendering for this frequent primal cry of anguish. The "Day of YHWH" is a common image in the Hebrew Scriptures. It can describe the sudden "visitation of God" upon the people, for either blessing or punishment, or a future time that sees the consummation of God's reign and the absolute cessation of all attacks upon it.

† The Hebrew word, *Shaddai*, is frequently translated "the Almighty," under the assumption that it derives either from the word *shadad*, which means "burly" or "powerful," or from *shadah*, which means "mountain," making the name mean "God of the mountains." There is growing opinion, however, that Shaddai may derive from the word *shad* or "breast"—thus El Shaddai may be a feminine image of God meaning "the Breasted God" or "the One who Nourishes." Then again, since mountains are frequently shaped like breasts, perhaps these two interpretations are not mutually exclusive.

2:1 Blow the shofar* in Zion!
 Sound the alarm on my holy mountain!
 Let all the people of the land tremble!
 For the Day of YHWH is coming—it is near—
2 a day of darkness and gloom,
  a day of fog and dense clouds.
 A vast and countless horde appears
  like soot spread over the hills;
 it is like something never known before,
  nor will be seen in ages to come.
3 Their vanguard is a consuming blaze;
  their rear-guard is a devouring fire.
 Ahead of them, the countryside is like the Garden of Eden;
  behind them is a desolate wasteland.
 Nothing escapes them!
4 They look like horses,
  they gallop like stallions.
5 With a racket like rumbling chariots
  they leap over the mountain tops,
 like crackling flames burning up straw,
  like a vast army in battle array.
6 People tremble at their sight;
  every face turns pale.
7 They charge like warriors in combat,
  they scale walls like soldiers.
 Each squad pursues its objective,
  never swerving to the right or left.
8 Never jostling each other,
  they move straight ahead;
 like flying arrows, they continue their pursuit,
  never breaking ranks.
9 They hurl themselves at the city.
  They leap upon its walls.
 They climb through windows
  like thieves in the night.
10 The earth trembles at their approach;
  the heavens shudder,
 sun and moon grow dim,
  and the stars withhold their brightness.

---

* The shofar is the ram's horn, frequently translated "trumpet." It summoned warriors to attention in battle, and called the people together for worship.

¹¹ YHWH roars, leading this horde,
with innumerable regiments forming the army;
countless are those who do God's bidding.
Great and terrible is the Day of YHWH!
Who can endure it?

ও   ও   ও

¹² "But know this," says YHWH:
"Return to me with all your heart,
with fasting, weeping, and mourning.
¹³ Tear open your heart,
not your clothes!"
Return to YHWH your God,
who is gracious and deeply loving as a mother,
quick to forgive, abundantly tender-hearted—
and relents from inflicting disaster.*
¹⁴ Who knows? God may come back, relent,
and leave a blessing behind—
grain and drink offerings†
for YHWH your God.
¹⁵ Sound the shofar in Zion!
Order a fast! Proclaim a solemn assembly!
¹⁶ Gather the people!
Purify the community!
Assemble the elders!
Gather the children—even infants at the breast!
Let the bridegroom leave his bedroom
and the bride her canopied bed!‡
¹⁷ Let the priests, the ministers of YHWH,
stand weeping between the portico and the altar
and say, "Spare your people, YHWH!

---

* This verse has an abundance of feminine imagery for God. The phrase "deeply loving" here translates the Hebrew word *rachum*, which derives from the word for "womb"—God is showing a mother's love. This is echoed by the word "tender-hearted" in the next line; usually translated "merciful," the Hebrew word *chesed* means devoted kindness. It is also the word for "stork," for the tender care she shows her young. Finally, the word for "relent" can mean "to be deeply moved," and has the same root as the word for "womb" used earlier.

† In other words, if God spares the people from the plague of locusts, there may yet be enough food left to give some of it back to God as an offering of thanksgiving.

‡ The Torah allowed for recently married couples to be exempt from certain mandatory services, such as military obligation, for a year. That newlyweds are summoned from their bed presupposes a time of great urgency that would override normal considerations.

Don't let your heritage become an object of ridicule,
  a byword for the Nations!
Don't let the peoples say,
  'Where is their God?' "

¹⁸ Then YHWH will be stirred on behalf of the land,
    and will take pity on the people.
¹⁹   YHWH will answer and say:

My people—I will send you grain, new wine, and oil,
  enough to satisfy you completely.
I will no longer allow you to be exposed
  to the taunts of the Nations.
²⁰ I will remove the northern army* from you
    and banish it into a land arid and waste;
  its vanguard I will throw into the eastern sea,
    its rear-guard into the western sea.†
  Their stench and foul smell will rise,
    for YHWH has done great things.
²¹ Forget your fear, my beloved land!
    Rejoice and be glad, for YHWH has done great things.
²² Forget your fear, you beasts in the field!
    The wilderness pastures will once again
    be carpeted in green,
  trees will bear fruit again,
    and the fig and the vine will give you their full yield.

²³ Rejoice, Children of Zion! Rejoice!
    Be glad in YHWH your God,
  who sends you rain—
    the autumn and spring rains as of old—
    and a new spring crop.
²⁴ The threshing floors will be heaped with grain,
    the vats will overflow will new wine and oil.
²⁵ I will repay you for the years that were eaten away‡
    by the locust swarm, the winged locust,
  the scavenger locust, and the bark-stripping locust—
    my great army, which I sent against you.

---

* The locust horde.
† The "eastern sea" is the Dead Sea; the "western sea" is the Mediterranean.
‡ This suggests that the plague of locusts was not limited to a single season.

²⁶ You will eat your fill and be satisfied,
and praise the name of YHWH your God,
who has dealt wondrously with you!
My people will never again be put to shame!
²⁷ You will know that I am in the midst of Israel,
and that I, YHWH, am your God,
and there is no other.
My people will never again be put to shame!*

3:1–4:21

After that, I will pour out my Spirit on all humankind.†
Your daughters and sons will prophesy,
your elders will have prophetic dreams,
and your young people will see visions.
² In those days, I will pour out my Spirit
even on those in servitude,
women and men alike.

³ I will show signs in the heavens and on the earth,
blood and fire and pillars of smoke—
⁴ the sun will be turned to darkness,
and the moon to blood‡—
at the coming of the great and terrible Day of YHWH.
⁵ But everyone who calls on the name of YHWH
will be rescued.
For there will be a remnant on Mount Zion
and in Jerusalem—
this is YHWH's promise.

---

* Here we follow the Hebrew verse numbers; many English translations continue chapter 2 where the Hebrew begins chapter 3; and begin chapter 3 where the Hebrew begins chapter 4.
† Literally, "all flesh," perhaps indicating humanity's frailty in contrast to the power of God's Spirit. Note that "Spirit," or *ruach*, always expresses the divine feminine. At this point, the prophecy of the "Day of YHWH" takes a sudden turn: from the armies of locusts to the armies arrayed against Judah and Jerusalem, from the temporal to the apocalyptic. The Spirit is given to old and young, women and men, slave and free, explicitly encompassing even the most marginalized people in society and making them prophets and visionaries.
‡ The "blood red" color could be caused by fires, volcanic dust, sandstorms, or other atmospheric phenomena.

Anyone who invokes the name of YHWH
  will be among that remnant.

ભ ભ ભ

⁴·¹ Look! In those days and at that time,
  when I restore the fortunes of Judah and Jerusalem,

² I will gather all the Nations
  and bring them down to the Valley of Jehosphaphat—
  which means "YHWH has judged"—
and there I will judge them
  on behalf of my people and my heritage Israel,
  because they scattered them among the nations.
They divided my land among themselves,

³   cast lots for my people,
traded boys for prostitutes,
  and sold girls for wine to drink.

⁴ What are you doing to me, Tyre and Sidon
  and all the regions of Philistia?
Are you exacting vengeance for something?
  If you are exacting vengeance,
I will turn your actions back upon your own heads
  swiftly and speedily.

⁵ For you took my silver and gold,
  and carried my precious treasures into your temples.

⁶ You sold the people of Judah and Jerusalem to the Greeks,
  removing them far from their own country.

⁷ But now I will rouse them to leave
  the places to which you sold them,
  and I will turn your actions back upon your own heads.

⁸ I will sell your daughters and sons
  into the hands of the people of Judah,
and they will sell them to the Sabeans,*
  to a nation far away.
  YHWH has spoken!

⁹ Tell all the Nations
  to prepare for war!
Then awaken your warriors!
  Soldiers, advance! March swiftly!

---

* The Sabeans were influential merchants who followed the ancient caravan routes that traveled
through Arabia.

¹⁰ Hammer your plowshares* into swords,
   your sickles into spears.
Let even the weaklings say,
   "I am invincible!"

¹¹ Wake up, you surrounding nations, and assemble!
   YHWH, let your warriors descend upon them!
¹² Let the nations rouse themselves,
   let them march to the Valley of Jehoshaphat,
for I am going to sit in judgment there
   on all the nations around.
¹³ Swing the sickle,
   for the harvest is ready!
Come and stomp the grapes,
   for the winepress is full
and the vats are overflowing—
   so great is their evildoing!"

¹⁴ Horde after horde
   in the Valley of Decision!
For the day of YHWH is near
   in the Valley of Decision!
¹⁵ Sun and moon grow dark,
   the stars withhold their brilliance.
¹⁶ YHWH roars from Zion,
   God's voice is heard from Jerusalem!
Heaven and earth tremble!†

But YHWH will be a shelter for the people of God;
   a stronghold for the children of Israel.
¹⁷ You will learn then that I, YHWH, am your God,
   and I dwell on Zion, my holy mountain.
Jerusalem will be a holy place,
   no foreigner will ever invade it again."
¹⁸ When that day comes,
   the mountains will run with new wine
and the hills flow with milk,
   and all the river beds of Judah
   will run with water.

---

* A plowshare is a sharp steel wedge, the bottommost part of a plow, that cuts loose the top layer of soil.
† These verses echo the language used earlier to describe the locust invasion.

A fountain will spring from the Temple of YHWH
to water the Wadi of the Acacia Trees.*

¹⁹ Egypt will become a desolation,
Edom will be a desert waste
because of the violence done to the children of Judah,
whose innocent blood they shed in their country.
²⁰ But Judah will be inhabited forever,
and Jerusalem for all generations.
²¹ I will avenge their blood and let none go unpunished,
and YHWH will dwell in Zion.

---

* Traditionally, "the Valley of Shittim." Acacia trees are usually found in extremely arid locations, where they can survive better than other trees. The stream's ability to revive the driest and most barren places near Jerusalem is a symbol for God's restoration and refreshment of the people.

amos

*T*he words of amos, a sheep breeder
from Tekoa.*

These are the visions Amos had of Israel in the time of Uzziah ruler of Judah and of Jeroboam ben-Joash, ruler of Israel, two years before the earthquake.

² Amos said:

YHWH roars from Zion,
and thunders from Jerusalem!
The shepherds' pastures will dry up
and the summit of Carmel will crumble.

---

* Tekoa was a town in the hill country of Judah, built by the first ruler of Judah, Rehoboam, a century and a half earlier. Amos preached between 760 and 750 B.C.E. Archaeological digs in the area have found evidence of a powerful earthquake during this period. Amos, who explicitly separates himself from the professional prophetic guild by stating that he is a sheep breeder, proclaims God's judgment on the northern realm, Israel; except for the oracle in 2:4, his theological and political perspective has very much a Judean slant, with God promising to "restore David's fallen house" in chapter 9.

³ Thus says YHWH:

> For the three atrocities of Damascus—no, four!*—
> I will not relent:
> Because they threshed Gilead
> with iron threshing sledges,
⁴ I will hurl fire on the house of Hazael
> to burn up Ben-Hadad's palaces;
⁵ I will break the iron gates of Damascus,
> and cut down the inhabitants of the Valley of Aven
> and the sceptered ruler of Beth-eden,
> and the people of Aram will be exiled to Kir.

⁶ Thus says YHWH:

> For the three atrocities of Gaza—no, four!—
> I will not relent:
> Because they have exiled an entire population
> as slaves to Edom,
⁷ I will hurl fire on the walls of Gaza
> and burn its palaces;
⁸ I will cut down the inhabitants of Ashdod
> and the sceptered ruler of Ashkelon.
> Then I will turn my hand against Ekron
> until the last of the Philistines is dead,
> says the Sovereign YHWH.

⁹ Thus says YHWH:

> For the three atrocities of Tyre—no, four!—
> I will not relent:
> Because they have deported entire nations as slaves to Edom
> and have violated the treaty of the alliance,†
¹⁰ I will hurl fire on the walls of Tyre
> and burn up its royal residences.

¹¹ Thus says YHWH:

> For the three atrocities of Edom—no, four!—
> I will not relent:

---

* This is a common literary construction, especially in Hebrew wisdom literature; it means "atrocity after atrocity."
† Hiram, the ruler of Tyre during Solomon's reign, had made a "pact of equals" with Solomon and called him "brother."

Because they pursued their treaty partner with the sword,
   suppressing all compassion
   and letting their rage storm unchecked,
12   I will hurl fire on Teman
   to burn up the royal residences of Bozrah.

13   Thus says YHWH:

For the three atrocities of the children of Ammon—no, four!—
   I will not relent:
Because they disemboweled the pregnant women of Gilead
   during an invasion to extend their own territory,
14   I will set fire to the wall of Rabbah
   and burn up its royal residences;
amid the sound of war cries on the day of battle,
   loud as a gale wind on a stormy day,
15   their ruler will go into exile, with their officials,
   says YHWH God.

2·1 Thus says YHWH:

For the three atrocities of Moab—no, four!—
   I will not relent:
Because they burned the bones of the ruler of Edom
   and desecrated them,
2   I will hurl fire on Moab
   and burn up the royal residences of Kerioth,
and Moab will die amid chaos,
   amid the sound of war cries and the blare of the shofar.
3   I will cut down their governor inside the city
   and slaughter all their officials at the same time,
   says YHWH.

4   Thus says YHWH:

For the three atrocities of Judah—no, four!—
   I will not relent:
Because they rejected the Law of YHWH
   and failed to keep its precepts,
because they were led astray
   by the false gods of their ancestors,
5   I will hurl fire on Judah
   and burn up the royal residences of Jerusalem.

⁶ Thus says YHWH:

> For the three atrocities of Israel—no, four!—
> I will not relent:
> because they sold the innocent for silver,
> and the needy for a pair of sandals;*
> ⁷ because they trample the heads of poor people into the dust
> and push the land's humble off the road;
> because both father and son go to the same Temple prostitute,
> thus profaning my holy Name,
> ⁸ having sex beside any altar
> on garments taken as collateral;
> because they drink wine in the house of their God,
> wine bought with the fines they imposed.
> ⁹ You did all these things
> even though I overthrew the Amorites when they attacked—
> warriors tall as cedars and strong as oaks!
> I destroyed them,
> both fruit above the ground and root below.
> ¹⁰ And I brought you out of the land of Egypt
> and led you through the desert for forty years
> so that you could take possession of the Amorite country,
> ¹¹ and raised up prophets from your children
> and Nazirites from among your young—
> is this not true, you Children of Israel?
> —it is YHWH who speaks!
> ¹² But you forced the Nazirites to drink wine†
> and ordered the prophets not to prophesy!
> ¹³ So I will press you down
> as a cart is pressed down when it is overloaded with grain.
> ¹⁴ The fastest runners won't be able to hide,
> the strong will find no strength,
> warriors will not be able to rescue themselves.
> ¹⁵ The archers will not stand their ground,
> the swift will not escape,
> not even those on horseback—

---

* Poor people often took out loans at exhorbitant interest rates, with lenders accepting their coats and shoes as collateral. The Torah required that the garments be returned before nightfall, but these loan sharks kept the clothing anyway. They levied huge fines as penalties for missed payments, and impoverished borrowers who defaulted on the loan altogether were sold into slavery—often for a relatively small price.

† Nazirites, or religious devotees, took a vow to abstain from alcohol.

16   the bravest warriors will flee unarmed on that day
        —it is YHWH who speaks.

:1–6:14

Listen, people of Israel! This is the oracle that YHWH speaks against you,
against the whole family that I brought out of the land of Egypt:

2   You alone are the people I cared for
            among all the families of the earth.
        This is why I call you to account
            for all your sins.
3   Can two travelers take the road together
            if they have not first met?
4   Does the lion roar in the jungle
            if it has no prey?
        Does a young lion growl in its den
            if it has captured nothing?
5   Does the bird fall to the ground ensnared
            if no trap was set for it?
        Does the net spring up from the ground
            unless it is to capture something?
6   Can the shofar sound in the city
            without alarming the citizens?
        Does misfortune come to a city
            if YHWH didn't send it?
7   YHWH does nothing
            without revealing those plans to the prophets.
8   The lions roar—who can help feeling afraid?
            YHWH speaks—who can refuse to prophesy?
9   Proclaim it in the royal residences of Assyria
            and in the royal residences in the land of Egypt!
        Say: Assemble on Samaria's mountain*
            and witness the shameful deeds in that city—
        witness the oppression inside its walls!

---

* This is Mt. Gerizim, the site of an ancient temple to Baal and, in later years, a temple to YHWH, in
direct competition with the Temple at Jerusalem.

33 mos 3

10 They know nothing of fair dealing—
        it is YHWH who speaks—
    they cram their fortresses full
        through violence and extortion.
11 So Sovereign YHWH says this:
        An enemy will overrun your land!
    That enemy will strip you of your splendor,
        and plunder your fortresses.
12 Thus says YHWH:
    Like a shepherd rescuing a couple of legs
        or a bit of an ear from the lion's mouth,
    so will these children of Israel who dwell in Samaria be rescued—
        with just the corner of a bed, or part of a couch.
13 Listen!
    Warn the House of Leah and Rachel and Jacob!
        —It is the Sovereign YHWH who speaks, the God of Israel.
14 On the day I punish Israel for its atrocities
        I will pass judgment on the altar of Bethel.
    The horns of the altar will be broken
        and smashed on the ground.
15 I will wreck both the winter residence
        and the summer residence.
    The house of inlaid ivory will be destroyed;
        the house of beautiful ebony will vanish
        —it is YHWH who speaks.

4:1 Listen to this word, you rich cows of Bashan*
        living in the mountain of Samaria:
    You defraud the poor, steal from the needy,
        and call out, "Bring me another drink!"
2   The Sovereign YHWH swears this in holiness:
    The days are coming
        when you will be dragged out in baskets,
        every last one of you in fish baskets.†

---

* Bashan, in northern Israel, was celebrated for the richness and fertility of its pasture land; its livestock were known for being strong, fat, and healthy. Psalm 22 speaks of the "strong bulls of Bashan," and Ezekiel talks of Bashan's "fatlings." Amos is comparing the wealthy of Samaria, who grew wealthy by oppressing the poor and who luxuriated in their opulence, with fatted cows who would soon be led to slaughter.
† In the ancient world, fish were tightly packed in baskets for transport to market; Amos is saying that people will be "packed like sardines," as it were, in the mass deportations during the exile. Jeremiah 16:16 and Habakkuk 1:15 also employ fishing metaphors to describe the exile.

3   You will be taken out of the city
       through the nearest breach in the wall,*
    to be flung onto the nearest dung heap.
    —It is YHWH who speaks.

4   Come to Bethel and sin!
       Come to Gilgal, and sin even more!†
    Offer your sacrifices the next morning
       and your tithes on the third day.

5   Burn your thank offering of leavened bread
       and announce your freewill offering in a loud voice—
    those are the things that make you happy,
       children of Israel!
    —It is YHWH who speaks.

6   So I left you with empty stomachs (but clean teeth!) in your towns;
       I left you without bread in your villages.
    Still you never returned to me
    —it is YHWH who speaks.

7   I withheld the spring rains,
       three months from the harvest;
    I let rain fall on one town and not another,
       one field got rain, and the next dried up.

8   Two or three towns would stagger
       into the next town for drinking water,
    and still you never came back to me
    —it is YHWH who speaks.

9   I struck you with blight and rot,
       and withered your gardens and vineyards.
    Locusts devoured your fig and olive trees,
       and still you never came back to me
    —it is YHWH who speaks.

10   I sent you a plague
       like Egypt's plague;
    I slaughtered your young warriors with the sword,
       while your horses were captured for plunder;
    I filled your nostrils with the stench of your camps;
       and still you never came back to me
    —it is YHWH who speaks.

11   I overthrew you as I overthrew Sodom and Gomorrah,
    and you were like a brand snatched from the blaze.

---

* That is, without even the dignity of passing through the city gates.
† Bethel and Gilgal were the centers of worship for the northern realm.

And still you never came back to me
  —it is YHWH who speaks.
12 I assure you, O Israel,
  This is my plan for you,
and because I will do this to you,
  prepare to meet your God, Israel!
13 Look—it is YHWH who formed the mountains
  and created the winds,
whose intentions are revealed to humankind,
  who makes both dawn and dusk,
who walks on the top of the heights of the world—
  whose Name is YHWH, God Omnipotent!

5:1 Listen to the word I speak against you.
  It is a dirge, O House of Israel:
2 You have fallen, never to rise again,
  once-innocent Israel—
abandoned on your own soil,
  with no one to lift you up!
3 For thus says the Sovereign YHWH:
The city that used to put a thousand in the field
  will be left with a hundred,
and the one which used to put a hundred
  will be left with ten.
4 Thus says YHWH to the House of Israel:
  Seek me and live!
5 Don't seek Bethel,
  don't go to Gilgal,
  don't journey to Beersheba!
Gilgal will be exiled
  and Bethel brought to nothing.
6 Seek YHWH and live!
Or God will rush like a fire on the House of Joseph,
  and no one in Bethel will be able to put out the flames.
7 Ah, you who turn justice to wormwood,*
  and bring righteousness to the dust—
8 seek the One who made the Pleiades and Orion,
  who turns the dusk to dawn, and day to the darkest night,

---

* A perennial symbol of bitterness, affliction, and punitive suffering, wormwood is an aromatic plant that produces a bitter extract used in flavoring certain wines, and as a medicine to expel intestinal worms. The Greeks called it absinthion, which means "undrinkable"; absinthe, the famous green liqueur of France that contained wormwood, is banned in many countries because of its toxicity.

who summons the waters of the sea
and pours them over the land—
seek YHWH!

9 YHWH rains down destruction on the strongholds
and brings ruin to the fortress.

10 You hate the arbiter who sits at the city gate*
and detest the one who speaks the truth.

11 Rest assured: since you trampled on the poor,
extorting inhumane taxes on their grain,
those houses you built of hewn stone—
you will never live in them;
and those precious vineyards you planted—
you will never drink their wine.

12 For I have noted your many atrocities,
and your countless sins,
you persecutors of the righteous,
you bribe-takers,
you who deny justice
to the needy at the city gate!

13 That is why the prosperous moan in times like this,
for such times bring disaster.

14 Seek good and not evil,
so that you may live,
and so that YHWH God Omnipotent
may truly be with you as you have been claiming.

15 Hate what is evil, and love what is good;
maintain justice at the city gate,
and it may be that YHWH God Omnipotent
will take pity on the remnant of Joseph.

16 For thus says YHWH God Omnipotent:
There will be dirges in every public square;
in every street, wails of "Woe is me! Woe is me!"
Farmers will be called upon to lament,
not just the professional mourners:

17 there will be wailing in every vineyard,
for I will pass through your midst,
says YHWH God.

18 You who wish for the Day of YHWH to come—
why do you want it?

---

* The court in each town was located at the city gate, where elders would sit as judges and settle disputes. Honest arbiters were despised by the wealthy because they could not be bribed.

What will the Day of YHWH mean to you?
It will be a day of darkness, not light!
19 It will be like running from a lion
only to meet a bear,
or like getting home safe at last,
only to get bitten by a snake hiding in the corner!
20 Rest assured: the Day of YHWH will be darkness, not light.
It will all be gloom, without a single ray of light.
21 I despise and reject your feasts!
I am not appeased by your solemn assemblies!
22 When you offer me burnt offerings,
I reject your oblations,
and refuse to look at your sacrifices of fattened cattle!
23 Spare me the racket of your chanting!
Relieve me of the strumming of your harps!
24 Rather, let justice flow like a river,
and righteousness flow like an unfailing stream.
25 Did you bring me all these sacrifices and grain offerings
during your forty years in the wilderness, house of Israel?*
26 Now you will carry off Sakkuth and Moloch
and Kiyyun your star god,
those idols you have made for yourselves,
27 for I will drive you into exile far beyond Damascus,† says YHWH!
God Omnipotent is my name!
6·1 Woe to you who live in luxury in Zion,
and to you self-important people on the mountain of Samaria,
you distinguished leaders of the nation,
in whom the House of Israel places its hope!
2 Cross over to Calneh and see,
go on from there to Hamath the great,
then down to Gath in Philistia.
Are you better off than these realms?
Is their territory larger than yours?

---

* In fact, the Israelites did offer sacrifices and grain offerings while they wandered in the desert. The point, however, seems to be that God places a much higher priority on justice and compassion for the poor than on a carefully codified system of religious observation—true obedience of the heart rather than an outward show of piety.

† In 721 B.C.E., less than thirty years after Amos preached, the northern realm of Israel was conquered by the Assyrians and its people taken into captivity, exiled to northern Assyria and the regions south of the Caspian Sea, never to return; these are the "ten lost tribes" of Israel (the large Jewish population in southern Russia is likely composed of their descendants). The road to Assyria ran through Damascus, Israel's neighbor to the north.

3   Yet you try not to think about the Day of Woe,
        and you hasten the reign of violence!
4   Lying on ivory beds and reclining on their couches,
        they dine on lambs from the flock,
        and young calves from the stalls.
5   They hum to the tune of the harp,
        and fancy themselves musicians like David.
6   They drink wine straight from the bottle,
        and anoint themselves with the finest oils.
        But they show no care for the ruin of Joseph!
7   So they will be the first to be exiled—
        they will recline no more at festive banquets!
8   The Sovereign YHWH swears it—
        it is YHWH God who speaks, God Omnipotent!
    I detest the pride of Jacob;
        I hate its royal residences.
    I will abandon the city
        and all it contains.
9   If ten are left in a single house,
        they will die.
10 Only a few will escape
        to carry the bones out of the house.
    And if one person calls to another in the house,
        "Is there anyone left with you?"
    the other will reply,
        "No! Hush! The name of YHWH must not be mentioned!"
11 For you see, YHWH alone orders it:
        the great house will be smashed to pieces,
        the small house to splinters.
12 Do horses gallop on rocks?
        Do people plow the sea with oxen?
    Yet you have turned justice into a poisonous weed,
        and the fruit of righteousness into wormwood.
13 You are happy over Lo-Debar,
        and you brag, "It was by our own strength
        that we took Karnaim!"*
14 But I will raise up a nation against you, O House of Israel.
        —It is the Sovereign YHWH who speaks, God Omnipotent.

---

* Lo-Debar and Karnaim are locations in northern Israel, but they are also puns: Lo-Debar means "nothing," and Karnaim means "horns," which are symbolic of strength. This verse could be rendered, "You are happy over nothing, and you brag, 'It was by our own strength that we gained strength!'"

A nation that will pursue you from the Pass of Hamath
right down to the Arabah river.

7:1–9:15

*t*his is what the Sovereign YHWH showed me:
 I saw a swarm of locusts
  at the time when the second crop started to grow,
 a swarm of full grown locusts,
  after the ruler's harvest was over.
2 After they had devoured the foliage of the land,
  I said, "O Sovereign YHWH! Forgive us, I beg you!
 How can Jacob survive, being so small?"
3 And YHWH relented—
  "This will not happen," YHWH said.
4 This is what the Sovereign YHWH showed me:
  The Sovereign YHWH summoned fire to punish.
 It had devoured the great Deep
  and was already encroaching on the pastures.
5 Then I said, "Please stop, O God, I beg you!
  How can Jacob survive, being so small?"
6 And YHWH relented.
  "This will not happen either," said YHWH.
7 This is what the Sovereign YHWH showed me:
  God was standing by a wall, a plumb line* in hand.
8 "What do you see, Amos?" YHWH asked me.
  "A plumb line," I said.
 Then God said to me,
  "Look, I am going to measure my people Israel by plumb line.
 I will no longer excuse their atrocities.
9 The high places of Isaac will be ruined,
  the sanctuaries of Israel destroyed.
 With sword in hand,
  I will attack the House of Jeroboam."

---

* A plumb line is a line with a small weight such as lead attached to it, used by builders to determine
a true vertical line.

¹⁰ Amaziah the priest of Bethel then sent this message to Jeroboam ruler of Israel: "Amos is plotting against you in the midst of the House of Israel. The country can no longer tolerate what he keeps saying. ¹¹ For this is what he says, 'Jeroboam will die by the sword, and Israel is going into exile from its land.' "

¹² Amaziah told Amos, "Go away, seer! Go back to the land of Judah. Earn your bread there. Do your prophesying there. ¹³ We want no more prophesying in Bethel. This is the royal sanctuary, the national Temple!"

¹⁴ Amos answered Amaziah: "I am no prophet. Nor am I the disciple of a prophet. I was a shepherd, and gathered figs for food. ¹⁵ But YHWH took me from herding the flock, and said to me, 'Go, prophesy to my people Israel.' ¹⁶ So listen to the word of YHWH! You say: 'Do not prophesy against Israel. Utter no oracles against the House of Isaac.' ¹⁷ Very well, this is what YHWH says: 'Your spouses will be forced to take the most demeaning work, your children will fall by the sword, your land will be parceled out by measuring lines, and you yourself will die on unclean soil. And Israel will go into exile, far from its own land.' "

8:1   This is what the Sovereign YHWH showed me:
      a basket of ripe figs.
2   God said, "What do you see, Amos?"
      "A basket of ripe figs," I replied.
      Then YHWH said to me:
      "The time is ripe for my people, Israel.
      I will no longer tolerate their atrocities.
3   The singers in the Temple will wail that day:
      'So many corpses scattered anywhere. Hush!' "
      It is the Sovereign YHWH who speaks.
4   Listen to this, you who live off of the needy
      and oppress the poor of the land,
5   you who say, "If only the New Moon were over
      so we could sell our grain,"
      and "When Sabbath is over,
      we will sell our wheat
      charging higher prices for smaller portions,
      tilting the scales in our favor.
6   That way, we can buy the poor for silver
      and the needy for a pair of sandals—
      and even make a profit on the chaff of the wheat!"
7   YHWH swears by the Pride of Jacob,*
      "I will never forget a single thing you have done."

---

* The Pride of Jacob is the land itself.

8   Will not the land tremble because of this,
      and all who dwell in it mourn?
    Will the land not rise up like the Nile,
      rising and sinking like the river of Egypt?
9   "That day—
      it is the Sovereign YHWH who speaks—
    I will make the sun set at noon,
      and darken the earth in broad daylight.
10 I will turn your feasts into funerals
      and all your happy songs into dirges.
    I will have your loins all in sackcloth,
      your heads all shaved.
    It will be a day of mourning, as for a dead child—
      all of this on that bitter day!
11 The time is coming—
      it is the Sovereign YHWH who speaks—
    when I will send famine on the land:
      not a famine of bread, or a drought of water,
      but a famine of hearing no word from YHWH.*
12 People will stagger from sea to sea
      and wander from north to east
    seeking revelation from YHWH,
      but will not find it.
13 That day,
      beautiful young women and strong young men
      will faint from thirst.
14 All who swear by the Shame of Samaria—†
      those who swear, 'By your god's life, Dan!'
    and, 'By your Beloved's life, Beersheba!'
      these will all sink, never to rise again."

9:1 I saw God standing at the side of the altar.
    "Strike the top of the pillars," God ordered,
    "and let the roof come down
      on the heads of all assembled there.
    Anyone left I will slay with a sword.
      No one will escape! No one will survive!
2   If they burrow their way down to Sheol,
      my hand will haul them out!

---

* Amos is prophesying an end to divine revelation.
† The "Shame of Samaria" refers to the worship of Ba'al-Hadad (the god) and Ashtoreth (the Beloved).

If they ascend to the heavens,
    I will bring them down!
³   If they try to hide on top of Mount Carmel,
    I will track them down and catch them.
If they try hiding from my sight at the bottom of the sea,
    I will command the serpent to bite them.
⁴   If they are carried off into captivity by their enemies,
    I will order the sword to slaughter them there.
My eyes will be on them for their misfortune,
    not their good."
⁵   It is the Sovereign YHWH Omnipotent!
Who touches the land and makes it tremble
    and all the inhabitants of the land mourn?
Who makes the land rise up like the Nile
    and then subside like the river of Egypt?
⁶   Who built the high dwelling places in the heavens
    and supported its vaulted dome over the earth?
Who commands the waters of the sea
    and pours them over the land?
    —It is YHWH!
⁷   "Aren't the children of Ethiopia the same to me
    as you are, children of Israel?
    —It is YHWH who speaks.
I brought Israel out of the land of Egypt,
    but I also led the Philistines in their own exodus from Caphtor,
    and brought the Aramaeans out of Kir.
⁸   Now I turn my eyes onto this sinful nation,
    and I will wipe it off the face of the earth.
But I will not destroy the House of Jacob completely—
    it is YHWH who speaks.
⁹   For now I will issue orders
    and shake out the House of Israel among all the nations,
as grain would be sifted with a screen
    to make sure not a single pebble gets through.
¹⁰ All the sinners among my people
    will perish by the sword—
all who brag, 'No misfortune will ever touch us,
    or even come anywhere near us!'
¹¹ On that day, I will set up again
    the fallen tent of David.
I will mend its tears, restore its ruins,
    and rebuild it strong as it was in the days of old,

¹² so that they can conquer the remnant of Edom
and all the nations that belonged to me.
It is YHWH who speaks,
YHWH who will carry this out!
¹³ The days are coming—
it is YHWH who speaks—
when the plower will overtake the reaper,*
when the mountains will run with new wine
and the hills all flow with it.
¹⁴ I will restore the fortunes
of my people Israel.
They will build the ruined cities and live in them,
plant vineyards and drink the wine,
dig their gardens
and eat their own produce.
¹⁵ I will plant them in their own land,
and they will never again be uprooted
from the land I have given them.
It is YHWH your God who speaks."

---

* In the blessing to come, crops will be so abundant that the harvest will not be finished before it is time to plow the fields again.

obaÒiah

*t*he *v*ision o*f* obaÒiah.*

I received a message from Sovereign YHWH.
A messenger was sent among the nations, saying,
"Rise up! Let us march against them in battle!"

Thus says YHWH concerning Edom:

2 I will diminish you among the nations.
You will be utterly despised.
3 Your arrogant heart has lead you astray,
you who live in mountain clefts,

---

* Obadaiah means "servant of YHWH." Scholars believe it was written immediately after the destruction of Jerusalem in 586 B.C.E. The Edomites—descendants of Esau, Jacob/Israel's brother—cooperated with Babylon in despoiling Judah during the Babylonian exile and overtook Judean territory. Obadiah refers to the Day of YHWH as the time Edom would be punished, and looks toward a time when the exiles would return and Mount Zion would again be glorious. The first part of Obadiah is a direct parallel with Jeremiah 49:7-22, indicating either that Obadiah borrowed from Jeremiah or that they both draw on the same tradition.

whose home is in the heights,
   you say in your heart,
   "Who is able to bring me down to the ground?"
4 Though you soared like the eagle,
   and built your nest among the stars,
I will still fling you down again—
   it is YHWH who speaks.
5 If thieves came to rob you,
   or intruders came during the night,
   they would steal only as much as they needed!
And if grape gatherers came to your fields,
   they would still leave some gleanings for you—
   that's how completely you'll be destroyed!
6 And how Esau will be plundered,
   their hidden treasures ransacked!
7 All your allies will drive you back,
   to the borders of the land.
Your fine friends will deceive and overpower you;
   those who ate your bread will set traps for you.
They'll say,
   "Where is your wisdom now?"
8 When that day arrives—
   it is YHWH who speaks—
I will remove the sages from Edom,
   and leave no wisdom on Esau's mountain.
9 Your warriors, O Teman, will loose their courage,
   and no one will survive on Esau's mountain.*
10 For the outrage done to Jacob your sibling,
   you will be swallowed up in disgrace
   and you will vanish forever.

11 That day—you stood there aloof
   while strangers carried off Jacob's wealth;
when foreigners passed through the gates
   and cast lots for Jerusalem,
   you behaved like the rest of them.
12 How could you gloat over your sisters and brothers
   on the day of their tribulation?

---

* Teman was a major city in Edom; it was the name of one of Esau's grandchildren. "Esau's mountain"
is Mount Seir, which was actually a mountain range rather than a single mountain.

How could you exult over the children of Judah
    on the day of their devastation?
How could you heckle them so loudly
    on the day of their anguish?
13 How could you march through the gate of my people
    on the day of their destruction,
or join in the gloating
    when disaster overtook them,
or pillage their treasures
    on the day of their heartbreak?
14 How could you stand at the crossroads
    to slay people while they were escaping?
How could you betray the survivors
    on the day of their anguish?
15 As you have done, so will it be done to you!
    Your deeds will recoil on your own head.
The Day of YHWH is near
    for all the nations!
16 You will drink that cup on my holy mountain—
    and all the nations will drink from it in turn!
They will drink and drink until their speech is slurred
    and they will become as though they had never been.

17 But a remnant will survive on Mount Zion,
    and it will be a holy remnant.
The House of Jacob will dispossess
    those who had dispossesed them.
18 The House of Jacob will be a fire,
    the House of Joseph a blaze—
and the House of Esau will be stubble!
    They will set it on fire and burn it down,
and no member of the House of Esau will survive.
    It is YHWH God who speaks.
19 And they will occupy the Negev and the Mount of Esau,
    as well as Shephelah and Philistia.
They will occupy the land of Ephraim and the land of Samaria,
    Benjamin along with Gilead.
20 The exiles from this army,
    the warriors of Israel,
will occupy the land of the Canaanites
    as far as Zarephath;

and the exiles from Jerusalem now in Sepharad*
    will occupy the towns of the Negev.
[21] Victorious, they will climb Mount Zion
    and judge the Mount of Esau.
And the sovereignty will belong
    to YHWH.

---

* That is, Spain. Sephardic Jews have their roots in Spain, Portugal, North Africa, and the Middle East. Most American Jews today are Ashkenazic, descended from Jews who emigrated from France, Germany, and Eastern Europe in the mid- to late-1800s, although most of the early Jewish settlers of this country were Sephardic.

Jonah

***T**he word of yhwh came to Jonah
ben-Amittai*:

² "Get up! Go to the great city of Nineveh right now. Raise a cry against
it! Tell them that I know all about their crimes."

---

* For many years, *Jonah* was thought to have been written in the 8th century B.C.E. by the prophet
mentioned in II Kings 14:25. Most scholars today reject this, and place the date somewhere between
400 and 200 B.C.E. For one thing, the book is not written in an 8th century literary style; for another,
it completely lacks historical detail (the name of the ruler of Nineveh, for instance), suggesting that
the author wasn't writing about contemporary events: one of the features of most prophetic writings
is the awareness of the historical events in which the prophet is living.

Two details of the story should be kept in mind. The first is that Ninevah is a city of non-Jews, yet
they are open to the message of a universal God; the book provides a nice balance for the frequently
nationalistic message of most of the prophets. Most ancient religions were based on "national
gods"; when one nation defeated another, its gods defeated the other nation's gods, and thus the
gods' territory was expanded as well as the nation's. But, as *Jonah* indicates, YHWH is not bound
by national boundaries, and cares for all peoples. Some scholars suggest that this—a moral God
transcending national boundaries—was the breakthrough Jewish contribution to world religion.
The second point is that prophecy is paradoxical. In order for Jonah's prophecy to be fulfilled, the
people of Nineveh would have to ignore him; if they listened and repented, the prophesy would
not be fulfilled. Jonah's anger at Nineveh's repentance (and God's words to him in reply) underscore
two contrasting definitions of prophecy: predicting events versus calling listeners to a change of
heart. Jonah's understanding of prophecy is limited to the former, whereas God's response points
to the true nature of prophecy.

³ But Jonah decided to run away from YHWH, and set out for Tarshish instead. He went down to Joppa and found a ship bound for Tarshish. He paid the fare and boarded the ship bound for Tarshish, in order to get away from YHWH.

⁴ But YHWH unleashed a violent wind on the sea, and the storm was so great that it threatened to break up the ship. ⁵ The frightened sailors, every one of them, appealed to their gods. Then they threw the cargo overboard to lighten the ship. Jonah, however, went below, laid down in the hold, and fell fast asleep. ⁶ The captain found Jonah and said, "How can you sleep at a time like this? Get up! Call on your god! Maybe your god will spare a thought for us, and not leave us to die."

⁷ The crew, meanwhile, said to one another, "Come on, let us cast lots to find out who is responsible for bringing this evil on us."* So they cast lots, and the lot fell to Jonah. ⁸ So they said to him, "You have brought all this misfortune on us—tell us, what is your business? Where do you come from? What is your country? What is your nationality?"

⁹ Jonah said, "I am a Hebrew, and I worship YHWH, the God of heaven, who made the sea and the land."

¹⁰ The sailors were seized with terror at this and said, "What have you done?" They learned that Jonah was trying to escape from YHWH—he told them the whole story.

¹¹ Then they said, "What are we to do with you, to make the sea grow calm for us?" For the sea was growing rougher and rougher.

¹² Jonah replied, "Take me and throw me into the sea, and then it will grow calm for you. I can see that it's my fault this violent storm happened to you."

¹³ The sailors rowed vainly in an effort to reach the shore, but the sea grew still rougher for them. ¹⁴ Then they called on YHWH and said, "Please, O YHWH, don't let us perish for taking this person's life. Don't hold us guilty of innocent blood; for you, O YHWH, acted as you have thought right." ¹⁵ And taking hold of Jonah they threw him into the sea, and the sea grew calm once more. ¹⁶ At this the sailors were seized with dread of YHWH; they offered a sacrifice to YHWH and made their vows.

^{2:1} Then YHWH sent a huge fish to swallow Jonah, and he remained in the fish's belly for three days and three nights. ² From the belly of the fish he prayed to YHWH, his God, and said:

---

* It is likely that they used small colored stones; in the ancient Middle East, casting lots was used as a means of divination to receive guidance from the gods about a particular situation; it was also a popular gambling game. Here it is likely that a number of similarly colored stones were put into a sack with one stone of a different color; everyone would draw one stone, and Jonah happened to draw the distinctive one.

3 "Out of my despair I cried to you
and you answered me.
From the belly of Sheol I cried,
and you heard my voice.
4 You threw me into the Deep,
into the heart of the sea,
and floods overwhelmed me.
All your waves, your torrents,
washed over me.
5 And I said, 'I am banished from your sight!
Will I ever again look upon your holy Temple?'
6 The waters surrounded me right by my throat,
the Deep enclosed me;
seaweed was wrapped around my head.
7 I sank down to the roots of the mountains;
the vaults of the earth closed me in forever.
But you raised my life
back up from the pit, YHWH my God!
8 As my soul was ebbing away,
I remembered YHWH, my God,
and my prayer came before you
in your holy Temple.
9 Those who cling to worthless idols
forsake their own wellbeing.
10 But I will sacrifice to you
with a song of thanksgiving.
I will fulfill the vow I made.
Deliverance comes from YHWH!"

¹¹ Then God spoke to the fish, and the fish vomited Jonah onto the shore.

3:1–4:11

the word of YHWH came a second time to Jonah: ² "Get up! Go to the great city of Nineveh and preach to them as I told you to do."

³ Jonah set out and went to Nineveh in obedience to the word of YHWH. Nineveh was a city large beyond compare:* it took three days to cross it.

---
* Literally, "a city great to God."

⁴ Jonah moved on into the city, making a day's journey. He proclaimed, "Only forty days more, and Nineveh is going to be destroyed!"

⁵ So the people of Nineveh believed God; they proclaimed a fast and dressed in sackcloth, from the greatest to the least. ⁶ When the news reached the ruler of Nineveh, he rose from his judgment seat, took off his royal robes and dressed in sackcloth, and sat down in ashes. ⁷ A decree was then proclaimed throughout Nineveh, by decree of the ruler and the ruler's ministers, as follows: "Citizens and beasts, herds and flocks, are to taste nothing! You must not eat anything, and you must not drink any water. ⁸ You must all dress in sackcloth and call on God with all your might; you must all renounce your sinful ways and the evil things you did. ⁹ Who knows, maybe God will have a change of mind and relent! Perhaps God's burning wrath will be withdrawn so that we don't perish!"

¹⁰ God saw their efforts to renounce their evil behavior. And God relented by not inflicting on them the disaster that threatened them.

4:1 But Jonah grew indignant and fell into a rage. ² He prayed to YHWH and said, "Please, YHWH! Isn't this exactly what I said would happen, when I was still in my own country? That's why I left and fled to Tarshish: I knew that you were a God of tenderness and compassion, slow to anger, rich in kindness, relenting from violence. ³ Now, YHWH, please take my life! I'd rather be dead than keep on living!"

⁴ Then YHWH said, "What gives you the right to be angry?"

⁵ Jonah then left the city and sat down to the east of it. There he made a shelter for himself and sat down under the shade to see what would happen to the city. ⁶ Then YHWH God sent a castor oil plant* to grow up over Jonah to shade his head and soothe his indignation. Jonah was delighted with the castor oil plant. ⁷ But at dawn the next day, God sent a worm to attack the castor oil plant and it withered. ⁸ And after the sun had risen, God sent a scorching east wind. The sun beat down on Jonah's head so that he was overcome and begging for death, and said, "I'd rather be dead than go on living!"

⁹ God said to Jonah, "What gives you the right to be upset about the castor oil plant?"

He replied, "I have every right to be angry, to the point of death!"

¹⁰ YHWH replied, "You feel sorrow because of a castor oil plant that cost

---

* The castor oil plant has been used from ancient times medicinally, usually as a purgative; there is likely a symbolic connection with the great fish that "vomited" Jonah back up on shore. It also grows up to ten feet tall, which would have provided Jonah with some pleasant shade.

you no labor, that you did not make grow, that sprouted in a night, and that perished in a night. [11] Is it not right, then, for me to feel sorrow for the great city of Nineveh, in which there are more than 120,000 people who cannot tell their right hand from their left, to say nothing of all the animals?"

micah

*t*he woRð of *y*hwh that came to micah
of Moresheth* in the time of Jotham, Ahaz, and Hezekiah, rulers of Judah.
His visions concerned Samaria and Jerusalem.

² Listen, people, all of you!
   let the earth and all that is in it pay attention!
   The Sovereign YHWH will give evidence against you—
   the Sovereign One from the holy Temple
³ comes down from the divine realm
   and walks upon the high places of the earth!
⁴ The mountains melt along the way
   and valleys are torn open

---

* The prophet Micah, who prophesied during the time of Isaiah of Jerusalem, was apparently well-respected by the ruler and the nobility, which gave him unusual entrée and allowed him to criticize the economic aristocracy with greater power. During this period, while Assyria was threatening to destroy the northern realm of Israel, Micah was calling for a change of heart for people in the southern realm, lest they suffer a similar fate.

like wax beside a flame,
like torrents eating away a hillside:
⁵ all this for Jacob's rebellion
and Israel's sin.
What is the rebellion of Jacob?
Isn't it Samaria?
And where are Judah's shrines to other gods?
Aren't they what Jerusalem has become?*

⁶ "I intend to make Samaria a ruin in open country,
a place where vines will be planted," says YHWH.
"I will pour its stones into the valley,
and lay bare its foundations."
⁷ All its idols will be shattered,
and the earnings of its temple prostitutes consumed by fire;
its statues will be broken into pieces,
for they were bought with wealth from ritual prostitution,
and will bring them even more money.
⁸ This is why I will mourn and lament,
go barefoot and naked,
howl like a jackal,
and screech like an owl!
⁹ For Samaria's disease† is incurable;
and now the infection has come to Judah.
It knocks at every door of my people,
and reaches even into Jerusalem.
¹⁰ Don't tell Gath about it,
and don't let them see you weep in Acco;
but in Beth-leaphrah
sit down in the dust.‡
¹¹ You who live in Shaphir, "Pleasantness,"
will go into captivity in nakedness and shame.

---

* Micah is saying that Judah is in danger going the way of Samaria, which erected numerous "high places" or hillside shrines to Baal-Hadad, Ashtoreth, and other gods.
† The worship of other gods.
‡ This section, to the end of the chapter, is full of puns, and prophesies the transfer of the western part of Judah to Philistine control by the Assyrians. Gath sounds like the Hebrew word for "tell," while Acco sounds like the word for "weep." Gath was one of five Philistine cities at the Judean border, and Micah doesn't want Philistines rejoicing in Israel's misfortune; Acco was a town in the north mentioned in the book of Judges as one of the places from which the Israelites did not drive out the Canaanite inhabitants, so they would also be happy at Israel's downfall. Beth-leaphrah, "House of Dust," is one of the towns of Judah mentioned by Micah where he is calling for mourning and repentence. In this section of the text, we include an English translation of the town names—in some cases this is the actual meaning of the Hebrew word; in others, a homonym, a pun crafted by Micah.

You who live in Zaanan, "Going Out,"
　　will be unable to go out of your walled city.
You, Beth-ezel, "House of Removal,"
　　will mourn as your supports are removed.
¹² You who live in Maroth, "Bitterness,"
　　will be desperate for something good,
　　for evil will come down from YHWH
　　　　to the very gate of Jerusalem.
¹³ Hitch the chariot to the horses and flee,
　　you people of Lachish,* "Team of Horses"!
You were the ones who led innocent Zion into sin—
　　you are the source of Israel's rebellion!
¹⁴ Therefore you must provide a dowry
　　for Moresheth-Gath, "Gath's Betrothed."†
Beth-Achzib, "Deceptive," will be to Israel's rulers
　　like a stream that disappoints when it's needed most.
¹⁵ Once again a dispossessor will come you,
　　inhabitants of Mareshah, "Possession,"
　　and the "glory of Israel" will flee to Adullam.‡
¹⁶ Cut off your hair in mourning
　　for the children that were your joy.
Shave your heads bald like the vulture,
　　for your children have gone from you into exile.

²:¹ Woe to those who plot trouble,
　　who lie in bed planning evil!
When morning comes they carry it out,
　　because they're the ones in power.
² They see a field and they seize it,
　　a house, and they take it over.
They defraud people of their homes,
　　then extort them of their land as well.
³ "Therefore," says YHWH,
　　"I am planning disaster for this family,
　　a yoke you cannot remove from your necks,

---

* Lachich was a fortified city at the northern border of Judah and the base of Assyrian operations; it would have been among the first cities of Judah to be influenced by Jeroboam's worship of other gods.
† Moresheth, which had at one time been controlled by Gath (hence the name), was Micah's hometown. Here Lachish, the protectorate, will be forced to give Moresheth-Gath away in "marriage" to a foreign power.
‡ Adullam, which means "Justice of the People," was the place where David hid in the caves after fleeing from his enemies. The "glory of Israel" refers to the country's leadership.

a yoke so heavy you will be unable to walk upright—
    it will be an evil time.
⁴ On that day they will taunt and humiliate you,
    and sing a mocking lament* about you:
'We are utterly despoiled,
    for our people's land changes hands.
It is taken from us;
    our fields are parceled out to apostates!' " †
⁵ No one in YHWH's community
    will ever again give them an allotment.‡
⁶ "Stop prophesying," your prophets say.
    "Stop prophesying about these things!
No shame will overtake us!
⁷ Can the House of Jacob be indicted?
    Can YHWH have run out of patience?
Are these God's doings?" they say.

"But aren't my promises intended
    for those who walk on the right road?" asks YHWH.
⁸ "You evildoers have become an enemy to my people,
    stripping the cloaks from travelers who felt safe
    as if they were your spoils after a war,
⁹ driving the women of my people from their pleasant homes,
    and robbing their children of my glory forever, saying,
¹⁰ 'Up! Get out!
This is no resting place for you!'
You defile yourselves
    with the extortionate pledges you exact from them.§
¹¹ If some windbag went about telling lies, saying,
    'I preach in favor of wine and liquor,'
    that would be the prophet for people like you!
¹² But you, House of Jacob, I will gather you together;
    I will gather up the remnant of Israel.
I will guard them like a flock of sheep in their fold,
    like sheep safe in their pasture,
    a noisy multitude.

---

* The Hebrew reads, *"naha, nehi, nihyah,"* or "lament with a lamentation of lamentations"—though since it is called a humiliating taunt, it sounds suspiciously like "nyah, nyah, nyah!"

† This is irony—the speakers are themselves apostates.

‡ When judgment passes and the people are restored, the greedy who disregarded the ancient land allotments will not be allowed to participate in the redistribution of the land.

§ The Law of Moses forbade taking pledges for loans that would be a hardship on the borrower, but loan sharks would routinely take the borrowers' cloaks (v. 8) as collateral, and seize their houses (v. 9) when the loan couldn't be repaid on time.

13 One will make a breach and lead the way;
    the rest will break it open further
    and leave as if through a gate.
    Their ruler will pass before them
    with YHWH at the head."*

Í said, "Now listen, you leaders of the House of Jacob,
    rulers of the House of Israel,
you should know how to judge rightly,
2   yet you still hate good and love evil;
you skin my people,
    stripping them to the bone.
3 You devour the flesh of my people,
    flay their skin and crush their bones,
then chop them up for the kettle,
    more meat for your stewpot.
4 Someday you'll cry out to YHWH,
    but God will not answer you.
God will look the other way
    because of all the crimes you've committed."

5 Thus says YHWH:
"You prophets who lead my people astray,
    who cry 'peace' when they have something to eat,
but declare war against those
    who have nothing to put in their mouths—

---

* Most Middle Eastern sheepfolds were a stone fence. After the sheep were led into the fold for the night, the shepherd would seal the entrance with rocks or debris, often sleeping across the threshold. In the morning, the shepherd went to the fence and shoved the rocks out of the way, making a breach in the wall that the sheep pushed through, widening the opening. Then the shepherd—the breach-maker or "breaker" (Hebrew *poretz*)—would lead the sheep back out into green pasture. Verse 13, ending as it does with a triumphal march led by God, has been viewed by many commentators as a prophecy about the return of the people of Israel from exile; others, including a rabbinic midrash, have seen it as a messianic prophecy, with Elijah as the *poretz*. Yet the "breaking forth" of the sheep was not a singular event, but an everyday occurrence for a flock that, as in verse 12, has already been gathered together into a sheepfold. In light of this, the "triumphal march" becomes Micah's vision of the ideal society: the people, safe and secure from outside threats, are led forth into green pastures each morning by their shepherd, a just and caring ruler, with God—like the Angel of YHWH in the days of old—leading them all.

         micah 3

6   you will have nightmares, not visions;
     you'll have darkness, not prophetic light.
  The sun will set for the prophets;
     your day is no more."
7   Seers and diviners will be humiliated
     and overcome with shame;
  they'll put their hands over their mouths,
     because God no longer speaks through them.
8   But I am full of strength by YHWH's Spirit,
     full of justice and courage,
  to declare the crimes of Jacob and Israel
     to their faces:
9   Listen, you leaders of the House of Jacob,
     rulers of the House of Israel,
  you who loathe justice
     and pervert all that is right,
10   you who build Zion with bloodshed
     and Jerusalem with violent injustice!
11   Her leaders sell their verdicts for bribes,
     her priests accept fees for their rulings,
     her prophets practice divinations for money.
  Yet they rely on God, saying,
     "Isn't YHWH in our midst?
     No disaster will overtake us!"
12   Because of you,
     Zion will become a plowed field,
  Jerusalem a heap of rubble,
     and the Temple mount overgrown with brush.

4:1   But at the end of days, the mountain of YHWH's Temple
     will be established as the most important mountain
  and raised above all other hills—
     all nations will stream toward it.
2   Many people will come and say:
     "Come, let us climb YHWH's mountain
     to the Temple of the God of Jacob,
  that we may be instructed in God's ways
     and walk in God's paths."
  Instruction* will be given from Zion
     and the word of YHWH from Jerusalem.

---

* Literally, *Torah*, the Law or Teaching, the complete revelation of God's mind and heart.

3   YHWH will judge between many peoples
     and arbitrate between mighty and distant nations;
  They will beat their swords into plowshares,
     and their spears into pruning hooks;*
  one nation will not raise the sword against another,
     and never again will they train for war.†

4   People will sit under their own vines and fig trees
     with no one to make them afraid.
  The mouth of YHWH Omnipotent has spoken.

5   Though all the nations walk in the names
     of their own gods,
  we will walk in the Name
     of YHWH our God forever and ever.‡

6   "On that Day," says YHWH,
     "I will gather in the lame of the flock,
  and retrieve the sheep who had strayed§—
     the people whom I afflicted.

7   Out of the lame I will make a remnant,
     and from the outcasts, a mighty nation.
  YHWH will reign over them from Mount Zion
     from now on and forever.

8   And you, watchtower of the flock,
     citadel of the people of Zion,
  your former sovereignty will be restored,
     the dominion of beloved Jerusalem."

9   Why are you now crying out in distress?
     Have you no ruler? No counselor?
  Is that why your pain seizes you
     like a woman in labor?

10   Writhe and cry out, Zion,
     like a woman in labor,
  for now you must leave the city
     and live in open country.

---

* A plowshare is the sharp blade of a plow that cuts the earth and creates a furrow; a pruning hook is a device that looks like a pole with a curved knife on it, used by gardeners to reach and prune the tallest trees and vines.

† Micah 4:1-3 is a nearly verbatim quotation of Isaiah 2:2-4, which suggests perhaps that Micah was a student of Isaiah of Jerusalem.

‡ To "walk in the name of" someone is to accept their authority over one's life.

§ Or possibly, "who had been driven away." God is taking the broken, the outcasts, the dwellers on the fringes of society, and making them into the nucleus of a new people.

You will go to Babylon,
  and there you will be rescued;
there YHWH will ransom you
  out of the power of your enemies.
¹¹ Now many nations
  are mustered against you!
"Let Jerusalem be desecrated!" they say,
  "Let us feast our eyes on the ruins of Zion!"
¹² But they don't know YHWH's thoughts,
  and they fail to understand God's purpose.
For God will gather them together
  like stalks of grain on the threshing floor:
¹³ "Up, Zion my daughter, and thresh them!
  For I will give you horns of iron and hooves of bronze,
  and you will trample many nations!"*
You will dedicate to YHWH
  the plunder you take from them,
and devote their treasures
  to the Sovereign of the whole earth.
¹⁴ But for now, withdraw behind your walls,
  people of the Walled City;
they've laid a siege against us,
  and Israel's ruler is struck on the cheek with a scepter.
5:1 †"As for you, Bethlehem in Ephrathah," says YHWH,
  "small as you are among Judah's clans,
from you will come a ruler for me over Israel,
  one whose goings out‡ are from times long past, from ancient days."

---

* Threshing floors were used to separate grain from its chaff. The cut stalks of grain were spread on the threshing floor, and oxen (to which Jerusalem is being likened here) were used either to trample the stalks, or to pull a threshing sledge, a heavy board with sharp stone or metal runners on the bottom, like a sled, that would break the heads of grain from their stalks. The broken stalks were then tossed in the air with a winnowing fork; the wind would blow the chaff away, and the grain fell into a pile. Most threshing floors were communal, located on hilltops or in open fields, and often used as landmarks or meeting places.

† The Hebrew manuscripts begin chapter 5 here, but in most English translations, it begins with the previous verse, so there is a one-verse discrepancy through the end of the chapter.

‡ "Goings out" could refer to either the origins (perhaps lineage) or the activities (perhaps type of government) of the ruler. When the phrases "from times long past" and "from ancient days" occur elsewhere in the scriptures, they refer sometimes to ancient eras of the world, and sometimes to the formative period in Israel's history; "from ancient days" could also be translated "from eternity." The reference to Bethlehem signifies a ruler of Davidic lineage.

² But God will give them over to their enemies*
until the time when she who is in labor† has given birth;
then the remnant of the ruler's sisters and brothers
will return to the Children of Israel.
³ The ruler will rise up to shepherd them in the strength of YHWH,
by the power of the Name of YHWH, their God.
They will live in security, for now the ruler's greatness
will reach to the ends of the earth.
⁴ They'll say, "This at last is the one
who will be our peace!
When Assyria invades our land
and tramples our fortresses
we will raise up against the invaders
seven—no, eight!—shepherds,
leaders of the people.
⁵ They will shepherd Assyria with the sword,
the land of Nimrod with drawn sword.
Our ruler will deliver us from the Assyrians,
when they invade our land,
and encroach on our frontiers!"
⁶ Then the remnant of Jacob,
surrounded by many peoples,
will be like the dew that YHWH sends,
like showers on the grass that do not depend on human effort
or wait with longing for any mortal to provide for them.‡
⁷ The remnant of Jacob among the nations,
surrounded by many people,
will be like a lion among the animals of the forest,
like a young lion among flocks of sheep,
trampling them and eating ravenously,
with no one daring to rescue the prey.

⁸ "Your hand will prevail over your adversaries,
and all your enemies will be cut down.

---

* Or possibly, "leave them helpless" or "abandon them." This likely refers to the Assyrian invasion that was close at hand.

† Many understand this to be suffering Jerusalem, though knowing the close relationship between Micah and Isaiah of Jerusalem, it could refer to the young woman of Isaiah 6:14 who gives birth to Immanuel ("God Is With Us"). The Children of Israel are the northern tribes, and the "remnant of the ruler's sisters and brothers" are the southern tribes, suggesting a future reunification.

‡ Dew and rain come from God and don't depend on human agency to bring them to earth; by the same token, the remnant will have God's power and won't need to depend on other nations for their help.

⁹ In that day," says YHWH,
     "I will cut off your horses from among you
     and destroy your chariots;
¹⁰ I will destroy the walled cities of your land
     and demolish all your strongholds;*
¹¹ I will cut off magical practices from your hand,
     and you will have no more fortunetellers;
¹² I will destroy your idols
     and remove your sacred pillars from your midst,
  and you will bow down no longer
     to the work of your hands;
¹³ I will uproot your sacred Asherah poles from among you,
     and destroy your towns.
¹⁵ And in anger and wrath I will execute vengeance
     on the nations that do not listen."

6:1–7:20

Ⓗear now what YHWH says:

"Come, plead your case before the mountains,
     and let the hills hear your voice!
² Listen to YHWH's indictment, you mountains
     and you enduring foundations of the earth;
  for YHWH has a dispute with the people,
     and is putting Israel on trial.
³ My people, what have I done to you?
     How have I wearied you?
     Give me an answer!
⁴ For I brought you up from the land of Egypt,
     and redeemed you from the house of slavery;
  and I sent Moses to lead you,
     and Aaron, and Miriam!
⁵ My people, call to mind the plans
     devised by the ruler Balak of Moab,
     and how Balaam ben-Beor answered him!

---

* In other words, war will be nonexistent, so they will need neither horses and chariots for offensive battle, nor walled cities and strongholds for defense.

Remember the journey from Shittim to Gilgal,
and recall how YHWH brought you justice!"

6 "What shall I bring when I come before YHWH,
and bow down before God on high?" you ask.
"Am I to come before God with burnt offerings?
With year-old calves?
7 Will YHWH be placated by thousands of rams
or ten thousand rivers of oil?
Should I offer my firstborn for my wrongdoings—
the fruit of my body for the sin of my soul?"
8 Listen here, mortal:
God has already made abundantly clear
what "good" is, and what YHWH needs from you:
simply do justice,
love kindness,
and humbly walk with YHWH.

9 Your voice, YHWH, cries out to the city—
and it is sound advice to tremble before your Name!
"Hear me, O tribe,
and those assembled in the city!
10 Will I forget the dishonest gain
hoarded away in your dishonest house,
or the accursed short bushel
with which you cheat your neighbor?
11 Can I acquit those with dishonest scales
and bags of fraudulent weights?
12 Your wealthy are full of violence,
your citizens are liars with forked tongues!
13 But now I inflict severe punishment on you,
bringing you ruin for your sins:
14 you will eat, but not be satisfied—
your stomach will always be empty;
you will become pregnant, but not deliver;
and if you bear a child, I will give it to the sword.
15 You will sow, but not reap;
you will press the olives, but not use the oil;
you will tread the grapes, but not drink the wine.

16 You have kept the precepts of Omri
     and all the practices of Ahab;
     you have adopted all their practices.*
     So I will lay you utterly waste;
     your citizens will be objects of derision,
     and other nations will mock you."

7:1 Woe is me!
     I've become a searcher for leftover fruit,
     a gleaner after the grape harvest:
     I find not even a single cluster to eat,
     not even an early fig that I so long for.
2   The faithful have vanished from the land;
     not one honest person is left.
     All who remain lie in wait for blood;
     and they hunt one another with nets.
3   Their hands are skilled in doing evil;
     the official and the judge demand bribes,
     and the powerful dictate whatever they wish—
     and everyone scurries to make it happen.
4   The best of them are like briars,
     the most upright like thorn hedges.
     But their day of reckoning has arrived—
     finally they will be confounded!
5   Don't trust your friends,
     don't rely on your loved ones;
     be careful of what you say
     to the one who lies in your embrace—
6   for son treats father with contempt,
     daughter defies mother,
     daughters-in-law battle mothers-in-law:
     your enemies are your own household.
7   But as for me, I will look to YHWH
     and wait for the God who will save me;
     my God will hear me.
8   Don't gloat over me, my foe:
     though I have fallen, I will rise;
     though I live in darkness,
     YHWH is my light.

---

* Ahab was famous for corruption and oppression.

9 Because I have sinned against YHWH
  I must bear the divine anger,
until God champions my cause
  and rights my wrongs.
Then God will bring me out into the light
  and I will rejoice to see God's justice.
10 When my enemies see this,
  they will be covered with shame;
they will say to me,
  "Where is YHWH, your God?"
I will gloat over them,
  and they will be trampled underfoot
  like mud in the street.
11 "The day is coming for you to rebuild your walls," says YHWH.
  "Your frontiers will be extended that day,
12 a day when your people will return to you
  from Assyria to Egypt, from Egypt to the Euphrates,
  from sea to sea and from mountain to mountain.
13 But the earth will be desolate because of its inhabitants,
  because of what they did."
14 Shepherd your people with your staff, O God,
  the flock that belongs to you!
Now they dwell alone in a forest
  surrounded by meadows;
let them pasture in fertile Bashan and Gilead
  as in the days of old!
15 As in the days when you brought us up from Egypt,
  show us marvelous things!
16 The nations will watch and be ashamed,
  despite all their power!
They will put their hands to their mouths in awe,
  they'll cover their ears and cower!
17 Let them lick the dust like serpents,
  like things that crawl on the ground.
They will come trembling from their strongholds
  to YHWH our God, full of fear and dread.
18 What god can compare to you?
  You take away guilt,
  you forgive the sins of the remnant of your people.
You don't let your anger rage forever,
  for you delight in mercy and steadfast love.

¹⁹ In your love, take us back!
   Conquer our iniquities,
      throw all our sins to the bottom of the sea.
²⁰ Grant Jacob your faithfulness
      and Abraham your mercy,
   as you swore to our ancestors
      in days long ago.

nahum

1:1–3:19

an oracle about nineveh.* the book of
the vision of Nahum and Elkosh.

² YHWH is a jealous and vengeful God!
  YHWH the avenger is full of wrath;
YHWH takes vengeance on foes
  and stores up fury for God's enemies.
³ YHWH is slow to anger—but immense in power!
  Most surely YHWH will not leave the guilty unpunished!
God's way is in whirlwind and storm,
  and the clouds are the dust of God's feet.
⁴ God rebukes the sea and makes it evaporate,
  and dries up all the rivers.

---

* Nineveh was the capital of the tyrannical and oppressive Assyrian empire. This prophecy was given
  sometime between 650 and 612 B.C.E. Assyria became vulnerable after successive attacks, first by by
  the Scythians and then by the Medes; a coalition between them finally succeeded in bringing down
  the empire, and after the flooding Tigris broke down part of Nineveh's wall in 612, the Medes and
  Scythians were able to besiege the capital. Within five years Nineveh was completely destroyed.

Bashan and Carmel wither,
    and the bloom of Lebanon fades.
5 The mountains quake before God,
    and the hills melt;
the earth heaves before God,
    the world, and all who live in it.
6 Who can stand before God's indignation?
    Who can stand the heat of God's anger?
God's wrath is poured out like fire,
    and it breaks the rocks into pieces.
7 YHWH is good,
    a stronghold in a day of troubles,
protecting those who take refuge in God,
8   even in rushing flood.
YHWH will make a full end of all enemies,
    and pursue them into the darkness.
9 Why do you plot against YHWH, Nineveh?
    God will make an end of you—
no enemy rises against God a second time!
10 You are tangled like thorns,
    drunk like drunkards,
    and you will be consumed like dry straw.
11 From you, Nineveh, one has gone out
    who plots evil against YHWH,
    of one mind with Belial.*

12 These are the words of YHWH to Judah:
"Though your enemies were strong and numerous,
    they will be cut down and disappear.
And though I have afflicted you,
    I will afflict you no longer.
13 Now I will break the yoke from your necks
    and snap the ropes that bind you."
14 Nineveh, this is what YHWH has ordained for you:
    children will no longer be born to you!
From the temple of your gods
    I will remove your idols and images.
I will prepare your grave,
    for you are utterly worthless.

---

* Belial became a proper name—an epithet of Satan, or at least a principal demon—rather late; most texts translate the Hebrew *beliyyaal* as "worthlessness," though it may derive from the name of the Babylonian goddess Belili.

2:1 *How welcome upon the mountains
    are the feet of one who brings good news,
    who announces peace!†
Celebrate your pilgrim feasts, Judah,
    and fulfill your vows!
Never again will the evildoers overrun you;
    they will be totally destroyed.
2 The Hammer is coming against you, Nineveh!
Take to the ramparts,
    keep a watch on the road,
brace yourselves,
    summon all your strength!
3 YHWH will restore the pride of Jacob and Israel alike,
    for pillagers despoiled them and ravaged their vines.
4 The shields of their warriors are bright red,
    and all their warriors are dressed in scarlet;
their steel chariots flash as they are thrown into battle,
    and the cavalry chafe for action.
5 The chariots storm through the streets
    and rush to and fro through the city
like torches,
    like the zigzag of lightning.
6 The ruler calls out the officers,
    stumbling to defend their place at the wall,
    setting up their movable shield tower.‡
7 The floodgates of the river are opened,
    the palace is deluged and its foundations melt.
8 Its standing columns collapse and wash away,
    while its attendants moan like doves,
    beating their breasts.
9 Nineveh is like a pool of water ebbing away.
    A cry goes up, "Stop! Stop!"
    but no one turns back.
10 Plunder the silver! Plunder the gold!
    The treasures are endless, valuables by the ton.

---

* This is the last verse of chapter 1 in many versions; we follow the numbering of the Hebrew text, so there is a one-verse discrepancy through the end of chapter 2.
† A direct quotation from Isaiah 52:7. "Second Isaiah," the author of that passage, was a contemporary of Nahum.
‡ This is a wheeled protective shield or mantelet to cover the soldiers from arrows and spears from above, often giving them time to advance their seige on the city by building a rampart or breaking through the city walls. The Neo-Assyrians used two kinds of these shields: small, hut-like shelters that could be carried by a few soldiers, and larger, tower-like structures with wheels.

¹¹ The palace is pillaged and emptied and ruined;
     hearts melt, knees buckle,
   bodies tremble, and every face is pale!
¹² See what has become of that den of lions,
     that cave where the lion cubs lived,
   where lion, lioness, and cubs prowled,
     with no one to frighten them!*
¹³ The lion tore its prey for the cubs,
     and for the lioness it broke its victim's neck;
   it filled it lair with prey,
     its dens with torn flesh.
¹⁴ "But now, as you see, I am against you,"
     says YHWH Omnipotent;
   "I will set fire to your chariots,
     and the sword will devour your young lions.
¹⁵ You will no longer prey upon the land,
     and the voices of your envoys will no longer be heard."

^{3:1} Woe to bloodstained Nineveh,
     steeped in deceit, plunder, and violence!
² Crack of whip, rumble of wheels,
     galloping horses and bounding chariots!
³ Charging cavalry, flashing swords, glittering spears!
     Numberless wounded, piles of corpses, staggering losses—
   they stumble over the dead—
⁴ all because Nineveh sold itself, beautiful and faithless,
     maven of deadly charms,
   enticing the nations with its beauty
     then teaching them all to worship its false gods,
     bewitching people everywhere.
⁵ "No wonder I stand against you,"
     says YHWH Omnipotent.
   "I will tear off your clothing
     and expose your nakedness,
   I will show nations your true nature
     and empires your shame.
⁶ I will pelt you with filth,
     hold you in contempt, and make you a public show.
⁷ All those who see you will recoil and say,
     'Nineveh is a ruin!'

---

* The Assyrians often depicted themselves as lions, particularly in royal inscriptions.

But who will mourn for you?
Where can I find someone to comfort you?"
8 Are you more secure than Thebes,
sitting on the Nile, surrounded by water,
with the river as its rampart,
water as its wall?
9 It counted on Ethiopia and Egypt,
powerful without limits;
Somalia and Libya were its allies.
10 But even Thebes was taken captive and went into exile,
and its infants were dashed to death in the streets;
lots were cast for its nobles
and its leaders were thrown into chains.
11 Now you, Nineveh, will drink the cup of wrath
until you are overcome;
you too will flee for refuge from the enemy.
12 All your fortifications are like the first ripe figs—
shake the tree, and they fall into the mouth of the eater.
13 Your warriors are weaklings,
and there is no one to defend your walls!
The gates of your land stand open to your enemies—
fire has burned down your barred gates!
14 Draw water for the siege
and strengthen your forts—
knead the mortar, trample the clay,
and make mudbricks to rebuild your walls!
15 But even then the fire will consume you,
and the sword will cut you down;
it will devour you like locusts.
Locusts! —You have mutiplied like locusts,
increased your numbers like grasshoppers—
16 you have more merchants than the stars of heaven!
Locusts! —The locust sheds its skin and flies away,
17 and your sentries are just like them—gone!
Your marshals are like locusts
that settle on stone fences on a cold day—
but when the sun rises, they fly away,
and no one knows where they went!
18 Your shepherds are asleep, O ruler of Assyria,
your leaders slumber;
your people are scattered all over the mountains,
with no one to gather them.

¹⁹ Your injury is incurable,
   your wound is fatal.
All who hear the news
   clap their hands in joy.
For who has not felt
   your relentless cruelty?

habakkuk

The oracle that habakkuk* the prophet received in a vision.

2   How long, YHWH, am I to cry for help
      while you do not listen?
    How long will I cry "Oppression!" in your ear
      and you do not save?
3   Why do you make me look upon injustice?
      Why do you countenance tyranny?
    Outrage and violence—this is all I see!
      All is contention, and discord flourishes.
4   The law loses its hold,
      and justice never shows itself.

---

* The prophet Habakkuk was active in Judah during the first part of "the Babylonian crisis," that is, the rise of Chaldea (or neo-Babylonia), shortly before the battle of Carchemish in 605 B.C.E. This first section takes the form of a dialogue between the prophet and God.

The corrupt triumph over those who are righteous,
and justice is perverted once again.

⁵ YHWH says, "Cast your eyes over the nations, take a look,
and be amazed, astonished.
For I am doing something in your days
that you would not believe
even if a messenger came and told you.*
⁶ For now I am stirring up the Chaldeans,
that fierce and fiery people
who march miles across the country
to seize the houses of others—
⁷ a people feared and dreaded:
their 'might makes right'; they make their own rules.
⁸ Their horses are swifter than leopards,
fiercer than wolves in the dark;
their cavalry gallop on,
their cavalry fly from afar,
like eagles swooping down to catch their food.
⁹ All of them come for plunder, all of them,
their faces scorching us like an east wind;
they scoop up prisoners like sand.
¹⁰ They are a people that scoff at rulers
and mock at leaders.
They laugh at fortresses,
and raise siegeworks to capture them.
¹¹ Then the wind changes and they are gone;
they ascribe their strength to their gods.†"

¹² YHWH, you are eternal!
My God, my Holy One, you do not die!‡
YHWH, you appointed them as instruments of justice;
my Rock, you commissioned them to punish us.
¹³ Your eyes are too pure to countenance evil,
you cannot look on at tyranny.
Why then do you look with favor
on the treacherous?*

---

* We would say, "You wouldn't believe it even if you saw it on the news."
† Or possibly, "Their strength is their only god."
‡ The Hebrew says, merely, "No die," so it could also be translated, "We will not die" or "You will not let us die."
§ "The treacherous" refers to the Chaldeans, and specifically to Nebuchadnezar, the greatest and most powerful of all the Babylonian rulers.

Why do you keep silent
while the wicked swallow those who are more righteous?
¹⁴ They treat humankind like fish in the sea,
like creeping things without a ruler over them.
¹⁵ They catch them on their hooks,
gather them in their nets,
or drag them in their trawls—
so they make merry and rejoice,
¹⁶ offering sacrifices to their nets,
and burning offerings to their trawls
for providing them with luxury and lavish food.
¹⁷ Their nets are forever open,
and they will continue to slaughter the nations unceasingly.
²·¹ I will stand on my watchtower,
and take up my post on my battlements,
watching to see what God will say to me,
what answers God will make to my complaints.

² YHWH replied, "Write down this vision,
inscribe it legibly on tablets
so that a herald can easily read it,
³ since this vision will stand as a witness
to the appointed time of judgment;
it gives faithful testimony
about a time that will come.
If it is slow in coming, wait for it—
for come it will, without fail."

⁴ Look—those whose hearts are corrupt
will faint with exhaustion,
while those who steadfastly uphold justice
will live.*

---

* The Hebrew is undeniably murky in this verse, made all the more troublesome because of its fame. St. Paul quoted the second half of this verse several times, and some feel it formed the basis for much of his theology of justification by faith. But much controversy surrounds the Hebrew word that ends the first part of the verse. Many scholars derive it from a root word meaning "to swell," yielding translations like "their soul is puffed up, and not upright within them" or "as for the proud, their spirit is not right within them." However, we feel this is a scribal error, and believe it comes from a word that means "will faint, be exhausted" (or, as the New Jerusalem Bible puts it, "will succumb"). This also restores the parallelism that the second half of the verse demands. In addition, the word usually translated "by faith" ("those who are righteous by faith will live," in many versions) actually means "in faithfulness, steadfastness, or firmness"—not, in this case, belief or trust in God. And "the righteous" are, particularly in the Prophets, those whose lives are directed toward righting wrongs and working against social injustice.

5   Moreover, greed* is treacherous, the arrogant do not endure.
     They open their throats wide as the grave;
     like death, they never have enough.
    They gather all the nations for themselves,
     and collect all peoples as their own.
6   Surely with taunts and insults
     the people will turn on them, and say:

"Woe to you robbers!
   At last justice has caught up with you!
Now you will be justly punished
   for your oppression and extortion.
7   Your creditors will suddenly rise up,
     and the collection agents will hound you!
   Then you will be their plunder,
     like the spoils of war.
8   Since you plundered many nations,
     all that remains of the peoples will plunder you;
   for you shed human blood and ravished the countryside,
     the city and all who dwell in it!

9   "Woe to you who grossly exploits others
     for the sake of your own house,
   building a nest on a height
     to be safe from the onset of disaster!
10   You contrived to bring shame on your house—
     by making an end of many peoples, you made your own end.
11   The stones will cry out from the wall,
     and the rafters will answer them.

12   "Woe to you who build a town on bloodshed,
     and found a city on crime!
13   Isn't it the will of YHWH Omnipotent that the people labor
     only to see their work go up in flames,
    and all the toiling of nations come to nothing?
14   The earth will be as full of the knowledge of YHWH's glory
     as the waters fill the sea!†

---

* Following the Dead Sea Scrolls; the traditional Hebrew text has "wine."
† That is, recognition of God's sovereignty will someday be universal; until then, human labor and accomplishment will all be for nought.

¹⁵ "Woe to you who make your neighbors drink,
   upending your wineskin until all are drunk,
   just so you can see them naked!*
¹⁶ Now you will become drunk—with ignominy, not with glory!
   Your turn to drink and expose yourself!†
The cup of YHWH's right hand will come around to you,
   and your shame will exceed your glory.
¹⁷ You will be overwhelmed by the same violence
   you used when you deforested Lebanon,
terrified by the same ruthlessness
   with which you destroyed the wild animals there,‡
because of the bloodshed and violence you inflicted
   on cities and their inhabitants over the earth.

¹⁸ "What use is a carved idol,
   since it was carved by human hands?
What use is a molten image,
   since it teaches lies?
Why trust in what you have made with your hands,
   an idol that cannot speak?
¹⁹ Woe to you who say to a piece of wood, 'Wake up!'
   or to a dumb stone, 'On your feet!'
Plated it may be with gold or silver,
   but not a breath of life in it.
²⁰ But YHWH is in the Holy Temple:
   let all the earth be silent in God's presence."

---

* The Chaldeans were particularly violent in their attacks on neighboring countries, and the aftermath for those overrun was both disorienting and humiliating; here it is being likened to drunken exploitation and sexual humiliation.

† Literally, "show yourself to be uncircumcised," which has a dual connotation: display to the world that you are not part of God's covenant, and be the object of mockery and derision.

‡ Nebuchadnezzar despoiled the cedar forests to get wood for new building projects, and overhunted the wilderness so excessively that it was tantamount to extermination.

A prayer of Habakkuk the prophet;
a wild musical rant.

2   YHWH, I have heard of your renown;
     your work, YHWH, inspires me with awe.
  Revive it in our time, reveal it in our time;
     in your wrath, remember to be merciful.
3   Eloah* is coming from Teman,
     and the Holy One from Mount Paran.†

The congregation responds freely.‡

  Divine glory covers the sky,
     and God's praise fills the earth—
4   a brilliant light with rays flashing forth,
     concealing the very power of God.
5   Pestilence marches before the Holy One.
     and plague follows behind.
6   When God stands, the earth quakes;
     when God looks down, the nations panic.
  The everlasting mountains crumble
     and the ancient hills collapse
     along God's age-old pathways.
7   The tents of Ethiopia are wrecked,
     the tent curtains of Midian tremble.
8   YHWH, are you angry with the rivers?
     Is your wrath against the floods?
  Did you rage against the sea§
     when you mounted your steeds
     and rode your chariots to victory?

---

* "God" is the usual translation of *'elohim*, which is a plural; *'eloah* is the singular form of the word, and is usually reserved for other nations' gods, or is used in poetry as a deliberate archaism.

† Teman and Paran are locations in the region of Edom, southeast of Israel but north of the Sinai peninsula. Habakkuk is seeing God coming to help Judah from the direction of Mount Sinai, following the path that the Israelites took as they wandered in the wilderness.

‡ This is our rendering of the rather cryptic word *selah*, a word found frequently in the book of *Psalms* that literally means "lift up." Some scholars believe that this "lifting up" indicated a pause in the music, or perhaps a musical interlude when singers were silent; others believe it denoted a crescendo or even a diminuendo. We believe that *selah*, which almost always appears at emotional high points in the psalms, denoted a pause in the singing during which the congregation was invited to freely add their own praises, blessings, or heartfelt interjections, as is done today in the worship services of a number of traditions—hence our rendering of the phrase as a direction to the congregation, to "lift up" their voices in reply to the poet's words.

§ Hebrew *Neharim* and *Yam*, personifications of the watery Deep, were names of ancient sea monsters whom YHWH battled at the beginning of time. Here, however, they stand beside many other features of the land that tremble as God arises to set things right.

⁹ You uncover your bow,
   you ply its string with arrows.

The congregation responds freely.

You split the earth with streams.
¹⁰ The mountains shiver when they see you;
   great floods sweep on their way,
the Deep roars aloud,
   its waves reaching to the sky.
¹¹ Sun and moon stay in their houses,
   avoiding the flash of your arrows,
   the gleam of your glittering spear.*
¹² Raging, you stride the earth;
   in anger you trample the nations.
¹³ You come forth to save your people,
   to deliver your anointed;
you have razed the evildoer's house,
   bared its foundations to the rock.

The congregation responds freely.

¹⁴ With your shafts
   you pierce the heads of their leaders.
But like a whirlwind they try to sweep us away,
   shouting joyfully as if they were devouring the poor in secret.†
¹⁵ So you tread the sea with your horses
   as the mighty waters foam.
¹⁶ I hear that roar, and my body quakes;
   my lips quiver at the sound;
weakness overcomes my limbs,
   and my feet totter in their tracks;
I long for the day of disaster
   to dawn over our attackers.
¹⁷ The fig tree has no buds,
   the vines bear no harvest,
the olive oil fails,
   the fields produce no yield,
the sheep vanish from the fold,
   and there are no cattle in the stalls.
¹⁸ But I will rejoice in YHWH,
   I will exult in God my Savior.

---

* "Glittering spear" and "arrows" are euphemisms for lightning.
† That is, without any opposition.

¹⁹ My sovereign YHWH is my strength!
     God makes my feet as agile as a deer's,
     and teaches me to walk on the heights.*

*This prayer is for the choir leader,
to be accompanied by stringed instruments.*

---

* The word here translated as "heights" is *bamah*, "high places," but it is frequently translated as "shrines." The earliest places of worship were hilltops and mountains; later, artificial mounds or elevated platforms were built, generally under green trees. Later still the platforms were built in cities, and the *bamah* came to indicate the shrines erected upon the platforms, or even portable sanctuaries. Here the construction is interesting: it is a feminine possessive, so it could be rendered "my high places"—perhaps meaning that God teaches us to worship in our inner temple, the soul.

zephaniah

The word of yhwh that was addressed
to Zephaniah ben-Cushi ben-Gedaliah ben-Amariah ben-Hezekiah, during
the reign of Josiah ben-Amon, ruler of Judah:

2   I will sweep away everything
     from the face of the earth,
     says YHWH.
3   I will sweep away humans and animals,
     birds of the air and fish of the sea!
    I will make evildoers stagger,
     and wipe humankind from the face of the earth,
     says YHWH.
4   I will raise my hand against Judah
     and against all those who dwell in Jerusalem;
    I will wipe out every last vestige
     of Baal worship in this place,
    even the names of the idolatrous priests
     who served alongside the priests of YHWH—

⁵ those who worship the host of heaven
    in secret, from their rooftops,
those who worship YHWH
    but swear oaths to Milcom,*
⁶ turn their backs on YHWH,
    neither seeking YHWH nor turning to God.
⁷ Remain silent in the presence of Sovereign YHWH,
    for the Day of YHWH is near.
YHWH has prepared a sacrifice
    and set apart those invited.
⁸ On the day of YHWH's sacrifice,
    I will punish the ministers, the royal officials,
    and assimilationists who dress in foreign attire.
⁹ On that day I will punish those
    who dance on the Temple terrace†
and fill YHWH's house
    with violence and fraud.
¹⁰ On that day, says YHWH, a cry will be heard
    from the Fish Gate,
a scream from the Second Quarter,
    a loud crash from the hills.
¹¹ Those dwelling in the Lower Town will wail,
    for all the merchants are destroyed
    and all weighers of silver are all wiped out.
¹² When that time comes I will search Jerusalem with lamps,
    and punish those who are complacent in their sin,‡
who say in their hearts,
    "YHWH has no power for good or for evil."
¹³ Their wealth will be plundered,
    their households looted.
They will build houses and never live in them,
    plant vineyards but never drink their own wine.

ର ର ର

¹⁴ The great Day of YHWH is near
    and coming fast!

---

* Milcom, also known as Molech, was the god of the Ammonites (present-day Jordan); his religious rites often involved child sacrifice.
† This was a ritual associated with Dagon, a Philistine god.
‡ Literally, "those who let their sediment thicken," like thick sediment that turns wine into syrup.

How bitter the sound of the Day of YHWH,
   the day of the warrior's war cry!
¹⁵ That day will be a day of wrath,
   a day of distress and agony,
a day of ruin and of devastation
   a day of darkness and gloom,
   a day of cloud and fog,
¹⁶ a day of trumpet roar and battle cry
   against fortified towns and high corner towers.
¹⁷ I will bring such distress on the people
   that they will grope like the blind
   because of their sins against YHWH.
Their blood will be poured out like dust
   and their flesh like dung;
¹⁸ neither their gold nor their silver
   will save them.
On the day of YHWH's wrath,
   in the fire of divine jealousy,
   all the earth will be consumed.
For YHWH intends to destroy—
   yes, destroy—
   all who dwell in the land.
^{2:1} Humble yourselves, you shameless nations,
   be humble,
² before you are driven away to disappear like fodder,
   before the burning anger of YHWH comes upon you,
   before the day of YHWH's anger comes upon you.
³ Seek YHWH,
   all you living humbly on the land,
   you who obey God's laws!
Seek integrity, seek humility,
   that perhaps you may find security
   on the day of the anger of YHWH.

2:4-15

⁴ _G_aza will be deserted, Ashkelon a waste;
   the citizens of Ashdod will be evicted before noon,
   and Ekron will be uprooted.

⁵ Woe to you who live on the coast,
  you people of Crete!
The word of YHWH is against you,
  Canaan, land of the Philistines,
and I will destroy you completely,
  and leave you without inhabitants!
⁶ The seacoast will become pastures
  a home for shepherds and folds for sheep,
⁷ and the coast will belong
  to the remnant of Judah.
They will pasture their flocks by the sea
  and lie down in the evening in the houses of Ashkelon,
for YHWH their God will turn to them,
  and restore their fortunes.

⁸ I heard Moab's insults, the taunts of the Ammonites,
  how they slandered my people and usurped their territory.
⁹ For this, as I live—
  it is YHWH Omnipotent who speaks, the God of Israel—
Moab will become like Sodom
and the children of Ammon like Gomorrah:
a land of nettles, a heap of salt, eternal desolation.
  What is left of my people will plunder them,
    the remnant of my nation will dispossess them.

¹⁰ This will be the retribution for their pride, for they insulted the people of YHWH Omnipotent and invaded their land. ¹¹ YHWH will bring terror on them and starve all the gods of the earth. Then the nations in all the coasts and islands will worship God, each in their own land.

¹² You Cushites also will be slain
  by the sword of YHWH.

¹³ YHWH will point to the north and destroy Assyria,
  making Nineveh a waste, arid as a desert.
¹⁴ Flocks will gather there
  along with every kind of wild animal.
The horned owl and the vultures will roost there;
  the owl will hoot at the windows,
the raven croaks on the threshold;
  and its cedar work will rot.
¹⁵ This is the city that took pride in its security, and said,
  "I and I alone am supreme"!

And what is it now but a waste, a refuge for wild animals,
at which every passer-by jeers and mocks.

3:1-20

TROUBLE is coming to the rebellious, the defiled,
the tyrannical city!*
2   They heeded no warning voice,
took no rebuke to heart;
they did not put their trust in YHWH,
nor did they draw near to their God.
3   The leaders among them were roaring lions,
their rulers wolves of the plains
that left nothing over till morning.
4   Their prophets are braggarts and imposters;
their priests profane the holy sanctuary
and do violence to the Law.
5   But YHWH in their midst is just and honorable,
and never does wrong;
morning after morning God makes the law known,
each dawn unfailingly;
yet these wrongdoers
know no shame!

6   I have cut off the nations,
their battlements are in ruins;
I laid their streets waste,
so that no one could use them;
their cities have been made desolate,
without people, without inhabitants.
7   I said, "But surely Jerusalem will fear me,
they will accept corrections;
surely the punishment I brought upon the nations
won't be lost on them."
But they were all the more eager to make
all their deeds corrupt.

---

* The city in question is Jerusalem.

⁸ Therefore wait for me, says YHWH,
   wait for the day I stand up to accuse you;
I have decided to assemble nations
   and gather governments together
in order to pour my wrath on them,
   all my burning anger;
the whole world will be consumed
   by the fire of my jealousy.
⁹ Then I will restore pure lips to all peoples,
   that they may invoke YHWH by name
   and serve God with one accord.
¹⁰ My worshipers, dispersed beyond the river Cush,
   will bring offerings to me.
¹¹ When that day comes,
   your rebellious deeds will no longer earn you shame,
for I will remove your proud boasters from your midst,
   and you will cease to strut on my holy mountain.
¹² In your midst I will leave a humble and lowly people,
   and they will find refuge in the name of YHWH.
¹³ Those left in Israel will do no wrong and tell no lies;
   no words of deceit will pass their lips;
they will graze and lie down to rest
   with no one to terrify them.

ରଃ   ରଃ   ରଃ

¹⁴ Shout for joy, fair Zion;
   shout, Israel, be glad!
   Rejoice with all your heart, fair Jerusalem!
¹⁵ YHWH has averted your punishment
   and swept away your foes.
Israel, YHWH is among you as ruler;
   never again need you fear disaster.
¹⁶ On that day this must be the message to Jerusalem:
   Fear not, Zion, let not your hands hang limp in despair,
¹⁷ for YHWH your God is in your midst,
   a warrior to keep you safe;
who will rejoice over you and be glad of it;
   who will show you love once more,
and exult with songs of joy
¹⁸   and soothe those who are grieving.

At the appointed time I will take away your cries of woe
and you will no longer endure reproach.
19 When that time comes,
I will deal with all who oppress you;
I will rescue the lost and gather the dispersed.
I will win for my people praise and renown
throughout the whole world.
20 When that time comes,
I will gather you and bring you home.
I will win for you renown and praise
among all the peoples of the earth,
when I restore your fortunes before your eyes.
It is YHWH God who speaks.

haggai

In the second year of Darius the ruler, on the first day of the sixth month,* the word of YHWH came through the prophet Haggai to Zerubbabel ben-Shealtiel, the high commissioner of Judah, and to Yehoshua ben-Yehozadak, the high priest.

² "YHWH Omnipotent declares: These people say that the time has not yet come to rebuild the Temple of YHWH.† ³ But YHWH, through the prophet

---

* The prophecy is given during a New Moon festival near the firstfruits harvest, when the size of the grain harvest to take place in November will be fairly evident.

† In 539 B.C.E., Cyrus, the first ruler of the Persian empire, allowed the Jews of the Diaspora to return to Judea, and provided financial support for them, encouraging them to rebuild the Temple in Jerusalem. But the work of rebuilding their lives after exile was difficult, and work on the Temple, though begun shortly after 538, soon ground to a halt. In 520, during the reign of Darius, the third ruler of Persia, the prophet Haggai gave five addresses urging the Jewish leaders to assume responsibility for the project and finish it. While the people were busy reestablishing their own standard of living, they put off rebuilding the Temple, and Haggai demanded that they reverse their priorities. In large measure because of Haggai's urging, the Temple (called the Second Temple to distinguish it from the Temple of Solomon) was completed in 515.

Haggai, asks, ⁴ Is this a time for you to live in your paneled houses, when this House lies in ruins?

⁵ "Now, YHWH Omnipotent says, reflect carefully how things have gone for you. ⁶ You have sown much and harvested little; you eat but never have enough, drink but never have your fill, put on clothes but do not feel warm. You earn wages only to put them in a purse riddled with holes. ⁷ That is why YHWH Omnipotent says to reflect carefully how things have gone for you!

⁸ "So go to the hill country, cut timber, and rebuild the Temple. Then I will take pleasure in it, and be glorified there, says YHWH. ⁹ You've been expecting much, but getting little. When you brought in the harvest, I would destroy it with a breath. And why? asks YHWH Omnipotent. —Because while my House lies in ruins, you are busy with your own houses, each one of you! ¹⁰ That is why the sky withheld the rain and the earth its yield. ¹¹ I called down a drought on land and hills, on wheat, on new wine, on oil and on all the produce of the ground, on people and cattle and all the labor of your hands!"

¹² Now Zerubbabel ben-Shealtiel, and Joshua ben-Jehozadak, the high priest, and all the remnant of the people paid attention to the voice of YHWH their God and to the words of the prophet Haggai, because YHWH had sent him to them. And the people were filled with awe before YHWH.

¹³ Haggai, the messenger of YHWH, gave YHWH's message to the people: "I am with you—it is YHWH who speaks."

¹⁴ And YHWH roused the spirit of Joshua ben-Jehozadak, the high priest, and the spirit of all the remnant of the people; and they came and set to work on the Temple of YHWH Omnipotent, their God. ¹⁵ This was on the twenty-fourth day of the sixth month.

ↄ҃ ҃ↄ ↄ҃

²·¹ In the second year of Darius the ruler, ² on the twenty-first day of the seventh month,* the word of YHWH came through the prophet Haggai and told him, ² "Speak to Zerubbabel ben-Shealtiel, the high commissioner of Judah, and to Joshua ben-Jehozadak, the high priest, and to all the remnant of the people. Ask them, ³ 'Who is there left among you who saw this Temple in its former glory? And how does it look to you now? Doesn't it seem like nothing in comparison? ⁴ But take courage now, Zerubbabel!—it is YHWH who speaks. Courage, High Priest Joshua ben-Jehozadak! Courage, all you

---

* The people started working on the Temple twenty-four days after Haggai began prophesying (1:15), having waited until the firstfruits harvest was completed. As this chapter opens, nearly a month more has passed; this prophecy takes place on the last and greatest day of the Feast of Tabernacles, when all the people of Israel are commanded to come to Jerusalem and worship.

people of the country!—it is YHWH who speaks. To work! I am with you—it is YHWH Omnipotent who speaks—[5] as I promised I would be when you came out of Egypt, and my Spirit remains among you. Don't be afraid! [6] For YHWH Omnipotent says this: A little while now, and I am going to shake the heavens and the earth, and the sea and the dry land. [7] I will shake all nations, and the treasures of all the nations will flow in,* and I will fill this Temple with glory, says YHWH Omnipotent. [8] Mine is the silver, mine the gold! says YHWH Omnipotent. [9] The new glory of this Temple is going to surpass the old, says YHWH Omnipotent, and in this place I will give peace,† says YHWH Omnipotent.' "

ରଃ   ରଃ   ରଃ

[10] On the twenty-fourth day of the ninth month,‡ in the second year of Darius, the word of YHWH came through Haggai the prophet. [11] YHWH Omnipotent told him to ask the priests for a ruling on the law:

[12] "If someone carries consecrated meat in a pocket of a garment, and the garment touches bread, stew, wine, oil, or food of any kind, does such food become holy?"

The priests answered, "No, it does not."

[13] Haggai continued, "But what of a person who is ritually unclean after having contact with a corpse—if that person touches any of these things, does such food become unclean?"

The priests answered, "Yes, it does."

[14] Haggai then said, "It is the same with this people, the same with this nation as I see it—it is YHWH who speaks—the same with everything they turn their hands to: everything they offer here is unclean.§

[15] "Think back. Before one stone was laid on another in the Temple of YHWH, [16] what state were you in? You would come to a twenty-measure heap and find only ten; you would come to a fifty-measure wine vat to draw off fifty measures and find only twenty. [17] It's because with blight and mildew and hail I struck you and everything you turned your hands to—but still

---

The King James version translates this phrase, "and the desire of all nations shall come," which many commentators have seen as a messianic prophecy.

"Give peace" could be translated "grant prosperity."

Three months have now passed since the people began rebuilding the Temple. Meanwhile, the grain harvest has taken place, and the fields have been plowed though not yet replanted for the following year. Haggai uses the occasion to announce that God will turn the curse into a blessing and that, from this time forward, the ground will yield a harvest sufficient for all the people's needs.

Haggai reminds the people that once again living in their land and offering sacrifices will not make their offerings acceptable so long as they themselves are unclean through neglect of the Temple. As commentator Joyce G. Baldwin puts it, "The ruined skeleton of the Temple was like a dead body decaying in Jerusalem and making everything contaminated."

you would not return to me! says YHWH. ¹⁸ Think back to how things were on the twenty-fourth day of the sixth month,* when you began restoration of the Temple of YHWH.

¹⁹ "The seed for next year is still in the barn, isn't it? And the vine and the fig tree, the pomegranate and the olive, as of now they bear no fruit. But from today onward, I will bless you."

C℞   C℞   C℞

²⁰ On the twenty-fourth day of the month the word of YHWH came a second time to Haggai: ²¹ "Speak to Zerubbabel, the high commissioner of Judah. Say this: 'I am going to shake the heavens and the earth. ²² I will overturn the judgment seats of entire countries and destroy the power of the rulers of the nations. I will overthrow their chariots and charioteers, and bring down their horses and riders; they will fall to the sword of their own comrades.

²³ " 'When the day comes,' says Yhwh Omnipotent, 'I will take you, Zerubbabel ben-Shealtiel, my servant—it is Yhwh God who speaks—and make you my signet ring.† For I have chosen you,' says Yhwh Omnipotent."

---

* The Hebrew says "ninth month," but this is a scribal error; Haggai is clearly referring to the sixth month, three months earlier, when the work of restoration began.

† The signet ring was a symbol of royal authority. It was used by a ruler or the ruler's representative to seal important documents, proof that the decree had come from the ruler and no one else.

zechariah

In the second year of darius, in the eighth month, this message from YHWH came to the prophet Zechariah ben-Berechiah ben-Iddo:*

² Tell the people, "YHWH was exceedingly angry with your ancestors." ³ Tell them, "These are the words of YHWH Omnipotent: If you return to me, I will return to you, says YHWH Omnipotent. ⁴ Don't be like your ancestors! When the prophets of old said, 'These are the words of YHWH Omnipotent: Turn back from your evil behavior and your evil actions,' they refused to listen or pay attention to me, says YHWH. ⁵ Where are your ancestors now? And the prophets, do they live forever? ⁶ Did not my words and my orders, with which I charged my servants the prophets, overtake your ancestors?

---

* Zechariah prophesied in Jerusalem around 520 B.C.E., a contemporary of Haggai, during the Babylonian captivity; the first part of the book (ch. 1-8) was almost certainly written by Zechariah, and is full of apocalyptic imagery strongly reminiscent of the visions of Daniel and Ezekiel. However, the second part (ch. 9-14), known as Second Zechariah, was written by an unnamed prophet in the late fourth and early 3rd centuries B.C.E. and contains two oracles about the restoration of Israel.

YHWH was stirred to anger against your ancestors. So they repented, and said, 'YHWH Omnipotent dealt with us as our behavior and our actions deserved.' "

ભ ભ ભ

⁷ On the twenty fourth day of the eleventh month, the month of Shebat, in the second year of Darius, this message from YHWH came to the prophet Zechariah ben-Berechiah ben-Iddo:

⁸ I saw a vision during the night: I saw a rider on a bay horse that stood among the myrtle trees in the ravine; nearby were three other horses, bay, sorrel,* and white. ⁹ I asked the angel who had brought me the vision,† "Please, what do these represent?"

The angel replied, "I will show you what they are."

¹⁰ Then the rider standing among the myrtles said, "They are those whom YHWH sent to patrol the earth."

¹¹ They then gave their report to the Angel of YHWH‡ standing among the myrtles: "We have been patrolling the earth, and the whole world is at peace."

¹² Then the Angel of YHWH said, "Sovereign YHWH, how long will you withhold your compassion from Jerusalem and the towns of Judah, on which you have vented your wrath these seventy years?"

¹³ In reply, YHWH spoke kind and comforting words to the angel who had brought me the vision.

¹⁴ The angel who had brought me the vision said, "Proclaim this: 'I am very jealous for Jerusalem and Zion, says YHWH Omnipotent, ¹⁵ but I am deeply angry with the nations that are enjoying their ease, because although I was angry only slightly, they overdid the punishment.§

¹⁶ " 'Therefore these are the words of YHWH: I will return to Jerusalem with compassion; my Temple will be rebuilt there, says YHWH God Omnipotent, and the measuring line will be stretched over Jerusalem.' ¹⁷ Proclaim further: 'These are the words of YHWH Omnipotent: My cities will again brim with prosperity. Once again YHWH will comfort Zion; once again God will choose Jerusalem.' "

---

* A bay horse is reddish brown, usually with a black mane and tail; sorrel is a lighter brown with more orange or yellow in the color.

† Literally, "the messenger (i.e., angel) who was talking with me."

‡ It is unclear whether we are to infer that the rider is now revealed to be the Angel of YHWH, or if the Angel is a separate individual. The Angel of YHWH, as opposed to other angelic messengers, is generally addressed and referred to as if it were the visible manifestation of God (but see verses 12 and 13, where YHWH and the Angel are clearly distinguished from one another).

§ In other words, the other nations were instruments of God in punishing Judah, but their actions were not commensurate with the level of God's anger.

2:1 * I looked up and saw four iron horns.† 2 I asked the angel who brought me the vision what they were, and the angel replied, "These are the horns that scattered Judah, Israel and Jerusalem." 3 YHWH then showed me four blacksmiths. 4 I asked what they were coming to do, and the angel said, "Those horns scattered Judah so completely that no one could hold up their head; but these blacksmiths came to rout them, overthrowing the horns that the nations raised against the land of Judah to scatter its people."

5 I looked up and saw someone carrying a measuring line. 6 I asked where was the person was going, and the angel replied, "To measure Jerusalem and discover its breadth and length." 7 Then, as the angel who brought me the vision was going away, another angel approached the first angel and said, 8 "Run to that youngster‡ and say, 'Jerusalem has so many people and so much livestock in it that its walls will not be able to contain them. 9 I myself will be a wall of fire all around it,' says YHWH, 'and a glorious presence within it.

10 " 'Away, away! Flee from the land of the north,' says YHWH, 'for I dispersed you to the four winds of heaven,' says YHWH God. 11 'Away! Escape, you people of Zion who live among the Babylonians.' "

12 These are the words of Sovereign YHWH, who sent me on a glorious mission to the nations who plundered you: "Whoever touches you touches the apple of my eye!§ 13 I will wave my hand over them, and they will become plunder for those they enslaved." You will then know that YHWH Omnipotent has sent me!

14 "Shout aloud and rejoice, people of Zion! I am coming, I will make my dwelling among you," says YHWH God. 15 Many nations will give their allegiance to YHWH on that day and become God's people, and God will dwell in your midst. Then you will know that YHWH Omnipotent sent me to you. 16 YHWH will claim Judah as God's own portion in the holy land, and will once again choose Jerusalem. 17 Silence, all mortal flesh! Be silent in the presence of YHWH, who has been bestirred once again and come forth from the holy dwelling place!

---

* The Hebrew text starts chapter 2 here, whereas many English translations begin chapter 2 with our verse 5.
† Horns are a symbol of strength; here they represent military powers. The four horns, like the four blacksmiths, represent other nations. The number four symbolizes the world; Judah's enemies, like the blacksmiths who rescue it (e.g., Cyrus of Persia), come "from the four directions," as it were.
‡ Zechariah, not the person measuring the city.
§ The English idiom, "the apple of my eye," has been used since the ninth century to mean someone who is most precious to us, though few people realize that "apple" actually referred to the pupil because both are small spheres and because in that era, apples were a precious commodity. The Hebrew text actually reads "gate of the eye," but in Hebrew, "gate" also denoted the pupil, which was considered one of the most treasured—and most vulnerable—parts of the body. So the English colloquialism expresses the Hebrew idiom remarkably well.

³·¹ Then God showed me Yehoshua the high priest* standing before the Angel of YHWH, with the satan† standing at the Angel's right hand, harassing Yehoshua about various things. ² And the Angel of YHWH said to the satan, "May YHWH silence you, Satan! May YHWH, who chose Jerusalem, silence you. Isn't Yehoshua a stick snatched from the fire?"

³ Standing before the Angel, Yehoshua's clothes were covered in excrement. ⁴ The Angel said to the attendants, "Help him take off those filthy clothes!"

Addressing Yehoshua, the Angel said, "I have taken away your guilt, and I will clothe you in splendid priestly robes!" ⁵ Then, to the attendants, "—and put a clean turban on his head!" They dressed Yehoshua as instructed them, as the Angel of YHWH stood nearby.‡

⁶ The Angel of YHWH gave Yehoshua this solemn charge: ⁷ "These are the words of the YHWH Omnipotent: If you walk in my ways and keep my ordinances, you will govern my Temple and watch over my courts, and I will give you free access among those who are in attendance here.§ ⁸ Listen, High Priest Yehoshua—you and your colleagues seated here before you are a sign that I am going to bring my servant, the Branch.

⁹ "Here is the stone which I set before Yehoshua, a cornerstone on which are seven eyes. Look, I will engrave an inscription on it, says YHWH Omnipotent, and in a single day I will wipe away the guilt of this land. ¹⁰ On that day, says YHWH God Omnipotent, you will invite each other to come and sit under your own vines and fig trees. "

⁴·⁴ Then I asked the angel of YHWH who talked with me, "What are these things?"**

⁵ The angel replied, "Don't you know what they are?"

"No," I replied.

---

* This is Yehoshua ben-Jehozadak, mentioned in Haggai 1:1. Yehoshua (usually translated Joshua) means "Yhwh is Deliverance" or "Savior"; in later Hebrew and Aramaic, Yehoshua was generally shortened to Yeshua, the Greek form of which is Jesus.

† "Satan" means "adversary" or "accuser," and was depicted throughout the Hebrew scriptures not as the progenitor of evil but as the prosecuting attorney in the heavenly courts. It was not so much an individual personage ("Satan") as a role or job ("the satan"), with the word usually taking the definite article.

‡ Yehoshua's disgusting clothing, the satan's harrassment of him, and the image of him as a "stick snatched from the fire" before it is completely burned all testify to his unfitness to be high priest—and, symbolically, of Judah's sad state during the Babylonian captivity: sent into exile because of apostasy, yet snatched from the fire in the nick of time. His purification is emblematic of the purification of the land and the restoration of its people.

§ This prophecy indicates the elevated role the high priest would play after the people returned from exile, especially since the monarchy would never be reinstated.

** Verses 1-3 of chapter 4 became displaced at some point over the centuries. They properly belong after verse 10, so we have placed them there.

⁶ The angel said, "This is the word of YHWH concerning Zerubbabel:* Neither by force nor by strength, but by my Spirit! says YHWH God Omnipotent. ⁷ How does a mountain, the greatest mountain, compare with Zerubbabel? It is no higher than a plain. Zerubbabel will pull out the keystone to shouts of: 'All blessings be upon it!' "

⁸ This word came to me from YHWH: ⁹ "Zerubbabel with his own hands laid the foundation of this Temple; with his own hands he will finish it. Then you will know that YHWH Omnipotent sent me to you. ¹⁰ No one should despise a day of small beginnings! These seven eyes will rejoice when they see Zerubbabel writing the inscription on the cornerstone—they are the eyes of YHWH, and they range over the whole earth."

⁴·¹ The angel who talked with me returned and roused me as someone is roused from sleep, ² then said, "What are you seeing?"

I answered, "I see a menorah made entirely of gold with the bowl for its oil sitting on top. It holds seven lamps, and there are seven pipes for the lamp on top of it. ³ There are also two olive trees standing by it, one on the right and one on the left."

¹¹ Then I asked the angel, "What are these two olive trees on the right and on the left of the lampstand?" ¹² I asked further, "And what are the two sprays of olive beside the golden pipes which discharge the golden oil?"

¹³ The angel said, "Do you know what they mean?"

"No, your excellency," I answered.

¹⁴ "These are the two dignitaries consecrated with oil† who attend the Sovereign of all the earth."

⁵·¹ Again I raised my eyes, and this is what I saw: a flying scroll. ² The angel who was talking to me said, "What can you see?"

I replied, "I can see a flying scroll; it is thirty feet long and fifteen feet wide."

³ The angel told me, "This is the 'Curse' which goes out over the whole land; for according to the writing on one side, every thief will be swept away, and according to the writing on the other side, every perjurer will be swept away. ⁴ I have sent it out, says YHWH God Omnipotent, and it will enter the house of the thief and the house of the one who swears false oaths by my Name; it will stay inside the house and demolish it, both timber and stone."

---

* Zerubbabel was the governor of Judaea under whom the rebuilding of the Temple at Jerusalem took place.
† Literally, "sons of fresh oil," in keeping with the olive tree imagery. The two are Yehoshua the high priest and Zerubbabel the governor; traditionally, only the high priest and the ruler were anointed for service.

⁵ The angel who talked with me came out and said, "Look at this thing that is approaching."

⁶ I asked what it was, and the angel said, "The thing that is approaching is a large bushel basket."* The angel added, "It is a symbol of the people's guilt throughout the land."

⁷ Then its cover, which was made of lead, was lifted, and sitting inside the bushel was a woman. ⁸ The angel said, "This is Wickedness," and thrust the woman down into the bushel and pressed the leaden weight down onto the opening.

⁹ I looked again and saw two women coming forth with the wind in their wings—for they had wings like those of a stork—and they lifted up the bushel between earth and sky. ¹⁰ I asked the angel who talked with me where they were taking the bushel, ¹¹ and it answered, "To build a temple for 'Wickedness' in the land of Shinar; once the temple is ready, the bushel will be set on its rightful pedestal there."

6:1 I looked again and saw four chariots coming out between two mountains, which were mountains of copper. ² The first chariot had bay horses, the second black, ³ the third white, and the fourth piebald—all strong and vigorous.

⁴ I asked the angel who talked with me, "What are these?"

⁵ It answered, "These are the four winds of heaven. After attending the Sovereign of the whole earth, they are now going forth. ⁶ The chariot with the black horses is going to the land of the north, the white horses are going west, the piebald ones are going to the south lands. . . ."† ⁷ They came forth with strength, eager to set off and range over the whole earth. "Go," the angel said, "range over the whole earth," and they did so.

⁸ Then the angel called me to look, and said, "Those going to the land of the north given rest to my spirit there."

⁹ The word of YHWH came to me: ¹⁰ "Receive the gifts from the exiles Heldai, Tobiah, and Jedaiah who have returned from Babylon, and go that same

---

* Noted Hebrew scholar Thomas McDaniel believes, with excellent lexical support, that this phrase should be translated, "This thing is a mobile shrine," and that the phrase "a woman" in verse 7 should be translated "the first lady," that is, a manifestation of the Goddess. He sees this shrine as the Babylonian counterpart to the Ark of the Covenant, or to the sacred palanquins used to transport a deity in Shinto festivals. This shrine is being carried to Shinar, or Babylon, where a temple would be built for it—suggestive of the shrines located on top of Babylonian ziggurats. McDaniel also notes that the Hebrew word for "Wickedness," with a different vowel pointing, becomes "Their Help"—so the female figure hidden in the shrine had her rightful place of worship in Shinar, though not in Judah. For her legitimate devotees, she was "Their (Shinar's) Help," but when the shrine became a cult center in Judah, it was "a symbol of the people's guilt."
† Some text seems to be missing here, presumably that the bay horse went east.

day to the house of Josiah ben-Zephaniah. ¹¹ Take the silver and the gold and make a crown; place it on the high priest, Yehoshua ben-Jehozadak, ¹² and say, "These are the words of YHWH Omnipotent: Here is a person whose name is The Branch; he will branch out from where he is, and will rebuild the Temple of YHWH. ¹³ It is this person who will rebuild the Temple, and when finished will wear royal insignia, sit on the judgment seat, and rule. A priest will also sit on the judgment seat and there will be harmony between them.* ¹⁴ The crown will serve as a memorial for Heldai, Tobiah, Jedaiah, and Josiah ben-Zephaniah in the Temple of YHWH.

¹⁵ "Workers will come from far away and work on the rebuilding of the Temple of YHWH; so you will know that YHWH Omnipotent sent me to you. This will come about if you listen with diligence to YHWH your God!"

⁷·¹ In the fourth year of the reign of the ruler Darius, the word of YHWH was addressed to Zechariah. On the fourth day of the ninth month, the month of Chislev, ² the town of Bethel sent Sharezer and Regem-Melech and their attendants to entreat the favor of YHWH. ³ They were to say to the priests of the Temple of YHWH Omnipotent and the prophets, "Am I to continue to lament and fast in the fifth month as I have these many years?"†

⁴ Then this word of YHWH Omnipotent came to me and said, ⁵ "Say to the people of the land and the priests: When you fasted and lamented in the fifth and seventh months these past seventy years, was it for my sake that you fasted so faithfully? ⁶ And when you ate and drank, was it not to please yourselves? ⁷ Didn't YHWH proclaim the following message through the prophets of old, while Jerusalem was still populous and peaceful, as were the towns around it, and there were people settled in the Negev and the Lowlands?" ⁸ The word of YHWH to Zechariah continued, ⁹ "Didn't I tell them, 'Thus says YHWH Omnipotent: Administer true justice; show kindness and mercy to one another; ¹⁰ do not oppress the widowed or the orphaned, the resident alien or the poor, and do not plot evil against one other'? ¹¹ But they refused to listen; they turned a stubborn shoulder and

---

* This passage as provoked much debate. Many scholars feel that there is text missing, as the person being crowned should be Zerubbabel; we have already seen Zerubbabel and Yehoshua depicted as the two olive trees, both anointed for service, and Zerubbabel was identified in 3:8 as being the one to build the Temple. Other scholars view Yehoshua as a "priest-king"—one individual serving in two capacities—with the "harmony" being between the two offices; they see Yehoshua serving as the archetype of a future messiah.

† This fast was undertaken on the anniversary of the destruction of Solomon's Temple seventy years earlier. The seventh month mentioned in verse 5 refers to the assassination of Gedaliah, governor of Judah, soon after the Temple was destroyed. The people of Bethel—which means "House of God," and which was the first home of the Ark of the Covenant before moving to the Temple in Jerusalem—want to know if they need to continue the ritual remembrance of the first Temple now that Zerubbabel is rebuilding it.

stopped their ears in order not to hear. [12] They were adamant in their refusal to accept the Law and its teachings which YHWH Omnipotent sent by the spirit through the prophets of old. [13] Since they did not listen when I called, I would not listen when they called. [14] I scattered them out among all the nations unknown to them, leaving their land deserted behind them, so that no one came and went. So their pleasant land turned into a desert."

[8:1] The word of YHWH Omnipotent was addressed to me as follows:

[2] YHWH Omnipotent says this:
I burn with jealousy for Zion,
    I am fiercely jealous for it.
[3] YHWH says this:
I am returning to Zion
    and I will dwell in the midst of Jerusalem,
which will be called the faithful city,
    and the mountain of YHWH Omnipotent, the Holy Mountain.
[4] YHWH Omnipotent says this:
Old women and old men will again
    sit in the squares of Jerusalem
each leaning on holding staffs
    because of their advanced years.
[5] And the squares will be filled
    with girls and boys playing happily.
[6] YHWH Omnipotent says this:
If this resembles a miracle to the remnant of this people,
    will it also seem a miracle to me? says YHWH.
[7] YHWH Omnipotent says this:
Now I will save my people from the east countries
    and the west countries.
[8] And I will return them
    to live in Jerusalem.
They will be my people and I will be their God
    in faithfulness and integrity.

[9] YHWH Omnipotent says this: May your hands be strong, you who today hear these words spoken by the prophets, who were present when the foundations for the house of YHWH Omnipotent were laid, so that the Temple can be rebuilt. [10] Before that time there was no hiring of people or animals; because of enemies, no one could go about their business safely. I had set every person against everyone else. [11] But now, with the remnant of this people, I am not as I was in the past. It is YHWH Omnipotent who speaks. [12] For I mean to spread peace everywhere; the vine will produce its fruit, the earth its bounty, and the heavens its dew. I am going to bestow

all these blessings on the remnant of this people. ¹³ Just as once you were a curse among the nations, you House of Judah and later the House of Israel, so now I mean to save you, and you will become proverbial as a blessing. Courage! Do not lose heart!

¹⁴ YHWH Omnipotent says this: Just as I once resolved to inflict evil on you when your ancestors provoked me, says YHWH Omnipotent, and as I did not then relent, ¹⁵ so now I have another purpose, and I intend in the present day to confer benefits on Jerusalem and on the House of Judah. Do not fear. ¹⁶ These are the things you must do. Speak the truth to one another; administer sound and true justice in your courts. ¹⁷ Do not plot evil against each other, and do not love false oaths; for all this is what I hate. It is YHWH who speaks.

¹⁸ The word of YHWH Omnipotent was addressed to me as follows: ¹⁹ "YHWH Omnipotent says this. The fast of the fourth month, the fast of the fifth, the fast of the seventh and the fast of the tenth are to become gladness and happiness and days of joyful feasting for the House of Judah. But love the truth and justice."

²⁰ YHWH Omnipotent says this: There will be other peoples yet, and citizens of great cities. And the inhabitants of one city will go to the next and say, ²¹ "Come, let us go and entreat the favor of YHWH, and seek YHWH Omnipotent. I myself am going." ²² And many people and great nations will come to seek YHWH Omnipotent in Jerusalem and to entreat the favor of YHWH.

²³ YHWH Omnipotent says this: In those days, every Jewish person will have ten Gentiles—people from nations of every language—grabbing them by the sleeve and saying, "We want to go with you, since we have learned that God is with you."

9:1–14:21

*a*n oracle. Because the eyes of humanity, and all the tribes of Israel, are upon YHWH, the word of YHWH is against the land of Hadrach; this burden comes to rest on Damascus, ² and Hamath, which borders it, and Tyre and Sidon, though they are very wise.

> ³ Tyre itself built a rampart, and heaped up silver like dust,
> and gold like the dirt of the streets.

⁴ But YHWH will take from it all it possesses,
and break its sea power
and the city itself will be destroyed by fire.
⁵ Seeing this, Ashkelon will be terrified,
and Gaza seized with trembling, as will Ekron,
at the ruins of its prospects;
the ruler will disappear from Gaza
and Ashkelon remains abandoned.
⁶ A mixed race will settle in Ashdod,
and I will cut down the pride of the Philistines.
⁷ I intend to take the blood out of the mouths
and their abominations from between their teeth.
They too will become a remnant of YHWH
and be like a family in Judah,
and Ekron will be like the Jebusite.
⁸ I will take my stand near my house
like a sentinel guarding against prowlers;
the tyrant will pass this way no more
for now I take notice of their suffering.
⁹ Rejoice in heart and soul, daughter of Zion!
Shout with gladness, daughter of Jerusalem!
Look! Your ruler comes to you; victorious and triumphant,
humble, riding on a donkey,
on a colt, the foal of a donkey.
¹⁰ The ruler will banish chariots from Ephraim
and horses from Jerusalem;
the bow will be banished.
The ruler will proclaim peace for the nations;
the empire stretching from sea to sea,
from the River to the ends of the earth.
¹¹ As for you, due to the blood covenant with me,
I am returning your prisoners from their waterless pit.
¹² Return to your stronghold, O prisoners of hope!
Today I declare that I will give you back double!
¹³ For my bow is strung, Judah;
I laid the arrow to it, Ephraim;
I will stir up your children, Zion,
against your children, Greece,
and wield you like a warrior's sword.
¹⁴ YHWH will appear over them,
with arrows flashing forth like lightning;

YHWH will sound the trumpet,
   and advance like the storm winds of the south.
15   YHWH Omnipotent will protect them;
   God's sling stones will devour, and prevail,
and they will be roaring drunk as if with wine,
   soaked in it like the horns of an altar.
16   On that day YHWH their God will save them,
   God's own, like a flock.
For they are the precious stones in a crown,
   which sparkle throughout the land.
17   What wealth is theirs, what beauty!
   They will produce young men like new grain,
   and young women like new wine.*
10.1 Ask for rain from YHWH in the season of spring rains,
   from YHWH who creates the storm clouds,
who gives you showers of rain,
   the vegetation in the field to everyone.
2   For the idols speak delusions
   and the diviners see lies;
the dreamers tell false dreams,
   and get empty consolation.
Consequently the people wander like sheep;
   they suffer for lack of a shepherd.
3   My anger burns hot against the shepherds,
   and I will punish the leaders of the flock.
Yes, YHWH Omnipotent will take care of the flock,
   the House of Judah,
   and will transform it into war horses,
4   From Judah will issue the cornerstone,
   from Judah the tent peg;
from Judah the battle bow,
   from them every commander.
5   Together they will be like warriors in battle,
   trampling the foe in the mud of the streets;
they will fight, for YHWH is with them,
   and they will humiliate the cavalry.
6   I will strengthen the house of Judah,
   I will save the house of Joseph.

---

* This sentence could also be translated, "Grain (i.e., beer) will make the young men cheerful, and new wine the young women."

I will bring them back for I have compassion on them,
    and they will be as though I had not rejected them;
    for I am YHWH their God, and I will answer them.
⁷ Then the people of Ehpraim will become like warriors,
    with hearts gladdened as if by new wine.
Their will see it and rejoice,
    their hearts will praise God.
⁸ I will signal for them and gather them in,
    for I have redeemed them,
    and they will be as numerous as before.
⁹ Though I scattered them among the nations,
    they will continue to remember me,
    and rear their children and return.
¹⁰ I will return them from the land of Egypt,
    and return them from Assyria;
I will bring them to Gilead and to Lebanon,
    until there is no more room for them.
¹¹ They will pass through the sea of distress,
    and the waves of the sea will collapse
    and the Nile will dry up.
The pride of Assyria will be laid low,
    and the scepter of Egypt will depart.
¹² I will make them strong in YHWH
    and they will walk proudly in my Name,
    says YHWH.

11:1 Open your doors, Lebanon,
    so that the fire can devour your cedars!
² Wail, cypress, for the cedar has fallen,
    and the glorious trees are ruined!
Wail, oaks of Bashan,
    for the thick forests have been felled!

³ The wailing of the shepherd is heard,
    their glorious pastures are no more.
The roaring of the young lions rings out;
    the thickets of the Jordan are laid waste.

⁴ This is how YHWH spoke to me: "Pasture the sheep bred for slaughter,
⁵ whose buyers kill them and go unpunished, whose sellers say of them,
'Thanks be to YHWH, for now I am rich.' Even their shepherds feel no pity
for them. ⁶ For I will no longer have pity on the land's inhabitants, says

YHWH. I am about to put everyone under the power of the shepherds and their ruler, and when the land is crushed I will not rescue them from their hands."

⁷ So I became a shepherd to the flock destined to be slaughtered, especially the most unfortunate sheep. I took two staffs: one I called Favor and the other Unity, and so I looked after the flock.

⁸ In a single month I got rid of three shepherds.* I had lost patience with the flock, and they came to abhor me.

⁹ Then I said to them, "I will not be your shepherd anymore. Any that are to die, let them die; any that are missing, let them stay missing; and the rest can devour each other." ¹⁰ I took my staff called Favor and snapped it in two, annulling the covenant YHWH made with all the nations. ¹¹ So it was annulled that day, and the dealers who watched me knew that this was a word from YHWH.

¹² I said to them, "If it suits you, give me my wages; otherwise, keep them."

Then they weighed out my wages—thirty pieces of silver.

¹³ YHWH said to me, "Throw it into the treasury."

I took the thirty pieces of silver—the princely sum at which I was paid off by them!—and threw them into the house of YHWH, into the treasury. ¹⁴ Then I broke in two my staff called Unity, annulling the family ties between Judah and Israel.

¹⁵ YHWH said to me, "Equip yourself once more as a shepherd, but a worthless one. ¹⁶ For I am about to install a shepherd in the land who will neither care about any that are missing, nor search for those who have strayed off, nor heal the injured, nor nurse the sickly, but will eat the flesh of the fat beasts and throw away the broken bones.

¹⁷   "Trouble is coming to the worthless shepherds
            who desert their flocks!
        May the sword strike their arms
            and their right eyes!
        May their right arm wither entirely,
            and may their eyes be totally blinded!"

12·1 An oracle. The word of YHWH about Israel. It is YHWH who speaks, who spread out the heavens and founded the earth and formed the spirit

---

* The "month" may be euphemistic, and may refer to the last three rulers of Judah—Jehoiakim, Jehoiachin, and Zedekiah—who succeeded one another in rapid succession (though their combined reigns actually lasted about 22 years).

of humankind within them: ² I am about to make Jerusalem an intoxicating cup for all the nations pressing around it; and Judah will be caught up in the seige of Jerusalem. ³ On that day, when all the nations of the earth are gathered to attack it, I will make Jerusalem a rock too heavy for any people to remove, and all who lift it will grievously hurt themselves. And all the nations of the world will come together against it. ⁴ On that day, say YHWH, I will strike every horse with panic, and its rider with madness. But on the horse of Judah I will keep a watchful eye, when I strike every horse of the peoples with blindness. ⁵ Then the clans of Judah will say to themselves, "The inhabitants of Jerusalem have strength through YHWH Omnipotent, their God."

⁶ On that day I will make the families of Judah like a burning brazier in woodland, like a burning torch among the sheaves. They will consume all the surrounding nations, right and left, while the people of Jerusalem remain safe in their city. ⁷ YHWH will set free all the families of Judah first, so that the glory of David's line and of the citizens of Jerusalem may not surpass that of Judah.

⁸ On that day YHWH will shield the inhabitants of Jerusalem; on that day the weakest of them will be like David, and the line of David, like the angel of YHWH going before them.

⁹ On that day I will set about the destruction of every nation that attacks Jerusalem, ¹⁰ but I will pour a spirit of pity and compassion on the house of David and the inhabitants of Jerusalem. Then they will look on me, the one they pierced, they will mourn for the pierced one, as one mourns for an only child, and weeps bitterly for it, as one mourns over a first born. ¹¹ On that day the mourning of Jerusalem will be as great as the mourning for Hadad-rimmon in the plain of Megiddo. ¹² The land will mourn, each family by itself—the family of the house of David by itself, the women mourning separately from the men; the family of the house of Nathan by itself, the women mourning separately from the men; ¹³ the family of the house of Levi by itself, the women mourning separately from the men; the family of the house of Shimeites by itself, the women mourning separately from the men; ¹⁴ and all the families that are left, each by itself, the women mourning separately from the men.

13:1 On that day a fountain will be opened for the house of David and the inhabitants of Jerusalem, to cleanse them from sin and impurity.

² On that day, says YHWH Omnipotent, I will cut off the names of the idols from the land, so that they will be remembered no more, and also I will remove from the land the "prophets" and the spirit of uncleanness.*

---

* "The prophets" here are the false prophets; the "spirit of uncleanness" is ritual impurity and the worship of other gods.

³ And if any "prophets" appear again, their fathers and the mothers who bore them will say to them, "You will not live, for you speak lies in the name of YHWH." And their fathers and the mothers who bore them will run them through with a sword when they prophesy. ⁴ On that day, every one of the "prophets" will be ashamed of their visions when they prophesy; they will no longer put on a prophet's hairy garment* in order to deceive the people, ⁵ but each one of them will say, "I am not a prophet, I am a tiller of the soil; for the land has been my possession since my youth." ⁶ And if anyone asks them, "What are these wounds on your chest?" they will answer, "The wounds I received in the house of my friends."

⁷　Awake, O sword, against my shepherd,
　　against the person who is my associate,
　　says YHWH Omnipotent.
　Strike the shepherd, and let the sheep be scattered—
　　I will turn my hand against the little ones.
⁸　In the whole land, says YHWH,
　　two-thirds of them will be cut off and will die,
　　and one-third will be left alive.
⁹　And I will put this third into the fire,
　　refine them as one refines silver,
　　and test them as gold is tested.
　They will call on my Name,
　　and I will answer them.
　I will say, "These are my people";
　　and they will say, "YHWH is our God."

14·1 Look, the Day of YHWH is coming—and spoils that were taken from you will be divided among you once again.

² First, I will gather all the nations to make war on Jerusalem; the city will fall, the houses ransacked, and the women raped. Half of the city will go into exile, but the remainder of the population will not be moved from the city.

³ Then YHWH will go forth and fight against those nations as when fighting on the day of battle. ⁴ On that day, YHWH's feet will rest on the Mount of Olives, which faces Jerusalem from the east. The Mount of Olives will be split in half from east to west, forming a huge gorge. Half of the Mount will recede northward, the other half will recede southward. ⁵ And the Valley of Hinnom will be blocked, for the new valley between them will reach

---

* Elijah and Elisha both wore animal skins; after the nation divided into northern and southern realms, a professional prophetic guild emerged, and the prophets often donned cloaks of animal hair as a sign of their office, much as shamans might wear a ceremonial headdress in honor of their power animal.

as far as Azal. It will be blocked as it was by the earthquake in the time of Uzziah the ruler of Judah. And YHWH my God will come to you, attended by all the holy ones.*

⁶ When that day comes there will be neither heat nor cold nor frost. ⁷ It will be continual daylight—only YHWH knows when it will be—and there will be no distinction between day and night. Even in the evening there will be light.

⁸ On that day, whether in summer or in winter, running water will issue from Jerusalem, half flowing to the eastern sea and half flowing to the western sea. ⁹ YHWH will become ruler over the whole world; on that day, all will worship† one God, and all will call God by the same name—YHWH.† ¹⁰ The whole land will become like the Arabah from Geba to Rimmon south of Jerusalem. But Jerusalem will stand high in its place, and be full of people from the Benjamin Gate to the point where the former gate stood, to the Corner Gate, and from the Tower of Nananel to the ruler's winepresses. ¹¹ Jerusalem will be inhabited, and never again will it be placed under the sacred ban and doomed to destruction; all who will live there will be secure.

¹² YHWH will strike with all the nations who waged war against Jerusalem with this plague: their flesh will rot while they still are on their feet, their eyes will rot in their sockets, and their tongues will rot in their mouths. ¹³ On that day, a great panic from YHWH will fall on them, so that each will seize the hand of a neighbor, and the hand of the one will be raised against the other. ¹⁴ Even Judah will fight at Jerusalem.

And the wealth of all the surrounding nations will be gathered up—gold, silver, and garments in great abundance.‡ ¹⁵ And a plague like this plague will fall on the horses, the mules, the camels, the donkeys, and whatever animals may be in their camps.

¹⁶ Any survivors among the nations which fought against Jerusalem will go up annually to worship the Ruler, YHWH Omnipotent, and observe the Feast of Tabernacles. ¹⁷ Should any of the families of the earth not go up to Jerusalem to worship the Ruler, YHWH Omnipotent, no rain will fall on them. ¹⁸ If the Egyptians do not go up and enter the city, then the same disaster will overtake it as that which YHWH will inflict on any nation that does not go up to keep the feast. ¹⁹ This will be the punishment that will befall Egypt and any nation that does not go up to keep the Feast of Tabernacles.

---

* "Holy ones" here could mean righteous people, or angels.
† Literally, "on that day, it will be YHWH alone and YHWH's name alone."
‡ These are the spoils spoken of in 14:1.

²⁰ In that day, "Sacred to YHWH" will be inscribed even on the horses' bells; the cooking pots in YHWH's Temple will be as holy as the basins in front of the altar, ²¹ and every cooking pot in Jerusalem and Judah will be holy to YHWH Omnipotent, so that all who sacrifice may come and use them to boil their sacrificial meat.* And there will no longer be merchants in the Temple of YHWH Omnipotent in that day.

---

* This is the essence of the messianic era: a time when all of creation, even the most mundane household items, are understood as being sacred and imbued with God's presence; the image of "every cooking pot in Judah" being available to worshipers to boil their sacrificial meat indicates that God will be as fully present in the villages and homes of poor people as in the Temple itself.

malachi

an oracle.* the word of yhwh to israel
through Malachi.†

2   I have loved you, says YHWH.
        But you ask, "How have you shown your love?"
    Esau and Jacob were brothers, weren't they? replies YHWH.
        Yet I loved Jacob, 3 but hated Esau.‡
    I have reduced Esau's hill country to a waste,
        and their ancestral land to desert pastures.
4   Whenever Edom says,
        "We are beaten down, but let us rebuild our ruined homes,"

---

* The Hebrew for "oracle" is *massa*, a technical term in prophetic literature indicating a message from God, is from a verb meaning "to carry." It literally means "burdensome message," that is, one with ominous content.
† The name means "my messenger."
‡ In covenant language, "love" and "hate" are synonymous with "choose" and "reject."

YHWH Omnipotent* replies,
　　If they rebuild, I will tear them down!
They will be called "Country of Evildoers"
　　and "The People of YHWH's Anger."
5　Your own eyes will see it,
　　　and you yourselves will say,
　　"YHWH's greatness reaches beyond　'
　　　the confines of Israel!"
6　Children honor their parents,
　　　and laborers their overseer.
　　If I am a parent, where is the honor due to me?
　　　If I am an overseer, where is the respect due to me?
　　　says YHWH Omnipotent.
　　　Yet you priests despise my Name!
　　"How have we despised your Name?" you ask.
7　　　—By offering polluted food on my altar!
　　"How have we polluted it?" you ask.
　　　—By saying that YHWH's table isn't worthy of respect!
8　When you offer a blind animal,
　　　you say there's nothing wrong with it,
　　and when you offer an animal that is lame or diseased,
　　　you say there's nothing wrong with it!
　　If you brought such a gift to your governor,
　　　would the governor welcome you, or show you favor?
　　　says YHWH Omnipotent.
9　And now you plead and implore God's favor—
　　　"Be gracious to us!"
　　This is what you have done—
　　　do you think God will accept any of you?
　　　says YHWH Omnipotent.
10　Oh, that someone among you would shut the Temple doors,
　　　so that you would stop lighting pointless fires on my altar!
　　I take no pleasure in you, says YHWH Omnipotent,
　　　and I will accept no offering from your hands!
11　For from the rising of the sun to its setting
　　　my Name is honored among the nations,
　　　says YHWH Omnipotent.

---

* "Omnipotent" here translates *tsva'ot*, which means "of hosts" or "of the armies," and can refer to
earthly armies, angelic forces, or even stars in the sky. The word is often translated "Almighty,"
and is a picture of universal power and authority, indicating that all created beings and forces are
under God's dominion.

¹² But you profane it when you say
　　that YHWH's table is polluted,
　　and its food isn't worthy of respect!
¹³ "How tiresome it all is!" you sniff,
　　says YHWH Omnipotent.
　　You bring animals that are injured or deformed or diseased,
　　　and these you bring as your offering!
　　Shall I accept them from your hands?
　　　says YHWH.
¹⁴ A curse on the cheater
　　who promises me a choice animal from the flock,
　　yet pays the vow with something damaged!
　　For I am a great Ruler, says YHWH Omnipotent,
　　and my Name inspires awe among the nations.
²·¹ And now, you priests,
　　this decree is for you:
² unless you listen to me and take it to heart
　　to give honor to my Name, says YHWH Omnipotent,
　　I will lay a curse on you.
　　　I will turn your blessings into a curse;
　　　in fact, I've done so already, for you pay no heed.
³ I will deprive you of the shoulder,* fling offal in your faces—
　　the offal from your pilgrim feasts—
　　and I will banish you from my presence.
⁴ Know this—that I issued this decree against you
　　so that my covenant with Levi will endure,
　　says YHWH Omnipotent.
⁵ My covenant with Levi was one of life and peace,
　　and I gave him the duty of reverence.
　　Levi revered me and lived in awe of my Name.
⁶ Because Levi, a priest, gave true instruction,
　　and no word of injustice fell from his lips,
　　Levi walked in harmony and uprightness with me,
　　and turned many people from evildoing.
⁷ For the faithful hang on the words of the priests
　　and seek knowledge and instructions from them,
　　for they are called to be messengers of YHWH Omnipotent.
⁸ But you turned aside from that path—
　　you caused many to stumble with your instructions!

---

* The shoulder was the part of the sacrificial animal given to the priests in return for their service at the altar; depriving them of this is a symbolic rejection of their priesthood.

You have corrupted the covenant of Levi,
   says YHWH Omnipotent.
⁹ So I in turn made you contemptible and vile to the whole people
   because you did not keep to my path
   but showed partiality in the way you administered the law.

aRE we all not the daughters and sons of God?*
   Did not one God create us?
Why, then, do we break faith with one another
   and defile the covenant of our ancestors?
¹¹ Judah broke faith,
   and detestable things are done in Israel and in Jerusalem.
In turning to a foreign god,†
   Judah violated the sacred place that YHWH loves.
¹² May YHWH banish from the tents of Jacob any who do this,
   whether nomads or settlers,‡
   even though they bring offerings to YHWH Omnipotent!
¹³ And that's something else you do:
   you weep and moan to trying to get God's attention,
      drowning YHWH's altar with tears,
   but God still refuses to look at your offerings
      or accept them from you with pleasure.
¹⁴ You ask why?
   It is because YHWH has borne witness against you
      on behalf of the spouse you loved from your youth.
   You broke faith even though you were partners,
      espoused by solemn covenant.
¹⁵ Did God not make you one,
      belonging to God in both body and soul?

---

* Here the prophet speaks his own thoughts rather than speaking for God.
† Literally, "in marrying the daughter of a foreign god." Marriage is a metaphor of Judah's idolatry, of being unfaithful to YHWH and "marrying" itself to pagan gods.
‡ This phrase is highly disputed, prompting nearly as many variations as there are biblical translations, such as "tempter and tempted," "teacher and scholar," "witness and advocate," "root and branch." The phrase may literally mean "those who awaken and those who answer."

And what does the One seek
>but daughters and sons, God's own progeny?
So keep watch on your spirit,
>and let none of you be unfaithful
>to the spouse of your youth.
¹⁶ "Couples who divorce in a spirit of hate,"
>says YHWH, the God of Israel,
"cover each other with garments of violence,"
>says YHWH Omnipotent.
So keep watch over your spirit,
>and do not be unfaithful.

2:17–4:5

*Y*ou have wearied YHWH with your talk.*
>"How have we wearied you"? you ask.
By saying that all evildoers are good in the eyes of YHWH,
>and that God is pleased by them,
or by asking,
>"Where is the God of justice?"
^{3:1} Well, pay attention!
>I am sending my Messenger†
>to prepare the way for me;
the One you seek‡ will suddenly come to the Temple,
>the Messenger of the Covenant whom you long for will come,
>says YHWH Omnipotent.
² But who can endure the day of that Coming?
>Who can stand firm when that One appears?
That day will be like a smelter's fire,
>a launderer's soap.
³ The One will preside as refiner and purifier,
>purifying the Children of Levi,
>refining them like gold and silver—

---

* From here to the end of the book, God is once again the speaker.
† "My messenger" is the same word as the name Malachi, though here it would appear to refer to someone different than the prophet.
‡ Literally, "the *Adonai* you seek." Adonai, usually translated "lord," refers to the Messenger of the Covenant. Ancient Hebrews viewed this Messenger as a messianic figure, though New Testament writers saw "the one who prepares the way" and "the Adonai who will refine the corrupt priesthood and make them true ministers of God again" as two different people.

then they will once again
 make offerings to YHWH in righteousness.
⁴ Then the offerings of Judah and Jerusalem
 will be pleasing to YHWH as they were in former days,
 in years long past.
⁵ I will appear before you in court,
 to testify against the sorcerers, adulterers, and perjurers,
against those who cheat the hired laborers of their wages,
 and oppress the widow and the orphan,
who rob foreigners of their rights
 and have no respect for me, says YHWH Omnipotent.
⁶ No—I, YHWH, do not change,
 and you, children of Jacob, are not ruined yet!
⁷ Ever since the days of your ancestors
 you turned aside from my statutes and did not keep them.
If you return to me,
 I will turn back to you, says YHWH Omnipotent.
You ask, "How can we return?"
⁸ —Dare a human being defraud God? Yet you defraud me!
You ask, "How have we defrauded you?"
 —In your tithes and offerings!
⁹ There is a double curse on all of you,
 your entire nation,
 because you defraud me!
¹⁰ Bring the entire tithe into the storehouse*
 so there be food in my house!
Put me to the test,
 says YHWH Omnipotent,
and see if I do not open windows in the sky
 and pour so much blessing on you
 that you cannot contain it!
¹¹ I will keep pests from destroying the produce of your soil,
 and prevent your vines from dropping their fruit,
 says YHWH Omnipotent.
¹² All nations will call you happy,
 for yours will be a land of delight, says YHWH Omnipotent.
¹³ You use harsh words about me, says YHWH.
 "How have we spoken against you?" you ask.

---

* This was the Temple warehouse, where grain, oil, and wine was stored so that poor people would have a supply of food, which operated rather like our modern food pantries for the homeless.

14 You've said, "It is useless to serve YHWH.
    What do we gain from God by observing all the rules
    and walking in humble submission?
15 Arrogant people are the blessed ones;
    evildoers prosper all the time,
    they flout God, and come to no harm."
16 But those who revered YHWH talked together,
    and YHWH listened and took note.
    A record* was written before God
    of those who stood in awe of YHWH and honored God's Name.
17 They will be mine, says YHWH Omnipotent,
    my own possession on the day I am preparing,
    and I will have compassion on them
    as a parent has compassion on an obedient child.
18 Then once again you will be able to distinguish
    the righteous person from the evildoer,
    the servant of YHWH
    from the person who does not heed God.
4:1 The Day is coming, burning like an oven,
    when all the arrogant and all the evildoers will be stubble;
    the Day that comes will burn them up, says YHWH Omnipotent,
    and it will leave them neither root nor branch.
2 But for you who revere my Name,
    the sun will rise, a sun of justice,
    with healing in its rays.
    You will go out leaping
    like calves released from their stall.
3 And you will trample on those who are corrupt,
    for they will be ashes under the soles of your feet,
    on the Day when I act, says YHWH Omnipotent.
4 Remember the teaching of my servant Moses,
    the statutes and ordinances
    that I commanded Moses at Horeb for all Israel.
5 Know this: I will send you the prophet Elijah
    before the great and terrible Day of YHWH comes,
    and he will reconcile parents to their children
    and children to their parents,
    so that, when I come,
    I need not strike the land with utter destruction.

* Literally, "a scroll of remembrance."